"What an achievement! John Oswalt's volumes on 1–2 Kings showcase the characteristics that make him one of the best commentators of his generation: the integration of exegetical insights into an explanation of the whole passage in a way that brings out the message of Scripture. Pastors and students will no doubt treasure Oswalt's commentary."

—ANDREW T. ABERNETHY, professor of Old Testament, Wheaton College

"Oswalt is a gifted translator, astute interpreter, and an even better writer. Few rival his ability to speak plainly about even the most complex truths. Oswalt leverages that skill to craft a commentary that productively wrestles with the Hebrew text without leaving anyone behind. Students, pastors, and scholars will find this commentary interesting, pleasant to read, and judiciously thorough. Oswalt's love for Scripture and care for the church shine through on every single page."

—MICHELLE KNIGHT, associate professor of Old Testament and semitic languages, Trinity Evangelical Divinity School

"In this superb commentary Dr. Oswalt demonstrates that 1 and 2 Kings provide much more than a historical and political background for the books of Isaiah (his specialty) and the rest of the prophetic books in our canon. He opens by reminding readers that the key to the message of 1 Kings is found not in tedious summaries of kings' reigns but in the living voices of prophets who served as the divinely inspired conscience in their courts and to the nation[s]. Assessing the flow of Israel's history through the lens of the Torah (Deuteronomy), the composers of these books were truly 'prophets in the train of Moses' (Deut 18:15–22). Dr. Oswalt is at his interpretive best when he contrasts the theological world of orthodox Yahwism divinely revealed to prophets and righteous kings (of whom there were few) and the spiritually bankrupt worldview of idolatrous nations around Israel and the neo-pagans within the chosen people. This commentary on Scripture reads and writes with prophetic passion; this is evangelical and biblical scholarship for the church at its finest."

—DANIEL I. BLOCK, Gunther H. Knoedler Professor Emeritus of Old Testament, Wheaton College

"The book of Kings is a critical voice in the Old Testament. Not only does it document Israel's occupation of the Promised Land during the later part of the Iron Age, but it explains the tragedy of the Babylonian exile and the demise of the Northern Kingdom. And as one reads through this text, they quickly realize that this is a complicated landscape. Internal and external pressures converged and affected God's people as they struggled to be faithful in that very turbulent era. Consequently, to make sense of all this, you need someone who is not only theologically sensitive but also well versed in history, culture, and the institutions of the ancient Near East. John Oswalt is one of those scholars who can not only give the proper attention to these variables but can also hold them in balance with his distinguished theological acuity. This is an impressive two volume work. His translations are well informed by his linguistic and text-critical acumen. His historical awareness and expertise in the prophetic institution allows him to penetrate the text and arrive at deeper insights for those scenes where prophetic figures dominate. But, without a doubt, his theological contributions are what give this project its distinctive flair. If you've read Oswalt's work, this project will not surprise. He never fails to move beyond the historical and scholarly conversations to consider the theological import of whatever he's discussing. For those who believe that discussions about the book of Kings have been tainted by bland historical-critical conversations, this commentary offers an up-to-date, well-informed voice that bucks those trends and challenges some of the most dominant assumptions. If the book of Kings is of any interest, you will do well to heed this contribution."

—David B. Schreiner, associate professor of Old Testament and inductive biblical studies, Asbury Theological Seminary

2 KINGS

EVANGELICAL EXEGETICAL COMMENTARY

2 KINGS

John N. Oswalt

General Editor
Tremper Longman III

Senior Old Testament Editor
David T. Lamb

2 Kings
Evangelical Exegetical Commentary

Lexham Academic, an imprint of Lexham Press
1313 Commercial St., Bellingham, WA 98225
LexhamPress.com

Print ISBN 9781683598343
Digital ISBN 9781683598350
Library of Congress Control Number 2024951385

Series Editor: Tremper Longman III, David T. Lamb, JoAnna M. Hoyt
Lexham Editorial: Derek Brown, Lynsey M. Stephan, Mandi Newell
Cover Design: Brittany Schrock
Typesetting: ProjectLuz.com

25 26 27 28 29 30 / IN / 12 11 10 9 8 7 6 5 4 3 2 1

Contents

Commentary Editors

Previous Commentary Editors

Acknowledgements

Three persons have been of inestimable help in the preparation of this commentary. They are my research assistants: Jonathan Beck, Keith Cooper, and Scott Engebretson. They have searched out bibliography material, reviewed articles, and generally prepared the ground for me. I might have been able to complete the work without their help, but it would have taken unimaginably longer to do so. Thank you, gentlemen, for the gifts of your time, your labors, and your good spirits throughout.

It was initially possible to employ these men because of the generosity of Dr. and Mrs. James Reed and Mr. and Mrs. Burt Luce. These good friends of a lifetime have believed in my work and encouraged me again and again along the way. Thank you.

Dr. William Barrick, Old Testament editor of the Evangelical Exegetical Commentary, invested countless hours in editing, revising, and improving the manuscript. I am very grateful for his contributions.

I am also grateful for the careful work of Dr. David Lamb, who succeeded Dr. Barrick, who added further improvements.

Jessi Strong, along with other editors at Lexham Press have invested many hours in improving the manuscript. I am grateful to her, and them, for their help in bringing this project to fruition.

Editor's Preface

The Bible is true in everything it intends to teach. At the same time, it is not always clear—which means it is not always obvious what it intends to teach, thus the need for commentary. The Evangelical Exegetical Commentary intends to help scholars, pastors, and laypeople understand Scripture in order to inform their understanding of God, motivate them to faithful action, and encourage their faith. We have recruited some of the best evangelical scholars to explore the meaning and application of the various books of the Old and New Testaments. Experts in the best sense of the word, they are doing their scholarship in the service of the church. They share a high regard for the Bible as God's Word, having honed their skills in biblical scholarship over decades of study.

The present commentary series is, first of all, *evangelical*. As the title of the series suggests, our contributors write from an evangelical perspective. While evangelicalism can be defined and exemplified in more than one way, evangelicals are united in recognizing the primary authority of Scripture for our knowledge of God and as a guide to faithful living.

The Evangelical Exegetical Commentary is also *exegetical*. The emphasis is on the original meaning of the text, starting with a close reading of the original languages in their original context. The biblical books, after all, were not written directly to us today, but to the faithful who were contemporary with the authors. Still, the fact that the church recognizes these books as canonical means that though they may not have been written *to* us, they were written *for* us.

Our hope and prayer, as editors and as contributors, is that these commentaries will help you so understand Scripture to inform your minds but also to stimulate your imaginations, to fire your emotions with faith, and to cultivate faithful obedience of God.

Tremper Longman III, General Editor

David T. Lamb, Senior Old Testament Editor

JoAnna M. Hoyt, Assistant Old Testament Editor

Andreas J. Köstenberger, Senior New Testament Editor

Benjamin L. Gladd, Assistant New Testament Editor

Abbreviations

AASOR	Annual of the American Schools of Oriental Research
ÄAT	Ägypten und Altes Testament
AB	Anchor Yale Bible
ABD	D. N. Freedman, ed., *The Anchor Yale Bible Dictionary*
ABQ	*American Baptist Quarterly*
ABR	*Australian Biblical Review*
AbrN	*Abr-Nahrain*
ACCSOT	Ancient Christian Commentary on Scripture. Old Testament
ACEBT	*Amsterdamse Cahiers voor Exegese en bijbelse Theologie*
AD	anno Domini
AJBI	*Annual of the Japanese Biblical Institute*
AJSL	*American Journal of Semitic Languages and Literatures*
AJT	*Asia Journal of Theology*
Akk.	Akkadian
ALQ	*Ancient Library of Qumran*
ALUOS	*Annual of Leeds University Oriental Society*
AnBib	Analecta Biblica
ANE	Ancient Near East(ern)
ANEP	J. B. Pritchard, ed., *The Ancient Near East in Pictures relating to the Old Testament*
ANET	J. B. Pritchard, ed., *Ancient Near Eastern Texts Relating to the Old Testament*, 3rd ed.
AOAT	Alter Orient und Altes Testament
AOOT	*Ancient Orient and Old Testament*
AOTC	Abingdon Old Testament Commentaries
ARAB	D. E Luckenbill, ed., *Ancient Records of Assyria and Babylonia*
ASORDS	American Schools of Oriental Research Dissertation Series
ASTI	*Annual of the Swedish Theological Institute*
AsTJ	*Asbury Theological Journal*
ASV	American Standard Version
ATANT	Abhandlungen zur Theologie des Alten und Neuen Testaments
ATD	Das Alte Testament Deutsch
AThR	*Anglican TR*
ATJ	*Ashland Theological Journal*
AUSS	*Andrews University Seminary Studies*

BA	*Biblical Archaeologist*
BAR	*Biblical Archaeology Review*
BASOR	*Bulletin of the American Schools of Oriental Research*
BBR	*Bulletin for Biblical Research*
BBVT	Berliner Beitrage zum Voderen Orient
BC	before Christ
BDB	F. Brown, S. R. Driver, and C. A. Briggs, eds., *Hebrew and English Lexicon of the Old Testament*
BEATAJ	Beiträge zur Erforschung des Alten Testaments und des Antiken Judentums
BETL	Bibliotheca Ephemeridum Theologicarum Lovaniensium
BHS	*Biblia Hebraica Stuttgartensia*
BI	*Biblical Illustrator*
Bib	*Biblica*
BibInt	*Biblical Interpretation*
BibInt	Biblical Interpretation Series
BibOr	Biblica et Orientalia
BibSp	*Bible and Spade*
BIOSCS	*Bulletin of the International Organization for Septuagint and Cognate Studies*
BJRL	*Bulletin of the John Rylands Library of Manchester*
BJS	Brown Judaic Studies
BKAT	M. Noth and H. W. Wolff, eds., Biblischer Kommentar, Altes Testament
BLS	Bible and Literature Series
BN	*Biblische Notizen*
BR	*Biblical Research*
BRev	*Bible Review*
BSac	*Bibliotheca Sacra*
BSOAS	*Bulletin of the School of Oriental and African Studies*
BT	*Bible Translator*
BTB	*Biblical Theology Bulletin*
BWANT	Beiträge zur Wissenschaft vom Alten und Neuen Testament
BZ	*Biblische Zeitschrift*
BZAW	Beihefte zur Zeitschrift für die alttestamentliche Wissenschaft
CAD	*The Assyrian Dictionary of the Oriental Institute of the University of Chicago*
CAH	Cambridge Ancient History
CANE	J. Sasson, *Civilizations of the Ancient Near East*. 4 vols.
CBAT	The Complete Bible, an American Translation
C BC	Cambridge Bible Commentary
CBQ	*Catholic Biblical Quarterly*
CBQMS	Catholic Biblical Quarterly Monograph Series
CC	Continental Commentaries
CDT	*Cuadermos de Teologia*

CEB	Common English Bible
CEV	Contemporary English Version
CH	Code of Hammurabi
CJB	Complete Jewish Bible
ConBOT	Coniectanea Biblica: Old Testament Series
Cor BC	Cornerstone Biblical Commentary
COS	W. W. Hallo, ed., *The Context of Scripture*
CTAT	D. Barthélemy, ed., *Critique Textuelle de l'Ancien Testament*
CTJ	*Calvin Theological Journal*
CTM	*Concordia Theological Monthly*
CTQ	*Concordia Theological Quarterly*
CTSR	*Chicago Theological Seminary Register*
CurBR	*Currents in Biblical Research*
CurTM	*Currents in Theology and Mission*
CV	*Communio Viatorum*
DBI	*Dictionary of Biblical Imagery*
DCH	*Dictionary of Classical Hebrew,* ed. D. J. A. Clines, Sheffield, 1993–2011
DDD	K. van der Toorn et al., eds., *Dictionary of Deities and Demons in the Bible*, 2nd ed.
DJD	Discoveries in the Judean Desert
DSD	*Dead Sea Discoveries*
DTT	*Dansk teologisk tidsskrift*
EHAT	Exegetisches Handbuch zum Alten Testament
ErIsr	Eretz-Israel
EstBib	*Estudios biblicos*
ESV	English Standard Version
ETL	*Ephemerides Theologicae Lovanienses*
ETR	*Etudes théologiques et religieuses*
EV	English version(s)
EvQ	*Evangelical Quarterly*
EvT	*Evangelische Theologie*
ExpTim	*Expository Times*
FAT	Forschungen zum Alten Testament
FCB	Feminist Companion to the Bible
FOTL	Forms of the Old Testament Literature
FRLANT	Forschungen zur Religion und Literatur des Alten und Neuen Testaments
GKC	E. Kautsch and A. Cowley, eds., *Gesenius' Hebrew Grammar*
Gk.	Greek
GNT	Good News Translation
GTJ	*Grace Theological Journal*
HALOT	L. Koehler, W. Baumgartner, and J. J. Stamm, *The Hebrew and Aramaic Lexicon of the Old Testament,* trans. and ed. M. E. J. Richardson et al., 4 vols.

HAR	*Hebrew Annual Review*
HBT	*Horizons in Biblical Theology*
HCOT	Historical Commentary on the Old Testament
Heb.	Hebrew
HKAT	Handkommentar zum Alten Testament
HR	*History of Religions*
HS	*Hebrew Studies*
HSM	Harvard Semitic Monographs
HTR	*Harvard Theological Review*
HUCA	*Hebrew Union College Annual*
HUCM	Monographs of Hebrew Union College
IB	*Interpreter's Bible*
IBC	Interpretation: A Bible Commentary for Teaching and Preaching
IBHS	B. K. Waltke and M. P. O'Connor, *Introduction to Biblical Hebrew Syntax*
ICC	International Critical Commentary
IEJ	*Israel Exploration Journal*
Int	*Interpretation*
ITC	International Theological Commentary
IVPDOTHB	*Intervarsity Press Dictionary of the Historical Books*
JANER	*Journal of Ancient Near Eastern Religions*
JANES	*Journal of the Ancient Near Eastern Society*
JAOS	*Journal of the American Oriental Society*
JB	Jerusalem Bible
JBL	*Journal of Biblical Literature*
JBQ	*Jewish Bible Quarterly*
JCS	*Journal of Cuneiform Studies*
JETS	*Journal of the Evangelical Theological Society*
JFSR	*Journal of Feminist Studies in Religion*
JHebS	*Journal of Hebrew Scriptures*
JHS	*Journal of Hellenic Studies*
JJS	*Journal of Jewish Studies*
JNES	*Journal of Near Eastern Studies*
JNSL	*Journal of Northwest Semitic Languages*
JPOS	*Journal of the Palestine Oriental Society*
JQR	*Jewish Quarterly Review*
JR	*Journal of Religion*
JRSSup	Journal of Religion & Society: Supplement Series
JRT	*Journal of Religious Thought*
JSJ	*Journal for the Study of Judaism in the Persian, Hellenistic and Roman Periods*
JSNTSup	Journal for the Study of the New Testament Supplement Series
JSOT	*Journal for the Study of the Old Testament*

JSOTSup	Journal for the Study of the Old Testament Supplement Series
JSS	*Journal of Semitic Studies*
JTS	*Journal of Theological Studies*
KHC	Kurzer Hand-Commentar zum Alten Testament
KJV	King James Version
LASBF	*Liber Annuus Studii Biblici Franciscani*
LD	Lectio Divina
LHBOTS	Library of Hebrew Bible/Old Testament Studies
LTJ	*Lutheran Theological Journal*
Luc. & G[L]	Luciani
LXX	Septuagint
MQR	*Michigan Quarterly Review*
MSJ	*Master's Seminary Journal*
MT	Masoretic Text
MTSR	*Method and Theory in the Study of Religion*
NAB	New American Bible
NAC	New American Commentary
NASB	New American Standard Bible
NEA	*Near Eastern Archaeology*
NEchtB	Neue Echter Bibel
NedTT	*Nederlands theologisch tijdschrift*
Neot	*Neotestamentica*
NIB	*The New Interpreter's Bible*, 12 vols., Nashville: Abingdon Press, 1994–2004
NIBC	New International Biblical Commentary
NICOT	New International Commentary on the Old Testament
NIDOTTE	W. VanGemeren, ed., *New International Dictionary of Old Testament Theology and Exegesis*
NIV	New International Version
NIVAC	NIV Application Commentary
NJB	New Jerusalem Bible
NJPS	New Jewish Publication Society Version
NKJV	New King James Version
NLT	New Living Translation
NRSV	New Revised Standard Version
NT	New Testament
NTS	*New Testament Studies*
OBO	Orbis Biblicus et Orientalis
OBT	Overtures to Biblical Theology
Occ.	occurance
OEANE	E. Meyers, ed., *Oxford Encyclopedia of Archaeology in the Near East*
OG	Old Greek
OL	Old Latin
OLA	Orientalia Lovaniensia Analecta

Or	*Orientalia (NS)*
OT	Old Testament
OTG	Old Testament Guides
OTL	Old Testament Library
OTP	J. H. Charlesworth, ed., *The Old Testament Pseudepigrapha*. 2 vols.
OtSt	Oudtestamentische Studiën
PAAJR	*Proceedings of the American Academy of Jewish Research*
PEQ	*Palestine Exploration Quarterly*
Presb	*Presbyterion*
PRSt	*Perspectives in Religious Studies*
RB	*Revue Biblique*
REB	The New English Bible, Revised
RefR	*Reformed Review*
RelEd	*Religious Education*
RelSRev	*Religious Studies Review*
ResQ	*Restoration Quarterly*
RevExp	*Review and Expositor*
RevistB	*Revista bíblica*
RevQ	*Revue de Qumran*
RevScRel	*Revue des sciences religieuses*
RHA	*Revue hittite et asianique*
RHR	*Revue de l'histoire des religions*
RJ	*Reformed Journal*
RSV	Revised Standard Version
SB	Sources bibliques
SBJT	*Southern Baptist Journal of Theology*
SBLDS	Society of Biblical Literature Dissertation Series
SBLMS	Society of Biblical Literature Monograph Series
SBLSP	*Society of Biblical Literature Seminar Papers*
SBT	Studies in Biblical Theology
ScEs	*Science et esprit*
S-CJ	*Stone-Campbell Journal*
ScrHier	Scripta Hierosolymitana
SCS	Septuagint and Cognate Studies
SEÅ	*Svensk exegetisk årsbok*
SemeiaSt	Semeia Studies
SHANE	Studies in the History of the Ancient Near East
SHBC	Smyth & Helwys Bible Commentary
SHCANE	Studies in the History and Culture of the Ancient Near East
SJOT	*Scandinavian Journal of the Old Testament*
SJT	*Scottish Journal of Theology*
SK	*Skrif en kerk*
SOTSMS	Society for Old Testament Studies Monograph Series

SR	*Studies in Religione*
SSN	Studia Semitica Neerlandica
STDJ	Studies on the Texts of the Desert of Judah
StPB	Studia Post-Biblica
STRev	*Sewanee Theological Review*
SwJT	*Southwestern Journal of Theology*
Syr.	Syriac
TANE	J. B. Pritchard, *The Ancient Near East: An Anthology of Texts and Pictures*
TDOT	G. J. Botterweck et al., eds., *Theological Dictionary of the Old Testament*
Tg.	Targum
Them	*Themelios*
Theol	*Theologica*
ThTo	*Theology Today*
TJ	*Trinity Journal*
TLOT	E. Jenni and C. Westermann, eds., *Theological Lexicon of the Old Testament*, trans. M. Biddle
TOTC	Tyndale Old Testament Commentaries
TQ	*Theologische Quartalschrift*
TR	*Theological Review*
TRu	*Theologische Rundschau*
TS	*Theological Studies*
TTZ	*Trierer theologische Zeitschrift*
TWOT	R. L. Harris et al., eds., *Theological Word Book of the Old Testament*
TynBul	*Tyndale Bulletin*
TZ	*Theologische Zeitschrift*
UF	*Ugarit-Forschungen*
Vulg.	Vulgate
VT	*Vetus Testamentum*
VTSup	Supplements to Vetus Testamentum
WBC	Word Biblical Commentary
WMANT	Wissenschaftliche Monographien zum Alten und Neuen Testament
WTJ	*Westminster Theological Journal*
WUNT	Wissenschaftliche Untersuchungen zum Neuen Testament
ZAW	*Zeitschrift für die alttestamentliche Wissenschaft*
ZDPV	*Zeitschrift des Deutschen Palästina-Vereins*
ZIBBC	J. Walton, ed., *Zondervan Illustrated Bible Backgrounds Commentary*, 5 vols.
ZRGG	*Zeitschrift für Religions- und Geistesgeschichte*
ZTK	*Zeitschrift für Theologie und Kirche*

Technical Abbreviations

abs.	absolute
acc.	accusative
ca.	circa
cf.	confer, compare
chap(s).	chapters
conj.	conjunction
const.	construct
ed(s).	editor(s)
e.g.	exempli gratia, for example
esp.	especially
etc.	et cetera, and the rest
fem.	feminine
gen.	genitive
i.e.	id est, that is
impf.	impf.
inf.	infinitive
K	*ketiv*
lit.	literally
masc.	masculine
mg.	marginal note
MSS	manuscripts
obj.	object
par.	parallel(s)
pass.	passive
pf.	perfect
pl.	plural
prep.	preposition
ptcp.	participle
Q	*qere*
sg.	singular
subj.	subject
t.	times
v(v).	verse(s)
vb.	verb

Introduction to the Books of Kings

Overview

The books of 1–2 Samuel and 1–2 Kings give us a history of the kingdom of Israel from its beginnings at the end of the Late Bronze Age until its final disappearance with the destruction of Jerusalem in 586 BC. The LXX reflects this understanding by labeling the four books 1–4 Reigns. That being said, it is clear that originally there were only two books: Samuel and Kings. It is theorized that the LXX translators divided each of the originals into two books because Greek has more letters than Hebrew and a single scroll could not accommodate the entire book in each case. The artificiality of the division is especially marked in the case of Kings, where the account of Ahaziah is begun at the end of 1 Kings but continued and concluded in the first chapter of 2 Kings. Clearly, the compilers of the material intended for the readers to see the plot as a unity from the accession of Solomon, until the report of Jehoiachin's release from prison in Babylon.

When Ulfilas (AD 310–370) completed his translation of the Bible into Gothic, he did not include Samuel and Kings; and it is thought that he omitted them because it might encourage Gothic aggressiveness![1] It must be admitted that there is much in the books which might be construed in that way. When compared to other holy books of the world, these accounts seem to have a remarkably human and warlike tone. Mahatma Gandhi is reported to have told the American missionary E. Stanley Jones that he could not accept the Bible as having a divine origin because it was so full of "stories" rather than philosophical discourses or self-standing divine pronouncements.[2]

Yet it is very plain that the Bible's use of historical narrative as a means of conveying the writers' understanding of God is entirely intentional. The transcendent God could not convey his nature in the recurring cycles of nature, for he is not nature. Rather, the writers tell us that he broke into the unique, non-recurring events of time and space, and there communicated himself and his nature to distinct human beings. That being so, it became

1. P. C. Comfort, *A Commentary on the Manuscripts and Texts of the New Testament* (Grand Rapids: Kregel, 2015), 122.

2. As reported by Dr. David Seamands, missionary to India and associate of Dr. Jones.

absolutely vital for the records of what he had said and done to be recorded faithfully and accurately. His self-revelation is not to be found in collections of generalized propositions at a distance from ordinary life. Rather, he is to be known in his interactions with real people in real-life situations.

When we read the book of Kings, we do not read a religious tractate in which the human characters are one-dimensional figures used merely as foils to facilitate the propagation of a message. These are multi-dimensional persons with their own distinctive qualities and foibles. At the same time the purpose is clearly not merely to tell an engaging story. A very clear religious point is being made, with the central character being Yahweh. But, the great success of the book is that the religious purpose does not swamp the narrative power of the story, while the story never escapes from the service of that purpose.

The purpose is to demonstrate that Israel's destiny as a nation could never be understood apart from their adherence to two covenants with Yahweh: the Sinaitic/Moasic covenant and the Davidic covenant, with primary emphasis on the first. This is the underlying storyline: if the stipulations of the covenant are kept, prosperity and security follow; if they are not kept, loss and ultimately dissolution are inescapable. This point means that the historical record is often not as full as we might like. Some rulers, like Omri and Jeroboam II, who were clearly significant figures from a general historical viewpoint, are glossed over with only a few sentences (1 Kgs 16:21–28; 2 Kgs 14:23–29). This is so, because everything they did during their reigns only added up to a minus in the column of covenant keeping. On the other hand, we hear a great deal about three kings: Solomon, Hezekiah, and Josiah (11, 4, and 2 chapters respectively). We hear a great deal of Solomon because he sets the stage for all that is to follow, both positively and negatively. On the one hand, he illustrates all the positive benefits of covenant keeping and on the other, when he failed to keep the covenant, he sows the seeds not only for the dissolution of his empire and the division of the kingdom, but also for the final dissolution of the nation. In telling Solomon's story, the narrator very deftly interweaves the positive and negative strands with a bare minimum of editorial comment. An attentive reader will recognize the strands without being told where to look for them.[3] Solomon also illustrates the aspects of the Davidic covenant in that he fulfills Yahweh's promise that David will have a descendant on his throne, but also that this promise does not exempt the Davidic monarch from the effects of disobedience.

Hezekiah and Josiah show that even after a depressingly consistent downward pattern of disobedience and punishment, the story need not have

---

3. A good deal of attention has been given to the attempt to separate a wholly positive Solomonic source from a wholly negative one and studying how these must have been combined. I think this approach fails to credit the narrator with an appropriate level of creativity and subtlety. For a discussion see Eric Seibert, *Subversive Scribes and the Solomonic Narrative: A Rereading of 1 Kings 1–11* (London: T&T Clark, 2006).

ended as it did. Hezekiah is the bright light coming after the final destruction of the northern kingdom. After no less than nineteen northern monarchs—not one of whom kept the Sinaitic covenant and all of whom followed the pattern of Jeroboam I and not the pattern of David—Hezekiah's behavior and experience showed that God would still care for his own when they did follow in David's footsteps and kept the terms of the covenant. Likewise, after Judah had been led down the same path as the northern kingdom by Hezekiah's son Manasseh, Josiah, Hezekiah's great-grandson, showed how it should have been and what might have been if the two covenants had been followed.

Besides the three blocks devoted to Solomon, Hezekiah, and Josiah, there is another large block of material that is devoted to a relatively short period of time: 1 Kings 17–2 Kings 13, nineteen chapters covering about seventy years (870–800 BC). In contrast, the next eighty years are covered in only slightly more than three chapters. What accounts for this striking disproportion? The nineteen chapters are dealing with what could have resulted, not in merely disobeying the covenant, but in its actual repudiation and the consequent repudiation of Yahweh himself. There was a genuine possibility during the reign of Ahab of Israel that the Canaanite god, Baal, could have become the god of Israel, and as a result of intermarriage between the house of Ahab and the house of David, the god of Judah as well. That this did not happen was the result of the ministry of the prophets Elijah and Elisha. I use the singular "ministry" advisedly. Although there were two prophets, their ministry was really one, with Elisha bringing to completion what Elijah had set in motion. The result of this prophetic ministry was that the Baal revolution was quashed, and Yahweh remained the God of Israel. Sadly, this did not mean that obedience to the Sinaitic covenant was restored, but it did mean that the revelation contained in the covenant and the related writings was not lost but saved for the future.

The mention of Elijah and Elisha brings forward another topic that must be introduced in this overview: the significance of the prophets in the historical experience of Israel. I have said above that God's speech was central to the biblical revelation. This phenomenon must be underlined. Yahweh, of all the so-called gods of the ancient world, was the speaking God. Many years ago, James Barr in criticizing the "Biblical Theology Movement," which made much of revelatory events in Israel's experience, pointed out that the Bible says much more about God's speech that it does his actions.[4] While God is certainly revealed in the roaring thunderstorm and in the soaring mountains, the central means of his revelation is through speech (cf. Ps 19). Again, this is expressive of his transcendent personhood. He is not seen best in the great recurrences of nature, but in his unique face-to-face communications with

4. James Barr, "Revelation Through History in the Old Testament and in Modern Theology," in *New Theology No. 1*, ed. by Martin E. Marty and Dean G. Peerman (New York: Macmillan, 1964), 60–74.

distinctive persons. No place is this seen more poignantly than in Exodus where he talks with Moses and, in fact, conveys the entire covenant to Moses in speech (see esp. Exod 33:9–11).

Here in Kings, prophets speaking for God are something of a thread running through the book from end to end. We begin with the prophet Nathan who is instrumental in ensuring that Adonijah does not usurp the place which Yahweh had promised to Solomon (1 Kgs 1:11–31; see 2 Sam 12:24–25) and end with Huldah's explanation that the book discovered in the temple was indeed the word of God. In between Nathan and Huldah, an anonymous prophet reveals the coming division of the united kingdom as a result of Solomon's sin (1 Kgs 11:29–39). Likewise, a prophet announces God's judgment on the idolatry introduced by Jeroboam I (1 Kgs 13:2–3), even to the extent of naming the future king Josiah who would destroy Jeroboam's altar. Then the prophet Ahijah himself, who on God's behalf gave the northern tribes to Jeroboam, predicts the destruction of Jeroboam's house (1 Kgs 14:7–16) and even the destruction of the entire northern kingdom (vv. 15–16).

These latter statements illustrate a critical feature of Israelite prophecy. Pagan prophecy is rooted in the concept of determinism. Everything that happens in time is determined by what happens outside of time in the invisible realm. A person's fate can be declared at the time of his or her birth on the basis of the position of the stars on the natal day. Thus, a prophet is either someone who is highly trained and can discern the patterns which indicate the unchangeable future, or someone who is possessed by a god and thus given insight into what is decreed to take place. But in Israel, the future is not determined. This is so because Yahweh is a person, not a force, and he deals with us as persons with all the dynamics that personal relationship involves. Thus, Ahijah's first announcement to Jeroboam was that Yahweh would give him a house as secure as David's (1 Kgs 11:38). But for that to happen required that Jeroboam would keep the covenant as David had done. In short, the future is dependent on human responses to divine initiatives. Because Jeroboam broke the covenant, the future was different than what had been predicted. The same is true in Ahijah's final message when he said that Israel would be destroyed. Was that a predetermined fact that would happen regardless of human choices, or alternatively, would there be no real choices because of that predetermination? The answer to both questions is "No." Israel did not have to fall. If Jeroboam's successors had followed in David's footsteps instead of Jeroboam's, history would have been different: Israel would not have fallen.

This is why historiography has been almost exclusively a practice in the Western world that has been shaped by the Bible. If one concludes that humans have no real choices, then an analysis of those choices, the reasons for them, and the results of them make no sense at all. This is true whether one believes the gods make the determinations or one's heredity and environment do. If real choices and the accountability for those choices are not possible, history writing will not exist.[5] For these reasons I suggest that it is the prophets who are responsible for history-writing in Israel. This topic will be discussed in more detail below.

The prophetic story continues with a man named Jehu who spoke judgment on Baasha (1 Kgs 16:2–4). Then, after the Elijah/Elisha block of material, the prophet Jonah appears in 2 Kgs 14:25 with a word of hope, namely that Yahweh "had not said he would blot out the name of Israel from under heaven" (v. 27). Here one has the impression that even the partial obedience to Yahweh that Jehu had offered was still bearing fruit in the reign of Jeroboam II, Jehu's great-grandson.[6]

Somewhat surprisingly there is no mention of prophets during the northern kingdom's final spasms after the assassination of Jeroboam's son Zechariah (2 Kgs 15:8–11). This period would have been during the ministries of Amos and Hosea. With the exception of Isaiah (2 Kgs 19:2), and Jonah (2 Kgs 14:25) the narrator makes no mention of any of the writing prophets. Perhaps this omission was because they did not fit in with his intent to work with historical sources.

The function of the prophets is underlined in the summary of Israel's sins found in 2 Kgs 17:7–23. Their task had been to warn the people of the consequences of choosing to break Yahweh's commandments and to call them to turn around (repent) and start keeping those commands. The clear implication is that despite the long history of disobedience, if at any moment there had been a genuine long-lasting turning back to Yahweh and to his covenant, the threatened end would not have come. But that was not to be, and the prediction of Ahijah to Jeroboam I's wife was finally fulfilled.

As mentioned above, the only "writing prophet" referred to in the book is Isaiah (apart from the passing reference to Jonah in 2 Kgs 14:25). Isaiah appears in context with Hezekiah. The narrative about Hezekiah and Isaiah is almost a duplicate of that which appears in Isa 36–39, prompting almost all commentators to hold that the Kings version is the original which was

---

5. The great Greek historians, Thucydides and Herodotus, were under the influence of the Greek philosophers who were struggling against determinism. But when that influence waned following the death of Aristotle, historical writing went into a steep decline. See R. G. Collingwood, *The Idea of History* (Oxford: Oxford University Press, 1946), 15–45; W. G. Hardy, *Origins and Ideals of the Western World: Lessons from our Heritage in History* (Cambridge, MA: Shenkman Publishing, 1968), 202–4, 240–44.

6. This blessing would fit perfectly with the picture of Yahweh given elsewhere in the Bible. "His anger is for but a moment, his favor is for a lifetime" (Ps 30:5 [Heb. 6]). The smallest effort in obedience will bear fruit far out of proportion; this is the character of Yahweh.

later incorporated into the book bearing Isaiah's name.[7] Be that as it may, the point is unmistakable: trust in and obedience to God—as a result of listening to his revealed words—will bring deliverance and blessing.

But whatever changes in Judah's attitudes and behavior may have taken place during Hezekiah's reign, they were clearly not of a permanent nature because when Hezekiah's son Manasseh reversed everything his father had done, there was no national protest. Once again, however, the protest came from the prophets (2 Kgs 21:10–15). There is a solemn note in these words; they lack any conditionality at all. "Because Manasseh ... has made Judah to sin with his idols ... I will forsake the remnant of my special possession ... ." This is the same note that appears in the final prophetic announcement found in the book, that of Huldah. There is no hope for the nation; "... my anger will be kindled against this place, and it will not be quenched" (2 Kgs 22:17). But true to the gracious and compassionate nature of Yahweh, the penitence of Josiah was enough to deliver him from seeing the destruction of his nation. This was not in response to his later attempts to cleanse the nation from its sins, but simply because of his anguish when he heard the words of Moses recorded in the book of Torah that was read before him. The Yahweh of the book of Kings is not an implacable tyrant who is determined to have his way no matter what the circumstances. He is willing to forgive anyone, anywhere, anytime, if they will truly turn around.[8]

Textual Attestation

The Hebrew text of Kings that appears in the MT is well preserved. This is the text that was standardized by scribes working in Galilee during the second half of the first millennium AD and now preserved in the Leningrad Codex dated to AD 1008. Leningrad is believed to be the work of the ben Naptali family, whereas the Aleppo Codex, dated about AD 925 is believed to be the work of the ben Asher family. The Aleppo Codex, damaged in the fire that destroyed the Aleppo synagogue in 1948, is reputed to have some slightly better readings than Leningrad, but it is not readily available.[9]

---

7. I do not agree with this conclusion. Rather, I believe that the material first appeared in Isaiah and was copied into Kings with some additions and deletions. To label Isa 36–39 a "historical appendix," as many do, is to fundamentally misunderstand the structure of Isa 7–39. For the argument see the commentary below.
8. This point of view is contested by some commentators (e.g., Brueggemann, 559–60) who note that Judah was sent into exile because of the sins of Manasseh. See the discussion below under Themes: The Kingship of Yahweh.
9. Emanuel Tov, *Textual Criticism of the Hebrew Bible*, 2nd rev. ed. (Minneapolis: Fortress, 2001), 46–7.

About twenty-eight identifiable fragments of Kings manuscripts have been discovered at Qumran, but most are so small and contain so little text that it is very difficult to use them for text critical purposes.[10]

While the Greek translation known as the Septuagint (LXX) was probably completed in Alexandria, Egypt by 125 BC, no copies from that time are extant. The two primary texts which contain the Greek translation of Kings are Vaticanus (first part of the fourth century AD) and Alexandrinus (fifth century AD). The text of Kings is mixed, with 1 Kgs 2:12–21:29 appearing in the so-called Old Greek (OG, which supposedly closely reflects the original) and 1 Kgs 22:1–2 Kgs 25:30 in the so-called *kai ge* text, possibly related to the recension of Theodotion.[11, 12]

The LXX translation of Kings, unlike those of the Torah and some of the Prophets, exhibits a relatively large number of variations from the MT. There are several examples of verses or even whole paragraphs being transposed. There are also several passages that do not appear in the MT at all. Besides these, there are a significant number of verbal differences. John Gray (45) opines that the Hebrew text must have been "fairly fluid" when the Greek translation was made. This reflects the opinion of many scholars today that when the Greek differs from the MT it is not because of the translators' choices, but because the Hebrew text they were translating was different. This opinion seems to be supported by evidence from Qumran.[13]

---

10. *Discoveries in the Judean Desert, III* (Oxford: Oxford University Press, 1962), 172.

11. Several recensions are known to have been produced in the early Christian centuries, all of which to one degree or another sought to bring the Greek text more in line with the Hebrew text. Theodotion was one of these. Unfortunately, we do not have complete copies of any of them. For a discussion see James D. Shenkel, *Chronology and Recensional Development in the Greek Text of Kings*, HSM 1 (Cambridge, MA: Harvard University Press, 1968), and M. Christine Tetley, *The Reconstructed Chronology of the Divided Kingdom* (Winona Lake, IN: Eisenbrauns, 2005), 14–29. The kaige text type is identified in this way because *kai ge* is its customary way of rendering the Heb. וְגַם (*wᵉgam*).

12. The history of the LXX is extremely complex and has been made so by one of the great scholarly works of antiquity. This was Origen's Hexapla (AD 230–240), a six-columned copy of the OT, sparked by the discrepancies between the LXX, the Bible of the Christians, and the Hebrew Bible used by the Jews. It included the recensions of Aquila, Symmachus, Theodotion, the Hebrew text, the LXX, and a Greek text corrected to the Hebrew. There were probably only six copies of the original, and all have been lost. Unfortunately, the corrected Greek text was widely copied, and we do not know today how much of the present LXX actually reflects the corrected text. See Melvin K. H. Peters, "Septuagint," in *ABD*, 5:1093–1104.

13. But Marvin Sweeney says, rightly I think, that many of "the differences represent an interpretation of the underlying Hebrew or stylistic modifications intended to produce an aesthetically pleasing Greek rendition of the text," 37.

That being so, there is general agreement that in almost all cases the MT reflects the better text. Wiseman (59) citing extensively D. W. Gooding, a Greek scholar, holds the LXX to represent a text that is derivative from the MT, and inferior to it.[14]

Not all agree, however, one of those being Shenkel, who argues that some readings are superior to MT.[15] But these superior readings are very few.[16] One of the evidences of this is the number of times the Vulgate and the Syriac versions agree with MT against LXX, which must be more than ninety percent of the time. This is somewhat surprising for the Vulgate and very surprising for the Syriac. When Jerome moved to Palestine to complete his revision of the Old Latin, which had been essentially a translation of the LXX, it seems apparent that the MT was already emerging as the standard Hebrew text. Jerome clearly had access to this Hebrew text. Thus, while Jerome's Vulgate usually follows LXX, reflecting his Old Latin *Vorlage,* it will from time to time agree with the MT. But to find it almost always going against the LXX, as it does here in Kings, is unusual, to say the least. Even more surprising is the almost total agreement of the Syriac with MT. This is so because it is generally agreed that the Syriac Peshitta is a translation from the Greek text.

What we should make of these facts is a matter of some dispute. Is it possible that the Vulgate as well as the Peshitta are dependent upon an LXX recension like Aquila that had been brought into line with the proto-MT? Or is the present text of Vaticanus a corruption of an earlier LXX? While both of these are conjectures, the fact is that the ancient versions are solidly in support of the MT.[17]

Authorship and Composition

Ideally it would be best to separate the topics of authorship and composition but in the case of Kings that is not a possibility. The reason for this is that the text does not identify the author and therefore one's decisions about composition necessarily affect any opinions at which one might arrive as regards authorship.

The first recorded opinion on this subject is that of Jerome, the translator of the Latin Vulgate (ca. 385 BC). He, noting the great similarities between the end of Kings and the end of Jeremiah, suggested that Jeremiah

14. D. W. Gooding, *Relics of Ancient Exegesis: A Study of the Miscellanies in 3 Reigns 2*, SOTSM 2 (Cambridge: Cambridge University Press, 1976).

15. Shenkel, *Chronology and Recensional Development in the Greek Text of Kings*, 110.

16. Note how relatively rarely *CTAT* chooses an LXX reading over the MT.

17. In order to make this clear to the reader, the textual notes (in the digital version) will call attention to the Vulgate and Syriac support for the MT. This will become very repetitive, but it is data that should not be overlooked.

had been responsible for the final edition of the book. That opinion was shared in the middle ages by Ravanel, the Jewish scholar.[18] With the rise of the Documentary Hypothesis concerning the authorship of the Pentateuch, with its supposed four documents: J, E, D, and P, there were various attempts in the late nineteenth and early twentieth centuries to apply the same approach to the so-called Historical Books: Joshua through Kings.[19] That is, there was a search conducted for written sources lying behind the present text which had been disassembled and reassembled to result in the present text. By and large, these attempts did not succeed, none of the suggestions gaining anything like the acceptance given to the JEDP theory in the early twentieth century. Thus, as the twentieth century progressed there were a variety of positions regarding the authorship and composition of these books.

All this changed in 1943 with the publication of Martin Noth's *Uberlieferungsgeschichtliche Studien*[20] in which he proposed that a single person writing during the exile composed a single work comprised of Deuteronomy, Joshua, Judges, Samuel, and Kings. Using the lawbook constructed by seventh century prophets and "discovered" in 621 BC when the temple was being renovated at the mandate of Josiah as a backbone, this single person (hypothesized by Noth) incorporated and reworked older traditions around the "Deuteronomic" philosophy of history with a particular goal of showing how it was that the chosen people of the Exodus became the outcasts of the Assyrian and Babylonian exile. Thus, Noth believed that the final composition took a profoundly negative view of both the Israelite and Judean kings, holding them to be responsible for the tragic result.

This proposal found a great deal of support, partly in view of its correct recognition that all four of the books: Joshua, Judges, Samuel, and Kings, do indeed reflect the "Deuteronomic" outlook. As mentioned above, that outlook involves the following idea: when the nation obeyed the terms of its covenant with Yahweh—exclusive worship of Yahweh, denial of all forms of idolatry, and treating one another according to the ethical standards called for in the covenant—the nation would be blessed. On the other hand, if those terms were disobeyed, the nation would be cursed.

The idea that the five books, starting with Deuteronomy and ending with Kings, form a single composition (often referred to as "The Deuteronomic History" [DtrH]) found almost immediate acceptance among scholars. However, how it arrived in that form has not gained the same unanimity. The first to raise a question was Frank Cross who, noting that the tone of the composition is not wholly negative toward kingship, especially Davidic kingship, proposed that there were two recensions of the composition, the

18. b. Baba Batra 15a.

19. For a summary, see R. K. Harrison, *Introduction to the Old Testament* (Grand Rapids: Eerdmans, 1969) 302–307.

20. 2nd ed. (Tübingen: Mohr, 1957). An English translation of pp. 1–110 appeared as *The Deuteronomistic History*, JSOTSup 15 (Sheffield: JSOT Press, 1981).

first of which appeared during or just after the reign of Josiah. This recension would have argued that in Josiah the Davidic dynasty had returned to its roots in David and in his single-hearted loyalty to Yahweh and his covenant, and that there was hope for the future.[21] Then, when those hopes were dashed through Josiah's sons, and the unthinkable, exile from the land, occurred, the exilic writer recast the text, giving it the more pessimistic tone that it now ostensibly has. Thus, there now two authors, or an author and an editor.

But Cross's observations opened a floodgate, and in the years since 1973, a plethora of proposals have been put forward.[22] Included among these are a three-recension model. In this view, the first complete composition occurred during the time of Hezekiah, when the northern kingdom had fallen and the country was in some sense "reunited" again under the rule of the good Davidide Hezekiah. Furthermore, for the first time since Solomon, the temple was the only officially sanctioned place of worship as Deuteronomy had specified. So, the composition would have seen the story coming right again, with the future a hopeful one.[23] In particular, the book of Kings would have seen the story coming right, with Hezekiah being the true son of David, that Solomon had proven not to be.[24] Of course, the story would not have ended with Isaiah's grim prediction that Hezekiah's progeny would be eunuchs in the court of Babylon (2 Kgs 20:18). On this understanding such a comment would have only appeared in the exilic edition.

But did the composition only begin to take form in or after the time of Hezekiah? Others, of whom André Lemaire is one, have argued that it did not. He has proposed something of a "rolling recension" growing out of a collection of sources, many of them administrative, possibly reaching as far back as Saul. As these were compiled and copied, he suggests, there were possibly documents of a more synthetic, historiographic nature included. He sees the formation of what he calls "the Nimshide apology" [the account of how the dynasty of Jehu ben-Nimshi replaced the Omride dynasty] as playing

---

21. Frank Moore Cross, "The Themes of the Books of Kings and the Structure of the Deuteronomistic History," in *Canaanite Myth and Hebrew Epic: Essays in the History of the Religion of Israel* (Cambridge: Harvard University Press, 1973), 274–89.
22. For a handy summary see Gary N. Knoppers, "Theories of the Redaction(s) of Kings," in *The Books of Kings: Sources, Composition, Historiography and Reception*, ed. Baruch Halpern and André Lemaire (Leiden: Brill, 2010), 69–88.
23. On this understanding, the views that were eventually to be stated explicitly in the book of Deuteronomy were already beginning to be formed.
24. For a brief statement of this thesis, see Iain W. Provan, *Hezekiah and the Books of Kings: A Contribution to the Debate about the Composition of the Deuteronomic History*, BZAW 172 (Berlin: Walter L. DeGruyter, 1988). Benjamin D. Thomas, *Hezekiah and the Compositional History of the Book of Kings*, FAT/II 63 (Tübingen: Mohr Siebeck, 2014) has a much fuller treatment. For a contrary opinion, see Nadav Na'aman, "Was an Early Edition of the Book of Kings Composed during Hezekiah's Reign?" *JSOT* 31, no. 1 (2017): 80–91.

a significant part in the formation and the shaping of the whole.[25] Marvin Sweeney (15–32) seems to agree in general with Lemaire's view as he speaks of the Josianic edition, the Hezekian edition, the Jehu history, and the Davidic-Solomonic history. However, he seems to go beyond Lemaire in seeing more conscious historiographic analysis in the later two than Lemaire does.[26]

A recent entry into the crowded field is that of Brian Petersen, who presents a detailed argument that it was the priests of Anathoth, beginning with Abiathar (the confidant of David) and concluding with Jeremiah, who are responsible for the writing of the Deuteronomic History.[27] He believes that Abiathar was responsible for the core of the present Deut 1 through 1 Kgs 2, that his descendants at Anathoth maintained the running account now found in the remainder of Kings, and that the final editor was the prophet/priest Jeremiah from Anathoth, with the likely help of his scribe, Baruch.

Peterson rightly tackles one of the central issues in the entire discussion: the date of the book of Deuteronomy, correctly labeling it the "linchpin" in the DtrH discussion.[28] If the scholarly consensus that Deuteronomy only came into existence as a book shortly before its "discovery" in the temple in 621 BC is right, then none of the four books of Joshua–Kings could have existed in their present form before that date. They could not because, as noted above, the Deuteronomic philosophy of history runs through all of them. But this creates great problems. Are we to think that the books existed in some form before 621? If so, what would that form have been without the Deuteronomic story line shaping them? On the other hand, if we are to think that the books were only loose collections of traditions which have been given their present shapes by Deuteronomic editors/authors writing between 609 and 560, why are they so different from each other? Should they not display much more uniformity in style and structure? For the fact is that the books differ from each other rather markedly. The style of Joshua is rather formal and pedantic, whereas Judges is much more colorful and racy. At the same time Judges is marked by a more formal structure with its repetition of what may be called the "Judges cycle" standing between the introductory and

25. André Lemaire, "Towards a Redactional History of the Book of Kings," in *Reconsidering Israel and Judah: Recent Studies on the Deuteronomic History*, ed. Gary N. Knoppers and J. Gordon McConville, SBTS 8 (Winona Lake, IN: Eisenbrauns, 2000), 446–61. See also Baruch Halpern and André Lemaire, "The Composition of Kings" in *The Book of Kings: Sources, Composition, Historiography and Reception*, ed. by Baruch Halpern and André Lemaire (Leiden: Brill, 2010), 123–53.

26. See also Marvin A. Sweeney, *King Josiah of Judah: The Lost Messiah of Israel* (Oxford: Oxford University Press, 2001).

27. Brian Neil Peterson, *The Authors of the Deuteronomic History: Locating a Tradition in Ancient Israel* (Minneapolis: Fortress Press, 2014).

28. Peterson, *The Authors of the Deuteronomic History*, 61–74, 121–32. He finds no reason to doubt "that Moses played a major role in contributing to the 'proto' form of the book of Deuteronomy" (132).

concluding chapters. Again, when Samuel and Kings are compared, we find the narrative style of Samuel continuing through 1 Kgs 2, but from 1 Kgs 3 onward, a considerably dryer, more formal style begins to prevail. In short, each of the four books exhibits its own structure and style, different from the others, but all displaying the same central theme: obedience to the God of the covenant equals success, while disobedience to him equals disaster.

The issue then becomes whether the Deuteronomic theme was imposed on already-existing books that lacked the theme, thus creating a somewhat unified corpus, or whether these four books all grew up semi-independently, having somewhat differing purposes, but all sharing almost unconsciously the same philosophy of history, the one first articulated by Moses in his final declarations to his people. With Peterson, I suggest that this latter alternative better fits the data than does the former. Have they finally been collected together and edited to tell the story of Israel from the point of its entering the promised land until its forcible expulsion from the land? Certainly. However, a study of the attempts to determine what was original and what is the work of editors does not encourage one to believe that any unanimity has been reached, or perhaps, even can be reached. This means that attempts to interpret the books on the basis of certain hypothetical sources which have been extracted from the whole by scholarly skill must necessarily be idiosyncratic at best. If we are to gain an understanding of the message which the authors/editors intended, it must be by interpreting the books as they now exist, and in the larger canonical context in which they now exist.

If we conclude with Peterson that the books of Deuteronomy, Joshua, Judges, and Samuel were in existence largely in their present form by the time of David's death—who was responsible for them, and what impulse led to their creation and editing? Our answer to that question will then have a direct bearing on the authorship and composition of Kings. Clearly, Kings was not complete until 562–560 BC.[29] But its inclusion as part of the four-book series and its very explicit focus on the Deuteronomic theme argues that the impetus that brought the previous books into existence was continuing in Kings.

The inclusion of the four books in the Neviim, or "Prophets" section of the Hebrew canon has a direct bearing on our question. To those reared on the English Bible, whose canonical divisions follow those of the LXX, it seems very strange that these "Historical Books" should be included in a section with Isaiah, Jeremiah, Ezekiel, and The Twelve (the Minor Prophets). But in fact, that inclusion is very instructive. It tells us that for the Israelites their historical experience from their entry into the land until their expulsion from it was inextricable from the life and work of the prophets; persons who

29. Awil-Marduk (who released Jehoiachin) only reigned for two years before being killed in a coup d'etat. The fact that the book mentions nothing about subsequent monarchs of Babylon makes it reasonable to think that the writing ended with his reign.

told them what Yahweh, whose name means I AM, who had given them the covenant, had to say to them.[30] So, from Moses' Song in Deut 32 to the ominous words of Huldah in 2 Kgs 22, it was that call from Beyond to live according to his plan that shaped Israel's understanding of itself. Here, I believe, is the impetus for writing the history of Israel's nation. The prophets point to an open future, one that will be shaped by the nation's response to Transcendent Reality as carried out in the most mundane of daily choices. The future is not determined, nor is it merely the expression in different form of what has happened before and will happen again. No, there is progression or retrogression, but never merely repetition. So, if Yahweh is to be known in his interaction with humans in their historical experience, it becomes vital to record that experience, *and to evaluate it* according to the standard given by Yahweh. Here is where one moves from chronicling to writing history. In chronicling, one records what happened as a series of discrete events without much, if any, attempt to see how those events might be related. Historical writing takes the long view, seeking to understand relationships, and looking for implications.

Joshua was in a unique position to see the long view. Over some four generations he had the opportunity to see the relationship between choices and outcomes in the context of a single standard of evaluation: obedience to a coherent set of expectations. He had lived through the plagues, the exodus, Kadesh-Barnea, the wilderness, and the occupation of the land. Moreover, he knew the voice of God; he was a prophet (Josh 13:1). Who better then to begin this great interpretation of the Israelite experience?

This suggestion that it was the prophets who wrote Israel's history gains explicit support from 1 and 2 Chronicles where we are told that the events of the lives of David, Solomon, Rehoboam, and Abijah were recorded in the writings of the prophets Samuel, Nathan, Gad, Ahijah, Shemaiah, and Iddo (1 Chr 29:29; 2 Chr 9:29; 12:19; 13:22). Whereas court recorders and secretaries could keep day-books and chronicles, they were not positioned to analyze and synthesize the data from an outside, even transcendent, point of view. The prophets were so positioned. While it is tempting to assign the book of Judges to a well-known person like Samuel, it is just as likely, and perhaps more so, that some prophet, or group of prophets that are unknown to us (as Iddo is otherwise) could have begun to record the all-too-predictable effects of Israel's vacillating obedience to Yahweh. It is likely that Samuel himself did begin the history that is recorded in the book(s) carrying his name, and that some other(s) (Nathan?) carried it out to its conclusion.[31]

---

30. Wiseman's comment is very apropos: "Prophecy is a history-creating force" (23).

31. While I am grateful to Peterson for his work in demonstrating the likelihood that the books of Deuteronomy, Joshua, Judges, and Samuel were substantially complete by the death of David, it does not seem likely to me that Abiathar and his fellow priests at Anathoth were the chief editors/authors of the collection. I take this position for two reasons. The first is the one stated above, namely, that the

When we come to Kings itself, there are two questions that present themselves: (1) what is the relation of Samuel and Kings, and (2) when was the book written? On the first question, the absence of any clear introduction is a major issue, as is the stylistic similarity of 1 Kgs 1 and 2 to 2 Sam 9–21 and 24. This latter point led Leonhard Rost to propose that there was once a document which he called "The Succession Narrative" that has now been incorporated into the two books with a later summary of David's reign and a statement about the origin of the temple location, 2 Sam 21–24, inserted into it at a later date.[32] While Rost's proposal has gained a wide measure of acceptance, it has also generated a good deal of debate.[33] This is not the place to go into a detailed analysis of the proposal, except to say that those who question whether 1 Kgs 1 and 2 are really a part of the narrative (such as Sweeney[7]) seem to me to have a good case. It might be better to say that 2 Sam 11–20 deals with the effects of David's sin with Bathsheba rather than with the succession. To be sure, those effects had a direct bearing on the succession, but we may question whether the account is first of all about the succession or not.

This raises a question about the style of chapters 1 and 2 of 1 Kings. Many years ago, Cyrus Gordon made the trenchant observation that there is such a thing as "heroic style." This style is colorful and direct, focuses on individual achievements, characteristics, and foibles, and praises craftiness and insight more than brute force, etc.[34] He further observed that in the eastern Mediterranean, it seems to have been characteristic of the Late Bronze Age,

---

prophets are those most likely to be interested in keeping such a record, precisely because of their prophetic utterances and the question as to how those utterances would be responded to or not, and what the outcomes of those responses were. My second reason for doubting the suggestion is that the priesthood in general in the OT is not depicted as including those who are the most likely to be sensitive to what God is doing in history. In fact, they are often indicted for leading their people into false worship (Exod 32: 2–4;1 Sam 2:27–29; Zech 7:4–6; Mal 1:6–8). It appears that they loved religion, but not necessarily Yahweh. This is not intended as a blanket indictment of all the priests. Clearly there were those like Phineas (Num 25:10–14) and Jehoiada (2 Kgs 12:2) who loved and served Yahweh, but as a class they seem to me more interested in worship than in the One being worshipped.

32. Leonhard Rost, *The Succession to the Throne of David*, trans. Michael C. Rutter and David Gunn (Sheffield: Almond Press, 1982).

33. The following is a brief selection: R. N. Whybray, *The Succession Narrative: A Study of II Samuel 9–20, I Kings 1 & 2* (Napierville, IL: A. R. Allenson, 1968); Serge Frolov, "Succession Narrative: A 'Document' or 'A Phantom,'" *JBL* 121 (2002): 81–104; Joseph Blenkinsopp, "Another Contribution to the Succession Narrative Debate (2 Samuel 11–20, 1 Kings 1–2)," *JSOT* 38 (2013): 35–58; John Van Seters, "A Revival of the Succession Narrative and the Case Against It," *JSOT* 39 (2014): 3–14.

34. Cyrus Herzl Gordon, *Before the Bible: The Common Backgrounds of Greek and Hebrew Civilization* (New York: Harper & Row, 1962).

and disappeared rather suddenly with the coming of the Iron Age. This is the style of Judges, much of 1 and 2 Samuel, and of 1 Kgs 1 and 2. This leads me to suggest that the similarity of 1 Kgs 1 and 2 to 2 Sam 9–24, excepting chaps. 21 and 22,[35] is not so much due to *source* as to authorial *style*. This is not necessarily to suggest a single author of Judges–1 Kgs 2, but it is to suggest that those who wrote this material did indeed write during the Late Bronze Age and had similar stylistic predilections.

If that is true, why the change in style in 1 Kgs 3 and forward? If my suggestion is correct that Nathan the prophet was responsible for the continuation of the book of Samuel after Samuel's death (and by extension, 1 Kgs 1 and 2), then it would follow that someone else steps in for 1 Kgs 3 and following. Interestingly, there is still a bit of heroic flavor in chap. 3, but it disappears in chap. 4, never to return in the same way again. Perhaps, it is Ahijah, named in 2 Chr 9:29, who becomes the narrator at this point. And perhaps it is from him that the negative comments about Solomon come.

We cannot leave this topic without addressing the issue as to whether Samuel and Kings were originally thought to be one book (something the LXX points to with its labelling them together as "The Book of Reigns" in four parts). Iain Provan argues for this, claiming that Kings lacks an introduction.[36] However, B. D. Thomas, arguing as does Provan for a Hezekian recension, presents a strong argument against the two books having been written as one.[37] He makes two valid points. First, he points out that the two books are different both in structure and style, and second, he argues that the uses of chronology and moral judgment are different in Samuel and Kings.[38] While his arguments on the latter point are highly technical and I do not agree with all of them, his point that Samuel is more interested in the Davidic covenant than in the Mosaic one is important. When all is said and done, I would argue that just as Genesis and Exodus are meant to be read together without considering them a single book, so Samuel and Kings are meant to be read together. Just as Genesis provides critical information that Exodus assumes, so does Kings assume Samuel. Similarly, just as Genesis starts a story that is incomplete and begs for continuation, so does Samuel. This is a vital point for our interpretation of the book of Kings. How does Kings continue the Samuel story, and how does the story as begun in Samuel affect our reading of Kings? Kings continues the story of kingship in Israel as begun in Samuel, and what the two books tell us is that Yahweh is the king of Israel. They tell us that Yahweh's purposes, his good purposes, are not going to fail. Saul failed, David failed, Solomon failed, and every king of Israel failed (because its first king, Jeroboam, poisoned the well at the outset,

35. Note that chaps. 9 and 10, and 21 and 24, which generally are not included in the Succession Narrative, still share the heroic style.

36. Provan, *Hezekiah and the Books of Kings*, 162–63.

37. Thomas, *Hezekiah and the Compositional History of the Book of Kings*, 208–28.

38. Thomas, *Hezekiah and the Compositional History of the Book of Kings*, 227–28.

and no one following him had the courage to cleanse it). In Judah there were some good kings, but every one of them failed as well. Asa failed, Jehoshaphat failed, Hezekiah failed, and Josiah failed, the very best that Judah had to offer failed, but Yahweh does not fail! How can we say that given the grim story that unfolds in Kings? It is because of the way Samuel tells us how to read that story. In Samuel one disaster after another unfolds, from the failure of the Elide priesthood all the way to David's arrogant census. Yet in every instance, Yahweh is able to bring good out of what seems hopeless. When the two books are read together, we come to Kings' suggestive conclusion ready to say, "So how is Yahweh going to redeem this one?"[39]

By this point it should have become clear that I do not believe with House (38–39), or Wiseman (53–54), or for that matter, Noth,[40] that there is a single author of Kings. It seems highly likely that there was a final editor who compiled earlier work and inserted comments where necessary to give the work its final form, but he (or she) was only bringing to a conclusion a process that had been going on for some 500 years. The recovery of the Torah scroll in 621 BC might well have prompted Jeremiah to clarify and highlight earlier points, but it would not have involved creating speeches for the characters that they did not speak. However, it does seem unlikely to me that the *very* final editor was Jeremiah. The problem with Jeremiah as the final editor is the *terminus ad quem* of 560 in light of the comment about Jehoiachin in 2 Kgs 25:27–30 (and Jer 52:31–34). If Jeremiah was forcibly taken to Egypt in 585 as Jer 43 tells us was the case, it does not seem to me that he would have been in a position to hear that news and incorporate it into the final form of the book. On the other hand, perhaps Jeremiah had done most of the work, and Baruch, who might have taken the proto-MT version of Jeremiah with him to exile in Babylon would have been in position to add the final material to both Kings and Jeremiah.[41]

There are two primary reasons why I cannot accept the proposal for a single author. The first is that it requires a feat of research at a time when such research would have been impossible. If we tentatively accept that such an author was working in Mizpah, the new provincial capital after Jerusalem's destruction, where could the author have gone to consult primary sources? Samaria had been gone for 140 years. Even if we hypothesize that some of the Israelite records had survived the Assyrian destruction and reached Jerusalem, a tenuous hypothesis, what happened to them during two successive sieges

39. A. Graeme Auld, *Life in Kings: Reshaping the Royal Story in the Hebrew Bible* (Atlanta: Scholars Press, 2017) has argued that there was once a historical narrative he calls "The Book of Two Houses," which dealt with the story of the houses of David and Yahweh, with remnants of it to be found in the overlapping accounts found in Samuel, Kings, Chronicles, and Isaiah.

40. See the earlier discussion of Noth's views above.

41. Richard Friedman, *Who Wrote the Bible?*, 2nd ed. (New York: HarperSanFrancisco, 1997), 147–49 argues for the authorship of Baruch.

and the subsequent destruction of Jerusalem by Babylon? What is the point of the references to the chronicles of both Israel and Judah when those chronicles have almost certainly been given to the fire? Why refer to them at all when they were no longer available? The presence of the references to the state archives with the clear implication that more information is available to the interested reader is either disingenuous or it was factually true at the time of the writing. The disappearance of these references from the time of Josiah onward tells us that these records were not available at the time when the material was written, namely between 609 and 586 BC, but that they had been available when the previous notices were written.

The unique reference to "The Book of the Acts of Solomon" (1 Kgs 11:41) suggests to me that this is a prophetic work that is not merely a chronicle but an account in which choices and relationships are analyzed in the light of Yahweh's words. This would have given impetus to what became an ongoing process of recording the history of Israel/Judah. Now that these "acts" were being incorporated into this prophetic work and were no longer separate documents, the court chronicles became the sources for extra information (1 Kgs 14:19, 29).

The second reason I doubt single authorship is found in the previous statements. The clear implication of the material is that the Deuteronomic standard had been in place from the outset of the process, from Joshua onward, but was brought into special prominence by the reign of Solomon (cf. Deut 17:16–17 and 1 Kgs 10:23–11:6), and thus, it became the standard whereby every successive king was judged. If this was not the case, if the standard was a new idea imposed on the data by the author after 621 BC, why had the data been preserved at all up to that point? Rather, this data had been preserved through the centuries by court prophets who were very different from the typical court prophets of the day. Far from working to discern the omens that would guarantee the king's success, these persons were seeking to help the king conform to the character and will of Yahweh so that the king would indeed succeed. With that purpose in mind, it would have made a great deal of sense to record what Yahweh had said both at the moment, and previously, and to evaluate the kings' response to his word and what the outcome had been. While the covenant terms of Exod 20–23 could have given some impetus to that effort (particularly, as noted above, the first two commandments) it is Deuteronomy's particular emphasis upon the singularity of Yahweh as compared to the idol-gods and the impact of conformity with that truth on continued residence in the land that would have made the study of the kings' behavior most poignant.

To sum up, I would argue that the book(s) of Kings was composed over a 400-year period with a single prophetic perspective giving it coherence. It is conceivable that parallel work was done in Israel and Judah by prophets who shared the same kind of motivation. It is also conceivable that the initial synchronism, utilizing court records, may have begun in the northern kingdom and was then incorporated in the southern accounts, perhaps as late as the time of Hezekiah.[42] It is also possible that 1 Kgs 17–2 Kgs 10:27, the narratives of Elijah and Elisha through the Jehu revolution, may have existed as a separate document that was incorporated into the synchronistic report. It does seem likely to me that there was a major edition of the work in the time of Hezekiah, bringing together the work that had been carried on in the two kingdoms. But exactly what the written forms were before that time and what shaping occurred in that editing process seems to me well beyond the capacity of any modern efforts to reconstruct. The lack of unanimity among the several proposed reconstructions supports that opinion. It is not so clear to me that there would have been a full-scale Josianic edition. As mentioned above, there may have been some sharpening in view of the recovery of the Torah, but if my supposition that the main lines of Deuteronomic thought had been in the narrators' minds all along is correct, the kind of substantial reworking that those who think Deuteronomy was only written in the time of Josiah would require would, in fact, not be required.

Setting

Political

When David had succeeded Saul, about 1000 BC, the Levantine coast of the Mediterranean was coming to the end of the upheavals that had attended the coming of the migrating groups whom the Egyptians had labeled "The Sea People." The origins of these groups are unknown, although they were all from the west. They first appear on the northeast Mediterranean coast where they appear to be responsible for the destruction of the city of Ugarit in the late fourteenth century BC. Shortly thereafter their presence is recorded in Asia Minor where they ultimately bring down the Hittite Empire. Finally, they appear in the Egyptian delta about 1200 BC. The Egyptians were able to repulse them, but with the last gasp of that great cultural energy that had made Egypt the envy of all it neighbors for 2,000 years. The repulsed migrants rebounded to the southeastern coast of the Mediterranean where they established the Philistine cities.[43] At the same time all of this was happening the Kassite Empire which had controlled Mesopotamia for nearly

---

42. It has long been noted that the accession notices of the northern kings differ from those of the southern kings, particularly in the fact that the mothers of the southern kings are listed in the notice, while no such information is given for the northern kings. Exactly what this says about the process is uncertain, but at the minimum it points to a difference in the sources, and the care with which the source information was handled.

43. The Hebrew term from which the English "Philistine" is derived is פְּלֶשֶׁת (*pᵉlešeṯ*) which appears to be a transliteration of the Egyptian *pršt* (*r* and *l* interchanged), which is translated "sea people."

400 years was going into decline for reasons that are not clear.[44] The upshot of all this was that the balance of power that had existed in the 1300s BC among Egypt, the Hittites, and the Kassites was replaced by complete chaos in which warlords had free rein, consistent with the picture we see in the book of Judges, and one that probably underlies the book of Joshua as well.

In that context, any group that could get itself organized into an effective force had an opportunity to become a power in the region. That is what we see in the book of Samuel. People who were weary of warlords were ready for kingship, for someone who could not only exercise enough power to protect his people from brigands but could energize his people in such a way to project power outward. Saul had an opportunity in that direction, but ultimately fell prey to his own inner demons. David is portrayed as such a person, a person who could attract great loyalty to himself, who could unite the two Israelite factions— all Israel and Judah"[45]— and could galvanize his men into an effective fighting force.

Thus, when Solomon comes to the throne in 1 Kings 1, Israel is the dominant force in the southern Levant. Israel is in a position to control the trade routes of Egypt and South Arabia on the one hand, and Syria and northern Mesopotamia on the other, with no effective opposition. Thus, the riches attributed to Solomon are not at all out of the question. In spite of certain historians who would make David a tribal chieftain and Solomon the mayor of a small city state, there is nothing in the extra-biblical evidence that mitigates against the biblical claims and much that argues in favor of it.[46]

In the same way, the internal collapse of the Israelite "mini-empire" (as reported in 1 Kgs 11–12) is consistent with the evidence. There were no nations in the ANE in 930 BC (the approximate date of Solomon's death) who were in a position to bring down such a well-established kingdom.

To be sure, the Libyan King Seshonq (biblical Shishak), who was ruling Egypt by this time, was able to take advantage of the ensuing weakness of the now-divided kingdom(s) to sack both of them some five years after the

---

44. The details of the Kassite Empire are very poorly known because almost no written records have been recovered.

45. When used with Judah, "all Israel" seems to stand for "all the rest of Israel." This language appears first in 1 Sam 18:6 where it is said that "all Israel and Judah loved David." 2 Sam 5:5 says that David reigned over Judah for seven years and over "all Israel and Judah" for thirty-three years. But "Judah" is distinguished from "Israel" already in Josh 11:21.

46. See Kenneth A. Kitchen, *On the Reliability of the Old Testament* (Grand Rapids: Eerdmans, 2003), 107–37. For an example of the current tendency to deny any historical accuracy to the biblical accounts, see Lester L. Grabbe, *1 & 2 Kings: History and Story in Ancient Israel* (London: Bloomsbury, 2017).

death of Solomon (1 Kgs 14:25–28),[47] but he did not have the power to do so while Solomon was alive. During that time, the most the Libyans could do was to provide amnesty and encouragement for rebels (1 Kgs 11:14–25, 40).

Israel's collapse left a vacuum waiting to be filled. The power that was to fill that vacuum was Assyria. Located on the Tigris River some 400 to 450 miles north of the Persian Gulf, the cities of this region had long been contenders for power with those in southern Mesopotamia, of which Babylon had become dominant. During the period before the collapse during the Late Bronze period, Assyria had been kept in check by the Hittites to the west and the Kassites to the southeast. Now with both of those gone and Israel no longer a factor to be considered, Assyria's ambitions had no limitations upon them. Thus, the period between 930 and 610 BC, also identified as Iron I, can be called the Assyrian Age, for during this 300-year time span, Assyria became the dominant force in the Near East. Whatever may have been the Assyrians' original designs, they ultimately came to control the entire trade chain reaching from the Persian Gulf to Egypt, a great crescent-shaped swath of territory sweeping up the Euphrates out across the northern edge of the desert to Tadmor (Palmyra) and Damascus, and down along the Mediterranean coast to Memphis and Thebes. Also included were the cities of northern Mesopotamia where the former Hurrian Kingdom of Mitanni had been located as well as the eastern parts of the old Hittite Empire.

For the first seventy-five years of the divided kingdom(s), as Assyria began to slowly expand, it was only a looming force in the background. It was apparently during the reign of Omri (1 Kgs 16:21–28; 885–874 BC) that Israel and Assyria first began to come into direct contact because one hundred years later the Assyrians were still referring to the northern kingdom, Israel, as "the house of Omri."[48]

By 860 BC the Assyrians had reached the northeast coast of the Mediterranean and were headed south. The only thing standing between them and Egypt were eight small countries of which Solomon's empire had once been composed: Syria (Damascus), Phoenicia (Tyre and Sidon), Israel (Samaria), Ammon (Rabbah), Moab (Dibon), Edom (Bosrah), Judah (Jerusalem), and the Philistines. No one of them could stand up to the Assyrian might, so several of them joined together in a coalition and confronted the Assyrians at a site called Qarqar on the Orontes River, north of the Lebanon/Anti-Lebanon mountain range. King Ahab of Israel was a major participant in the coalition. While the Assyrians claimed a crushing victory, the fact that their westward expansion largely ceased for some eighty years

47. Although it is not reported in Kings, Shishak's own report actually makes more of the sacking of Israel than it does that of Judah. Possibly the reason the narrator does not include that information is that he wants to emphasize the stripping of Solomon's temple so shortly after its building. See the discussion of Shishak in "Egypt, Egyptians," *IVPDOTHB*, 243.

48. See *ANET*, 284, 285.

suggests that the coalition may have taken a higher toll than the Assyrians admitted.[49]

The diminution of the Assyrian westward thrust meant that the former coalition partners were now free to tear at each other. For Israel, it was Syria that became the enemy, and it was in his attack on Syrian forces at the critical crossroads of Ramoth-Gilead in the Transjordan that Ahab met his death (1 Kgs 22:29–38), perhaps during the same year as the battle at Qarqar.

For Judah, it is clear that Assyria was not considered an immediate threat. Furthermore, there had been a state of warfare between Judah and Israel throughout much of Asa's reign. It was only with the accession of Omri in 886/85 BC, during Asa's thirty-first year, that the hostility began to ease. Eventually, during Asa's son Jehoshaphat's reign the relationship became one of amity, and some suggest that Judah actually became a vassal of Israel (Sweeney, 259). The marriage of Jehoshaphat's son, Jehoram, to Ahab's daughter Athaliah certainly argues for a very close relationship, as does the friendship of the grandson of Jehoshaphat, Ahaziah, and Ahab's son Jehoram (2 Kgs 9:16).

During this entire period and into the ensuing one in which Jehu destroyed the dynasty of Omri and set up his own dynasty, the major threat and challenge to both Israel and Judah were their neighbors, whether Moab (2 Kgs 3:4–27), Syria (2 Kgs 6:8, 24; 7:28; 12:17–18; 13:17), or Edom (14:7).

Between about 775 and 745 BC Assyria was ruled by two kings (Ashur-dan III, Ashur-nirari V) who were not aggressive toward their neighbors. This was during the reigns of Jeroboam II of Israel and Azariah/Uzziah of Judah. In both cases they were able to regain control of territories that had not been under the control of their respective countries since the days of Solomon: in the case of Israel, Syria was conquered all the way north to Hamath (2 Kgs 14:28), and in the case of Judah, control of Edom was gained all the way south to the port of Elath on the Red Sea (2 Kgs 14:22).

But none of this peace was to last, because a series of kings came to the throne of Assyria beginning in 745 BC who would more than make up for any

---

49. The Assyrian report, the only one extant, appears in Shalmanezer's Monolith Inscription located near the modern town of Kurkh in southeastern Turkey. For a picture of the relief, see *ANEP*, 153. The translation may be found in *ANET*, 278–97. See Barry J. Beitzel, *The Moody Atlas of Bible Lands* (Chicago: Moody Press, 1985), 132–33 for a discussion of the battle and its significance for biblical chronology. The absence of any mention of this important event in Kings is a clear indication of the disciplined intent of the narrator or narrators (for a discussion of authorship, see above). Recognizing the complexity of the issue, for ease of reading, I will refer in what follows to "the author" and use masculine pronouns to refer to this person. He is not writing a general history of the two kingdoms. Rather, he is narrating the connection between the attitudes of the kings to Yahweh and his covenant and the success or failure of their leadership. Only matters that bear on that purpose are narrated.

lack of aggressiveness on the part of their immediate predecessors. Beginning with Tiglath-pileser III in 745 BC and continuing through Ashurbanipal, who died in 629, one Assyrian tyrant after another marched south along the great coastal highway devastating everything in their path until even Thebes in far southern Egypt was reached. Along the way they crushed and annexed every nation in their way, except Judah, notably. Israel lost everything north of the Jezreel Valley to Tiglath-pileser almost at once, and during the next twenty years went through seven different kings and five different dynasties in a futile attempt to stave off disaster (2 Kgs 15:8–31; 17:1–6).

As a part of that effort, Pekah, king of Israel (739–731 BC) and Rezin, king of Syria, attacked Judah, planning to replace Ahaz, king of Judah (735–715) with someone else (2 Kgs 16:5–9). Possibly this was because they wanted Judah to join them in a coalition against Assyria and Ahaz—probably put on the throne with his father by a pro-Assyrian faction—had refused to do so. Ahaz, rather like a mouse being attacked by two other mice, hired the cat to defend him. He sent a large amount of money to Tiglath-pileser to persuade him to do what the Assyrian was surely already intent on doing, attack Israel and Syria. In 732, the Assyrians did so. Damascus was destroyed, and Israel, already truncated with the loss of Galilee and now the Transjordan, had only another decade to live. The end came in 722/21 under Shalmanezer II (2 Kgs 17:3–6). However, Shalmanezer died before the work of Samaria's destruction and the exile of the city's most capable citizens could be completed. That work was completed by Shalmanezer's successor, Sargon II.[50]

Judah was not immediately in the enemy's sights because the Judean territory was east of the coastal plain and the highway leading to Egypt. Still, while it was the Philistines who were most in jeopardy, the Judeans knew that once the Philistine cities were taken, their own hour would not be far behind; the Assyrians could not afford to leave an unconquered force in their rear while they pressed on south toward Egypt. Thus, when Sargon died in 705 BC with subsequent upheavals in the Assyrian court, the Judean King Hezekiah, who had succeeded his father Ahaz, evidently thought he saw an opportunity for preemptive action. Like Pekah and Rezin he would form a coalition consisting of Judah, the Philistines, and Moab. He went so far as to imprison the king of the Philistines, who, like Ahaz, had evidently resisted the idea.

---

50. When Sargon's annals were first discovered and read in the late nineteenth and early twentieth centuries AD there was some consternation among biblical scholars since the Bible seems to have Shalmanezer destroying Samaria and exiling its inhabitants, whereas Sargon claimed to have done these things. Initially, it was argued the Bible was wrong, but a closer look at the sources has led to the position now current as reported above. See John Bright, *A History of Israel*, 3rd ed. (Philadelphia: Westminster Press, 1981), 275. Note that while the text is explicit that Shalmanezer began the attack (2 Kgs 17:3), it then says only that "the king of Assyria" was the one who destroyed the city and exiled the people (17:6).

But any hope that the struggles in the Assyrian court might result in a weaker Assyria were in vain. The successor was Sennacherib who spent three years subduing the uprisings that had taken place at other places in the empire, and finally turned his attention to the west in 701 BC. It did not take him long to dispense with the coalition, to devastate Judah, and force the release of the Philistine king. The final holdout before his taking of Jerusalem was the great fortress city Lachish, some twenty-five miles southwest of Jerusalem.[51] Hezekiah, rather like his father, sent a large sum of money to the Assyrian emperor, begging him to withdraw (2 Kgs 18:13–16), but Sennacherib refused, instead sending one of his chief officers to demand the surrender of Jerusalem. Hezekiah, encouraged by the prophet Isaiah, refused to do that, daring to believe that Yahweh would deliver the city. The Bible reports that Yahweh did so, with most of the Assyrian army dying in one night and Sennacherib departing for home (2 Kgs 19:35–37). Most modern historians deny the validity of the biblical claim. But the fact is that Jerusalem was not captured, and Hezekiah was not put to death, the normal fate of any rebel city and its rebel king. It is also significant that although Sennacherib was on the throne of Assyria for another nineteen years and was quite active in other parts of his empire, he never campaigned in the west, where Egypt was wide open to him, again.

That being so, Judah could still not avoid the fact that both Israel and Philistia were now Assyrian military provinces. Thus, it seems that Hezekiah's young son Manasseh, who came to the throne in 696 BC was under the influence of the pro-Assyrian faction in the Judean court (2 Kgs 21:1). At any rate, he became a faithful Assyrian vassal for the next fifty years, through the reigns of Sennacherib and Esarhaddon, and into the reign of Ashurbanipal. Not only was he a political follower, but as the Bible indicates, and Assyrian documents confirm, he adopted the Assyrian (and ancient Near Eastern) worldview as well (2 Kgs 21:2–9).[52]

During Manasseh's lifetime, Assyria reached its final goal, Egypt, with Esarhaddon taking Memphis in 672 BC, and Ashurbanipal reaching as far south as Thebes and holding it for about a decade after 664. But the distance from this high point to the disappearance of Assyria from the world scene is surprisingly short. Babylon had always been a thorn in Assyria's side, always rebelling whenever the chance presented itself. Now, with Ashurbanipal's forty-year long reign, and perhaps a certain ennui after reaching its goal, Assyria seemed to lose momentum, and Babylon was ready to seize the initiative. Nabopolassar, a Chaldean strongman who had seized control of Babylon, formed an alliance with the Medes from the Zagros mountains to the east of the Mesopotamian valley, and set out to destroy Assyria. He achieved his goal within just twenty years of Ashurbanipal's death. The city of Asshur fell in 614, and Calah and Nineveh in 612, the latter after a siege of only

---

51. For images of the Lachish seige, see ANEP, 371–74, 129–32.

52. *ANET*, 289–90.

three months. The remnants of the Assyrian army fled westward, but in 609 at Harran they were forced to stand and fight. The Ethiopian Pharaoh, Necho, had come north to help, apparently trying to keep a weak Assyria between him and the surging Medo-Babylonian force. But the Assyrians and the Egyptians suffered a devastating defeat, and with that the Assyrian empire that had been the dominant political element in the Near East for 300 years ceased to exist.

The Babylonians took the southern, and richest, part of the Assyrian empire, while the Medes took the northern part. However, the Egyptians under the Ethiopian Pharaoh Necho would not give up the opportunity to try to keep control of the Levant as a buffer between them and the Medes and Babylonians. Nabopolassar's son, Nebuchadnezzar, put an end to that hope when he decisively defeated the Egyptians at Carchemish in 605 BC. He immediately moved to assert his control of the entire Levant, including Judah.

In the chaotic twenty years between 625 BC and 605, much had happened in Judah. Manasseh's infant grandson Josiah, placed on the throne after the assassination of his father Amon in 639 (2 Kgs 21:3–4), had come to maturity, begun repair of the temple (22:3–7), found the Book of the Torah, and horrified by what he found there, had begun to try to expunge from Judah the effects of his grandfather's long reign (22:8, 11; 23:1–25). However, in 609 he was killed at Megiddo by Pharaoh Necho (23:29). Apparently, Josiah was trying to prevent Necho from reaching Harran, although why that would have been the case is not spelled out. The Judean people passed over Josiah's first-born son Jehoiakim and placed his younger brother Jehoahaz on the throne (22:31). Perhaps they did this because he was anti-Egyptian. At any rate Necho dethroned him, sent him to exile in Egypt, and put Jehoiakim, Jehoahaz' older brother, on the throne as Egypt's vassal (23:33–34). That situation lasted until 605 when, with Necho's defeat by Nebuchadnezzar, Jehoiakim changed allegiances and became a Babylonian vassal (24:1).

However, it appears that in 601 BC Nebuchadnezzar somewhat overreached in attempting to conquer Egypt itself, and suffered a stinging defeat, requiring him to withdraw to Babylon to recover and rearm. Whatever effect this event may have had on other vassals, it emboldened Jehoiakim to break his covenant with Babylon and to withhold tribute. It was a false hope. Jerusalem was almost immediately besieged by other Babylonian vassals, and eventually the revived Babylonian army itself arrived, and Jerusalem surrendered in 598. The king who actually surrendered and was taken into exile with the rest of the royal family was Jehoiachin, Jehoiakim's son. Jehoiakim died under circumstances never fully explained in the Bible.

The Babylonians put yet a third son of Josiah, Zedekiah, on the Judean throne, but the Bible never considers him a valid king. He is depicted by the Bible as someone lacking in both principles and wisdom, someone who is continually swayed one way and the other by what he perceives to be the prevailing public opinion. In the end he was convinced to rebel against Babylon and experienced the typical results of repeated rebellion: destruction of the capital city and death to the rebel king and all his supporters.[53]

The Babylonian empire was to a great extent the creation of one man: Nebuchadnezzar. From 605 BC until his death in 562 he ruled absolutely, built widely, and his empire seemed completely secure. But almost immediately upon his death, the signs of dissolution began to appear, with one weak ruler succeeding another in short order, until Cyrus the Persian brought the entire tottering edifice down in 539. It is tempting to think that the release of Jehoiachin from prison by Awil-Marduk (Evil-merodach, 2 Kgs 25:27) at the beginning of his reign in 560 may have been an attempt to gain supporters for himself in what he already saw as perilous circumstances. But there is no indication in the record of his motivation for the action.

Religious

The two key evidences of covenant keeping in the book of Kings are: 1) exclusive worship of Yahweh, and 2) no worship of idols, whether of Yahweh or any other god. These are, of course, the first two commandments (Exod 20:3–6), so it is appropriate that they should be given pride of place. But it is too easy to gloss over the central importance of these. They are expressive of the diametrically opposite worldview of the biblical writers from that of the neighboring peoples. The fact that there are still only three religions that espouse these views, Christianity, Judaism, and Islam, all of which stem from the Old Testament, gives some indication as to how radical they are.

The religions of the ANE, up to and including those of Greece and Rome, are remarkably similar. They hold that there are many gods, that the gods are to be identified with the psycho-socio-physical forces of the cosmos, that because of this identification the gods can be manipulated through the visible world, that the gods are profoundly sexual, that all existence is cyclical, that good and evil are eternal entities constantly at war with each other within

---

53. The Assyrians had perfected a three-staged approach to conquering a city and the Babylonians adopted it. In the first stage, the imperial army arrives in a location and "offers" an alliance, one which involves a high tribute. The people accept the alliance, really having no other option. But sooner or later they revolt and withhold the tribute. This sets in motion the second stage when the imperial army arrives to besiege the city. The besieged eventually surrender and renew their covenant, allowing the conqueror to pick the next king, and impose a larger tribute. Again, revolt is inevitable because the country is being stripped of all its assets. This brings on the third stage: the imperial army once again returns to besiege the city, but the besieged know that terms of surrender will not be offered. They must hold on, hoping that perhaps the empire will suffer some event that might cause the siege to be lifted. If not, the city will eventually fall with death and destruction to follow, and with the country becoming a province of the empire, ruled by a military governor. For an extended discussion see Amélie Kuhrt, *The Ancient Near East c. 3000 – 330 BC*, 2 vols. (London: Routledge, 1995), 2.478–83.

the cosmos, that there is no single standard of ethics (ethics being primarily defined by the pragmatic needs of a given culture), that life is without purpose except to survive with a maximum of comfort, security, and pleasure, that acquisition of power over the environment, divine, human, and natural, is necessary to achieve the aforementioned ends, and that the absolute is power, conceived of abstractly and impersonally.[54]

Why was there this degree of uniformity? It was because all of these neighboring cultures shared the conception that this psycho-socio-physical cosmos is all there is to reality. There is nothing other than it. To be sure, there is an invisible spirit component in the cosmos, and indeed, it is that component that seems to control the cosmos. But, in order to gain control of it, something that is necessary if we are to achieve the ends of comfort, security, and pleasure, we must have some understanding of it. In order to do so, we assume that the invisible world is continuous with the visible one. Therefore, we can reason from the visible to the invisible by analogy. What are the gods like? They are like humans, only larger in every way. They are better than we are, but also worse; they are strong, but also weak; they are dependable, but also fickle; they are wise, but also foolish. Since the cosmos is incredibly diverse, there must be many gods. Since the cosmos is not moving to any discernible end, neither is existence. Since the cosmos functions in an endless cycle, so does existence. Since the cosmos is without personality, individual personhood is of no real significance. By starting with the same data (i.e., the cosmos), and by following the same path of reasoning (i.e., analogy), all the ancient religious thinkers came to the same place, whether Sumerians in 3000 BC or Romans in AD 300.

The Bible disagrees at every point. There is tremendous pressure on biblical scholars today to minimize this point, to find all the places of commonality between the Bible and the other religious literatures of the ancient world. Certainly, there are such commonalities; it would be impossible for there not to be since the Israelites and early Christians were full participants in the culture of their times. That is not surprising. What is surprising is the remarkable differences, differences that are unique to the Bible. If biblical religion emerged from ancient paganism by a process of slow evolution, as many modern thinkers assert, then why are there not many other examples of such emergence, even if they take another form than that of the Bible? But there are none. All the religions of the ancient world, with the exception of the three mentioned above, share the same central convictions. This argues

---

54. See Yehezkel Kaufmann, *The Religion of Israel: From its Beginnings to the Babylonian Exile*, trans. Moshe Greenberg (Chicago: University of Chicago Press, 1960), 7–59; Thomas Molnar, *The Pagan Temptation* (Grand Rapids: Eerdmans, 1987), 5–50; John N. Oswalt, *The Bible Among the Myths* (Grand Rapids: Zondervan, 2009), 47–62; Wolfram von Soden, *The Ancient Orient: An Introduction to the Study of the Ancient Near East*, trans. Donald G. Schley (Grand Rapids: Eerdmans, 1994), 173–202.

against the Bible having started in the same place as all the others and slowly reaching a point unlike all the rest.

What is the biblical worldview? It is that this psycho-socio-physical world is *not* all there is to reality. This is the watershed. Indeed, there are really only two worldviews: the biblical one and the other one. Either this cosmos is all there is to reality, or it is not all there is to reality.

The Bible alone maintains the latter. We may label this view transcendence: there is reality that transcends this cosmos. Some thinkers speak of the invisible spirit realm as transcendent, but that is to misuse the term.[55] That realm is simply one more aspect of the cosmos that is continuous with the others: humanity and nature. The fact that all these religions believe that the spirit, or divine, realm can be controlled by manipulating the human and natural realms shows that the spirit realm does not transcend the others.

But Yahweh does transcend everything in the cosmos. The Bible holds that he is the Creator (not the originator, as is the chief god in all the so-called "creation myths") who utterly transcends his Creation. Thus, he is One, it not possible for several things all to transcend each other.[56] He cannot be identified with any created thing. He cannot be manipulated through or with any created thing. Hence, imitative magic is forbidden in the Bible. God is not gendered and does not function in any sexual way.[57] He is not a force with a human-like mask, as are the gods; rather, he is fully and profoundly personal. Thus, individual personhood is of ultimate significance (this is the reason for writing history). Life has purpose, namely deepening fellowship with the Creator in which we come to share his unique character. Since the absolute is not faceless power, but a person, acquisition of power is not the goal, but godly, holy character is. Since there is a purpose in existence, it is possible to measure progress; existence is not an endless cycle, but linear.

In the Bible there is an absolute standard of ethics, the ethics of the Creator, ethics he calls on us to share. Unlike the gods, whose characters are

---

55. See, for instance, Rudolf Otto, *The Idea of the Holy*, trans. J. W. Harvey (Oxford: Oxford University Press, 1926).

56. As is evident from all the other non-biblically derived religions, monotheism cannot be maintained without a belief that the divine is not continuous with the cosmos. The nineteenth century idea that monotheism is the logical conclusion of the progress of thought from animism to polytheism, etc. is, in fact, not defensible.

57. If Yahweh is not gendered, why is he regularly, and exclusively, referred to in male terms? It is not because, as some maintain, Israel was a uniquely male-dominated society. It is because of Yahweh's personhood. That being the case, the neuter cannot be used. Neither could some mix of feminine and masculine terms be used, since no human person is both sexes at once. Finally, the transcendent God could not be referred to in exclusively female terms for two reasons: (1) the almost complete identification of the goddesses with fertility themes, and (2) the fact that the child emerges from the mother's body, a view of cosmic origins that is inimical to transcendence.

simply those of humans written large, the character of Yahweh is unique. He is not both dependable and fickle, but absolutely dependable. He is not both loving and hateful, but *is* love. He is not both right and wrong, but does right in every circumstance, even to his own disadvantage. He is not both good and evil, but only good; evidenced by the repeated "O give thanks to Yahweh, for he is good; his unfailing love is forever" (Ps 106:1; 107:1; 109:5 and a dozen other times). Thus, to make God in our image (whether physical or spiritual) is to get things exactly backward. He is attempting to transform us into his image.

All of this means that the issue with which the book of Kings is dealing is not merely a matter of religious preferences, or national religions. The very nature of reality is at stake. It is not merely a matter of picking out one of the many gods and giving exclusive allegiance to him. It is to recognize that Yahweh, I AM, is unique, in a category utterly separate from the spirits inhabiting the cosmos, of whom there are many. In the same way, making an idol of Yahweh is not merely a matter of making the invisible visible. It is to deny transcendence, and in so doing cut the root of truth. In fact, idolatry is the fullest and most effective expression of the other worldview: a natural object is given human form and inhabited by a "divine" spirit. That is the world view of continuity, the continuity among all the elements of the cosmos, all the elements of reality. It is to make inseparable that which *must* be separated. It is to make the transcendent amenable to human control. By doing things to/for my idol, I therefore delude myself into thinking that I am doing something to/for God. But it is not true. Yahweh cannot be controlled or manipulated. He can only be trusted and surrendered to.

But there is the problem, the problem that pursued both the kingdoms of Israel and Judah, and eventually left them helpless before the vicious covetousness of the kingdoms of this world. The problem is that we humans are terrified of losing control of our lives. This transcendent I AM asks too much; he asks us to entrust our comfort, pleasure, and security into his hands, believing he can provide them more effectively than we can by ourselves. Instead of providing for ourselves as the center of our little universe, or, alternatively, simply losing ourselves in the mass around us, absolving ourselves of all responsibility, he asks us to "walk" with him, devoting ourselves to the needs and rights of others, while focusing on the development of character like his. As that is too much for most of us, so it was too much for most of the Israelites, starting with their kings.

So, when Solomon built shrines for the gods of his pagan wives (1 Kgs 11:7–8), he was not merely committing a minor peccadillo, he was tearing apart the very fabric of reality. He was crossing that continental divide from transcendence to continuity, from the biblical worldview to the pagan worldview. In the same way, when Jeroboam represented Yahweh as a golden bull (1 Kgs 12:28), he was not merely making a little "slip-up," but was destroying the ground of biblical faith. Yahweh cannot be identified with anything created. Do that, and the game is lost. But much more than a game is at stake here; it is the very nature of reality.

This is why nineteen of the forty-seven chapters of the book(s) (1 Kgs 17–2 Kgs 13) are fully focused on the ministries of two prophets, Elijah and Elisha, spanning only about eighty years (out of a total of 400). Now the issue is not merely a tacit acceptance of the anti-biblical world view, but an outright acceptance of that fiction along with an accompanying repudiation of the truth. Would Baal, embodiment of the view that this cosmos is the sum-total of reality, replace Yahweh—the transcendent One—as the god of Israel, with the almost certain following of Judah? In short, would all that Yahweh had been seeking to inculcate in human thinking through the descendants of Abraham for a millennium be for naught? Would he have to start over again with a new Abraham? That is what was at stake in the Baal crisis. It was not simply a question of one god versus another; it was the correct view of reality versus the false view of reality.

This explains the miracles of Elijah, and especially Elisha, related in 2 Kgs 1–8. These are often dismissed as legends that are ancillary to the main account of the kings of Israel upon which it is thought the text should have focused.[58] But in fact, these narratives are fundamental to the key point being made, namely, that Yahweh, standing outside of the cosmos, is free to break into it and do things that the forces resident in the cosmos do not have the freedom to do. Such evidence as this was a key part of the argument that the view of reality inherent in the Baal cult is in fact wrong. It is telling that the king, probably Ahab's grandson, Jehoash, was fascinated with what Elisha had done, and wanted to hear more about it (2 Kgs 8:4). These miracles were not random fireworks designed to titillate the gullible; they were part of a life and death campaign between truth and falsehood, one that was won by truth, although by the narrowest of margins.[59]

Theological and Practical Emphases

Several of the main emphases of Kings have already been mentioned, but it will be helpful to list them and discuss them in more detail here.

The Kingship of Yahweh

While the ostensible subject of the book(s) of Kings is Solomon and the nineteen kings of Judah[60] and the nineteen kings of Israel, that is clearly not the case. The real subject of the book is Yahweh, the King. He is the one about whom the book circles. This point is made in the recurring judgment that

58. See, for instance, Gray, 371–77; Montgomery and Gehman, 39–41.

59. For a fuller discussion of this subject, see my *The Bible Among the Myths* (Grand Rapids: Zondervan, 2009).

60. Leaving out Athaliah but including Zedekiah.

appears in connection with the accession formulae. How is a king's rule to be assessed? It is assessed in terms of the king's adherence to the commands of the King. Either "he did what was right in the sight of Yahweh" (וַיַּעַשׂ הַיָּשָׁר בְּעֵינֵי יהוה, *wayya ʿaś hayyāšār bᵊ ʿênê yhwh*) or "he did what was evil in the sight of Yahweh" (וַיַּעַשׂ הָרַע בְּעֵינֵי יהוה, *wayya ʿaś hāra ʿ bᵊ ʿênê yhwh*). The first example of this is found in reference to Solomon (1 Kgs 11:6).[61] After eleven chapters detailing Solomon's accomplishment, the devastating words come: "He was not careful to keep Yahweh's commands" (וְלֹא שָׁמַר אֵת אֲשֶׁר־צִוָּה יהוה, *wᵊlō ʾ šāmar ʾēṯ ʾăšer-ṣiwwâ yhwh*; 1 Kgs 11:10). Forty years of rule are dismissed in just five Hebrew words. The result was the tearing away of the kingdom from Solomon. Yahweh is the one who rules in this world, not the Solomons, no matter how competent those persons may be in administration or how much wealth and splendor they have accumulated.

The judgment passed on Rehoboam (1 Kgs 14:22–24) is interesting because it does not blame the covenant breaches directly on the king, but rather on the people. The strong implication is that the king was not strong enough, or perhaps willing enough, to prevent the people from doing what their King had specifically commanded them not to do, namely recognize and worship other gods, particularly in ways that deny the Creator's right to define what is right and what is wrong.[62]

Throughout the book, the record of king after king is evaluated according to one standard, the standard of Yahweh. Thus, many kings whom the world might call successful or effective are called to the bar of the covenant terms of their covenant Lord, and there are judged to have been a failure. Tragically, in the entire book, out of thirty-nine kings there are only seven, all Judeans, of whom it is not said, "they did evil in Yahweh's sight."[63] They are Asa (1 Kgs 15:11), Jehoshaphat (22:43), Joash (2 Kgs 12:2), Amaziah (14:3), Azariah (15:3); Hezekiah (18:3), and Josiah (22:2). Yet, even these, every one of them, when held up to the white light of Yahweh's perfection failed in some way. What is that saying? It is saying that if we put our hope in human leadership, it will fail us. The dream of nineteenth century humanists, that humans will bring in the kingdom of God, was blown apart

---

61. The statement appears here but it is not in an accession formula (as is usual), chiefly because there is not one for Solomon. As noted above, it is possible that this particular form began in the northern kingdom and was later duplicated in the south with adaptations.

62. The term "abomination" (תּוֹעֵבָה, *tô ʿēḇâ*; 1 Kgs 14:24) defines anything that is contrary to Yahweh's design of the Creation, i.e., his מִשְׁפָּט, *mišpāṭ*. When cult is designed to manipulate the forces of this world, submitting them to our control, abomination is often the result.

63. Although the precise phrase is not applied to either Elah or Jehu, Both are condemned. It is twice said of Jehu that "he did not turn away from the sins of Jeroboam: (2 Kgs 10:29, 31). Likewise, it is said of Elah, "because of all the sins Baasha and his son Elah had committed and caused Israel to commit (1 Kgs 16:13).

by the shattering realities of the twentieth century (e.g., WWI, WWII, the Holocaust, Hiroshima). Yahweh alone can bring in his kingdom. But that truth was already clearly displayed in the book of Kings 2,500 years ago. Yahweh alone is fit to be King, and it is by his standards that everyone on this earth is judged, from the highest status to the lowest.

But this King is "tender and gracious, slow to get angry, and overflowing with unfailing love" (רחוּם וְחַנּוּן אֶרֶךְ אַפַּיִם וְרַב־חֶסֶד וֶאֱמֶת, *raḥûm wᵊḥannûn ʾerek̲ ʾappayim wᵊrab̲-ḥesed̲ we ʾĕmet̲*; Exod 34:6). One of the frequent characteristics of great kings and leaders is a terrible temper that can lash out in a moment, devastating everyone in front of them. That is not true of Yahweh, particularly the Yahweh revealed in this book. Above all, Yahweh's patience is seen in the fact that the story of his people takes 400 years to reach its denouement. The covenant stated that the occupation of God's land and experience of his presence was dependent upon that covenant's fulfillment (Lev 26:1–13; 2 Kgs 21:8), and that if the terms of the covenant were persistently broken, that occupation and that presence were forfeited (Lev 26:27–33). Clearly, the terms began to be broken while the Israelites were still at Sinai and, with few exceptions, were broken consistently from then on. Yet, the exceptions were rewarded much more than might have been expected from the stated terms of the covenant. That is the case in Kings. How grievous was Solomon's failure. The builder of the temple of Yahweh falls by building temples for Chemosh, for Molech, and for Asherah (1 Kgs 11:5, 7). Surely the fall of a person of such attainments should be judged especially harshly. But the God of compassion determines to defer the judgment for a generation (1 Kgs 11:12). After a fall like that, certainly the full judgment of exile and alienation would have been well-merited, but it was not to be.[64] Again, in the case of Ahab, a bad man if ever there was one ("there was none who sold himself to do evil in the sight of Yahweh like Ahab," רַק לֹא־הָיָה כְאַחְאָב אֲשֶׁר הִתְמַכֵּר לַעֲשׂוֹת הָרַע בְּעֵינֵי יהוה, *raq lōʾ-hāyâ k̲ᵊ ʾaḥ ʾāb̲ ʾăšer hit̲makkēr la ʿăśôt̲ hāra ʿ bᵊ ʿênê yhwh*; 1 Kgs 21:25), Yahweh generously offered to defeat the armies of Syria for him not only on one occasion, but two (1 Kgs 20:13, 28). In the end, when Ahab repented of what he had done to Naboth, Yahweh deferred the destruction of the Omride dynasty for two generations. Throughout the sad story of the Omride dynasty winding its way down to its end, the miracles of Elijah and Elisha speak again and again

64. Note that here (11:36) and again in 15:4 and 2 Kgs 8:19, when Davidic kings have failed to obey Yahweh, he defers judgment so that the "lamp" of David would not be extinguished. In the latter case, the sin is especially egregious since the Davidic monarch has not merely done evil but has "followed the ways of the kings of Israel, as the house of Ahab had done" (וַיֵּלֶךְ בְּדֶרֶךְ מַלְכֵי יִשְׂרָאֵל כַּאֲשֶׁר עָשׂוּ בֵּית אַחְאָב, *wayyēlek̲ bᵊd̲erek̲ malk̲ê yiśrā ʾēl ka ʾăšer ʿāśû bêt̲ ʾaḥ ʾāb̲*; 2 Kgs 8:18). Nevertheless, "Yahweh did not want to destroy Judah" (וְלֹא אָבָה יְהוָה לְהַשְׁחִית אֶת יְהוּדָה, *wᵊlōʾ- ʾāb̲â yhwh lᵊhašḥît̲ ʾet̲-yᵊhûd̲â*; v. 19) because of his promise to David. Justice would take a back seat to love.

of healing, restoration, provision, and raising of the dead. Life is in the hands of the King, and if the human kings are taking their kingdoms into sickness, deprivation, desolation, and death, the King can do the opposite for all those who will recognize his Lordship.

But is this King genuinely compassionate and restorative? There are those who would say that in the end, when even Judah had gone the way of the northern kingdom (2 Kgs 21:13), Yahweh's patience ran out and he determined to destroy Judah in spite of the fact that the people, following Josiah's lead, had repented of Manasseh's sins (2 Kgs 23:26–27). But the text nowhere says the people repented. It says that Josiah renewed the covenant, and the people "stood in the covenant" (וַיַּעֲמֹד כָּל־הָעָם בַּבְּרִית, *wayya ʿămôḏ kol-hā ʿām babbᵊrîṯ*; v. 3). Modern versions read more into the phrase than is justified (ESV "joined in the covenant"; NIV, NLT "pledged themselves to the covenant"). I suspect the phrase means "they acquiesced in the covenant." In any case this is much less than what the people did at Sinai (Exod 24:1–6), or at Shechem (Josh 24:21–27). But whatever that phrase means, it is clear that no real repentance took place apart from that of Josiah (and an unnamed few others), because as soon as Josiah is dead, the people obviously make no objection whatsoever at the reinstatement of Manasseh's evil practices by Josiah's sons (e.g., see Ezek 8:1–18).

Then why does the text say that the end came as a result of Manasseh's sins (2 Kgs 24:3–4)? The point is that after the very hopeful signs of genuine renewal during Hezekiah's reign, Manasseh set the very opposite pattern into place, and notwithstanding the momentary exception for about a dozen years during Josiah's reign, that pattern prevailed for more than one hundred years. Indeed, Judah fell because of Manasseh's sins which Judah enthusiastically participated in. But even then, had there been a true national repentance that took hold and changed the complexion of the nation, the God of compassion may well have extended Judah's life (see Jer 36:2–3, 7; but 36:23–24).

This revelation of the compassion of the King has a very important bearing on the enigmatic final paragraph of the book. The narrator does not tell us how he wants us to read the paragraph. Is it just a historical appendix, a footnote? There are those who insist we should see it in that light (so Cogan and Tadmor, 329–30). On the other hand, there are others (famously Von Rad[65]) who see it in a much more positive light. I suspect that the passage has been left intentionally ambiguous. We ask the narrator, "Is this release a hopeful sign or not?" His answer is, "It all depends." Depends on what? The response of the exiles. If they will respond in faith and trust, believing that in the end the King's חֶסֶד (*ḥeseḏ*), unfailing love, will prevail over legalistic justice, and refuse to become assimilated to Babylonian culture, then it is a very hopeful sign. On the other hand, if they succumb to despair, then this release is indeed merely a historical footnote. The future, he says, as indeed

65. Gerhard von Rad, *Old Testament Theology*, trans. D.M.G. Stalker (NY: HarperCollins, 1967), 1:343.

the whole book says, is in God's hands, but also in yours. What will you do with it?[66]

The Primacy of the Word of Yahweh

While it is by no means unique to Kings, the theme of Yahweh speaking to his people cannot be overlooked in the book. Some forty times the phrases "Yahweh said" or "Yahweh says" (יהוה אָמַר, *yhwh ʾāmar* or וַיֹּאמֶר יהוה, *wayyōʾmer yhwh*; e.g. 1 Kgs 8:12, 18) occurs, and "God said" (וַיֹּאמֶר אֱלֹהִים, *wayyōʾmer ʾĕlōhîm*; e.g. 1 Kgs 3:5) occurs an additional five times. Alongside those are twenty-three occurrences of "the word of Yahweh" (דְּבַר יהוה, *dᵉbar yhwh*; e.g. 1 Kgs 2:27) among which are fifteen of the twenty-nine total occurrences in the Bible of "according to the word of Yahweh" (כִּדְבַר יהוה, *kidbar yhwh*; e.g. 1 Kgs 12:24).[67] The point to be made here is that the concept that the Transcendent One reveals himself and his will through speech communication is absolutely central to the biblical view of reality. The idea that the gods could speak in free conversation with ordinary human beings was not believed by a majority of the ancient world. This is not surprising when we understand that the gods are cosmic forces wearing human-like personas. Speech is characteristic of *persons* and the gods are not personal. To be sure, the gods are imagined to be analogous with humans; therefore, they speak among themselves, but only on rare occasions do they speak to humans.

That is not the case in the Bible and particularly in Kings. God is everywhere speaking. Normally he does so through those who are accredited in some way as prophets, but that is not always the case. So, for instance, in 1 Kgs 3 Yahweh spoke to Solomon in a dream (v. 5). Likewise in chap. 9, we are told that God spoke through a dream (v. 2). In chap. 11 he is represented as speaking directly (v. 11). Yet, God speaks to Jeroboam through the prophet Ahijah.

These multiple examples of Yahweh speaking reinforce the previous theme. It is not what the kings of Israel and Judah say that is important for understanding what is happening in the country, but rather what the true King has to say. Things happen according to what he has said will happen. Judgments fall as he has said they will. The significance of persons and events is determined by what Yahweh says about them. He is not known through the great voiceless forces of nature, but by what he says. Jesus was speaking about physical sustenance in Matt 4:4, but the broader point certainly applies in the book(s) of Kings: humans live by every word that comes out of the mouth of God.

So Rehoboam must give up his plans to forcibly reunite the country (1 Kgs 12:24) because the division had been according to Yahweh's word, and the prophet who had spoken Yahweh's word to Jeroboam with authority died

66. Three times Yahweh declares he wants to preserve a "lamp" for David (2 Sam 21:17; 1 Kgs 11:36; 2 Kgs 8:19). Is this yet one more expression of that motif?

67. There is one occurrence of "the word of God" (דְּבַר הָאֱלֹהִים, *dᵉbar hāʾĕlōhîm*) in 1 Kgs 12:22.

because he flouted the authority of that same word (13:26). Jeroboam's son died, as indeed did his whole family line, just as Yahweh had said through Ahijah (14:18; 15:29). A similar message was spoken against Baasha and came to pass just as it was spoken (16:12). Elijah did what God told him to do, the cruse of oil did not fail, just as he said it would not, etc., etc. Throughout the book, the fulfillment of God's word occurs right to its end when we see Josiah defiling the bones of Israel's idol-priests (2 Kgs 23:16) just as the man of God, speaking for God, had said to Jeroboam some 300 years earlier (1 Kgs 13:2). This history of Israel and Judah is unintelligible apart from the God who speaks.

But not only does God speak; people speak with him. As has been said above, the biblical God is a person who desires a relationship with persons, and deep relationships are impossible without speech communication. Accordingly, God asks Solomon what he wants, and Solomon replies in a most significant way (1 Kgs 3:4–9). We see it in the experience of Elijah, as this man of God not only receives messages from him, which he obeys or passes on, as the case may be, but also speaks back to him with petitions (e.g., 17:20), and complaints (19:10). But the greatest example in Elijah's life is on Mt. Carmel, where the prophets of Baal have spent the day in ritualistic behavior designed to move Baal to action and have failed. What is Elijah's response? It is simply to engage in communication with Yahweh; it is to pray, nothing more (18:36–37).

Another moving example of prayer in this book is that of Hezekiah when confronted by the Assyrians with the demand that he should surrender the city of Jerusalem into their hands (2 Kgs 19:15–19). The prophet Isaiah had encouraged Hezekiah not to accede to the demand, and when faced with a recurrence of the demand, Hezekiah prays a profound prayer in which he affirms Yahweh's uniqueness and asks that Yahweh will deliver the city so that his uniqueness would be demonstrated to the world. The Judean monarch shows that he has grasped the key theological theme of the book, but also demonstrates that he knows the key to the divine/human experience: personal relationship.

The greatest example of prayer in the book is found in Solomon's prayer dedicating the temple (1 Kgs 8:9–53). Here Solomon prays at length to God, and what he says is quite surprising on the surface. This temple is going to be and already is, a place dedicated to ritual behavior, particularly the rituals of sacrifice. Solomon himself would cause thousands of animals to be sacrificed on the temple altar (vv. 62–63); yet in his prayer he never refers to the temple as a place of ritual. What does he refer to it as is a house of prayer. He asks repeatedly that Yahweh will hear and answer the prayers that are made to him in reference to this place. Yahweh is the God who speaks and who delights to be spoken with. Sacrifices do not in themselves accomplish anything, but speech coming from a devoted and penitent heart will always touch the heart of God.

This is a place to consider what may be called a minor theme in Kings. Whereas Brueggemann (2–3) considers the temple to be a major preoccupation of the narrator(s), Wiseman (25) contends that temple worship is not a main theme of the book. Which is correct? There is a sense in which both are correct, and I think Solomon's prayer gives us the key. In the sense that the temple is the representation of Yahweh's "name," that is, his character and nature, it is very important; the amount of space given to its construction and furnishings in chaps. 5–7 tell us that. But it has no significance in itself. To imagine that its rituals will somehow accomplish something in themselves, or that the possession of "God's house" will necessarily procure God's favor for Jerusalem and Israel is, in fact, to fall prey to pagan thinking. This is where Solomon's prayer is so important. Relationship with God based on faith in his "name"—his loving, dependable, and good character—and rooted in a repentant, submissive will, and expressed in loving and faithful communication between Yahweh and his worshipper is what the temple must represent. To the extent that what takes place in the temple complex reflects that relationship, the temple will be under God's protection, but the moment it becomes a place where covetous humans attempt to manipulate divine favor, the temple will be a place of profound disgust to God. This is seen immediately in Yahweh's response to Solomon's prayer in 1 Kgs 9: so long as Israel does worship Yahweh alone, the temple matters, but as soon as Yahweh becomes merely one more of the gods, the temple is meaningless.[68] This is illustrated in the repeated robbing of the temple, either by an enemy such as Shishak (less than a generation after the complex had been built; 1 Kgs 14:25–28), or by the Judean kings themselves (15:18; 2 Kgs 12:18; 18:16). Far from being some sort of magic talisman that will protect Judah and Jerusalem, the temple cannot even protect itself. In the final sacking described in 2 Kgs 25:13–17 all the objects described in such loving detail in 1 Kgs 7 are summarily broken up and carried off. They are of no account to Yahweh.

The significance of prophecy

The previous theme of God's word is directly related to this theme. We have already commented on the significance of the location of Joshua–Kings in the Prophets section of the Hebrew canon, and their being labeled "the Former Prophets." The prophets who spoke Yahweh's word and called people and

68. One of the difficult interpretive questions has to do with "the high places" (בָּמוֹת, *bāmôṯ*; see the excursus on high places on p. 459). Up until Hezekiah it is regularly said of the good kings of Judah that they did not remove the high places. Presumably these were places where Yahweh was worshipped, and not pagan shrines (see e.g., the statement that Elijah repaired the altar of Yahweh on Mt. Carmel; 1 Kgs 18:30). Thus, although they would not have been in full compliance with the Deuteronomic ideal that Yahweh's "name" would only be honored in one place, these kings are not condoning the worship of idols.

kings alike to account based on that word, were at the very heart of Israel's historical experience. Israel was what it was, and became what it did, as a direct result of the ministries of these men and women. That is especially true in the book(s) of Kings. No fewer than fifteen prophets are mentioned in the book, ten of them by name: Nathan, Ahijah, Shemaiah, Jehu, Elijah, Elisha, Micaiah, Jonah, Isaiah, Huldah. It is also interesting that the phrase "man of God" (אִישׁ אֱלֹהִים, *ʾîš ʾĕlōhîm*; e.g., 1 Kgs 13:1) in reference to prophets is much more frequent in Kings than it is the rest of the Bible: fifty-five occurrences out of the total of seventy-five. To be sure, fully thirty-seven of those fifty-five appear in the Elijah/Elisha narratives, but it is still a remarkable phenomenon.[69] These persons were not merely marked as those who represented deity to the world; they were people who were marked by a unique relationship with God. It seems significant that it is a "man of God," Shemaiah, who warns Rehoboam not to attack Israel (12:22–24), and it is an unnamed "man of God" who confronts Jeroboam for his breaches of the covenant (13:1–3). Here at the outset of the two kingdoms the emphasis is not on the "profession" of prophetism, but on the One for whom these men speak. Likewise, this seems to be the sense of the recurring use of the term in reference to Elijah and Elisha. This two-fold ministry in defiance of Baal was carried out not so much by inspired speakers, as by two men who were emissaries of Yahweh, like David and Moses.

It has become a cliché to declare that the prophets of Israel were not so much "foretellers" as they were "forthtellers." That is, the Israelite prophets, especially the so-called "writing prophets," spent more time naming the sins of the people and their leaders and calling them back to faithfulness to their covenant with Yahweh than they did predicting the future. There is a great deal of truth in that statement, and to a very significant degree it set the Israelite prophets apart from what we know of prophets elsewhere in the ancient world, where telling the future seems to have been a main function.[70]

However, it is wrong to minimize the predictive element in Israelite prophecy and to make it appear that this aspect is of little significance. Part of the reason that some have downplayed this element is that they do not believe genuine prediction of the future is possible. For these persons, all supposed predictions actually occurred after the fact. Predictions are a religious fiction designed to convince the hearers or the readers of whatever "truth" is being taught.[71] Such a position as this does not take into account the unique nature of the biblical historical literature. It fails to recognize that the main explanation for writing about history in Israel is precisely

69. Six occurrences in Chronicles, five in Samuel, two in Judges and Nehemiah, and one each in Deuteronomy, Joshua, Psalms, Ezra, and Jeremiah. Moses, 6x; Samuel, 4x; David, 3x; Shemaiah and Igdaliah 1x each; and anonymous 4x.

70. See my "Is There Anything Unique in the Hebrew Prophets?" *BSac* 172 (January-March 2015): 67–84.

71. See Gray, 326; Fritz, 150; Montgomery and Gehman, 260–61.

because of the predictive word of God. The prophet said that Solomon's kingdom would split into two unequal parts because of Solomon's sin. Did that actually happen? Was God's word fulfilled? If so, how? How was the human element involved in the fulfillment, etc.? Prediction and fulfillment tie together the past, present, and future in precisely the ways in which history writing is interested. But it will often be said that the Israelites had no real interest in what actually took place; rather, they were trying to show that their god, Yahweh, was superior to someone else's god, so they claimed that he had foretold some event. One problem with this view is that it is difficult to find another people group in the ancient world who took that approach to demonstrating the superiority of their god. Why was it only Israel who did? Furthermore, if one is attempting to show the superiority of one's god, it seems counterproductive to have him predicting his nation's defeat, as is the case with Israel. In fact, it is precisely because Yahweh transcends time and space that these kinds of claims are possible. Thus, it seems reasonable that it is the prophets who would be moved to investigate and then report whether and how the divine word they proclaimed had been fulfilled. Without the prophetic prediction there would be little interest in studying that event when it occurred. The occurrence of the prediction invites one to investigate how it was, and through what human choices, the fulfillment actually took place.[72]

The importance of covenant

Two covenants run through Kings as point and counterpoint. They are interwoven in a unique way, with one surfacing and then the other: the Sinaitic covenant (Exod 20:1–23:33) and the Davidic covenant (2 Sam 7:5–16; the term "covenant" does not appear here, but it seems clear that is what Yahweh's promise amounts to). The Sinaitic covenant set the terms for Israel's life: Yahweh is God alone, not to be identified with this world in any way, and his unique character was to be mirrored in how his covenant people treated each other and the world Yahweh had given them. Their character was to be the same as his: holy. As covenant partners with Yahweh they would be permitted to live in and possess his land, the land of Canaan.

However, when Israel, now a significant people group, did possess that land, as reported at the end of the book of Joshua, that only fulfilled two of the three promises to Abraham. How were Abraham's descendants to become a blessing to all the world, and how was the world to be blessed through them (cf. Gen 12:3; 22:18)? This issue became especially problematic after the people had gotten the land, as the Judges account tells us. They had gotten what they wanted, so there was no longer any motivation to obey the covenant in order to secure future blessings; they had lost their sense of the future, and thus forgot their covenant bond, and fell into a downward spiral

72. DeVries has a very cogent statement about the importance of historical writing in Israel (xxx–xxxv).

of violence and moral corruption. The Davidic covenant became the means of fulfilling that third promise and restoring a future perspective. It was through the rule of David that Israel could bless the world. But that would require perseverance and faithfulness; the Davidic house would need to be preserved if that blessed rule was to be achieved.

But the Davidic covenant did not stand alone; it assumed that the Davidic monarchs would keep the Sinaitic covenant as David had. That had already appeared in the provision for kingship (should it become necessary) that Moses had included in his restatement of the covenant terms on the plains of Moab (Deut 17:18–20). The monarch was expected to have his own copy of the Torah, with which he was to be very familiar. To be sure, the dynasty would continue, that was God's promise, but any member of the dynasty who did not keep the terms of the Sinaitic covenant would be subject to Yahweh's judgment (2 Sam 7:14).

In Kings, the Davidic covenant is in the forefront. Solomon knows himself to be the son that Yahweh had promised to David (1 Kgs 3:6; 8:19), but the Solomon we see is full of ambiguity: his accession to the throne is marred by intrigue and violence (chaps. 1 and 2), and chap. 3 (the chapter which celebrates his wisdom) begins with his marriage to a non-Israelite, the princess of Egypt. Yet, we are told that he loved God, and God evidently kept his promise to bless him with a long life (1 Kgs 3:3, 13–14). But we can only wonder at the narrator's point of view as he explains Solomon's arrangements with Hiram, the Phoenician king, his use of forced labor, and his evident excesses. Much like the narrator of the book of Judges, he leaves us—knowing the Sinaitic covenant—to draw our own conclusions. We need not posit two different authors, one wholly positive toward Solomon, and one wholly negative, whose works have been cut apart and rather clumsily stitched together. Rather, we can think of a single person who is using annals and other reports faithfully, but in their juxtaposition is making points that are more powerful for their subtlety. He is revealing to us, the readers, the trends that will reach their climax in 1 Kgs 10:23–11:14. The representative of the Davidic dynasty is confronted with the Sinaitic covenant and found wanting.

This will be the recurring theme throughout the book: did the king "walk as David walked" (cf. 1 Kgs 3:14) which was according to the Sinaitic covenant? David's heart was "perfect" (שָׁלֵם, *šālēm*, i.e., undivided; 11:4) toward Yahweh. He was solely devoted to Yahweh (11:6), and to Yahweh's will (so also Asa, 1 Kgs 15:14; and Hezekiah, 2 Kgs 20:3; cf. Deut 10:12–13). The tragedy of the northern kingdom is that its first king set the pattern of defiance regarding the Sinaitic covenant right at the outset (1 Kgs 12:25–33) and every king after him followed in Jeroboam's footsteps, not David's.

But in Judah, the hold that the Davidic promise had on the imagination of the people is clear. There is no other explanation, humanly speaking, for the duration of that dynasty across some 400 years, through assassinations, revolutions, and attempted subversions. In Israel to the north, there were nine different dynasties in just 250 years (although four of them were during the last twenty years). But in Judah there was only one. This is not to say that all seventeen of these Davidic monarchs fully followed David's example of covenant love for Yahweh. In fact, it is only said of three of them that they "walked" in such a way: Asa, Hezekiah, and Josiah (1 Kgs 15:11; 2 Kgs 18:3; 22:2). Several others, Jehoshaphat, Joash, Amaziah, Azariah, and Jotham, are said to have emulated their fathers or mentors in doing what was right,[73] although in Amaziah's case it is specified that his behavior was not up to David's standard (14:3). Three Davidic kings, Jehoram (8:18), his son Ahaziah (vv. 26–27), and Ahaz (16:2–3) are said to have followed in the way of the kings of Israel, and of Ahaz, it is specifically said that he did not follow the ways of David. As for Manasseh, he was said to have fallen even below the standard of the northern kings and have sunk to the level of the Canaanites whom Yahweh had expelled from his land (21:2–6).

Yet, through all of this, Yahweh kept his promise. There were tragic results of individual failures, as he had said would be the case, but the results of the three who followed David were vital for the survival of the nation and the faith. Asa, followed by his son Jehoshaphat, gave Judah both political and spiritual stability in the years when the north, Israel, was experiencing chaos, both politically and spiritually. When Jeroboam was introducing the Yahweh idols at Bethel and Dan, Asa was tearing down the idols his mother (or grandmother) had erected. When Baasha destroyed the dynasty of Jeroboam, and then had his own dynasty destroyed by Zimri (whose rule lasted all of one week), who was replaced by the contesting kings Omri and Tibni, the dynasty of David continued steadily onward in Judah. These sixty-two or sixty-three years under only two monarchs, both of whom were loyal to the Sinaitic covenant, put Judah on a base that made it able to survive what was about to come on them as a result of a foolish alliance with the house of Omri.[74]

If Asa's rule came at a critical moment in the history of Judah, Hezekiah's came at an even more critical one. The northern kingdom had fallen and become an Assyrian province; the Assyrian "border" was now six miles north of Jerusalem. Hezekiah's father, Ahaz, had made a career of catering to the Assyrians to the extent of emulating their worship (2 Kgs 16:10–18). Was Judah about to be swallowed up in the Assyrian empire without even so much as a whimper? Was there anything to be done to preserve the nation and the faith? Everything said no. Yet Hezekiah, utterly loyal to Yahweh, convinced of his transcendence, would not bow to the forces around him. There had been no one like him in faith, not even Asa, since David. And that faith would be tested to the limit. What Hezekiah's reign meant for Judah was

---

73. 1 Kgs 22:42; 2 Kgs 12:2; 14:3; 15:3, 14.

74. It is hard to avoid the conclusion that while Jehoshaphat was a good man and a covenant loyalist, he was not very perceptive. His inability to see where an alliance with Ahab and the marriage of his son Joram to Ahab's daughter (and Omri's granddaughter) would lead provides primary evidence of his imperceptivity.

that Judah would have another hundred years of existence, years when the works of Isaiah, Micah, Nahum, Habakkuk, Zephaniah, and Jeremiah would be produced and would find rootage in the hearts and minds of faithful men and women. The vision of the one Holy God would not succumb to the apparently overwhelming evidence against it that the Assyrian empire posed.

Then there was Josiah. I do not agree that at some point it was thought that Josiah was a David *redivivus* who would somehow restore the kingdom.[75] Perhaps there were some in Judah who hoped for that, but I do not believe the present book would have us believe that, nor do I believe that there is evidence that there was once an edition of the book that taught such a thing. Rather, the book tells us that the sins into which Manasseh led the people were such that the only thing that could be hoped for was some mitigation of the effects of what was now all but inescapable.[76] As I have argued above, the mass of the people, as the book of Jeremiah shows, were far too settled into the paganism that Manasseh had promoted for fifty years to be moved by the "fanaticism" of this one king. What Josiah did was to prepare the faithful for the survival of what lay ahead. At this moment when it appeared that the biblical faith in the transcendent Yahweh was a chimera at best, this good man dared to shout, "No!" He showed people what would have to happen if the faith was to survive: there would have to be genuine heart-wrenching repentance not so much for their own sins as for those of the nation. There would have to be an unequivocal destruction of anything that compromised Yahweh's holy transcendence, that made him part of this world. There would have to be repudiation of the ways in which the northern kingdom had walked for 200 years. Nothing less than the severest iconoclasm would be enough. In this way Josiah, as the last significant son of David, would repudiate what the first son of David, Solomon, had begun.[77] Could his actions change the outcome of the story? Not at all. Things were much too far gone for that. But unquestionably, again as seen in Jeremiah, there were a remnant of the people whose faith would have been fired by what they saw this great man doing, and the faith would be such as even to survive two horrifying

---

75. As per Cross, "The Themes of the Books of Kings and the Structure of the Deuteronomistic History," 274–89. Also Sweeney, *King Josiah of Judah: The Lost Messiah of Israel* (Oxford: Oxford University Press, 2001).

76. It will be said that the pronouncements of doom resulting from Manasseh's sins were inserted by the exilic author/editor who is trying to explain why Josiah's reform did not have its desired effect. But the assumption that the "Josianic edition" could not have contained such statements is based on the false assumption that literary pieces must have been completely uniform in their outlook. As I have said above, the book does not tell of a "Josianic reform." It tells us of a historic interlude when we get a glimpse of what might have been, but nothing more.

77. Jehoahaz, Jehoiakim, Jehoiachin, and Zedekiah are almost footnotes. With the death of Josiah, the story is effectively ended and these four kings are really figures in an epilogue.

sieges and a fifty-year exile. What if there had not been a Josiah? Surely God's plans for the world would not have been thwarted, but would they have had to go in another entirely different direction? We do not know, nor do we need to speculate because there *was* a representative of the Davidic covenant who would not give in, who was absolutely loyal to the Sinaitic covenant as none of his predecessors, not even Hezekiah, had been. The catalogue of things that Josiah destroyed (2 Kgs 23:4–14) gives some indication of how far from the Sinaitic covenant Judah had gone, and how drastic the measures were going to have to be for any who wished to remain in that faith. In Josiah's narrative here at the end of the book, although it was too late to save the nation, we see that if the combination of Davidic covenant and Sinaitic covenant had been followed from the outset, it would have led Judah and all Israel to divine blessing. As the book stands, we are left to wonder, much in the vein of Ps 89, has God repudiated the Davidic covenant? Or will he somehow, some way, manage to fulfill it in ways we could not otherwise imagine? If we read Kings in the light of Samuel, surely that must be a possibility.

Chronology

The careful recording of the lengths of reigns and the synchronisms between the reigns of the Judean and the Israelite kings has been a source of both fascination and consternation for a long time. Simply adding up the numbers given results in major discrepancies. In the north the total number of years given for the period from the death of Solomon until the destruction of Samaria amounts to 237 years. But we know from synchronisms with other nations that this period cannot be longer than 208 years. When we add up the years for the Judean monarchs during this same period the discrepancies are even worse (255 years). On the other hand, there is a reasonably close correlation between the total regnal years for the Judean kings from the fall of Samaria to the fall of Jerusalem and the chronology as now understood.

Prior to the middle of the twentieth century it was not uncommon to point to these problems as evidence that the Israelites had no real interest in accurate historical reporting, and that the numbers were not at all accurate or reliable.[78] That position changed fairly radically with the publication of a doctoral thesis for the University of Chicago by Edwin Thiele in 1951.[79] The book is now in its third edition, and although it has its detractors, the majority of scholars have come to agree that far from the numbers being fanciful, they have been recorded with great accuracy. Thiele showed that three factors

78. See the discussion in Montgomery and Gehman, 45–57.

79. Edwin R. Thiele, *The Mysterious Numbers of the Hebrew Kings*, 3rd ed. (Grand Rapids: Kregel, 1994). See also Gershon Galil, *The Chronology of the Kings of Israel and Judah* (Leiden: Brill, 1996), who generally agrees with Thiele, but offers some helpful corrections.

must be taken into account. The first is whether the first year of the reign is post-dated or antedated, i.e., does a partial year of reign count as a full year, or is the reign counted as beginning in the next year? The second factor is when the new year was said to begin, in the fall or the spring. The third factor involves co-regencies. Thiele showed that if we understand Judah and Israel as taking varying positions at different times on the first two factors, and if we allow for several co-regencies, especially in Judah, the numbers work out with astonishing accuracy. The one major issue that resists easy resolution has to do with the dates of Hezekiah. The solution that Thiele has proposed seems much too complex (see the "Commentary" below).

Probably the most controversial of Thiele's proposals has to do with the co-regencies.[80] We only have reasonably clear evidence of one, that of Azariah (who is also called Uzziah) and his son Jotham. Second Kings 15:5 tells us that Azariah was confined to the palace because he had contracted leprosy and that his son Jotham "ruled the people of the land" (שֹׁפֵט אֶת־עַם הָאָרֶץ, *šōpēṭ ʾeṯ- ʿam hā ʾāreṣ*). There is also circumstantial evidence for a coregency between Azariah and his father Amaziah. Amaziah had foolishly challenged the Israelite king Jehoash to battle and was defeated and captured. It appears very likely that during Amaziah's captivity his teen-aged son was put on the throne, where he remained after his father was released (14:12–14, 21–22). But beyond these two accounts, the text is silent on the several other co-regencies that have been proposed. In most cases, they are very plausible, but they are still conjectural.[81]

Outline

- I. THE SOLOMON NARRATIVE 1:1–11:43
  - A. Established on the throne 1:1–2:46
    - 1. Solomon made king instead of Adonijah 1:1–53
      - a. Abishag is brought to court 1:1–4
      - b. Adonijah attempts to make himself king 1:5–10
      - c. Nathan and Bathsheba remind David of his oath 1:11–31
        - i. Nathan informs Bathsheba of her danger 1:11–14
        - ii. Bathsheba confronts David 1:15–21

---

80. Hobbs, for one, finds the evidence for them too weak (xliii). He also, with Sweeney, believes that more account should be taken of the LXX chronology which differs markedly from the MT (40–44). Sweeney says "The MT presents an impossible chronology," and sees the LXX system as being more consistent (43). However, another explanation for the LXX chronology is that the translators did not understand the complexities of the system that appears in the MT and sought to adjust the numbers to make sense, see Gray (45).

81. Commentators as diverse as Gray (57) and Wiseman (27) accept the likelihood of co-regencies.

iii. Nathan confronts David 1:22–27
iv. David responds to Bathsheba 1:28–31
d. David makes Solomon King 1:32–53
i. David's instructions 1:32–37
ii. David's instructions carried out 1:38–40
iii. The report reaches Adonijah 1:41–48
iv. Adonijah's fall 1:49–53
2. David's charge to Solomon 2:1–12
a. The King as covenant officer 2:1–4
b. David's directions for Solomon 2:5–9
c. Summary of David's reign 2:10–12
3. Solomon secures his kingship 2:13–46
a. Adonijah's foolish request 2:13–22
b. Solomon deals with the conspirators 2:23–35
c. Shimei's execution 2:36–46
B. Solomon's wisdom 3:1–4:34 [MT 5:14]
1. Introduction: unfortunate beginning 3:1–3
2. Yahweh gives wisdom to Solomon 3:4–15
3. A wise ruling 3:16–28
4. Wisdom in administration 4:1–28 [MT 5:8]
a. Solomon's officials 4:1–6
b. Solomon's administrative districts 4:7–19
c. Extent of Solomon's dominion 4:20–28 [MT 5:8]
5. Summary 4:29–34 [MT 5:9–14]
C. Solomon's building projects 5:1 [MT 5:15]–9:28
1. Preparations 5:1–18 [MT 5:15–32]
a. Negotiations with Hiram 5:1–12 [MT 5:15–25]
b. Laborers for the temple 5:13–18 [MT 5:26–32]
2. Building the temple 6:1–38
a. The floor plan of the temple 6:1–10
b. Yahweh's conditions 6:11–13
c. Furnishing and decorating the temple 6:14–38
3. Solomon builds his palace 7:1–12
4. The furnishings of the temple 7:13–51
5. Dedicating the temple 8:1–66
a. The ark is brought to the temple 8:1–13
b. The introduction 8:14–21
c. Solomon's prayer: opening 8:22–30
d. Solomon's prayer: the petitions 8:31–53
e. Solomon blesses the people 8:54–61
f. The dedication of the temple 8:62–66
6. Yahweh's judgments regarding the Temple 9:1–9
7. Solomon's further activities 9:10–28
D. Solomon's fame and splendor 10:1–29

1. The queen of Sheba visits Solomon 10:1–13
2. Solomon's riches 10:14–29

E. Solomon's downfall and death 11:1–43
1. Solomon's sins 11:1–10
2. Judgment on Solomon 11:11–40
a. Announcement of judgment 11:11–13
b. Adversaries in the empire 11:14–25
c. Rebel in the kingdom 11:26–40
3. Solomon's death 11:41–43

II. THE DIVIDED MONARCHY 1 Kings 12:1–2 Kings 17:41
A. Rehoboam to Ahab 12:1–16:28
1. Jeroboam and the secession 12:1–14:20
a. The kingdom is divided 12:1–24
b. Jeroboam's sin 12:25–33
c. A man of God prophesies against Jeroboam 13:1–34
i. Judgment on Jeroboam's cult 13:1–10
ii. The death of the man of God 13:11–34
d. Judgment on Jeroboam's house 14:1–20
2. Rehoboam, Abijam, and Asa 14:21–15:24
a. Rehoboam 14:21–31
b. Abijam 15:1–8
c. Asa 15:9–24
3. Jeroboam's successors 15:25–16:28
a. Nadab 15:25–32
b. Baasha 15:33–16:7
c. Elah 16:8–14
d. Zimri 16:15–20
e. Omri 16:21–28

B. The house of Ahab and the ministries of Elijah and Elisha 1 Kgs 16:29–2 Kgs 13:25
1. Elijah 1 Kgs 16:29–2 Kgs 1:18
a. Elijah and Ahab 1 Kgs 16:29–22:40
i. Ahab's opening regnal account 16:29–34
ii. Elijah and the great drought 17:1–18:46
(a) Elijah announces the drought 17:1
(b) Elijah at the Wadi Kerith 17:2–7
(c) Elijah cared for by the widow of Zarephath 17:8–16
(d) Elijah and the widow's son 17:17–24
(e) Elijah's confrontation with Baal 18:1–46
(i) Elijah presents himself to Ahab 18:1–19
(ii) Elijah states the challenge 18:20–24
(iii) The contest on Mt. Carmel 18:25–38
(iv) The response to the contest 18:39–46
iii. Elijah and Yahweh at Horeb 19:1–21

(a) Elijah escapes to Horeb 19:1–8
(b) Yahweh reveals himself and his plans 19:9–18
(c) The selection of Elisha 19:19–21
iv. The final events of Ahab's reign 20:1–22:40
(a) The struggle with Ben-hadad 20:1–43
(i) The first battle 20:1–22
(ii) The second battle 20:23–34
(iii) Prophetic condemnation of Ahab 20:35–43
(b) Naboth's vineyard 21:1–29
(i) Naboth's vineyard taken 21:1–16
(ii) Elijah's condemnation of Ahab 21:17–29
(c) Micaiah's prophecy and Ahab's death 22:1–40
(i) Micaiah's prophecy against Ahab 22:1–28
(ii) Ahab's death 22:29–38
(iii) Ahab's closing regnal summary 22:39–40
b. Jehoshaphat 22:41–50 [MT 51]
c. Elijah and Ahaziah 1 Kgs 22:51 [MT 52]–2 Kgs 1:18
2. Elijah and Elisha 2 Kgs 2:1–25
a. Elijah's flight to heaven 2 Kgs 2:1–11
b. Elisha's first miracles 2:12–25
3. Elisha 2 Kgs 3:1–13:25
a. Elisha's miracles 3:1–8:6
i. The attack on Moab 3:1–27
ii. The widow's oil 4:1–7
iii. The Shunamite woman and her son 4:8–37
iv. Miracles of provision 4:38–44
v. Two miracles of restoration 5:1–6:7
(a) The healing of Naaman 5:1–27
(i) Naaman and Elisha 5:1–19
(ii) Gehazi and Naaman 5:20–27
(b) The floating axe head 6:1–7
vi. Elisha and the Syrians 6:8–7:20
(a) The abortive attempt to capture Elisha 6:8–23
(b) Famine in Samaria 6:24–7:20
vii. The Shunamite's land restored 8:1–6
b. The end of the dynasty of Omri 8:7–11:21
i. The appointment of Hazael 8:7–15
ii. Jehoram king of Judah 8:16–24
iii. Ahaziah king of Judah 8:25–29
iv. The Jehu revolution 9:1–10:36
(a) Jehu's coronation 9:1–13
(b) The deaths of Joram and Ahaziah 9:14–29
(c) The death of Jezebel 9:30–37
(d) The destruction of Ahab's family 10:1–17

(e) The killing of the servants of Baal and the destruction of his temple 10:18–29
(f) Final comments on Jehu and his reign 10:30–36
v. Athaliah and Joash 11:1–21 [MT 12:1]
c. The reign of Joash 12:1–21 [MT 12:2–22]
i. The restoration of the temple 12:1–16 [MT 2–17]
ii. The end of Joash's reign 12:17–21 [MT 18–22]
d. Jehoahaz, Jehoash, the death of Elisha, and the end of Syrian dominance 13:1–25
i. Jehoahaz, king of Israel 13:1–9
ii. Jehoash and the death of Elisha 13:10–21
iii. Relief from Syria 13:22–25
C. Amaziah to the fall of Samaria 14:1–16:20
1. Amaziah of Judah 14:1–22
2. Jeroboam II 14:23–29
3. Azariah of Judah 15:1–7
4. Zechariah and Shallum 15:8–16
5. Menaham and Pekahiah 15:17–26
6. Pekah 15:27–31
7. Jotham of Judah 15:32–38
8. Ahaz of Judah 16:1–20
D. The fall of Samaria 17:1–41
1. Hoshea 17:1–6
2. Reasons for the exile 17:7–23
3. Samaria resettled 17:24–33
4. A reflection on religious conditions in resettled Samaria 17:34–41
III. JUDAH ALONE 18:1–25:30
A. Hezekiah 18:1–20:21
1. Hezekiah's opening regnal account 18:1–12
2. Hezekiah versus Sennacherib 18:13–19:37
a. Hezekiah's attempt to pay Sennacherib to withdraw 18:13–16
b. Sennacherib's messenger 18:17–37
i. The Rab-shaqeh's first address 18:17–25
ii. The Israelite party's request 18:26
iii. The Rab-shaqeh's second address 18:27–37
c. Hezekiah's anguish and Yahweh's response 19:1–7
d. Sennacherib's letter and Hezekiah's prayer 19:8–19
e. Yahweh's response 19:20–34
f. The destruction of the Assyrian army 19:35–37
3. Hezekiah's illness and recovery 20:1–11
4. The embassy from Babylon 20:12–21
B. The reign of Manasseh 21:1–18

- C. The reign of Amon 21:19–26
- D. The reign of Josiah 22:1–23:30
    1. Josiah's accession 22:1–2
    2. The discovery of the book of the Torah 22:3–20
    3. Josiah's reforms 23:1–27
    4. Josiah's death 23:28–30
- E. Judah's final days 23:21–25:30
    1. Jehoahaz 23:21–35
    2. Jehoiakim 23:36–24:7
    3. Jehoiachin 24:8–17
    4. Zedekiah 24:18–25:7
    5. The destruction of Jerusalem and Judah 25:8–21
    6. The death of Gedaliah 25:22–26
    7. Favor shown to Jehoiakim 25:27–30

Selected Bibliography

Cross, F. M. "The Themes of the Books of Kings and the Structure of the Deuteronomistic History." In *Canaanite Myth and Hebrew Epic*. Cambridge: Harvard University Press, 1973.

Gooding, D. W. *Relics of Ancient Exegesis: A Study of the Miscellanies in 3 Reigns 2*. SOTSMS 2. Cambridge: Cambridge University Press, 1976.

Grabbe, L. L. *1 & 2 Kings: An Introduction and Study Guide: History and Story in Ancient Israel.* T&T Clark Study Guides to the Old Testament. London: Bloomsbury T&T Clark, 2017.

Halpern, B., and A. Lemaire, eds. *The Books of Kings: Sources, Composition, Historiography and Reception*. VTSup 129. Leiden: Brill, 2010.

Halpern, B., and A. Lemaire. "The Composition of Kings." In *The Book of Kings: Sources, Composition, Historiography and Reception*, ed. Baruch Halpern and André Lemaire, 123–53. VTSup 129. Leiden: Brill, 2010.

Knoppers, G. N. "Theories of the Redaction(s) of Kings." in *The Books of Kings: Sources, Composition, Historiography and Reception*, ed. Baruch Halpern and André Lemaire, 69–88. VTSup 129. Leiden: Brill, 2010.

Lemaire, A. "Towards a Redactional History of the Book of Kings." In *Reconsidering Israel and Judah: Recent Studies on the Deuteronomic History*. ed. Gary N. Knoppers and J. Gordon McConville, 446–61. SBT 8. Winona Lake, IN: Eisenbrauns, 2000.

Leuchter, M., and A. Klaus-Peter, eds. *Soundings in Kings: Perspectives and Methods in Contemporary Scholarship.* Minneapolis, MN: Fortress Press, 2010.

McConville, J. G., "The Old Testament Historical Books in Modern Scholarship." *Them* 22, no. 3 (1997): 3–13.

McKenzie, S. L. "The Books of Kings in the Deuteronomistic History." In *The History of Israel's Traditions: The Heritage of Martin Noth*, ed. Steven L. McKenzie and M. Patrick Graham, 281–307. JSOTSup 182. Sheffield: Sheffield Academic, 1991.

———. *The Trouble with Kings: The Composition of the Book of Kings in the Deuteronomistic History*. VTSup 42. Leiden: Brill, 1991.
Na'aman, N. "Was an Early Edition of the Book of Kings Composed during Hezekiah's Reign?" *JSOT* 31, no. 1 (2017): 80–91.
Nelson, R. D. *The Double Redaction of the Deuteronomic History*. Sheffield: JSOT Press, 1981.
Noth, M. *The Deuteronomic History*. JSOTSup 15. Sheffield: JSOT Press, 1981.
Peterson, B. N. *The Authors of the Deuteronomistic History: Locating a Tradition in Ancient History*. Minneapolis, MN: Fortress Press, 2014.
Provan, I. *Hezekiah and the Books of Kings*. BZAW 172. Berlin: Walter de Gruyter, 1988.
Römer, T. and A. de Pury. "L'historigraphie deutéronomiste (HD): Historie de la recherché et enjue du débat." In *Israël construit son histoire*, ed. Albert de Pury et al., 9–120. Monde de la Bible 34. Geneva: Labor et Fide, 1996.
———. *The So-Called Deuteronomic History: A Sociological, Historical, and Literary Introduction*. London: T&T Clark, 2005.
Shenkel, J. D. *Chronology and Recensional Development in the Greek Text of Kings*. HSM 1. Cambridge, MA: Harvard University Press, 1968.
Tetley, M. C. *The Reconstructed Chronology of the Divided Kingdom*. Winona Lake, IN: Eisenbrauns, 2005.
Thomas, B. D. *Hezekiah and the Compositional History of Kings*. FAT 2/63. Tübingen: Mohr Siebeck, 2014.
Weinfeld, M. *Deuteronomy and the Deuteronomic School*. Oxford: Clarendon Press, 1972.

Commentary Bibliography

Barnes, William H. *1–2 Kings*. CorBC. Carol Stream, IL: Tyndale House Publishers, 2012.
Benzinger, I. *Die Bücher der Könige*. KHC 9. Freiburg: J. C. B. Mohr, 1899.
Brueggemann, Walter. *1 & 2 Kings: A Commentary*. SHBC. Macon, GA: Smyth & Helwys, 2000.
———. *1 Kings*. Knox Preaching Guides. Atlanta: John Knox Press, 1983.
———. *2 Kings*. Knox Preaching Guides. Atlanta: John Knox Press, 1982.
Buis, Pierre. *Le Livre des Rois*. SB. Paris: Librairie Lecoffre, J. Gabalda, 1997.
Burney, Charles Fox. *The Book of Judges, with Introduction and Notes, and Notes on The Hebrew Text of The Books of Kings, with An Introduction and Appendix*. Library of Biblical Studies. New York: KTAV Pub. House, 1970.
Cogan, Mordechai. *1 Kings: A New Translation with Introduction and Commentary*. AB. New York: Doubleday, 2001.
———, and Hayim Tadmor. *II Kings: A New Translation*. Garden City, NY: Doubleday, 1988.
Cohn, Robert L. *2 Kings*. Berit Olam. Collegeville, MN: Liturgical Press, 2000.

Conti, Marco, Gianluca Pilara, and Thomas C. Oden. *1–2 Kings, 1–2 Chronicles, Ezra, Nehemiah, Esther.* ACCSOT 5. Downers Grove, IL: Intervarsity Press, 2008.

Dawes, Stephen B. *1 & 2 Kings.* People's Bible Commentary. Oxford: Bible Reading Fellowship, 2001.

DeVries, Simon John. *1 Kings.* WBC 12. Nashville, TN: Thomas Nelson Publishers, 2003.

Fretheim, Terence E. *First and Second Kings.* Westminster Bible Companion. Louisville, KY: Westminster John Knox Press, 1999.

Fritz, Volkmar. *1 & 2 Kings.* CC. Minneapolis, MN: Fortress, 2003.

Gray, John. *I and II Kings: A Commentary.* 2nd, fully rev. ed. OTL. Philadelphia: Westminster Press, 1970.

Hens-Piazza, Gina. *1–2 Kings.* AOTC. Nashville, TN: Abingdon, 2006.

Hentschel, Georg. *1 Könige.* NEchtB 10. Würzburg: Echter, 1984.

———. *2 Könige.* NEchtB 11. Würzburg: Echter, 1985.

Hobbs, T. R. *2 Kings.* WBC 13. Waco, TX: Word Books, 1985.

———. *1, 2 Kings.* Word Biblical Themes. Dallas, TX: Word Pub., 1989.

Hochberg, Reuven, A. J. Rosenberg, and Rashi. *I Kings, A New English Translation.* Judaica Books of the Prophets. New York: Judaica Press, 1980.

House, Paul R. *1, 2 Kings.* NAC 8. Nashville, TN: Broadman & Holman Publishers, 1995.

Jones, Gwilym H. *1 and 2 Kings: Based on The Revised Standard Version.* New Century Bible Commentary. Grand Rapids: W.B. Eerdmans Pub. Co., 1984.

Kittel, Rudolf. *Die Bücher der Könige, Übersetzt und Erklärt.* HKAT 5. Göttingen: Vandenhoeck, 1900.

Klostermann, August, and Hermann Leberecht Strack. *Die Bücher Samuelis und der Könige.* Nördlingen: C.H. Beck, 1887.

Konkel, August H. *1 & 2 Kings.* NIVAC. Grand Rapids: Zondervan, 2006.

Laffey, Alice L. *First and Second Kings.* New Collegeville Bible Commentary. Collegeville, MN: Liturgical Press, 2011.

Leithart, Peter J. *1 & 2 Kings.* SCM Theological Commentary on the Bible. London: SCM Press, 2006.

Long, Burke O. *1 Kings: With an Introduction to Historical Literature.* FOTL 9. Grand Rapids: Eerdmans, 1984.

———. *2 Kings.* FOTL 10. Grand Rapids: Eerdmans 1991.

Long, Jesse C., Jr. *1 & 2 Kings.* College Press NIV Commentary. Joplin, MO: College Press Publishing Company, 2002.

Monson, John. "1 Kings." *ZIBBC* 3:2–109.

Montgomery, James A., and Henry Snyder Gehman. *A Critical and Exegetical Commentary on The Books of Kings.* ICC. Edinburgh: T&T Clark, 1951.

Mulder, M. J., and John Vriend. *1 Kings 1–11.* HCOT. Leuven: Peeters, 1998.

Nelson, Richard D. *First and Second Kings.* IBC. Atlanta: John Knox Press, 1987.

Noth, Martin. *Könige.* BKAT 9. Neukirchen-Vluyn: Neukirchener Verlag, 1968.

Oswalt, John N. *The Book of Isaiah, Chapters 1–39*. NICOT. Grand Rapids: Eerdmans,1986.

———. *The Book of Isaiah, Chapters 40–66*. NICOT. Grand Rapids: Eerdmans, 1994.

Petersen, David L. *1 & 2 Kings*. OTG. Sheffield: Sheffield Academic, 1997.

———. "2 Kings." *ZIBBC* 3:110–219.

Petersen, David L., and Beverly Roberts Gaventa. *The New Interpreter's Bible One Volume Commentary*. Nashville, TN: Abingdon.

Provan, Iain W. *1 and 2 Kings*. NIBC. Peabody, MA: Hendrickson, 1995.

Rice, Gene. *Nations Under God: A Commentary on The Book of 1 Kings*. ITC. Grand Rapids: Eerdmans, 1990.

Robinson, J. *The First Book of Kings*. CBC. Cambridge: University Press, 1972.

———. *The Second Book of Kings*. CBC. Cambridge: Cambridge University Press, 1976.

Šanda, Albert. *Die Bücher der Könige: Übersetzt und Erklärt*. 2 vols. EHAT 9. Münster: Aschendorff, 1911.

Seow, Choon-Leong. "The First and Second Books of Kings." Pages 1–296 in vol. 3 of *NIB*. Edited by Leander E. Keck. Nashville, TN: Abingdon, 1994.

Slotki, I. W., and Ephraim Oratz. *Kings: Hebrew Text & English Translation*. Rev. ed. Soncino Books of the Bible. London: Soncino Press, 1990.

Smelik, K. A. D. *1 Koningen*. Belichting van Het Bijbelboek. Brugge: Katholieke Bijbelstichting, 1993.

Sweeney, Marvin A. *First and Second Kings: A Commentary*. OTL. Louisville, KY: Westminster John Knox Press, 2007.

Thenius, Otto. *Die Bücher der Könige*. Leipzig: Weidmann, 1849.

Vos, Howard Frederic. *1, 2 Kings*. Bible Study Commentary Series. Grand Rapids: Zondervan, 1989.

Walsh, Jerome T., and David W. Cotter. *1 Kings*. Berit Olam. Collegeville, MN: Liturgical Press, 1996.

Wiseman, D. J. *1 and 2 Kings: An Introduction and Commentary*. TOTC 9. Downers Grove, IL: InterVarsity Press, 1993.

Würthwein, Ernst. *Die Bücher der Könige*. 2nd ed. ATD 11. Göttingen: Vandenhoeck und Ruprecht, 1984.

The House of Ahab and the Ministries of Elijah and Elisha (1 Kgs 16:29–2 Kgs 13:25)

Outline

II. The Divided Monarchy 1 Kings 12:1–2 Kings 17:41
- B. The house of Ahab and the ministries of Elijah and Elisha 1 Kgs 16:29–2 Kgs 13:25
  - 1. Elijah 1 Kgs 16:29–2 Kgs 1:18
    - a. Elijah and Ahab 1 Kgs 16:29–22:40
    - b. Jehoshaphat 22:41–50 [MT 51]
    - c. Elijah and Ahaziah 1 Kgs 22:51 [MT 52]–2 Kgs 1:18
  - 2. Elijah and Elisha 2 Kgs 2:1–25
    - a. Elijah's flight to heaven 2 Kgs 2:1–11
    - b. Elisha's first miracles 2:12–25
  - 3. Elisha 2 Kgs 3:1–13:25
    - a. Elisha's miracles 3:1–8:6
      - i. The attack on Moab 3:1–27
      - ii. The widow's oil 4:1–7
      - iii. The Shunamite woman and her son 4:8–37
      - iv. Miracles of provision 4:38–44
      - v. Two miracles of restoration 5:1–6:7
        - (a) The healing of Naaman 5:1–27
          - (i) Naaman and Elisha 5:1–19
          - (ii) Gehazi and Naaman 5:20–27
        - (b) The floating axe head 6:1–7
      - vi. Elisha and the Syrians 6:8–7:20
        - (a) The abortive attempt to capture Elisha 6:8–23
        - (b) Famine in Samaria 6:24–7:20
      - vii. The Shunamite's land restored 8:1–6
    - b. The end of the dynasty of Omri 8:7–11:21
      - i. The appointment of Hazael 8:7–15
      - ii. Jehoram king of Judah 8:16–24

iii. Ahaziah king of Judah 8:25–29
iv. The Jehu revolution 9:1–10:36
(a) Jehu's coronation 9:1–13
(b) The deaths of Joram and Ahaziah 9:14–29
(c) The death of Jezebel 9:30–37
(d) The destruction of Ahab's family 10:1–17
(e) The killing of the servants of Baal and the destruction of his temple 10:18–29
(f) Final comments on Jehu and his reign 10:30–36
v. Athaliah and Joash 11:1–21 [MT 12:1]
c. The reign of Joash 12:1–21 [MT 12:2–22]
i. The restoration of the temple 12:1–16 [MT 2–17]
ii. The end of Joash's reign 12:17–21 [MT 18–22]
d. Jehoahaz, Jehoash, the death of Elisha, and the end of Syrian dominance 13:1–25
i. Jehoahaz, king of Israel 13:1–9
ii. Jehoash and the death of Elisha 13:10–21
iii. Relief from Syria 13:22–25

Selected Bibliography

Angel, H. "Hopping Between Two Opinions: Understanding the Biblical Portrait of Ahab." *JBQ* 35, no. 1 (2007): 3–10.

Battenfield, J. R. "YHWH's Refutation of the Baal Myth through the Actions of Elijah and Elijah and Elisha." In *Israel's Apostasy and Restoration: Essays in Honor of Roland K. Harrison*, ed. A. Gileadi, 19–37. Grand Rapids: Baker, 1988.

Brodie, T. L. *The Crucial Bridge: The Elijah-Elisha Narrative as an Interpretive Synthesis of Genesis-Kings and A Literary Model for the Gospels.* Collegeville, MN: Liturgical Press, 2000.

Bronner, L. *The Stories of Elijah and Elisha as Polemics against Baal Worship.* Leiden: Brill, 1968.

Brueggemann, W. *Testimony to Otherwise: The Witness of Elijah and Elisha.* St. Louis, MO: Chalice Press, 2001.

Cohn, R. L. "The Literary Logic of 1 Kings 17–19." *JBL* 101 (1982): 333–50.

Coote, R. B, ed. *Elijah and Elisha in Socioliterary Perspective.* SemeiaSt. Atlanta: Scholars Press, 1992.

DeVries, S. J. *Prophet Against Prophet: The Role of the Micaiah Narrative (I Kings 22) in the Development of Early Prophetic Tradition.* Grand Rapids: Eerdmans, 1978.

Gros Louis, K. R. R. "Elijah and Elisha." In *Literary Interpretations of Biblical Narratives*, ed. K. R. R. Gros Louis, J. S. Ackerman, and T. S. Warshaw, 177–90. Nashville: Abingdon, 1974.

Jobling, D. "The Syrians in the Book of the Divided Kingdoms: A Literary/Theological Approach." *BI* 11 (2003): 531–42.
Lightbourn, F. C. "The 'Story' in the Old Testament." *AThR* 21 (1939): 94–102.
Morrison, C. E. "Handing on the Mantle: The Transmission of the Elijah Cycle in the Biblical Versions." In *Master of the Sacred Page: Essays in Honor of Roland E. Murphy, O. Carm., on the Occasion of His Eightieth Birthday*, ed. R. E. Murphy, K. J. Egan, and C. E. Morrison, 109–29. Washington, DC: Carmelite Inst., 1997.
Otto, S. "The Composition of the Elijah-Elisha Stories and the Deuteronomic History." *JSOT* 27 (2003): 487–508.
Overholt, T. W. "Elijah and Elisha in the Context of Israelite Religion." In *Prophets and Paradigms: Essays in Honor of Gene M. Tucker*, ed. G. M. Tucker and S. B. Reid, 94–111. JSOTSup 229. Sheffield: Sheffield Academic, 1996.
Steck, O. H. *Überlieferung und Zeitgeschichte in den Elia-Erzählungen.* WMANT 26. Neukirchen-Vluyn: Neukirchener, 1968.
Sweeney, M. A. "Prophets and Priests in the Deuteronomic History: Elijah and Elisha." In *Israelite Prophecy and the Deuteronomistic History: Portrait, Reality, and the Formation of History*, ed. M. R. Jacobs and R. F. Person, Jr., 35–49. Atlanta: SBL Press, 2013.
Wallace, H. N. "The Oracles Against the Israelite Dynasties in 1 and 2 Kings." *Bib* 67 (1986): 21–40.
Wendland, E. R. "Elijah and Elisha: Sorcerers or Witch Doctors?" *BT* 43 (1992): 213–23.
White, M. C. *The Elijah Legends and Jehu's Coup.* BJS 311. Atlanta: Scholars Press, 1997.

Elijah and Ahaziah (1 Kings 22:51 [MT 52]–2 Kings 1:18)

Translation

22:51 [MT 52] Ahaziah the son of Ahab began to rule over Israel in Samaria
in the seventeenth year of Jehoshaphat, king of Judah, and he ruled for two
years. **52 [MT 53]** He did evil in Yahweh's eyes, walking in the way of his
father and the way of his mother, and in the way of Jeroboam, son of Nebat,
who caused Israel to sin. **53 [MT 54]** He served Baal and prostrated himself
to him, and he provoked Yahweh in the same way his fathers had done.

2 Kings 1:1 (Now Moab had rebelled against Israel after Ahab died.)
2 Ahaziah fell through the lattice in his upper chamber which was in Samaria
and was injured. So he sent messengers and said to them, "Go and inquire
of Baal-zebub, the god of Ekron, whether I will survive this injury." **3** The
angel of Yahweh spoke to Elijah the Tishbite, "Get up, and go up to meet the
messengers of the king of Samaria and say to them, 'Is there no God in Israel
that you are going to inquire of Baal-zebub, the god of Ekron?' **4** Therefore,
thus says Yahweh, 'As for the bed on which you are, you will not get up from

it, for you will surely die.' " So Elijah went. **5** The messengers returned to him
and he said to them, "Why have you returned?" **6** They said to him, "A man
came up to meet us and he said to us, 'Go, return to the king who sent you
and say to him, "Thus says Yahweh, 'Is it because there is no God in Israel
that you are sending to inquire of Baal-zebub, the god of Ekron? Therefore,
the bed on which you are lying,[1] you will not get up from it, for you will
surely die." ' " **7** He said to them, "What sort[2] of man was it who came up
to meet you and spoke these words to you?" **8** They said, "A hairy man with
a leather loincloth fastened on his hips." "It is Elijah the Tishbite," he said.
9 So he sent a captain of fifty with his fifty to him. Now he was sitting on the
top of a hill. He said to him, "Man of God, the king says, 'Come down.' " **10**
Elijah answered and said to the captain of fifty, "If I am a man of God, let fire
fall from heaven and devour you and your fifty." Then fire fell from heaven
and devoured him and his fifty. **11** Again he sent to him another captain of
fifty and his fifty. He answered and said to him, "Man of God, thus says the
king, 'Hurry down.' " **12** Elijah answered and said to them, "If I am a man of
God, let fire fall from heaven and devour you and your fifty." Then the fire
of God fell from heaven and devoured him and his fifty. **13** Again he sent a
third captain of fifty and his fifty. So the third captain of fifty went out and
came. But he fell on his knees before Elijah and pleaded with him and said to
him, "Man of God, please let my life and the lives of these, your servants, be
precious in your sight. **14** Look, fire from heaven fell and devoured the first
two captains of fifty and their fifties. But now make my life precious in your
eyes." **15** The angel of Yahweh spoke to Elijah, "Go down with him; do not
be afraid of him." So he arose and went down with him to the king. **16** He
said to him, "Thus says Yahweh, 'Because you sent messengers to inquire
of Baal-zebub, the god of Ekron – is it because there is no God in Israel to
inquire of his word? Therefore, the bed upon which you went up there, you
will not go down from, for you will surely die.' " **17** So he died according to
the word of Yahweh which Elijah spoke, and Joram reigned after him in the
second year of Jehoram,[3] son of Jehoshaphat, because he had no son. **18** The
remainder of the things which Ahaziah did, are they not written in the book
of the events of the days of the Kings of Israel.

Textual Notes

53.a. אִמּוֹ: Gk. "the ways of Jezebel his mother"; Vulg. and Syr. with MT.

53.b. וּבְדֶרֶךְ: Gk. "in the sins of"; Vulg. and Syr. with MT.

---

1. Here and again in v. 6 "the bed on which you are" is placed in an emphatic position in the sentence.
2. Heb. מִשְׁפָּט, *mišpāṭ*.
3. It has become conventional to use the short form of Jehoram: Joram, to distinguish the northern king from the southern king of the same name.

54.a. הַבַּעַל: Gk. "the Baals"; Vulg. and Syr. with MT.

54.b–b. אֲשֶׁר־עָשָׂה אָבִיו: Gk "according to all that had been done before him"; Vulg. and Syr. with MT.

2.a–a. בְּבַעַל זְבוּב אֱלֹהֵי עֶקְרוֹן: Gk. "the goddess Baal, the fly-god of Ekron"; Vulg. "Beelzebub; Syr. "Baal-zebub." Same readings in vv. 3, 6, and 16.

3.a. הַתִּשְׁבִּי: Gk. and Vulg. add "saying"; Syr. with MT.

3.b. מַלְאֲכֵי: Gk. adds "Ahaziah"; Vulg. and Syr. with MT.

4.a. וְלָכֵן: Gk. reads "Not so for"; Vulg. and Syr. with MT. So also in vv. 6 and 16 below.

4.b–b. מוֹת תָּמוּת: Gk. reads "there by death you will die"; Vulg. and Syr. "you will surely die" with MT. So also in vv. 6 and 16.

4.c. אֵלִיָּה: Gk. adds "and spoke to them"; Vulg. and Syr. with MT.

5.a. אֵלָיו: Vulg. and Syr. "to Ahaziah"; Gk with MT.

6.a. הַמֶּלֶךְ: Syr. "the man"; Gk and Vulg. with MT.

6.b–b. כֹּה אָמַר יְהוָה: Syr. omits; Gk and Vulg. with MT.

6.c. לָכֵן: Syr. adds "thus says the LORD"; Gk and Vulg. with MT.

9.a. אֵלָיו: Gk. adds "and came"; Vulg. and Syr. with MT.

9.b. וְהִנֵּה: Gk. reads "Elijah"; Vulg. and Syr. with MT.

9.c. וַיְדַבֵּר: Gk. adds "the captain of 50"; Vulg. and Syr. with MT.

9.d. דִּבֶּר: Gk. reads "has summoned you"; Vulg. and Syr. with MT.

11.a. וַיָּשָׁב: Gk. reads "The king proceeded"; Vulg. and Syr. with MT.

11.b. וַיַּעַן: Gk. reads "He went up and the captain of 50"; Vulg. and Syr. omit. *CTAT* (376) considers MT most likely.

12.a. אֲלֵיהֶם: Gk. and Syr. "to him"; Vulg. omits. A good case can be made for either alternative.

12.b. הָאֱלֹהִים: Gk. and Vulg. omit "of God"; Syr. with MT. *CTAT* (377) considers MT probable.

13.a–a. וַיָּשָׁב וַיִּשְׁלַח שַׂר־חֲמִשִּׁים שְׁלִשִׁים: Gk. "The king proceeded still to send a third leader, a captain of fifty"; Vulg. with MT; Syr. "He sent again to him a third time, a captain of fifty." MT best explains the others.

13.b–b. וַיַּ֫עַל וַיָּבֹא שַׂר־הַחֲמִשִּׁים הַשְּׁלִישִׁי: Gk. "So the third captain of fifty went out"; Syr. "So the captain of fifty went up"; Vulg. "So he came."

13.c–c. וַיִּתְחַנֵּן אֵלָיו וַיְדַבֵּר אֵלָיו: Gk. "spoke to him and said"; Vulg. and Syr. "and said." The second "to him" of MT seems added.

13.d–d. תִּיקַר־נָא נַפְשִׁי וְנֶפֶשׁ עֲבָדֶיךָ אֵלֶּה חֲמִשִּׁים בְּעֵינֶיךָ: Vulg. "Do not despise my life and the lives of your servants who are with me"; Syr. "Let my life and the lives of these fifty servants of yours who are standing before you be precious in your sight"; Gk. with MT. MT best explains the others.

14.a–a. וְעַתָּה תִּיקַר נַפְשִׁי בְּעֵינֶיךָ: Gk. "the life of your servants"; Vulg. "I beg, 'Have pity on my life' "; Syr. with MT. As above.

15.a. מִפָּנָיו: Gk. "them"; Vulg. omits; Syr. with MT.

16.a. וַיְדַבֵּר: Gk. "Elijah"; Vulg. and Syr. with MT.

16.b. יַעַן: Gk. "Why"; Vulg. and Syr. with MT.

16.c–c. הַמִבְּלִי אֵין־אֱלֹהִים בְּיִשְׂרָאֵל לִדְרֹשׁ בִּדְבָרוֹ: Gk. omits; Vulg. and Syr. with MT.

17.a. וַיִּמְלֹךְ: Gk. inserts v. 18 here. Vulg. and Syr. with MT.

17.b. יְהוֹרָם תַּחְתָּיו: Vulg. and Syr. (as well as Lucian) add "his brother"; Gk. reads "the son of Ahab". *CTAT* (378–9), considers MT probable.

17.c–c. בִּשְׁנַת שְׁתַּיִם לִיהוֹרָם: Gk. omits and reads instead "over Samaria 12 years until 18th year of"; Vulg. and Syr. with MT.

17.d–d. כִּי לֹא־הָיָה לוֹ בֵּן: Gk. omits; Vulg. and Syr. with MT.

Commentary

As mentioned above, this sub-unit is the final illustration of Yahweh's power at work in Elijah. Commentators (Fritz, 229; Hobbs, 4) are divided over whether it should be considered a single unit or a composite. But even many of those who take it to be composite recognize that it is a literary unity, with the evidence of literary artistry manifest throughout, especially in the latter portion, 2 Kings 1:2–17.[4] The fact that 1 Kings ends and 2 Kings begins in the middle of Ahaziah's regnal narrative illustrates the fact that Kings was originally considered to be one book, and that the division into two books was more mechanical than thoughtful. It first appears in the LXX, only appearing in Hebrew with the Bomberg Bible in 1516 AD, with a note that this is the way "foreign speakers" divide the books (Cogan and Tadmor, 22).

4. Christopher T. Begg, "Unifying Factors in 2 Kings 1:2–17a," *JSOT* 10 (1985): 75–86.

A possible reason for the division at this point is the parenthetical mention of the Moabite rebellion (2 Kings 1:1), which Ahaziah's successor Jehoram tried unsuccessfully to quell (2 Kings 3:4-27). In many ways this event was a watershed for the northern kingdom, in that it decisively signaled the end of any Israelite empire. From this point on, even recognizing the temporary recovery under Jeroboam II (796–752 BC), the road for the northern kingdom was one of diminishment.

1.22:51 [MT 52] "two years" (בִּשְׁנַת שְׁבַע, *bišnaṯ šᵉḇa*ʿ) reflects the characteristics of the dating system in use at that time (see the section on Chronology in the Introduction]). Although Ahaziah reigned during two calendar years, his actual reign was less than twelve months. It was for this reason that although Moab rebelled during his reign, it was left to his brother who succeeded him to attempt to deal with it.

52–53 [MT 53–54] These two verses contain the standard condemnation found in the opening regnal formula of all the northern kings,[5] that is, that he walked in the path laid down by Jeroboam at the beginning of the northern kingdom. But something more is added here: he walked "in the way of his father and his mother" (בְּדֶרֶךְ אָבִיו וּבְדֶרֶךְ אִמּוֹ, *bᵉḏereḵ ʾāḇîw ûḇᵉḏereḵ ʾimmô*), that is, Ahab and Jezebel, with the result that, unlike Jeroboam, who worshipped Yahweh although in idolatrous form, Ahaziah "served Baal and prostrated himself to him" (וַיַּעֲבֹד אֶת־הַבַּעַל וַיִּשְׁתַּחֲוֶה לוֹ, *wayyaʿăḇōḏ ʾeṯ-habbaʿal wayyišᵉttaḥăweh lô*) (i.e., worshipped him). There is no pretense about serving Yahweh, even though he had decisively proven that he, and not Baal, was God (1 Kgs 18:39). This explains much of what takes place in the subsequent encounter between Elijah and Ahaziah.

2 Kings 1:1 Cogan and Tadmor (21) point out that the typical word for political revolt is not the one used of Moab here. Rather, it is פשׁע, *pšʿ*, "transgress," which appears most commonly in legal and cultic contexts. Perhaps its use here is intended to convey the idea that the relationship between Israel and Moab was felt to be more than merely a political one. It may also reflect the fact that Moab proper was located south of the Arnon River, whereas the territory north of the Arnon, which Moab took away from Israel in its rebellion, had historically been the land belonging to the northern tribe of Reuben (cf. Num 32:37). The Moabite king, Mesha, recorded his victory on a stela, which has been recovered.[6]

2–17 This engaging narrative is, as Brueggemann (284) has pointed out, a conflict between two kings, a human one and the Divine One. That being

5. Exceptions are Elah (1 Kgs 16:8–10; but see v. 13) and Shallum (2 Kgs 15:13–14) whose reign lasted one month.
6. See *ANET*, 320–21.

so, although Ahaziah never quite realizes it, the conclusion of the encounter is foregone. Interestingly, after being identified in v. 2, Ahaziah is not named again in the unit. He is simply "the king of Samaria" (מֶלֶךְ־שֹׁמְרוֹן, *melek-šōmᵊrôn;* v. 3) and after that "the king" (הַמֶּלֶךְ, *hammelek* ; vv. 6, 9, 11, 15).[7] The "king of Samaria," with his messengers (vv. 2, 3, 5), has ranged himself against the King of Heaven, who also has a messenger (vv. 3, 15; ["angel" and "messenger" are both translations of the Heb. word: מַלְאָךְ, *mălʾāk*]). There can only be one outcome of such a conflict: the human king will lose.[8]

One of the interesting literary features of the piece is the use of "up" (עלה) and "down" (ירד). Ahaziah has gone *up* (עלה) onto a bed, and he will never *come down* (ירד) from it (6, 16). Elijah is commanded by the king's captains of fifty to *come down* (ירד) from the hill on which he is (9, 11), but he refuses until directed to do so by Yahweh's messenger (15). In the next chapter, Elijah will be taken *up* (עלה, 2 Kgs 2:11) to life, from which he will not *come down.*

2 The narrator has little interest in the event in which Ahaziah was injured and gives only the sparest description of it. He tells us that the "lattice" (הַשְּׂבָכָה, *haśśᵊbāk*) was a feature of "the upper chamber" (עֲלִיָּה, *ʿăliyyâ*), but we do not know what that term defines (Syr. calls it "a balcony," but that is obviously a guess). It was apparently an opening of some sort in the room that could be found on the flat roofs of houses from that period (cf. 1 Kgs 17:19, 23; 2 Kgs 4:10; 23:12), and Ahaziah fell out of it or through it, injuring himself seriously enough to raise questions about his recovery.[9]

"Baal-zebub" (בְּבַעַל זְבוּב, *bᵊbaʿal zᵊbûb*) has occasioned a great deal of comment (e.g., Cogan and Tadmor, 25), partly because this is the only occurrence of the name in the Bible. As it stands, it means "Baal of the flies," a very odd appellation. When this is coupled with the location of his shrine: Ekron, serious questions are raised. If Ahaziah was a Baal-worshipper, which he was, why would he not send to Baal himself at one of his major shrines? The occurrence of the title "Beel-zebul" in the New Testament (Matt 12:24; Mark 3:22; Luke 11:15), where he is called "the prince of demons," and the appearance of *zbl* in Ugaritic with the meaning of "prince," has been the

---

7. Several times Ahaziah is not identified at all, but simply indicated by a third person masculine pronoun. In these cases, the versions, as well as modern translations, often feel compelled to supply "the king," or "Ahaziah" as the subject or object (cf. NIV, vv. 5, 7, 11, 13, 16).

8. Robert L. Cohn, in his "Convention and Creativity in the Book of Kings: The Case of the Dying Monarch," *CBQ* 47 (1985): 603–16, argues that this was a "type-scene" (*à la* R. Alter), one of four dealing with a king who died. However, as Cogan and Tadmor point out, there are too many differences of style and ideology for this to be merely a type-scene from a later era (28).

9. Sweeney recalls the "lucky" arrow that killed Ahab, and wonders if this incident was similar in being not quite accidental (269).

occasion for some interpreters to argue that this was the original meaning of the title: "Prince Baal." The Hebrew, then, has changed *zebul* into *zebub*, in keeping with its well-known practice of replacing objectionable terms with pejorative ones (cf. "Ishbosheth," "man of shame," 2 Sam 2:8, for "Ishbaal," "man of the lord," 1 Chr 8:33).

However, this still does not explain going to Ekron, and some other commentators (e.g., Wiseman, 192) are not convinced that the title has been changed.[10] They point out that flies were often seen to be objects of healing and appear in various places as amulets. Thus, it is possible that this particular manifestation of Baal at Ekron was understood to have particular healing powers and that this explains why he was sought out.[11]

"Inquire" translates the term דָּרַשׁ, *dāraš* which denotes a formal religious request (cf. Gen 25:22). It is different from שָׁאַל, *šāʾal,* "to ask" which might have been used (cf. Josh 9:14), and which has less formal, cultic overtones. In this, Ahaziah was doing something forbidden in the Torah. As such, he was fulfilling the description of him by the narrator in 1 Kings 22:54: serving and worshipping his god Baal. When Jeroboam's son was ill, he sent his wife to the Yahwistic prophet Ahijah (1 Kgs 14:1–2). Now, in a similar situation, as an indication of how far the Israelite kingship has fallen, it is Baal who is being inquired of. Ahaziah's actions showed that, whatever he might have said, he did indeed believe that there was "no God in Israel" (אֵין־אֱלֹהִים בְּיִשְׂרָאֵל, *ʾên-ʾĕlōhîm bᵊyiśrāʾēl*), just as Yahweh's messenger declared (v. 3).[12]

3 "The angel of Yahweh" (מַלְאַךְ יהוה, *malʾak yhwh*): The messenger of the Divine King tells the prophet how to respond to the messengers of the human king. This phrase only occurs four times in Kings, with three of them in connection with Elijah (1 Kgs 19:7; 2 Kgs 1:3, 15; 19:35).

"Elijah, the Tishbite" (אֵלִיָּה הַתִּשְׁבִּי, *ʾēliyyâ hattišbî*): Once again, as at the beginning of the Elijah narrative (1 Kgs 17:1), it is specified that the prophet came from Tishbe, on the east side of the Jordan. As noted in the "Commentary" there, this may be a way of underlining Elijah's social location, as not being part of the royal establishment, or a Samarian insider.

As noted above "Baal-zebub, god of Ekron" may have been noted as having particular healing abilities. The angel's rhetorical question, "Is there no God in Israel… ?" (הַמִבְּלִי אֵין־אֱלֹהִים בְּיִשְׂרָאֵל, *hamibbᵊlî ʾên-ʾĕlōhîm bᵊyiśrāʾēl*), subtly points out a central facet of biblical theology: Yahweh is not fragmented into different functions at different places; he is one God, the

---

10. See K. Arvid Tangberg, "A Note on Baʿal Zēbūb in 2 Kgs 1:2, 3, 6, 16," *SJOT* 6 (1992): 293–96 for a brief review of the options and an argument to retain Baal-zebub.

11. The LXX translation "the goddess Baal, the fly god of Ekron," while raising interesting gender questions, supports the "flies" interpretation.

12. It is ironic that in a similar situation, the Syrian king Ben-hadad "inquires" of Elisha, "the man of God."

same in all places. He is able to do his full work in any place, so it would not be necessary to travel forty-five miles to Ekron to find help and hope.

4 Verse four contained the accusation, and this verse contains the pronouncement of judgment. The pronouncement ends with what amounts to a royal death sentence: "You will surely die" (מוֹת תָּמוּת, *môṯ tāmûṯ*) (cf. Gen 2:17; 1 Sam 22:16; 1 Kgs 2:37; Ezek 3:18; 33:8, 14).

5–6 "Why have you returned?" (מַה־זֶּה שַׁבְתֶּם, *ma-zze šaḇtem*): Not enough time had elapsed for the messengers to have made the roundtrip to Ekron, and to have remained there long enough to receive the desired oracle. The messengers faithfully report the message, although without the messenger formula, "thus says Yahweh" (כֹּה אָמַר יהוה, *kōh ʾāmar yhwh*).

7–8 Ahaziah is clearly suspicious. Perhaps he had been with his father on Mt. Carmel or at Naboth's vineyard when the "man of God" had shown up to embarrass, or worse, condemn, the king. So he asked what this man looked like.[13] When he was told the details about this mysterious man: "hairy" (בַּעַל שֵׂעָר, *baʿal śēʿār*), and with a "leather loincloth" (אֵזוֹר עוֹר, *ʾēzôr ʿôr*), he immediately recognized that it was Elijah. Several commentators (e.g., Cohn, 6; Provan, 170) suggest that the literal "lord of hair" is intentionally used to contrast with the god's title "lord of flies." The NIV "garment of hair" is not likely, depending more on the NT description of John the Baptist (cf. Mark 1:6). It seems more likely that, like a Nazirite, Elijah had never cut his hair (cf. Num 6:5).[14]

9 Ahaziah's reactions are significant: first, there is no sign of contrition or repentance. Second, he seems to think that if he can capture the prophet, he can somehow force him, perhaps on pain of death, to amend the sentence. Third, he recognizes that this is no ordinary prophet, so he sends what he apparently thinks is an overwhelming force to accomplish his purpose. He is wrong on all three counts.

---

13. The word here translated "sort of" (KJV "manner of," ESV "kind of," NRSV "sort of") is מִשְׁפָּט, *mišpaṭ*, which is usually translated "justice," or "judgment." Long (283) suggests it is used intentionally here in a kind of wordplay. However, this need not be the case, for the larger sense of the word is "pattern" or "order." Thus, we are told that Solomon built the temple according to its *mišpaṭ* (1 Kgs 6:38; see also Exod 26:30), and that those brought in to populate Israel after the Assyrian exile worshipped according to the *mišpaṭ* of the nations (2 Kgs 17:33–34). So Ahaziah was asking only what the pattern of the man's appearance was.

14. Sweeney, however, opts for "garment of hair" citing the four references to "cloak" in the Elijah/Elisha narratives (1 Kgs 19:13, 19; 2 Kgs 2:8, 13–15) and the mention in Zech 13:4 of a prophet's "garment of hair" (270). But "lord of hair" says nothing about a "cloak" or "garment." See Cogan and Tadmor, 26.

Elijah had said that Ahaziah will not be able to go down from his bed. Here "the king," speaking through the captain of an impressive troop of fifty men,[15] commands the prophet with one imperious Hebrew word (רֵדָה), "Down!"[16] In the historical books the title "man of God" (אִישׁ הָאֱלֹהִים, *'îš hā 'ĕlōhîm*), with which the captain addressed Elijah, seems to be reserved for prophets who were not professionals and were not part of the establishment (see, for example 1 Kgs 11:29 as opposed to 1 Kgs 13:1). Both Elijah and Elisha are regularly referred to in this way.[17]

Elijah clearly understood that if he went down, he would be in danger of losing his own life (note the assurance given in v. 15). These fifty men were not merely an escort. Thus, it was a case of the life of the King's (i.e., Yahweh's) one man, or the lives of the king's fifty men. In this contest of power between the two kings, the outcome could be predicted: the king's men would be the losers. Elijah did not come down, but fire did, and the captain and his fifty died. Elijah was indeed a "man of God," a certified representative of the Sovereign of the World, whether Ahaziah and his captain thought so or not.

11–12 We are hard-pressed to understand how Ahaziah could be obtuse enough not to learn the lesson of the previous event. But, like the pharaoh of the exodus before him, it is evident that his pride, his "hard heart" would not allow him to do so. After all, he was king! But we would at least expect him to "up the ante," as it were, and send a larger force. But the only change is that this time the captain's imperious command has two words, "Hurry! Down!" (מְהֵרָה רֵדָה, *mᵉhērâ rēḏâ*). Tragically for his obedient soldiers, the contest could have no other outcome than the first one. The power of the earthly king had no chance against the power of the heavenly one.

The connection of this incident with the one on Mt. Carmel is apparent: the God who answers by fire is God. The house of Omri seems not to have learned its lesson from that first incident, so now it is forced to encounter this truth even more poignantly.

13–14 If there were any remaining question concerning Ahaziah's stubbornness or his inability to reason, it is laid to rest by his third repetition of the same strategy that had failed twice before. He simply seems incapable of drawing the obvious conclusion. The third captain, however, his life hanging by a thread, was not so thick-headed. Whatever message his king may have given to him, he had his own message, one that was based in reality. There was no contest between the God whom this "man of God" served and the

---

15. This was an important military unit; see 1 Sam 8:12; Isa 3:3.

16. Long believes that Elijah is on Mt. Carmel, but there is nothing in the text to indicate that (283).

17. When other persons speak of Elijah or Elisha, they call them "prophets" (נְבִיאִים, *nᵉḇî 'îm*) but when the author refers to them, they are "the man of God." The only exception is in 9:1, for which there is no obvious explanation.

petty "king of Samaria." If this captain and his men were to survive, it would simply be because Elijah would grant the captain's plea for grace and consider their lives "precious" (יקר, *yqr*). Here was the kind of recognition and submission that Ahaziah should have offered at the outset, but which his pride and idolatry prevented him from giving.

15 Not only did God grant the captain's plea, but now the thing the king had been demanding all along took place. Throughout the account, the place of the "angel of Yahweh" has been most significant. This is not a contest between Elijah and Ahaziah. Elijah is simply the representative; Ahaziah is dealing with Yahweh whom he has tried to ignore and replace with Baal. So here, Elijah goes down, not at Ahaziah's command, but at Yahweh's. He need not be afraid anymore: these fifty men will not be taking Elijah's life since he has given theirs back to them. He can go with them confidently.

16 Whatever Ahaziah may have hoped to accomplish by bringing Elijah to the palace, his attitude had rendered all in vain. Elijah's message was no different from what he had delivered to the messengers in the beginning (vv. 3–4). Nothing had changed in Ahaziah's heart, so nothing changed in the judgment rendered against him.

17–18 As the MT stands now, the typical closing regnal formula is disordered. Typically, what is now v. 18 would lead off and 17a would follow. What is now 17b would not appear here, but would be part of the opening regnal formula for Jehoram.[18] LXX is apparently attempting to deal with these issues when it moves 18 to follow the notice of Ahaziah's death in v. 17, and then starts v. 18 with 17b, and adds to it a good deal of material from MT 3:1–3.

Perhaps the MT organization is to be explained by two factors. First, the editor wants to put the announcement of Ahaziah's death immediately after the judgment oracle in v. 16. Second, he wants to include the information that Ahaziah was not succeeded by his own son, because he had none. In order to do that, he had to incorporate some of the regnal information about Jehoram.

But this regnal information creates its own problems because it does not agree with the chronology found in 3:1. That one, stating that Joram began to reign in Jehoshaphat's eighteenth year accords well with 1 Kings 22:51 [MT 52] which says that Ahaziah began to reign in Jehoshaphat's seventeenth year (see the "Commentary" on Ahaziah's reign above on 1 Kgs 22:51 [MT 53]). Second Kings 8:16 further complicates matters by saying that Jehoram of Judah began to reign in Joram of Israel's fifth year! Thiele proposed to solve the problem with a coregency between Jehoshaphat and his son Jehoram.

18. This probably explains the very anomalous appearance of a petuhah between 17a and 17b. Normally this symbol functions to mark the end of one major unit and the beginning of another. But here it probably is saying that what follows it does not normally appear in this location.

Thus, 2 Kgs 8:16 would refer to the year when Jehoram of Judah became king in his own right, whereas 1:17 would refer to the second year of his co-regency with Jehoshaphat.[19]

Biblical Theology Comments

This passage, the last prophetic encounter in Elijah's life, underlines the central theme of his life, the Yahweh – Baal crisis. Although it is evident that the Israelites had taken a syncretistic approach to the worship of Yahweh for a long time, this situation was different. Now there was a clear move to replace the worship of Yahweh with the worship of Baal. Sponsored as it was from the very palace, and with a high degree of energy, this was a genuine threat. Ranged against it was this one visible figure. To be sure, Elijah was *not* the only worshipper of Yahweh, as Yahweh had made plain to Elijah during their encounter at Horeb (1 Kgs 19:18). The presence of Micaiah in Samaria (1 Kgs 22) also demonstrates the point. Yet Elijah was the lonely "point man," as it were. It fell to him to demonstrate that Baal is not God, and Yahweh is. That was the intention at Mt. Carmel, and it is again here. As Isaiah was to say it a century later, "Yahweh is God alone, there is no other" (Isa 46:9). This conflict is between the man of Yahweh and the man of Baal, and Baal is shown to be an empty container at every point: he has no word to speak, and he has no power to save. The man of Yahweh has but to speak a word, and two elite military forces are wiped out, reducing the commander of the third to abject pleading. To worship the powers of this world is to make oneself as meaningless and valueless as they are (cf. Pss 115:8; 135:18).

Throughout the Bible, fire is the symbol of God's presence (e.g., the burning bush, Exod 3:2–4; the pillar of fire, Exod 13:21; the seraphim ["burning ones"], Isa 6:2; Mt. Carmel, 1 Kgs 18:24, 38). It is thus expressive both of his blessing and his judgment. For those who recognize his transcendent reality and submit to it, his fire is a blessing (Isa 6:7). But for those who arrogantly refuse to recognize that reality, it is a deadly force (Lev 10:1–2), as it was in this account. We tend to look on this event as the arbitrary act of the vengeful prophet and his vengeful god. To be sure, not everyone who refuses to submit to Yahweh so immediately feels the negative side of his fiery presence. Yet the fact remains, every one of us must confront that presence either to our eternal blessing or to our eternal destruction. Thus, what took place here, as was the case with Aaron's sons, Nadab and Abihu (Lev 10:1–2), was not something arbitrary, but merely the immediate application of an eternal reality.

---

19. E. R. Thiele, *The Mysterious Numbers of the Hebrew Kings,* rev. ed. (Grand Rapids: Eerdmans, 1965), 69–70. Gershon Galil, *The Chronology of the Kings of Israel and Judah* (Leiden: Brill, 1996), 38–39 disagrees with Thiele's dates, saying that "Thiele attempts to take on more than he can handle." However, he still assumes that there was a coregency between Jehoshaphat and his son Joram. See Table 10 in Galil, on p. 45.

Yet we may ask, why the immediacy in this case? Since no explanation is given in the text, caution is advisable. But perhaps it is because of the terrible seriousness of the situation. Although Ahab was dead, Jezebel was not, and the conflict between Baal and Yahweh was far from settled. Jezebel's son, who "served Baal and prostrated himself to him" (1 Kgs 22:53 [MT 52]) was on the throne, acting as if there was no God in Israel. Could this Baal-worshipper take the life of Yahweh's prophet in his hands through the use of military force? No he could not; Yahweh is God alone.

Application and Devotional Implications

Throughout its history, the church has contended that pride is the deadliest of the deadly sins. In general, Christians have not believed this supposition and instead, take the sins of the flesh far more seriously. Be that as it may, the church's teaching is correct, as the Bible makes plain again and again (cf. Prov 8:13; 16:18; Luke 18:14). Pride is the human usurpation of the place that only the transcendent God can take. It is a failure to recognize the simple truth: I am not ultimate in the universe. Yet every human has been and will be, guilty of this sin at some point in our lives, if not in much of our lives. It is a mark of our fallenness. That being the case, what must be our stance before God? It is beautifully illustrated in this account. It is the stance of humility and contrition, as exhibited in the third captain of fifty. It was not exhibited by Ahaziah. After all, he was king. So what if this hairy prophet of Yahweh had delivered a negative oracle concerning him? He was king and would soon take care of the situation, much as his mother had taken care of the situation with Naboth (1 Kgs 21:7).

Neither was that stance exhibited by the first captain of fifty, or more remarkably, by the second. These were military men who had risen to responsible and powerful positions. They were used to having their commands obeyed instantly. In their circumscribed worlds, they were ultimate; hard, proud men who would have their way in every circumstance.

Not only does this narrative demonstrate the character of pride, it also demonstrates how pride corrupts the mental processes. Ahaziah never did get the message. He should have gotten it from the moment he heard the oracle, as Hezekiah was to do a century later (2 Kgs 20:2–3). But he did not. Neither did he get it when not one, but two, of his military companies was destroyed. As a result, he ordered a third into the same situation. We tend to discount the narrative at this point. Surely no one would be this foolish. But we fail to account for the power of pride. For Ahaziah to admit that Yahweh was God, and that he was not, was simply unthinkable.

Fortunately for him and his men, the third captain's pride had not corrupted his thought processes. He recognized his mortal peril and sacrificed his pride on the altar of good sense, abasing himself and pleading for mercy. He recognized that he was in no place to demand anything from this man and his God. This is the stance which we all must take in the presence of the all Holy. It is the *only* stance which we creatures can take.

But notice what takes place next. Not only does Yahweh spare the lives of the third group, but the original demand is granted: Elijah comes down from his hilltop and goes with the captain and his men to confront the king. Now, of course, he goes not as captive, but as the life-giver. This is entirely characteristic of the Yahweh portrayed in the Bible. Let us demand that he produce whatever for us, and that is the surest way to be certain that it will not happen. Recognize that we can demand nothing from him, that we merit death, and we will find not only our requests, but our desires, granted. As Isaiah 57:15 says,

> For this is what the high and exalted One says—
> he who lives forever, whose name is holy:
> "I live in a high and holy place,
> but also with the one who is contrite and lowly in spirit,
> to revive the spirit of the lowly and revive the heart of the contrite."

Selected Bibliography

Fensham, F. C. "Possible Explanation of the Name Baal-Zebub of Ekron." *ZAW* 79 (1967): 361–64.

Korchin, P. "Suspense and Authority Amid Biblical Hebrew Front Dislocation." *JHS* 15 (2015): 1–46.

Elijah and Elisha (2 Kings 2:1 [MT 52]–2 Kings 2:25)

In this chapter we see the transition between the two prophets with the conclusion of Elijah's ministry and the opening of Elisha's. The way in which the material is structured emphasizes that their ministry is really one. Elisha is not only Elijah's "first-born son," but also his double. The visual illustration of this joint ministry is Elijah's mantle. Elijah used it to divide the waters of the Jordan so that he and Elisha could cross over. Then when Elijah left it behind Elisha picked it up and used it to divide the waters so he could pass back to the west. Although Elijah and Elisha display different personalities, yet their concern is the same, the destruction of the institutionalized Baal cult and the demonstration that Yahweh alone is God.

Elijah's Flight to Heaven (2 Kings 2:1–11)

Translation

1 Now when Yahweh was about to take up Elijah in a whirlwind to heaven, Elijah and Elisha went from Gilgal. **2** Elijah said to Elisha, "Stay here, please, because Yahweh has sent me to Bethel." But Elisha said, "As Yahweh lives, and as you yourself live, I will not forsake you."[20] So they went down to Bethel.

---

20. This is a typical condensation of the oath form, the full form of which would read something like, "I swear on the life of Yahweh and your life, may I die if I forsake you."

3 The sons of the prophets who were in Bethel came out to Elisha and said
to him, "Do you know that today Yahweh is going to take your master from
over you?" He said, "Yes, I do[21] know. Be quiet." **4** Elijah said to him, "Elisha,
please stay here, for Yahweh has sent me to Jericho." But he said, "As Yahweh
lives and as you yourself live, I will not forsake you." So they went to Jericho.
5 The sons of the prophets who were in Jericho approached Elisha, and said
to him, "Do you know that Yahweh is today going to take your master from
over you?" He said, "Yes, I do know. Be quiet." **6** Elijah said to him, "Please
stay here, because Yahweh has sent me to the Jordan." He said, "As Yahweh
lives, and as you yourself live, I will not forsake you." So the two of them
went on. **7** Fifty men of the sons of the prophets went and stood at a distance
while the two of them were standing at the Jordan. **8** Elijah took his cloak,
folded it, and struck the water. It was divided on each side and the two of
them passed over on dry ground. **9** When they had passed over, Elijah said
to Elisha, "Ask what I shall do for you before I am taken from you." Elisha
said, "Let there be a double portion[22] of your spirit on me, please." **10** He
said, "You have asked a hard thing; if you see me taken from you, so it will
be to you. If not, it will not be." **11** As they were walking along, walking and
conversing, there was a chariot of fire and horses of fire. They separated the
two of them, and Elijah went up in a whirlwind to heaven.

Textual Notes

2a. שֵׁב: Syr. "Wait for me" (so also vv. 4 and 6); LXX and Vulg. with MT.

3a. רֹאשֶׁךָ: Syr. and Vulg. "over you." LXX with MT.

6a. הַיַּרְדֵּנָה: LXX and Vulg. "as far as"; Syr. with MT. (Heb. has locative ה).

8a. בֶּחָרָבָה: LXX "into the wilderness"; Vulg. and Syr. with MT.

Commentary

These verses compose the second part of the transitional segment composed of 1 Kings 22:51 [MT 52]–2 Kings 2:25. The first part (1 Kgs 22:51 [MT 52]–2 Kgs 1:18) was focused on the final event in Elijah's ministry, while the third part (2 Kings 2:19–25) introduces Elisha's ministry. This middle portion covers the transition itself, telling how Elijah was translated from earth, and how Elisha was installed as his successor. Chapter two is remarkable in that it occurs between Ahaziah's closing regnal formula (1:17–18) and Jehoram's opening regnal formula (3:1–3). The only other occurrence of such a phenomenon, where material occurs outside of the chronological structuring of the book is the account of Elisha's death (2 Kgs 13:14–21). These two oddities underline the importance of Elisha's ministry in the war against Baalism.

---

21. The subject "I" is emphasized here and also in v. 5.

22. Lit. "a double mouth" (פִּי־שְׁנַיִם, *pî-šᵉnayim*).

Second Kings 2:1–18 is structured in a broadly chiastic way.[23] There is the journey to the Jordan (vv. 1–7), the miraculous crossing of the Jordan (v. 8), Elijah's ascension (vv. 9–12), the miraculous crossing of the Jordan (vv. 13–14), and the journey from the Jordan (vv. 15–18). All this seems designed to reinforce the point that Elisha is, in every sense, the true successor of Elijah.

The many parallels with chapter 1 suggest that the author intends for us to associate the two chapters. For instance, three times Ahaziah sends troops to apprehend Elijah, and Elisha three times refuses to be left behind. There are three groups of "sons of the prophets" (בְּנֵי־הַנְּבִיאִים, *bᵉnê-hannᵉḇî ʾîm*), one at Bethel, and two at Jericho, as there are three troops of soldiers. There are fifty men in each of Ahaziah's three troops, and there are fifty "sons of the prophets" at Jericho, and it seems they have another fifty to send on the search for Elijah. It is fire that destroys the first two troops, and it is a chariot and horses of fire that separate Elijah from Elisha. While some scholars separate chapters one and two (e.g., House, 252) these numerous parallels suggest that the two chapters should be read together, thus emphasizing the unity of the ministries of the two prophets.[24]

Another important observation concerning the unit is its obvious allusions to Moses and Joshua. The crossing of the Jordan without wetting their feet can only be alluding to the crossing of the Reed Sea under the leadership of Moses and the crossing of the Jordan under the leadership of Joshua. Philip Satterthwaite picks up on this and uses it to make a good case that these allusions give us the key to understanding the ministry of Elisha in chapter 3–8 (see further below).[25] There was hope that as a new Joshua, Elisha could lead his people back to pure worship of Yahweh. Tragically, that hope did not come to fruition.

1–2 Verse one leaves no doubt about what will comprise the central event of the unit: Elijah's translation to heaven. But at the same time, by telling the reader what is going to happen to him at the outset, it seems to rule out the idea that the purpose of the narrative is to reveal that. So what is the unit's purpose? It is to show how Elisha came to succeed Elijah. We have known

23. Cohn (11) and Long (288) both emphasize this structure, extending it through both chapters 1 and 2, believing that it begins with Elijah moving from Mt. Carmel to Samaria in chap. 1 and ending with Elisha doing the same thing. However, there is no mention of either Mt. Carmel or Samaria in chap. 1. Thus, the proposal of that larger chiasm seems strained to me.

24. See below on 2:19–25 for an argument why these two miracles should not be considered merely the first two in the succession of Elisha's miracles.

25. Philip E. Satterthwaite, "The Elisha Narrative and the Coherence of 2 Kings 2–8," *TynBul* 49 (1998): 1–28. On the connections with Moses, see R. P. Carroll, "The Elijah Elisha Saga: Some Remarks on Prophetic Succession in Ancient Israel," *VT* 19 (1969): 400–15.

that Elisha was to succeed him since chapter 19 of 1 Kings, but we have not known how it would occur.

That being said, we may ask why the succession should happen in such a dramatic fashion? Why did Elijah not simply die and Elisha carry on in his place? Why was there not a more "natural" succession? Perhaps the reason is the dramatic nature of the challenge being faced. As mentioned above, the very position of Yahweh as the God of Israel was being challenged. This was a war, and war can necessitate unusual measures. Thus, it may be that the point is that there is really a single ministry stretching from Elijah through Elisha, with no recognizable break between them, during which the "enemy" could regather his forces. There was no period of uncertainty while the old man was slowly dying and it was not quite clear how, or how well, the young man might take up the reins. Elijah is suddenly out of the picture, and Elisha is immediately in it.

The storm (or whirlwind; סְעָרָה, *sᵊʿārâ*) that was to take up Elijah is a frequent manifestation of Yahweh in the OT. He appears in the storm (Job 38:1; 40:6; Isa 29:6; Zech 9:14), and he regularly uses it as an instrument of judgment (Ps 83:15 [MT 16]; Jer 23:19; 30:23).

There is some uncertainly about the location of the Gilgal mentioned here. This is primarily occasioned by the statement in v. 2 that "they went down" to Bethel. The Gilgal referred to in Joshua (e.g., 5:9–10), although still not positively located, must have been in the Jordan Valley not far north of Jericho. From such a location, the direction west to Bethel is definitely "up," since Bethel is located on the central ridge north of Jerusalem.[26] An alternative was proposed as early as G. A. Smith who suggested an Arab village named Jiljilia just off the main highway between Bethel and Shechem for this Gilgal.[27] The problem with this proposal is two-fold: (1) it is the Gilgal of Joshua that would fit the allusions to Joshua referred to above, along with Bethel and Jericho; (2) there seems a clear possibility that Bethel and Gilgal were chosen by Elijah as sites to visit because of the paganized Yahwism that had come to be practiced at these ancient and venerable locations (cf. Amos 4:4; 5:5; Hos 4:15; 9:15; 10:15). In this context, note that Jericho had recently been rebuilt in a way that fulfilled Joshua's ancient curse (1 Kgs 16:34).[28]

Likewise, there is considerable uncertainty about Elijah's motivation in asking Elisha not to accompany him on his journey (2, and again in vv. 4 and 6). Some, like Cohn (12), think Elijah wanted to spare Elisha the pain

26. Presumably the recognition of this problem accounts for the LXX reading in v. 2 "they came to Bethel."

27. Smith, *Historical Geography of the Holy Land* (London, 1894; repr., New York: Harper, 1966), 318.

28. For the interesting suggestion that "down" is a theological term and not a geographic one, see Joel S. Burnett, "'Going Down' to Bethel: Elijah and Elisha in the Theological Geography of the Deuteronomistic History," *JBL* 129 (2010): 281–97.

that his departure would bring. Others, like Long (289), who generally takes a less charitable view of Elijah, wonder if he was reluctant to hand over his power to Elisha.[29] In view of the less-than-commanding tone of his initial invitation to Elisha (1 Kgs 19:19–21), I wonder if he wanted to avoid any possibility that Elisha would take up this burden under pressure. He wanted to be certain that Elisha was doing this freely and without any compulsion except that which would come from Yahweh. (Note that Elisha's initial call was equally indeterminate [1 Kgs 19:19–21].) Thus, the old prophet gives his protégé three opportunities to "back out." If he took them, that would be the proof positive that he was not God's man.[30]

But Elisha did not take the opportunity. Rather, in the strongest of terms he affirmed that he was ready to take up the challenge. Putting himself under a curse, he swore on the life of Yahweh himself, as well as that of his master, that he would never "leave" (or "abandon"; עָזַב, *ʿzb*) his master. A contemporary way of saying this might be "I swear on Yahweh's life and yours that I will never leave you. May he strike me dead if I ever do." That kind of unswerving commitment to Yahweh and to Elijah, as Sweeney (272) says, "demonstrates that Elisha is a worthy successor of Elijah."[31]

3 It is interesting that at each of the locations where Elijah was "sent" (שָׁלַח, *šlḥ*) there were "sons of the prophets". Prior to this, there had only been one reference to this group, found in 1 Kings 20:35 where the prophet who condemned Ahab for letting Ben-hadad go is identified as being a member of the group. From this point on, the rest of the references, ten in all, are all associated with Elisha.[32] The significance of this fact is debated. While many have argued that this was some sort of prophetic "guild," R. R. Wilson has argued that they were dispossessed followers first of Elijah and then Elisha.[33] They would have been outcasts from both the political and the religious establishments of the northern kingdom. Barnes (200) calls them "lay supporters." Perhaps Elijah's itinerary was planned for the purpose of encouraging these prophets at the ancient sites that were being venerated for all the wrong reasons (see above).

---

29. Jesse Long, *1 & 2 Kings*, College Press NIV Commentary (Joplin, MO: College Press, 2002), 289.

30. The use of the enclitic נָא, *nāʾ* with the imperatives gives them more the tone of a request than a command. Note also the use of Elisha's name in v. 4.

31. For a similar understanding, see John Weidenaar, "The Dedication of Elisha," *RJ* 5 (1955): 1–3.

32. Outside of this chapter, there are six other occurrences: 2 Kgs 4:1, 38 (2x); 5:22; 6:1; 9:1.

33. R. R. Wilson, *Prophecy and Society in Ancient Israel* (Philadelphia: Fortress, 1980), 141, 202. For further discussion, see the helpful excursus in Hobbs, 25–26.

In both Bethel and later in Jericho (v. 5) "the sons of the prophets" seem anxious to know whether Elisha knows what is about to happen.[34] Perhaps they did not want him to be going into the situation blind. They may also have wanted to know whether, as Elijah's supposed successor, he was gifted with prophetic insight. If he did not know what they knew, that could raise serious questions about his fitness for the task.

The phrase "from over your head" (מֵעַל רֹאשֶׁךָ, *mēʿal rōʾšeḵā*) is significant, pointing as it does to the immanent change in Elisha's status. He would no longer be able to shelter under the hand of his "master" (אָדוֹן, *ʾāḏôn*) with its protection from responsibility. Now there would be no one above him, and the full responsibility for his choices and proclamations would be his alone.

Elisha's response to the query in both instances is extremely terse, just three words in Hebrew (אֲנִי יָדַעְתִּי הֶחֱשׁוּ, *ʾănî yāḏaʿtî heḥĕšû*): "Yes, I do know. Be quiet." It is obvious that he does not want to talk about the matter. Perhaps his questioners were inclined to ask for more information, which might be embarrassing for Elijah, who was undoubtedly present. In any case, it was not their business to know more.

6 As Cohn (12) argues, "So the two of them went" (וַיֵּלְכוּ שְׁנֵיהֶם, *wayyēlᵉḵû šᵉnêhem*), as opposed to "Elijah went" in verse one, seems to argue that Elijah is now satisfied that Elisha will not leave him and is content for them to travel together from here on.

7–8 "Stood at a distance" (וַיַּעַמְדוּ מִנֶּגֶד מֵרָחוֹק, *wayyaʿamḏû minneḡeḏ mērāḥôq*) suggests something of the awe of the occasion. Undoubtedly the fifty men (see above on connections with chap. 1) were intensely curious about what was going to take place. But something restrained their curiosity, and they held back. Presumably they did see what happened next, though. They saw Elijah take his cloak, fold it,[35] and, as Moses struck the Nile with his staff (Exod 7:17), strike the Jordan. The result was like when Moses held his staff over the Reed Sea: the waters parted on each side (Exod 14:21–22) and "the two of them passed over on dry ground" (וַיַּעַבְרוּ שְׁנֵיהֶם בֶּחָרָבָה, *wayyaʿaḇrû šᵉnêhem beḥārāḇâ*). It seems likely that at this point they passed out of the sight of the watchers. Nonetheless, it would have been apparent to all that Yahweh's power was being demonstrated again. For further discussion, see the "Biblical Theology Commentary" below.

34. Cf. those who were warning the apostle Paul about what would happen to him when he reached Jerusalem (Acts 20:23). Like Elisha, Paul pressed on regardless.

35. This is the only place where this vb. (גלם) occurs. A possible noun form appears in Ezek 27:24 which could give the sense of a "wrapped garment." The sense of the LXX εἰλέω (*eileo*) is "to roll, twist or fold."

9 It is in keeping with the nature of the event that Elijah would ask if there should be some parting gift that he could give to his successor. But Elisha's request was both startling and prescient. He asked to be given the place of the first-born son of a father. Upon the father's death his estate was divided into equal portions, and the firstborn received two of these (Deut 21:17; lit. "two mouths"). But what was Elijah's estate? What was his chief possession? Elisha understood very well: it was the Spirit of Yahweh. Elijah had not done what he had done or said what he had said on his own account. It was only, in the language of Judges 6:34, that the Spirit had "clothed" Elijah. Elisha is not asking for twice as much of the Spirit as Elijah had, but to be the true heir of the man he saw as his "father."

10 But, as Elijah said, this was a "hard" (קשׁה, *qšh*) request, because although Elisha had said "your spirit" (רוּחֲךָ, *rûḥăḵā*), the spirit that was upon Elijah was not his, but the Spirit of Yahweh, and as such, was not his to grant. The Spirit was not a possession of his that he could dispense at will. Yahweh will be possessed by no one. He is the Giver, and he gives only as he chooses.[36] However, Yahweh could choose to grant Elisha's request, and if he did so choose, the evidence would be "sight." If Elisha should "see" (ראה, *rʾh*) Elijah "being taken from" (לֻקָּח מֵ, *luqqāḥ mē*) him, that would be the evidence that Elisha was indeed Elijah's true son. This is an entirely appropriate sign, because the vocation of a prophet in Israel was to see and hear what Yahweh was doing and intended to do.

11 The climactic moment came "as they were walking, walking and speaking" (וַיְהִי הֵמָּה הֹלְכִים הָלוֹךְ וְדַבֵּר, *wayhî hēmmâ hōlᵉḵîm hālôḵ wᵉḏabbēr*). As with much in this narrative, the narrator does not tell us why he does certain things, and this is one of them. Why does he tell us that the "chariot of fire and horses of fire separated the two of them" (רֶכֶב־אֵשׁ וְסוּסֵי אֵשׁ וַיַּפְרִדוּ בֵּין שְׁנֵיהֶם, *reḵeḇ- ʾēš wᵉsûsê ʾēš wayyap̄riḏû bên šᵉnêhem*) during a moment of intimate relationship? I suspect it is to underline the point that is being made by this unit: although Elijah and Elisha were different people and operated differently, they were one in spirit, and were so right to the very end of their relationship. This war on Baal was unitary from start to finish; what Elijah began Elisha would finish without a break between them.

Several commentators point out that the text does not say, contrary to popular opinion, that Elijah "went up" (עלה, *ʿlh*) in the fiery chariot (Brueggemann, 297; Sweeney 274, etc.). He "went up" as v. 1 said, "in a whirlwind" or "windstorm" (בַּסְּעָרָה, *bassᵉʿārâ*). The horses and chariot simply

36. Notice that it is Yahweh, not Moses, who puts "some of the Spirit that is upon" Moses upon the 70 elders (Num 11:25). Likewise, it is Yahweh who placed the Spirit upon Joshua (Num 27:18) and on Saul (1 Sam 10:6). See also Isa 42:1 where Yahweh announces that he has "put my Spirit on" his Servant.

separated the two men. Three things should be pointed out here. First, the use of storm seems to be a direct refutation of the power of Baal, who was considered to be the god of the storm. Second, the use of fire directly recalls not only the fire that destroyed Ahaziah's two troops of fifty (1:10, 12), but also the fire that confirmed Yahweh as sole God on Mt. Carmel (1 Kgs 18:38–39). Third, although cavalry was coming into use as the dominating military instrument at this time, for some hundreds of years previously the chariot, pulled by a team of horses, had been the ultimate weapon. It is thus a symbol here, especially coupled with fire, of Yahweh's overwhelming power.[37] Neither Baal, nor the Israelite descendants of Omri, nor any other powers of earth, stand any chance against him.[38]

Biblical Theology Comments

The clear allusions to both Moses and Joshua in this unit are intended to point the reader's attention in two directions: backwards and forwards. In terms of backwards, the call is to remember Israel's history and what it had taught. For one thing, history had established that Israel was the chosen possession of Yahweh. Without his gracious adoption of them as his people and his deliverance of them from the hand of the pharaoh of the exodus, in particular in the Reed Sea crossing, they would not exist. How then could they now simply turn away from him to a god who had neither affection for, nor investment in, them?

The second thing that history taught was the incredible power of Yahweh, again, as it culminated in the Reed Sea crossing. As Exodus 12:12 makes explicit, the plagues upon Egypt were an attack on the Egyptian gods. Whatever the Egyptians thought was life-giving in this world was shown to be only death-dealing. The power of life and death is solely in the hands of Yahweh. What possible power could Baal and his Omride clients now have to justify supplanting Yahweh as Israel's God? The people of Israel were clearly suffering from a terminal case of amnesia, one that would result in their sharing the fate of the pharaoh if they did not come to their senses.

But Yahweh's love and power had not only been demonstrated at the exodus, alluded to in Elijah's action; they had also been demonstrated in the conquest, beginning with the crossing of the Jordan under the leadership of Joshua, something alluded to by the action of Elisha. What people and which gods had been able to stand up against the all-conquering Yahweh

37. In two places Yahweh is said to ride in a chariot through the heavens (Ps 104:3; Hab 3:8). In several others he is said to "ride" in the heavens, which probably assumes a chariot (Pss 18:10 [MT 11]; 68:4 ([MT 5]; Isa 19:1), an allusive appropriation of mythic language for communicative purposes.

38. In 2 Kgs 6:8–23 when the king of Syria, intending to capture the prophet, has surrounded Dothan with a force of horses and chariots, Yahweh instead surrounds that force with his own force of fiery chariots and horses.

when the people would be faithful to him? The answer was none. Against all the odds Yahweh had led his rabble of a people to victory against a highly sophisticated, and militarily superior culture. Once again it had to be asked, why would the present people abandon a God like that?

But the lessons did not only recall the past; they also pointed ahead, asking, "If a people faithful to Yahweh and his covenant experienced deliverances like that in the past, why could that not happen again in our day?" The message of the prophets was a remarkable one. They could speak of the future with certainty, but at the same time acknowledge that their words were contigent on the response of the people. They were unlike the pagan diviners, whose clients paid them to look into what they imagined was an inescapable fate that lay ahead, one that could not be avoided, but only prepared for. For Yahweh there is no such thing as fate; he is always ready to turn aside an announced judgment for any who repent. Jonah knew this, and it grated on him intensely (Jonah 4:1–3).

So here, as Elijah strode across the bed of the Jordan, the future beckoned in the light of the past. In spite of all the apostasy in Israel, the God who did not destroy his people in the desert, but led a second generation across this same river to victory, would surely hear a repentant people and restore them to himself. The price of that repentance might be very high indeed, involving the chastisement of the Syrians, and the blood of the house of Omri, but if there really was a repudiation of Baal and a wholehearted return to the terms of the covenant, Yahweh would receive them with open arms.[39]

It seems likely that Elijah's mysterious departure, unique in the biblical accounts,[40] is what accounts for the proliferation of Elijah legends during the Second Temple period, including the tradition of leaving an empty chair for him at the Passover meal. However, there is warrant for the idea that "Elijah" would herald the coming of the Messiah. That warrant is found in the final verses of the book of Malachi, the final prophet in the canonical order. There we see in the context of the promise of a day when "the sun of righteousness" will rise, either to destroy the wicked, or to heal "those who fear my name," that "I will send the prophet Elijah to you" before that day comes (Mal 4:1–6 [MT 3:19–24]). These statements are clearly alluded to by the NT writers and by Christ himself with respect to John the Baptist (Matt 3:4 [cf. 2 Kgs 1:8]; 11:10, 14; Luke 1:17).

Although Moses is said to have died, the place of his grave is unknown (Deut 34:5–6). This fact, coupled with Elijah's strange departure, may explain why it was Moses and Elijah who met and talked with Jesus at his transfiguration, as representatives of the Law and the Prophets (Mark 9:4–5), and why popular tradition identifies them as the two witnesses in Revelation 11:3–13.

---

39. See Satterthwaite, "The Elisha Narrative," for fuller exploration of these themes.
40. Only Enoch is similar, but the terse statement in Gen 5:24 "then Enoch was no more, for God took him" is nothing like what is described here of Elijah.

Application and Devotional Implications

Elijah's inference that the Spirit was not a possession of his to dispense at will calls to mind the statement in James 5:17 that Elijah was an ordinary human being, and that he did not have superhuman powers. James' point is to emphasize the power of prayer and that anyone can avail themselves of that power, but the point can and should be enlarged upon. Neither Elijah, nor Elisha after him, accomplished what they did because they were, like some cartoon figure, possessed of superpowers. They were ordinary human beings through whose lives the Breath of God was blowing. One indication of this fact is the evident differences in the two men's personalities. Elijah was a solitary figure who appeared and disappeared in a somewhat mysterious way. Elisha was much more gregarious, moving in and out of the royal court with ease. Where Elijah seems to have been rough, Elisha was smooth. What was it that they had in common? The Spirit of God.

Humans today may be filled with that same Spirit, and though entirely ordinary, may live extraordinary lives. This is the good news of the gospel of Christ: not merely that we may be declared innocent from sin, but that every believer has the Holy Spirit living in him or her, and may be filled with that Spirit if they will allow him to do so. Will they do things that are so remarkable that the actions call attention to themselves? Perhaps. But perhaps not. Nevertheless, such persons will clearly transcend the norm for human life in love, in works of charity, in integrity, even in simple goodness. In this sense, they will be like Elisha, having received from their Father the best possible inheritance, a double portion of his Spirit (cf. Eph 1:13–14).

Selected Bibliography

Beek, M. A. "The Meaning of the Expression 'The Chariots and Horsemen of Israel.' " *OtSt* 17 (1972): 1–10.

Cohn, R. L. "Reading in Three Dimensions: The Imperative of Biblical Narrative." *Religion and Intellectual Life* 6 (1989): 161–72.

Davis, D. R. "The Kingdom of God in Transition: Interpreting 2 Kings 2." *WTJ* 46 (1984): 384–95.

Fox, E. "The Translation of Elijah: Issues and Challenges." In *Bible Translation on the Threshold of the Twenty-First Century: Authority, Reception, Culture and Religion*, ed. Athalya Brenner and Jan Willem van Henton, 156–69. Sheffield: Sheffield Academic, 2002.

Lundbom, J. R. "Elijah's Chariot Ride." *JJS* 24 (1973): 39–50.

O'Brien, M. A. "The Portrayal of Prophets in 2 Kings 2." *ABR* 46 (1998): 1–16.

Rice, G. "Elijah's Requirement for Prophetic Leadership 2 Kings 2:1–18." *JRT* 59/60 (2006): 1–12.

Walfish, R. "Ruth and Elisha: A Comparative Study." *JBQ* 41 (2013): 236–42.

For studies of Luke's use of the Elijah/Elisha narratives see:

Brodie, T. L. "The Departure for Jerusalem (Luke 9:51–56) as a Rhetorical Imitation of Elijah's Departure for the Jordan (2 Kgs 1:1–2:6)." *Bib* 70 (1989): 96–109.

Evans, C. A. "Luke's Use of the Elijah/Elisha Narratives and the Ethic of Election." *JBL* 106 (1987): 75–83.

Elisha's First Miracles (2:12–25)

These two miracles, one positive and one negative summarize Elisha's ministry. Although he brought about the curse that Yahweh pronounced on the house of Ahab (1 Kgs 21:20–24) by means of his anointing of Jehu (2 Kgs 9:1–13), his ministry also had continual overtones of hope for new life, and both these elements are demonstrated in the material that follows.

Translation

12 Elisha was watching and crying out, "My father, my father, the chariotry of Israel and its horsemen." But he did not see him again. He took hold of his clothes and tore them in two pieces. **13** Then he picked up the cloak of Elijah that had fallen from him, and went back and stood on the bank of the Jordan. **14** Then he took Elijah's cloak that had fallen from him, and struck the water, and he said, "Where is Yahweh the God of Israel?" When he too struck the water, it was divided on two sides, and Elisha passed over. **15** Now the sons of the prophets who were in Jericho saw him at a distance and they said, "The spirit of Elijah has rested on Elisha." So they came to meet him and fell down on the ground in front of him. **16** They said, "There are with your servants fifty strong men. Please let them go and look for your master lest the Spirit of Yahweh has taken him up and cast him on one of the mountains or in one of the valleys." He said, "Do not send them." **17** But they pressed him until he was embarrassed, so he said, "Send!" So they sent the fifty men and they searched for three days, but they did not find him. **18** They returned to him while he was staying in Jericho, and he said to them, "Didn't I tell you not to go?"

19 The men of the city said to Elisha, "See, the setting of the city is good, as my lord sees, but the water is bad and the land is sterile." **20** He said, "Take a new jar, and put salt in it." So they took one to him. **21** He went out to the outflow of the water and scattered the salt there, and said, "Thus says Yahweh, 'I have healed these waters. There will no longer be death and sterility from there.' " **22** The water was healed until this day according to the word of Elisha which he spoke.

23 He went up from there to Bethel. As he was going up on the road some young boys came out from the city and mocked him and said to him, "Go up[41], Baldie; go up, Baldie." **24** He turned around and looked at them and cursed them in the name of Yahweh. Then two bears came out of the

41. Cogan and Tadmor translate "Be off," and cite several references in support (38). However, in all the occurrences they cite עֲלֵה, *ʿălê,* "go up," is followed by מֵעַל, *mēʿal,* which does not occur here.

forest and tore to pieces forty-two of the lads. **25** He went from there to Mt. Carmel and then went back to Samaria.

Textual Notes

12a. אָבִי: LXX lacks the first person pronoun in both cases; Vulg. and Syr. with MT.

14a. הַמַּיִם: LXX and Vulg. add "and it did not part"; Syr. with MT. See the "Commentary" below.

14b. אַף־הוּא: LXX transliterates Heb. אַף־הוּא as αφφω; Vulg. attaches it to the question and translates "even now", perhaps reading אֵפֹא. Syr. with MT reading it with the following clause, "he also." See *CTAT* (379-80), for a lengthy discussion, ultimately opting for MT with reservations.

16a. וַיַּשְׁלִכֵהוּ: LXX add "in the Jordan"; Vulg. and Syr. with MT.

16b. הַגֵּיָאוֹת: LXX reads "hills"; Vulg. and Syr. with MT.

Commentary

This unit, paralleling 1 Kings 17:1–24, where Elijah's prophetic power was demonstrated, displays two selected miracles of Elisha's that establish his prophetic credentials. But these two events also, by their juxtaposition, demonstrate the possibilities of Elisha's prophetic ministry: blessing or curse.[42] Thus, they are not merely the first of Elisha's miracles oddly separated from the rest by Jehoram's regnal account. Rather, they are intended to be representative of all the rest of his ministry.[43]

In both cases, the descriptions are quite terse, leaving us with a number of unanswered questions. Commentators (e.g., Gray, 477–81) have sought to provide answers to many of these questions, but the narrator has probably been terse for a reason. He does not want the details to obscure the point being made: this Elisha is the fully accredited successor to Elijah, and his ministry is "set for the rising and falling of many" (cf. Luke 2:34).

12 Elisha's cry[44] "My father, my father, the chariot and horsemen of Israel" (אָבִי אָבִי רֶכֶב יִשְׂרָאֵל וּפָרָשָׁיו, *ʾāḇî ʾāḇî rekeḇ yiśrāʾēl ûpārāšāyw*) could be taken in that sense: "My father, I have seen the almighty power of Yahweh," or it could be that he meant it as something of a lament, "My father, you have been the representative of the power of Yahweh." This seems to be the way in which King Jehoash used it at Elisha's death (13:14). This latter instance

42. See Rachelle Gilmour, *Juxtaposition and the Elisha Cycle*, LHBOTS 594 (London: Bloomsbury, 2014), 95–103.

43. So Satterthwaite, "The Elisha Narrative," 9–10.

44. The text uses participles to express some of the immediacy and intensity of the moment. "Watching this happen, he was crying out... ."

suggests the possibility that the phrase may have been a stock one at that time, used when someone significant died. But perhaps it is more likely that it had become known that Elisha had used it at Elijah's translation, and that the king then used it of Elisha in memory of that event.

The explicit statement that Elisha tore his clothes "in two" (לִשְׁנַיִם, *lišnayim*) suggests that this is more than a gesture of mourning,[45] but also represents his sense of the division that has taken place: Elijah is no longer on earth, and Elisha is; a fiery chariot stands between them. No longer is Elisha merely an assistant to the man whose spiritual power exceeded the power of horses and chariots; now the responsibility rests squarely on his shoulders. His old life, like his old clothes, is gone forever.

13 As an expression of this new reality, Elisha picks up "Elijah's cloak that had fallen off him" (אֶת־אַדֶּרֶת אֵלִיָּהוּ אֲשֶׁר נָפְלָה מֵעָלָיו, *ʾet-ʾadderet ʾēliyyāhû ʾăšer nop̄lâ mē ʿālāyw*)." What an expressive phrase that is. Elijah no longer needed his cloak, the one he had thrown over Elisha (1 Kgs 19:19), the one he used to try to hide his face from God (1 Kgs 19:13), the one he had used to divide the Jordan, and we can see him almost absent-mindedly shrugging it off as he is whirled away into the skies. But Elisha does need it. Here again is the theme of this unit. The ministries of Elijah and Elisha are a seamless whole. The power by which Elijah had served was none other than the one by which Elisha will serve. As Elisha wrapped that cloak around his shoulders, how he must have remembered that day when the wild-haired man had met him at the end of a furrow and had thrown it over his same shoulders. He had seen Elijah, his "father," translated, so now with his "father's" cloak about him, he could be confident of being his true heir, and filled with the same Spirit.

14 While the essential point of this verse is quite clear, it is not so clear exactly what is being said. This is largely because of the Hebrew phrase אַף־הוּא (*ʾap̄-hû ʾ*) at the beginning of the second main clause of the sentence. By any standard it is awkward, especially when it is coupled to a second statement that Elisha struck the water. A number of solutions have been put forward, extending at least as far back as the LXX, which adds "and it did not part" (καὶ οὐ διέστη, *kai ou diestē*) after the first occurrence of "he struck the water." On this understanding, it was only after calling upon Yahweh, and striking the water a second time that the waters parted. While few commentators believe the text should be emended to follow the LXX,[46] many believe the interpretation is correct.[47] That is, Elisha struck the water with Elijah's cloak, but nothing happened. The cloak itself had no magical power. Then, in words somewhat reminiscent of Elijah's query to Ahaziah,

---

45. On tearing clothes as a sign of mourning or extreme distress, see Gen 37:29, 34; Judg 11:35; 2 Sam 1:11; 13:31; Job 1:20; 2 Kgs 11:14, etc.

46. Vulgate follows the LXX, but Syr. does not.

47. Cogan and Tadmor call the LXX reading "exegetical" (33).

"Is there no God in Israel?" (1:3, 16), Elisha cried out, "Where is Yahweh, the God of Elijah?" (אַיֵּה יהוה אֱלֹהֵי אֵלִיָּהוּ, *ʾayyē yhwh ʾĕlōhê ʾēliyyāhû*), a sign of his recognition that it is only as a result of Yahweh's sovereign action that miracles occur. Then when he struck the water again, they parted.

However, this interpretation requires doing something with the troublesome *ʾap̄-hû*, such as moving it to the beginning of the main clause and reading it as אֵפוֹ (*ʾēp̄ô*), resulting in reading such as the NIV: "Where *now* is the LORD, the God of Elijah?"[48] A much simpler approach is to understand the phrase as "he too" referring to Elisha's having done the same thing as Elijah had done. This was the approach of KJV followed by NAS and is reflected in the translation above. That is, in the first and only time that Elisha struck the water he understood that it was not Elijah's cloak, but Elijah's God, who would part the waters. The cloak was but the symbol of the reality. The second main clause simply confirms that when Elisha struck the water as Elijah had, the same thing occurred.

15–18 As Cohn (15) correctly observes, these verses establish without question the distinction between Elisha and the sons of the prophets. They could not see what had happened to Elijah, but they clearly could see that in returning to them, Elisha had just done what Elijah had done before them. Clearly, the same Spirit that had been on Elijah was now resting on Elisha. Their act of obeisance indicated their recognition that the man who had come back to them was a different one from the one they had insistently questioned previously.

Yet, they were not quite certain. If Elisha told them what had happened to Elijah, they were not quite ready to believe it. Perhaps the רוּחַ, *rûaḥ*, the wind of God, had merely swept him up and dropped him someplace else.[49] Evidently, they were used to Elijah's disappearing from one place and showing up in another (cf. 1 Kgs 18:12), and they were not quite ready to grant that Elisha's prophetic insight would carry that far. So, they had a fifty-man troop (chap. 1!) that they could send in search of Elijah. Elisha assured them the search would be useless and would not give permission for one to be made. But they pressed him to the point where he was "embarrassed" (בֹּשׁ, *bōš*)[50] to keep on insisting. So he let them go, and after three days it was they who were embarrassed, coming back to admit that the old prophet was nowhere

---

48. The only thing the LXX translators knew to do with it was to transliterate it and leave it. See the "Textual Note" above.

49. For the understanding of *rûaḥ* as wind here, see Robert B. Chisholm, Jr., "The 'Spirit of the Lord' in 2 Kings 2:16," in *Presence, Power and Promise: the Role of the Spirit of God in the Old Testament*, ed. David G. Firth and Paul D. Wegner (Downers Grove, IL: IVP Academic, 2011), 306–17.

50. Lit. "ashamed" (בֹּשׁ). He was not ashamed of the position he was taking. Rather, he was ashamed to keep refusing them. Eng. "embarrassed" captures the sense better.

to be found. Elisha's insight, his vision, was confirmed. He was indeed the successor to Elijah.

19–22 This miracle, almost certainly performed at the spring now known as ʿAin es-Sultan, next to the mound of Jericho, established that Elisha could speak a word of blessing. Just as Moses was able, with the use of a stick, to turn bitter water sweet so could Elijah, with the use of salt, make bad water good. That was Moses' first miracle after the crossing of the Reed Sea, and this was Elisha's first miracle after crossing the river. The similarity between the two cannot be coincidental.

Again, it is hardly coincidental that the first place Elisha went after crossing the Jordan was Jericho, just as Joshua's was. But whereas Joshua's presence resulted in a curse upon any who would rebuild the city (Josh 6:26), Elisha's work was to make it inhabitable again. Could it be that through Elisha, Israel, under a curse for its idolatrous ways, could yet be healed and restored to Yahweh?

20–21 Although a "new jar" (צְלֹחִית חֲדָשָׁה, *ṣᵉlōḥîṯ ḥăḏāšâ*) and "salt" (מֶלַח, *melaḥ*)[51] were used in the act of purifying the water, Elisha makes it very clear that it was not they, nor any power intrinsic to him, that accomplished the task. Yahweh, speaking through the prophet specifies, "I have healed these waters" (רִפִּאתִי לַמַּיִם הָאֵלֶּה, *rippi ʾṯiy lammayim hā ʾēlleh*). Just as was made plain when Elisha returned across the Jordan, it is only as Yahweh works through his man that anything is accomplished. Jesus was to make a similar point concerning his own miracles (John 10:25).

23–24 This incident was especially distasteful to older commentators, among whom Gray (479) is one of the most irate, calling it "a puerile tale" with "no serious point." Recent writers (e.g., Provan, 175), more prone to see the account in its context, have been more measured. Yet, we still wish for more details. Who were these mockers, and what was their motive? Was there more justification for Elisha's action than appears on the surface? But as with the previous incident, the narrator is not interested in satisfying our curiosity. He only wants to make the point that this man Elisha has the power of heaven at his command, a power that can bless, but also one that can curse. That being so, Israel, and the Omrides in particular, should take notice.

23 If the narrator is very sparing of details, there are some clues here that should not be overlooked. The event took place on the road to Bethel—the place that throughout the book of Kings is known as the center of Israel's apostasy (1 Kgs 12:29–33; 13:1–4; 2 Kgs 10:29; 17:28)—the place where

---

51. There are almost as many explanations as to why the waters are "bad" (רָעִים, *rā ʿîm*) and why a new jar and salt were used as there are commentators. But all are speculative, and as such, not very profitable.

Yahweh had twice met the patriarch Jacob (Gen 27 and 35). This was a place that was no friend to a prophet of Yahweh, as Amos was to learn in the next century (Amos 7:12–13). Thus, it seems no accident at all that it was from this place that this jeering group issued forth. Notice that there were forty-two of them (v. 24). As Wiseman (198) says, this looks more like "an organized mob" than merely a loose-knit group of troublemakers. But children? The difficulty here is in the indeterminacy of the Hebrew terms being used. The term נַעַר, *na ʿar* translated "boy" above, can refer to anyone up to the age of thirty,[52] whereas קָטָן, *qāṭān,* translated "young," can also mean "small," and "insignificant."[53]

What was the content of the "young boys' " 'mockery? Again, we are left to wonder. Were they just telling him to go away? Or were they daring him to go on up into the city, perhaps to confront an even more hostile crowd? Or were they daring him to fly up into heaven as they may have heard Elijah had done? We do not know. Likewise, we do not know why they fastened on the prophet's baldness? Was he tonsured as a holy man? Or was it just that natural baldness makes a man appear less virile than one with a full head of hair? All of the proposals just mentioned can be found in one or another commentary, and all are possible (although not all at the same time!). But I say again that this is not the point. The point is that the divine power resting upon this man, and at his disposal, is not something to be taken lightly. To mock the representative of the Court of Heaven, as Israel was to do (see 2 Chr 36:16) was to invite disaster. The covenant that results in blessing when kept, is the same covenant that brings curse when it is broken.

Again, note that the curse was given "in the name of Yahweh" (בְּשֵׁם יהוה, *bᵉšēm yhwh*). Whatever might happen to these lads, it would not be as a result of the prophet's magical powers. It would be because Yahweh's name and power rested upon him. The immediacy of the fulfillment of the curse underlines how dangerous it is to treat Yahweh lightly. Within a few years, the house of Omri would be as thoroughly destroyed as those boys were. Yahweh is not an idol who can be manipulated so as to supply our needs. He is all-loving, but he is also all-powerful, and to live in defiance of his character and nature is as deadly as it is to pick up a live electric wire.[54]

25 Elisha's itinerary from Jericho to Bethel to Mt. Carmel to Samaria can hardly be coincidence. It is tempting to see it as a recapitulation of Elijah's travels, as begun in chapter one; however, as pointed out above, Carmel and Samaria are inferences there, and are not explicitly stated (e.g., Ahaziah could have been in Jezreel). Furthermore, if that were the point, then Gilgal should have been included in Elisha's journey. It is better to understand that Bethel

52. So House (260n23), citing 1 Sam 16:11; 2 Sam 14:21; 18:5.

53. BDB, 881–82.

54. Provan notes that animals appear elsewhere in Kings as instruments of divine judgment: 1 Kgs 13:20–28; 20:36 (175).

and Carmel were chosen because on the one hand, Bethel represented Israel's apostasy and on the other, Carmel spoke of Yahweh's triumph (1 Kgs 18). Thus, Elisha finally came to Samaria with those two issues clearly underlined. Would apostasy, especially as represented now in the open worship of Baal in preference to Yahweh, win, or would Israel's ancient faith promulgated through Moses and Joshua, and fully vindicated through Elijah, win?

Selected Bibliography

Alexandre, J. "Des Enfants et du Pain: Deux Récits de Purification dans le Cycle d'Élisée: II Rois 2,19–25 et 4,38–44." *Foi et Vie* 104 (2005): 36–47.

Bodner, K. *Elisha's Profile in the Book of Kings: The Double Agent* (Oxford: Oxford, 2013).

Carr, A. D., "Elisha's Prophetic Authority and Initial Miracles (2 Kings 2:12–25)." *Evangelical Journal* 29 (2011): 34–44.

Irwin, B. P. "The Curious Incident of the Boys and the Bears: 2 Kings 2 and the Prophetic Authority of Elisha," *TynBul* 67 (2016): 23–35.

Kissling, P. J. *Reliable Characters in the Primary History: Profiles of Moses, Joshua, Elijah and Elisha.* JSOTSup 224; Sheffield: Sheffield Academic, 1996.

Mercer, M. K. "Elisha's Unbearable Curse: A Study of 2 Kings 2:23–25." *Africa Journal of Evangelical Theology* 21 (2002): 165–98.

Sperber, D. "Weak Waters." *ZAW* 82 (1970): 114–16.

Ziolkowski, E. J. "The Bad Boys of Bethel: Origin and Development of a Sacrilegious Type." *HR* 30 (1991): 331–58.

Elisha (3:1–13:25)

This material covers the conclusion of the ministry of Elijah and Elisha that began with the introduction of Elijah in 1 Kings 17. It is divided into two parts: 3:1–8:6 and 8:7–13:25. In the first part Elisha is the central character, and we see him doing a series of miracles that on the surface appear to be somewhat miscellaneous. But in fact, as we will see below, they fit together to give a final demonstration to the house of Omri (Omri, Ahab, Ahaziah, and Joram) of Yahweh's power and care. The miracles are overwhelmingly positive, and suggest that even at this late date, if there were a genuine turning back to Yahweh in whole-hearted trust, there could be restoration, and the dire possibilities inherent in Yahweh's instructions to Elijah in 1 Kings 19:15–17 could be averted. However, that was not to be.

In some ways, we see the ultimate outcome already in chapter three. Although 3:2 tells us that Joram was not as bad as his father and mother, he still "clung" (דָּבֵק, *dāḇēq*) to the sins of Jeroboam, which centered on the bull-idols at Bethel and Dan. It is perhaps because of this equivocal following of Yahweh that he is prone, as soon as trouble develops, to question Yahweh's goodness (3:10). That tendency comes to the fore during the siege by Ben-hadad (chap. 6), when Joram attributes the disaster to Yahweh, and more particularly to Elisha; and like his brother Ahaziah tried to kill Elijah, he sought to do the same to Elisha. He could not believe in Yahweh's ultimate goodness nor in his intention to redeem his people. Perhaps he had the fundamentally pagan idea that the gods are to be manipulated for human benefit, but never trusted.

At any rate, it is apparent by chapter eight that the judgment on the house of Omri that Elijah had predicted (1 Kings 21:21–22) could no longer be averted. Yahweh had spared the dynasty when he brought about Ahab's death, and even when he visited the curse on Ahab's son Ahaziah, but now with Ahab's second son, Joram, it was to come to its end.

The second segment (8:7–13:25) describes that end. It was set in motion by the carrying out of the other two parts of Yahweh's instructions of Elijah: the anointing of Hazael of Syria (8:7–15) and Jehu of Israel (9:1–13). Some commentators (Walsh, 278) believe that Elijah was at fault for not carrying out those two things during his own lifetime. However, there is no indication in the accounts of the rest of Elijah's life that that was the case. He anointed Elisha, and clearly communicated the rest of the directive to him, because Elisha saw that it was carried out. One of the things these details indicate is the essential unity of the ministry of Elijah and Elisha (see further in the "Commentary" on 2:1–18 above). They are clearly separate individuals, with distinct characters, yet from 1 Kings 17 to 2 Kings 13, they have one task: to confront the domination of Baal that was being promoted not only in Israel, but also in Judah, and to defeat it. It began on Mt. Carmel (1 Kgs 18) and ended with the destruction of the temple of Baal in Jerusalem and the restoration of Yahweh's temple there (2 Kings 11, 12), and it is essentially one undertaking from beginning to end.

Surprisingly, after the anointing of Hazael and Jehu, Elisha disappears from the narrative until chapter thirteen. This is unexpected since he was so prominent in chapters three through eight. No reason is given for this, but it is probably because once he had set the machinery of destruction in motion there was nothing else to do but let it run its course, as it did with terrible inexorability. Chapters nine and ten detail the destruction of not only Omri's dynasty, but everyone associated with it. Then chapter eleven takes the massacre to Judah, but there it is Omri's granddaughter Athaliah who tries to exterminate the dynasty of David, only herself to die at the hands of her grandson Joash's guards.

Elisha's return to the narrative in chapter 13 is a fitting recap of his entire career, a bittersweet encounter with an Israelite king. Jehu had not lived up to his promise: he had destroyed the power of Baal, as resident in the Omride dynasty, but he had not gone all the way back to the pure worship of Yahweh. Thus, the word to him from Yahweh (through Elisha?) is that while his dynasty would endure to the fourth generation, it would *only* endure to the fourth generation (10:30). Elisha had lived through two of those generations to see Jehu's grandson on the throne of Israel. It would be easy for a dying old man, seeing the incompleteness of his work, and knowing that the Jehide dynasty would not last, to be bitterly glad for whatever trouble might befall Jehoash. But that was not the case; without any caveat he offered victory over the Syrian invaders, but then had to accept the less-than-extravagant trust that the Israelite king was able to put forth.

The final comment on Elisha's ministry is found in the bizarre little incident reported in 13:20–21. A body was hurriedly thrown into Elisha's tomb, and when it touched Elisha's remains the man sprang to life. Elisha's ministry had been to offer life and death (cf. Deut 30:19), but throughout his life his cry, like that of Moses, was, "Choose life!"

Selected Bibliography

Bodner, K. *Elisha's Profile in the Book of Kings: The Double Agent*. Oxford: Oxford, 2013.

Bronner, L. *The Stories of Elijah and Elisha as Polemics Against Baal Worship*. Leiden: Brill, 1968.

Gertel, E. "Moses, Elisha and Transferred Spirit: The Height of Biblical Prophecy? Part II." *JBQ* 30 (2002): 171–77.

Miller, J. M. "The Elisha Cycle and the Omride Wars." *JBL* 85 (1966): 441–54.

Moore, R. D. *God Saves: Lessons from the Elisha Stories*. JSOTSup 95; Sheffield: JSOT Press, 1990: 11–68.

Elisha's Miracles (3:1–8:6)

As mentioned above, these miracles are a demonstration to the house of Omri that it has a choice of life or death before it. The miracles are largely positive showing that in spite of their sponsorship of Baal worship that has brought the dynasty to the brink of extinction, that is not Yahweh's desired purpose. He would preserve the dynasty if they would repent and turn to him. The king with whom Elisha deals is Ahab's son Jehoram (or Joram). He is clearly conflicted in his feelings about Elisha. While he shows a certain fascination with the prophet and his works (8:1-6), he is also ready to blame Elisha whenever there is trouble (6:31–33).

The incidents in which Elisha figures are the attack on Moab (3:1–27); the widow's oil (4:1–7); the Shunammite woman (4:8–37); the deadly stew (4:38–44); the healing of Naaman (5:1–27); the recovered axehead (6:1–7); the Syrian king's attempt to capture Elisha (6:8–23); the failed Syrian siege of Samaria (6:24–7:20); and the Shunammite woman's return (8:1–6)

The Attack on Moab (3:1–27)

More than is the case with Elijah, Elisha's narrative is composed largely of miracle reports. On the surface these miracles seem somewhat miscellaneous, but there are three recurring themes that unite them. One is the power and influence of Yahweh. In the end these are the miracles of Yahweh *through* Elisha more than they are the miracles of Elisha.

The second theme is the fraught relationship between Elisha and Jehoram, the king of Israel, and son of Ahab. We find him at the end of the account plying Gehazi for stories of Elisha's miracles (8:4), and yet there was a point where the king was determined to kill the prophet (6:31). The problem was that Elisha was in no sense a court prophet whose task was to make the king a success. Rather, he was a man of God whose task was to bring the king to account.

The third theme is the one of life and death. Death is ever threatening, but the prophet is ever bringing victory over death wherever possible. This begins immediately in chapter three when Jehoram believes Yahweh has called them out to destroy them (3:10), but Elijah brings life-giving water. It continues through the widow's oil and the Shunammite woman's son (4), etc. God's purpose is to give life. That gift is not in the hand of Baal or Asherah, only Yahweh's.

Translation

1 Joram, son of Ahab, became king over Israel in Samaria in the eighteenth
year of Jehoshaphat, king of Judah, and he ruled twelve years. **2** He did evil
in the eyes of Yahweh, although not like his father and his mother. He took
away the pillar of Baal which his father had made. **3** However, he clung to
the sins of Jeroboam, son of Nebat, with which he made Israel sin, and did
not turn away from them.[55] **4** Now Mesha, king of Moab, was raising sheep,
and he would supply[56] to the king of Israel 100,000 lambs and the wool of
100,000 rams.[57] **5** When Ahab died, the king of Moab rebelled against the
king of Israel. **6** King Joram went out from Samaria at that time and mustered
all Israel. **7** He then went[58] and sent to Jehoshaphat, king of Judah, saying,
"The king of Moab has rebelled against me. Go with me to Moab to make
war." He said, "I will go—I am yours, my people are yours, and my horses
are yours."[59] **8** He said, "Which way shall we go?" He said, "The way of the
wilderness of Edom." **9** So the king of Israel, the king of Judah, and the king
of Edom went, and they went around on a journey of seven days. But there
was no water for the camp or for the animals that were in their train.[60] **10** The
king of Israel said, "Oh, no! Yahweh has called us[61] three kings to give us into
the hand of Moab." **11** Jehoshaphat said, "Is there no prophet of Yahweh here
that we may inquire through him?" One of the servants of the king of Israel
answered and said, "Elisha, son of Shaphat, who poured water on the hand

---

55. Heb. 3ms.; typical in this case. See GKC (§133*p*).
56. Frequentive; see *IBHS* (§34.2.3).
57. For this construction, see GKC (§131*k*).
58. הלך, *hlk* is functioning as an auxiliary verb, giving more immediacy to the statement. See GKC (§113*x*).
59. Lit. "I am like you, my people are like yours, and my horses are like yours."
60. Lit. "at their feet," indicating those following, cf. 1 K 20:10; Judg 4:10; 1 Sam 25:27; 2 Sam 15:16, 17. See Cogan and Tadmor, 45.
61. See *IBHS* (§17.4.2c) for a "deictic" use of the demonstrative pronoun.

of Elijah is here." **12** Jehoshaphat said, "The word of Yahweh is with him." So king of Israel, Jehoshaphat, and the king of Edom went down to him. **13** Elisha said to the king of Israel, "What do I have to do with you? Go to the prophets of your father and the prophets of your mother." The king of Israel said to him, "No, because Yahweh has called us three kings to give us into the hand of Moab." **14** Elisha said, "On the life of Yahweh of Heaven's Armies, before whom I stand, were it not for the presence of Jehoshaphat whom I regard, I would neither look at you, nor see you. **15** But now get me a musician."[62] When the musician played, the hand of Yahweh was upon him. **16** He said, "Thus says Yahweh, 'Make this wadi into nothing but trenches.'[63] **17** For thus says Yahweh, 'You will not see wind and you will not see rains, but this wadi will be full of water and you will drink, you, and your livestock, and your animals.' **18** This is a light thing in the eyes of Yahweh; he will give Moab into your hand. **19** You will strike every fortified city and every choice city;[64] every good tree you will fell, and all the springs of water you will stop up and every good piece of land you will ruin with stones." **20** In the morning, when the offering was being given, all at once there was water coming from the direction of Edom and the land was filled with water.

21 Now Moab had heard that the kings had come up to make war on them. Everyone old enough to put on armor was called out, and they stood on the border. **22** They rose early in the morning and the sun rose on the water and Moab saw the water opposite them as red as blood. **23** So they said, "This is blood! The kings have attacked each other and each one has struck the other. To the spoil, Moab!" **24** So they came to the camp of Israel, but Israel rose up and struck Moab, and they fled from them. So they went in, entering and striking Moab.[65] **25** They threw down cities, and each man threw his stone on every good piece of land and covered it. They stopped up every spring of water and felled every good tree until only the stones of Kir-hareseth remained. The slingers surrounded it and struck it. **26** The king of

---

62. Reading וְהָיָה, *w^{e}hāyâ* as per GKC (§112*uu*).

63. The versions all support this traditional reading (cf. KJV, etc.) which takes עָשֹׂה, *ʿāśōh* to be an inf. abs. functioning as an emph. imp. (see GKC [§113*bb*] and *IBHS* [§35.5.1a]). Modern interpreters have preferred to read it as standing in place of a 1cs finite verb: "I will make" (see ESV, NIV, NRSV, etc.). JPS and NLT seem to take the term as functioning as a kind of passive form "will be made" and read "This wadi shall be full of pools." For the rendering "nothing but" or "full of" see GKC (§123*e*). See the "Commentary" below for further discussion.

64. See the "Textual Note" below. Cogan and Tadmor, noting that "fortified" and "choice" have only one different Heb. letter between them, and that Gk. omits "choice city," and that the phrase does not occur in the report in v. 25, they argue to omit it here (45). However, the phrase does appear in Vulg. and Syr. and it is equally likely that Gk. omits it to harmonize with v. 25.

65. For this translation, see "Textual Note" 24a–a. below.

Moab saw that the battle was too much for him, so he took 700 swordsmen and tried to break through to the king of Edom, but he could not. **27** So he took his firstborn son who would have succeeded him and offered him up on the wall as a whole burnt offering. A great rage came upon Israel and they withdrew from him and returned to the land.

Textual Notes

2a. אֶת־מַצְּבַת: Gk. and Vulg. "pillars"; Syr. with MT.

4a. נֹקֵד: Gk. transliterates.

4b. לְמֶלֶךְ־יִשְׂרָאֵל: Gk. adds "at the rising" (of the year?); Vulg. and Syr. with MT. *CTAT* (381) notes that MT is probable.

10a. הָאֵלֶּה: Gk. adds "passing by"; Vulg. and Syr. with MT.

12a. וִיהוֹשָׁפָט: Gk. and Vulg. add "king of Judah"; Syr. with MT. MT is harder reading.

13a–a. אֶל־נְבִיאֵי אָבִיךָ: Gk. omits "and the prophets of your mother"; Vulg. omits "prophets of"; Syr. with MT.

17a. וּמִקְנֵיכֶם: Gk[L] reads "your camp," but other Gk. MSS read "your possessions" with MT, as do Vulg. and Syr. See the "Commentary" below.

19a–a. וְכָל־עִיר מִבְחוֹר: Gk. omits; Vulg. and Syr. with MT. Gk. is perhaps harmonizing with v. 25.

24a–a. וַיַּבּוֹ בָהּ: MT Q is ויכו בה; Gk. "they entered Moab, going in and striking," seeming to argue for וַיָּבֹאוּ בֹא, arguing for MT K although altered for the lost *'alephs*; Vulg. "they came, who had conquered, and struck," Syr. "they continued attacking them and devastated," seeming to support MT Q. GKC (§113*x*) supports the Gk. reading, explaining the lost *'alephs* as "avoiding the hiatus." *CTAT* (382) gives marginal support to that reading.

25a–a. עַד־הִשְׁאִיר אֲבָנֶיהָ בַּקִּיר חֲרֶשֶׂת: Gk. "they left the stones of the wall overturned"; Vulg. "until only earth remained of the walls"; Syr. "until the stones of the wall of the capital city were demolished." MT best explains the other readings (so also *CTAT*, 383).

Commentary

This chapter is a fitting introduction to chapters 3–13, as it portrays Joram, the last king of the Omride dynasty and Elisha's interaction with him. It depicts a man who tries to play both sides and succeeds in winning neither and it shows the independence of the prophet who will finally bring him down (by inaugurating another dynasty that will have its own issues).

The chapter raises many questions that commentators and scholars have wrestled with, with varying degrees of success. Among these are: how much is the reader intended to read this chapter in the light of 1 Kings 22; what is Jehoshaphat's role in the events; how are we to understand the apparent failure of Elijah's prophecy; and most of all, what are we to make of the strange, terse final verse—whose anger caused the Israelite armies to withdraw? As with chapter two, the narrator is not at pains to answer all these questions, and that is a part of the narrative's fascination. However, we should not allow these issues to deter us from the main points the narrator is clearly making. First, although Joram is willing to recognize Yahweh, the Omride dynasty has by no means repudiated Baalism and turned to trust in Yahweh. Second, Elisha's ministry, while not limited to the royal court, will always have the court in view. Third, there can be no doubt that Elisha is the one through whom the authority and power of Yahweh will be manifested, not only in Israel, but in Judah as well.

There are three subdivisions in the chapter: vv. 1–3, Joram's opening regnal information; vv. 4–20, the expedition to punish Moab and the consequent water crisis; vv. 21–27, the attack on Moab and its outcome.

1–3 This standard formula includes: (1) the name of the king ... Joram, (2) whose son he was ... Ahab's, (3) when he began to reign in correlation with his contemporary in Judah ... eighteenth year of Jehoshaphat,[66] and (4) how long he reigned ... twelve years (v. 1). It then moves to the phrase that appears in the regnal summary of every one of the northern kings, with the exception of the insignificant reigns of Elah (1 Kgs 16:8) and Shallum (2 Kgs 15:13): "he did evil in the eyes of Yahweh" (וַיַּעַשׂ הָרַע בְּעֵינֵי יהוה, *wayyaʿăśe hāraʿ bᵊʿênê yhwh*). What follows next, though, is somewhat surprising, because we are told that, unlike his brother Ahaziah (1 Kgs 22:52–53 [MT 51–52]), Joram did not fully follow in the footsteps of his father and mother. With one exception, however, we are not told what that meant. The exception is that "he took away the pillar of Baal which his father had made" (וַיָּסַר אֶת־מַצְּבַת הַבַּעַל אֲשֶׁר עָשָׂה אָבִיו, *wayyāsar ʾet-maṣṣᵊbat habbaʿal ʾăšer ʿāśâ ʾābîw*) (v. 2). We do not know whether this pillar was inside Ahab's temple to Baal (1 Kgs 16:32). If so, he did not actually destroy it because there were still such pillars in that temple when Jehu destroyed that building (2 Kgs 10:26–27).[67]

Perhaps we should not be completely surprised if Joram varied from the behavior of his parents and his brother, since he had at least heard what took place on Mt. Carmel and had certainly seen what had happened to his father and his brother. Yet, he clearly did not turn away from the worship of Baal to the worship of Yahweh, and as v. 3 tells us, whatever Yahwism he did acknowledge was still the paganized form that his predecessor Jeroboam had instituted, one that betrayed the essential truth of biblical religion: Yahweh is

66. See the "Commentary" on 1:17.
67. On the pattern of other pillars known in this region, it may have had a bas-relief of the deity on it with some sort of inscription below. For a photograph of possible examples, see *ANEP* 136, 139.

absolutely other than his creation. The degree of his commitment to a paganized view is indicated in the use of the word "clung" (דָּבֵק, *dāḇēq*). That is, he hung on to the bull-idols and the rituals and the pagan concepts behind it all with the same kind of fervency that Solomon "clung to" (דָּבַק, *dāḇaq*) his pagan wives (1 Kgs 11:2). This is the more poignant, because Deuteronomy 10:20 and 13:4 climax their lists of what it means to follow Yahweh with the injunction to "and to him you will cling" (וּבוֹ תִדְבָּק, *ûḇô ṯiḏbāq*).

4–5 Moab was located in Trans-Jordan along the lower southeast side of the Dead Sea, between the Arnon River in the north, and the Zered in the south.[68] It had been subjugated by David (2 Sam 8:2) and had remained a vassal of Israel after the division of the kingdom. The totality of its subjugation is probably intended to be conveyed by the very large numbers used here.[69]

As was often the case in the ANE, the death of an overlord, such as that of Ahab at Ramoth-gilead (1 Kgs 22:29–35), was a signal for vassals to attempt to break free, and that is what took place here. Mesha, king of Moab, saw his chance and seized it.[70] Apparently Ahaziah, in his short reign of less than a year, and then with his injury, was in no place to deal with the revolt, so it was left to his brother who succeeded him. Just as in the summary statement in 1:1 above, the term used for rebellion is not the normal one. Rather, it is פשׁע, *pšʿ*, which normally has the idea of "transgression," or violation of the terms of a relationship. This is the term that is used of the northern tribes separating from the southern (1 Kgs 12:19), as well as of Edom and Libnah breaking away from Judah (2 Kgs 8:20, 22). It may indicate that at least for

68. See "Moab" *ABD* 4:882–93.

69. Similar kinds of very large numbers appear in the Assyrian annals, when the Assyrian kings described the amount of booty they captured in their various conquests. See *ANET*, 276.

70. We have a report of this rebellion from the Moabite perspective on one of the earliest finds of an extra-biblical inscription relating to biblical events. The is the so-called Moabite Stone, also know as the Mesha Stele, now in the Louvre (for a photograph, see *ANEP* 74). Discovered in 1868, it is a self-congratulatory piece describing how the Moabite king, Mesha, broke away from Israel, and then proceeded to capture the Israelite territory (Reuben) north of Moab. Since its purpose is self-congratulation, it does not mention the events reported in this chapter. That it makes no mention of driving off the Israelite armies may suggest that that event was more of an embarrassment to him than any real victory. For discussions of the relation between the stone and this account, see Joe M. Sprinkle, "2 Kings 3: History or Historical Fiction," *BBR* 9 (1999): 247–70; Philip D. Stern, "Of Kings and Moabites: History and Theology in 2 Kings 3 and the Mesha Inscription," *HUCA* 64 (1993): 1–14.

the narrator, there was a closer covenantal relationship between these groups than mere subjugation.[71]

6–9 If no action had been taken against Mesha during the year of Ahaziah's kingship, Joram undoubtedly knew, as soon as he became king, that the time for action was "now" (perhaps reflected in "at that time," [בַּיּוֹם הַהוּא, *bayyôm hahû*] v. 6). He is reported to have done two things in preparation. First, he "mustered" (פקד, *pqd*) [72] his army, and second, he called on his ally, or perhaps vassal,[73] Jehoshaphat, for assistance. Jehoshaphat's response was immediate agreement, using the same words that he had spoken to Ahab before the battle at Ramoth-gilead (1 Kgs 22:4). Almost certainly Joram did a third thing, and that was to consult with his prophets. It is highly unlikely that any king in those days would go to war without such consultation (e.g., 2 Sam 5:19, 23–24). This could explain his wails in vv. 10 and 13 (see the "Commentary" there) and it might also underlie Elisha's biting comment in v. 13. It is not out of the question that the statements in v. 8 where no subjects are identified beyond 3ms pronouns may actually reflect the question to the prophets and their answer.

In any case, the opinion of some commentators (e.g., Provan, 182) that Jehoshaphat is at fault for not asking for a prophetic word before they set out on the campaign (as he had done with Ahab, 1 Kgs 22:7) seems unjustified. It is likely that Joram would have assured Jehoshaphat that he had made inquiries and that they had been favorable. Jehoshaphat, who is often presented in the text as a good man, but somewhat gullible and naïve (cf. 1 Kgs 22:30) would have accepted such assurances at face value.

The shortest way to Moab from Samaria and Jerusalem was to cross the Jordan at Jericho and proceed directly south. But if we accept Mesha's claims recorded on his stone, he had captured and fortified the former Israelite cities located in Reuben north of him. This would have made an attack by the direct route very difficult: Mesha would have been armed and ready. Thus, the much more difficult route south through Judah and around the south

---

71. Reflecting this idea, the Vulg. reads "transgressed his covenant that he had with the king of Israel."

72. Heb. פָּקַד, *pāqad* has a wide range of meanings, from "visit," to "appoint." It seems to reflect the activity of a commanding general. Thus, it can mean to "muster" troops as well as to "number" them.

73. We do not know for certain what the relationship was between Judah and Israel during the Omride dynasty. Omri clearly made alliances with the nations around him, as seen in the marriage of his son Ahab to the Tyrian princess Jezebel. Since Athaliah, the daughter of Ahab and Jezebel who was married to Jehoshaphat's son Jehoram, is also called "the daughter (granddaughter?) of Omri," this suggests that the alliance between Israel and Judah at least had its roots in Omri's diplomacy. So it is not clear whether this was a parity-treaty between equals (so Wiseman, 185), or a vassal treaty with Israel as the dominant partner (most other commentators).

end of the Dead Sea through the arid Arabah of Edom made sense. The combined army would have been attacking Moab from the rear, as it were.

The idea of the circuitous journey is conveyed in the phrase "and they went around" (וַיָּסֹבּוּ, *wayyāsōbbû*) (v. 9). This is not to say that they got lost, but simply that they went around to the south side of Moab. Gray (485) believes that they went up the escarpment on the east side of the Arabah, and through the mountains there until they could attack Moab from the southeast. This would have certainly taken all of seven days. But it is also possible that it simply took that long to travel from Samaria, pick up the Judeans wherever they mustered, collect the Edomite[74] vassals of Judah, and lead the army around the end of the sea.

Why the army ended up without water is an open question. Perhaps they thought the journey would not take so long and did not take enough for that eventuality. In any case, they were in dire straits, much as their forebears were repeatedly in that waterless region (cf. Exod 17:2; Num 20:2).

10–14 Joram's response to the crisis was despair and suspicion. As mentioned above, it is likely that he had gotten a favorable response concerning his journey from his prophets, who probably, like his father's prophets, were comfortable doing divination in the name of Baal or Yahweh, or both, as the case might be. Now, what has happened? Were his prophets deceived, as his father's had been (1 Kgs 22)? Had Yahweh actually led them into this desert to destroy them? Can Yahweh be trusted at all?[75] This is a man who does not know Yahweh.

Jehoshaphat's response is much more quiet and measured. He is neither despairing nor suspicious. He does not question Yahweh's motives in this crisis, but, using almost the same words he had with Ahab, seeks for Yahweh's guidance.[76] It is as though he is saying that before they blame Yahweh for their present circumstances, they should see what he might have to say about those circumstances.

---

74. The ruler of Edom at this time was a deputy appointed by Judah (1 Kgs 22:47 [MT 48]). However, that he should be called a "king" here need not be troublesome. That term was notoriously flexible. Note that the rulers of each of the Canaanite cities were also called "kings" (Josh 10:1; 12:1).

75. Note a similar response to the crisis in 6:33. Joram assumes the worst from Yahweh.

76. The parallels with 1 Kgs 22 have led some commentators to propose that it is a "doublet"; one original event now multiplied into two (Montgomery and Gehman, 367). Others, taking a lead from R. Alter, propose that there is a schematic ("type-scene") to be used when a narrator is wishing to tell a certain kind of story (Barnes, 218). Cogan and Tadmor take the more reasonable position that the similarities can be accounted for by assuming that disciples of Elijah and Elisha told and re-told the accounts of their masters and that the similarities arose in the retellings (59–60).

It is noteworthy that Joram did not know that Elisha was in the company. Rather, it is one of the king's servants[77] who is privy to this vital information. This is indicative of the fact that the true prophet in Israel was typically a peripheral figure who was not in "the center of things," and thus, not usually within the purview of the elite. Provan (185) notes the multiple instances where it is a servant or someone else of the lower classes who recognizes the prophets.[78]

Why Elisha was present in this instance is something of a mystery. While it would have been normal for the armies of other nations to have a diviner in the company, this is the only occurrence in the Bible where a prophet was present.[79] Had Yahweh alerted Elisha that his presence would be needed in this case? We do not know, but he was there in the moment of crisis.

If there were any question about Joram's relation to Yahweh, Elisha's reaction to him lays the matter to rest. In a way very similar to Elijah's confrontation with Ahab (1 Kgs 18:18), the prophet makes it very clear that Joram's attempts to keep a foot in the Baal camp and one in the Yahweh camp as well simply will not do. Elisha tells that king that they have nothing in common and that if he wants a word, he ought to go back to those paganized prophets of his father and mother (whom, as mentioned above, he probably consulted at the outset). In fact, if Jehoshaphat, for whom the prophet has "regard" (lit: פְּנֵי...נֹשֵׂא, *pᵉnê ... nōśēʾ*), were not present, he (Elisha), would not even look at Joram, much less speak a word for Yahweh to him. The prophet strengthens this assertion with an oath in which he invokes "Yahweh of Heaven's Armies" (יהוה צְבָאוֹת, *yhwh ṣᵉḇāʾôṯ*) (as Elijah had done earlier, 1 Kgs 18:15). This had been the favorite term throughout the books of Samuel[80] used to describe the limitless power of Yahweh to accomplish his purposes. Its use here places Elisha firmly in the camp of those who revere Yahweh in that way.

This tension-filled encounter sets the stage for us, the readers, as we work our way through the next chapters. Apart from the brief contact when Elisha delivers the Syrian army to Samaria as reported in 6:21–23, Joram and Elisha never meet again. The die is cast here, and despite all the deliverances that will occur between this event and the anointing of Hazael in chapter eight, nothing will occur that will change the attitude nor the fate of the Omrides.

15–20 The reference to a "musician" (מְנַגֵּן, *mᵉnaggēn*) (v. 15) here has suggested to some that this was a typical practice among Israelite prophets who sought to be possessed by God in order to get a message from him, as is known in other ancient cultures (e.g., Gray, 486–87). However, this is not typical.

---

77. The term could refer to one of the king's officers or to a body-servant. In any case, it is not the king.

78. U. Simon, "Minor Characters in Biblical Narrative," *JSOT* 46 (1990): 11–19.

79. See H. W. F. Saggs, *The Greatness That Was Babylon* (New York: Hawthorne Books, 1962), 347.

80. 1 Sam 1:3, 11; 4:4; 15:2; 17:45; 2 Sam 6:2, 18; 7:8, 26, 27.

It is the only example, apart from the anomalous example of Saul (1 Sam 10:5–6), who was not seeking any message, and who seems to have been susceptible to music in any case (1 Sam 16:23). It is not possible to draw any conclusions from this single example. Of much more significance are the numerous occasions (especially in Jeremiah) where the Israelite prophet is not in a trance but in dialogue with Yahweh.

"Make this wadi full of ditches" (עָשֹׂה הַנַּחַל הַזֶּה גֵּבִים גֵּבִים, *ʿāśō hannaḥal hazze gēḇîm gēḇîm*) corresponds to the instructions Elijah gave to the widow of Zarephath (1 Kgs 17:13–14) and to the ones which Elisha would give to the widow in 2 Kings 4:3–6.[81] That is, in all three instances the person should take actions in faith before the fact, believing that Yahweh would indeed do what he had promised. In all three cases, if Yahweh did not act, the participants would be shamed. In this case, it certainly seems an act of futility to dig catchments in a dry wadi. Catchments for what? On the other hand, if Yahweh showed again that he is the source of water, and not Baal (1 Kgs 18:44–46), and sent water roaring down that wadi, when it passed those "ditches" would be full of water.

The statement that they would "see neither wind nor rain" (לֹא־תִרְאוּ רוּחַ וְלֹא־תִרְאוּ גֶּשֶׁם, *lōʾ-ṯirʾû rûḥa wᵉlōʾ-ṯirʾû gešem*) (v. 17) suggests that the device Yahweh would use to fulfill his promise is a cloudburst occurring far away in the mountains that in an arid land only manifests itself miles away when, without warning, wadis run full of water. This is no way alters the miraculous nature of what took place. The miracle is that it occurred at just this time, as predicted.

Then Elisha goes on to declare that if they think this giving of water is a great thing, Yahweh does not, but will go on to do something greater: he will make Moab helpless before them; "he will give Moab into your hand" (וְנָתַן אֶת־מוֹאָב בְּיֶדְכֶם, *wᵉnāṯan ʾeṯ-môʾāḇ bᵉyeḏkem*). It is at this point, knowing the outcome of the account, namely, that Israel withdrew from Moab without capturing the capital city, that we are tempted to ask if this is a

---

81. This is the reading adopted by the KJV as is found in the versions. (See the "Textual Note" above.) However, since the opening infinitive absolute can be understood in several different ways, modern interpreters have generally chosen some other reading that seems to them to better fit the context. Of these, "I will make ..." (Fritz, 243) is the least supportable grammatically. Better is Cogan and Tadmor's (45) "This wadi shall produce pools..." (see also Sweeney, 277). But Cogan and Tadmor's comment that "this reading is preferable because if humans dig the pools, that leaves no room for the supernatural" misses the point made above. Perhaps the infin. was used instead of the imper. to invest the command with some idea of continuing action, such as "Start digging ... ."

failed prophecy, or perhaps an intentionally deceptive one.[82] However, note that it is *not* said that Israel will subjugate Moab. It is simply said that Moab will come under Israel's power, its "hand." Furthermore, while it is said that Israel will devastate the land, nothing is said about what they should do with captives or spoil (as for instance, 1 Sam 15). It is explicitly not said that Israel will recapture the land. In fact, everything that Elisha predicted was fulfilled exactly as he said it. Did these words lead Joram to expect more would happen than it did? Perhaps, but he had already made up his mind to attack. Elisha's words did not deter him, but neither did they move him to do anything other than what he had already planned. Thus, we can say that this prophecy was neither false nor deceptive. It did not lead Joram into a predetermined fate, as Ahab's prophets did, nor did it fail in any way.

That being said, we must consider the words of v. 19. Why would Elisha, speaking for Yahweh, command such a vicious and thorough devastation of the land (especially in view of the command of Deut 20:19 not to cut down trees[83]). But did he? Despite the assertions of several commentators (Sweeney, 283, and Cogan and Tadmor, 46, among them) that these are commands, that conclusion is not at all clear (so Wiseman, 201). What is clear is that the verbs are *not* imperatives. They are perfect verbs with *waw* consecutive, giving them a future narrative sense. They *can* be translated with "shall," but it is equally likely, or in my view, more likely, that they should be understood as indicatives "you will," as NIV and NLT render them. Thus, just as Elisha reported with grief what Hazael would do (8:12), so he reports what the combined Israelite/Judean/ Edomite army would do in the frenzy of battle. It is not what Yahweh wants them to do, but it is what they will do.

Verse 20 reports the fulfillment of the prediction. It may be significant that it occurred "in the morning when the offering was being made" (בַבֹּקֶר כַּעֲלוֹת הַמִּנְחָה, *babbōqer ka ʿălôṯ hamminḥâ*). That is, it is when Yahweh was being honored that his word through Elisha was fulfilled. "From the direction of Edom" (מִדֶּרֶךְ אֱדוֹם, *midderek ʾĕḏôm*) indicates that the rain had fallen to the west of them and the water was flowing eastward.

21–25 The grammar points to a new section of the narrative, as well as to a new focus, "Moab." During the week when the armies of Israel, Judah, and Edom were marching, the news reached Mesha that if he had been preparing for an attack from the north, he must quickly change his attention

82. See Jesse R. Long, Jr., "Unfulfilled Prophecy or Divine Deception? A Literary Reading of 2 Kings 3," *S-CJ* 7 (2004): 101–17, for an argument for divine deception. For a view agreeing with the position taken above, see Raymond Westbrook, "Elisha's True Prophecy in 2 Kings 3," *JBL* 124 (2005): 530–32. For yet another position, that Israel lacked sufficient faith, see Robert B. Chisholm, Jr., "Israel's Retreat and the Failure of Prophecy in 2 Kings 3," *Bib* 92 (2011): 70–80.

83. Gray's suggestion that Deut 19:20 only applies to the conquest of Canaan seems strained to me (488).

through one hundred eighty degrees to the south. He recognized the crisis and enlisted every able-bodied man (lit. "belting a belt and up";[84] חֹגֵר חֲגֹרָה וָמַעְלָה, *ḥōgēr ḥăgōrāh wāma ʿlâ*) and rushed them to the border. Under those conditions the Moabite army was on the verge of chaos, needing only a spark to set it off. That spark was the sight, just at sunrise, of what looked like blood covering the ground of the enemy camp. It could only mean one thing: the three rival nations: Israel, Judah, and Edom, had fallen out with each other and engaged in mutual slaughter, leaving tons of spoil lying around for the first one to get there. Every man for himself!

It was in that disorganized form that the Moabite hordes fell on the Israelite camp, only to find the Israelites far from dead. Whatever might have been their surprise, the Israelites stood their ground, and very quickly their organization turned the battle into a rout. This seems to be the point of the uncertain phrase at the end of v. 24. The consonantal text in Hebrew (וַיַּבוֹ־בָהּ וְהַכּוֹת,) is best understood as a *waw* consecutive plus imperfect, followed by an infinitive absolute of the same root בוא, *bw* ʾ. This understanding is supported by the infinitive absolute of נכה, *nkh* that follows. The combination gives a sense of ongoing immediacy.[85]

Verse 25 reports that the combined army did as Elisha had predicted they would, visiting complete devastation on the land until they reached Kir-hareseth, the capital city.[86] There they were required to mount a siege, with a focus on "slingers" (הַקַּלָּעִים, *haqqallā ʿîm*), who could shoot stones at the defenders on the walls as well as over the walls into the city itself. Clearly the siege was succeeding, since Mesha felt the need to try to break through the siege lines with a picked group of 700 swordsmen (v. 26). We are told that he chose to attack the Edomite lines,[87] presumably because they were weaker than the Judean or Israelite ones, but he could not succeed even there, and that drove him to his last desperate measure.

The degree to which child sacrifice was actually carried out in the ANE has become more a matter of controversy in recent years. It used to be said that it was very common, especially among the Phoenicians. That position

---

84. Gray suggests that this phrase distinguishes a boy (clothed only in a loose shirt) from a man (having a belt around his waist) (489). But elsewhere, to "gird oneself" often indicates arming oneself (*HALOT* 1.291), and the context certainly points in that direction here. "And upward" means "and older."

85. See the "Textual Note" 24a–a.

86. This site is normally identified with Kerak, located eleven miles east of the Dead Sea and seventeen miles south of the Arnon gorge. However, Brian C. Jones, "In Search of Kir Hareseth: A Case Study in Site Identification," *JSOT* 16 (1991): 3–24, has argued, especially on the basis of references in Isaiah and Jeremiah, that it should be located farther north, in the vicinity of Heshbon.

87. There is no textual support for Gray's (484, n. d) suggestion that "Edom" should be emended to "Aram".

has been challenged;[88] however, there is no question that the practice did occur. Presumably Mesha sacrificed the crown prince to Chemosh as his very best offering, begging the god to intervene on his behalf. What happened next has provoked intense speculation. But we should not miss what is not said; it is not said that the Moabite army rallied from its near-defeat (because of the power of Chemosh) and drove the Israelite army away. The Israelite army "withdrew" (נסע, *ns'*). But what was the "rage" (קֶצֶף־גָּדוֹל, *qeṣep̄-gāḏôl*) that came upon Israel so that they did withdraw? Was it that the Moabites went berserk and the Israelites melted away before them? Was the rage from Yahweh because Joram had led them into this situation where such a deplorable thing could occur? Was it from Jehoshaphat and Edom against Joram for leading them into the situation? Was the atrocity such a shock to the Israelite army they lost courage and slunk away? Was it some sort of pestilence? All these and more have been proposed, with none receiving majority support.[89] Among them, the idea of shock to the Israelite army has received slightly more support. This may be prompted by the Gk. "great regret" (μετάμελος μέγας, *metamelos megas*).[90] But whatever our conclusion on that issue, the key point is that the final defeat of the Omrides has begun. Not only have they lost Moab, but they have not recovered Reuben. The downward slide has begun.

Biblical Theology Comments

The hostility of both Elijah and Elisha to the Omrides should be understood in the light of the seriousness of the issue at hand. This was not merely a question of the superiority of one god over another. Nor was it a question of a foreign god: Baal, as opposed to the Israelite God: Yahweh. What was at stake was the whole biblical world view. When Elijah had called Israel to the top of Mt. Carmel it was not to a contest to see which god was greater; it was a contest to determine which one was God (1 Kgs 18:21). That was a shocking concept in that milieu which thought: of course there were many gods, one for each entity in the cosmos, whether physical, psychological, social, or political; where could anyone get the idea that there was only one god? Both Elijah and Elisha believed in transcendence, the idea that the Deity

---

88. See Franceska Stavrakopoulous, *King Manasseh and Child Sacrifice: Biblical Distortions of Historical Realities* (Berlin: de Gruyter, 2004); Henry B. Smith Jr., "Caananite Child Sacrifice, Abortion and the Bible," *JMT* 17 (2013): 90–125 reviews the data and reaffirms the older position.

89. For two reviews, see J. B. Burns, "Why Did the Besieging Army Withdraw," *ZAW* 102 (1990) 187–194; Scott Morschauser, "A 'Diagnostic' Note on the 'Great Wrath Upon Israel' in 2 Kings 3:27," *JBL* 129 (2010): 299–302.

90. Note REB "There was such great consternation among the Israelites that... " See Sweeney's discussion in support of this view (284).

is not of this world, and is not part of it. That being so, there could only be One who transcends all other beings.

This was the problem with Jeroboam's idols: they were a fundamental betrayal of Yahweh's transcendence. Idolatry is the clearest expression of the belief that the gods are co-extensive with the creation. The idol is typically in the form of something created, whether human or animal, made of a physical material, and thought to be inhabited by a spirit. It seems like a small thing, but once take that small step, and everything about biblical religion collapses. It does so because everything about it is predicated on divine transcendence. Because Yahweh is transcendent, he cannot be manipulated by ritual. Because he is transcendent, he can know the future. Because he is transcendent, he can do things that are truly new, that have never happened before. Because he is transcendent, he does not operate sexually. Because he is transcendent, his character and nature are not merely human nature, written large, and the list goes on. That Joram clung to his bull-idols of Yahweh meant that he was not an adherent of Yahwism, but its bitter enemy, whether he knew that or not.

Elisha's command to dig ditches in a dry wadi is very consistent with the rest of the Bible, beginning at least as far back as Noah, commanded to build a huge boat, when, as far as the text is concerned, he had never seen rain (Gen 2:6; 6:13–14). Abraham was commanded to start off on a journey whose end he did not know (Gen 12:1). In the same way, Abraham sent his servant off to find a girl whom they did not know for certain existed (Gen 24:7). Moses went to Egypt believing that one day he would lead his people in worship on the very mountain where he had met Yahweh in a burning bush (Exod 3:12). The list continues and the idea is developed in Hebrews 11 with its great catalog of the faithful.

What this all defines for us is the nature of faith: not merely believing something that you do not know to be a fact but taking deliberate action on the basis of that belief. Thus, again and again, biblical signs are not given in order to persuade people to act. Rather, like Moses's sign of the mountain, they are given to confirm that the faithful act was justified, *after the fact*. This then is the nature of Christian faith. We will know that our faith was justified when we rise with Christ on the last day. But until then we act in the conviction that he will come and will establish his kingdom in a new heaven and a new earth (Isa 65:17–25; Rev 21:1–5). We energetically dig ditches in dry wadis, in the assurance that they will one day be filled with water.

Selected Bibliography

Briggs, W. "The Preservation of Prophecy in the *Jewish Antiquities*: Josephus' Account of Elisha's Prophecy during the Campaign against Moab." *JSJ* 47 (2016): 508–31.

Brueggemann, W., and C. D. Hankins. "The Affirmation of Prophetic Power and Deconstruction of Royal Authority in the Elisha Narratives." *CBQ* 76 (2014): 58–76.

DeVries, S. J. "The Three Comparisons in 1 Kings 12:4b and its Parallel in 2 Kings 3:7b." *VT* 39 (1989): 283–306.
Gass, E. "Topographical Considerations and Redaction Criticism in 2 Kings 3." *JBL* 128 (2009): 65–84.
Long, B. O. "2 Kings 3 and Genres of Prophetic Narrative," *VT* 23 (1973): 337–48.
Walsh, J. T. "The Organization of 2 Kings 3–11." *CBQ* 72 (2010): 238–54.

The Widow's Oil (4:1–7)

Translation

1 A certain[91] woman from the wives of the sons of the prophets cried out to Elisha, saying, "Your servant, my husband, is dead, and you yourself know that your servant was one who feared Yahweh. Now the creditor is coming to take my two children to be his slaves. **2** Elisha said to her, "What shall I do for you? Tell me what you have in the house." She said, "Your handmaid has nothing in the house except a juglet of oil." **3** He said, "Go outside and ask for vessels from all your neighbors, empty vessels; don't stint. **4** Then go in and close the door behind you and your sons. Pour into all these vessels and set aside the full [ones]." **5** She went from him and closed the door behind her and her sons. As they were bringing, she was pouring.[92] **6** When the vessels were full, she said to her son, "Bring me another vessel." He said to her, "There is no other vessel." The oil stopped. **7** She went and told the man of God, and he said, "Go, sell the oil and repay your debts, and you and your sons can live[93] on the remainder."

Textual Notes

1a. מִנְּשֵׁי בְנֵי־הַנְּבִיאִים: Gk. lacks "wives of the"; Vulg. lacks "from the sons of"; Syr. with MT. MT best explains the others.

2a. לְכִי: *ketiv* is an archaic form of the 2fs pronoun. *Qere* (לָךְ) is the later form. See also vv. 5 and 7.

2b. שָׁמֶן: Gk. and Vulg. add "with which I anoint myself"; Syr. with MT. The addition is probably a gloss.

3a. כֵּלִים: Vulg. lacks. Gk. and Syr. with MT.

7a. בְּנֵיכִי: The versions read the conjunction "and" with *ketiv*. This is the better reading.

---

91. For this use of the numeral "one," see *IBHS* (§15.2.1b).
92. On this construction, see GKC (§116*u*); for "pouring," see *IBHS* (§28.3a), reading with the *qere*.
93. The verb is 2fs, but it is not uncommon to have a singular vb. with a compound subject.

Commentary

This is the first of eight accounts of miracles performed by Elisha. While some interpreters dismiss these as a somewhat miscellaneous collection of fanciful legends, others see them as purposefully collected and organized. As such, they make the point that what happened to Israel under Joram was not foreordained and inescapable but was the result of an intentional refusal to avail himself and themselves of the divine grace and power that was exampled again and again in Elisha's ministry.[94]

The four accounts collected in chapter four establish the fact that Yahweh, not Baal, is the one who can provide the necessities of life, such as oil for the needy, food for the hungry, children to the childless, and life in place of death. What reason could there possibly be to continue to worship a powerless god, when the true God is making himself available not only to the poor (1–7), but also to the rich (8–37), not only to his prophets (38–41), but also to the people in general (42–44).[95]

1 The contrast between this incident and the one that preceded it is striking. We go with Elisha from consorting with kings in one of the significant political-military events of the day to a widow, one of the least powerful people in the society. Yahweh's concerns are no less for the last and the least than they are for the powerful and the momentous. Very possibly it was financially perilous to be among "the sons of the prophets" in the midst of a society saturated with Baalism, and that may have been the reason the woman's husband had left her in debt upon his death.[96] The practice of debt slavery was known throughout the ANE, and although the biblical legislation limits the period of that slavery to six years (Exod 21:2–3, 7), the loss of her sons (more economically profitable than enslaving her) would not only be emotionally devastating, but economically as well, since they were her only support. Her use of the participle "he was one who feared" (הָיָה יָרֵא, *hāyâ yārēʾ*) instead of the simpler verb "he feared" may perhaps indicate that she wanted to leave no doubt that her husband had been completely faithful to Yahweh, and that she was therefore qualified for Elisha's action on her behalf.

2 Once again, the contrast with chapter three is apparent in Elisha's reaction to this woman as compared to his reaction to Joram. Here there is no "What do I have to do with you?" but simply the quiet question: "What can I do for you?" (מָה אֶעֱשֶׂה־לָּךְ, *mâ ʾeʿěśe-llāḵ*), followed immediately by straightforward instruction. This humble woman merits respect where the king did not.

---

94. For examples of the latter position see especially Gilmour, "Juxtaposition and the Elijah Cycle," and Satterthwaite, "The Elisha Narrative."

95. Long points out the similarities with the Elijah narratives in 1 Kgs 17: oil, flour, life to a dead son, multiplication of bread (309).

96. The legendary association of this man with Obadiah (1 Kgs 18:3–4, so Josephus [Ant. ix.4.2] and the Targum [Targum Jonathan 2 Kings 4:1]) lacks external support.

The term translated "juglet" (אָסוּךְ, *ʾāsûḵ*) occurs only here. It may have been a small flask used for anointing (so Wiseman, 202, as well as Cogan and Tadmor, 56). If so, its smallness would compare with the small bit of oil and flour that the widow of Zarephath had (1 Kgs 17:12). In both cases, the point is that the smallness of our resources impose no limits whatsoever on what Yahweh can do with them. Yet, at the same time, the small resource that she had was not pushed aside, instead it was used by God to perform the miracle. Again, this is a note of respect.

3 As with the command to dig ditches (see 3:16 and the "Commentary" there), the widow is to take action before the fact. She is to go out and "ask for vessels [for youself]" (שַׁאֲלִי־לָךְ כֵּלִים, *šaʾălî-lāḵ kēlîm*) from her neighbors, and not a few! That could only have raised a lot of questions from the neighbors, but she did it, and as a result of that faith in action, the miracle occurred.

4–6 Again, we are presented with a detail in the narrative that invites questions, but for which no answer is provided. Why was the woman told to go indoors with her sons and "shut the door" (סָגַרְתְּ הַדֶּלֶת, *sāgart haddeleṯ*)? Commentators have speculated at some length, but any conclusion has to be very tentative, especially since other miracles were done in full view. Perhaps the most likely explanation has to do with those curious neighbors. Had they seen all this happening, it would have been the wonder of the day. But God was not interested in creating fireworks; he was only interested in providing for the needs of a destitute woman.

The phrase, "As they were bringing vessels, she was pouring" (הֵם מַגִּשִׁים אֵלֶיהָ וְהִיא מֵיצָקֶת, *hēm maggišîm ʾēlêhā wᵉhîʾ mêṣāqeṯ*) gives a bit of the sense of urgency and excitement of the moment. As fast as one vessel filled up, another was pushed into place and the oil just kept coming until all of a sudden there were no more vessels and the oil stopped! Perhaps we are intended to wish that she and the boys had collected more vessels, but if so, it is only an inference, because the text does not pass any word of judgment (unlike 13:18–19).

7 Although the prophet was identified by name in v. 1, he is now identified as "the man of God." The narrator wishes to leave no doubt in our minds as to the role and character of this man. Again, we are impressed by the simple and straightforward tone of Elisha's instructions to her. There is nothing of condescending or overbearing in what he says. Although it has just been demonstrated that great spiritual power flows through him, he has no need to make a display of it. We sense that he is simply glad to be of assistance to "common folk."

Biblical Theology Comments

Yahweh's use of our small resources is an important theme in the Bible. We think of the shepherd's staff that was in Moses's hand (Exod 4:2), or of David's musical ability (1 Sam 16:18), or of Mary's womb (Luke 1:31), or of the boy's five loaves and two fish (John 6:9). This willingness to involve us in his work is a mark of Yahweh's respect for us. He does not need any human resources to accomplish his work. After all, he created the cosmos simply by the power of his Word. Yet he condescends to us and gives us a significance beyond anything we could ever deserve. It is a testimony to the value that he places upon us that just as a good parent delights in involving their child in their work, and making use of what little they can provide, so does the heavenly Father.

Selected Bibliography

Berman, J. "The Legal Blend in Biblical Narrative (Joshua 20:1–9; Judges 6:25–31; 1 Samuel 15:2; 28:3–25; 2 Kings 4:1–7; Jeremiah 34:12–17; Nehemiah 5:1-12)," *JBL* 134 (2015): 105–25.

Chirichigno, G. C. *Debt Slavery in Israel and the Ancient Near East.* JSOTSup 141; Sheffield: JSOT Press, 1993.

The Shunammite Woman and Her Son (4:8–37)

Translation

8 One day[97] Elisha passed by Shunem and a wealthy woman was there and
she prevailed on him to take a meal. So whenever he passed he turned aside
to eat there. **9** She said to her husband, "Look, I know that he is a holy man
of God, who is passing by us continually. **10** Please, let's make a small walled
room for him on the roof, and let's put a bed, a table, a chair, and a lampstand
in it, so that when he comes to us, he can turn aside here." **11** One day he
came there and turned aside to the room and laid down there. **12** He said to
Gehazi, his servant, "Call this Shunammite woman." So he called her and she
stood before him. **13** He said to him, "Please say to her, 'Now you have gone
to all this trouble for us. What should[98] we do for you? Can we speak[99] to the
king for you, or to the commander of the army?' " She said, "I am dwelling in
the midst of my people." **14** He said, "What should we do for her?" Gehazi
said, "In fact, she has no son and her husband is old." **15** He said, "Call her."
So he called her and she stood in the doorway. **16** He said, "At this season
next year,[100] you will be embracing a son." She said, "No, my lord, man of
God, don't lie to your handmaid." **17** But the woman conceived and bore a
son at that time the next year, as Elisha had said to her.

18 The child grew and one day he went out with his father to the reapers.
19 He said to his father, "My head, my head!" He said to the servant, "Carry
him to his mother." **20** So he carried him and brought him to his mother. He
sat on her lap until noon and died. **21** She went up and laid him on the man
of God's bed. She closed him in and went out. **22** She called her husband and

---

97. See GKC (§126*s*) for this construction.
98. See GKC (§114*k*) for this construction.
99. See *IBHS* (§36.2.3f).
100. Lit. "at the time of life." There are several possible translations; see the "Commentary" below.

said, "Please send one of the servants to me and one of the donkeys. I will run to the man of God and come back." **23** He said, "Why are you going to him today? It is neither a New Moon nor a Sabbath." She said, "It's all right." **24** She saddled the donkey and said to her servant, "Drive and go. Don't slow down for my riding unless I tell you to." **25** So she went and came to the man of God on Mt. Carmel. When the man of God saw her approaching, he said to Gehazi his servant, "Look, it is our[101] Shunammite! **26** Run to meet her and say to her, 'Is it well with you? It is well with your husband? Is it well with the child?' " She said, "It is well." **27** She came to the man of God on the mountain, and she took hold of his feet. Gehazi came to push her away. But the man of God said, "Let her alone, because her life is very bitter for her, and Yahweh has hidden it from me and not revealed it to me." **28** She said, "Did I ask for a son from my lord? Did I not say, 'Don't deceive me?' " **29** He said to Gehazi, "Tuck up your robe and take my staff in your hand and go. If you meet a man, don't greet him, and if he greets you, don't reply to him. Put my staff on the boy's face." **30** But the boy's mother said, "I swear on Yahweh's life and yours that I will not go without you!" So he got up and went after her. **31** Gehazi went before them and put the staff on the boy's face, but there was no sound nor any sign of life. So he went back to meet him and told him, saying, "The boy has not awakened." **32** Elisha came to the house and there was the boy lying dead on his bed. **33** He went in and closed the door behind the two of them and he prayed to Yahweh. **34** Then he went and laid down on the child and put his mouth on his mouth, his eyes on his eyes, his hands on his hands and crouched over him, and the child's flesh became warm. **35** He went back into the house and walked this way and that. Then he went up and crouched over him. The boy sneezed seven times and opened his eyes. **36** He called Gehazi and said, "Call our Shunammite." He called her and she came to him. He said, "Pick up your son." **37** She came and fell at his feet, and prostrated herself on the floor. Then she picked up her son and went out.

Textual Notes

8a. שׁוּנֵם: Syr. "Shiloh"; Gk. "Souman"; Vulg. "Sunam"; MT. "Shunem." Syr. reads "Shilomite" throughout.

8b. עָבְרוֹ: Gk. "After enough entrances"; Vulg. and Syr. with MT.

10a. קִיר: All versions lack *qîr*. See the "Commentary" below.

13a. לוֹ: Syr. reads "And he said to her"; Gk. and Vulg. with MT. Syr. avoids the complex interchange and omits the opening "And he said to him, 'Please say.' " See the "Commentary" below.

---

101. For this use of the deictic, see *IBHS* (§17.4.2c).

13b–b. חָרַדְתְּ אֵלֵינוּ אֶת־כָּל־הַחֲרָדָה הַזֹּאת: Gk. reads "You have amazed us with all this amazement"; Vulg. "You have diligently done all this ministry for us"; Syr. "You have shown us all this respect." MT best explains the others.

16a–a. לַמּוֹעֵד הַזֶּה כָּעֵת חַיָּה: Gk. "at this season, when the time is ripe"; Vulg. "at this time, in this very hour"; Syr. "About this season." So also v. 17. MT best explains the others.

16b. אַתִּי: *ketiv* is the more archaic form (see GKC §32*h*).

16c–c. חֹבֶקֶת בֵּן: Vulg. "you will have a son in your womb"; Gk. and Syr. with MT.

16d–d. אִישׁ הָאֱלֹהִים: Gk. lacks "man of God"; Vulg. and Syr. with MT, although Syr. throughout reads "prophet of God." *CTAT* (384) considers MT probable.

17a. אֱלִישָׁע: Syr. adds "and she was with child"; Gk. and Vulg. with MT.

21a. וַתִּסְגֹּר: Vulg. and Syr. add "the door"; Gk. with MT.

23a–a. אַתִּי הֹלַכְתִּי *ketiv* preserves the archaic forms of 2fs. However, GKC (§90*n*) considers the second to be an error.

23b–b. וַתֹּאמֶר שָׁלוֹם: Syr. reads "But the Shilomite gave orders"; Gk. and Vulg. with MT.

24a. לִרְכֹּב: Gk. reads "mount"; Vulg. "go"; Syr. "dismount." All are interpretive of MT.

25a–a. וַתֵּלֶךְ וַתָּבוֹא: Gk. reads "Come and you shall go and come to"; Vulg. and Syr. with MT.

25b–b. אִישׁ הָאֱלֹהִים: Gk. reads "Elisha" (so also v. 27); Vulg. and Syr. with MT in both vv.

28a–a. לֹא תַשְׁלֶה אֹתִי: Gk. "Do not go astray with me"; Syr. "Do not ask a son for me"; Vulg. with MT.

29a. וַיֹּאמֶר: Gk. adds "Elisha"; Vulg. and Syr. with MT.

30a. וַיָּקָם: Gk. adds "Elisha"; Vulg. and Syr. with MT.

31a. לִפְנֵיהֶם: Gk. "before her"; Vulg. and Syr. with MT.

33a. וַיָּבֹא: Gk. adds "the house"; Vulg. and Syr. with MT.

35a–a. וַיְזוֹרֵר הַנַּעַר: Gk. omits; Vulg. "the lad yawned"; Syr. with MT.

COMMENTARY

This delightfully detailed story continues the emphasis upon Yahweh's power over life and death. Although the god Baal is not mentioned, there could be no mistaking the polemic in the charged atmosphere of both Israel and Judah at this time. It is Yahweh who provides, not Baal; Yahweh who gives life, not Baal, and any worship of Baal can only end in death.

The contrast between the destitute woman of vv. 1–7 and the "wealthy woman" (אִשָּׁה גְדוֹלָה, *ʾiššâ gᵉḏôlâ*) here is unlikely to be coincidental. Although Yahweh has a special affinity for the widow and the orphan, those at the top of the social scale are no less needy when one comes to the elemental issues of life and death. Nor is Yahweh less concerned about their well-being (שָׁלוֹם, *šālôm* is at the center of this account, vv. 23, 26).

There are numerous parallels with 1 Kings 17:17–24 and Elijah's resuscitation of the widow's son there: placing the body on a bed in an upper chamber; prayer to Yahweh; the prophet lying on the child; and restoring the child to the mother. Yet, there are enough differences to argue against taking the two accounts as different versions of the same events (see Cogan and Tadmor, 59–60).[102] Rather, the point is to emphasize once more that Elisha has indeed received the spirit of Elijah, and that their two ministries are really one in their focus and intended effect.

The picture drawn of the Shunammite woman is a remarkable one: she is depicted as resolute, decisive, and determined, but also reverent, respectful, and hospitable. She is not likely to be taken advantage of, but neither is she hard and self-centered. She is an altogether remarkable woman, not least for the deep assurance of her faith.

8–10 Shunem was located on the north side of the Jezreel valley at the foot of Mt. Tabor, about five miles north of the royal summer capital Jezreel (on the south side of the valley), and fifteen miles east of Mt. Carmel. As such, it would have been near the east-west trade route leading from the Jordan Valley to the Mediterranean coast, and this would explain the prophet's "continually" (תָּמִיד, *tāmîḏ*) passing that way.

The text describes the woman as "great" which probably implies not only wealth but significance. By the end of the account we will have additional reasons to think her great. Her forcefulness is on display immediately as she "prevails upon" (וַתַּחֲזֶק־בּ, *wattaḥăzeq-ḇ*) Elisha to stop and eat in her home. We think of Abraham's insistence upon hosting the three travelers (Gen 18:1–5). Like that event, this one too would result in a rather shocking birth announcement (Gen 18:10).

The relationship between the woman and her husband is interesting. She defers to him, both here and later, when she requests the servant and donkey (v. 22), something that the mores of the time would have required, but he is

102. E.g., note that in this case the woman recognizes Elisha's status ("holy man of God") before the fact, whereas the widow of Zarephath only does so after the fact.

not depicted as being active in any way. She has the idea for the room and its furnishings, and the clear implication is that she is the one who saw that the work was carried out. She is not the man's chattel.

The text describes the construction as an upper chamber with a "wall" (קִיר, *qîr*), but all the versions lack "wall." Perhaps they did not know what to do with the idea. Nevertheless, all commentators take "wall" to be original. Probably the word is used to specify that this would be a permanent construction, and not merely an awning stretched between poles to give some shade on the flat roof on a summer afternoon. The motivation for her request is not given. Perhaps it was merely an extension of the hospitality that prompted her first request. However, her description of Elisha as "a holy man of God" (אִישׁ אֱלֹהִים קָדוֹשׁ, *ʾîš ʾĕlōhîm qādôš*) suggests that it was done out of reverence for him and his ministry. Again, a remarkable woman.

11–13 The second "one day" (הַיּוֹם, *hayyôm*) introduces the second section of the narrative, one that will extend through v. 17. It introduces an event that obviously occurred after the prophet had enjoyed this hospitality for some time and had created a desire in him to somehow repay the favor. The story is recounted with several touches that give it a special air of authenticity. We are here introduced to Gehazi, who will especially figure in the conclusion of the Shunammite incident in chapter 8.[103] Gehazi is instructed to act as go-between for the austere prophet and his hostess. After she had been called to the roof, she still stood at a distance, and the prophet spoke to her through his servant (vv. 12–13). This would have been according to the protocol of the time. Only when she was expressly asked did she come and stand "in the doorway" (בַּפָּתַח, *bappātaḥ*) of the room (v. 15).

The word used in v. 13 has raised a question about what exactly was being said. The verb חָרַד, *ḥārad* has the meaning "to tremble, be anxious, terrified."[104] The present translation (with the majority) takes it that she had been anxious to care for Elisha well. Sweeney and some others think that it refers to the trembling awe with which she viewed the prophet. I wonder if that is quite consistent with the picture the narrative draws of this woman. In any case Elisha did not take for granted what she had done and wanted to recognize it. His offer to intercede for her with the king or the army commander indicates that although he was not a regular at the court (see above on chapter three) he did have influence there. What he could do for her (and her husband?) is not specified, although having someone speak a good word for you to people in power is never a bad thing. The reference to

---

103. It had been noted that there is a similarity in the spelling of Gehazi with Isaiah's sarcastic description of Judah as a "valley of vision" (גֵּיא חִזָּיוֹן, *gêʾ ḥizzāyôn*) in Isa 22:1 (see BDB, 161). Although the appropriateness of that appellation for Gehazi is clear, there are enough differences in the spelling to make the identification unlikely.

104. *HALOT* 1:350. See "Textual Note" 13b–b. for the variety of translations in the versions.

the army commander suggests that perhaps her husband was responsible to supply a certain number of armed men, and perhaps Elisha might be able to reduce the requirement (Cogan and Tadmor, 57).

The woman's response: "I am dwelling in the midst of my people" (בְּתוֹךְ עַמִּי אָנֹכִי יֹשָׁבֶת, *bᵊtôḵ ʿammî ʾānōḵî yōšāḇeṯ*), seems to be both gracious and firm if we understand it. It is neither blunt nor obsequious. She appears to be saying that she is not in need of any special assistance because she (and her husband) have the support of the tribe and clan structure in which they live. Here again is the mark of the woman's character. Many would leap at a chance to gain special favors from such a holy man, especially if they could tell themselves they had somehow earned the consideration. Not her.

14–17 But Elisha is not to be put off. Surely there is something he can do to express his gratitude. Interestingly, it is Gehazi who must tell him that the woman does indeed lack something. As will be demonstrated again in v. 27, to be a prophet is not to possess the gift of "second sight." The prophet is an ordinary human who only knows what God chooses to reveal to him.[105] So Gehazi must tell Elisha that this woman is childless and that her husband is old. In short, she is facing the prospect of becoming a childless widow, a situation where all her wealth will do her little good.

Here is something Elisha can give his benefactress. Now he calls her to him and using words which only appear elsewhere in Genesis 18, tells her that she will have a child.[106] Although he does not evoke the name of Yahweh, the connection with the Genesis passage makes it very clear to us the readers that it is indeed the power of Yahweh that will make this possible. In fact, it is to be wondered if Elisha knew the Genesis passage and used this language intentionally. The woman's reaction is startling, and again indicates that this is not some sort of "set piece" conforming to a literary pattern. It also once again speaks of the character of the woman. This is not some artificial saint replying with sugared piety. This is a real woman who cannot believe her ears. Whatever her reverence for Elisha, she is not at all sure, though he be "my lord, man of God" (אֲדֹנִי אִישׁ הָאֱלֹהִים, *ʾăḏōnî ʾîš hā ʾĕlōhîm*), that he can fulfill the outrageous promise he has just made. How unkind of him to have made such a promise if it should fail. This carefully developed lead-in makes the narrator's laconic words in v. 17 all the more powerful. In fact, the conception and birth were just "as Elisha said to her" (אֲשֶׁר־דִּבֶּר אֵלֶיהָ אֱלִישָׁע, *ʾăšer-dibber ʾēlêhā ʾĕlîšāʿ*). The giving of life is prerogative of Yahweh alone, and he keeps his promises.

105. On this point see Yairah Amit, "A Prophet Tested: Elisha, the Great Woman of Shunem, and the Story's Double Message," *BI* 11 (2003): 279–94.

106. Cogan and Tadmor argue persuasively that the intertextual comment in Gen 17:21 "will bear to you by this time next year" should define עֵת חַיָּה, *ʿēṯ ḥayyâ* (Gen 18:10, 14; 2 Kgs 4:16, 17) which would normally be rendered "time of life" (spring?) (57).

18–21 The third "one day" (הַיּוֹם, *hayyôm*) (v. 18) introduces the final climactic section of the story (vv. 18–37). Yahweh can give life, but can he restore it, when the vicissitudes of existence in this world have snatched it away? The answer is a resounding yes. The child, though grown larger, is still a boy. Out in the field with his father, he suffers sudden pain in his head, and the father, taking no responsibility, as throughout the account, sends him to his mother (v. 19). He dies in her lap (v. 20).[107]

The best explanation for what the mother did next is that she did not want anyone to know the boy was dead. She took him to the out-of-the-way room on the roof "and closed him in" (וַתִּסְגֹּר בַּעֲדוֹ, *wattisgōr baʿădô*). From what occurs in vv. 22 and 23, it is apparent that she did not even tell her husband. If anyone found out the boy was dead, then the whole machinery of mourning would be put into motion. But that was not going to happen before she had a chance to appeal to the man who had given this boy to her in the first place. The boy was not really dead until, if, and when the man of God should fail, and she did not believe he would.

22–24 The woman's comments to her husband are very light. She wants a servant and a donkey so she can "run" (רוץ, *rwṣ*) over to the prophet's location and back. She must have done this before, because her husband is not at all curious that she is going (a remarkably obtuse man), but only that she is going on this day, not a festival day, when she must have been accustomed to make the journey before. She responds with a single word: שָׁלוֹם, *šālôm*, which might be translated in contemporary speech as "It's okay." Evidently that is all the husband needed, and he complied with her requests.[108] She did not wait for the servant to saddle the donkey, but did it herself, telling him to "drive" (נְהַג, *nᵉhag̱*) the donkey mercilessly and not to worry about whether she could keep her seat or not. Obviously, with fifteen miles to Carmel and back, this was no time for dawdling.

25–28 Another indication of Elisha's humanity (see above on v. 14) is that he had no intimation why the woman was coming (unlike Samuel with Saul, 1 Sam 9:15–16; or Ahijah with Jeroboam's wife, 1 Kgs 14:5). Evidently in this case advance intelligence was not necessary. Nevertheless, as soon as he saw her coming, he clearly had a premonition that something was wrong. Why would she be coming so rapidly on this ordinary day? She had said to her husband that everything was well when she obviously did not want to talk to him about the situation. Now to Gehazi's three-fold question about wellness (v. 26), she again answered the same way. She had no interest in chatting, and

107. Again, the narrator is very laconic. The details of the event are not important; rather, it is what Elisha, and Yahweh, will do about it.

108. Wiseman, following Keil, makes the attractive suggestion that given the state of religion in the country, it may have become common for the faithful to meet with the prophets for worship on the festival days (204).

this time Gehazi was not going to be the go-between. She needed the man of God and no one else. When this woman, of all women, fell down and took hold of his feet, Elisha knew that the situation was dire. Officious Gehazi tried "to push her away" (לְהָדְפָּהּ, *lᵉhodpāh*), but Elisha would not let him. In this moment protocol was abandoned. How could Elisha not respond to her need, whatever it was? Once again, the woman's words are surprising, and ring with authenticity: "If you were going to let me in for this, why did not you just leave me alone. I did not ask for this son" (4:28, paraphrased). The fact of life is: the sweeter the joy, the deeper the sorrow. She had organized her life well on a level plane, and now this man had plunged her to the depths by raising her so high.

29–31 Elisha realized at once what had happened. If he did not have divinely given information, he was unusually sensitive. He realized that not a moment could be lost and sent Gehazi immediately to lay his "staff" (מִשְׁעֶנֶת, *miš'enet*) on the boy's mouth.[109] Commentators differ over the reason for this action. Did Elisha think that was all that was necessary, that his staff, like Moses', had miraculous powers (Gray, 498)? Or did he simply want the most immediate possible action to be taken while he and the woman were still on the way (Hobbs, 52)? In any case, it looks as though the woman thought he might not come with her, and with an oath just like the one Elisha swore to Elijah (2 Kgs 2:2, 6), she refused to leave without him. Somehow, she understood that personal presence and not miraculous powers are essential to Yahweh's activity in the world. Again, we meet the laconic narrator: "Elisha got up and went after her" (וַיָּקָם וַיֵּלֶךְ אַחֲרֶיהָ, *wayyāqom wayyēlek 'aḥărêhā*).

It was a good thing that he did, because although Gehazi obeyed Elisha's commands to the letter, so far as we know, the action was ineffective. Just as the rituals of the prophets of Baal had produced "no sound and no response" from their god (1 Kgs 18:31), neither had the staff produced any such thing from the boy (v. 31). Once again, the point is that Yahweh's power cannot be captured by any mechanical means. It is only available in the context of personal relationships.

32–37 Verse thirty-two makes the situation starkly real: "there was the boy lying dead on his (Elisha's) bed" (וְהִנֵּה הַנַּעַר מֵת מֻשְׁכָּב עַל־מִטָּתוֹ, *wᵉhinnē hanna'ar mēt muškāb 'al-miṭṭāṯô*). This boy was dead, as had been underlined by Gehazi's failure, and this was the crisis moment. Either Yahweh would demonstrate his power now, or all was lost. Again, "and the door is closed on

109. The KJV's "Gird up your loins" is a lit. translation of חֲגֹר מָתְנֶיךָ, *ḥăgōr moṯnêkā*. It speaks of pulling the hems of one's robe up and tucking them into the belt, so that one's legs would not become tangled in the robe while running. That injunction and the one not to stop to exchange greetings with anyone, underline Elisha's sense of urgency. For a discussion of this element of the account, see Reuven Chaim (Rudolph) Klein, "Gehazi and the Miracle Staff of Elisha," *JBQ* 45 (2017): 103–10.

the two of them" (וַיִּסְגֹּר הַדֶּלֶת בְּעַד שְׁנֵיהֶם, *wayyisgōr haddeleṯ bᵉ ʿaḏ šᵉnêhem*). While that may mean Elisha and the boy, I suspect that it is Elisha and Gehazi, and that the details of what happened next were reported by Gehazi afterwards to all who would listen (as in chap. 8). As with Jesus and Jairus' daughter (Luke 8:51), Elisha closed the door because this was no place for a curiosity seeker.[110]

As Elisha had learned from Elijah, the first thing to do was to pray to Yahweh (1 Kgs 17:20; 18:42). This was not Elisha's business, but Yahweh's. Then "he laid down on" (יִשְׁכַּב, *yiškaḇ*) the boy, touching eye to eye, mouth to mouth, and hand to hand.[111] A great deal has been written on this action (paralleling that of Elijah in 1 Kgs 17, but not repeating it exactly), examining whether it was some sort of magical ritual.[112] There is nothing in the text to indicate that this was the case. Note the variety of actions that Jesus took when performing his miracles, sometimes merely speaking (John 4:50), and at other times touching (Mark 1:41), or acting in some other way (John 9:6). But, as here, there is nothing to suggest that he was following some prescribed set of actions. See the "Biblical Theology Comments" below for further discussion.

Several commentators (e.g., Gray, 499; Cohn, 33) suggest that Elisha's walk through the house (v. 35) was to regather his forces after the previous exertions. But it may also have been simply a pause to see whether the prescription had taken effect. When he returned, it had not, so he repeated the activity. The result was dramatic: "and the boy sneezed seven times and the boy opened his eyes" (וַיְזוֹרֵר הַנַּעַר עַד־שֶׁבַע פְּעָמִים וַיִּפְקַח הַנַּעַר אֶת־עֵינָיו, *wayzôrēr hannaʿar ʿaḏ-šeḇaʿ pᵉʿāmîm wayyip̄qaḥ hannaʿar ʾeṯ-ʿênāyw*). "Sneezing" is probably significant as it expresses the return of breath to the body. Likewise, "seven" is probably significant as the number expressing perfection. This boy, through the power of Yahweh, is most fully alive.

Once more in vv. 36 and 37, we meet the laconic narrator. The primary point has been made: Yahweh, working through his prophet, has the power of life and death in his hands. Baal is nowhere to be seen, neither to be feared nor worshipped. That point made, there is nothing to do but wind up the story. Gehazi should "call our [lit: this one] Shunammite" (קְרָא אֶל־הַשֻּׁנַמִּית הַזֹּאת, *qᵉrāʾ ʾel-haššunammîṯ hazzōʾṯ*), who was undoubtedly waiting on the

110. Note that Jairus, like this woman, was also intent on having Jesus come to his child's side (Luke 8:41).

111. The second vb. in the sentence, "crouched" (גהר, *ghr*) occurs only here (and again in v. 35) and in 1 Kgs 18:42, when Elijah crouched down in prayer. This suggests that the prophet did not lie flat on the small boy but crouched over him. Given the parallel with Elijah, it may also suggest something of the intensity of Elisha's praying in that moment.

112. For a recent treatment, see Bob Becking, "'Touch for Health...': Magic in II Reg 4,31–37 with a Remark on the History of Yahwism," *ZAW* 108 (1996): 34–54.

tenterhooks of hope and fear. She comes, cautiously (?), exultantly (?), and Elisha has just two words for her in Hebrew. But in those terse words there is a certain tenderness. It is not a colorless, "The child's alive," but, "Take your son up [into your arms]" (שְׂאִי בְנֵךְ, *śᵊ ʾî ḇᵊnēḵ*). She is speechless, first falling to the ground in adoration, then gathering up her son, and rushing (?) out.

Biblical Theology Comments

In the ancient world childlessness was a major issue. It is hard for us to grasp this in a world that must face over-population in a serious way. It is also hard to grasp the depth of the problem when many couples today seriously consider whether children are worth the trouble and expense. We are often more interested in preventing conception and birth than achieving it. But in those days, to die without children was to be as if one had never lived. Furthermore, children were an economic boon. Sons could work in the fields, daughters could be married to neighbors whose inheritance might be joined to her family's, and all in all the future could be considerably brighter with children. This is why so much attention was given to ensuring fertility, and why gods and goddesses of fertility were so prominent in the worship of the ancient world. This then, threw the question of Yahweh's preeminence into sharp relief. If he was not the god of the storm, or of rain, or of vegetation, or of sexual potency, could he really do anything about this massive issue?

This is almost certainly why all three of the first mothers of Israel: Sarah, Rebecca, and Rachel, are seen to be childless until the intervention of Yahweh. Could he, from his position as Transcendent Creator, deal with this problem, and grant the prayers of his desperate people? Yes, he could and he can, in abundant ways. The issue of barrenness reemerges at a time that might be labeled, "the beginning of the prophetic era," with Samuel's mother Hannah, and climactically, it appears again at the beginning of the Messianic era, with Elizabeth. Yahweh is the Giver of Life.

In thinking about the significance of Elisha's actions in the resuscitation of the boy, a comparison with the biblical understanding of sacrifices is in order. The sacrifices were commanded in detail in the first six chapters of Leviticus, yet again and again, prophets condemned the activity (Isa 1:10–15, Amos 5:21–24; Micah 6:6–8; Mal 1:10). Although some early critics took this as evidence that Leviticus postdated these prophets, that can no longer be maintained. What the prophets were condemning was the prevailing attitude toward ritual in the surrounding world. That was the idea that the rituals were effective in themselves, that the performance of them would guarantee the desired results.

But there was a different understanding of ritual in the Bible, one that stems from the idea of Yahweh's transcendence. Because he is transcendent, nothing that is done here on earth will automatically affect him. He can only be moved in personal interaction. However, as humans, for whom physicality is a given, we need ways to image personal reality. Thus, giving a lamb that could be sold for a good deal of money, as a way of concretizing my total devotion to God is very helpful in cementing that devotion. On the other hand, if my daily behavior shows that I am not devoted to God at all, giving a lamb, far from insuring God's favor, can only disgust him. So, it seems highly unlikely that Elisha's actions (or Elijah's before him) were thought to produce any kind of necessary results. If they demonstrated total reliance on Yahweh for life, well and good. If they represented a pagan approach to life, the belief that what is done in the visible part of the cosmos is necessarily repeated in the invisible, how were they different from the prophets of Baal?

The implications of this account could have had great meaning for the exiles as they looked at their situation. In many ways they were like the Shunammite. God had come to them unbidden and given them life out of the sterility of father Abraham and mother Sarah. They had not been looking for it, he simply came to them with incredible promises. And those promises had been magnificently fulfilled. From just two had come a great nation, living in its own land, ruled by great kings. But what then? Death had come calling. Great empires had swept over them and left them lifeless as a nation. Could God give them life again if they were as persistent as the Shunammite? This story would have said to them that he most certainly can. And as we know, he has done it, and through them, he is seeking to raise the whole world from the dead, just as he has raised his own Son.

Application and Devotional Implications

The Shunammite's story can be ours. We see in her several qualities that should be characteristic of us. In the crisis, she did not become frantic, but she knew just what had to be done, and she did it with urgency. She knew where the only possible source of hope lay – the man of God, and she would not be content with anything less than his presence. He alone would do. What does this say to us? First of all, it should remind us that there is only one cure for our crises: the Man of God. Jesus Christ is our intercessor, and no one else will do, especially not the Gehazis of this world. Furthermore, while we must have that same kind of urgency and single-mindedness in our prayers, we need not become frantic in our emotions. We can rest in the certainty of his concern and his ability. Finally, we can go directly to the Man himself: Jesus. His blood has procured for us direct access to the throne, and in Christ we have the very presence of Yahweh: Jesus is LORD!

Selected Bibliography

Brodie, T. L. "Luke 7:36–50 as an Internalization of 2 Kings 4:1–37: A Study in Luke's Use of Rhetorical Imitation." *Bib* 64 (1983): 457–85.

Van Dijk-Hemmes, F. "The Great Woman of Shunem and the Man of God: A Dual Interpretation of 2 Kings 8–37." In *Feminist Companion to Samuel and Kings,* ed. Athalya Brenner, 218–30. Sheffield: Sheffield Academic, 1994.

Kalmanofsky, A. "Women of God: Maternal Grief and Religious Response in 1 Kings 17 and 2 Kings 4." *JSOT* 36 (2011): 55–74.

Plate, S. B. and E. M. Rodrigues Mangual, "The Gift that Stops Giving: Hélène Cixous' 'Gift' and the Shunammite Woman." *BI* 7 (1999): 113–32.
Rice, G. "A Great Woman of Ancient Israel (2 Kings 4:8–37; 8:1–6)." *JRT* 60–63 (2008): 69–85.
Shields, M. E. "Subverting a Man of God; Elevating a Woman: Role and Power Reversal in 2 Kings 4." *JSOT* 18 (1993): 59–69.
Simon, U. "Elisha and the Woman of Shunem: The Miracle Worker Needs Guidance from Beneficiary of his Miracle." In *Reading Prophetic Narratives,* trans. L. J. Schramm, 227–62. Indianapolis: Indiana University Press, 1997.
Walters, S. D. "All is Well." *CTJ* 47 (2012) 192–214.

Miracles of Provision (4:38–44)

Translation

38 Elisha returned to Gilgal, and there was a famine in the land. The sons of the prophets were sitting before him. He said to his servant, "Put on the large pot and boil stew for the sons of the prophets." **39** One of them went out into the field to gather herbs and found a wild vine. He gathered wild gourds from it, filling his cloak. Then he came and cut up the gourds into the pot of stew, but they[113] did not know. **40** They poured it for the men to eat. Now as they were eating the stew, they cried out, "There is death in the pot!" **41** He said, "Get some flour," and he put it[114] in the pot. Then he said, "Pour it out for the men to eat," and there was nothing harmful in the pot.

42 A man came from Baal Shalishah and brought to the man of God bread of the firstfruits, twenty loaves of barley, along with grain still in the husk.[115] He said, "Give it to the people so they can eat." **43** The one serving him said, "How can I give this to 100 men?" He said, "Give it to the people so that they can eat, for Yahweh has said, 'Eat, and leave some over.' " **44** So he put it before them and they ate and left some over, just as Yahweh had said.

Textual Notes

39a. וַיָּבֹא: Gk. lacks; Vulg. "went back"; Syr. with MT.

---

113. Vulg. and Syr. have "he," and this is very possible, in which case Heb. כִּי, *kî* should be read as "because," rather than "but" as here. Gk. supports MT, which is fairly significant.

114. Gk. and Syr. translate this vb. (וַיַּשְׁלֵךְ, *wayyašlēḵ*) as an imperative, thus taking it as part of Elisha's quoted command. Vulg. does not but inserts "and when they brought it" between the quotation and "he put it." All three are trying to smooth out the rough MT. But this kind of ellipsis is fairly typical of the text in this section of the book.

115. The rendering "fresh grain in his sack" is based on the Vulg. which may be based on an emendation (see BDB, 502). Perhaps it is "fresh grain in the husk", so Sweeney (292) and others.

39b. יָדָעוּ: Vulg. and Syr. "he did not know what it was"; Gk. with MT.

40a. וַיִּצְעֲקוּ: Gk. and Syr. "He"; Vulg. with MT.

41a–a. וַיֹּאמֶר וּקְחוּ־קֶמַח וַיַּשְׁלֵךְ אֶל־הַסִּיר: Gk. and Syr. "Take some flour and throw it into the pot." Vulg. "Take some flour." When they brought it, he threw it into the pot." MT best explains the others.

41b. וַיֹּאמֶר: Gk. adds "to Gehazi the servant"; Vulg. and Syr. with MT.

42a–a. וְכַרְמֶל בְּצִקְלֹנוֹ: Gk. "fruitcakes"; Vulg. "new grain in his sack"; Syr. "new wheat rubbed from ears in a cloth." Heb. צקלון is a *hapax legomenon* and its meaning is disputed. See the note on the "Translation" above.

44a–a. וַיִּתֵּן לִפְנֵיהֶם: Gk. lacks; Vulg. and Syr. with MT.

Commentary

These two narratives complete the series of four miracle accounts begun at 4:1. Together, the four narratives demonstrate three things: (1) they show that Elisha, the man of God, is indeed the successor of Elijah, (2) they make it clear that the power of Yahweh flows effortlessly through him, (3) it is evident that the power of life and death is in the hands of Yahweh and no other, certainly not Baal.

The two interwoven themes in the chapter are providence and resurrection: Yahweh provides for human need, for persons of all ranks and stations—he cares. But the deepest need of all is our need for life; death mocks us at every turn, yet it cannot defeat Yahweh. He is the Life-Giver. The interweaving is clear in these last two accounts. Famine and death stalk the land. But through his prophet Yahweh provides both food and deliverance from death.

38 Commentators are divided over the location of Gilgal here. Some, especially in the light of the reference to Baal Shalishah in the second narrative (see there), believe that it must be the one located in Ephraim (see the "Commentary" on 2:1–2) (so Wiseman, 205). However, in the light of the importance in Israel's religious history of the Gilgal located near Jericho, it seems to me most likely that this is the one being referred to here (so also Fritz, 253). It may be for that very reason that a company of prophets was located there, to try to counteract the subversion of the ancient site to a paganized Yahwism (see Hos 4:15). Probably "the sons of the prophets sitting before him" (וּבְנֵי הַנְּבִיאִים יֹשְׁבִים לְפָנָיו, *ûḇᵊnēy hannᵊḇîʾîm yōšᵊḇîm lᵊpānāyw*) indicates some sort of teaching session.

The "famine" (הָרָעָב, *wᵊhārāʿāḇ*) referred to here is probably the one mentioned in 8:1 that extended over seven years. Provan (190) points out that this is just what might be expected in a land that had broken its covenant with Yahweh (Deut 28:21–24; 1 Kgs 17:1; Amos 4:7–10). Yahweh gives rain and abundance, not Baal.

39 Perhaps it was because of the scarcity of food that one of the company was looking for something—anything—to put in the pot. There is a consensus (so Gray, 500; Konkel, 417; Cogan and Tadmor, 58) that the "gourds" (פַּקֻּעֹת, *paqquʿōṯ*) that he found were the fruit of *citrillus colocynthus*, a plant that grows in the area around Jericho, and is known for its very strong laxative qualities. It is also very bitter to the taste. As noted above on the "Translation," the textual data may be read in two ways: "because he did not know" (the fruit was poisonous), or "but they did not know" (he had put the gourds in the pot). They seem equally possible.

40 Probably the bitter taste of the gourds signaled that there was something wrong with the stew, to the point of making it inedible. What it was no one knew, and so they assumed the worst: "Death is in the pot!" (מָוֶת בַּסִּיר, *māweṯ bassîr*). Indeed, if taken in sufficient quantity, the fruit, also known as "Apple of Sodom" can cause death. But the primary reason for the reference here is to underline one of the themes of the chapter: death is our constant enemy, and only Yahweh can defeat it.

41 As with the other crises in this chapter, Elisha is both calm and decisive. He knows where the source of both hope and power lies. He calls for flour, puts it in the pot, and commands the prophets to eat it.[116] Sure enough, there is nothing wrong with the stew now. While various suggestions are made as to what the effect of the flour might have been on the cut-up gourds, that is not the point. The point is that in the hands of the man of God, evil (רָע, *rāʿ*) has been turned to good, death to life.

42 Although it is not certain that this event occurred in the same time and place as the previous, the use of a little food to feed many argues that we are intended to read it in the context of previous mention of famine, and that, in turn, suggests the same time and place. There is some disagreement about the location of Baal Shalishah (Khefar Thilth or Khirbet el-Marjame), but both are in the central hill-country, northwest of Bethel, and some distance from Gilgal near Jericho.[117] The mention of "firstfruits" (לֶחֶם בִּכּוּרִים, *leḥem bikkûrîm*) is significant, both because when harvest was just beginning the

---

116. Note that in contrast to the suggestion that has been made in regard to 3:15 that Israelite prophets, as elsewhere in the ANE, sought to receive God's guidance through the medium of a trance, in this chapter there is no evidence of this. The prophet was in such immediate contact with Yahweh, that he knew what Yahweh was directing immediately.

117. This has prompted some commentators (e.g., Wiseman, 219) who take it that both these accounts refer to the same place and thus, that the Gilgal of v. 38 must be located in Ephraim. However, in my opinion the arguments presented above are stronger, and the location of Baal Shalishah need not undercut them. See Cogan and Tadmore, 59.

famine would be at its most severe, and the gift would be most precious,[118] and because firstfruits should normally be given to the priests (Lev 23:10). This means that the man has bypassed the priests at Bethel to bring his gift to Elisha whom he clearly was recognizing as more deserving of his devotion, respect, and affection than were the pagan functionaries at the official sanctuary.

Elisha was immediately concerned for his followers and saw an opportunity to meet their needs. His compassion reflected that of Yahweh. His words, "Give it to the people so they can eat" (תֵּן לָעָם וְיֹאכֵלוּ, *tēn lāʿām wᵊyōʾkēlû*) are very similar to those spoken by Jesus centuries later (Matt 14:16) and reflect the same kind of selfless concern.

43–44 The somewhat unusual terminology "the one serving him" (מְשָׁרְתוֹ, *mᵊšorṯô*; lit. "the one ministering to him") has suggested to several interpreters (e.g., Wiseman, 219) that this is an oblique reference to Gehazi (Gk. specifically identifies him in v. 41, Γιεζι, *Giezi*). If so, we realize that this disciple is like the disciples of Jesus in seeing only impossibilities instead of possibilities (Mark 6:37).

Elisha repeated his words, and then added that the command was from Yahweh. It may be significant that this reference to Yahweh's instruction comes here in this final account of the four miracles. In the previous three, Elisha's actions were depicted as being taken on his own initiative (although perhaps the reference to prayer to Yahweh in 4:33 is intended to suggest that he received instructions in response to that prayer). But perhaps the reference here, almost casually given, is intended to alert us to the understanding that all that Elisha did was in response to Yahweh, with whom the prophet was in constant communication.

Again, the reference to what was left over from the miraculous feedings in the Gospel accounts reflects what took place here (Matt 14:20; Mark 6:43; Luke 9:17). Yahweh does not merely provide necessities, he provides in abundance if we will place our trust in him and not in the powers of this world.

Two Miracles of Restoration (5:1–6:7)

Sweeney (296) has observed that the *wayyômer* form (lit: וַיֹּאמְרוּ, *wayyōʾmᵊrû*) which begins 6:1 indicates literary continuity with what precedes it. This observation is supported by the Masoretic punctuation which places a setumah after 5:19 and 5:27 and a petuhah after 6:7. Setumah marks a minor paragraph break, while petuhah marks a major one. This recognition that the two accounts are intended to be read together proves helpful in answering the question why the ax-head miracle is placed where it is, between two

118. The festival of firstfruits occurred 50 days after Passover, at the end of the barley harvest and at the beginning of the wheat harvest (Num 28:26). This would typically occur sometime in May on our calendar.

rather consequential narratives dealing with the Syrians (5:1–27; 6:8–7:20). Both events: the healing of Naaman and the raising of the ax-head, speak of Yahweh's power in his creation, in particular, his ability to restore both what is diseased and what is lost. The breadth of this ability is highlighted by the contrast between the greatness of Naaman and the lowliness of the hapless junior prophet. There is also a literary contrast, between the richly developed account of Naaman, and the terse simplicity of the ax-head story. There is also a revelation of divine concern both for a man who at the beginning of his story only knows Yahweh as a local god of Israel, as well as for a man who is a devoted follower of his. When the account of Gehazi's greed is placed between the two accounts, there is an added dimension. Gehazi's lie about the needy sons of the prophets (5:22) contrasts with the actual divine provision that had resulted in the group needing expanded living space (6:1). Yahweh does not need lies to care for his own. There is also a strong contrast between Gehazi, who proceeds on his own to take care of himself, and the sons of the prophets, who bring their proposal to Elisha both for his approval and his accompaniment. It is a contrast between self-serving and submission. Finally, the picture of Elisha in the two accounts is illuminating. With the great Syrian general, the prophet is "the man of God," who until the end speaks through a messenger, and even in the end is somewhat distant. With the prophets he is directly involved and available. Thus, we gain a fuller picture of the man by reading the two accounts together. His demeanor reflects what is said of Yahweh in Psalm 18:27 "You save the humble, but those whose eyes are haughty you bring down."[119]

The Healing of Naaman (5:1–27)

This account is one of the best-known stories in the Bible. This fact is understandable in view of both its literary richness and its theological significance. With a minimum of words, it gives the reader character portraits of several people, including the Syrian general, Naaman, the little girl who gave him hope, the Israelite king, Elisha, the man of God, and Gehazi, his greedy servant. There are revealing comments, and intriguing plot twists. Gray (502), citing Gressman, points out that Naaman is proud when sick, but humble when healed, that the noble pagan is a leper at the beginning while the servant of Yahweh's prophet is a leper at the end, and that the master, Elisha, is unselfish, whereas the servant is greedy. Overall, the narrative, which shows some interesting parallels with 4:8–37, functions to teach two interrelated things. First, it is one more assertion that Yahweh is not one of the gods, nor even chief of the gods, but the *only* God. Although this truth was lost on the Omride kings, it was not lost on the general of their chief enemy. Second, the account makes the point, both through Elisha and through Gehazi, that the power being exercised through Elisha was not his, and thus, something for

119. For further discussion of the connections between the two accounts, see Gilmour, 156–62.

which he was to be compensated. Rather, it was Yahweh's power and could not be bought. But while these are the major points, there are a myriad of others, on which see the "Commentary" below. This rich complexity is one of the features that has made the account so enduring.

There is little doubt that vv. 1–27 constitute a unit.[120] There is also broad agreement about the structure of the narrative: the healing, in which Naaman is the main character (vv. 1–19), and Gehazi's response, in which he is the main character (vv. 20–27). The main alternative to seeing the unit as having two parts is exemplified by Cohn (35), who sees it as tripartite (1–14; 15–19; 20–27). The main objection to this view (which separates Naaman's healing from his response) is that the three parts are not equal in length to each other. Instead, vv. 1–14 and vv. 15–19 are sub-divisions of vv. 1–19.

Naaman and Elisha (5:1–19)

Translation

5:1 Naaman, commander of the army of the king of Syria,[121] was a great man before his lord, honored by him, because Yahweh had given victory to Syria. The man was a great hero—a leper.[122] **2** Raiding bands had gone out from Syria and had taken captive from Israel a little girl who waited[123] on Naaman's wife. **3** She said to her mistress, "Would that[124] my lord would wait on the prophet who is in Samaria. Then he would heal[125] him from his leprosy." **4** So he went and told his lord, saying, "The girl who is from the land of Israel said such and such." **5** The king of Syria said, "Go on[126] and go, and I will send a letter to the king of Israel." So he went, taking in his hand ten talents of silver, 6,000 pieces of gold and ten changes of clothing. **6** So he brought the letter to the king of Israel. It said, "And now, when this letter comes to you, here I have sent to you, Naaman, my servant, that[127] you might heal him from his leprosy." **7** Now when the king of Israel had read the letter, he tore his clothes and said, "Am I God to kill and bring to life that this fellow is sending to me to heal a man of leprosy? Indeed, know and see that he is

---

120. Even those who would see it as a composite agree that those component parts have been welded into a literary whole.

121. Heb. אֲרָם, *ʾărām*. Ancient Aram, with its capital at Damascus, was roughly contiguous with modern Syria.

122. Heb. מְצֹרָע, *mᵉṣōrāʿ*: a term referring to a wide range of skin diseases, but probably not to what is called "leprosy" today. See the "Commentary" below.

123. Lit. "was before" (לִפְנֵי, *lip̄nê*); see v. 1. See also vv. 9 and 16.

124. As Cogan and Tadmor point out, the only other occ. of this particle (אַחֲלֵי, *ʾaḥălê*) in the Bible is in Ps. 119:5, but it has now been found in Ugaritic (64).

125. The only occ. of the consonants אסף, *ʾsp* with the meaning of "to heal." Normally "to gather" or "to add to."

126. Using הָלַךְ, *hālak̲* as an auxiliary vb. See *IBHS* (§34.5.1a).

127. See *IBHS* (§32.2.3c) on the use of a *waw* + pf. to express logical basis.

seeking an occasion[128] against me." **8** When Elisha, the man of God, heard that the king of Israel had torn his clothes he sent to the king, saying, "Why have you torn your clothes? Let him come to me that he may know there is a prophet in Israel." **9** So Naaman went with his horses and chariots and waited at the door of Elisha's house. **10** Elisha sent him a messenger, saying, "Go[129] and wash seven times in the Jordan and your flesh will return to you and you will be clean."[130] **11** Naaman became angry and went away, saying, "Look here, I said, 'Surely he will come out and stand and call on the name of Yahweh, his god, and wave his hand over the place and heal the leprosy.' **12** Are not the Abana and Pharpar, rivers of Damascus, better than all the waters of Israel? Could I not wash in them and be clean?" He turned and went away in a fury. **13** His servants approached and spoke to him and said, "My father,[131] had the prophet said some great thing to you, would you not have done it? How much more, when all he has said to you is, 'Wash, and be clean.' " **14** So he went down and dipped in the Jordan seven times according to the word of the man of God and his flesh returned like that of a little boy, and he was clean. **15** He went back to the man of God, he and all his military escort, and waited on him and said, "Now I know that there is no God in all the earth, except in Israel. So now accept a gift[132] from your servant." **16** He said, "I swear on the life of Yahweh, whom I serve, that I will not take a thing." He urged him to take something, but he refused. **17** Naaman said, "If not, let two mule-loads of earth be given to your servant, because your servant will no longer offer a burnt offering or a sacrifice to any other god than Yahweh. **18** But in this matter, may Yahweh forgive your servant, when my lord goes into the house of Rimmon, to worship there leaning on my arm, and I worship in the house of Rimmon, when I worship in the house of Rimmon, may Yahweh forgive your servant in this matter." **19** He said to him, "Go in peace." So he went from him a short distance.[133]

---

128. There are only two examples of this root (אנה) having this meaning; here in the *hithpael* form (מִתְאַנֶּה, *mit̲ʾanne*), and as a verbal noun in Judg 14:4.

129. הָלוֹךְ, *hālôk̲*: An inf. abs. functioning as an emphatic imperative. See GKC (§113*bb*).

130. טְהָר, *ṭ*ᵉ*hār*: An imperative of intent. See GKC(§110*i*).

131. The absence of a conditional particle probably explains the Gk. reading: "The prophet has said a great thing to you, will you not do it." So also ESV. However, the odd word order, obj. (דָּבָר גָּדוֹל, *dāb̲ār gād̲ôl*) + subj. + (הַנָּבִיא, *hannāb̲îʾ*) + vb. (דִּבֶּר, *dibber*), suggests the possibility of an implied question in the subjunctive mood. So both Vulg. and Syr. Furthermore, "wash and be clean" is not a "great thing."

132. Lit. "blessing" (בְּרָכָה, *b̲*ᵉ*rāk̲â*). For this use see also Gen 33:11; Josh 15:19; 1 Sam 30:26.

133. There is no grammatical reason for combining vv. 19 and 20 as do many modern translations. Furthermore, the setumah argues explicitly against it. On the other hand, the brief final clause certainly sets the stage for what follows.

Textual Notes

1a. מֶלֶךְ: Gk. lacks "king"; Vulg. and Syr. with MT.

4a–a. וַיָּבֹא וַיַּגֵּד לַאדֹנָיו: Gk. "she went and she told her lord"; Vulg. "Naaman went and he told his lord"; Syr. "they went and they told her lord." MT best explains the others.

8a–a. אִישׁ־הָאֱלֹהִים: Gk. omits; elsewhere it replaces "man of God" with "Elisha" (vv. 14, 15); Vulg. and Syr. with MT throughout.

9a–a. בְּסוּסוֹ וּבְרִכְבּוֹ: Gk. "his horse and his chariot"; Vulg. "his horse and his chariots"; Syr. "his horses and chariots"; MT "his horse (*ketiv*), his horses (*qere*), and his chariot." Perhaps the original was singular in both cases, but both understood as collective: "he came with horse and chariot."

11a. יְהוָה: Gk. lacks "Yahweh"; Vulg. and Syr. with MT.

12a. אֲבָנָה: Vulg. and Syr. "Amana," a confusion of labial consonants, with either one possibly original.

12b. כֹּל: Gk. adds "the Jordan and"; Vulg. and Syr. with MT.

13a–a. וַיְדַבְּרוּ אֵלָיו וַיֹּאמְרוּ: Gk. and Vulg. "they said to him"; Syr. with MT.

13b. אָבִי: Gk. lacks; Vulg. "my father"; Syr. "our lord."

13c–c. דָּבָר גָּדוֹל הַנָּבִיא דִּבֶּר אֵלֶיךָ הֲלוֹא תַעֲשֶׂה וְאַף כִּי־אָמַר אֵלֶיךָ רְחַץ וּטְהָר: Gk. reads "The prophet has said a great thing to you; will you not do it? Even because he said to you, 'Wash and be clean.' " Vulg. and Syr. both make the first sentence conditional. GKC (§159*cc*) takes **אָבִי** as some sort of conditional particle, but as per **13b.** above, both Vulg. and Syr. translate it as an honorific, while Gk. omitting it, does not give the sentence a conditional sense (except for Luc.).

13d–d. דָּבָר גָּדוֹל הַנָּבִיא דִּבֶּר: GKC (§142*f*) notes the rarity of the obj.-subj.-vb. construction, laying special emphasis upon the obj.

18a–a. לַדָּבָר הַזֶּה: Gk. omits; Vulg. and Syr. with MT.

18b. בְּהִשְׁתַּחֲוָיָתִי: Gk. and Vulg. "when he worships"; Syr. with MT.

19a–a. כִּבְרַת־אָרֶץ: The versions do not know what to do with this phrase: Gk. "a debratha [translit. of Heb.] of the land"; Vulg. "a choice land for a time"; Syr. "a little way." Modern translations link it with the following verse, but the setumah is against such a reading.

Commentary

1 This verse presents the first main character of the narrative in very fulsome terms. Naaman, the Syrian army commander (שַׂר־צָבָא, *śar-ṣəḇāʾ*), is an effective leader, victorious in battle, honored by his king, an altogether heroic figure.[134] There are just two unexpected features in the description: first, credit for his victories is given to Yahweh, the God of Israel. Upon reflection, however, this should not be surprising in the biblical context. The biblical writers know that whatever happens in the world, Yahweh is ultimately responsible for it. Naaman does not know this yet, but he will. Perhaps the Syrian victory at Ramoth-gilead (1 Kgs 22:36) is particularly in mind here.

The other surprising thing in the description is handled consummately by the narrator. After seventeen Hebrew words of praise concerning Naaman, there is just one last word, a word that trumps all the rest: "a leper" (מְצֹרָע, *mᵉṣōrāʿ*). Although this is almost certainly not Hansen's Disease, since that terribly disfiguring illness is not known before the second century BC in Egypt, it was clearly one of the several irritating and mildly disfiguring diseases dealt with in detail in Lev 13–14. Some of these were evidently contagious, and they were all worrisome because of their tendency to spread unaccountably. They were most troublesome because they rendered a person unclean, and thus not able to participate in the important religious ceremonies.[135]

2–3 Clearly, we are expected to feel the extreme contrast between the great Naaman and "the little girl" (נַעֲרָה קְטַנָּה, *naʿărâ qᵉṭannâ*). Their situations could hardly be more diverse. He is a captain, she is a captive; he is a male, she is a female; he is great, she is little; he is grown up, she is a child; he is honored, she is a slave. Yet, he is helpless before his affliction, and she has the key to his only hope. This is typical of the reversals of the Bible. Much of what we humans think is great and productive is really of very little worth in the economy of heaven, while what is truly worthwhile, we often dismiss as insignificant and unimportant. Jesus' famous statement that it is only as we become like little children that we can enter the kingdom of heaven underlines the point (Matt 11:25; 18:3).

Although the description of the girl is sketchy at best, interpreters have expanded her story largely.[136] This is somewhat justified since her part, though small, is of central importance. Had she, through either despair or vengeance, kept quiet, we would never have heard of either her or Naaman. Furthermore, her complete faith in the ability of "the prophet who is in Samaria" (הַנָּבִיא אֲשֶׁר בְּשֹׁמְרוֹן, *hannāḇîʾ ʾăšer bᵉšōmᵉrôn*) (did she even know his name?) must have been compelling. To the Omride kings, Elijah and Elisha had been

---

134. That he is called "a great man" (אִישׁ גָּדוֹל, *ʾîš gāḏôl*) reminds us forcibly of the "great lady" (אִשָּׁה גְדוֹלָה, *ʾiššâ gᵉḏôlâ*) from Shunem (4:8–37). In both cases their greatness masked a fundamental need that they were unable to provide for themselves.

135. See "Leprosy," *ABD* 4:277–84.

136. Jean Kyoung Kim, "Reading and Retelling Naaman's Story (2 Kings 5)," *JSOT* 30 (2005): 49–61; Esther Menn, "A Little Child Shall Lead Them: The Role of the Little Israelite Servant Girl (2 Kings 5:1–19)," *CTM* 35 (2008): 340–48.

troublemakers, whose power only served to embarrass the rulers, but this child knew that the power they wielded was for blessing, and that it was available to anyone, anywhere.

4–5 Throughout these miracle accounts we have seen that the narrator makes extensive use of ellipses. He is intent on keeping the story moving. So it is here. Obviously Naaman's wife told him what the servant girl said, but all we hear is Naaman telling the story to the king, and even then the details are not repeated. Nor do we hear of any discussion of pros and cons. The king simply urges him to go, assuring him that he will send a "letter" (סֵפֶר, *sēp̄er*) of introduction with him. Furthermore, he will send a huge amount of money along as well. When we consider that Omri only paid two talents of silver for the site of Samaria (1 Kgs 16:24), we get some sense of the immensity of the amount.[137] All of this speaks to how important Naaman was to the king of Syria, but it also speaks of how desperate they both were to find some solution for this disfiguring and embarrassing condition. It also speaks of their perhaps, unwilling, recognition of Yahweh's power, something Israel's kings had tended to discount (cf. Ahaziah, 2 Kgs 1).

Apparently, there was some sort of semi-peaceful relationship between Syria and Israel at this time. The large amount of money being sent to Israel suggests that Syria was not in a dominant role over Israel. Wiseman (206) suggests that the Syrian king may have been Ben-hadad III, referred to in 8:7.[138] But the fact that he is nowhere named (nor is the king of Israel) is surely the narrator's way of saying that these great men were really of no significance in comparison with the power of Yahweh.

6–7 The text's report of the royal letter that Naaman presented to the (un-named) king of Israel is completely authentic. The letter would have begun with stereotyped greetings and good wishes, with "and now" (וְעַתָּה, *wᵊ ʿattâ*) marking the transition to the real purpose of the letter. The narrator has dispensed with the "boilerplate" and moved directly to that purpose. Again, so much is conveyed in a few words. The girl did not said anything about the king in Samaria, but only about the prophet. However, in the typical understanding of prophecy in the ancient world, the prophet would have been a royal functionary, working for the king. So of course, the king of Syria would have sent Naaman to the king of Israel for that king to do the work ("and that you might heal him" [וַאֲסַפְתּוֹ, *wa ʾăsap̄tô*]) by commanding his lackey to perform some amazing feat that he was apparently capable of.

---

137. Approximately 1,000 pounds of silver, and between 100 and 200 pounds of gold.

138. Perhaps Syria had exhausted itself enough in its first two encounters with Ahab (1 Kgs 20) that even with Ahab's death in his attack on Ramoth-gilead, they did not have the strength to capitalize on the victory. Note that Joram had felt secure enough about his northern and eastern borders that he had no qualms about taking an army far to the south in his attempt to bring Moab back under his control (2 Kgs 3).

This was a matter of one power speaking to another power with the trappings of great wealth undergirding it all.

Unfortunately, the king of Israel does not seem to have had as much information as the little girl had. When confronted with the Syrian's demand, it evidently never occurred to him that although he was not "God who could kill and bring to life" (הָאֱלֹהִים ... לְהָמִית וּלְהַחֲיוֹת, *ha'ĕlōhîm ... ləhāmîṯ ûləhaḥăyôṯ*),[139] there was someone in his kingdom who did have the authority to dispense that divine power. Here is the blindness of power: everything in this man's world circled around him, and whatever did not, did not exist. So, knowing that he could not heal Naaman himself, and not knowing any of his stable of prophets who could do such a thing, it simply did not occur to him to think of the crazy man Elisha. Not having the right answer to his problem, he therefore jumped to the wrong answer: this Syrian king knew he could not do what was requested and was trying to maneuver him into a position where he could not help but give offense, thus giving the Syrian a pretext to attack Israel. In distress over the certainty that whatever he did it would be wrong, "he tore his clothes" (וַיִּקְרַע בְּגָדָיו, *wayyiqra' bəgāḏāyw*), something he was to do again with more reason in the not-too-distant future (6:30).

8 Elisha's location at this time is uncertain. The little girl had located him "in Samaria" (v. 3) and that is undoubtedly where Naaman had gone to speak to the king of Israel, and it seems easiest to think that Elisha had "heard" (שְׁמֹעַ, *šəmōa'*) about the king's distress because he was in that vicinity. On the other hand, the events before and after this have him in Gilgal or at least in the vicinity of the Jordan (4:38; 6:4). That location would make the most sense given the command for Naaman to wash in the Jordan. For the Syrian commander to go from Samaria to the Jordan and back again seems to ask too much. So perhaps Elisha's "hearing" what the king had done was of a supernatural nature, like his "being with" Gehazi when he lied to Naaman (5:26).

Elisha's question to the king is very pointed. It is to say, "You would not have needed to do that if you had known 'there is a prophet in Israel' (יֵשׁ נָבִיא בְּיִשְׂרָאֵל, *yēš nāḇî' bəyiśrā'ēl*), as this man is shortly to 'know' (ידע, *yd'*)." Because of the king's blindness, he had done something entirely unnecessary. This suggests that if indeed he, Joram, had taken steps against the dominance of Baal (3:2), that his mother was pressing for, he still had no sense of the transcendent uniqueness of Yahweh, as represented in the ministries of Elijah and Elisha. Yahweh was one of the gods, so Elijah and Elisha did not stand out among all the other religious functionaries in the land.

Elisha's prediction: "he will know there is a prophet in Israel" speaks to that very point. Naaman would know much more than that, would he not? He would know there is no God except Yahweh. Why does Elisha not say that? There were certainly many prophets in Israel, and Naaman would have known that. But what he did not know that just as there is only one Yahweh,

---

139. Cf. Deut 32:39; 1 Sam 2:6.

so Elisha was not just any prophet. Naaman would know that Elisha was not just any prophet, but as the one divinely accredited by the One Deity, he would stand out from all the rest. Naaman would go home knowing what Joram only lately learned (8:1–6), if at all: there is a prophet in Israel.

9–12 Again, the narrator does not burden us with unnecessary details. He does not tell us where Elisha was, nor how the Israelite king conveyed the information to Naaman, nor what instructions he may have given him. Naaman simply shows up outside of Elisha's door in a panoply of horses and chariots. If Elisha was in the area of Samaria, he must not have been in the city proper, because he was in a place accessible to horses and chariots. On the other hand, if he was in Gilgal, this would not have presented a problem.

The language here is somewhat ironic. To "stand before" (עמד, *ʿmd*) (v. 9) is typically to "wait upon" in the sense of "serve" (so v. 16). But clearly this great man has not come to serve Elisha, nor does he come to wait as a humble supplicant, as his words quoted in v. 11 make clear. He is waiting for Elisha to come to him, recognizing the signal honor Naaman is offering him in even coming to him at all. But Elisha's response (v. 10) is much the same as it was to the Shunammite. He sends "a messenger" (מַלְאָךְ, *mal ʾāḵ*) with a very curt message. Assuming that this messenger is Gehazi, it is possible to see how the man could have begun to have an inflated estimate of himself. After all, the prophet's work here, as with the Shunammite, was only done through him. One can imagine a certain condescending note in the messenger's voice as he addresses the great man.

"Seven" appears here again (v. 10), reminding the reader of the Shunammite's son's seven sneezes (4:35). The number also appears in Lev 14:7 where the leper is sprinkled with blood seven times and then pronounced clean. The association of the number with totality is common in the scripture, most especially in the seven days of creation (Gen 1).

It is not hard to understand why Naaman was insulted (v. 11). He was not used to being treated so cavalierly, nor was the prescription at all what he expected. *Wash* (רחץ, *rḥṣ*) ... *and be clean* (וּטְהָר, *ûṭ hār*) sounds suspiciously like folk medicine, as Brueggemann (333) observes, or even like a religious ritual of cleansing. Where was the incantation that would demonstrate the prophet's magical skills and engage his Yahweh god's healing ability?

Even in ancient days, before so much of its water was drawn off for irrigation, the Jordan would not have been very impressive. Flowing in its jungle of vegetation (Zech 11:3), it would have seemed more of a creek than a river. The two rivers of Damascus, the Abana[140] and the Pharpar, (v. 12) flowing as they did off the Amanus and Hermon mountains respectively, would have been much more impressive, especially if one thought of them in the spring, overflowing with snowmelt. Naaman can be forgiven for thinking that if it

140. Heb. *qere*, אֲמָנָה "Amana." Probably what is now called the Barada. The Pharpar is probably Wadi al'Awaj. It has a tributary now known as Wadi Barbar.

had to be water, at least it could be impressive water, something more fitting for his station in life.

13–14 As elsewhere in these narratives (cf. 3:11; 4:14), it is often the servants who seem more in tune with reality than their masters.[141] Perhaps it is because they are not so blinded by power and status. So here Naaman's servants in effect remind their master that it would be foolish to have come all this way, and not at least try what the prophet had directed. No, he had not given the great man a comparably "great thing" (דָּבָר גָּדוֹל, *dāḇār gāḏôl*) to do, but at least he should try the humble thing. If it failed, nothing would be lost but his dignity, and what if it succeeded? Fortunately for him, Naaman listened to the voice of wisdom.

"And his flesh was restored" (וַיָּשָׁב בְּשָׂרוֹ, *wayyāšoḇ bᵉśārô*) means that his body was restored to its non-diseased condition. But more than that, it was "like the flesh of a little boy" (כִּבְשַׂר נַעַר קָטֹן, *kiḇśar naʿar qāṭōn*). The fact that the terms used for "little boy" are exactly parallel to those for the "little girl" (v. 2; נַעֲרָה קְטַנָּה, *naʿărâ qᵉṭannâ*) can hardly be coincidental. What the little girl knew, the "little boy" now knows. In fact, much more than his body had been healed, as his interactions in the next verses make plain. The arrogance that had made him the center of his world had been washed away.

15–16 It was a different Naaman who came back to the prophet's house. Yes, he still had his military escort with him, but he did not come expecting the prophet to stand before him; now "he stood before him" (יַעֲמֹד לְפָנָיו, *yaʿămōḏ lᵉpānāyw*) (i.e., *waited on* Elisha). He now knows that "there is a prophet in Israel" (v. 8), but he knows something even more important, something that the king of Israel did not know: "there is no God in all the earth, except in Israel" (אֵין אֱלֹהִים בְּכָל־הָאָרֶץ כִּי אִם־בְּיִשְׂרָאֵל, *ʾên ʾĕlōhîm bᵉḵol-hāʾāreṣ kî ʾim-bᵉyiśrāʾēl*). At least one person, and he a foreigner, has gotten the point of this entire narrative, going all the way back to 1 Kings 17. How did he arrive at this conclusion? Why did he not merely conclude that Yahweh was greater than all the other gods? Provan (192–193) suggests that it was the healing at a distance, obviously not by the prophet, that convinced him. But I suspect that it was in some way connected with the destruction of his pride. To be willing to go down into that muddy creek not once, but seven times, to take the risk of being seen as a fool; to, in effect, throw himself at the feet of this God in abject dependence, and to have Yahweh not humiliate him, but respond with kindness and without being magically manipulated, did something to Naaman's thinking. This God clearly is not merely a representation of one of the powers of this world, as are all the other things called "god." He is God alone. Did he grasp all the far-reaching implications of that

141. The use of "my father" (אָבִי, *ʾāḇiy*) here strikes some as overly familiar. GKC (§159*cc*) says that it is "unquestionable" that it is a corruption of a conditional particle. But see 1 Sam 24:11; 2 Kgs 2:12; 6:21; 13:14.

insight? Of course not. But his following requests show that he did indeed intend to follow through with some of its implications.

His first request was to give his benefactor a "gift" (בְּרָכָה, *bᵉrāḵâ*). We may not make too much of the wording, since protocol might well cloak "payment" in buffered terms such as "gift." Nevertheless, when we look at the three other places where *bᵉrāḵâ* "blessing" is used in this way (Gen 33:11; Josh 15:19 [//Judg 1:15]; 1 Sam 30:26), they are indeed gifts rather than compensation. Nevertheless, Elisha, now speaking directly to his supplicant, refuses with his typical oath on the life of Yahweh (v. 16; cf. 2:2; 3:14). He will not permit even a hint of the idea that he somehow dispenses the power of Yahweh and can be compensated for that. He would accept gifts given to him personally (4:10, 42), but nothing directly related to Yahweh's power flowing through him.

17–19 If Elisha will not accept a gift, perhaps he will give gifts. Naaman, identifying himself as Elisha's "servant" (עֶבֶד, *ʿeḇeḏ*), asks for two mule-loads of Israelite earth. Old ways of thinking die hard, and the thought that Yahweh, the God of Israel, was in some magical way linked to the soil of Israel was fixed in his mind. So, if he were to worship Yahweh as the One God, he would need to do so on Israelite soil. We would like to see him recognize that if Yahweh is the only God in the universe he can therefore be worshipped anywhere in his universe, but—we are still grateful for Naaman's determination to worship no other god. He is going to match his actions with his confession.

His final request is clearly stated with a good deal of repetitive diffidence. While earlier commentators tended to emend the text to get rid of some of its repetitiveness, most recent ones recognize that the narrator is skillfully representing the man's anxiety (see the discussion in Cogan and Tadmor, 65).[142] Naaman is faced with a dilemma: now that he is ritually clean, his king will expect him to accompany him when he "worships" (הִשְׁתַּחֲוָה, *hištaḥăwâ*; lit. "prostrates himself") Baal-hadad (i.e., Rimmon[143]). Can Elisha give him Yahweh's absolution if he has to prostrate himself before Baal-hadad, while presumably praising Yahweh in his heart?

The prophet's response to both these requests is very enigmatic: "Go in peace" (לֵךְ לְשָׁלוֹם, lēḵ *lᵉšālôm*). Some commentators (e.g., Long, 327, citing 1 Sam 1:17) take it to be a positive affirmation, others (e.g., Fritz, 260) understand that the requests, particularly the latter, are neither granted nor precluded. I think the latter is more likely. Elisha is not giving Naaman some sort of blanket "pass" for deception. Nor is he falling prey to any renewed suggestion that Yahweh's power, now of forgiveness, is his to dispense. On the other hand, he is not demanding that the new "convert" settle at once

142. Cohn has observed that the statement has a chiastic structure (39).

143. This is apparently a biblical parody on the title "Ramman," or "Thunderer," an epithet of Baal-hadad. Rimmon is a term for "pomegranate."

all the issues his new faith will raise. Rather, he bids him go without anxiety, believing that God will lead him aright if he will only follow faithfully.

Biblical Theology Comments

Elisha's similar treatment of Naaman and the Shunammite speaks to the issue of human pride. The church, throughout its history, has rightly designated pride as the deadliest of sins. So long as a creature considers itself to be in the place of God, which is, in reality, what pride consists of, there is no hope of redemption. This is so because pride deprives us of any knowledge of a need for redemption. The most vivid picture of pride and its results is found in Isaiah 14:4–21. Particularly since John Milton's appropriation of the title "Lucifer" for Satan, this powerful poem has been thought to be a description of Satan. However, the text is actually describing human pride. It aspires to heaven, but in refusing to grant preeminence to Yahweh, it only brings itself down into hell. Thus, when Elisha refused to give either the "great lady" or the "great man" the kind of deference they expected, he was actually doing them a favor, reminding them that they were not God, and were actually needy people, in need of divine grace.

Ritual cleanness was a major concern in the ancient world. The demonic was a source of such uncleanness, as was death. For the pagan, the problem was that ritual was ineffective where uncleanness was present. For the Hebrew, ritual effectiveness was not the issue, nor was the presence of the demonic, for transcendence had cut that nerve. It was sin that defiled and led to death, and the effect was to bar the unclean one from the presence of God (see Ps 51). This spiritual uncleanness was the real issue, and the spreading skin diseases were symbolic of it. The structure of the book of Leviticus points in this direction. Nadab and Abihu, Aaron's sons, decided that it was not necessary to obey Yahweh precisely (Lev 10:1–4). After all, he was only God. They did not understand that all the rituals were designed to teach how radically, transcendentally, holy Yahweh is. He wishes to have fellowship with us, but that can only be on his terms, not ours. Thus, it is no accident that, within the structure of Leviticus, the teaching on clean and unclean (with all their associated symbols) comes between the moment of Nadab and Abihu's death and the return to instructions about the cult in Leviticus 16. Chapters 11–15 are a parenthesis attempting to make the point that the priests had not understood: sin, particularly the sin of disobedience, defiles us in the presence of God, and requires a radical cleansing if his presence is to give us life rather than death.

Application and Devotional Implications

As Joram demonstrated, spiritual blindness leads to wrong conclusions and unnecessary actions. The Syrian king was not looking for an excuse to go to war against Israel, and there was no need for Joram to be distressed. If he had only remembered Elisha, he could have sent Naaman on his way immediately, and slept easily. But he did not realize the huge resource that was available to him and so was terrorized. For persons today, the principles are the same. Many of us, when crises fall upon us, not having cultivated the practice of prayer in ordinary days, have no God to turn to. We assume the worst both of the distant God and of those whom we may see as provoking the crisis. We fall prey to our worst fears and succumb to all kinds of stress-related illnesses and neuroses. But if we know we have Jesus Christ interceding for us at the right hand of the Father, we could lay our fears in his lap, knowing he is adequate for anything that might come to us.

Through much of the church's history (and in many parts of the world today), Naaman's concerns have been very real. When does the believer need to stand against false religions and leave no doubt about the issue? And when does a person, without surrendering his or her faith not need to flaunt it? These have been real concerns for followers of Yahweh through the ages. In some cases, as with the three men whose story is recorded in the book of Daniel (3:13–18), there can be no compromise. Where the faith of Yahweh is particularly being challenged, the only recourse is to stand and be counted for him. But in other cases, where a direct challenge is not being mounted, it seems possible not to make an issue of one's faith. That seems to have been the case with Esther. There is no judgment rendered against her for not publicly declaring and practicing her Jewish faith. Of course, in the end circumstances required her to make a choice, and she did (Esther 4:12–16), but up until then it seems she was not forced into a public declaration.

Selected Bibliography

Effa, A. "Prophet, Kings, Servants, and Lepers: A Missiological Reading of an Ancient Drama." *Missiology* 35 (2007): 305–13.

Maier III, W. A. "The Healing of Naaman in Missiological Perspective." *CTQ* 61(1997): 177–96.

Nwaoru E. O. "The Story of Naaman (2 Kings 5:1-19): Implications for Mission Today." *Swedish Missiological Themes* 96 (2008): 27–41.

Gehazi and Naaman (5:20–27)

Translation

20 Gehazi, the servant of Elisha, the man of God, said, "Now look, my lord has spared Naaman, this Syrian, by not taking from him what he had brought. By the life of Yahweh,[144] I am going to run after him in order to[145] get something from him." **21** So Gehazi pursued Naaman and when Naaman saw someone running after him, he jumped down from the chariot to greet him and he asked, "Is all well?" **22** He said, "All is well. My lord sent me saying, 'Just now,[146] there came to me two lads from Mt. Ephraim from the sons of

144. Heb. כִּי־אִם, *kî ʾim*; a strong assertion, especially in the context of an oath. Cf. GKC (§163*d*); Judg 15:7; Jer 51:14.

145. *IBHS* (§32.2.3c).

146. GKC (§136*d*).

the prophets. Please give them a talent of silver and two changes of clothes.' "
23 Naaman said, "Please take two talents." He pressed him and he tied two
talents of silver in two bags[147] along with two changes of clothing and put
them on two of his servants, who carried them before him. **24** He came to
the hill and took (it) from their hands and arranged[148] (it) in the house and
sent them off, and they went. **25** He came and stood in front of his lord, and
Elisha said to him, "Where[149] did you come from, Gehazi?" He said, "Your
servant has not been anywhere." **26** He said, "Did my heart not go when the
man turned from his chariot to meet you?[150] Is this the time to take silver
and to take clothes and olive groves and orchards and flocks and herds and
menservants and maidservants? **27** The leprosy of Naaman will cling to you
and to your descendants forever." He went out from him as white as snow.

Textual Notes

20a. אִישׁ־הָאֱלֹהִים: Gk. omits; Vulg. and Syr. with MT.

21a. וַיִּפֹּל: Gk. "turned around" (cf. v. 26); Vulg. "leapt down"; Syr. "got down." MT best explains the others.

21b–b. וַיֹּאמֶר הֲשָׁלוֹם: Gk. omits (homoioarchton with following); Vulg. and Syr. with MT.

23a. הוֹאֵל: Gk. lacks; Syr. "I am willing"; Vulg. with MT.

23b–b. וַיִּפְרָץ־בּוֹ וַיָּצַר כִּכְּרַיִם כֶּסֶף: Gk. reads "he accepted it in"; Vulg. and Syr. with MT.

24a. אֶל־הָעֹפֶל: Gk. reads "darkness," apparently reading אפל instead of עפל; Vg. "evening"; Syr. "the secret place." MT as the harder reading best explains others.

24b. וַיֵּלֵכוּ: Gk. omits; Vulg. and Syr. with MT.

26a. וַיֹּאמֶר: Gk. Adds "Elisha"; Vulg. and Syr. with MT.

26b. הָלַךְ: Gk. and Vulg. add "with you"; Syr. "told me." MT is the harder reading.

---

147. This term (חֲרִטִים, *ḥărīṭîm*) only occurs here and in Isa 3:22 where "satchel" or "purse" seems suggested.

148. The term is פקד, *pqd* which can mean "to muster" or "appoint" (as well as "visit," "bless," and "judge").

149. On the contraction (*ketiv* and *qere*) see *IBHS* (§18.4e n.29).

150. The lack of an interrogative particle is not a barrier to taking this sentence as a question (with Gk. and Vulg.). See GKC (§150*c* n.1).

26c–c. הַעֵת לָקַחַת אֶת־הַכֶּסֶף וְלָקַחַת בְּגָדִים וְזֵיתִים: Gk. reads "Even now you accepted silver and even now you accepted clothes and will you receive from him"; Vulg. "You took silver and you took clothes and would you buy"; Syr. with MT. Apparently both Gk. and Vulg. misread the opening העת as a 2ms indep. pron. 6QReg shows the presence of the interrogative ה (*he*). *CTAT* (387) considers MT probable.

Commentary

The contrast between Gehazi and Naaman is drawn in stark colors in this segment. Both had needs: Naaman went to the prophet, but Gehazi sought to meet his needs for himself. Naaman began as a leper and Gehazi ended as a leper. Naaman went from arrogance to humility, but Gehazi from arrogance to lies. Naaman found wholeness (שָׁלוֹם, *šālôm*) whereas Gehazi destroyed relationships, while professing *šālôm.*

There is also a powerful contrast between Gehazi and Elisha. Whereas Elisha, recognizing that the work was not his, but Yahweh's, refused with an oath to take anything, even when he was pressed. Gehazi asserted with the same oath that he, who had done nothing, would get something, and allowed himself to be pressed to take more.

The upshot is that Gehazi's failings cause both Elisha and Naaman to stand out in brighter relief: we see more clearly what had taken place in Naaman's life and we recognize more forcefully what it is that motivates Elisha. In both cases, we see men who were willing to place their needs in the hands of Yahweh, something Gehazi, and Israel, were unwilling to do. We also see that being an instrument of Yahweh's power does not relieve one from manifesting Yahweh's character.[151]

20 Gehazi's attitude toward Naaman is telling. Instead of rejoicing over the wonderful miracle that had taken place and the profound change that had occurred in Naaman, he can only think that *this Syrian* has gotten off scot-free. Had the little Israelite girl had a similar attitude toward her master this story would never have been told. Clearly, Gehazi did not want to be dependent on whatever generosity people were moved to shower on Elisha and his servant (4:42). Neither did he want to be dependent on Elisha's largesse. He wanted "something in the bank," as it were, and if his lord was too lofty to take something, he "by God" (the import of his oath) was not. The terrible irony of the same oath coming from Gehazi's mouth that had come from Elisha's (v. 16), but with the opposite intent, is not lost on the reader. We ask what the foolish servant has just called down upon himself.

21–23 This is a different Naaman than the one who haughtily stood in his chariot outside Elisha's door waiting for the prophet to come out and speak to

151. See Sweeney who says the purpose of the account is to show that the miraculous cannot be separated from the moral (300).

him. Seeing "someone running" (רָץ, *rāṣ*) from Elisha's direction, he instantly dismounted[152] and anxiously asked if everything was alright back there. The use of שָׁלוֹם, *šālôm* recalls its use in 4:26 where it was Elisha, through Gehazi, anxiously asking about the Shunammite woman's well-being. Just as there, the response is, "All is well." But of course, in both cases that was a false answer. There a little boy was dead, and the mother was determined to get through to the man who was her only hope. Here Gehazi was about to embark on a lie about his master and did not want anything to impede the smooth functioning of the lie. There the purpose of the misrepresentation was to arrive at a greater good; here it was to promote a greater evil.

One must admire Gehazi's cunning. He was not asking for himself, oh, no. Neither had his master had a change of heart and was now asking something for himself. Naaman, so overjoyed at the שָׁלוֹם, *šālôm* (body and soul) that was now his, would probably have acceded to either request, but still he might have wondered why Elisha changed his mind. But to the prophet's request that Naaman provide him the means to be generous to a couple of penniless lads from that group devoted to the service of the Yahweh who had healed him, the Syrian would certainly give without a second thought.

That is exactly what he did, even pressing Gehazi to take *two* talents (one for each boy?), something to which the liar probably reluctantly, but graciously, acquiesced. Naaman was so delighted to have some way of expressing his gratitude that he even wrapped the talents in bags and sent two of his servants to carry them.[153]

24 Several commentators have noted the succession of five verbs in this sentence (e.g., Cohn, 41). Everything was working out perfectly. Each step followed the next like clockwork. They got back to the city[154] without trouble. Then before they got within sight of Elisha, he relieved the servants of their burdens, sent them back to their master and artfully hid his theft "in

---

152. The Heb. term is נפל, *npl* "fell." It also appears in Gen 24:64 where Rebekah dismounts from her camel, also precipitately, it seems. Later in 5:26, when the manner of dismounting is not important, it is simply said that he "turned from on" (מֵעַל... הָפַךְ, *hāpak ... mēʿal*).

153. While it is not specified that these were Naaman's servants, it seems unlikely that Gehazi would have had servants of his own, or even if he had, would have risked their possible disclosure of his secret.

154. It is not entirely clear what an "ophel" (עֹפֶל, *ʿōpel*) is (as it was obviously not to the versions [see the "Textual Note"]). Some believe it to be the central acropolis found in many ancient cities. If that is what it was, that would argue that Elisha's residence was in Samaria (see the "Commentary" above on 5:8). But it is not clear that this is what is meant by the *ʿōpel* in Jerusalem (cf. Neh 3:26, 27; 11:21). Perhaps it simply refers to the mound which constituted many ancient cities after centuries of destruction and rebuilding on the same spot.

the house" (בַּבָּיִת, *babbāyiṯ*). Presumably this was the house where he lived with Elisha, so his hiding would have to be artful indeed.

25–27 In fact, all Gehazi's cunning and artfulness were worthless, and one wonders, since he had evidently lived with Elisha for some time, how he could be so obtuse as not to realize who he was dealing with. Perhaps he was misled by Yahweh's not revealing the Shunammite's situation in advance (4:27) into believing that might apply here too. False hope. The language used in v. 25 to describe Gehazi's meeting with Elisha is not the same that we have seen at least twice before in this chapter. It is not to stand before[155] in the sense of "wait upon" (either temporally [v. 9] or professionally [v. 16]), but almost to stand *over* (וַיַּעֲמֹד אֶל־אֲדֹנָיו, *wayya ʿămōḏ ʾel- ʾăḏōnāyw*;"and he stood in front of his master").[156] It suggests a certain bluster on Gehazi's part. But if it was bluster, it would shortly be blown away. Elisha's mild question about his servant's recent whereabouts might be construed as the prophet's giving his servant one last opportunity to admit what he had done and seek forgiveness. But if that was the case, it was not to be. Too often in life, one lie leads to another, and that is what happens here: Gehazi denies he has been anywhere except there in the house.

If the ultimate tone of Elisha's response is harsh, its opening is almost plaintive. Did not Gehazi realize that he was on his master's "heart" (לֵב, *lēḇ*), and that where he was, his master's heart was there too? I believe "heart" is used intentionally, and that it is not merely a synonym for "spirit" as some modern versions suggest. If that had been the intent, "spirit" could have been used. Here "heart" is indicative of the whole person, including intellect, will and emotions: Elisha himself was there. What form that consciousness took is an unanswerable question, but Elisha is saying that he saw and felt the incident as clearly as if he had been there in the flesh.

"Is this the time" (הַעֵת, *ha ʿēṯ*) may refer to the famine. That is, when other people are suffering and dying, is this the time to make yourself rich? The additional listing of items besides the silver and the clothes has strong overtones of Samuel's list of the oppressions of the typical king (1 Sam 8:14–17), but it is also representative of the Deuteronomic expression of the abundance of a good land (Deut 6:11; Josh 24:13; Neh 9:25). It is as though Elisha is rhetorically asking, "Why stop with a demand for silver and clothes? Why not ask for everything the good life could give you? If you have needs, and have to lie to get them supplied, why not go for it all?"[157]

---

155. Heb. לִפְנֵי, *lip̄nê*. Note that *lip̄nê* is twice used by itself in the chapter to express serving (vv. 1, 2).

156. Heb. אֶל, *ʾel*. See 1 Sam 17:51.

157. The LXX has Gehazi "accepting" (λαμβάνω, *lambanō*) the things as opposed to the MT's "taking" (לקח, *lqḥ*) them. D. P Obrie, "'Is This a Time to Accept … ?': Simply Moralizing (LXX) or an Ominous Foreboding of Yahweh's Rejection of

There is a certain dreadful symmetry in the conclusion. Since Gehazi wanted Naaman's stuff, he can have his leprosy also. As mentioned above, this is not Hansen's Disease, nor is it one of the skin diseases that required quarantine, as per Leviticus 13–14 (cf. 8:1–6). But it was disfiguring ("white as snow"; כַּשָּׁלֶג, *kaššāleḡ*).[158]

Biblical Theology Comments

The similarity of this event to that of Achan (Josh 7:1–26) is striking. There the Israelite soldier took spoils from Jericho that belonged to the true victor in that battle: Yahweh. Here Gehazi took compensation for himself for what only Yahweh had done. What Achan took is very similar to what Gehazi took: clothes and silver (as well as gold). The point is clear. In both cases, it was Yahweh who accomplished the task. Thus, it was not appropriate that those who were mere instruments should be compensated for something they had not done.[159] In the case of Achan, the offense was the more serious because the spoil of Canaan had been designated as *herem* (חרם, *ḥrm*), that is, the property of God alone. That was not a war of occupation, but a carrying out of divine justice. However, the essential point is the same: we cannot arrogate to ourselves what rightfully belongs to Yahweh. If he chooses to give it to us, that is his prerogative, but we cannot tear it from his hands.

Application and Devotional Implications

It has often been observed that the tenth commandment is something of a mirror image of the first commandment. When we covet, we effectively make created things into our gods. We think that if we had the possessions of someone richer, then our desires would be satisfied, never realizing that our desire is for fellowship with our transcendent Creator, and that nothing else can fill that particular void. Thus, we spend our lives stretched out, grasping for something more. Those two talents of silver and those two beautiful robes, would they satisfy what was driving Gehazi? No, there would have to be orchards, and vineyards, and … , and … , and there would never be enough. It is only when we have found our fulfillment in God through Christ that there is enough. With him, whatever we have is enough. That is the point of the opening verse of Psalm 23: because Yahweh is my Shepherd, I will have enough, whatever that may amount to.

Israel (MT)?" *VT* 46 (1996): 448–57, argues that this is to reduce what is intended to be a diatribe against rapacious Israel to mere moralizing.

158. Cogan and Tadmor suggest that the simile may speak of dead skin flaking off (66). See also Num 12:10.

159. Perhaps Gehazi had come to have some inflated view of his own importance. After all, he had been the prophet's representative to both the "great lady" of Shunem, and the "great man" of Syria. Indeed, the prophet's word had only functioned through him.

Closely coupled to the sin of covetousness is the deep-seated desire for independence. We have a dread of being dependent on others for anything. Unquestionably, that desire has its deepest roots in our refusal to be dependent on God. Nietzsche called it "the will to power," but we might also label it "the will to be God."[160] This is the profound truth of Genesis 3. We do not want to submit to anyone else, and we do not want to be dependent on anyone else. Gehazi wanted something to call his own. He did not want to be dependent on Elisha, and he did not want to be dependent on Yahweh. In a small way that is illustrated in the account of the giving of the manna in Exodus 16. There was enough for that day alone. It was not possible to gather enough for tomorrow; whatever you did not use that day would rot. Should we not plan; should we not be prudent? Certainly we should, but the point is our attitude. Do we continually remember that God is the provider of our needs, not we ourselves? If we do not, then providing for our needs will become ultimate, and God will become simply our "blessing machine"—a profoundly pagan approach to religion. Furthermore, once providing for our needs is ultimate, truth must be the first victim. It is so because, the proposition that I and my needs are ultimate is a lie. Like Gehazi, the only way to get what we want is to lie. The only hope is to make Yahweh ultimate, to commit our ways and our wants to him, and then we can afford to live with that most expensive of commodities, truth.

Selected Bibliography

Brodie, T. L. "Towards Unraveling the Rhetorical Imitation of Sources in Acts: 2 Kgs 5 as one Component of Acts 8:9–40." *Bib* 67 (1986): 41–67.

Brueggemann, W. "2 Kings 5: Two Evangelists and a Saved Subject." *Missiology* 35 (2007): 263–72.

Cohn, R. L. "Form and Perspective in 2 Kings 5." *VT* 33 (1983): 171–84.

Ngan, L. L. E. "2 Kings 5" *RevExp* 94 (1997): 589–97.

Smith, W. A. "Naaman and Elisha: Healing, Wholeness, and the Task of Religious Education." *RelEd* 89 (1994): 205–19.

The Floating Ax Head (6:1–7)

Translation

6:1 The sons of the prophets said to Elisha, "Look, the place where we are living under your authority[161] is too constricted for us. **2** Let us go to the Jordan, and let each man take a timber and we will make ourselves a place to live there." And he said, "Go." **3** One of them said, "Please consent to go with your servants," and he said, "Indeed, I[162] will go." **4** He went with them and they came to the Jordan and cut down trees. **5** It so happened that one of them was felling a timber, and the iron ax-head fell into the water. He

160. Friedrich W. Nietzsche, *The Will to Power* (New York: Random House, 1967).

161. Heb. לְפָנֶיךָ, *lᵉpānêḵā*, "before you." For similar usage see, 5:1, 2.

162. The 1cs pron. is in an emphatic position.

cried out and said, "Oh, no, my lord, it was borrowed!" **6** The man of God said, "Where did it fall?" He showed him the place. He cut off a stick and threw it in there and made[163] the iron ax-head float. **7** He said, "Pick it up for yourself," and he reached out his hand and took it.

Textual Notes

5a. וְאֶת־הַבַּרְזֶל: GKC (§117*m*) considers this particle which is normally an accusative indicator to be an error. *IBHS* (§10.3.2b) says it is here used to mark the subject of an intransitive vb. The versions all take "iron" to be in the nominative case.

5b. וַיֹּאמֶר: Gk. omits; Vulg. and Syr. with MT.

5c. אֲהָהּ:Vulg. "Alas, alas, alas"; Syr. "I beg you"; Gk. with MT.

5d. אֲדֹנִי: Gk. "lord"; Vulg. and Syr. with MT.

6a–a. וַיָּצֶף הַבַּרְזֶל: Syr. "it stuck in the hole of the ax-head"; Gk. and Vulg. with MT.

6b. וַיָּצֶף Gk. and Vulg. "it floated" (not causative as in MT).

Commentary

As mentioned in the introduction to 5:1–6:7, the two units (5:1–27; 6:1–7) are to be read together with both of them revealing Yahweh's power to restore what is lost: in the first (5:1–27), lost health, and here, a lost ax-head. The second part of that first unit (5:20–27) shows that that power is not exercised in isolation from God's moral character, and a similar point is made here, as will be commented upon below.

1–2 As noted above, the explicit location of this event in the Jordan Valley suggests that Elisha may have been resident there for the previous events (5:1–27) as well. Commentators disagree over how to understand the Hebrew ישב, *yšb*, whether as "living" (Gray, 511) or more literally "sitting" (Long, 333; Cogan and Tadmor, 69). If it is the former, as here, then the group are living together communally, and their living space has become too constricted.[164] If it is the latter, then it is their meeting space that needs to be enlarged.

---

163. MT is *hiphil* (causative). Gk. and Vulg. take the axe head itself as the subject ("it floated"). MT is probably preferable as emphasizing that the prophet caused it to happen. This vb. only appears here and in Deut 11:4 and Lam 3:54.

164. Note the very similar wording in Isa 49:20, one of only five occs. of the word (צרר, *ṣrr*) in this form (צַר, *ṣar*).

While the trees that still grow in profusion along the Jordan are not by any means large lumber-producing trees,[165] they would provide wood[166] that was substantial enough for shelters, and such shelters would be satisfactory in the hot, dry climate of the Jordan Valley.

The direct conversation between Elisha and the representative of the prophetic group is in contrast to the prophet's more distant contacts with the Shunammite (4:12) and Naaman (5:10). He is clearly more open with his disciples who were not "great" people (so also the widow of the prophet in 4:1–2, and the prophets in 4:38–41, and 42–44).

3–4 It is not clear why the men were so eager for Elisha to accompany them, but perhaps it was simply because they were glad of any opportunity to have him with them, whether in some sort of formal teaching session, or in the world of work. The same situation seems to have applied with Jesus (Mark 2:15). In any case, Elisha appears to have been glad for the invitation, and accepted it with alacrity.[167] As events unfolded, his presence was a reason for thanks.

5–7 Although ax-head is quite certain, the text simply says "the iron fell off" (הַבַּרְזֶל נָפַל, *habbarzel nāp̄al*). This is analogous to our calling the instrument used to smooth clothes "an iron." In this case, "the iron" was an instrument for *felling* (מַפִּיל, *mappîl*; "one felling") a timber, but instead of *felling*, it *fell* (נָפַל, *nāp̄al*) into the water. Although we do not know how these cutting instruments were formed, it is likely that they were much like our axes, with a wooden handle and a metal head. Apparently, the iron head flew off.

Although this was a couple of centuries after the Philistine monopoly on iron mentioned in 1 Sam 13:19–21, iron tools would still have been very costly to produce and to maintain. We can imagine the owner allowing this man to borrow his ax only with dire warnings. Now it is lost, and the borrower is faced with somehow making good for the loss. The covenant is very clear about a borrower's responsibility (Exod 22:9–14), so this person, who probably had little if any income with which to purchase a replacement, was in serious straits.[168] But his first response was the right one: he cried out to his lord, who was the man of God. Like all the persons from the widow of Zarephath onward, with the exception of Gehazi, this man presented his need to God through the man of God. With the decisiveness seen throughout

165. On the wild growth in the valley, see Jer 49:19; 50:44.

166. Hobbs notes that קוֹרָה, *qôrâ*, here variously translated as "beams," "logs," and "poles," is uncommon enough (four occs. counting this one) to preclude dogmatism in the translation (76). In Gen 19:8 it is commonly translated "roof."

167. Note the emphasized pronoun, lit: "*I*, I will go" (אֲנִי אֵלֵךְ, *ʾănî ʾēlēḵ*).

168. Wiseman says that the tool was "begged" or "asked for" (שָׁאוּל, *šāʾûl*) and not necessarily "borrowed" (222). But unless the man was under the burden of replacement, it is hard to understand why he would have made that point to Elisha.

these accounts, a decisiveness springing from direct acquaintance with the divine source, Elisha took action. It is interesting that he had to be told where the iron had fallen. Clearly the kind of clairvoyance that enabled him to see what Gehazi had done (5:26) was not simply an ability of his to be used indiscriminately (see 4:27 and the "Commentary" there) but was given by God when necessary.

Once again, the prophet throws something into the water (2:21; 4:41). And again, we are not told the significance of the act. Some commentators[169] suggest that he used the "stick" (עֵץ, *ʿēṣ*) to maneuver the ax-head where it could be reached, or even to put it in the head to raise it. Others[170] reasonably dismiss this, arguing that the whole point of this account, as well as the others in this series, is to emphasize Yahweh's miraculous power. This power is demonstrated, not only to show that Yahweh can provide the fertility and abundance that Baal cannot, but also to heal and restore Israel. If they would stop emulating Gehazi, trying to meet their own needs through manipulation, and turn to him, that healing and restoration could be theirs.

As Cohn (43) observes, this miracle closes like all the others thus far with the prophet giving the supplicant a command to do something (4:7, 36, 41, 43; 5:19). In each case, more evidently in some, but present in all, is an indication not only of the divine power that has been displayed, but of the divine compassion: the widow is to provide for herself; the Shunammite is to cradle her son in her arms; the prophets are to eat not only harmless food but plenty of food; Naaman is to go in wholeness and serenity, both in body and soul. Here the prophet is to "pick it up for yourself" (הָרֶם לָךְ, *hārem lāḵ*). That is, it is his again to use and return. The lost thing is not merely restored; it is restored to the one who lost it, by the God whose heart goes out both to the lost, and to the loser. No place is that made more clearly than in the series of Jesus' parables in Luke 15. Only Gehazi, not having lost anything, but having gained something illicitly, is given no command. There is nothing for him to do, as there would not be for Israel, but to live with the results of his grasping.

Selected Bibliography

Cummings, J. T. "The House of the Sons of the Prophets and the Tents of the Rechabites." In *Studia Biblica,* ed. E. A. Livingstone. Vol. 1: 119–26, JSOTSup 11 (Sheffield: Sheffield University, 1978).

Elisha and the Syrians (6:8–7:20)

In this segment we move onto the larger stage of international events with two incidents in which Elisha and the king of Israel are involved with the continuing threat of the Syrians. The two incidents are not contiguous in

169. E.g., Gray, 511.

170. E.g., Brueggemann, 341–42.

time, as 6:23, with its statement that "Syrian raiders did not come into the land of Israel anymore" (וְלֹא־יָסְפוּ עוֹד גְּדוּדֵי אֲרָם לָבוֹא בְּאֶרֶץ יִשְׂרָאֵל, *wᵉlōʾ-yāsp̄û ʿôḏ gᵉḏûḏê ʾărām lāḇôʾ bᵉʾereṣ yiśrāʾēl*) makes clear. Rather they are two incidents which have been brought together by the author to illustrate the point that while Yahweh is the God of Israel, his power is not restricted to Israel, but has an international scope.[171]

As has been the case throughout these accounts of Elisha's miracles, the narrator's art is evident in these reports as well. There is humor, pathos, satire, and engaging detail. We, the readers, are drawn into the narrative, and find ourselves both empathizing and making judgments, just as the narrator intends. We find the king of Israel, presumably Joram, present again, after an absence since chapter three, and again, he does not come off very well. He is not depicted as a powerful figure who is directing affairs, but as a chip on the water, tossed to and fro by conflicting currents. Power is in the hands of Yahweh, and it is he who is directing matters. Joram recognizes this truth, but can only see Yahweh as vindictive and cruel, not as the One whose ultimate desire is restoration, deliverance, and health.[172]

Selected Bibliography

Labarbera, R. "The Man of War and the Man of God: Social Satire in 2 Kings 6:8–7:20." *CBQ* 46 (1984): 637–51.

The Abortive Attempt to Capture Elisha (6:8–23)

Translation

8 At that time the king of Syria was fighting[173] with Israel and he would counsel with his officers, saying, "My encampment[174] will be at a certain place." **9** The man of God would send to the king of Israel, saying, "Keep from going by this place because the Syrians are going down there." **10** The

171. Gilmour (*Juxtaposition and the Elisha Cycle,* 173) suggests that the second account has been selected to enhance our understanding of Elisha's miraculous powers, with his ability not only to see present reality (6:8–23), but also the future (6:24–7:20).

172. Satterthwaite (*The Elisha Narrative,* 20–23) sees the two accounts as contrasting, with fairly good relations between the king and the prophet in 6:8–23, and the very opposite in 6:24–7:20. He thus wants to see a division between the two. However, that need not be the case, with the contrast being one of the literary devices that in fact holds the two together. See the "Commentary" below for further discussion.

173. For this rendering, see *IBHS* (§37.7.1b).

174. The ancient versions read the word here in a variety of ways, often taking it as an error for a similar word (נחת *nḥt*) in v. 9. However, as Sweeney (304–5) says, the very variety argues for the priority of the MT.

king of Israel would send[175] to the place about which the man of God told him. So he warned him and he saved himself not only once or twice. **11** The heart of the king of Syria was enraged,[176] so he called his officers and said to them, "Will you not inform me who among us is for the king of Israel?" **12** One of his officers said, "No, my lord, the king, but Elisha the prophet who is in Israel informs the king of Israel of the words you speak in your bedchamber." **13** He said, "Go and see where he is and I will send and take him." He was informed, saying, "He is in Dothan." **14** He sent there horses and chariotry and a strong force; they came by night and surrounded the city. **15** The attendant of the man of God rose early and went out and there was an army surrounding the city with horses and chariots. His servant said to him, "Oh, no, my master! What shall we do?" **16** He said, "Don't be afraid, for there are more with us than with them." **17** So Elisha prayed and said, "Oh, Yahweh, please open his eyes, that he may see."[177] Yahweh opened the servant's eyes and he could see, and there the hill was, full of horses and chariots surrounding Elisha. **18** They came down to him and Elijah prayed to Yahweh and said, "Please strike this nation with blindness." And he struck them with blindness, according to the word of Elisha. **19** Elisha said to them, "This is not the way, and this is not the city. Follow me and I will lead you to the man whom you are seeking." Then he led them toward Samaria. **20** When they reached Samaria, Elisha said, "Oh, Yahweh, open the eyes of these that they may see." Yahweh opened their eyes, and they saw, there they were[178] in the midst of Samaria! **21** The king of Israel said to Elisha when he saw them, "Shall I strike them,[179] shall I strike them, my father?" **22** He said, "You shall not strike them. Would you strike those whom you had captured with your sword and bow?[180] Put food and water before them so they can eat and drink and go to their lord." **23** So he made a great feast[181] for them and they ate and drank, and he sent them off and they went to their master. So Syrian raiders did not come into the land of Israel anymore.

175. Frequentative use of the vbs.; see GKC (§112*f*).

176. This word is not translated so forcefully in the versions: Gk. "perturbed"; Vulg. "troubled"; Syr. "sorely troubled."

177. A jussive; see *IBHS* (§34.2.1a).

178. "they were" is supplied for the English sense. They are not in Heb., which is much more elliptical.

179. Some interpreters (e.g., Cogan and Tadmor, 74), noting the clumsiness of the Heb. take this to be an error for an inf. abs. which would emphasize the main vb. Thus, "Shall I surely kill them?" See the commentary below.

180. In Heb. the subj. and vb. "you would strike" occur at the end of this sentence. GKC (§142*f* n.1) explains this odd placement as an attempt to achieve chiasm with the same vb. in the preceding sentence.

181. A *hapax legomenon*. Perhaps related to Akk. *Kirētu,* "festival, banquet."

Textual Notes

8a. אַלְמֹנִי: Gk. transliterates; Vulg. and Syr. translate.

8b. תַּחֲנֹתִי: Vulg. and Syr. "lie in wait"; Gk. with MT. *CTAT* (387) considers MT possibly original (Vulg. and Syr. harmonizing with v. 9).

9a–a. אִישׁ הָאֱלֹהִים: Gk. "Elisha" (so also vv. 10, 14); Vulg. and Syr. with MT throughout.

9b. נְחִתִּים: Gk. "hidden"; Vulg. and Syr. "lying in wait." *CTAT* (387) considers MT probable.

10a–a. וְהִזְהִירָהּ: Gk. "he avoided it"; Vulg. "he seized it and guarded it"; Syr. "he warned him about it"; MT best explains the others.

11a. מִשֶּׁלָּנוּ: Gk. and Vulg. "is betraying me"; Syr. with MT. *CTAT* (388) considers MT probable. See *IBHS* (§19.4a n.1). Probably a N. Palestinian dialectal form.

13a. הוּא: Gk. "this man"; Vulg. and Syr. with MT.

13b. וַיֻּגַּד: Gk. and Vulg. "They informed him"; Syr. with MT.

15a. נַעֲרוֹ: Gk. "the servant"; Vulg. lacks; Syr. with MT.

16a. אוֹתָם: Reading אִתָּם with the versions and with *K* in MSS.

17a. אֶת־עֵינָיו: Gk. "the eyes of the lad"; Vulg. and Syr. with MT.

17b. אֶת־עֵינֵי: Gk. "his eyes"; Vulg. and Syr. with MT.

17c–c. וְרֶכֶב אֵשׁ סְבִיבֹת: Gk. "and there was a chariot of fire surrounding"; Vulg. and Syr. with MT.

18. וַיַּכֵּם: Vulg. Adds "the Lord"; Gk. and Syr. with MT.

19a–a. לֹא זֶה הַדֶּרֶךְ וְלֹא זֹה הָעִיר: Gk. "this is not the city … the way"; Vulg. and Syr. with MT.

19b. זֹה: An Aramaic or N. Palestinian form.

20a–a. אֶת־עֵינֵי־אֵלֶּה: Gk. "their eyes"; Syr. "the eyes of these men"; Vulg. with MT.

21a. אֶל־אֱלִישָׁע: Gk. lacks "to Elisha"; Vulg. and Syr. with MT.

21b–b. הַאַכֶּה אַכֶּה אָבִי: Gk. "Striking shall I strike them, father?"; Vulg. "Shall I strike them, my father?"; Syr. "My father, shall I strike them, shall I strike them?"; MT best explains the others.

COMMENTARY

This narrative serves again to highlight the power of Yahweh as it flowed through Elisha. That power is superior to all human power, especially as typified by the two anonymous human kings. They are almost certainly Ben-hadad[182] and Joram,[183] but their identities are of no interest to the narrator. The point is to show that before Yahweh, and his prophet Elisha, all earthly power must bow. As it is, neither king comes off looking very good. The Syrian king, foolish enough to think that he can capture a man who knows what the king is saying in his bedroom (v. 12), receives his troops back as a very embarrassing gift, while the Israelite king is depicted as entirely dependent upon Yahweh's prophet both for protection and diplomatic wisdom.

Verses 8–10 describe the condition of on-going border war. The Syrians would lay ambushes for the Israelites, just as almost certainly the Israelites did for the Syrians. But the Israelites seemed remarkably effective at avoiding the Syrian traps. We, the readers, know why this was happening. It was because "the man of God" (אִישׁ הָאֱלֹהִים, *ʾîš hā ʾĕlōhîm*) (v. 9) was telling the king of Israel where not to go. The king was evidently unsure of the validity of the intelligence because he would send agents to check on it (v. 10). But in fact it turned out to be regularly—"not only once or twice" (לֹא אַחַת וְלֹא שְׁתָּיִם, *lōʾ ʾaḥat wᵉlōʾ šᵉtāyim*)—correct.

Some commentators wonder whether this activity on Elisha's part indicates a softening of his attitude toward the Omride kings, particularly in view of the radical turn of events in the following narrative (6:24–7:20). I do not think that Elijah was any less aware of Joram's real tendencies than were the prophets of Ahab's day when they offered that king divine protection from Syria (1 Kgs 20). Here, as there, this action represented Yahweh's care and concern for his people. It was also intended to demonstrate to the Omride kings that he was not their enemy, but that he was their friend, and that his judgments, when they came, were not intended to destroy them, but to cause them to abandon their pagan worship and turn to him alone. Unfortunately, it does not seem that any of Omri's descendants ever got that message.

At least one of the Syrian officers (perhaps Naaman?), also knew what was happening. Here is another instance where the lower levels in the hierarchy are more in touch with reality than the superior is (3:11; 5:3). The intelligence being given to the Israelite king was not the result of treachery,

182. For further discussion on Ben-hadad, see p. 147n208 on 6:24 below.

183. Some commentators (e.g., Gray, 516), taking the apparent ease with which the raiders reached Dothan as an indication of Israelite weakness, hypothesize that the event must have occurred later when Hazael had reduced Israel almost to a state of vassalage. But others (e.g., Fritz, 264) point out that this kind of back and forth raiding must have been a frequent affair between Israel and Syria throughout the ninth century.

but divinely given insight.[184] The occurrence of "inform" (נגד, *ngd*) in v. 11 is the first of eight occurrences in 6:8–7:20.[185] With its overtones of "revelation," the term is certainly being used to underline the whole theme of insight, understanding, and making known that is central to both these accounts. By contrast, the Syrian king seems to have had no insight at all. If we wish for an example of blindness, it is surely given to us in the Syrian king's idea that he can simply say "I will send and take" (וְאֶשְׁלַח וְאֶקָּחֵהוּ, *wᵊ ʾešlaḥ wᵊ ʾeqqāḥēhû*) (v. 13) for this man who already knows what the king is thinking. Ahaziah had had a similar idea, and the result was disastrous for those who tried to take Elijah (2 Kgs 1:10–12).

Dothan (v. 13) was located on the road from Jezreel, the Israelite kings' summer palace, located in the midst of the Jezreel Valley, to Samaria. It was about nine miles from Samaria in a straight line and about 12 miles by road. Dothan lay on the south edge of a fertile valley which gave access from the Jezreel Valley to the coastal plain.[186] Thus, it would have been fairly easy for a raiding party of "horses and chariots" (סוּסִים וְרֶכֶב, *sûsîm wᵊrekeḇ*) (v. 14) to have made a forced march through the night, crossing the Jordan near Beth-shean, and reaching Dothan at dawn, with the expectation of seizing their man, and hurrying back across the Jordan before the Israelites could mobilize to catch them. Fairly easy except for one glaring fact: Elisha.

Once again, the "attendant[187] of the man of God" (מְשָׁרֵת אִישׁ הָאֱלֹהִים, *mᵊšārēṯ ʾîš hā ʾĕlōhîm*), presumably Gehazi, serves as a foil to Elisha. He sees physical reality and is terrified (v. 15); but he cannot see spiritual reality, as Elisha can (v. 16). The Syrian armies have surrounded the city, but within their circle, "surrounding" (סְבִיבֹת, *sᵊḇîḇōṯ*) the actual mound ("the hill"; הָהָר, *hāhār*) upon which the city stood, were "horses and chariots of fire" (סוּסִים וְרֶכֶב אֵשׁ, *sûsîm wᵊrekeḇ ʾēš*) like those that had appeared when Elijah was taken up to heaven (2:11–12).[188] The spiritual reality was that Elisha, and Gehazi,

---

184. Some commentators (e.g., Gray, 515) suggest that the reference to "bedchamber" means that Elisha had spies in the Syrian court. But surely the whole point of the account is to demonstrate that Yahweh has the power to enable his servants to "see" and "reveal" what is not normally possible. On the meaning of "for the king of Israel" see Max Frederick Rogland, "Pro or Contra?; 2 Kings 6:11," *Presb* 27 (2001): 56–58.

185. 6:11, 12, 13; 7:9, 10, 11, 12, 15.

186. Brueggemann notes that the giving of this location, which has no particular relevance to the account, is "one of the concrete particularities that marks Biblical narrative" (345).

187. The word מְשָׁרֵת, *mᵊšārēṯ* is unusual enough that it has been proposed to emend it (cf. *BHS*). However, as Cogan and Tadmor note, there is no support for any emendation in the versions, and the term occurs with נַעַר *na ʿar* (as here in v. 15) elsewhere (4:34, 38; 2 Sam 13:17).

188. Rachel Gilmour, "A Note on the Horses and Chariots of Fire at Dothan," *ZAW* 125 (2013): 308–13.

were protected by Yahweh. Elisha saw this, but Gehazi could only see (v. 17) when Elisha specifically prayed that Yahweh would make this happen. Spiritual insight is a divine gift. That prayer did not always precede Elisha's miracles (see only 4:33) indicates that Elisha's access to divine power and insight was not a formulaic matter. The variety of ways in which these miracles occurred demonstrates the freedom and mutuality of the relationship between Yahweh and his man.

When the Syrian raiders moved forward to capture Dothan[189] they did not encounter fiery enemies, but they did encounter spiritual power against which they were helpless. Again, Elisha prayed. But this time it was to close eyes (v. 18). The term used here (סַנְוֵרִים, *sanwērîm*) is not the normal one for blindness (see Deut 28:28; Zech 12:4). This term only occurs here and in Genesis 19:11, with a probable meaning of "to dazzle with a bright light."[190] Thus some commentators suggest that the Syrians' vision was only distorted and give their ability to follow Elisha to Samaria as evidence of that. Be that as it may, they were blind enough that they did not know where they had come to until Elisha prayed for a third time, and their eyes were opened, and they realized with a shock that it was Samaria (v. 20).[191]

If the text of v. 21 is correct (see p. 137n179 on the translation), the Israelite king is presented as being in a flurry of excitement. His words are falling over each other. This is somewhat understandable. Elisha has come "out of nowhere," as it were, leading a considerable force of stupefied Syrians. What to do with a windfall like that? But surprise aside, we do not see someone in control of himself or the situation. He seems to blurt out the first thing that comes to mind: enemies? Kill them! It is possible, as Long (336) observed, that Joram remembers that his father was condemned for not killing Ben-hadad (1 Kgs 20:35–43) and wants to avoid the same fate. But that does not seem very likely. He is simply out of control. It is Elisha who is in control. He calmly informs the king that these Syrians are not his to do with as he wishes. He did not capture them, and he may not kill them. Verse 22 may be construed in two different ways. It may be taken as a question asking whether the king would have killed them if he had captured them, or it could be assuming a conditional element: would he kill them *as though* he had captured them? In either case, they are not his captives, they are Yahweh's, and Yahweh decrees that they should be fed and sent back to their king. Since the text does not explain the reason for this magnanimous act, commentators have been free

---

189. For אֶל, *'el*, normally "to," as "against" see 1 Sam 17:8; 2 Sam 23:21.

190. Cf. *HALOT* (760–61).

191. This is the third use of the particle הִנֵּה, *hinneh* in this passage (vv. 13, 15). Regularly translated as "behold" in KJV, it is often left untranslated in modern Eng. versions. It has a similar function to the phrase "and there was" emphasizing the discovery of something by the subject of the narrative. Its triple use here almost certainly has to do with the key theme of insight and revelation.

to propose a variety of explanations.[192] One or two points should be made, however. First, this was not "holy war" in which captives would be killed as a sacrifice to God. In ordinary warfare such as this is, captives could be expected to be ransomed or exchanged. In that context, they were too valuable a commodity to be destroyed. That is what is unusual here: nothing was gained from the possession of this "commodity." Second, in this context (6:8–7:20) where Yahweh is being "revealed" as God of the world, sending these men back would be a very direct message to the Syrian king: Yahweh is not only all-powerful, he is so powerful that he can afford to be beneficent. Thus, it is not surprising if that king concluded that raids were not going to be worth it (v. 23b), and that if he was ever going to defeat his Israelite enemies, he was going to have to do it with overwhelming force (6:24).

Biblical Theology Comments

As noted above, both this account and the following one, but especially this one, are about sight, insight, and the reporting of what has been seen. Here, Elisha is able to see where the Syrians will be hiding and to report (v. 12) their location to the king. The king of Syria wants his men to report (v. 11) to him who the betrayer is. Then he wants them to "see" (v. 13) where the prophet is, and the information is reported (v. 13) to him. Elisha's servant sees the enemy horses and chariots (v. 15), but he is unable to see the heavenly ones, until he is supernaturally enabled as a result of prayer (v. 17). The Syrians lose their ability to see as a result of prayer (v. 18) and do not regain it until again they are prayed for (v. 20). Then they see the man they are looking for, but it is too late.[193] The king of Israel sees them (v. 21) but chooses the wrong alternative of action. Then we may assume that the Syrian soldiers made a full report of what they had "seen" in Israel.

Throughout the Bible, this combination of insight, especially spiritual insight, coupled with the reporting of what has been seen, is a central idea. Joseph was supernaturally enabled to see what the pharaoh's dreams were about and to report to him what they meant (Gen 41:25). But beyond incidents like this (see also Dan 7:1), there is the entire fabric of thought.

---

192. E.g., Ronnie Goldstein, "The Provision of Food to the Aramean Captives in II Reg 6,22–23," *ZAW* 126 (2014): 101–05.

193. Cohn (44, followed by Long, 336) argues that the account is arranged chiastically around the theme of seeing, as follows:

A Syrian raids
 B King of Aram wishes to see
  C Yahweh opens eyes of Elisha's servant
   X Yahweh blinds eyes of Syrian army
  C' Yahweh opens eyes of Syrian army
 B' King of Israel sees
A' Syrian raids stop

Persons who were enabled to "see" what God was revealing about reality were expected to make known what they had seen. The Bible exists because of this combination: men and women were inspired both to see and tell. This is all stated most explicitly in the NT. So John is to be told what his disciples have seen and heard (Luke 7:22); the Son of Man bears witness to what he has seen and heard (John 3:32); the apostles could not help but speak about what they had seen and heard (Acts 4:20), nor could Paul (Acts 22:15). Finally, John expresses the point most clearly: that which we have seen and heard we proclaim to you (1 John 1:3). God has broken into the experience of his creatures, making his own nature and the nature of reality visible and they can do nothing else but to inform others what they have experienced.

Selected Bibliography

Brueggemann, W. "The Embarrassing Footnote," *ThTo* 44 (1987): 5–14.
Rhee, S. "Second Kings 6:8–23." *Int* 54 (2000): 183–85.

Famine in Samaria (6:24–7:20)

Translation

6:24 Now after this, Ben-hadad, king of Syria, gathered up all his army and went up and besieged Samaria. **25** There was a great famine in Samaria, and they continued besieging it until the head of a donkey was worth eighty pieces of silver, and a fourth of a qab of dove dung was worth five pieces.[194] **26** The king of Israel was passing by one the wall, and a woman cried out to him, saying, "Deliver, my lord, the king." **27** He said, "If[195] Yahweh has not delivered you, how can I deliver you? From the threshing floor? From the winepress?" **28** The king said to her, "What is your trouble?" She said, "This woman said to me, 'Give your son, and let us eat him today, and we will eat my son tomorrow.' **29** So we cooked my son and ate him. Then I said to her on the next day, 'Give your son so we can eat him' but she hid her son." **30** When the king heard the woman's words, he tore his clothes. Since he was passing by on the wall, the people saw, and there was sackcloth next to his skin underneath. **31** He said, "May God do so[196] and more to me if the head of Elisha ben Shaphat remains on him today."

32 Now Elisha was sitting in his house, and the elders were sitting with him. He had sent a man from his presence, but[197] before the messenger came

---

194. Most Eng. versions read "eighty shekels ... five shekels," but whereas "shekels" are specified in 7:1, 18, they are not here. The assumption is not unreasonable, but it is not explicit.

195. There is no conditional particle present; the conditionality is implied. See GKC (§§159*b*–*k*).

196. Perhaps accompanied by a gesture, so *IBHS* (§40.2.2a).

197. There is no conjunction in Heb. Whether the appearance of a conjunction in Vulg. and Syr. indicates the presence of a *waw* in their *vorlage*, or whether they only understood the conjunctive idea to be implied is unclear.

to him, he said to the elders, "Do you see that this son of a murderer has sent to remove my head? See here, when the messenger comes, bar the door and hold him out.[198] Is not the sound of the feet of his master behind him?" **33** While he was still speaking with them, here came the messenger down to him. He said, "This calamity is from Yahweh. Why should I put hope in Yahweh anymore?" **7:1** Elisha said, "Hear the word of Yahweh: thus says Yahweh, 'At this time tomorrow, a seah of flour can be had for a shekel, and two seahs of barley for a shekel in the gate of Samaria.' " **2** The officer upon whose hand the king leaned answered the man of God and said, "Even if[199] Yahweh makes windows in heaven, could this thing happen?" He said, "Look here, you are going to see it with your eyes, but you will not eat any of it."

3 Now four men who had leprosy were at the entrance to the gate. They said to each other, "Why are we sitting here until we die? **4** If we say, 'Let us go into the city,' famine is in the city and we will die there. But if we remain here, we will die. So now, come, let us defect to the camp of the Syrians. If they let us live, we will live, and if they kill us, we will only die."[200] **5** So they got up at twilight to go to the camp of the Syrians. They came to the edge of the camp of the Syrians and, look here, not a man was there! **6** The Sovereign[201] had made the Syrian army hear the sound of horses, and the sound of chariots, and the sound of a mighty force, and they said to each other, "Look here, the king of Israel has hired the kings of the Hittites and the kings of Egypt to come against us." **7** So they got up and fled in the twilights and left their tents and their horses and their donkeys, and the camp just as it was, and fled for their lives. **8** So these lepers, having come to the edge of the camp, went into a tent and ate and drank and gathered up silver and gold and clothes, and went and hid them. Then they went back and came to another tent, and they took from there and went and hid it. **9** Then they said to each other, "We should not be doing thus. Today is a day of good news. If we keep silent and wait until the morning light, we will be found guilty.[202] So now, come on, let us go and inform the house of the king. **10** So they went and called

---

198. Lit. "and press him by the door" (וּלְחַצְתֶּם אֹתוֹ בַּדֶּלֶת, *ûlᵉḥaṣtem ʾōṯô baddeleṯ*). Gk. "detain him at the door"; Vulg. "do not permit him to enter"; Syr. "push him outside."

199. For this construal of הִנֵּה *hinneh*, see *IBHS* (§40.2.1d); on the implied question, see GKC (§159*i*).

200. GKC (§112*ff*) says that the *wqtl* used in this way adds emphasis: "we can only die."

201. This is not the divine name. Many medieval MSS do have it. Unfortunately, it is impossible to tell what the ancient versions had before them, because they always represent both the divine name and *ʾadonai* with "Lord."

202. Lit. "guilt will find us" (מְצָאָנוּ עָוֺן, *mᵉṣāʾānû ʿāwwōn*).

to the gatekeepers[203] of the city and informed them, saying, "We went to the Syrian camp, and look, there is no one there, not a single human voice. But the horses are tied, and the donkeys are tied, and the tents are as they were." **11** The gatekeepers called[204] and informed the house of the king inside. **12** So the king got up in the night and said to his servants, "Let me inform you what the Syrians have done to us. They know we are famished, so they have gone out from the camp to hide in the field, saying, 'When they come out of the city, we will take them alive and go into the city.' " **13** Then one of his servants replied and said, "Let them take five of the remaining horses that remain in it—look, they are all like the mass of Israel that is finished—let us send them off and let us see."[205] **14** So they took two chariot horses and the king sent them out to the Syrian camp, saying, "Go and see."[206] **15** They went after them as far as the Jordan, and look, the whole way was full of clothes and implements they had thrown aside in their haste. So the messengers returned and informed the king. **16** The people went out and sacked the Syrian camp. So it happened that a seah of flour went for a shekel and two seahs of barley for a shekel according to the word of Yahweh.

17 Now the king appointed the officer on whose hand he leaned to be in charge of the gate and the people trampled him in the gate and he died as the man of God had said when the king came down to him. **18** It was when the man of God had spoken to him, saying, "Two seahs of barley will go for a shekel and a seah of flour for a shekel at this time tomorrow," **19** and the officer had replied to the man of God and said, "Even if Yahweh makes windows in heaven, could this thing happen?" He said, "Look, you are going to see it with your eyes, but you will not eat any of it." **20** And so it happened to him: the people trampled him in the gate and he died.

Textual Notes

25a–a. בִּשְׁמֹנִים כֶּסֶף: Gk. "50 shekels"; Vulg. and Syr. with MT.

26a. הוֹשִׁיעָה: Vulg. and Syr. add 1st person sing. pron.; Gk. with MT.

27a–a. אַל־יוֹשִׁעֵךְ יְהוָה: Gk. and Syr. "No, may the Lord deliver you"; Vulg. with MT.

---

203. Heb. "the gate" (שֹׁעֵר, *šōʿēr*) but the pl. pron. following (לָהֶם, *lāhem*) requires that it be construed as pl. ptcp. The consonantal text would require the addition of a י (*yodh*).

204. This vb. (וַיִּקְרָא, *wayyiqrāʾ*) is sing. in Heb. All the versions render it as a pl.

205. In MT "which remains in it, look, they are all like the mass of Israel" (נִשְׁאֲרוּ־בָהּ הִנָּם כְּכָל־הֶהָמוֹן יִשְׂרָאֵל אֲשֶׁר, *nišʾărû-ḇāh hinnām kᵉḵāl-hehāmôn yiśrāʾēl ʾăšer*) is repeated twice. Both Gk. and Vulg. omit the repetition, and although Syr. paraphrases the passage, it does not include the repetition either. It appears to be a clear dittography.

206. A possible alternative could be "two [men] mounted on horses."

27b–b. הֲמִן־הַגֹּרֶן אוֹ מִן־הַיָּקֶב: Gk. "Surely not from the threshing floor and not from the winepress"; Vulg. and Syr. with MT.

31. וַיֹּאמֶר: Vulg. Adds "the king"; Gk. and Syr. with MT.

31b–b. בֶּן־שָׁפָט: Gk. omits; Vulg. and Syr. with MT.

32a. בְּטֶרֶם Vulg. and Syr. add a conjunction; Gk with MT.

33a. יֹרֵד Vulg. and Syr. "came"; Gk with MT.

7:6a. וַאדֹנָי: Many Heb. MSS have ויהוה.

6b–b. אֶת־מַלְכֵי הַחִתִּים וְאֶת־מַלְכֵי מִצְרַיִם: Syr. reverses these; Gk. and Vulg. with MT.

8a. וַיַּטְמִנוּ: Gk. omits; Vulg. and Syr. with MT.

10a. אֶל־שֹׁעֵר: Gk. and Vulg. "gate"; Syr. "gatekeepers." Virtually all modern Eng. versions opt for "gatekeepers" on the basis of the plural suffix in the next clause.

10b–b. אִם־הַסּוּס אָסוּר וְהַחֲמוֹר אָסוּר: Gk. "a tied horse and a tied donkey"; Vulg. and Syr. with MT.

10c. וְאֹהָלִים: Gk. "their tents"; Vulg. and Syr. with MT.

11a. וַיִּקְרָא: The versions all construe this vb. as pl.

12a. הַמֶּלֶךְ: Vulg. omits; Gk. and Syr. with MT.

13a–a. אֲשֶׁר נִשְׁאֲרוּ־בָהּ הִנָּם כְּכָל־הֶהָמוֹן יִשְׂרָאֵל: Gk. and Vulg. omit; cf. Syr. MT probably a dittography. *CTAT* (389–90) considers the versions possibly correct.

14a. רֶכֶב: Gk. and Syr. "mounted"; Vulg. omits. *HALOT* (1233) understands רֶכֶב as mounted but mounted in a chariot.

17a. הַמֶּלֶךְ: Gk. "messenger" (cf. 6:33); Syr. "when he [the king?] came down as a messenger; Vulg. with MT.

19a. כַּדָּבָר: The versions all omit כ (cf. v. 2). MT probably an error.

20a. כֵּן: Vulg. adds "as was predicted" which seems to be supported by 6QReg; Gk. and Syr. with MT.

Commentary

This unit is the second of the encounters between the Syrians and Yahweh by means of Elisha (after 6:9–23). Like the first, it should have served to convince Joram of the absolute sovereignty of Yahweh and moved him to a full and complete surrender to Yahweh as the only God and the only hope of Israel. But there is no evidence that it did so. In fact, the doubt and resulting destruction of the officer "upon whose arm he [the king] leaned" (אֲשֶׁר־נִשְׁעָן עַל־יָדוֹ, *ʾăšer-nišʿān ʿal-yāḏô*) (7:2, 17) seems to be an ominous foreboding of the king's own attitude as well as his end and that of his dynasty.

There are four divisions in the unit: 6:24–31; 6:32–7:2; 7:3–16; 7:17-20. After the first sub-unit, each of the others is marked by a disjunctive *waw* attached to a noun at the beginning of a clause, marking a change in subject: Elisha, the four lepers, and the king. It rivals the story of the Shunammite for detail and narrative quality. It moves from tragedy to comedy and concludes with solemn force.[207]

As in the previous narrative (6:8–23), the recurrence of verbs of seeing (6:30, 32; 7:2, 13, 14, 19) and of the call to see: הִנֵּה, *hinneh* (7:2, 5, 6, 10, 15, 19) are intended to focus the reader's attention on the necessity of spiritual insight and the tragic lack of such a thing in the Omride dynasty.

6:24 It appears that "Ben-hadad" was a Syrian throne name, and that there are three persons bearing that name in the Bible. Ben-hadad I was a contemporary of Baasha of Israel and Asa of Judah (1 Kgs 15:18, ca. 900 BC). Ben-hadad III was a son of Hazael (2 Kings 13:3, 24–25) and contemporary with Jehoash of Israel and Joash of Judah (ca. 800 BC). The king mentioned here is Ben-hadad II, who would have been reigning ca. 850 BC.[208] If there was any reason for the siege apart from sheer aggression, it is not given.

25 The siege was having its desired effect, with the inhabitants being starved to the point where submission might be the only option. Most commentators[209] believe that "dove's dung" (חֲרֵי יוֹנִים, *ḥărê yônîm*) is the name given to a species of carob seed that is edible but has a very unpleasant taste. However, the point of the statement is to say that the starvation was so severe that even

207. Cogan and Tadmor compare the ending to that of a sermon (84n1).

208. Several commentators (e.g., Cogan and Tadmor, 84, and Gray, 518), note that the king of Israel is not named here, and believe that there were somewhat amicable relations between Syria and Israel during the time of Joram, have argued that these events must have taken place at the end of Jehoahaz' reign or at the beginning of the reign of Jehoash, when Syria regularly humbled Israel, and that this Ben-hadad is the one mentioned in 2 Kgs 13. However, these arguments are very inconclusive. Although Syria and Israel were allies in the battle of Qarqar in 854 BC, such alliances were notably fragile. Furthermore, Jehoash was able to defeat Ben-hadad several times (2 Kgs 13:25). It is clear in the overall context that we are intended to think of Joram. See Sweeney, 310.

209. E.g., Gray, 522; Fritz, 269; Long, 337; House, 278.

the most horrid things were being sold at incredible prices.[210] The following story of cannibalism only underlines the dreadful situation. Thus, the reference to dove's dung may be entirely literal.[211]

26–31 This segment is introduced by the narrative element וַיְהִי (*wayᵊhi*). Like many other biblical narratives, especially those in the book of Judges, the narrator achieves his effect with no moralizing or explanation. He tells the story in a straightforward way, so that we readers are horrified by the evident moral paralysis which the famine has inflicted on the woman in the account. She does not seem troubled that she and her companion have eaten her son, she is only outraged that the other woman has not fulfilled her side of the bargain and given up her son. The probability that the two boys were already dead and that it was the corpses that were to be eaten only slightly mitigates our shock.[212]

26–27 The king was probably looking over the state of the defenses, although it is a bit surprising that he was doing this for himself, and not through some agent. Perhaps he needed to get out of the palace and do something to get his mind off the awful prospect. The woman saw her chance to demand that the king do what kings were supposed to do: dispense justice. The verb translated here as "deliver" (הוֹשִׁיעָה, *hôšî ʿâ*) can also be translated "save" and may have been used intentionally by the narrator. In any case, it highlights the dilemma: the king cannot save his people; only *Yahweh* can do that. The king's despair is revealed in his outburst to the woman. Thinking she is asking for food, he rails at her. Where is he to get food? "From the threshing floor or from the winepress" (הֲמִן־הַגֹּרֶן אוֹ מִן־הַיָּקֶב, *hămin-haggōren ʾô min-hayyāqeḇ*)?

28–31 The king recovers himself enough to inquire more formally what the woman's request is, and the terrible truth is revealed. As Long (338) observes, Elisha had made the same inquiry to the Shunammite woman, and this fact highlights the difference between the prophet's ability to solve that woman's

---

210. There is no agreement about the volume of a kab. Rabbinic sources say it was one sixth of an ephah, but opinions about the volume of an ephah vary. The kab may have equaled about two quarts. The fact that in normal times the price of a slave was thirty shekels gives some idea of the inflated charges here. See Jonas C. Greenfield, "Dove's Dung and the Price of Food: The Topoi of II Kings 6:24–7:2," in *Storia e tradizioni di Israele: scritti in onore di J. Alberto Soggin,* ed. Danielle Garrone (Brescia: Paideia Editrici, 1991): 123–25.

211. So Hobbs, 79 and Provan, 202. Sweeney thinks it could be either possibility (311).

212. On this incident, see Gina Hens-Piassa, "Forms of Violence and the Violence of Forms: Two Cannibal Mothers Before a King (2 Kings 6:24–33)," *JFSR* 14 (1998): 91–104; Stuart Lasine, "Jehoram and the Cannibal Mothers (2 Kings 6:24–33)," *JSOT* 50 (1991): 27–53.

problem, and the king's inability to do anything for his people here.[213] His horror and despair over what has befallen his people causes the king to tear his tunic (v. 30), and because he was "walking on the wall" (עֹבֵר עַל־הַחֹמָה, *ʿōḇēr ʿal-haḥōmâ*) in plain view, the people could see that he was wearing "sackcloth" (שַׂק, *śaq*), a hair shirt, next to his skin. When this fact is taken together with his outburst in the next verse, it seems clear that he is an example of what the apostle James calls "a double-minded man" (Jas 1:8). On the one hand, he is wearing a classic symbol of repentance and penitence (see 1 Kgs 20:31; 1 Chr 21:16; Neh 9:1, Lam 2:10); yet, on the other, he determines to kill Elisha, taking the same oath his mother Jezebel had when she sought to destroy Elijah (1 Kgs 19:2). This latter fact raises the distinct possibility that he was not penitent at all but was simply in mourning over what he thought was imminent destruction (see Gen 37:34; 2 Sam 3:31; 21:10; Esth 4:1). In short, he was as helpless before what lay ahead as his people were.[214]

His outburst against Elisha (v. 31) is surprising, and again seems to indicate serious instability. Did he think that Elisha, having previously protected Israel from Syrian depredations, had failed in his responsibility? Or did he, in the classic stance of the person who distrusts Yahweh, think that this disaster had come upon him because Elisha, and more importantly, Yahweh, "had it in for" him? That was his position in chap. 3 and seems not to have changed materially since. Whereas a person of faith would humbly submit, believing that Yahweh has only good intentions toward him or her and would somehow work for good through this terrible thing (so Hezekiah, 2 Kgs 19:1–4,14–19), Joram could only lash out at the man who was, as House says (278), "his best friend." Obviously, he was not thinking clearly; what would killing Elisha accomplish, except cut off the king from his one potential source of help?

6:32–7:3 While this turmoil was taking place in the city. Elisha was quietly "sitting in his house" (וֶאֱלִישָׁע יֹשֵׁב בְּבֵיתוֹ, *we ʾĕlîšāʿ yōšēḇ bᵉḇêṯô*) with "the elders" (הַזְּקֵנִים, *hazzᵉqēnîm*). Perhaps the elders of the city understood what the king did not, namely that Yahweh's intentions toward them were good, and that they needed to hear from God as to how they should address the situation. But it is also possible that they were on the pattern of the elders in the book of Ezekiel who saw the prophet as something of a smooth-talking magician whose powers they could access (Ezek 14:1; 20:1). In any case, they were witnesses to Elisha's ability to see the future as he told them what was about to happen. The "son of the murderer [Ahab]" (בֶּן־הַמְרַצֵּחַ, *ben-hamᵉraṣṣēaḥ*) (1 Kgs 18:4) was about to follow in his father's and mother's footsteps and had sent a messenger to seize him. The elders are told by Elisha to bar the

213. For other refs. to cannibalism, see Deut 28:56–57; Lam 2:20; 4:10; Ezek 5:10.
214. Brueggemann points out that the king expresses no concern for the woman at all, but simply lashes out at Elisha (357).

door against the messenger until the king should arrive, the sound of whose footsteps were right behind the messenger's (v. 32).[215]

Since the antecedent of "he said" (יֹּאמֶר, *yō ʾmer*) is not defined in v. 33, it is not entirely clear whose words they are. Hobbs (80–81) thinks they are Elisha's, and while it is possible the first sentence might be his, it makes no sense for the question to be his. It seems clear that these are Joram's words, either spoken directly by him, or quoted by his messenger.[216] As discussed previously, Joram could only believe that Yahweh was against him. Thus, it was foolish to put any trust in him, as perhaps Elisha had been encouraging him to do. The word here translated "put hope in" is יחל (*yḥl*) which, along with קוה (*qwh*) and חכה (*ḥkh*), is regularly translated "wait." But unlike the English "wait," which merely speaks of spending time, all three of these words connote confident expectation. Thus, they are synonyms of "put hope in" and "trust."[217] Joram refuses to trust that Yahweh could, or would, do anything to help him (cf. Isa 30:18).

Elisha's response to this word of despair is an oracle of salvation introduced with the formal: "Hear the word of Yahweh; thus says Yahweh" (שִׁמְעוּ דְּבַר־יהוה כֹּה אָמַר יהוה, *šim ʿû dᵊbar-yhwh kō ʾāmar yhwh*) (7:1).[218] But what he promised seemed frankly impossible: could a seah (perhaps a bushel) of flour, or two seahs of barley possibly sell tomorrow for one eightieth of what a rotting donkey's head would sell today? If the king's right-hand man[219]

---

215. There is some confusion among interpreters here because this verse and the next mention the messenger (מלאך, *ml ʾk*) while the presence of the king can only be inferred from the reference to the king's officer in 7:2. However, in the recounting of the incident in 7:18, it is said the prophet spoke to the king (מלך, *mlk*). Thus, some recommend emending the text in v. 33 to *mlk*. But there is no textual evidence in support of such a change. We may imagine that just as Elisha said, the king was right behind his messenger, perhaps to ensure that the wily prophet did not get away from the messenger, that when the king arrived, the door was opened to him, Elisha made his pronouncement about the events of the next day, and the king was just superstitious enough to give him that day's grace. 2 Kgs 7:18 thus makes explicit what is implicit here.

216. NIV and NLT both supply "king"; whereas NRSV emends "messenger" to "king." See the previous note.

217. For יָחַל, *yāḥal* see Ps 42:5[6], 11[12]; 43:5; 130:5; Lam 3:21.

218. The only other place where this double form appears is Ezek 20:47.

219. The title is literally "the third" (הַשָּׁלִישׁ, *haššālîš*). It is not clear what the significance is. An older suggestion was that it is derived from the third man in the chariot, a spear man whose task was possibly to protect the archer and the driver. More recent commentators have tended to reject the idea, largely because the three-man chariot was not common in the ANE. Another suggestion is that this person is the third person in the hierarchy, perhaps only behind the prime minister. The ref. to "leaning on the hand of" is found only here and in 2 Kgs 5:18. In any case, a close confidant.

responded with mocking incredulity (v. 2), we can at least understand the reaction. It is not clear what was intended by "makes windows in heaven," (עֹשֶׂה אֲרֻבּוֹת בַּשָּׁמַיִם, *ʿōśe ʾărubbôṯ baššāmayim*). One possibility was that it referred to abundant rainfall resulting in bumper crops (cf. Gen 7:11). Another is that it spoke of God dropping supplies out of those windows. Yet another possibility is that it is simply speaking of something patently impossible. For example: "Even if God did something impossible, this thing you have said, Elisha, is still more impossible."[220] As mentioned above, it seems very likely that this officer who is so close to the king is to be understood as speaking the king's own sentiments. Elisha's response is just six words in Hebrew, two of which have to do with seeing: "Look here, you will see it, but you won't eat it!" (הִנְּכָה רֹאֶה בְּעֵינֶיךָ וּמִשָּׁם לֹא תֹאכֵל, *hinnᵉḵâ rōʾeh bᵉʿênêḵā ûmiššām lōʾ ṯōʾḵēl*). In short, he would gain no benefit from his experience. Again, we have to believe that this is a word for an unbelieving dynasty.

7:3–11 The narrator now changes from the rather grim and somber tones preceding to a lighter note. As has been frequent throughout these narratives, it is among those in the lower parts of society, and here, even among the outcasts, that genuine perception and insight occur.[221] The king has no good news of deliverance to share, and even when it comes, will not believe it, but these four, who have nothing more to lose, are the ones who have the chance to carry the unbelievable news of miraculous salvation.

It is not clear exactly where the lepers[222] were when the story begins. "The entrance to the gate" (פֶּתַח הַשָּׁעַר, *peṯaḥ haššāʿar*) (v.3) might be inside or out. The "gate" would have been a multi-level structure with three or more sets of doors on the lower level through which came the main access to the city. Between these sets of doors were chambers where troops could be stationed during an attack. There would also have been small sally-ports through which small groups of armed men could rush out for raiding attacks.[223] So these four men may have been in one of the chambers of the gate complex while they held their discussion. It seems unlikely that they would have been outside since they would already have been dead of starvation and exposure. So what to do (v. 4)? They could leave the gate and go back into the city, but that would only mean death; they could stay where they are, but that would mean death also. So why not go out through one of the sally-ports and defect[224] to the Syrians? What would be the worst that could happen?

See B. A. Mastin, "Was the *šālîš* the Third Man in the Chariot?" in *Studies in the Historical Books of the Old Testament*, VTSupp 30 (Leiden: Brill, 1979): 125–54.

220. On "windows of heaven" see Isa 24:18; Mal 3:10.

221. 2 Kgs 3:11; 5:2; 6:12; 7:13.

222. See the note on 5:1 for a discussion of this disease and what it entailed.

223. For a plan and photograph of such a gate, see Yigael Yadin, *The Art of Warfare in Biblical Lands,* 2 vols. (New York; McGraw-Hill, 1963), 2:370–71.

224. Lit. "fall." For this use of the word, see 1 Sam 29:3; Jer 38:19.

They would die. But maybe, just maybe, the Syrians would let them live. Why they thought that the Syrians would have any use for lepers is part of the humor of the situation.

"Twilight" (נֶשֶׁף, *nešep̄*) (v. 5)[225] could serve their purposes from two directions: it would be hard for the gatekeepers to see them going, and it would be equally hard for the Syrian sentries to see them coming. So they crept up to the "edge of the camp" (עַד־קְצֵה מַחֲנֵה, *ʿaḏ-qᵊṣēh maḥănē*), perhaps hoping to evade the sentries, when they made the shocking discovery: "Look, nobody's here!" (וְהִנֵּה אֵין־שָׁם אִישׁ, *wᵊhinnēh ʾên-šām ʾîš*). The narrator then has us step back from the shock while he gives us the explanation (vv. 6–7). This was Yahweh's doing. He had "made the camp of the Arameans [Syrians] hear the sound" (הִשְׁמִיעַ אֶת־מַחֲנֵה אֲרָם קוֹל, *hišmîaʿ ʾeṯ-maḥănē ʾărām qôl*) of an approaching army[226] and they had panicked, drawing a perfectly reasonable, but quite wrong, conclusion. The Syrians said, "Look" (הִנֵּה, *hinnēh*), but they really were blinded, and so they left everything as it was, not taking time to harness the chariot horses or load the donkeys "and fled for their lives" (וַיָּנוּסוּ בְנֶשֶׁף, *wayyānûsû ḇannešep̄*).

Our heroes, back at the edge of the camp (v. 8) apparently did not take any time to explore further and verify the situation but fell to at once. Their feverish haste is indicated by the appearance of no less than twelve verbs in this verse: (1) they came, (2) they went in, (3) they ate, (4) they drank, (5) they took, (6) they went, (7) they hid, (8) they came back, (9) they entered, (10) they took, (11) they went, and (12) they hid. We can almost hear them gasping for breath as they fall to the ground after the second hiding of the typical material/objects of wealth: silver, gold, and fine clothing (the same things Naaman brought with him to pay off Elisha; 5:5).

But then something dawned on them (v. 9): come morning the situation will be apparent to the whole city and they "will be found guilty" (וּמְצָאָנוּ עָווֹן, *ûmᵊṣāʾānû ʿāwwōn*)[227] of having kept this good news to themselves (along with who knows what else) all night. If there is to be any hope of not raising suspicions and thus keeping the valuables that they hid, they must sound the alert at once. They have seen something and now they must inform (נָגַד, *nāgad*, see the comments on 6:11–13) the king. Insight demands witness. So

225. For an argument that "first light" is intended, see Steven W. Holloway, "Antiochan Temporal Interpolations in 2 Kgs 6.24–7.20," *Bib* 78 (1997): 543–47.

226. By this time the once-great Hittite empire had been broken up into city-states in what is now northern Syria. These were quite capable of hiring themselves out as mercenaries. The Egyptians were much less available that far north at that time, but to people in a panic, logic is in short supply. For the demolition of the long-held theory that מִצְרַיִם, *miṣrayim,* "Egypt," should be emended to *muṣri*, a state in Cilicia (southern Turkey), see Cogan and Tadmor, 82.

227. Lit. "guilt will find us." This is the only time this noun is used as subj. of "find." For "sin" so used, see Num 32:23.

they went (v. 10) and informed the gatekeepers what they had "seen" (הִנֵּה, *hinneh*). The gatekeepers (v. 11) in turn informed the palace.

12–16 Now it is the king's turn to inform his courtiers and officers about what is going on. Unfortunately, he has it all wrong. His information, although plausible enough, is not based on sight, but upon speculation. As Cohn (52) points out, his "Let me inform you" (אַגִּידָה־נָּא לָכֶם, *ʾaggîḏā-nnāʾ lāḵem*) has the air of bluster about it. This is a man who needs to take charge of a situation that could shortly spin out of control. What he does not do is to take Elisha's prediction into account. It seems that he gave no more credence to it than his aide did. Thus, when faced with this incredible news, and feeling forced to give some explanation for it, he does not even consider the possibility that Yahweh has intervened in a miraculous way. Rather, he looks at it from a strictly naturalistic point of view.[228] He was ready to ascribe calamity to Yahweh, but it did not occur to him to think that blessing might come from him also.

Once again (v. 13), the solution must come, not from the leader, but from the lower ranks. One of the officers suggests that they could at least go and *see* (ראה, *rʾh*) what the actual situation was. Besides the apparent dittography in v. 13 (see p. 145n205–6 above on the translation of v. 13) there seems to be a discrepancy between it and v. 14. Verse 13 has the officer suggesting that "five of the remaining horses" be taken, whereas v. 14 says that they took "two chariot horses." If the text is correct (see n206 on the translation), perhaps it means that when they looked they could only find two horses, not five.

The scouts did "go and see" (לְכוּ וּרְאוּ, *lᵉḵû ûrᵊʾû*) (v. 14), and what they saw more than vindicated the four lepers. The route back to the Jordan was littered with things that had been abandoned as the panic became more severe the farther the Syrians went (v. 15). Two different routes were possible, one more direct, but more difficult, the other somewhat more circuitous, but easier. The direct route would be east to Shechem, then north to Tirzah, and east again down the Wadi Faria. The other would entail first going west then back northeast past Dothan and Jezreel to Beth-shean. This was the route the Syrian force that attempted to capture Elisha would have used both coming and going (6:8–23). Once again נָגַד, *nāgad* appears as the scouts return and inform the king of the real situation, as they have seen it. At this point the king lost all control of the city. The starving "people went out and sacked the Syrian camp" (וַיֵּצֵא הָעָם וַיָּבֹזּוּ אֵת מַחֲנֵה אֲרָם, *wayyēṣēʾ hāʿām wayyāḇōzzû ʾēṯ maḥănē ʾărām*) and as v. 17 makes clear, it was a stampede. The result was that Yahweh's word was fulfilled exactly as Elisha had said it. Flour and barley sold for a fraction of the cost at which detestable "food" had been selling. Yahweh had provided for his people.

---

228. Humanly speaking, the kind of ruse Joram imagined was very plausible. Joshua had done something similar at Ai (Josh 8:3–8); so also had Abimelech (Judg 9:42–45).

17–20 Here is the final character shift: "Now the king... " (וְהַמֶּלֶךְ, *wᵉhammelek*). We began with the king, then went to Elisha, then to the four lepers, and have now returned to the king. The king tried to keep control of the situation by putting the officer "upon whose hand he leaned" in charge of the gate. But in doing so, he signed the man's death warrant. What the officer had believed impossible he had seen to happen, and in happening he was crushed to death.

Commentators (e.g., Gray, 525) have suggested that since vv. 18–20 are so repetitive of what has been said already in the account they must be the work of a somewhat inept later editor. However, that need not have been the case. This becomes clear when we think of the probable function of the statements in the larger context. This incident is the last of the reports of Elisha's works on behalf of Yahweh in the context of the Omride dynasty. (See below on chap. 8 for the function of that chapter.) Thus, these verses may be seen as the final judgment on that dynasty (perhaps the reason why this final segment [17–20] begins with the king as subject). The dynasty had been given several revelations of Yahweh's incomparable power, as well as his desire to be benevolent to them. They had been encouraged to put their trust in him alone. But they had refused to do so. They had not truly seen what had been set before them, and they had not believed the message when they had been informed. Thus, the end had come. Elijah had announced it many years earlier (1 Kgs 20:20–21), but Yahweh had delayed it, and had graciously extended Elijah's ministry into that of Elisha, hoping for repentance and faith. But as these verses express in microcosm, there had been neither repentance nor faith, only mocking dismissal. The dynasty would die in a "stampede" (רמס, *rms*; cf. 2 Kgs 9–10).

Biblical Theology Comments

Throughout the Bible it is clear that suffering is inescapable. It is a given in this world as it is. Philosophers and theologians, as well as ordinary people, have wrestled with this fact for centuries. Several explanations can be offered, extending from divine predestination, through a world damaged by sin, to the denial of the existence of God. In fact, the Bible does not offer an explanation. This is most evident in the book of Job. Job demands that God explain himself, but God never does. He only asks Job if he, as a human, can explain the existence of the cosmos or if he could maintain it in existence. Obviously, the answer to both questions is "no," and Job humbly accepts the restoration that Yahweh offers.

If the Bible offers no explanation, it does offer a prescription. Suffering cannot be avoided, but it can be survived, and even overcome. The key, as it is indeed to every aspect of the human predicament, is in faith: belief resulting in action. The faith that the Bible calls for in regards suffering is two-fold. We are called to believe that Yahweh is all-powerful, and that he is good (or as the author of the book of Hebrews says, "the rewarder of them that seek him," Heb 11:6 KJV). It is clear that neither Joram nor the other members of his dynasty could believe either of these. They could not because they could never bring themselves to cast themselves unreservedly upon Yahweh. It is evident that both Ahab and Joram "believed" in Yahweh. That is, they believed he existed and that he should be revered in some sense. But it is equally evident that they never "believed" in him in that unreserved sense.

Thus, they are classic examples of what James calls "double-minded" (Jas 1:8). With one part of their "mind" they recognize the existence of Yahweh, but with another part of their "mind" they doubt his goodness. Thus, they are in a constant state of tension regarding him. Is he for them or against them? Does he really mean to do good to them or is he secretly plotting to destroy them? When he commands them to do something, is it really for their good, or is he secretly playing some other, deceptive game?

How different the picture painted by the apostle Paul in the eighth chapter of the book of Romans. In the first seventeen verses he portrays in the strongest terms a person who is single-minded. Through the power of the Holy Spirit (mentioned sixteen times) unleashed in the Christian believer's life, there is now a single "law" at work: "the law of the Spirit of life" (8:2). Such a person suffers just as much, and perhaps more, than other humans do, but with a completely different attitude. They no longer suspect that God is punishing them or that he "has it in for" them. They accept that suffering is part of a fallen world (vv. 18–23). But they find strength in their Savior to accept the suffering with grace, confident that Yahweh is so powerful and so good (as evidenced by what he has done for them in Christ) that he can accomplish good even through this trouble (v. 28). They wait in hope (vv. 24–25), confident that Yahweh will keep them and help them (vv. 29–30), even as he intercedes for them within his Triune nature (vv. 26–27). The result is the glad confidence that nothing, "no trouble, or hardship, or persecution or famine or nakedness or danger or sword" can "separate us from the love of Christ" (v. 35). This is the confidence of the single-minded human.

Selected Bibliography

Earl, D. "Moving beyond Grammatico-Historical Methods: The Value and Application of a Literary-Poetic Approach with Specific Reference to 2 Kings 6:24–7:20," *Evangel* 21 (2003): 66–77.

Lanner, L. "Cannibal Mothers and Me: A Mother's Reading of 2 Kings 6.24–7.20," *JSOT* 24 (1999): 107–16.

Matthews, V. H. "Taking Calculated Risks: The Story of the Cannibal Mothers (2 Kings 6:24–7:20)," *BTB* 43 (2013): 4–13.

The Shunammite's Land Restored (8:1–6)

Translation

8:1 Now Elisha had spoken to the woman the life of whose son he had restored, saying, "Get up, go, you and your household, and emigrate to wherever you wish,[229] because Yahweh has summoned a famine, and furthermore, it is coming for seven years." **2** So the woman got up and did according to the word of the man of God. She and her household went and stayed in the land of the Philistines for seven years. **3** It happened at the end of seven years that the woman returned from the land of the Philistines and she went to appeal to the king for her house and land. **4** Now the king was speaking to Gehazi, the servant of the man of God, saying, "Recount for me, please, all the great things which Elisha did." **5** It happened that while he was recounting to the king that he brought the dead to life, here was the woman whose son he had revived appealing to the king in regard to her house and land. So Gehazi said, "My lord, the king, this is the woman, and this is her son whom Elisha brought back to life." **6** So the king asked the woman and she confirmed it to him. So the king appointed an official for her, saying, "Restore all that belonged to her and all the revenue of her property from the day she left the land until now."

Textual Notes

1a. בָּא: Gk. takes as pf. 3ms "it came": Vulg. and Syr. take it as a ptcp. "it is coming."

2a–a. אִישׁ הָאֱלֹהִים: Gk. "Elisha"; Vulg. and Syr. with MT.

2b–b. שֶׁבַע שָׁנִים: Vulg. "many days"; Gk. and Syr. with MT.

3a. שָׂדָהּ: Gk. and Vulg. "fields"; Syr. with MT.

4a. אִישׁ־הָאֱלֹהִים: Gk. adds "Elisha"; Vulg. and Syr. with MT.

5a. הַמֵּת: Gk. reads "a dead son"; Vulg. and Syr with MT.

5b. הֶחֱיָה: Gk. adds "Elisha"; Vulg. and Syr. with MT.

5c. וְעַל־שָׂדָהּ: Gk. and Vulg. "fields"; Syr. with MT.

5d. אֲדֹנִי: Gk. "O Lord"; Vulg. and Syr. with MT.

6a. הַשָּׂדֶה: Vulg. "fields"; Gk. and Syr. with MT.

Commentary

This account concludes the discussion of Elisha's miracles on behalf of great and small, Israelite and non-Israelite, during the reign of Joram, the last of the Omride dynasty. Commentators differ widely as to its function and purpose. Hobbs (97) believes that it functions to redeem Joram's reputation in that he solves a problem created by Elisha. Brueggemann (365), on the other hand,

---

229. Heb. "now emigrate to where you will emigrate" (וְגוּרִי בַּאֲשֶׁר תָּגוּרִי, *wᵉgûrî ba ʾăšer tāgûrî*).

holds that its purpose is to demonstrate that Yahweh is in control of events through Elisha and not the king. Between these poles are a variety of similar and dissimilar opinions. I suggest, in line with Satterthwaite (23–26) and Cohn (55), that the incident has been consciously selected to conclude the series by underlining the authority of Elisha and bringing down the curtain on Joram.[230]

Elisha's absence from the account is significant, as is Joram's response. Elisha's last direct encounter with Joram was through his dead officer at the end of chapter 7. From that point he has nothing more to say to the man. In that vacuum, the king, who throughout his reign had manifested considerable ignorance of the prophet and his word, suddenly develops a new interest in who he was and what he did. But the best he can do is to engage the services of the less-than-ideal servant Gehazi to tell him about his master. Then, on the basis of the prophet's confirmed miraculous powers he, without a question, grants the appeal of the woman who had had direct contact with the great man. This is probably not a magnanimous act of justice, but the act of one who desperately hopes it is not too late to gain favor with the man who has indeed been the life of the kingdom. Unfortunately, it was too late.

1 Although Elisha is absent from the story proper, the account begins with, "Now Elisha" (וֶאֱלִישָׁע, *we ʾĕlîšāʿ*) fronted before the verb (דִּבֶּר, *dibber*). Though he is not present, he is the central character.[231] The "famine" (רָעָב, *rāʿāḇ*) mentioned here is possibly the same one mentioned in 4:38. It is also possible that it may have lain behind the famine in Samaria (6:25). However, the particular food shortage in the city there is explicitly attributed to the Syrian siege. We have no idea of the time sequence involved in Elisha's speaking to the Shunammite woman. Perhaps it was immediately after her son's restoration to life, or at some later date. In any case, it is a mark of the prophet's care for the woman and the fundamentally benevolent character of his ministry through the power of Yahweh. He sought to make life triumph over death whether by an instantaneous miracle or through a providential warning. If Yahweh brought hardship on the land as a result of its sins, his goal was not destruction, but repentance and refining (e.g., Amos 4:6–11).

2 The narrator gives us no explanation of the reason for the woman's choice to go to "the land of the Philistines." It may have been purely rational, given

230. Gilmour, *Juxtaposition and the Elisha Cycle,* 184–190 sees the function of the unit to be a softening of the character of Elisha and an improvement in the reputation of the king. But such an understanding contributes almost nothing to our understanding of the flow of the narrative, in particular as this unit stands between the judgment explicit in 6:24–7:20 and the appointment of Hazael in 8:7–15.

231. As Hobbs (101) points out *contra* Gray (529), there is no reason to think that this incident occurred after Elisha's death. Elisha did not make himself available to the king on demand.

that even when the rain does not fall in the highlands, it is rarely absent on the coastal plain, where the Philistines lived. On the other hand, since the Philistines, like the Syrians, were frequently the enemies of Israel and Judah (1 Sam 17:1; 2 Sam 28:4; etc.), her choice may have been prompted by Yahweh to demonstrate once more that he is the God of the whole world, not merely Israel. Such traveling to other areas to escape famine is a feature of the biblical narrative (Abraham, Gen 12:10; Jacob Gen 41:57: 46:1; Naomi and Abimelech, Ruth 1:1).

3 The lack of any mention of the woman's husband has been taken by many commentators (e.g., Hobbs, 100; Wiseman, 212) to indicate that he had died by this time and that she was a widow attempting to regain her husband's ancestral lands.[232] Cogan and Tadmor (88) dispute this, arguing that as a "great" woman (4:8), she had probably held the property in her own name, perhaps as an inheritance (Num 27:8). The appearance of the vb. צָעַק, *ṣāʿaq* "to cry, plead" here as well as in the woman's appeal to the king in 6:26 suggests that it is being used in a formal sense for the presentation of a legal case to the king, who was the court of last appeal. There is no indication of what had happened to her property. Many commentators (e.g., Fritz, 273) have taken it somewhat for granted that, having been left untended it had been forfeited to the crown, but as Cogan and Tadmor (88) have said, there is no indication of that. More logically, it would have been left in trust to another member of her tribe or clan, who perhaps now refused to part with it.

4–5 With the stage now set, we come to the heart of the story. The king, with Elisha absent, has suddenly developed an interest in this man whom he has overlooked and taken for granted through the years. Was he really the kind of miracle-worker that people were saying he was? Were there resources there that could be made better use of? Unfortunately, his only source of information was the less-than-reliable Gehazi. We can only imagine what Gehazi may have done to the stories and how he aggrandized himself in the telling. Or maybe he had been suitably chastened by his experiences and was now a humbler and more reliable witness.[233] It may well be that his account of reviving the dead boy was the climax of his stories, and that the king had become more than a little skeptical. But at that very moment (הִנֵּה, *hinnē*; ""behold!") the Shunammite woman and her son were ushered into the

---

232. It is tempting to relate the number *seven* here to the Sabbatical year (Lev 25:3–7), but there is no indication of that in the text, and the official restoration of ancestral lands only came in the Jubilee year (Lev 25:13-17).

233. The question of Gehazi's "leprosy" has caused some commentators to position this event before chap. 5, while others suggest he may have been healed at some time between the Naaman account and this one. Neither expedient is necessary. It is evident that the type of skin disease Naaman had had did not prevent him from carrying out official duties and so we may take it that the same was true for Gehazi.

audience chamber (or did she burst in?), and Gehazi could say, "Here is the evidence that I am not lying!" Notice that in the account thus far, "reviving the dead" (הֶחֱיָה אֶת־הַמֵּת, *heḥĕyâ ʾet-hammēt*) has appeared no less than four times. Life itself is in the hands of Yahweh and his prophet.

6 It was natural that the king would seek to verify Gehazi's claim with the woman herself, but when she did, he instantly "appointed an official" (וַיִּתֶּן־לָהּ הַמֶּלֶךְ סָרִיס, *wayyitten-lāh hammelek sārîs*)[234] to oversee her case and make sure that she not only got her property back, but also the sum of what the famine-stricken property might have produced during the previous seven years. This appointment of an official supports the idea that the land had not merely become crown property. In that case, the king could have simply ruled by fiat, and the matter would be finished.

As I suggested above, this act on Joram's part is not a sign of magnanimity. It was simple justice. What sets it apart is its instantaneity. It is not a response to the woman, but a response to Elisha's miraculous powers in front of Elisha's servant. This suggests that it is an attempt to regain the prophet's favor. As such, it was too late.

SELECTED BIBLIOGRAPHY

Jobling, D. "A Bettered Woman: Elisha and the Shunammite in the Deuteronomic Work." In *The Labour of Reading: Desire, Alienation, and Biblical Interpretation,* edited by Fiona C. Black, Roland Boer, and Erin Runions, 177–92. Atlanta: SBL, 1999.

Mommer, P. "Der Diener des Propheten: Die Rolle Gehasis in der Elisa-Überlieferung." In *Gottes Recht als Lebensraum: Festschrift für Hans Jochen Boecker,* 101–15. Neukirchener Verlag: 1993.

Mulzer, M. "Der Kranke und der Gesunde Gehazi: Zum Verhältnis von 2Kön 5 zu 2Kön 8,1–6." *BN* 153 (2012): 19–27.

Rice, G. "A Great Woman of Ancient Israel (2 Kings 4:8-37; 8:1-6)." *Journal of Religious Thought* 60–63 (2008): 69–85.

Roncace, M. "Elisha and the Woman of Shunem: 2 Kings 4:8–37 and 8:1–6 Read in Conjunction." *JSOT* 91 (2000): 109–27.

The End of the Dynasty of Omri (8:7–11:21)

With the appointments of Hazael (8:7–15) and Jehu (9:1–13), the final pieces are in place, as outlined by Yahweh to Elijah (1 Kgs 19:15–17), for the destruction of the house of Omri and humbling of a nation that had bowed at the feet of Baal. Between the two appointments we are told, almost in passing,

234. The Heb. term (סָרִיס), a loan word from Akk. is often translated "eunuch." That does not, however, seem to have been the term's exclusive meaning. It is used of the Egyptian Potiphar, but he had a wife (Gen 39:1, 7). For an extended discussion see Cogan and Tadmor on 9:32 (112).

of the reigns of two kings in Judah, Jehoram (8:16–24; 849–842 BC) and his son Ahaziah (8:25–29; 842–841 BC). These accounts are given as part of the overall chronological correlation between the two kingdoms (the reigns of the Judean kings occurring during that of Joram of Israel), but also because they were under the heavy influence of the Northern Kingdom, as witnessed to by the marriage of Jehoram to Athaliah, the daughter of Ahab and Jezebel (8:18), who was in turn the mother of Ahaziah (8:26).

Chapters 9–11, beginning with 9:14, detail the destruction of the Omride dynasty in Israel and of Athaliah, who had replaced her murdered son in Judah. The effect was finally to destroy organized Baal worship both in Israel (10:28) and in Judah (11:18). The crisis was past and there was no longer a chance that Baal would supplant Yahweh as the God of Israel. But in each case the reform was only partial: in the north, the idols continued to be worshipped in Bethel and Dan (10:29), and in the south, exclusive devotion to Yahweh waned after the death of Jehoiada, Joash's mentor (see 2 Chr 24:17–18). For these failures, Hazael, whom Elisha had helped to bring to power in Syria, was Yahweh's scourge to discipline the two nations (10:32–33; 12:17–18).

The Appointment of Hazael (8:7–15)

Translation

7 Elisha went to Damascus. Ben-hadad, king of Syria, was ill, and he was
informed, saying, "The man of God had come here." **8** The king said to
Hazael, "Take a gift in your hand and go to meet the man of God and inquire
of Yahweh through him, saying, 'Will I recover from this illness?' " **9** So
Hazael went to meet him and took a gift in his hand, every good thing of
Damascus, forty camel loads, and he came and stood before him and said,
"Your son, Ben-hadad, king of Syria, sent me to you, saying, 'Will I recover
from this illness?' " **10** Elisha said to him, "Go, say to him, 'You will surely
live.' But Yahweh has shown me that he will surely die." **11** He set his face
and fixed until he was embarrassed, and the man of God wept. **12** He said,
"My lord, why are you weeping?" He said, "Because I know that you will do
evil to the sons of Israel. Their fortresses you will set on fire; their young men
you will kill with the sword; their little ones you will throw on the ground;
and their pregnant women you will rip open." **13** He said, "But what is your
servant, a dog, that he should do this great thing?" Elisha said, "Yahweh
has shown me that you will be king over Syria." **14** He left Elisha and went
to his lord. He said to him, "What did Elisha say to you?" and he said, "He
said to me that you will surely recover." **15** But on the next day he took the
bedcover and dipped it into water and spread it over his face and he died.
And Hazael reigned in his place.

Textual Notes

7a. וַיֻּגַּד: Gk. and Vulg. "they reported"; Syr. with MT.

8a. מֵחֳלִי: Gk. and Vulg. "my sickness"; Syr. "sickness" with MT. (So also v. 9.)

10a. לא: The versions all read "to him" (לו) with *qere*.

10b. תִחְיֶה: Vulg. "you will be healed."

10c. יָמוּת: Gk. "you will surely die"; Vulg. and Syr. 3ms with MT.

11a–a. וַיַּעֲמֵד אֶת־פָּנָיו וַיָּשֶׂם עַד־בֹּשׁ: Gk. "He stood before his face and fixed until shame"; Vulg. "He stood before this one and he was troubled until his face flushed"; Syr. omits. MT best explains the others.

12a–a. אֵת אֲשֶׁר־תַּעֲשֶׂה לִבְנֵי יִשְׂרָאֵל רָעָה: Gk. "what evil you will do to the sons of Israel"; Vulg. and Syr. with MT. For אֲשֶׁר' introducing a noun clause, see *IBHS* (§38.8d).

13a. הַכֶּלֶב: Gk. adds "dead"; Vulg. and Syr. with MT.

13b. הַגָּדוֹל: Gk. lacks; Vulg. and Syr. with MT.

Commentary

This narrative, with its many intimate details that would have stemmed from Elisha's disciples (so Wiseman, 213), is arranged chiastically, as argued convincingly by Cohn (60).[235] Beginning with Ben-hadad's[236] sickness and ending with his death, its climax is the conversation between Elisha and Hazael in vv. 9b–13. The question of Elisha's integrity has engaged the attention of many commentators (e.g., Barnes, 247–8), but, as I will argue below, it is not the central issue. That issue is Yahweh's sovereignty in the world—making and deposing kings to serve his larger purposes.[237]

7 If we understand Elisha's action in going to Damascus in the way we are clearly intended to, as the fulfillment of Yahweh's directions to Elijah (1 Kgs 19:15), then Ben-hadad's illness was simply a concomitant circumstance.[238] The goal was to make Hazael the next king of Syria. As has been demonstrated

235. Contra Fritz, who following Würthwein, argues that 10b–13 were a later, intrusive addition (275).
236. For a discussion of the identity of this man, see the comment above on 6:24.
237. Cogan and Tadmor observe that there are no moralizing comments here explaining that Hazael is put in place to carry out Yahweh's judgments on Judah and Israel (92). But that is a feature of most of these prophetic narratives. The narrator generally allows his hearers/readers to draw their own obvious conclusions. This feature is reminiscent of the book of Judges.
238. Cogan and Tadmor's contention that this narrative and the one in 1 Kgs 19 are separate traditions with the first lacking its conclusion and this one lacking its opening instructions seems to me to fly in the face of the obvious intent of the narration to show that the ministries of Elijah and Elisha are one effort from beginning to end (92). See especially the comments on 2 Kgs 2.

repeatedly in these Elijah-Elisha narratives, Yahweh is the God of the whole earth. Thus, it is significant that Ben-hadad, who had repeatedly been the foil for Yahweh's activities in his seeking to demonstrate to Ahab and his descendants that he alone is God, should here acknowledge the power of Yahweh as mediated through "the man of God" (אִישׁ הָאֱלֹהִים, *ʾîš hā ʾĕlōhîm*).

8 This point is made more evident when we recognize that Ben-hadad's inquiry of Yahweh is identical to that of Ahaziah to Baal-Zebub (2 Kgs 1:2). It seems likely that the narrator has structured the two scenes intentionally so that the reader will grasp the irony. The king of Israel, whose God was Yahweh, had sent to Baal in a foreign land to ask his question, whereas here, the king of Syria, the land of Hadad (i.e., Baal), is asking his question of Yahweh, God of Israel and the world.

It is unclear what Hazael's position was in the court. He is not said to be Ben-hadad's son, and this is confirmed in the annals of Shalmaneser III, the Assyrian monarch, which report that Ben-hadad (called "Hadad-ezer") died and was replaced by Hazael, "a nobody" (i.e. a commoner).[239] Nonetheless, it is apparent that he was in Ben-hadad's inner circle and had his confidence. He was directed to make a formal inquiry (Heb. דָּרַשׁ, *dāraš*)[240] of Yahweh whether the king would or would not "live" (הַאֶחְיֶה, *ha ʾeḥyeh*) (i.e., "will I recover?") from this illness.

9 It is not clear how literally we are to take the description of the gifts that Hazael took to Elisha. The presence of the number "forty," which often expresses an indefinite totality, reinforces the idea that it was simply a very large amount, even excessive. What the prophet would have been expected to do with such an excess is not even hinted at. The idea that Yahweh might be in charge of what was taking place, and that his prophet did not need the compulsion of super-abundant payment seems not to have occurred to either Hazael or Ben-hadad.

10–13 The report of the conversation is powerful because of the way it conveys the emotions of the two men in such an economical use of language. Elisha tells Hazael that he may tell his master that he "will live" from the illness, but that Yahweh has shown him that the king "he will surely die" (כִּי־מוֹת יָמוּת, *kî-môṯ yāmûṯ*). In effect, although Hazael may tell his master what he wants to hear in regard to the illness, Yahweh has shown the prophet that the king is going to die from another cause altogether, one that is unrelated to his question. This is not a matter of prophetic integrity, or of a "lying spirit" as Long (352) would have it. What would the king have done differently if he

239. *ANET,* 280.

240. The term, which has a fairly wide range of connotations associated with "seeking," occurs thirteen times in the books of Kings with this particular connotation of seeking an answer to a specific question from a deity.

had been told he would die of this disease (which would indeed have been an untruth)? Elisha is concerned with Hazael, not Ben-hadad, and the truth or falsehood of what Hazael might say to his master was of little concern to the prophet. This is not an attempt to exonerate the prophet but simply to suggest that the truth or falsity of what he instructed Hazael to say to Ben-hadad is not of much consequence to what is taking place here.[241]

Of more consequence is the question whether Elisha, by his actions incited Hazael to assassinate Ben-hadad. The answer must be "no." Here we come to the interface between human freedom and divine foreknowledge (see the Biblical Theology Comments below). The fact that Elisha had been "shown" (הִרְאַנִי יהוה, *hir'anî yhwh*) (v. 13) that Hazael would become king of Syria did not mean that Elisha therefore caused Hazael to do what he did. Undoubtedly this incident was a contributing cause, but it was not the effective cause. The effective cause was Hazael's own choice, perhaps, for all we know, something that he had been considering for some time. (The fact that his coup was successful argues that plans had already been laid.)[242]

Since the subjects of the verbs "set" (יָשֵׂם, *yāśem*) and "embarrassed" (בֹּשׁ, *bōš*) in v. 11 are not defined, it has led to some uncertainty. Most commentators, as well as most modern translations, take Elisha to be the subject of "set" and Hazael the subject of "embarrassed." A few, for instance Hobbs (102), and Cogan and Tadmor (90), take Hazael to be the subject of both. But it seems likely that the majority are correct with the law of the prior antecedent in operation. Thus, Elisha, having pronounced that the king would die, and knowing how that would happen and what the consequences of the act would be, was overcome with emotion, and could say no more, simply staring at Hazael with a fixed gaze until the man became embarrassed. Finally, the prophet burst into tears.

Hazael was obviously unprepared for any of this and asked what the crying was about. Elisha responded in a way that is subtly poetic (v. 12), suggesting that this expression may have been a conventional one to express the horrors of war where the goal was not so much to defeat the enemy as to annihilate him (see Amos 1 for other descriptions of this kind of warfare). Hazael's response (v. 13) is not an expression of shock that Elisha would think him capable of doing such things, but rather a question about his worthiness

---

241. The *ketiv* and *qere* of לֹא, *lōʾ* in v. 10 suggest that the issue may have been a concern for scribes at some point in the transmission of the MT (see textual note above). *Ketiv* "… say, 'You will not recover' " vs. *qere* "… say to him, "You will recover.' " The versions and many MSS read with *qere*. It is suggested that *qere* was original and that someone altered it to *ketiv* in order to absolve Elisha from any charge of untruthfulness. For further discussion see C. J. Labuschagne, "Did Elisha Deliberately Lie: A Note on 2 Kings 8:10," *ZAW* 77 (1965): 327–28.

242. For a discussion see Lena-Sofia Tiemeyer, "Prophecy as a Way of Cancelling Prophecy: The Strategic Uses of Foreknowledge," *ZAW* 117 (2005): 329–50.

to do such a "great thing" (הַדָּבָר הַגָּדוֹל, *haddāḇār haggāḏôl*). The reference to his being a "dog" (כֶּלֶב, *keleḇ*) is in that vein. In 1 Sam 24:14; 2 Sam 9:8; 16:9, the phrase is "dead dog" (and so LXX here [harm.]), but the sense of unworthiness expressed is the same.[243] Clearly Hazael is not thinking of these acts as terrible ones from the Israelite point of view, but as great ones from the Syrian perspective. Regardless of Hazael's protest, Elisha makes his point specific: Hazael will be the next king; Yahweh has shown it to Elisha. Interestingly, Elisha did not anoint Hazael. Perhaps it was that he did not want to appear to give any trace of approval to those things he knew the Syrian would do.

14–15 Whatever may have been Hazael's state of mind and planning before this event, there can be little doubt that the experience galvanized him to action. Some commentators, e.g., Gray (532), do not believe that Hazael actually killed Ben-hadad, but that he was just found dead the next morning. This view depends in part on the understanding of the term here translated "bedcover" (מַכְבֵּר, *makḇēr*). The word only occurs here, and the root idea elsewhere (Amos 9:9) seems to suggest some sort of netted material.[244] On Gray's reading, this netting was hung around the king's bed and wetted to provide a kind of air conditioning. When a person went to check on the king in the morning, he was dead. But this does not accord with the context nor with the plain sense of the Hebrew text. Hazael dipped the cloth in water and "spread it over his face and he died" (וַיִּפְרֹשׂ עַל־פָּנָיו וַיָּמֹת, *wayyip̄rōś ʿal-pānāyw wayyāmōṯ*).

Biblical Theology Comments

The Bible clearly teaches that Yahweh knows the future while at the same time teaching that humans have real choices to make for which they are held responsible. For us humans, it is impossible for both these to be true at the same time. If God knows that something is going to happen, then it must happen and free choice is only an illusion; we are compelled to do what God knows. Mark Twain expresses this point of view in a grim short story entitled "The Mysterious Stranger." The mysterious stranger of the title meets two young boys and enthralls them with his ability to create miniature worlds. But then he destroys the creations on a whim and does not see why the boys are so upset at the destruction. He then tells the boys that one of them, whom he identifies, will drown the next day. The boys do everything in their power to prevent that drowning, but it happens anyway. The story is a moving diatribe against the God of the Bible as Twain understands him. On the other hand, it would seem that if humans really do have choices, then

---

243. In the Lachish ostraca, the term appears without the adjective, as here expressing the idea of unworthiness. *ANET*, 322.

244. A related term appears in 1 Sam 19:13, 16, but there, as here, it is a bedcovering and not evidently netted.

God's knowledge of the future must be limited. He only knows what *could* happen, not what will happen.

There have been various attempts to find a way around this apparent impasse. One of the more famous ones is attributed to St. Augustine, who explains that for God there is no time. Everything is "Now," and to know what is happening as it happens in no way preconditions the outcome of that activity.[245] The problem with this explanation is that since we humans are in time it is almost impossible for us to understand how such an eternal Now would function.

This highlights the problem, which is the limitations of human thinking. To attempt to reduce eternal verities to the limits of the human mind is to deny the transcendent reality of God. If his ways can be contained within the human mind, then he is no longer God, but the human mind is God. This has been the problem of humanity from the outset. We would be God and would determine what the terms of existence are. To do so is to condemn ourselves to complete meaninglessness, as modern philosophy has taught us. If humanity is the measure of all things, then all things are meaningless, as Qoheleth ("the preacher") learned long ago and reported in the book of Ecclesiastes.

What we must do is to allow the text to stand in its glorious contradictions. Does God know that Hazael is going to kill Ben-hadad, make himself king, and do terrible things to Israel and Judah? Yes. Does this absolve Hazael of the moral responsibility for his choices? No, it does not. Whatever we do, we must not reduce God's knowledge to our terms, nor dare we blame God for our sinful choices, and the culpability for them. A powerful example of these points is found in Isaiah 10:5–19. Assyria is a tool in God's hands in order to humble God's people, but that fact does not mean that Assyria will escape judgment for the terrible things they will do to God's people. The same thing is said of Babylon in Isaiah 47:4–7. Neither point may be relinquished in our desire to force our understanding of consistency on the Word of God.

Selected Bibliography

Unger, M. F. *Israel and the Arameans of Damascus*. London: J. Clarke, 1957: 64–76.

245. Augustine, *Confessions*, tr. R. S. Pine-Coffin (New York: Penguin, 1970), XI, 264–71.

Jehoram, King of Judah (8:16–24)

Translation

16 In the fifth year of Joram, son of Ahab, king of Israel, Jehoshaphat having been king of Judah,[246] Jehoram, son of Jehoshaphat became king over Judah. **17** He was thirty-two years old when he became king, and he ruled for eight years in Jerusalem. **18** He walked in the way of the kings of Israel according to what the house of Ahab did, because the daughter of Ahab was his wife, and he did evil in the eyes of Yahweh. **19** But Yahweh was not willing to destroy Judah on account of David his servant according to what he had said to him to give him a lamp for his sons[247] all the days. **20** In his days Edom revolted from under the hand of Judah and they made a king rule over them. **21** So Jehoram passed over to Zair and all his chariot forces with him. Arising at night, he struck Edom who had surrounded him and the chariot commanders, and the people fled to their tents.[248] **22** So Edom has revolted from under the hand of Judah until this day. Libnah also revolted at that time. **23** The remainder of the events surrounding Jehoram and all that he did, are they not written in the book of the chronicles of the kings of Judah? **24** Jehoram slept with his fathers and was buried with his fathers in the city of David and Ahaziah his son ruled after him.

Textual Notes

16a–a. וִיהוֹשָׁפָט מֶלֶךְ יְהוּדָה: Gk. and Syr. omit; Vulg. with MT.

16b. יְהוּדָה: Gk. and Syr. omit; Vulg. with MT.

17a. וּשְׁמֹנֶה: On the use of the sing. here see *IBHS* (§15.2.2b).

18a. עָשׂוּ: Vulg. "walked"; Gk. and Syr. with MT.

18b. בֵּית: Syr. "the sister"; Gk. and Vulg. with MT.

19a–a. כַּאֲשֶׁר אָמַר־לוֹ: Gk. "since he said"; Vulg. and Syr. with MT.

19b. לְבָנָיו: Gk. and Vulg. add "and"; Syr. periph. "to give an heir to his sons"; *CTAT* (391) MT is likely.

21a. לַיְלָה: Gk. omits; Vulg. and Syr. with MT.

---

246. This phrase is lacking in Gk. and Syr. Cogan and Tadmor (94) consider it a dittograph of the last phrase in the verse, but Sweeney (320), noting the *waw* that begins it, believes it to be a gloss. See "Commentary" below.

247. It has been proposed to emend "to his sons" to "before him," a change of only one letter in Heb. (see Gray, 533). However, the versions, including Syr. which paraphrases the v., all read "to his sons."

248. A notoriously obscure verse. Many commentators argue that the grammar is corrupt. See "Commentary" below.

21b–b. שָׂרֵי הָרֶכֶב: Syr. "his commanders with chariots"; Gk. and Vulg. with MT.

22a. יַד: Vulg. omits "hand"; Gk. and Syr. with MT.

24a. דָּוִד: Gk. adds "his father"; Vulg. and Syr. with MT.

COMMENTARY

While it would be normal to introduce the parallel Judean reign(s) after the death of the contemporary Israelite king, in this case Joram, the accounts of Jehoram and Ahaziah are brought forward here because the deaths of the three were simultaneous, or almost so. Jehoram died the year before Joram and Ahaziah were killed by Jehu.[249]

16 The regnal dates as given in this verse are complicated by the apparent contradiction found in 2 Kgs 1:17. That verse tells us that Joram became king in Jehoram's second year whereas this verse says Jehoram became king in Joram's fifth year! It seems likely that there was a coregency between Jehoshaphat and Jehoram which began two years before the end of Ahaziah of Israel's reign and ended with Jehoshaphat's death in Joram's fifth year.[250] Such a coregency might also explain the appearance of the rather odd "Jehoshaphat having been king of Judah" (וִיהוֹשָׁפָט מֶלֶךְ יְהוּדָה, *wîhôšāpāṭ meleḵ yᵊhûḏâ*) (see p. 166n246 above).

17 The absence of the mother's name here, a usual feature in the Judean regnal data, may indicate that she was dead by this time. Jehoshaphat's relatively long reign and Jehoram's relatively high age upon his accession lend support to such a hypothesis.

18 The denunciation of Jehoram, although not as detailed as that found in 2 Chr 21:2–11, is just as unsparing.[251] Far from doing what was right in the eyes of Yahweh, as David had done, as was said of his father and grandfather (1 Kgs 15:11; 22:43), "he walked in the way of the kings of Israel" (וַיֵּלֶךְ בְּדֶרֶךְ

249. Note that both the Israelite and the Judean kings were named Jehoram, and that both are sometimes spelled Joram without any clear pattern. We are here following a common convention for clarity's sake, consistently calling the northern king Joram and the southern Jehoram. The fact that they carry the same names, and that Jehoram's son was named Ahaziah, as Joram's father had been, is surely a sign of the close relationship between the two kingdoms, to the extent of probable vassalage of Judah to Israel.

250. See the comments above on 1:17–18. For discussion see Thiele, 65. Several commentators agree, including Cogan and Tadmor, 95, and Gray, 532na.

251. While some would say that the books of Kings show a bias toward Judah, as Wiseman points out here (216), when denunciation is warranted, there is no indication of such a bias.

מַלְכֵי יִשְׂרָאֵל, *wayyēlek bᵊderek malkê yiśrāʾēl*), most especially the house of Ahab, with the result that "he did evil in the eyes of Yahweh" (וַיַּעַשׂ הָרַע בְּעֵינֵי יהוה, *wayyaʿaś hāraʿ bᵊʿênê yhwh*). One of the contributing causes of this behavior is said to be his wife, the daughter of Ahab.[252] As we know her from chap. 11, this is Athaliah, a woman of remarkable determination. While we do not know whether her mother was Jezebel or not, she seems to have been equally devoted to Baal, and to have shared a similar strength of purpose. The murderous instinct she displayed toward the royal family as reported in 11:1 may give grounds to Josephus' claim that she was the one who incited Jehoram to a similar atrocity at the beginning of his reign (2 Chr. 21:4).[253] The marriage would have been contracted between Jehoshaphat and Ahab as a way of cementing an alliance between them (see 1 Kgs 22:4, and 2 Kgs 3:7), an alliance that may well have amounted to submission of Judah to Israel as a vassal. This might explain how the marriage came about: it may have been forced upon Jehoshaphat, as it is somewhat difficult to understand why this devoted follower of Yahweh would have agreed to it otherwise.

19 The sins of the house of Ahab, in which Jehoram was happily walking, were going to bring the dynasty of Omri to a bloody end. Would that be true for the dynasty of David as well? The answer is given in this verse. God had made a promise to David which he would not recant (2 Sam 7:16). This did not mean that David's descendants would not be subject to severe discipline if they sinned (2 Sam 7:14–15), as was certainly to be the case with Ahaziah, but God would not allow the "lamp"[254] (נִיר, *nîr*) of the family to be put out (see 2 Sam 14:7 for a similar metaphor), as Athaliah made every attempt to do.

20–22 Although, as before, the narrator does not make an explicit connection between Jehoram's sins and the losses described in these verses, there seems little doubt that this is the connection we are intended to make.

---

252. 2 Kgs 8:26, which names her the daughter of Omri, probably gave rise to the Syr. reading here, "the sister of Ahab." The most likely explanation of that statement is that בַּת, *bat* designates a female descendant and can mean granddaughter as well as daughter. But see Gray for the suggestion that she might have been born in Omri's old age and raised in the house of her brother Ahab, as though she were his child (534). For a discussion of the issues, see Reuven Chaim Klein, "Queen Athaliah: The Daughter of Ahab or Omri?" *JBQ* 42 (2014): 11–20.

253. *The Works of Flavius Josephus,* tr. W. Whiston (Philadelphia: International Press) n.d., 283.

254. The word here, as well as in 1 Kgs 11:36 and 15:4 in similar contexts to this, is נִיר, *nîr,* while "lamp" is נֵר, *nēr*. For this reason, and given an Akkadian cognate connoting dominion, some (e.g., Sweeney, 319n.a) argue that "dominion" should be read here. But the versions translate it as "lamp." (Syr. reads "heir," but that is surely an interpretation of "lamp." See Cogan and Tadmor for support of the traditional reading (95).

Jehoram had taken himself out of Yahweh's camp, and it is Yahweh who gives victory. Rule over Edom to the south of Judah was important to Judah because it gave them access to the Red Sea port of Ezion-geber (Elath), and thus control over the trade that entered the Levant through that port. But under Jehoram, that control would be lost and Edom would become a deadly rival to Judah. Given Jehoram's evident weakness, and possibly encouraged by Moab's success in breaking away from Israel, Edom saw its chance and took it. Previously, as 1 Kgs 22:48 has it, Edom had been governed by a deputy appointed by Judah, but that would no longer be the case.[255]

The identification of Zair is unknown. Many equate it with Zoar, probably at the south end of the Dead Sea (Gen 19:22; Deut 34:3), although Isa 15:5 seems to suggest it was in the territory of Moab. Others take it to be a site northeast of Hebron, but that presupposes an Edomite attack deep into Judean territory. The Greek transliteration (Σιωρ, *Siōr*) is the one it normally reserves for Seir, the Edomite city east of the Arabah rift. That is attractive, but it would require altering the first letter from one sibilant to another.[256] In any case, "passed over" (יַעֲבֹר, *ya ʿăḇōr*) probably connotes the crossing of a border into Edomite territory. From this point on, as noted on the translation above, the precise meaning of the verse becomes very obscure. Did Jehoram surround the Edomites, or did they surround him? Did he strike Edom and the Edomite chariot commanders, or did he strike the Edomites who surrounded him and the chariot commanders? What is proposed here seems most likely, but it is hardly certain. On this reading, Jehoram, having been ambushed by the Edomites, attacked at night and he and his chariot corps escaped the encirclement, leaving the rest of the army to fend for itself.[257] However we read the verse, it was a defeat, and Edom was lost to Judah from then on. Later Amaziah of Judah was able to inflict a defeat on Edom (2 Kgs 14:7), but there is no indication that he was able to bring Edom back into submission.

Not only was the revolt external, it was also internal. Libnah, one of the Levitical cities located in the low country on the border with the Philistines,[258] broke away. Chronicles reports that a coalition of Arabs and Philistines attacked Judah at this time (2 Chr. 21:16–17), so perhaps the inhabitants of this city became disaffected with what was going on in Jerusalem and joined the opposite side.

---

255. On the apparent contradiction of this statement with the ref. to "the king of Edom" in 3:9, see the "Commentary" there.

256. For a discussion, see "Zair," *ABD* 6:1038–39.

257. Wiseman argues that "to their tents" (לְאֹהָלָיו, *lᵊʾōhālāyw*) is not merely "to go home," but "to take flight" (216).

258. Beyond what is said above, the location is unknown. It was evidently in the neighborhood of Lachish and has been identified most often with Tell Bornat in that region.

23–24 The point having been made in the previous verses, nothing remains but to remove Jehoram from the pages of history with the standard death notice. Our narrator is content with that, but the Chronicler does not want us to miss the point and adds more details of the king's painful death and less than optimum burial site (2 Chr 21:18–20).

Selected Bibliography

Thiele, E. R. *The Mysterious Numbers of the Hebrew Kings.* Third edition. Grand Rapids: Zondervan, 1983: 99–101.

Ahaziah, King of Judah (8:25–29)

Translation

25 In the twelfth year of Joram, son of Ahab, king of Israel, Ahaziah, son of Jehoram, king of Judah became king. **26** Ahaziah was twenty-two years old when he began to reign and he reigned[259] one year in Jerusalem. The name of his mother was Athaliah, the granddaughter[260] of Omri, king of Israel. **27** He walked in the way of the house of Ahab, and he did evil in the eyes of Yahweh like the house of Ahab, for he was the son-in-law to the house of Ahab. **28** He went with Joram, son of Ahab, to fight with Hazael, king of Syria, in Ramoth-gilead and the Syrians smote Joram. **29** So Joram the king returned to Jezreel to recover from the wound the Syrians had inflicted[261] in Ramoth when he was fighting Hazael, king of Syria, and Ahaziah, son of Jehoram, king of Judah, went down to see Joram, son of Ahab, in Jezreel because he was ill.

Textual Notes

27a–a. כִּי חֲתַן בֵּית־אַחְאָב הוּא: Gk. lacks; Vulg. and Syr. with MT.

29a. אֲרַמִּים: Gk. lacks; Vulg. and Syr. with MT.

29b–b. מֶלֶךְ יְהוּדָה: Gk. lacks; Vulg. and Syr. with MT.

Commentary

25–27 Ahaziah, Jehoram's son, was the one on whom the ax would fall not only for his father's sins, but also for his own. Although he reigned for less than a year, perhaps only for a few months, the die was cast.[262] It is not said

259. See *IBHS* (§30.2.1b) who label this use of the pf. as "ingressive," indicating the beginning of a process.

260. See note p. 166n252 above.

261. *IBHS* (§31.1.1d n.5) identifies this impf. (יַכֻּהוּ, *yakkuhû*) as a "true preterite." GKC (§107*e*) says it indicates repeated action in the past.

262. 2 Kgs 9:29 says that Ahaziah began to reign in Joram's eleventh year, while here it is said to be the twelfth. Unless an error has occurred (see Cogan and Tadmor, 99), Thiele's suggestion (97, 101) that Judah had switched from accession year dating to

that he walked in the way of his father, as might be expected, but he is three times linked directly to "the house of Ahab" (בֵּית אַחְאָב, *bêṯ ʾaḥʾāḇ*). Here the tree of intermarriage bears its most bitter fruit. One can only wonder what might have been the result if this man had been allowed to live out a long reign. Evidently his mother Athaliah had a powerful influence on him.[263] While it is possible that he was the literal son-in-law of the Ahab family, the term has broader connotations, and may only be saying that he is related by marriage, namely the marriage of his mother and father. In any case the result was deadly.

28–29 Scholars debate the sense of "went with" (וַיֵּלֶךְ אֶת, *wayyēleḵ ʾeṯ*). Is it to be understood literally, that Ahaziah accompanied Joram into battle, as Jehoshaphat had accompanied him to Moab years earlier? Or does it only mean that he gave Joram his general support. The language "went down" (יָרַד, *yāraḏ*) (v. 29), while not impossible in reference to the journey from Ramoth-gilead to Jezreel, is usually applied to a journey from Jerusalem to someplace else. Gray (536) thinks that the situation in Judah, where it may be assumed there were struggles between Baal and Yahweh supporters, may have prevented him from undertaking a prolonged stay away from home, and only permitted a swift visit to the wounded Joram.

Ramoth-gilead,[264] located some 30 miles southeast of the Sea of Galilee, stood at a critical junction between the highway leading west through Beth-shean to the Mediterranean and the north-south King's highway leading from the port of Ezion-geber (Elath) to Damascus. Control of this cross-roads meant great commercial gain for whoever exercised that control. This is where Joram's father Ahab had met his death battling Hazael's predecessor Ben-hadad (1 Kgs 22:29–37), and it would continue to be a focus of the struggles between Israel and Syria in years to come.

Joram, wounded as his father had been, but apparently not mortally, had withdrawn to the nearest Israelite city of any size, Jezreel, which also happened to contain his summer palace, that happened to adjoin Naboth's vineyard. His mother was already there or had perhaps come there to be with him. Then Ahaziah arrived. A fateful gathering indeed.

The Jehu Revolution (9:1–10:36)

In these two chapters the terribly bloody end of the house of Ahab is reported in a very terse and unemotional manner. The narrative is gripping in its carefully detailed accounting of the thorough way in which Jehu carried out his mandate. As has been typical from 1 Kings 17 onward, there is a minimum of

---

Israel's non-accession year dating is the best explanation and seems to be confirmed through the rest of the synchronisms between the two kingdoms.

263. On Athaliah's relation to Omri, see p. 168n252 above.

264. "Ramah" as a sing. form seems to be a variant of "Ramoth" the pl.

moralizing. At the same time there can be no doubt that the narrator has a point of view, and we begin to wonder about that point of view when we see just how detailed the reports of the executions are. Can it be that the validity of the overall action is approved of, but the extent to which it is carried out is not? Of course, knowing the criticism stated in Hosea 1:4–5 may influence our reading. But at the same time, it is difficult to read this account without saying at some point, "Enough already!"

Regardless of our reactions to the violence, when we come to 10:28, we can breathe a sigh of relief that the institutional worship of Baal is broken and that Israel has a chance for a fresh start. But that sigh of relief is very short-lived. If Jehu had rebelled against the house of Ahab's sponsorship of Baal worship, he did not transcend the paganized Yahwism that had characterized Israel from Jeroboam on, and the remainder of chapter 10 (vv. 28–36) tells the sad story of an opportunity squandered and the results of it.

Selected Bibliography

Breytenbach, J. H. and Oberholzer, J. P. "2 Konings 9–10: 'N Beoordeling van die Jehuvertelling as Historiese Bron." *Hervormde Teologiese Studies* 48 (1992): 663–89.

King, A. M. "Did Jehu Destroy Baal from Israel: A Contextual Reading," *BBR* 27 (2017): 309–32.

Lamb, D. T. *Jehu and His Evil Heirs: The Deuteronomist's Negative Perspective on Dynastic Succession.* Oxford: Oxford, 2007.

Moore, M. S. "Jehu's Coronation and Purge of Israel." *VT* 53 (2003): 97–114.

Würthwein, E. "Die Revolution Jehus: Die Jehu-Erzählung in Altisraelitischer und Deuteronomistischer Sicht." *ZAW* 120 (2008): 28–48.

Jehu's Coronation (9:1–13)

Translation

9:1 Now Elisha the prophet called one of the company of the prophets and
said to him, "Tuck up your robe and take this jug of oil in your hand and go to
Ramoth-gilead. **2** You shall go there and look for Jehu the son of Jehoshaphat
the son of Nimshi. Go and make him get up from among his comrades and
bring him into an inner chamber. **3** Take the jug of oil and pour it on his head
and say, 'Thus says Yahweh, "I have anointed you king over Israel." ' Then
open the door and flee; do not wait." **4** So the young man, the servant of the
prophet, went to Ramoth-gilead. **5** He arrived, and there were the commanders of the army sitting together. He said, "I have a word for you, Commander."
Jehu said, "To whom, from among all of us?" He said, "To you, Commander."
6 So he got up and went into the house, and he poured the oil on his head,
and he said to him, "Thus says Yahweh, God of Israel, 'I have anointed you
king over the people of Yahweh, Israel. **7** You shall strike the house of Ahab,
your lord, and I will avenge the blood of my servants the prophets and the
blood of all the servants of Yahweh from the hand of Jezebel. **8** The house
of Ahab will perish, and I will cut off from Ahab every male, bound or free,

in Israel. **9** I will make the house of Ahab like the house of Jeroboam, son of Nebat, and like the house of Baasha, son of Ahijah. **10** As for Jezebel, dogs will eat her in the plot of Jezreel, and there will be no one to bury her.' " Then he opened the door and fled. **11** But Jehu went out to the servants of his lord and they[265] said to him, "Is it well?[266] Why did this madman come to you?" He said, "You yourselves know the man and his whining." **12** They said, "Liar! Tell us!" He said, "He said this and that to me, saying, 'Thus says Yahweh, "I have anointed you king over Israel." ' " **13** Immediately each man took his cloak and they spread them under him on the bare steps, and they blew the trumpet and said, "Jehu is king!"

Textual Notes

2a–a. בֶּן־יְהוֹשָׁפָט בֶּן־נִמְשִׁי: Syr. omits; Gk. and Vulg. with MT.

4a. הַנַּעַר: Gk. and Syr. omit; Vulg. with MT. Delete as dittograph? (But see GKC §127*g*).

6a. הַבַּיְתָה: Vulg. and Syr. "inner room"; Gk. with MT.

7a. וְהִכִּיתָה: Gk. "utterly destroy"; Vulg. and Syr. with MT. The Gk. usually translates אבד' (Hobbs, 109).

7b. אֲדֹנֶיךָ: Gk. adds "from before me"; Vulg. and Syr. with MT.

8a. וְאָבַד: Gk. "and from the hand of"; Vulg. and Syr. "I will destroy," reading as 1st person *hiphil.* MT best explains the others.

8b. וְהִכְרַתִּי: Gk. "you shall utterly destroy"; Vulg. and Syr. with MT.

10a. בְּחֵלֶק: Syr. reads "in the inheritance in Jezreel"; Gk. and Vulg. with MT.

11a. וַיֹּאמֶר: All the versions and many MSS read "they said."

13a–a. אֶל־גֶּרֶם הַמַּעֲלוֹת: Gk. "garem [translit.] steps"; Vulg. "under his feet"; Syr. "on a seat in the steps."

265. With all the versions; Heb. "he said" (וַיֹּאמֶר, *wayyōʾmer*).

266. This rendering reflects the variety of connotations of שָׁלוֹם, *šālôm* "to be whole." Note Vulg. "Is everything right?"; Syr. "Is all well?" A fully contemporary expression might be "Is everything okay?" At this point the issue is not about absence of conflict. In the following section, where this same phrase is repeated three times, that will become increasingly the case.

Commentary

We come now to the final act in the preparation for the destruction of the house of Ahab.[267] The last part of the instructions that Yahweh gave to Elijah at Mt. Horeb (1 Kgs 19:15–17) will be carried out here. There is no answer to the question why Elijah did not fulfill them himself, but if we think of Elijah and Elisha as the biblical text presents them, as "Siamese twins," then the question is moot; it is a single ministry, and here the injunction is fulfilled. It is not entirely clear whether Jehu was the chief commander of the Israelite army, but it seems unlikely that he was anything but, given the immediate accolade that the other commanders gave to him. It is also not clear why Yahweh chose Jehu for the task. Perhaps it was because he was one of those 7,000 who had not bowed the knee to Baal (1 Kgs 19:18). It may also have been that like the prophets, he was a bit crazy (vv. 11, 20; שׁגע, *šgʿ*), and could be counted on to have the daring to undertake the task.

1 The prophet chose not to involve himself directly in this anointing but sent one "from the company of prophets" (מִבְּנֵי הַנְּבִיאִים, *mibbᵉnê hannᵉbîʾîm*) to do the task. This kind of small historical detail, merely reported and not commented on, argues for the historicity of the narrative. When this fact is coupled with the instruction for the young man to do the deed, and leave at once (v. 3), it suggests that Elisha wanted to call the least possible attention to what was taking place. If a mere servant of the prophet appeared in the camp it would arouse much less suspicion than if the prophet himself were to make an appearance. It was important to get the thing over and done with, and not to allow any entanglements to drag out the process. Evidently Elisha knew what kind of a man Jehu was, and that once the anointing had taken place, he would act on it at once.

The command to "tuck up your robe" (חֲגֹר מָתְנֶיךָ, *ḥăgōr moṯnêḵā*) (cf. 1 Kgs 18:46; 2 Kgs 4:29) emphasizes the need to get the deed done as expeditiously as possible. The king must not find out what was afoot, and other people in the army, or the society in general, who might have other candidates to put forward if a coup was known to be in the air, must not either.

On "Ramoth-gilead," see on 8:29 above.

2 If Jehu was the commander of the army, then he would be recognizable to the servant, as seems to be the assumption here. It is not clear why he is identified both by his father and his grandfather. Since elsewhere the father's name is omitted entirely and he is only identified as the son of Nimshi (1 Kgs 19:16;

---

267. Although commentators often refer to the destruction of the dynasty of Omri, it is significant that the biblical writers do not think in those terms. Although Omri is not depicted as a good king, having walked "completely" in the ways (בְּכָל־דֶּרֶךְ, *bᵉḵol-dereḵ*) of Jeroboam (1 Kgs 16:26), it is Ahab who, having introduced institutionalized Baalism (under his wife's influence?), is cited as the real cause of the destruction of the dynasty.

2 Kgs 9:20), it may be that the grandfather was the more well-known.[268] As with the anointing of David (1 Sam 16:13) where the kingship was contested, this anointing was to be private, in the "inner chamber" (חֶדֶר בְּחָדֶר, *ḥeḏer bᵊḥāḏer*).[269] Again, it seems that the point is to present a *fait accompli* with a minimum of possibility for interference, uproar, and uncertainty.

3 There is disagreement among scholars over exactly what the young man was to say to Jehu, in that the instruction here is so much shorter that what he is reported to have said in vv. 6–10. The most common explanation is that the latter is a Deuteronomistic insertion, making sure that the reader connects Jehu with the judgment on Ahab. However, Provan (212, supported by Long, 362) has suggested that Elisha did indeed instruct the servant to make the longer statement, but that the narrator has shortened it here (as Jehu was to do in v. 12), in the interest of stressing that the act was to be done very quickly. It is also possible that the servant, being himself a prophet, was inspired to make the connection inescapable. At any rate, the man is to get in, perform the act, and then get out, not remaining for explanations with all their inevitable complications.

4–5 When the young man[270] arrived in the camp, he found the "commanders sitting together." Whether this was a casual gathering or a more formal council is not specified. The suggestion by Gray (p. 540) that they may have been plotting to overthrow Joram is interesting, but conjectural.[271] In any case, the prophet announced that he had a "word for you (sing.), Commander" (דָּבָר לִי אֵלֶיךָ הַשָּׂר, *dāḇār lî ʾēlêḵā haśśār*). That is, he clearly recognized Jehu and addressed himself to him. Jehu's response is interesting. It is almost as though he is saying, "Do you mean me, out of all of us?" as though he was attempting to avoid something uncomfortable that this man might have to say to him. But if that was the case, the prophet would not be deflected. His message was for Jehu alone.

---

268. In the annals of the Assyrian Shalmaneser III, to whom Jehu became a vassal in his first year (841 BC), Jehu is called "the son of Omri" (*ANET*, 280), but that probably only indicates an ignorance on the part of the Assyrians of the dynastic niceties of an insignificant kingdom on their western frontier. A hundred years later, they were still referring to Israel as "the house of Omri" (*ANET*, 285). Perhaps Omri had been king when the Assyrians first encountered Israel in the 880's, and they never bothered to update their information.

269. Ben-hadad had hidden from Ahab's forces in a similar place (1 Kgs 20:30).

270. There is a possibility that the second הַנַּעַר, *hannaʿar*, here translated as "the servant" is an error, but almost all commentators and Eng. versions take it to be original.

271. Sweeney (331–2) contends that the deteriorating military situation with Syria, now that Hazael was in command, was probably the real explanation of the coup. Supposedly Joram was not strong enough for the military leaders. Again, this is purely conjectural.

6–10 Note that Jehu was anointed "king over Yahweh's people" (מֶלֶךְ אֶל־עַם יהוה, *lᵉmelek̲ ʾel- ʿam yhwh*).[272] That phrase itself is significant. The people of Israel did not, could not, belong to Baal. They were Yahweh's, betrothed to him at Sinai, and he would do whatever was necessary to keep them from falling into the hands of some other lover. That being so, the house of Ahab could not be allowed to continue. In these verses the prophet draws together the ancient curses that had been pronounced upon the houses of Jeroboam (1 Kgs 14:10) and Baasha (1 Kgs 16:11) with those pronounced over the house of Ahab and Jezebel (1 Kgs 21:20–24). In so doing, he paints a picture of darkening gloom in which the sins of the former kings paved the way for the climactic sins of this family. In particular, it was the killing of *the prophets* that called down the divine wrath (cf. 1 Kgs 18:4, 13). Why should this act be singled out? Why not judge them for their attempt to make Baal the God of Israel? In fact, those murders were the most graphic expression of that attempt. These deaths were what made the effort the more damnable. So long as there were men (and women, no doubt) who were boldly condemning in the name of Yahweh what the monarchy was trying to do, the effort would be less than effective. Thus, the only thing to do had been, as was the case with Naboth and his vineyard, the draconian use of royal power to silence the offending voices. For this, Yahweh had no mercy. Not a single male would be left alive to carry on Ahab's line (v. 8).[273] Of course, the fact that the judgment had been delayed for a generation (1 Kgs 21:27–28) did indicate that mercy might be found even for these people. We can only wonder how the story might have been different if Ahaziah had believed Elijah and repented, or if, following him, Joram had believed Elisha and repented. But it was not to be. There is no evidence that Elisha was ever anything but a troublesome nuisance or a diverting oddity to Joram; he seems never to have been the voice of Reality itself, and so the end had come.

It is Jezebel for whom the most severe judgment was reserved. Her death would occur "in the plot of Jezreel" (בְּחֵלֶק יִזְרְעֶאל, *bᵊḥēleq yizrᵊʿeʾl*). It seems probable that Cogan and Tadmor (108) are correct when they say that this "plot" was none other than that which had once belonged to Naboth.[274] "The blood of all the servants of Yahweh from the hand of Jezebel" (דְמֵי כָּל־עֲבָדַי יְהוה מִיַּד אִיזָבֶל, *ûd̲ᵊmê kol- ʿab̲d̲ê yhwh miyyad̲ ʾîzāb̲el*) (v.7) probably has Naboth in mind, and the plurality of "servants" suggest that there may well have been others, like Naboth, whose adherence to Yahweh's covenant had in

---

272. Jehu is the only northern ruler to be anointed. Furthermore, like Saul and David, he was anointed by a prophet. These facts underline his significance and the significance of this moment. The action literally fulfills Yahweh's instructions to Elijah in 1 Kgs 19:16.

273. For a discussion of this traditional phrase, see above on 1 Kgs 21:21.

274. Syr. suggests this when it translates "the *inheritance* in Jezreel."

one way or another provoked the queen's wrath. Here the implication of the words in 1 Kings 21 is made explicit. Jezebel's body would be eaten by dogs, and thus, "there will be no one to bury (her)" (אֵין קֹבֵר, *ʾên qōḇēr*), a terrible fate in the ancient world, for one's spirit would be doomed to roam the earth.[275]

11–12 After the prophet had fled, Jehu went out and tried to act as though nothing significant had happened, even though the anointing oil was probably still glistening on his hair. After all, this was a prophet, a "madman" (מְשֻׁגָּע, *hamšuggāʿ*) by definition, as they themselves had called him.[276] Perhaps he was uncertain how his comrades would respond to what had happened. The description of them as "servants of his lord" (עַבְדֵי אֲדֹנָיו, *ʿaḇdê ʾăḏōnāyw*) gives some weight to the possibility that they might see him as a traitor.[277] But they would not be put off. In the banter of the "locker-room" they called him a liar[278] and demanded to know what had really happened. He waffled on the details of what had been said responding with something like, "this and that", but finally got to the point: he had been anointed ... king.

13 If Jehu had any question about the other officers' response to his anointing, it was instantly laid to rest. They tore off their cloaks and laid them on the steps[279] where he was standing. The significance of this act is unknown. Obviously, it is an act of adulation, but the reason why this particular activity was thought to express such emotion is unclear. There may be a parallel in Jesus' triumphal entry, but again the purpose is unclear. Barnes (255) cites Cato saying that Roman soldiers threw down their capes for him to walk on when he left military service. Perhaps our "red carpet treatment" is similar. This immediate response by the army is similar to that of the army when they heard that Zimri had usurped the throne, and immediately proclaimed their commander Omri to be king (1 Kgs 16:16). It suggests that there had been dissatisfaction with Joram, for whatever reason.

---

275. Cf. Isa 14:18–20; 22:16–18; Jer 8:2; 16:4, 6; 22:19; 25:33. See also the Mesopotamian curse: *ANET*, 538.

276. Prophets customarily acted, dressed, and spoke in an eccentric manner that appeared deranged to ordinary people (cf. Num 11:26–28; Isa 20:3; Jer 20:7–8; Ezek 4:4–5; Mark 1:6).

277. Their question, "Is it well?" (הֲשָׁלוֹם, *hăšālôm*) will be repeated several times in the chapter (2 Kgs 9: 17, 18, 19, 22). Here it was well, but in those instances, that was hardly to be the case. See Saul Olyan, "*Hašālôm*: Some Literary Considerations of 2 Kings 9," *CBQ* 46 (1984): 652–58.

278. Heb. שֶׁקֶר, *šeqer*, "something worthless, false," often applied to idols. For a similar expression see Jer 37:14.

279. The adj. modifying "steps" appears only here (גֶּרֶם, *gerem*), so its meaning is conjectural. "Bare" is the most commonly accepted suggestion. Gk. transliterates γαρεμ (*garem*); Vulg. "under his feet"; Syr. "on a seat in the steps."

Wiseman (221) points out that "Long live the king" seems to have been reserved for the acclamation of the general public (1 Sam 10:24; 2 Sam 16:16; 1 Kgs 1:34; 2 Kgs 11:12; 2 Chr. 23:11) and that this explains its absence here.

Selected Bibliography

Čapek, F. "Balancing Evidence about Jehu and Joash in Ancient Near Eastern Texts: Critical Assessment." *Communio Viatorum* 56 (2014): 23–34.

Garcia-Treto, F. O. "The Fall of the House: A Carnivalesque Reading of 2 Kings 9 and 10." *JSOT* 15 (1990): 47–65.

Schniedewind, W. H. "History and Interpretation: The Religion of Ahab and Manasseh in Book of Kings." *CBQ* 55 (1993): 649–61.

The Deaths of Joram and Ahaziah (9:14–29)

Translation

14 So Jehu, son of Jehoshaphat, son of Nimshi, conspired against Joram. (Joram and all Israel had been guarding Ramoth-gilead in front of Hazael, king of Syria. **15** But Joram the king had returned to be healed in Jezreel from the wounds which the Syrians had inflicted on him when he had fought against Hazael, king of Syria.) Jehu said, "If this is what you really want,[280] let no one escape from the city to inform those in Jezreel." **16** So Jehu mounted up and went in the direction of Jezreel, for Joram was lying there, and Ahaziah, king of Judah, had come down to see Joram. **17** Now a watchman was standing on the tower in Jezreel and he saw Jehu's crowd as he came, and he said, "I see a crowd." Joram said, "Get a horseman and send him to meet them, and say, 'Is all well?' "[281] **18** So a rider on horseback went to meet him and he said, "Thus says the king, 'Is all well?' " Jehu said, "What is wellness to you? Circle around behind me." The watchman reported, saying, "The messenger reached them, but he is not coming back." **19** He sent a second horseman, and he came to them and said, "Thus says the king, 'Is all well?' " Jehu said, "What is wellness to you? Circle around behind me." **20** The watchman reported, saying, "He reached them, but he is not coming back. And the driving is like that of Jehu, son of Nimshi, because he is driving madly." **21** Joram said, "Harness up!" So they[282] harnessed his chariot and Joram, king of Israel, and Ahaziah, king of Judah went out, each in his own chariot and they went to meet Jehu and came upon him in the plot of Naboth, the Jezreelite. **22** When Joram saw Jehu, he said, "Is all well, Jehu?" He said, "How can it be well as long as the prostitutions and sorceries of Jezebel your mother are so many?" **23** Joram wheeled his chariot

280. Heb. נֶפֶשׁ *nepeš,* more than just a casual wish.

281. The root שָׁלוֹם *šālôm* carries the idea of "wholeness." Thus, it can refer to one's health, or in this case, a state of well-being. In v. 26 below where it is translated "repay," it refers to satisfying a debt, making the situation whole.

282. Heb. "he," but Vulg. and Syr. and Gk^{B} read "they."

around[283] and fled, and he said to Ahaziah, "Treachery, Ahaziah!" **24** Jehu
drew his bow and struck Joram between the shoulders and the arrow came
out through his heart and he slumped down in his chariot. **25** He said to
Bidkar, third in charge, "Pick him up and throw him on the plot of land of
Naboth the Jezreelite! Remember when you and I were riders together following Ahab his father and Yahweh laid the pronouncement on him, **26** 'I
swear that as I have seen the blood of Naboth and his sons yesterday,' says
Yahweh, 'I will repay you on this plot.' So now pick him up and throw him
on the plot, according to the word of Yahweh." **27** Now Ahaziah, king of
Judah, saw and fled on the road to Beth-haggan, and Jehu pursued him and
said, "Strike him too!" And they struck him in the chariot on the Ascent of
Gur which is by Ibleam. He fled to Megiddo and died there. **28** His servants
took him in a chariot to Jerusalem and they buried him in his sepulcher with
his fathers in the city of David. **29** Ahaziah had become king over Judah in
the eleventh year of Joram, son of Ahab.

Textual Notes

15a. נַפְשְׁכֶם: Gk. adds "with me"; Vulg. and Syr. with MT.

15b. K לַגִּיד; Q לְהַגִּיד: Elision of the ה (*he*) is probably an example of colloquial speech.

16a. וַיִּרְכַּב: Syr. "rode in a chariot"; Gk. and Vulg. with MT.

16b. וַיֵּלֶךְ: Gk. "went down to"; Vulg. and Syr. with MT.

16c. שָׁמָּה: Gk adds "being healed in Jezreel from the arrows with which the Arameans shot him down in Rammath in the battle with Hazael the Aramean for he was powerful and a man of power"; Vulg. and Syr. with MT.

16d. יוֹרָם: Syr. adds "who was lying sick in Jezreel"; Gk. and Vulg. with MT.

19a. שָׁלוֹם: The versions all state this as a question. Either the interrogative particle is accidentally omitted from MT or the question was expressed through inflection (see GKC [§150*a*] citing 2 Sam 18:29).

20a–a. וְהַמִּנְהָג כְּמִנְהַג יֵהוּא בֶן־נִמְשִׁי כִּי בְשִׁגָּעוֹן יִנְהָג: Gk. "he that was bringing was bringing Jehu … because it was alternating back and forth"; Vulg. "the pace is like that of the pace of Jehu … because it is stepped headlong"; Syr. with MT.

21a. וַיֶּאְסֹר: Vulg., Syr., and Gk[B] " "they"; Gk. with MT.

21b. רִכְבּוֹ: Gk. "a chariot"; Syr. "chariots"; Vulg. with MT.

25a. שָׂא: Gk. lacks: Vulg. and Syr. with MT.

---

283. Heb. "Joram turned his hand"; see also 1 Kgs 22:34.

27a. גַּם־אֹתוֹ הַכֻּהוּ: Gk. "Him too, and he struck him"; Vulg. with MT; Syr. "Slay him too, and they slew him." Cogan and Tadmor (111) suggest that the reading now reflected in Syr. (with two forms of נכה, the imp. and the impf.), is closest to the original. The Gk. lost the first and MT the second. *CTAT* (392–93) considers MT possible but unlikely.

28a–a. וַיַּרְכִּבוּ אֹתוֹ עֲבָדָיו יְרוּשָׁלָֽמָה: Gk. "they put him in a chariot and brought him to Jerusalem"; Vulg. the same except "his chariot"; Syr. "they took him up and brought him to Jerusalem." Gray (549) says that the MT need not be emended but can be understood as "they drove him in a chariot."

Commentary

In this dramatic account we read of beginning of the end for the house of Ahab. Joram and his nephew Ahaziah meet their ends in a manner worthy of any novel. The suspense builds slowly and inexorably to its sudden end. We the readers know why Jehu is making his mad dash toward Jezreel: he is the anointed executioner. But hapless Joram and even more hapless Ahaziah have no clue. The general of the army is coming in a headlong dash, not even taking long enough to parley with messengers. Either the news is very good: Hazael has been routed, and Jehu is hurrying to make the announcement, or very bad: Israel has been defeated, and Jehu is running for his life. What apparently never entered either man's mind was that there might be treachery afoot. We wonder if, when they met him (or found him waiting?) on the plot of land that had been Naboth's vineyard, a first spark of alarm shot through Joram's mind, at least. But if it did, there was no question when they heard Jehu's loaded response to the innocent question.

It has taken nine verses to get to this point, but the falling of the terrible axe is narrated in just two. To be sure, the extermination of the dynasty will take the rest of this chapter, and two more, but in the sudden execution of Joram, the die is cast, and the rest follows with a deadly inexorability.

14–16 After the initial announcement of what is taking place: a conspiracy against Joram, the narrator reminds us what Joram's situation is. Cogan and Tadmor (108–9) judge that this is the original statement and the similar one in 8:28–29 is secondary. Others, take the opposite view. In these kinds of discussions so many assumptions are involved concerning how this literature arrived in its present form, that it is almost impossible to adjudicate the alternatives. It seems likely to me that if the accounts were first circulated orally, such a reminder as this of previous data would be quite normal, even necessary (see Hobbs, 112; House, 289).

The appearance of the Heb. נֶפֶשׁ, *nepeš*, "soul, self, mind," in Jehu's question to his comrades (v. 15) underlines the seriousness of the situation. Is this dangerous expedient *really* what they want, or is it only a passing fancy? See Gen 23:8 for a similar use of נֶפֶשׁ, *nepeš*. If they are committed, then the first step is not to allow Joram to be warned of what is coming to him. The next step is to mount up[284] and get to Jezreel immediately. Throughout the narrative, Jehu's decisiveness, often impetuous decisiveness, is evident. This may be another reason why Yahweh chose him.

17–20 The three-fold aspect of what is described here is reminiscent of Elijah's encounter with Ahaziah (1:9–16); Elijah's attempt to dissuade Elisha from following him (2:2–6); and Elisha's efforts to revive the Shunammite's son (4:29–35). While this may be evidence of literary structuring, it certainly achieves the desired aim of heightening the suspense and increasing the impact of the final event. The typical English rendering of the repeated question הֲשָׁלוֹם, *hašālôm* as "Is it peace?" (vv. 17, 18, 19, 22) is misleading in that it suggests that the question of conspiracy was in Joram's mind, and that he was asking whether Joram was coming with warlike intent. The clue to the correct understanding is in Jehu's comrades' use of the same terminology in v. 11. It is a neutral inquiry about the situation: "Is everything all right?"[285] It is simply a request for information about what has prompted this precipitous journey. But Jehu, in his repeated responses to the question utilizes the broader sense of the word to make it into a statement about the condition of the nation.

The word translated "crowd" (שִׁפְעַת, *šip῾aṯ*) (v. 17) has a rather indefinite meaning referring to "a mass of some sort." It suggests that what the watchman saw was more of a rabble than an organized military troop. It again speaks of the haste in which this was all done. We recall Elisha's instructions to his emissary to get in and get out as quickly as possible. Once the process was set in motion, it would be easy to get trampled, figuratively if not literally.

Both of the messengers sought to impress upon Jehu the authority of their position. Their question came directly from the king (vv. 18, 19). But Jehu was not impressed. His somewhat enigmatic question to them is on the order of, "What do you care?" And without slowing down, he peremptorily ordered them to fall in behind him. Did they simply respond to the voice of authority, or did they sense what this man was about? We do not know, and that is part of the fascination of the account.

21 When it was clear that this was Jehu, the general of the army, and that he could not even slow down enough to parley with the king's messengers, and then diplomatically send them on ahead of him to request an audience with

---

284. Cogan and Tadmor point out the difficulty in determining the precise connotation of the various uses of רָכַב, *rāḵaḇ* (109). It may be that initially it was connected with "mounting and riding a chariot" (מֶרְכָּבָה, *merkāḇâ*, "chariot"), but if so, the connotations evidently broadened as cavalry came into play. Thus, it is not entirely clear whether Jehu mounted a horse or a chariot. The later reference to "driving" (v. 20) suggests that it was a chariot. On the other hand, the root seems to be used in vv. 17 and 19 to refer to "a rider on horseback." See *HALOT* (3.1230–33).

285. See p. 177n277 on the translation above.

the king, Joram recognized that this was no time to stand on formality and that whatever was going on, it demanded immediate attention. But there is no indication yet that he recognized the danger in which he stood. Surely if he had, he would have barricaded himself in the fortress and thumbed his nose at the intruder outside, who was in no position to mount a siege. Instead, he and Ahaziah, full of curiosity, mounted their chariots and went out to their doom. They "encountered" (מָצָא, *māṣāʾ*) their man at a portentous spot: the piece of land that had once belonged to Naboth the Jezreelite. It is tempting, in view of vv. 25 and 26, to believe that Jehu, like any good general, had chosen his spot for the encounter, but the narrator does not satisfy our curiosity on the point. Perhaps we are to think of it as another instance of divine providence.

22–24 One last time Joram asks about the *šālôm* of the situation (in Ramoth-gilead?). But Jehu does not want to talk about that. It is Israel he wants to talk about, and nothing is well, or can be well, in Israel as long as "Jezebel, your mother," is alive. Her "prostitutions" (זְנוּנִים, *zənûnîm*) and "sorceries" (כֶּשֶׁף, *kešep̄*) are a reference to her worship of Baal. Israel was Yahweh's bride (Hos 2:19–20; Ezek 16:8) and for her to go after other gods was to prostitute herself (Hos 4:10–11; 6:10; Ezek 16:15, 20). That is what Jezebel had been leading Israel to do. Furthermore, sympathetic magic was an intrinsic part of the worship of the pagan gods. This was the supposed means to get the gods to supply the needs of the worshippers. But Israel was forbidden to engage in these practices. Yahweh is not part of this world and cannot be manipulated through this world. He can only be related to through trust and surrender (cf. Deut 18:10–14). So there was a breach between Israel and Yahweh, and there could be no well-being, no wholeness, for Israel while this sort of thing was going on.

Now the light came on for Joram, and perhaps it came home to him with a shudder what ground his chariot was standing on. Jehu was not here as his servant, his officer, but as his nemesis. Wheeling the chariot around,[286] and shouting to Ahaziah, he tried to escape, but it was futile. With a single sweep of his hand,[287] Jehu had his bow out, drawn, and released, and Joram was a dead man, shot through the heart, slumping to the floor of his chariot.

---

286. Long has noted the large number of parallels between this account and the one of Ahab's death in 1 Kgs 22:34–38 (367). One of the more striking is the appearance in both accounts of this phrase for turning a chariot: "he turned his hand" (וַיַּהֲפֹךְ יְהוֹרָם יָדָיו, *wayyahăpōḵ yᵉhôrām yāḏāyw*) here and in 1 Kings 22:34 (הֲפֹךְ יָדְךָ, *hăpōḵ yoḏḵā*). It is apparent that the narrator intends that we should associate the death of the son with the death of the father.

287. Heb. "He filled his hand with his bow" (מִלֵּא יָדוֹ בַקֶּשֶׁת, *millēʾ yāḏô ḇaqqešeṯ*).

25–26 Now we learn something for which we were not prepared. Jehu and his second in command[288] had been with Ahab[289] on that day, perhaps as much as twenty years earlier, when Elijah pronounced doom upon Ahab for the contrived murder of Naboth (and apparently "his sons" as well) and the judicial theft of his land. Here may be another reason for the choice of Jehu. He had had an experience as a young man that had marked him, and he had a conviction on some level that "the word of Yahweh" (דְּבַר יהוה, *dᵉḇar yhwh*) would be fulfilled. He could not have known then that it would be fulfilled through him, but he had evidently believed it would be somehow because he had never forgotten it.

There is no pretense here of a direct quote of Elijah's words to Ahab (they are not recorded in the form of an oath in 1 Kings 21:21–22), and if it was, it would be suspect, because it is highly unlikely that Jehu would have been able to recall the words verbatim after the passage of so many years. What we have is the gist of what had been said, and the sense is entirely congruent with the original. Elijah had said that the dogs would lick Ahab's blood on this ground, while in fact it was the dogs of Samaria that had licked it (1 Kgs 22:38), but now it is indeed Ahab's blood through his son's parallel death that would stain that ground. As the poet has said, "Though the mills of God grind slowly, they grind exceedingly small."[290]

27–29 Now we begin to see another side of Jehu. If he was decisive and impetuous, he was also implacable, a trait that will be more and more evident as the narrative continues to unfold. Ahaziah fled southward from Jezreel on the road to Beth-haggan, modern Jenin, about eleven miles south of Jezreel. He was apparently heading for either Jerusalem or Samaria. But a mile or two south of Beth-haggan, near Ibleam, his enemies caught up with him. Perhaps it was because Ahaziah was a grandson of Ahab through Athaliah that Jehu gave the command "Strike him too!" (גַּם־אֹתוֹ הַכֻּהוּ, *gam-ʾōṯô hakkuhû*). It may be argued that as a young man under the thumb of his mother, the very dedicated Athaliah, he could have done great harm had he lived, but it is still hard to believe that his death was really necessary. But Jehu's bloodlust was high, and there was no stopping him. A century later, Hosea spoke judgment on the house of Jehu "because of the blood of Jezreel" (Hos 1:4); it is to be wondered if the prophet had in mind this and other similar actions like it, explicable perhaps, but not really justifiable.

---

288. Heb. שָׁלִישׁ, *šālîš,* probably not the third man in the chariot. Possibly the third in command of the army, after Joram and Jehu. Or possibly Jehu's personal aide. See the discussion on 7:2.

289. Heb. צְמָדִים, *ṣᵉmāḏîm* (v. 25) connotes being teamed together in pairs. So "side by side" ESV, NRSV; "together in chariots" NIV; "together as a team" Hobbs, 117.

290. Friedrich von Logau, "Sinngedichte" III.ii.24, c. 1654. Translated by H. W. Longfellow in "Retribution," *Poetic Aphorisms,* 1846.

Wounded, Ahaziah seems to have realized he could not outrun his pursuers up the ascent of Gur, whose location is uncertain, but apparently up through the hills to Samaria and on down to the coast, so he turned to the northeast for a somewhat easier run along the rim of the Jezreel Valley to Megiddo, where he could reasonably hope news of the rebellion had not yet reached. He arrived at his destination, but died there.[291] His retainers, who were either with him in his flight, or more unaccountably, awaiting him in Megiddo, put his body in his chariot and transported him to Jerusalem for a burial befitting a king, even one who had only ruled a few months.

This latter fact probably explains the odd v. 29. Someone, noting that in light of the mismatching of accession years in the two kingdoms, Ahaziah seemed to have become king in the twelfth year of Joram, ruled a year, and yet died in the same year he became king.[292]

Biblical Theology Comments

It may be asked whether the house of Ahab was brought to an end over the worship of Baal or because of the greedy appropriation of Naboth's land. If we answer "yes" to the first, an answer that seems necessary in view of the tenor of the overall narrative, extending from 1 Kings 16:29 to this point, then we ask why it is that it was in connection with the judicial fraud that the specific pronouncement of the death of Ahab and the destruction of his dynasty was made (1 Kgs 21:20–22). The answer to these questions lies in the unique connection between the worship of Yahweh, the limits of royal power, the rule of justice, and the value of all persons.

In biblical religion, the fundamental principle is that Yahweh alone is God, that he is not part of this cosmos, that he has established the principles upon which the world operates (מִשְׁפָּט, *mišpāṭ*), that he values all people equally, and that his rule is motivated out of self-giving love. In Baal worship, as in all the other religions of the ancient world, except Israel's, the gods are part of this world and are to be manipulated through this world. The gods themselves are manipulative and their needs are primary. The king alone is the image of the divine in the world. Humans are the slaves of the gods.

In that light, what happened with Naboth's vineyard is a perfect illustration of the effects of Baal worship in everyday life. It is very interesting that Ahab, with a recrudescence of Yahwism still in his veins, felt forced to accept (although in a deep sulk) that if Naboth was unwilling to sell his land there seemed to be nothing to more to be done. Jezebel, on the other hand, could see no such limitation. If the king had a need (wanted something), then there

291. 2 Chr. 22:9 has him hiding in Samaria and executed by Jehu there. It does not seem possible to reconcile the two accounts.

292. Thiele accounts for this discrepancy as an indication that Judah changed to non-accession year dating (with Israel) at this time, and that the scribe here is adjusting the dating on that basis (68–69).

was no reason why, as a viceroy of the god, he could not manipulate justice to fulfill that need. It that entailed trampling on and destroying a mere human, what was the problem in that? The idea that the principles of Deity are—not need driven, are absolutely consistent, and are motivated solely for the good of his creatures, and that rules, such as land possession, are bound by these principles, was something absolutely foreign to Jezebel's way of thinking. Ahab's sin was that in spite of knowing better, he was quite willing to enjoy the benefits of the judicial murder without raising a hand to stop it.

So, was the house of Ahab destroyed for its worship of Baal, or for the murder of Naboth and his sons, and the theft of the family inheritance? The answer to both questions is "yes."

Selected Bibliography

Cronauer, P. *The Stories about Naboth the Jezreelite.* London: T&T Clark, 2005.

Na'aman, N. "Naboth's Vineyard and the Foundation of Jezreel." *JSOT* 33 (2008): 197–218.

Rofé, A. "The Vineyard of Naboth: The Origin and Message of the Story." *VT* 38 (1988): 89–104.

The Death of Jezebel (9:30–37)

Translation

30 Then Jehu came toward Jezreel, and Jezebel heard about it. She put dark cosmetics[293] on her eyes and dressed her hair and looked down from the window. **31** Then Jehu came through the gate, and she said, "Is it well, Zimri, murderer of his master?"[294] **32** Jehu lifted his face to the window and said, "Who is with me? Who?" Two or three[295] eunuchs looked down at him. **33** He said, "Throw her down!" and they threw her down. Some of her blood splashed on the wall and on the horses, and he trampled her. **34** Then he went in and ate and drank, and he said, "Take care of this cursed woman and bury her, for she was the daughter of a king." **35** So they went to bury her, but they could not find any[296] of her except the skull, the feet and the palms of the hands. **36** They returned and reported to him and he said, "It is the word of Yahweh which he spoke by the hand of his servant Elijah the Tishbite saying, 'On the plot in Jezreel dogs will eat the body of Jezebel. **37** The corpse of Jezebel will be dung on the surface of the field in the plot of Jezreel so that none can say, "This was Jezebel." ' "

293. *Kohl*, פּוּךְ, *pûk* is "powdered antimony." Widely used as eyeshadow in the ancient world. Cf. Jer 4:30.

294. On the shift from 2nd to 3rd person, see GKC (§144*p*).

295. GKC (§134*s*) identifies this construction as a way of indicating an indefinite number.

296. See GKC (§119*m*) for the partitive use of the prep. ב.

Textual Notes

31a. בַשַּׁעַר: Gk. "city"; Vulg. and Syr. with MT.

32a. הַחַלּוֹן: Gk. adds "and saw her"; Vulg. and Syr. with MT.

32b–b. מִי אִתִּי מִי: Gk. reads "Who are you? Come down with me." Vulg. and Syr. with MT. Gk. apparently duplicates Heb. אתי reading it first as "you" (2fs, אַתְּי) and second as "with me" (אִתִּי).

32c. שְׁלֹשָׁה: Gk. omits; Vulg. and Syr. with MT.

33a. שִׁמְטֻהוּ: Reading 3fs suffix with Q (שִׁמְטוּהָ) and all the versions. The 3ms K is possible a copyist's error with the following ו (*waw*).

33b. וַיִּרְמְסֶנָּה: The versions all read "they," presumably the horses, which Syr. makes explicit. See the "Commentary" below.

37a. וְהָיְת: *Ketiv* here represents the archaic form.

37b–b. בְּחֵלֶק יִזְרְעֶאל: G^L omits; Vulg. and Syr. with MT.

Commentary

30 The narrator continues his dramatic recital of the destruction of Ahab's house by telling of the ghastly death of Ahab's wife and Joram's mother, Jezebel. Evidently Jehu returned to Jezreel after the pursuit of Ahaziah, and Jezebel and heard about his return from within the confines of the harem. Whatever she was, Jezebel was no weakling. She would have heard of the death of her son and would have known that Jehu would not leave her alive. So she arrayed herself as the queen she was, and waited for his coming.[297] She would not die whining.

31 Apparently the harem looked down on the public square inside the gate, and when the usurper's chariot came through the gate, the defiant queen called down to him from her "window" (חַלּוֹן, *ḥallôn*). Her words, "Is it well?," (הֲשָׁלוֹם) mock the typical greeting that has already appeared five times since 9:11. She knows full well that everything is far from well, at least from her perspective. While she appears in all her regal dignity, she casts Jehu in the

297. Cogan and Tadmor (112) are right when they dismiss the idea that by putting on makeup and sitting in the window Jezebel thought she might be able to seduce Jehu or negotiate with him. Besides the fact that she would not have been a young woman by this time, her mocking reference to Zimri, certainly lays any such idea at rest. These were acts of defiance on the part of a person determined to go down fighting. For the alternative, see S. B. Parker, "Jezebel's Reception of Jehu," *Maarav* 1 (1978) 67–78. See also Anne Létourneau, "Jézebel: Généalogie d'une Femme Fatale," *ScEs* 66 (2014) 189–211.

role of an upstart who is doomed to failure. She does this with her allusion to Zimri, the captain of half the chariotry who destroyed the dynasty of Baasha. Zimri ruled for a grand total of seven days before committing suicide in view of the imminent victory of Omri, his general, who was the father of Ahab (1 Kgs 16:9–20). By comparing Jehu to Zimri, she not only declares him to be someone who has broken his oath of loyalty to his master, and is a murderer, but predicts that his reign would be just as insignificant and temporary as Zimri's had been. In this, she was wrong, for Jehu's dynasty, lasting almost exactly 100 years, would be the longest in Israel's history. But one cannot fault her for utilizing the best attack available to her at the moment.[298]

32 In the manner we have come to expect from Jehu, he does not even respond to Jezebel's mockery, but asks "who" (מִי, *mî*) is for him up there. Note that he does not ask *if* someone is for him, but in confidence assumes someone is, and only asks "who." The doubling of the interrogative pronoun (מִי) underlines the intensity of the question. Some of the eunuchs[299] who were in charge of the women of the harem looked out, evidently casting their vote merely by doing so. Like the one-word command that sealed Ahaziah's fate (v. 27), so here Jehu spoke Jezebel's end in a single Hebrew word (although it requires three English ones), "Throw her down!" (שִׁמְטוּהָ [Q], *šimṭûhā*). Much like the suddenness in the account of Joram's death (v. 24), so here, after the dramatic build-up, the actual moment of Jezebel's death is reported tersely. She is instantly out and down, striking the pavement with such force that her "blood splashed on the wall" (וַיִּז מִדָּמָהּ אֶל־הַקִּיר, *wayyiz middāmāh ʾel-haqqîr*) and also on the horses of Jehu's chariot. Without a moment's hesitation Israel's new king drove the chariot over her body to insure that she was dead.[300]

34–36 It seems certain that Jehu's next actions were calculated, although the narrator allows us to reach that conclusion on our own. The new king pays no attention to the dead queen, the one whose actions, according to v. 22, were at the heart of all that was taking place. But she is dead, and the king has other things to think about, such as the fact that he is hungry and thirsty. Some suggest that this was a display meal in the royal chambers in the course of which Jehu was securing the loyalty of Jezreel's leaders. That may be, but the disregard for the body of the woman who had dominated Israel for some

---

298. See Saul Olyan, "2 Kings 9:31 – Jehu as Zimri," *HTR* 78 (1985) 204–6.

299. In this case, as overseers of the harem, actually castrated. See above on 1 Kgs 22:9 and 2 Kgs 8:6 for discussion of this term in other contexts. See Cogan and Tadmor (112) for a full discussion.

300. As noted above on the text, the versions are unanimous in emending the Heb. sing. "he trampled" to a pl. "they trampled." However, with Cogan and Tadmor (112), there is every reason to go with the MT as it unsparingly depicts Jehu as being brutally decisive, which is entirely consistent with the way in which the text depicts him elsewhere.

thirty-five years could not have been accidental. It was a way of saying in the most decisive manner that that woman's influence simply did not exist anymore. It was also a display of audacious confidence. After all, the city was by no means secure. Yet, the conqueror calmly stops the proceedings to have lunch! Whether he actually felt that confident or not, the action could not have failed to communicate confidence to all who were looking on.

Eventually, Jehu, perhaps now thinking as a king, decides that the body of "the daughter of a king" should receive some respect even if she is "accursed" (הָאֲרוּרָה, *hā ʾărûrâ*), and dispatches servants to pick up the body and bury it. But they have waited too long. The dogs have been at the body, and there is nothing left but "the skull, the feet and the palms of the hands" (הַגֻּלְגֹּלֶת וְהָרַגְלַיִם וְכַפּוֹת הַיָּדָיִם, *haggulgōleṯ wᵉhāraḡlayim wᵉḵappôṯ hayyāḏāy-im*)[301] On hearing this, as with Joram, Jehu was reminded of what Elijah had said years before, and in a paraphrase of the prophet's pronouncement recalls what he had said.[302] What had taken place here had been the fulfillment of those dire words. Ahab, his wife, and his scion were dead, their blood licked by dogs, and their bodies eaten by dogs. While Ahab had been permitted a decent burial, his son and his wife were not; they were given over to the worst punishment that could be imagined in Israel. Because their bodies were not buried, their disembodied spirits, separated from their ancestors, were doomed to wander forever.

37 One of the reasons why Jezebel's body was to be dismembered by dogs and left unrecognizable in the field was so that no one could venerate her body or worship at her tomb: "This was Jezebel" (זֹאת אִיזָבֶל, *zōʾṯ ʾîzāḇel*). The phrase "as dung on the surface of the field" (כְּדֹמֶן עַל־פְּנֵי הַשָּׂדֶה, *kᵉḏōmen ʿal-pᵉnê haśśāḏe*) is a conventional one for unburied bodies and should not be made too much of here in regards Jezebel.[303] Of more significance is the repeated phrase "in the plot of Jezreel" (בְּחֵלֶק יִזְרְעֶאל, *bᵉḥēleq yizrᵉʿeʾl*) (cf. 9:10). The use of the word חֵלֶק, "plot" with reference to Naboth's land (9:21, 25, 26) makes it clear that its less defined use in 9:10 and here are still referring

301. Since יָד, *yāḏ*, "hand" could denote anything from the elbow downward, "the palms" (כַּפִּים, *kappîm*) here may denote what we would call the "hands." Hands, feet, and skulls were often the trophies of war and served for body counts.

302. Commentators (e.g., Gray, 548; Hobbs, 113; Cohn 71) have devoted a good deal of attention to attempting to determine exactly what Elijah said or did not say on the basis of Jehu's quotation of him. It seems to me that this is not necessary. Jehu is speaking from memory. The important point is that he is not making the prophet say something substantially other than what the text reported him to have said originally. What he predicted had indeed come to pass: the dynasty had come to its end in the very ways Elijah had said it would; Yahweh's word is completely reliable.

303. Ps 83:10; Jer 8:2; 9:22; 16:4; 25:33.

to Naboth's "plot" specifically. The disgraceful final disposition of Jezebel's body was due to her disgraceful treatment of Naboth and his sons.[304]

Selected Bibliography

Appler, D. A. "From Queen to Cuisine: Food Imagery in the Jezebel Narrative." *Semeia* 86 (1999): 55–71.

McKinlay, J. E. "Negotiating the Frame for Viewing the Death of Jezebel." *Biblical Interpretation* 10 (2002): 305–23.

The Destruction of Ahab's Family (10:1–17)

Translation

10:1 Ahab had seventy descendants in Samaria. Jehu wrote letters and sent
them to Samaria, to the princes of Jezreel,[305] to the elders, and to the guardians
of Ahab's descendants,[306] saying, **2** "And now when this letter reaches you, you
have the sons of your master with you, and chariotry and horses, and fortified
cities,[307] and weapons, **3** so you should choose the best and most appropriate
of the sons of your master and put him on the throne of his father and fight
for the house of your master." **4** They were extremely frightened, and said,
"Look, two kings could not stand before him, so how can *we* stand?" **5** So
the one who was over that house and the one who was over the city, and the
elders and the guardians sent to Jehu, saying, "We are your servants and all
that you say to us we will do. We will not make anyone king; whatever is good
in your eyes do." **6** So he wrote them a second letter saying, "If you are for me
and will obey me,[308] take the heads of the men,[309] the sons of your master, and
come to me at this time tomorrow in Jezreel." The sons of the king, seventy
men, were with the leading men[310] of the city, who were bringing them up.
7 When the letter reached them, they took the sons of the king and they
slaughtered seventy men and they put their heads in baskets and sent them
to him in Jezreel. **8** The messenger came and reported to him, saying, "They
brought the heads of the sons of the king." He said, "Put them in two heaps
at the entrance of the gate until morning." **9** Now in the morning he went
out and stood and said to all the people, "You are righteous. Look here, I

---

304. Jerome T. Walsh, "On היה in 2 Kings 9:37," *VT* 60 (2010): 152–53, and a reflection by Gary A. Rendsburg, "Notes on 2 Kings 9:36–37," *VT* 66 (2016): 317–23.

305. Gk. reads "Samaria"; Vulg. "city"; Syr. "Jezreel." This variety favors the MT (יִזְרְעֶאל, *yizrᵊ ʿeʾl*) as the original. See the "Commentary" below.

306. Reading with Gk, and Syr., Heb. lacks "descendants." Provan's suggestion that אֹמְנִים, *ʾōmᵊnîm* does not refer to "guardians" of the descendants, but should be translated "stalwarts" seems forced, especially in view of the unanimous reading of the versions as some form of guardian (217).

307. With all the versions. Heb. "city" (עִיר, *wᵊ ʿîr*).

308. Heb. "will listen to my voice" (לְקֹלִי אַתֶּם שֹׁמְעִים, *lᵊqōlî ʾattem šōmᵊ ʿîm*).

309. For the const. state used to introduce words in apposition, see GKC (§130*e*).

310. See *IBHS* (§14.5c) for this reading.

conspired against my master and murdered him. But who smote all these? **10** Know then that no word of Yahweh that Yahweh spoke concerning the house of Ahab will fall to the ground. Yahweh has done that which he spoke by the hand of his servant Elijah." **11** Jehu struck down all who remained from the house of Ahab in Jezreel, and all his nobles, and his friends, and his priests until no survivor remained to him. **12** Then he got up and went to Samaria. On the way, at Beth-eked of the shepherds, **13** Jehu encountered the brothers of Ahaziah, king of Judah. He said, "Who are you?" They said, "We are the brothers of Ahaziah, and we have come down to the children of the king and the children of the queen mother[311] to wish them well." **14** He said, "Take them alive!" So they took them alive and slaughtered them at the cistern of Beth-eked, forty-two men, of whom not one remained. **15** He went from there and encountered Jehonadab, son of Rechab, coming to meet him.[312] He blessed him and said to him, "Is your heart right,[313] as my heart is with yours?" Jehonadab said, "It is, it is!" "Give me your hand."[314] He gave him his hand and he took him up into the chariot. **16** He said, "Go with me and see my zeal for Yahweh," and he made him ride with him in his chariot. **17** He came to Samaria and struck down all the men belonging to Ahab in Samaria until he had destroyed him[315] according to the word which Yahweh spoke to Elijah.

Textual Notes

1a. סְפָרִים: Syr. "letter"; Gk. and Vulg. with MT.

1b. אֶל־שָׂרֵי: Gk. "princes of Samaria"; Vulg. "princes of the city"; Syr. with MT. MT likely because of the variety of readings *CTAT* (393). Barthelemy opines that the Jezreelite leaders may have gone to Samaria to consult.

1c. אַחְאָב: Gk. and Syr. add "of the sons of"; Vulg. with MT. GKC (§127*f*) supports Gk., but *CTAT* (394) considers MT likely.

2a. וְעִיר: All the versions read "cities." *CTAT* considers MT possibly correct (395).

---

311. Gk. reads δυναστευούσης, *dynasteuousēs*, "the woman who holds power," a literalistic reading of the Heb. word (הַגְּבִירָה, *hagg*ᵉ*ḇîrâ*). See the "Commentary."

312. Heb. lacks "coming" but the idea is contained in the gerundive function of the inf. const. (לִקְרָאתוֹ, *liqrā*ʾ*ṯô*). See *IBHS* (§36.2.3e).

313. Gk. adds μετὰ καρδίας μου, *meta kardias mou*, "with my heart," but this is unnecessary, as the sense is clear enough as the Heb. stands.

314. Reading with Cogan and Tadmor (114–15), and Sweeney (338). See the "Commentary" below.

315. Gk. and Syr. "them"; Vulg. "struck down ... up to every last one." MT's 3ms sg. direct object suffix, "him" (הִשְׁמִידוֹ, *hišmîḏô*) follows the law of the nearest antecedent, which is Ahab.

5a. וַאֲשֶׁר...אֲשֶׁר: Gk. "those"; Vulg. and Syr. with MT.

5b. עֲשֵׂה: Gk. reads "we will do"; Vulg. and Syr. with MT.

6a. אַנְשֵׁי: Vulg. and Syr. omit; Gk. with MT.

6b. וּבֹאוּ: Gk. and Syr. "and bring them"; Vulg. with MT.

6c. מְגַדְּלִים: GKC (§§118*p*, 131*h*) explain the lack of article as an indication of state or condition.

7a. וַיִּשְׁחֲטוּ: Gk. and Syr. read "they slaughtered them"; Vulg. with MT.

8a. לוֹ: Gk. Omits "to him"; Vulg. and Syr. with MT.

9a–a. וַיְהִי בַבֹּקֶר: Vulg. "When it grew light"; Gk. and Syr. with MT.

9b. וַיַּעֲמֹד: Gk. adds "in the gate of the city"; Syr. omits "stood"; Vulg. with MT.

9c. הִנֵּה: Syr. Omits; Vulg. "If"; Gk. with MT.

9d. וּמִי: Vulg. omits the disjunctive; Gk. and Syr. with MT.

12a–a. וַיָּקָם וַיָּבֹא וַיֵּלֶךְ: Gk. "he set out and went"; Vulg. "he arose and came"; Syr. with MT.

12b–b. הוּא בֵּית־עֵקֶד הָרֹעִים בַּדָּרֶךְ: Vulg. "When he came to the chamber of the shepherds on the way"; Syr. "on the way he destroyed the houses of the idols"; Gk. with MT.

14a. אֶל־בּוֹר: Gk. Omits; Syr. "and threw them into the pit"; Vulg. "in the pit." See the "Translation."

15a. רֵכָב: Gk. Adds "on the way"; Syr. adds "coming"; Vulg. with MT.

15b. וַיֹּאמֶר: Gk. adds "Jehu"; Vulg. and Syr. with MT.

15c. כַּאֲשֶׁר: Gk. Adds "with my heart"; Vulg. and Syr. with MT. *CTAT* (395) considers MT possibly correct.

15d–d. יֵשׁ וָיֵשׁ: Gk. reads "It is. And Jehu said, '"If it is, give…' "; Vulg. "It is. If it is, he said, give…"; Syr. "It is, it is. He said to him, Give… ." *CTAT* (395) considers MT certainly correct.

16a. לַיהוָה: Gk. adds "Sebaoth"; Vulg. and Syr. with MT.

Commentary

The first part of the narrative of Jehu's revolution (9:1–13) dealt with his anointing by the prophet and his coronation by his troops. The second part

(9:14–29) covered his killing of the principals: Joram, Ahaziah, and Jezebel. Now the circle is expanded by one more ring. This one takes in the entire dynasty of Ahab, just as Elijah had predicted it would (10:10, 17). A number of commentators (e.g., Fritz, 283, 285, 287; Gray, 548–49), following the lead of Noth in his original hypothesis of a Deuteronomic History composed during the exile to explain why the kingdoms of Israel and Judah had fallen, treat statements such as those appearing in these verses as editorial comments inserted long after the original narrative was spoken/written. Further thinking about the hypothesis has emended it considerably (see the Introduction). It is now thought by many that while this history (DH) did reach its final form in the exile, it was only the end product of a process that may have seen two or even three earlier versions. In this view, whatever we may think of the accuracy of the attribution to Yahweh of the causes of these events, those interpretations, rather than being a late redaction, may well have been a driving force in the creation of the narrative from its outset, serving to shape and mold it.[316]

The personality of Jehu as the narrator describes him continues to remain an enigma. Was he a deeply loyal follower of Yahweh, consumed with zeal for him (cf. 10:16)? Or was he a vicious opportunist, carried away with bloodlust, seizing on the Yahweh traditions to justify a clear-eyed grab for power? One of the things that makes this great literature is that as Jehu's story is narrated, it is very difficult to put the man into either category all the time. Jehu is not a one-dimensional "cardboard" character created by the author to be a vehicle for "author's message."[317] I suspect that he was one of those who had not "bowed the knee to Baal," and that he did see himself as Yahweh's sword to accomplish Yahweh's purposes, but that a failure to distinguish himself and his desires from Yahweh and his desires led him to baptize his own human failings with an aura of infallibility, thus justifying the most draconian and cruel measures.[318]

10:1–3 If the text is correct, while Jehu was dispatching Joram, Ahaziah, and Jezebel, "the princes of Jezreel" (שָׂרֵי יִזְרְעֶאל, *śārê yizrᵊʿeʾl*) escaped to Samaria

---

316. On the integration of historical narrative and theology in the Bible, see my *The Bible Among the Myths* (Grand Rapids, MI: Zondervan, 2009), 111–70.

317. I would suggest that this feature of biblical historical narrative is the direct result of the revelation of himself that Yahweh gave to Israel. He is transcendent, not of this world, and cannot be manipulated through the world. Telling your story as you would like it to be will not work for him. He is only known as he has acted and spoken in time and space, and if we are to know him, we must tell his story, and ours, *as they happened.*

318. It is significant that unlike the narrators in the cases of Asa, Jehoshaphat, Josiah, and Hezekiah, all of whom voiced their own approval of those kings' behaviors, that is not the case here. This narrator remains studiously silent about Jehu.

with the bad news.[319] This made Jehu's situation very precarious. He could not wait until securing Jezreel before addressing the crisis in Samaria. There were seventy descendants of Ahab in the capital city. That would include other brothers of Joram as well as Joram's own children. Although the number is almost certainly a round one,[320] it need not be considered outlandish. Kings were expected to engender as many children as possible as a sign of their virility. Here, where two generations are involved, seventy is not out of the question. If all of those descendants were allowed time to think carefully and organize themselves the results for Jehu could be dire.

So Jehu chose to force the hand of the leaders in Samaria, by writing "letters" (סְפָרִים, *sᵊpārîm*)[321] to them, calling them to take immediate (and precipitate?) action. The "And now" (וְעַתָּה, *wᵊʿattâ*) (v. 2) is typical of the opening of the body of a letter after a typically flowery introduction to the addressee(s).[322] The message is a model of restraint and implied self-deprecation. There is no threat or bluster. He says that they have all the resources they need (as opposed to his pitiful army?), as well as several good candidates for king, and that they need to get the "right one" on the throne immediately and be prepared to fight for him. The implication is that Jehu is not inclined to wait around. One way or the other, he is going to force the issue. Given his reputation as an impetuous "madman," that implication probably carried a lot of weight. His direction that the elders should choose "the best and most appropriate" (הַטּוֹב וְהַיָּשָׁר, *haṭṭôḇ wᵊhayyāšār*) of Ahab's descendants to be king (not just the next in line) would have almost certainly destroyed any possibility of unified action on the part of those worthies as they would be caught up in the struggle for dominance.

4–5 Having just received the shocking news of the horror that had taken place in Jezreel, and now receiving this demand for immediate action, the leaders in Samaria, including "he who is over the house and he who is over the city" (אֲשֶׁר־עַל־הַבַּיִת וַאֲשֶׁר עַל־הָעִיר, *ʾăšer-ʿal-habbayiṯ waʾăšer ʿal-hāʿîr*),

319. See note 300 on the "Translation" above. Several commentators agree with Gray (552–53) that "Jezreel" is an obvious error, since Jehu was in Jezreel at the time. However, the lack of unanimity among the versions suggests that Jezreel may be original and that some explanation for it, as above, may be possible.

320. Note Jacob's descendants in Gen 46:27; Gideon's sons in Judg 8:30; and Abdon's children in Judg 12:14. See F.C. Fensham, "The Numeral Seventy in the Old Testament and the Family of Jerubbaal, Ahab, Panamuwa, and Athirat," *PEQ* 109 (1977): 113–15.

321. The pl. suggests the possibility that multiple copies were sent, addressed to each of the groups named.

322. See above on 5:6.

that is, the prime minister of the kingdom,[323] and the prefect of Samaria, the very top officials, were panic-stricken.[324] They must make a decision at once, and without very good intelligence. Almost certainly they did not know how widespread the rebellion was, or what kinds of forces might be at Jehu's command. All they knew for certain was that Joram and Ahaziah were both dead and who was to say they would not be next. So they made a bet that the house of Ahab would be the loser and the house of Jehu would be the winner, and they would change horses and become "servants" (עֲבָדִים, *ʿăḇāḏîm*) of the winner. In view of what Jehu did when he came through the opened gates of Samaria later, it is very unlikely that their bet paid off in the end. As former servants of the house of Ahab, they probably did not escape. The blood on their hands was almost certainly eventually their own.

6–8 It seems very likely that the apparent ambiguity in the present text of v. 6 is original. The intent was clear enough: take those peoples' heads off! But just as in English, "head" (ראשׁ, *rōʾš*) in Hebrew can be used metaphorically, i.e., the "head" of a tribe, or the "head" of a household. So the officials are only told to "Take [which can mean "get"] the heads of" (קְחוּ אֶת־רָאשֵׁי, *qᵉḥû ʾeṯ-rāʾšēy*) that group of people and come to Jezreel.[325] Jehu could say, as he seems to in v. 9, that if these people in Samaria misunderstood what he wanted and murdered all these innocents, it was not his doing. The implication that the men were killed by the very ones who had raised them is a testimony to the heartlessness of humans when we think our own lives are at stake.

Jehu's response to the grisly trophies as recorded in v. 8 gives the lie to any denial of complicity he might make. As Hobbs (127) and others point out, there is no trace of shock or compassion displayed, nor even a modicum of human decency as might be shown in covering the heads. No, on the model of the Assyrian emperors, who piled the heads of the slaughtered citizens at the gates of conquered cities,[326] Jehu had the heads piled overnight at the gates of Jezreel so the inhabitants could have time to contemplate the likely fate of anyone who opposed the new king. Whatever Jehu may have been before this stage of his life, or whatever his relationship to Yahweh may have been, the trend being increasingly displayed is not an encouraging one. Man of God or heartless manipulator? Or some frightening combination of both?

---

323. Almost certainly this person was not just the "palace administrator," as some (e.g., NIV) have him. Rather he was a major official in the kingdom similar to the position of Joseph in Egypt (Gen 41:41–45; 47:13–26). See Isaiah 22:15–22; 36:3. See e.g., Brueggemann, 396, and Wiseman, 225. See Cogan and Tadmor "royal steward" (113).

324. The repetition of מְאֹד, *mᵊʾōḏ*, "very" should not be deleted. It is repeated for emphasis. See GKC (§123*e*).

325. Even if the reading found in Gk. and Syr.: "bring them," were thought to be original, it would not resolve the ambiguity.

326. Shalmaneser III, *ANET*, 277.

9 The interpretation of this verse is made difficult by the elliptical nature of the opening assertion, and by the question at the end of the verse. What does it mean when Jehu says the people are "righteous" (צַדִּקִים, *ṣaddiqîm*)? Does it mean they are innocent of wrongdoing, as the majority of English versions read? Or does it mean that they are competent to judge, as REB, and a few commentators take it? Sweeney (337) insists that it must be the former, because this is the term used in the law court (see Isa 5:23). But if so, what is Jehu saying, and why? Is he absolving them of guilt in what is taking place? On the surface, that seems magnanimous, but to what end? He forthrightly affirms his own guilt for conspiracy and regicide, but then, in spite of Sweeney's (337) claim to the contrary, he quite clearly denies any guilt for the deaths of Ahab's descendants, seeming to lay that on those who did the deed in Samaria, or perhaps on the basis of what follows in v. 10, on Yahweh (see below). But taking this verse by itself, what is he saying to the people of Jezreel? I offer the following possibility: "Don't blame yourselves for this gory spectacle. Yes, I set it all in motion by killing my master, but I did not kill these folks; their own caretakers did it. This thing has become a conflagration that will probably get a lot worse before it gets better, so hang on, and by the way, don't oppose me; that would not be good for your health."

10 Some would say that by his following statement about the fulfillment of Yahweh's word, he is laying the blame at Yahweh's feet. But he does not say that. He says the events are in fulfillment of what Yahweh had said, but he does not explicitly say that what he has done is justified because it is fulfilling what the prophet has said. It is more of an observation than a justification. That lack of an explicit connection, whether omitted by Jehu or the narrator, is important. It is possible to be doing God's will, but in ways that are quite contrary to God's ways.[327]

11 Jehu neutralized any who might yet have opposed him in Jezreel with his masterful three-part persuasion: (1) the threat of terrible fury that the pile of heads represented, (2) the assuaging of any responsibility for what might happen, and (3) the assertion that this was all the outworking of the divine word. As a result, he had no difficulty is erasing every vestige of Ahab's power in the city. As mentioned above, it certainly appears that in doing so he far exceeded his mandate from God. He not only destroyed the house of Ahab, but he also killed the nobles, friends, and priests who were not a part of the dynasty at all, and he did so with a thoroughness that will be reiterated several times in the remainder of the narrative: "no survivor remained" (עַד־בִּלְתִּי הִשְׁאִיר־לוֹ שָׂרִיד, *ʿad-biltî hiš ʾîr-lô śārîḏ*) (cf. 14, 17, 21). When the sword is unsheathed, it is very difficult to get it back into the scabbard again.

327. Peter D. Miscall, "Elijah, Ahab, and Jehu: A Prophecy Fulfilled," *Prooftexts* 9 (1989): 80 (cited by Jesse Long, 377) says Jehu remembered the past well and adapted his assertions about it to fit his present purposes.

12–14 Having finished his work in Jezreel, Jehu set out for Samaria. Along the way, at a spot whose location is uncertain, he came upon the brothers of Ahaziah, king of Judah. The place where he met them is identified as "Beth-eked of the shepherds" (בֵּית־עֵקֶד הָרֹעִים, *bêṯ- ʿēqeḏ hārō ʿîm*). It has traditionally been located on a high rocky promontory northeast of Jenin. But this is not on the way to Samaria from Jezreel, and it is certainly not on the way from Jerusalem to Samaria, so it seems probable that this identification is incorrect. If the location is uncertain, the purpose of these men's journey is also unclear. Hobbs (122) has argued that the שָׁלוֹם, *šālôm* in these men's greeting should actually be vocalized as a *piel* form which would render the meaning "to pay back." In other words, they had heard about the slaughter of Joram and Jezebel[328] and their children in Jezreel and were intending to wreak vengeance on the killers. On this reading, perhaps they were hiding out at the "out-of-the-way" Beth-eked, planning to ambush Jehu, but were found out. But that scenario does not fit the conversation reported in v. 13, which does not seem at all confrontational. Rather, it seems that the whirlwind of revolt was occurring so rapidly that they were not even aware of it. Perhaps they had come north one way while the body of their brother Ahaziah was going south by another way. On this reading, they were simply paying a friendly visit from one branch of the family to another[329] (some of them, at least, would have been children of Athaliah, Ahab's daughter), and have been inadvertently caught up in the whirlwind.[330] Once again, we see the brutally decisive Jehu in action. Once they answer his bluntly direct question about their identity, he instantly tells his men to capture them ("Take them alive" [תִּפְשׂוּם חַיִּים, *tipśûm ḥayyîm*]). Perhaps the strategy was to avoid a pitched battle (after all, there were forty-two of them) which might take some time and might result in some deaths among his own men, neither of which he could afford. Instead, the unsuspecting travelers were surrounded and disarmed, and then swiftly executed, either "by the cistern/pit" (אֶל־בּוֹר, *ʾel-bôr*) or perhaps "in" it (as in Syr.). It is significant that whereas the divine word is cited in connection with Jehu's other actions it is not cited here. While the connection of these men to the house of Ahab (through Athaliah) might be argued, no such argument is made, and we are left to wonder what the

328. Jezebel was הַגְּבִירָה, *haggᵉḇîrâ*, "the great lady," or "queen mother" referred to in v. 13. It is apparent that the position of the king's mother was one of great importance, both in Israel and Judah (cf. 1 Kgs 15:13; Jer 13:18; 29:2).

329. This reading would take שָׁלוֹם, *šālôm* as the text has it. They are "well-wishers." Vulg. and Syr. have "coming down to greet."

330. Given the traditional location of Beth-eked, Wiseman offers the creative suggestion that the men who had been at Jezreel, and, having left before the revolt had begun, were on their way home (226). While the grammar would allow this, there is nothing in the text that would point in this direction.

narrator would like us to think about the event. I suggest we are intended to draw the conclusion that Yahweh's avenger is out of control.

15–16 In these verses we are told of the forming of what may have been a significant alliance for Jehu, although that conclusion is more by inference, than by direct statement. For the third time in this extended narrative, the vb. מָצָא, *māṣā'* "to find," is used to describe a meeting. When used in this way it has the meaning of "to come upon."[331] So Joram and Ahaziah had come upon Jehu at Naboth's vineyard (9:21); Jehu had come upon the brothers of Ahaziah (10:13), and now he comes upon Jehonadab son of Recab. The results of the first two had been death, but this one would be blessing and friendship. The presumption is that this man is the same one mentioned in Jeremiah 35:6–8. There called Jonadab, he is identified as the ancestor of a clan who had laid on his descendants the obligation to refrain from any use of alcohol and to maintain a Bedouin lifestyle (cf. Jer. 35:6, 14–16). Jeremiah was directed to use them as an example of people who were doggedly faithful to a humanly originated covenant, in contrast to Judah who would not keep faith with their divinely originated one. On this basis, it is maintained by many that Jehonadab was a fanatical Yahwist who welcomed the bloody destruction of Ahab's house and of the Baalism that Ahab had supported. Some support for this view is garnered from the reference to his accompanying Jehu during the slaughter of those who served Baal (10:23). While it seems unquestionable that Jehonadab approved of the direction that Jehu was taking (v. 16), we cannot go much farther than that in estimating his motives. Nothing is said of Jehonadab's participation in Jehu's actions or even of his encouragement of his behavior. As for fanatical Yahwism, nothing is said of that. What we probably can say is that this man is representative of many others in the nation who were glad that because of Jehu's actions Israel's deadly direction away from Yahweh and into the arms of Baal was being arrested. What they felt beyond that is to say more than the text warrants.[332]

One of the problems for interpreting v. 15 lies in the indeterminacy of its pronouns. It is not at all clear when Jehu is speaking and when Jehonadab is. For instance, does Jehonadab bless Jehu (v. 15) or is it the other way around? Clearly it is Jehu who asks about Jehonadab's heart, but who asks for whose hand? Does Jehonadab respond by saying, "It is, it is! Give me your hand!" Or should we read, "It is, it is!" (And Jehu said,) "Give me your hand!"? Although these are intriguing questions, the different answers do not materially change our understanding of the significance of what is being said. Either Jehu blesses Jehonadab for coming out to offer encouragement, or

331. "to meet accidentally," see *HALOT* (2.619).

332. The suggestions that they were tinsmiths or that they were chariot-builders (on the basis of the consonants רכב, *rkb*) are not beyond the realm of possibility, but again, the text does not say either of these. For a discussion see R. S. Frick, "The Rechabites Reconsidered," *JBL* 90 (1971): 279–87.

Jehonadab blesses Jehu for undertaking this perilous task of destroying Ahab's influence. Then Jehu asks whether Jehonadab has the same concerns ("heart" [לֵב, *lēḇ*]) that he has. When Jehonadab assures the revolutionary leader in the strongest terms that he does indeed share those concerns, they clasp hands and Jehonadab joins Jehu in his chariot for the journey to Samaria. Jehu's question about Jehonadab's "heart" being *right* is somewhat ironic, because we have reason to wonder whether Jehu's heart is "right." It may indeed be right with Jehonadab's, but is it truly right with Yahweh? In the final analysis, the narrator will tell us it is not (10:31). He may have been very passionate ("zeal" [קִנְאָה, *qin ʾâ*]) for Yahweh (v. 16), but it was a passion for a Yahweh who had been formed by Israelite traditions (including idolatry), and apparently not by the Yahweh who had formed Israel at Sinai.

17 This verse is almost anti-climactic in its understated assertion that when Jehu came to Samaria he finished off any who remained of Ahab's house. Presumably he was just as thorough there as he had been at Jezreel, and the slaughter included anyone who was remotely connected with the dynasty, whether a blood-relative or not.

Selected Bibliography

Miller, J. M. "Fall of the House of Ahab." *VT* 17 (1967): 307–24.

White, M. "Naboth's Vineyard and Jehu's Coup: The Legitimation of a Dynastic Extermination." *VT* 44 (1994): 66–76.

The Killing of the Servants of Baal and the Destruction of his Temple (10:18–29)

Translation

18 Jehu gathered all the people and said to them, "Ahab served Baal a little; Jehu will serve him much. **19** So now all the prophets of Baal, all those serving him and all his priests, call to me. None shall be absent. For I have a great sacrifice to Baal. Any who are absent shall not live." But Jehu acted with cunning in order to destroy all those who were serving Baal. **20** Jehu said, "Sanctify an assembly for Baal." So they called it. **21** Jehu sent through all Israel, and all those who were serving Baal came. None remained who did not come; they went into the house of Baal and they filled the house of Baal from end to end.[333] **22** He said to the one who[334] was in charge of the wardrobe,[335] "Bring out clothing[336] for all those serving Baal." He brought out the clothing. **23** Jehu and Jehonadab ben Rechab went into the house of Baal, and he said to those serving Baal, "Search and see, lest there be with you any of the servants of Yahweh, but only those serving Baal." **24** They

---

333. Heb. פֶּה לָפֶה, *peh lāp̄eh* "mouth to mouth." See also 2 Kgs 21:16; Ezra 9:11.

334. On the use of אֲשֶׁר, *ʾăšer* as a substantive, see GKC (§138*e*).

335. The only occ. of this word (מֶלְתָּחָה, *meltāḥâ*). Meaning derived from context.

336. Heb. is sing. (לְבוּשׁ, *lᵉḇûš*), perhaps collective. The versions all translate with the pl.

went to make sacrifices and burnt offerings. Jehu had eighty men there on the outside. He had said, "If any man escapes from the men I am bringing into your hands, it is his life for his life." **25** Now when he finished making the burnt offering, Jehu said to the guards and the officers, "Go in and strike them down. Do not let a man come out." So they struck them with the edge of the sword. The guards and the officers threw (them aside)[337] and went into the inner cell[338] of the house of Baal. **26** They brought out the stele of Baal from the house of Baal and burned it. **27** So they demolished the stele of Baal and they demolished the house of Baal and made it into a latrine till today. **28** So Jehu exterminated Baal from Israel. **29** But as for the sins of Jeroboam, son of Nebat, with which he made Israel sin, Jehu did not turn aside from them: the calves of gold which were in Bethel and Dan.

Textual Notes

19a. כָל־נְבִיאָיו: Gk. reads "all you prophets," making "prophets" the subject of the imp. "call"; Vulg. and Syr. with MT.

19b–b. כָּל־עֹבְדָיו וְכָל־כֹּהֲנָיו: Gk. and Syr. "all his priests and all his servants"; Vulg. with MT. *CTAT* (396) considers MT probable.

19c. עֹבְדָיו: Throughout this section MT uses ptcps. for the servants of Baal ("those serving Baal"). Gk. renders this with "servants." It is not clear that this represents an original noun as a variant reading, as per *BHS.* However, many medieval Heb. MSS do have the noun form. Vulg. and Syr. seem to be reflecting the ptcp. when they translate with "worshippers." Interestingly, the noun form does appear in ref. to "the servants of Yahweh" in v. 23. It seems that the text is wishing to distinguish between the two groups.

19d. אַל־יִפָּקֵד...יִפָּקֵד: Gk. "none shall be inspected." This seems to represent a very literalistic reading of פָּקַד. Vulg. and Syr. "missing," which is the regular meaning of the *niphal* form. Cf. *HALOT* (955–58).

20a–a. קַדְּשׁוּ עֲצָרָה: Syr. and Tg. "Invite all the assembly to come to"; Gk. and Vulg. with MT.

21a. יִשְׂרָאֵל: Gk. inserts "saying"; Vulg. and Syr. with MT.

21b–b. וַיָּבֹאוּ כָּל־עֹבְדֵי הַבַּעַל: Gk. reads "Now all his servants and all his priests and all his prophets, let them not remain behind, because I am making a great sacrifice and whoever remains behind will not live." All the servants of Baal and all his priests and all his prophets came." Vulg. and Syr. with MT.

337. For the probable meaning, see the "Commentary" below.

338. Heb. עִיר, *ʿîr*, normally translated "city."

22a–a. וַיֹּצֵא לָהֶם הַמַּלְבּוּשׁ: Gk. reads "The keeper of the sacred robes brought them out for them." Vulg. and Syr. with MT.

24a. וַיָּבֹאוּ: Gk. "He"; Vulg. and Syr. with MT. *CTAT* (396) MT is likely.

24b. שְׁמֹנִים: Luc. "3000"; Syr. "380"; Gk. and Vulg. with MT.

25. עִיר: Luc. "sanctuary"; the other versions read "city" with MT. See the "Commentary" below.

26a–a. אֶת־מַצְּבוֹת בֵּית־הַבַּעַל: Gk. "the pillars of Baal"; Vulg. "the statue from the temple of Baal"; Syr. "the statue from the house of Baal." On the use of the pl. see GKC (§135*p*). *CTAT* (397) considers the pl. of the MT unlikely.

27a–a. וַיִּתְּצוּ אֵת מַצְּבַת הַבָּעַל: Gk. "pillars of Baal"; Syr. "image of Baal"; Vulg. "it." *CTAT* (397) considers MT sing. highly likely.

27b. הַיּוֹם: The versions all read "this day."

Commentary

If Jehu's earlier references to the prophecies of Elijah had painted him as a follower of Yahweh, the actions narrated here leave no doubt of that fact. Although he makes no reference to Elijah with respect to this destruction, the attentive reader will remember that the divine directives to appoint Hazael, Jehu, and Elisha in 1 Kings 19 were all in response to Elijah's lament over what the Baal worshippers had done to Yahweh and his worship (1 Kgs 19:14–18). Thus, Jehu's mission could not have been fulfilled until he had uprooted the institutionalized worship of Baal from the land and restored the worship of Yahweh to its rightful place.

That being said, the final comment in this segment, as contained in v. 29, tells us that the Yahwism to which Jehu was committed was the idolatrous form fostered by Jeroboam and his followers. Yes, he was going to remove the "foreign" religion of Baal from any possibility of dominating his country, but one has the sense that Jehu was not committed to Yahweh as much as he was to "the religion of Israel" and to "Israel's god," as opposed to "Tyre's god."

This might have something to do with the difference between Elijah's confrontation with Baal (1 Kgs 18) and Jehu's as reported here. Elijah was determined to demonstrate the absolute superiority of Yahweh and was quite willing to leave no question about where he stood. Jehu, on the other hand, seems only to have been concerned about destroying the influence of Baal and as the narrator points out in an unusual evaluative comment (v. 19), was willing to use deception to achieve his goal. While we should not offer a justification for Jehu's behavior which the text does not, it still might be imagined that Jehu felt the deception was necessary in order to accomplish the wholesale uprooting that was required. In any case, when he was done, there was no possibility that Baal would replace Yahweh as the God of Israel. The only question was, which Yahweh?

18–20 Presumably there were a number of questions in the air as the slaughter of Ahab's family gathered momentum. Was this coup politically based or religiously based, or both? Was Jehu simply a military strongman lusting for power, and using the words of Elijah to give some legitimacy to the takeover, or was he really a Yahwist with further reasons for his enmity with Ahab's dynasty than a mere power-grab? Undoubtedly, Jehu's insistence that he would be a more ardent follower of Baal than Ahab had come as a great relief to the Baal worshippers. The takeover *had* been merely a power-grab, and they could relax. When the new king then cemented his claim with the proclamation of great religious "assembly" (עֲצָרָה, *ʿăṣārâ*) there must have been a party atmosphere among that segment of the population, while any hopes the Yahwists might have entertained were smashed.[339]

It seems likely that whether Jehu intended it or not, the narrator wants us to recognize the double significance of the promise of a "great sacrifice" (זֶבַח גָּדוֹל, *zeḇaḥ gāḏôl*). There was indeed a sacrifice, but it was the Baal worshippers who were the offering, and it was only those who might "have been absent" (אֲשֶׁר־יִפָּקֵד, *ʾăšer-yippāqēḏ*) who would live (v. 19).

21 It is hard to estimate how many there were who filled the house of Baal to capacity because there is no archeological evidence yet found at Samaria to tell us how large this temple was. The lack of any such evidence is not surprising in view of the kind of demolition described in v. 27. Since Ahab, as was typical of kings in that day and time, would have built it in his relatively new capital city as a testimony to his power (1 Kgs 16:32), it presumably would have been a very large and impressive building. Nevertheless, we need not think that every person in Israel who had ever bowed the knee to Baal was housed inside the walls of that temple. That would have run into the tens, if not hundreds, of thousands. Rather, these would have been the leaders of the movement, those whose execution would be similar to cutting off the head of an animal: the rest of the body would shortly die without any necessary further action.[340]

22 The reason for investing the worshippers with festal "clothing" (לְבוּשׁ, *lᵉḇûš*) is not given, but perhaps it was to allay any remaining fears of those who might still be wondering about Jehu's sincerity. It is not known whether this was normal practice, or something out of the ordinary. If it was out of the ordinary it would perhaps underscore Jehu's claim to be more of a fanatic for Baal than even Ahab had been. Along with the next verse, neither of which

339. On the command to "sanctify an assembly," see Mic 3:5; Joel 1:14; 2:15.

340. Cf. the comments of Gamaliel in Acts 5:34–39. But Long trenchantly observes that when Jehoiada set out to accomplish a similar thing in Judah (2 Kgs 11:18) only the priest of Baal would die (382). Thus, we must ask again how much of Jehu's bloodletting was in service to Yahweh, and how much was simply bloodlust?

is strictly necessary to the plot, it lends an unmistakable air of verisimilitude to the narrative.

23 There is a potential anomaly in this verse: if Jehonadab was widely known as a follower of Yahweh, then what was he doing in the house of Baal when Jehu had said to put out all such persons? This suggests that he was not known in that way, at least among the Baal worshippers. Jehu's action seems designed to further undergird his devotion to Baal: no Yahwistic spies allowed!

24–25 These verses further undergird the impression gained thus far of Jehu's ruthless efficiency. Presumably the "guards and officers" (לָרָצִים וְלַשָּׁלִשִׁים, *lārāṣîm wᵉlaššālišîm*)[341] were the members of Jehu's bodyguard who had demonstrated their complete loyalty to him in the bloodletting thus far and who knew him well enough to know that he was quite capable of carrying out his drastic threat if any of Baal's devotees escaped. If we were to think of thousands of worshippers inside the building, then the number eighty for the executioners seems small. This is probably what lies behind the Syriac "380" and Lucianic "3000." However, even if there were several hundred people inside, a small disciplined force with some barring the doors, and with the victims perhaps encumbered with voluminous robes, could accomplish the terrible task without too much trouble. The elliptical "threw" (וַיַּשְׁלִכוּ, *wayyašliḵû*) (v. 25), lacking either a direct object or an indirect object, is problematic. Several commentators (e.g., Brueggemann, 399; Long, 381) take it to mean that they threw the bodies outside. But perhaps it simply refers to the violent nature of the event with bodies being hurled this way and that. Or perhaps it is as taken here, that the men had to throw bodies aside to get to the inner cell (עִיר, *ʿîr*)[342] where the idol was housed.

---

341. Heb. "runners and third men." The runners appear in similar situations elsewhere (1 Sam 22:17; 2 Sam 15:1; 1 Kgs 1:5; 14:27–28; 2 Kgs 11:4, 6), where they seem to have special responsibilities for guarding the king and the royal enclave. Here and in 1 Kgs 9:22 are the only times שָׁלִישִׁים, *šālîšîm* "third men," appears in the pl. Elsewhere (2 Kgs 7:2, 17, 19; 15:25) it appears in the sing. and refers to the special aide of the king. For a discussion see the "Commentary" on chap. 7 above.

342. Although it is generally agreed that this interpretation is correct, it has to be admitted that עִיר, *ʿîr*, "city" is nowhere else used in this sense. It has been plausibly suggested that perhaps it is an error for דְּבִיר, *dᵉḇîr*, "inner sanctuary," cf. 2 Chr 4:20. However, the ancient versions, with the exception of Luc., are unanimous in translating "city." See Cogan and Tadmor for a discussion, 116. Wiseman suggests that the soldiers went out into that part of the city where the temple was located to continue their depredations (228). But the next sentence referring to the bringing out of the stele of Baal seems to discredit that idea. Another suggestion is that as the ancient cities often had a central citadel, "city" is being used metaphorically here to refer to the innermost part of the temple.

26–28 It may be that the sacred object was a "stele" with the figure of the god inscribed on it in bas-relief, as the term מַצְּבוֹת, *maṣṣᵉḇôṯ* implies (see *TANE* 1, fig. 136 for an example), or it could be that the term is a euphemism for an actual idol. An idol would have probably been carved wood overlaid with precious metals, and so it could have been easily burned. On the other hand, a stone stele would have been heated in a fire and then had water poured over it so that it shattered. So much for Baal and all his power.

The repetition of "stele" (מַצְּבַת הַבָּעַל, *maṣṣᵉḇaṯ habbāʿal*) in v. 27 has caused some commentators (e.g., Gray, 558) to suggest that this one be emended to "altar" מִזְבֵּחַ, *mizbēaḥ* (see 11:18). But the versions give no countenance to the idea. Probably we should simply see the verse and the next as a resumptive conclusion. What they did to the idol—נתץ , *ntṣ* ("demolished")—they did to the temple as a whole, and the result was to exterminate Baalism as an organized cult in the land. While some question the translation "latrine" (מַחֲרָאוֹת, *maḥărāʾôṯ*), arguing that "dung-pit" might be better, the versions all render the text in this way.[343, 344]

28 In some ways this verse is reminiscent of 2 Samuel 11:27b. There the narrator had told the sordid story of David and Bathsheba and the murder of Uriah in remarkably dispassionate and neutral tones. But then with just five Hebrew words he gave the verdict. So here, we have had the tale of Jehu's sweeping victory culminating in the extermination of the Baal cult from Israel. But there is just one thing; what would replace the Baals? Would it be the Yahweh of Moses and Sinai? No, it would be the adulterated Yahweh of Jeroboam, son of Nebat. The point is made more poignant by the construction of the sentence: the long compound object: "the sins of Jeroboam with which he made Israel to sin" (חַטָּאֵי יָרָבְעָם בֶּן־נְבָט אֲשֶׁר הֶחֱטִיא אֶת־יִשְׂרָאֵל, *ḥăṭāʾê yārobʿām ben-nᵉḇāṭ ʾăšer heḥĕṭîʾ ʾeṯ-yiśrāʾēl*) is thrown into bold relief by putting it before the subject and the verb.[345] Thus, as in 2 Samuel, in a few words the narrator brings the story of the destruction of the dynasty of Ahab and of the Baalism he sponsored to a somewhat bitter end. Jehu had a great opportunity and he failed to make the most of it.

Selected Bibliography

Trebolle, J. "From 'Old Latin' through the 'Old Greek' to the 'Old Hebrew.' " *Textus* 11 (1984): 17–36.

343. Hobbs and others argue that the vowel pointing in "latrine" (מַחֲרָאוֹת, *maḥărāʾôṯ*) is that of מֹצָאוֹת, *mōṣāʾôṯ* "excrement" (130), but Wiseman finds the etymology doubtful (228).

344. The ref. to "this day" points to a *terminus ad quem* of 722 BC for the writing of this narrative since after that time Samaria had been largely destroyed.

345. See GKC (§143*b*).

Final Comments on Jehu and His Reign (10:30–36)

Translation

30 Yahweh said to Jehu, "Because you did well by doing right in my eyes
according to all that was in my heart that you did to the house of Ahab,
you will have sons sitting on the throne of Israel to the fourth generation."
31 But Jehu was not careful to walk in the instruction of Yahweh, God of
Israel, with all his heart, not turning aside from all the sins of Jeroboam with
which he made Israel sin. **32** In those days Yahweh began to cut Israel back
and Hazael struck them down on all the borders of Israel, **33** from the Jordan
toward the sunrise, all the land of Gilead, the Gadites, the Reubenites, and
the Manassites, from Aroer which is by the Wadi Arnon and Gilead and
Bashan. **34** The rest of the events surrounding Jehu and all that he did and
of his might, are they not written in the book of the chronicles of the kings
of Israel? **35** Jehu slept with his fathers and they buried him in Samaria, and
his son Jehoahaz reigned after him. **36** The days that Jehu was king over Israel
were twenty-eight years in Samaria.

Textual Notes

34. וְכָל־גְּבוּרָתוֹ: Gk. Adds "and all the alliances which he made"; Vulg. and Syr. with MT.

Commentary

Although Jehu was to rule for another twenty-eight years after his accession in 841 BC, the Bible has almost nothing to say about those years. Clearly, as elsewhere in these books, the interest is not in a comprehensive history, but a selective recounting of historical facts in support of the revelation of Yahweh. Thus, once it becomes clear that, after his extermination of institutionalized Baalism, Jehu is not going to produce a wholesale return to the covenant with Yahweh, there remains little to be said. From extrabiblical data, we know that the Assyrian Shalmaneser III attacked both Syria and Israel in 841 BC and inflicted defeats on both of them, claiming to have received large amounts of tribute from them both.[346] It can be surmised that after Jehu's wholesale destruction of Ahab's family, friends, and retainers, the forces of Israel would not have been in a position to mount much of a defense against the Assyrians. As for Hazael, he seems to have weathered the Assyrian attacks reasonably well until Shalmaneser's death in 824 BC after which he gained some breathing room and was able to attack Israel almost at will for the rest of his reign.

30–33 These verses continue the equivocal tone that was struck in vv. 28–29. Yes, from one point of view "you [Jehu] had done well" (הֱטִיבֹתָ, *hĕṭîḇōṯā*): he

346. On the well-known Black Obelisk, Jehu is depicted prostrating himself before Shalmaneser (*TANE* 1, fig. 100a). For these campaigns, see M. Elat, "The Campaigns of Shalmaneser III against Aram and Israel, *IEJ* 25 (1975): 25–35.

had carried out the destruction of the house of Ahab,[347] and was rewarded with a dynasty that would exceed in length the Omride dynasty that it replaced. But from another point of view, he had missed his opportunity to restore Israel fully to Yahweh. The statement that he "was not careful to walk in the instruction of Yahweh, God of Israel, with all his heart" (וְיֵהוּא לֹא שָׁמַר לָלֶכֶת בְּתוֹרַת־יהוה אֱלֹהֵי־יִשְׂרָאֵל בְּכָל־לְבָבוֹ, *wᵉyēhû ʾlō ʾšāmar lāleḵeṯ bᵉṯôraṯ-yhwh ʾĕlōhê-yiśrā ʾēl bᵉḵol-lᵉḇāḇô*) is significant because it is unique in the standard judgment of the northern kings. With the others, it is said that they did evil in the eyes of Yahweh, and walked in (or did not turn away from) the ways of Jeroboam, son of Nebat.[348] The unusual language here points to Jehu's commitment to Yahweh, unlike that of the descendants of Omri, but it also speaks regretfully of his failure to go all the way back to the scriptural instructions about the worship of Yahweh, a task that was incumbent on the king (1 Kgs 2:1–4; 9:1–9).

As a result, instead of Yahweh's being a protector of the nation, he became its enemy, himself cutting back the territory of the land through his instrument Hazael (v. 32). This point should be underlined. It was Yahweh who was performing the action, and Hazael was simply his tool. This point was first made through Elisha's appointment of Hazael. It was Yahweh who chose the man. Here for the first time, Israel began to lose its ancestral territory. Prior to this they had lost Moab (chap. 3), but Moab had been conquered territory. Now it was the lands of Reuben, Gad, and the half-tribe of Manasseh, land that Moses had allowed those tribes to settle (Num 32:28–30), that was lost. This territory, on the east side of the Jordan River, extended from the Arnon gorge in the south, which had been the historical border between Israel and Moab, northward through Gilead, which generally extends from the north end of the Dead Sea to the south end of the Sea of Galilee, and Bashan, which begins at the Yarmuk Gorge and extends northward onto the heights of Golan.[349] The territory was lost to Israel during the entire reign of Hazael (ca. 842–800 BC). We are told that Jehu's grandson Jehoash (798–782 BC) succeeded in recapturing the towns after Hazael's death (13:24–25), and that his great grandson, Jeroboam II (782–753 BC) recaptured the territory as far south as the Dead Sea (14:25). This was, of course, an interlude before Assyria took it all, beginning with Tiglath-pileser III's depredations in 734 BC.

34–36 These verses give us the standard death formula, with the exception that they include the years of Jehu's reign at this point, rather than at the beginning of the account where they would normally appear. This is probably

---

347. This should not be construed to say that Yahweh necessarily approved of the manner in which the injunction to destroy Ahab's house was carried out. See the "Application and Devotional Implications" below.

348. E.g., 1 Kgs 15:26, 34; 2 Kgs 13:2, 11; 14:24.

349. Deut 3:8–11.

because there is no normal accession formula for him, the narrative of his prophetic anointing taking that place.[350]

Biblical Theology Comments

Jehu is judged because he continued to endorse the idolatrous worship of Yahweh at Bethel and Dan. But the appointment of Hazael prior to the anointing of Jehu might suggest that the continued Yahwistic idolatry in Israel after Jehu's succession was a foregone conclusion. That is, if Hazael's role was to punish Israel for its idolatry and had already been appointed, then Jehu could not help but fail. This, of course, opens the age-old question as to whether divine foreknowledge abrogates human freedom (and responsibility). The simple answer is that it does not. On what basis do I say that? On the basis of Scripture. Clearly, although it is beyond our understanding, the fact that something is predicted does not invalidate responsibility for our choices. This is seen again and again in the Bible, most famously in the case of king Manasseh of Judah and the Babylonian exile (see the "Commentary" below). It is said that the exile occurred because of the sins of Manasseh (2 Kgs 21:10–15). Yet, the prophets continued to plead with the Judeans to repent of their sins, with the expectation that the exile need not occur (Zeph 3:6–7; Ezk 18:30, 32). This is the remarkable view of history that is found in the Bible. Human choice can change the future! So Isaiah could predict that after the remnant returned from exile, Jerusalem would never fall again (62:8). That is, *if* the people were faithful, it *need not* fall again. But since the people were not faithful, particularly in regards the recognition of their Messiah, it did fall again. So the answer to the question is that Jehu could have been completely faithful to Yahweh, and had he been, Hazael would not have been the destroyer he was.

Application and Devotional Implications

Throughout the account of Jehu's revolution, we have wrestled with the question of how to evaluate his actions. That question continues even into this final segment. Was Jehu a man of God simply fulfilling the divine mandate, or was he a brutal military man, bent on exterminating anyone who might threaten his ultimate power? As suggested above, there is no simple answer to these questions. To come down exclusively on one side or the other is to do damage to the scriptural witness. Clearly, Jehu knew what Elijah had said about the fate of Ahab's house because of their unfaithfulness to Yahweh, and in some sense was motivated by that knowledge. Furthermore, he was determined that Israel's long-time worship of Yahweh should not be supplanted by the "foreign" Baal worship.

350. The same thing is true for David (1 Kgs 2:11), Solomon (11:42), and Jeroboam (14:20), none of whom have normal accession formulae.

All of that is confirmed by the statement, presumably spoken by a prophet, in v. 30. Yahweh was pleased with the outcome of Jehu's coup; Jehu had destroyed the dynasty of Ahab and Yahweh would reward Jehu with a dynasty lasting 100 years, four generations, a very lengthy dynasty in Israel. But it is not an eternal dynasty such as was offered to Jeroboam I (1 Kgs 11:37–38), and we may ask why. I believe the answer is to be found in Hosea 1:4–5, probably spoken during the reign of Jeroboam II, the third generation Jehu dynast.[351] Jehu's dynasty would be punished "for the blood of Jezreel." What does that mean? It means that it is possible to do God's will with the wrong spirit and in the wrong way. Jehu did not need to slaughter anyone and everyone having anything to do with Ahab and his descendants (10:11), nor did he need to slaughter the worshippers of Baal (10:25).

What is that wrong spirit and wrong way? It is the way of one who is self-serving. It is the way of justifying what I want to do out of a consciousness of doing what God wants. Just because we are within the will of God does not mean that we are doing it the way God wants. The history of the Christian church and of other Christian institutions is littered with the sad results of people who were doing good things in cruel and selfish ways. Is God's kingdom furthered? Again, there is no simple answer. Yahweh, being the Creator, is able to take the most malformed things and bring good out of them. But why should he have to? Could we not come to the fulfillment of God's purpose for us forcefully and determinedly, but yet with the full knowledge of the how deeply self-reference can corrupt? This is the challenge for us as we contemplate this endlessly interesting story.

Selected Bibliography

Lamb, D. T. "The Non-eternal Dynastic Promises of Jehu of Israel and Esarhaddon of Assyria." *VT* 60 (2010): 337–44.

Mullen, E. T. "The Royal Dynastic Grant to Jehu and the Structure of the Books of Kings." *JBL* 107 (1988): 193–206.

Athaliah and Joash (11:1–21 [MT 12:1])

Translation

11:1 Now Athaliah was the mother of Ahaziah; when she saw that her son was dead, she proceeded[352] to kill all the royal sons. **2** Then Jehosheba, daughter of King Jehoram and sister of Ahaziah, took Joash, son of Ahaziah, and stole him—him and his nurse[353]—from among the sons of the king who were being

351. Or perhaps during the six-month reign of Zechariah, the last of the Jehu dynasts (15:8–12).

352. Understanding Heb. תָּקָם, *tāqām* "she arose" as an auxiliary vb.

353. The parallel passage in 2 Chr 22:11 reads "she put him and his nurse in the bedroom." The vb. (וַתִּתֵּן, *wattittēn*) is not present in the MT here, nor is it found in Gk. or Vulg. Syr. reads "she hid him and his nurse in her bedroom." A majority

killed in the bedroom, and they hid him from Athaliah so that he was not killed. **3** He was with her in the house of Yahweh hidden for six years while Athaliah was ruling the land.

4 In the seventh year Jehoiada sent and took the captains of the Carites and the guards[354] and brought them to him in the house of Yahweh. He imposed a covenant on them and made them swear an oath in the house of Yahweh. Then he showed them the son of the king. **5** He commanded them, saying, "This is the thing you must do: one third of you who are going on duty on the Sabbath are guards of the kings's house; **6** one third of you are in the gate of Sur, and one third in the gate behind the guards. You shall keep watch over the house alternately.[355] **7** The other two divisions of you going off duty on the Sabbath shall guard the house of Yahweh on behalf of the king. **8** You shall surround the king on all sides, each man with his weapons in hand; whoever comes into the ranks shall die; be with the king when he goes out and when he comes in." **9** So the captains did according to all that Jehoiada the priest commanded. Each one took his men, whether coming on duty on the Sabbath, or going off duty, and came to Jehoiada the priest. **10** The priest gave the captains the spears[356] and the quivers[357] belonging to King David that were in the house of Yahweh. **11** So the guards stood, each one with his weapons in hand, from the right side of the house to the left side, the altar and the house, around the king. **12** He brought out the son of the king and put the crown on him and the testimony and they made him king and anointed him; they clapped their hands and said, "Long live the King!"

13 When Athaliah heard the sound of the guards and the people,[358] she went to the people in the house of Yahweh. **14** She looked and there was

---

of commentators believe the MT reading is correct, and that the killing was taking place in the bedchamber. Cogan and Tadmor note the several instances where the places where murder occurred are specified: 11:20; 12:20 [MT 21]; 15:10, 14 (126).

354. On the use of the ל preposition to express the genitive relationship, see GKC (§129*b*); RJW (§270).

355. מַסָּח, *massāḥ* is a *hapax legomenon.* For this meaning, see *HALOT* (3.605). Gk. omits; Vulg. transliterates, and Syr. reads "from harm." Sweeney (346) reads "stragglers," while Cogan and Tadmor (127) identify it as a copyist's error that is meaningless.

356. MT sing. (הַחֲנִית, *haḥănîṯ*). The versions and 2 Chr 23:9 pl. Cogan and Tadmor (127–8) suggest an orig. fem. pl. ending וֹת, *-ôṯ*, was lost by haplography with the following וְאֶת.

357. Meaning uncertain (הַשְּׁלָטִים, *haššᵉlāṭîm*). Gk. "thirds" (apparently mistaking *ṭ* for *š*); Vulg. "arms"; Syr. "quivers." On the basis of DSS "quivers" is suggested. See Cogan and Tadmor, 128. See the "Commentary" below.

358. This phrase is problematic because הָרָצִין, *hārāṣîn* has final *n* instead of the normal final *m* of Heb. masc. pl. Furthermore, there is no conjunction between *hārāṣîn* and הָעָם, *hā ʿām.* This may be why Gk. and Vulg. translate "the sound of

the king beside the pillar according to the custom, and the captains and the trumpeters were beside the king and all the people of the land were rejoicing and blowing trumpets. Athaliah tore her clothes and shouted, "Treason, Treason!" **15** Jehoiada the priest commanded the captains, commanders of the army, and said to them, "Bring her out between the ranks and whoever come after her, will die by the sword," because the priest had said, "She must not be killed in the house of Yahweh." **16** They laid hands on her and she went by way of the entrance of horses into the king's house, and she was killed there.

17 Jehoiada made a covenant between Yahweh and the king and the people to become Yahweh's people, and between the king and the people. **18** All the people of the land went to the house of Baal and they tore it down, its altars and its images they broke completely, and Mattan the priest of Baal they killed before the altars. The priest put overseers[359] over the house of Yahweh. **19** He took the captains and the Carites and the guards and all the people of the land and they took the king down from the house of Yahweh and they went by way of the gate of the guard into the house of the king and he sat on the throne of the kingdom. **20** And all the people of the land rejoiced and the city was quiet, Athaliah having been killed with the sword in the house of the king. **21** **[MT 12:1]** Joash was seven years old when he became king.

Textual Notes

1a. וּרְאֲתָה: As Q (רָאֲתָה) indicates, the ו (*waw*) is problematic. GKC (§112*pp*) suggests that it may be a narrative indicator, as in Aramaic. Montgomery and Gehman (424) see it as an error, duplicating the *waw* at the end of the preceding word.

1b. בְּנָהּ: Gk. "sons"; Vulg. and Syr. sing. with MT.

1c. וַתָּקָם: Gk. omits; Vulg. and Syr. with MT.

2a. בֶּן־אֲחַזְיָה: Gk. "son of her brother"; Vulg. and Syr. with MT. Hobbs (134) comments that "her brother" and "Ahaziah" are identical except for the ז in Ahaziah. This is true, but it is very difficult to say which way the alteration went. Given the ms. support, it seems more likely that an original ז fell out in the Gk. reading.

2b. הַמְּמוֹתְתִים: The difference between K and Q (הַמּוּמָתִים) is between a *pulal* (K) and a *hophal* (Q). See *IBHS* (§27.1d) for a discussion of the difference

---

the people running" (so also 2 Chr 23:12); Syr. "the sound of the people, the people rejoicing."

359. Because of the great variety of connotations for פקד, *pqd*, it is difficult to determine the exact purpose for this action. Gk. "overseers"; Vulg. "guards"; Syr. "officers." See the "Commentary" below.

in connotation between *piel* and *hiphil*. Briefly, the former brings the object into a state or condition, whereas the latter causes an event to take place.

2c. אִתּוֹ: Syr. adds "she hid"; Gk. and Vulg. with MT. *CTAT* (398) considers MT likely.

2d–d. בַּחֲדַר הַמִּטּוֹת: Vulg. "dining room"; Syr. "her bed chamber"; Gk. with MT.

2e. וַיַּסְתִּרוּ: Gk. and Syr. "she hid"; Vulg. with MT. MT is the harder reading. Perhaps the indef. 3rd pl. is intended to function as a passive: "he was hidden."

4a. יְהוֹיָדָע: Gk. and Syr. add "the priest"; Vulg. with MT.

4b. K הַמֵּאיוֹת: Q (המאות) omits י (*yod*); so also in 9, 10, 15. Hobbs (134) suggests it may have been an aid to pronunciation.

4c–c. לַכָּרִי וְלָרָצִים: Gk. "Chorri and rasim"; Vulg. "soldiers"; Syr. "the guards and the runners."

4d. בְּרִית: Gk. adds "of the Lord"; Vulg. and Syr. with MT.

4e–e. בְּבֵית יְהוָה: Gk[B] and Syr. omit; Gk. "in the sight of the Lord"; Vulg. with MT.

5a. הַמֶּלֶךְ: Gk. adds "in the gateway"; Vulg. and Syr. with MT.

6a. סוּר: Gk. "of the roads"; Vulg. "Sur"; Syr. "Kersa."

6b. מַסָּח: Gk. omits; Vulg. "messa"; Syr. "from harm." The only occ. in Heb.; meaning unknown.

8a. אֶל־הַשְּׂדֵרוֹת: Gk. "saderoth"; Vulg. "to the precincts of the temple"; Syr. "within range."

8b. וֶהְיוּ: Gk. "And he was"; Vulg. "You shall be"; Syr. imp. with MT.

9a. הַכֹּהֵן: Gk. "the wise"; Vulg. and Syr. with MT.

10a. אֶת־הַחֲנִית: Versions and MSS read pl. MT a collective?

10b. וְאֶת־הַשְּׁלָטִים: Gk. "the thirds"; Vulg. "the arms"; Syr. "the shields."

11a. וְכֵלָיו: Gk. "his weapon"; Vulg. and Syr. with MT.

11b–b. לַמִּזְבֵּחַ וְלַבָּיִת עַל־הַמֶּלֶךְ סָבִיב: Gk. "by the altar and the house around the king"; Syr. "and they surrounded the altar and the king's house"; Vulg. with MT.

12a–a. אֶת־הַנֵּזֶר: Gk. "the nezer and the testimony"; Syr. "the crown on his head"; Vulg. with MT.

12b–b. וַיַּמְלִכוּ אתוֹ וַיִּמְשָׁחֻהוּ: Gk. "he made him king and he anointed him"; Vulg. and Syr. with MT.

13a–a. הָרָצִין הָעָם: Gk. "of the running of the people"; Vulg. "of the people running"; Syr. "of the uproar of the people as they rejoiced." The MT is difficult, both because of the ן (final-*nun*) on "runner" (or "one running") and because of the absence of a conjunction on "the people." *IBHS* (§7.4b) suggests that the ן (final-*nun*) is the remnant of an enclitic, and that might explain the Gk. and Vulg. readings. (Syr. tends to be periphrastic in 2 Kings). The common Eng. translation "the guards and the people" is hard to justify. Burney's suggestion (cited by Gray, 576) that the ן (final-*nun*) is an error, thus yielding "the guards of the people" is grammatically possible, but it is not clear what such a phrase would mean.

14a–a. עַל־הָעַמּוּד כַּמִּשְׁפָּט: Gk. "beside the pillar according to the judgment"; Vulg. "beside the judgment seat according to the custom"; Syr. "beside the pillar as was the custom of the kings."

14b. וְהַשָּׂרִים: Gk. and Vulg. "singers"; Syr. with MT. "Singers" has a שׁ (*shin*) instead of the שׂ (*sin*) of "princess" or "captains." In the context it is difficult to judge which is more likely to be original.

15a–a. אֶל־מִבֵּית לַשְּׂדֵרֹת: Gk. "from the inside to the saderoth"; Vulg. "outside the temple precincts"; Syr. "outside the ranks." GKC (§119*e*) explains the combination of preps. as yielding "forth between," and thus most Eng. translations.

15b. הָמֵת: An inf. abs. functioning as a jussive (cf. GKC §113*cc*). Gk. reads it as an intensifier "by death he will be put to death."

18a. K אֶת־מִזְבְּחֹתָו: Reading as pl. with Q.

19. וַיֵּשֶׁב: Gk. "they made him sit"; Vulg. and Syr. with MT.

Commentary

The scene now shifts. For much of the previous seventeen chapters (since 1 Kgs 15:25) the focus has been upon the northern kingdom. The only brief interludes have been 1 Kings 22:41–50 (Jehoshaphat) and 2 Kings 8:16–29 (Jehoram and Ahaziah). But even these treatments were rather cursory. The main story line has dwelt on the momentous events taking place in the north as the crisis of Baalism was being played out. Some have argued that this was because Judah was essentially a vassal of Israel during this entire period from the beginning of Omri's reign until the time of Jehu or even later.[360] However that may be, we are hardly prepared for the news we receive here. For some 65 years, while the north had been going through one dynastic crisis after another, Judah had enjoyed great stability and, under the rule of first Asa and then his son, Jehoshaphat, had, as far as the text is concerned, been firmly rooted in the exclusive worship of Yahweh (1 Kgs 15:11–15; 22:43, 46). To be sure, in 8:18 and 26 we were informed in passing that Jehoshaphat had been an ally, if not vassal, of Ahab (1 Kgs 22) and Joram (2 Kgs 3), and that the relationship had been sealed with a marriage between his son Jehoram and Ahab's daughter Athaliah. Furthermore, it is in connection with those announcements, that we are told that both Jehoram and his and Athaliah's son Ahaziah had "walked in the ways of the house of Ahab" (8:18, 27). But it was easy there to overlook the import of those statements for the life of Judah.

Now we learn that indeed Athaliah had been a force to be reckoned with, as we might have expected, given that her mother, or stepmother, was Jezebel. We also learn, although in passing, that just as the worship of Baal had become institutionalized in Israel, the same thing had taken place in or near Jerusalem. Given that both Asa and Jehoshaphat are said to have done much to put the worship of Yahweh on a firm footing this news is disconcerting, reminding us again that apostasy is only a generation or two away from even the most fervent devotion to Yahweh. On the other hand, this account also reminds us that genuine reform is possible in the face of the most difficult odds, if devotion, courage, and careful planning are allowed their head.

We are led to reflect on the impact of the northern kingdom upon the southern only here at the end of the story. What had gone on in the south during the previous twenty or thirty years is left to our imagination. The reason for the inclusion here seems clear: the impact of Ahab and his family had not been limited to Israel but had gone south across the border. Thus, any account of the extirpation of that impact was going to have to include Judah as well.

Again, as we have seen in the previous chapters, the tale is told with a great deal of literary skill. There is drama, suspense, action, and violence, all narrated with brevity and simplicity, and a minimum of narrator's comments. The account is organized with an introduction (1–3), the detailing and the accomplishment of the plans (4–12), the immediate outcome (13–18), and the ultimate outcome (19–21 [MT 12:1]).[361]

---

360. See Megan Bishop Moore and Brad E. Kelle, *Biblical History and Israel's Past* (Grand Rapids: Eerdmans, 2011), 297–305.

361. Reaching as far back as Wellhausen, it has been argued that the account is a combination of two or more original accounts, one reflecting Priestly concerns and the other more popular. See Gray, 565–69 and Fritz, 296–98 for a discussion. Cogan

1–3 As represented elsewhere in this book, the queen mother (גְּבִירָה, *gᵉḇîrâ*), from Bathsheba onward (1 Kgs 1) played an outsized role in the politics of the two kingdoms (most recently, Jezebel, 2 Kgs 10:13). So here, it is not Ahaziah's queen who takes action upon her husband's death, but his mother. The motivation for the brutal action Athaliah took is not stated. Sweeney (343–344) suggests, somewhat oddly, that it was to prevent one of Ahaziah's sons taking the throne, thereby making that woman the queen mother. He further suggests that it was only Joash and his mother Zibiah who were her targets. It is much more probable that Athaliah's motive was revenge. Her family and their dynasty had been destroyed in the north, and the destruction had almost certainly included many, if not all, of her own sons (10:13). If that was true, it is easy to imagine her thinking, "If my family is extinguished, then David's dynasty is going to go down with it. At least I can do that much."[362] If the slaughter of all the other wives' children and grandchildren might catch up a few of her own grandchildren, so be it. The picture is of a hard and determined woman without hope.

It is significant that although the author reports that Athaliah ruled for six years (v. 3), he does not grant her either an accession report or a death report. Clearly, he does not see her reign as being legitimate.[363] Like Jehu, she had usurped the throne; but unlike Jehu, who was carrying out Yahweh's will, she was seeking to defy his will.

The ironic contrast between the female would-be destroyer of the dynasty and the female savior of the dynasty is heightened when we learn that the contest is between the mother and the sister of the dead Ahaziah. Cogan and Tadmor (126) opine that Jehosheba was actually Athaliah's daughter, but one would expect that if the contrast was that pronounced, the point would have been made explicit. Thus, it seems likely that Jehosheba's mother was one of the other ladies of the harem. As a princess, she would have had full access to the harem, and if Chronicles is correct that she was the wife of the high priest Jehoiada (2 Chr 22:11), she would have had access to the living quarters in the temple as well. Her concern to preserve a scion of the Davidic dynasty could be explained by her marriage to a priest as well. From a more cynical point of view, the priests could wish to protect the dynasty because it was that dynasty that had built the Yahweh temple and hopefully had a stake in maintaining it. Less cynically, and I think more likely, they wished

---

and Tadmor argue for its unity (140). Hobbs shows that the criteria upon which the different hypothesized sources are constructed are inconsistent (135–36).

362. So also, Wiseman, 230.

363. Although the matter is debated, it seems possible that Athaliah's six years are included in Joash's forty. See Galil 47–48, *contra* Thiele, 71. "Six years" is interesting, because it is the number of imperfection, whereas "seven" (for Joash's first, v. 4) is perfect. See Job 5:19; Prov. 6:16.

to preserve the dynasty because it was their God, Yahweh, the Lord of the temple, who had given his guarantee to the Davidic dynasty.[364]

Some commentators think it unlikely that the boy could have been hidden from Athaliah in the temple, which was part of the royal complex, for as long as six years.[365] In reply, others, including Sweeney (345), argue that Athaliah, being a foreigner, could not go into the temple. That is not a strong argument. Clearly, she was able to go there without difficulty when she heard the uproar surrounding Joash's coronation (11:13). Furthermore, if she had any inkling the child was there, and if the priests tried to keep her out on the basis of her nationality, she could have sent the temple guards to do her bidding. It is much more likely that in her disdain for the Yahweh temple, she gave it the widest berth possible, quite content to allow it to subside into the ruins which Joash later sought to repair (12:6). Thus, irony comes into play again: if she had paid more attention to Yahweh, the news of her nemesis might have reached her ears; ignoring him, it did not.

4 Presumably, Jehoiada waited as long as he did ("the seventh year") to allow "the son of the king" (בֶּן־הַמֶּלֶךְ, *ben-hammelek̲*) to reach some level of maturity. He may also have needed that long to allow some of the plans to mature. It is noteworthy that Jehoiada is not identified by title until v. 9. This has led some to deny that he was a priest at all but was rather a royal official of some sort, and that his identification as a priest came only in a late redactional layer.[366] However, if that is the case it is difficult to explain his influence over the temple guards, or why the oath of loyalty they took was in the temple. Cogan and Tadmor (126) proposed an alternative that there was more to this particular part of the narrative, and that Jehoiada's title was given in an earlier portion that was omitted.

The captains (שָׂרֵי הַמֵּאיוֹת, *śārê hammē ʾyôt̲*, "princes of hundreds") might be referred to as "centurions," except that it would be anachronistic. But this was indeed their role. The typical hierarchy would be prince (or commander) of tens, fifties, hundreds, thousands (Exod 18:21), and the host (army) ("commander of the host"; 1 Sam 17:55). Thus a "commander of hundreds" would be a junior officer of considerable authority comparable to a captain in the U.S. Army. It is not known who the Carites were. Perhaps they can be identified with the "Carians" who stemmed from southeast Asia Minor, and who appear as mercenary soldiers in the armies of several ancient Near Eastern

---

364. Jehosheba's action is described as גָּנַב, *gānab̲*, that is kidnapping, a crime punishable by death (see Deut 24:7). But even apart from the teaching of the Torah, it is clear that she was risking her life in this attempt.

365. See Lowell K. Handy, "Speaking of Babies in the Temple," *Proceedings* 8 (1988): 155–65.

366. So Wolfgang Zwickel, "Priesthood and the Development of Cult," *The Books of Kings: Sources, Composition, Historiograpy and Reception,* eds. B. Halpern and André Lemaire (Leiden: Brill, 2010), 421.

countries.[367] Whether they are to be identified with the Kerethites[368] in David's bodyguard (2 Sam 15:18) is more debatable (although the Vulg. does make that identification in v. 19—here calling them simply "soldiers").[369] Regardless of their precise identification, these men, along with the הָרָצִים, *hārāṣîm*, "the guards" (see above on 1 Kgs 14:27–28; 2 Kgs 10:25), clearly served as the elite troops guarding the royal complex, including the temple and the palace.[370]

Evidently these military men had deep respect for Jehoiada. Again, this may be a reflection of the long period of time between Athaliah's murder of the children and the unveiling of "the son of the king." In his dealings with these men, the priest had evidently displayed devotion to Judah's God (not the foreign Baal), and a level of integrity and trustworthiness such that when he finally judged it was time to set his plan in motion, there is no evidence of quibbling or backpedaling on their part. They go into the temple, accept the covenant that Jehoiada lays on them,[371] and swear oaths of loyalty (both to Jehoiada and to Yahweh?) without one demur, as far as the record indicates. That must have been a moment of anxiety for the priest, but it passed without a hitch. Then, and only then, did he display his prize, the genuine son of the dead Ahaziah; the one living being with a right to David's throne.

5–9 The details found in these verses are both intriguing and confounding. In particular, it has been argued that v. 6 is a gloss produced by the mention of "a third" (הַשְּׁלִשִׁית, *haššᵉlišîṯ*) in v. 5. The evidence in support of this contention is found both in the fact that: (1) it is possible to read straight from the end of v. 5 into the beginning of v. 6, and (2) the presence of several unknown locations and at least one unknown word in v. 6. However, several commentators, including Hobbs (140) and Cogan and Tadmor (127), argue against the idea, suggesting that the very complexity argues for the verse's originality. As Konkel (500) indicates, it is only our distance that makes interpretation difficult; to those who knew the layout of the complex intimately, these directions would have been quite intelligible.[372]

---

367. See "Carites," *ABD* 1:872. See O. Masson, "Les nom des Cariens dans quelques langues de l'antiquité," *Mélanges É. Benveniste* (Louvain: Peeters, 1975): 407–14.
368. See "Cherethites," *ABD* 1:898–99.
369. Gray (571) and Wiseman (231) think so; others are less certain.
370. Chronicles, written several hundred years later, and concerned to retain the ritual purity of the temple, identifies them as "priests and Levites" (2 Chr 23:4). At the same time, it is not beyond the realm of possibility that the temple guards did have Levitical connections.
371. This is not a covenant of mutuality (see below on v. 17) indicated by the prep. ב "with," or בֵּין "between," but rather a covenant of obligation, indicated by the prep. ל "to, on."
372. For a rebuttal of the position that v. 6 is a gloss, see Gnana Robinson, "Is 2 Kings 11:6 a Gloss?" *VT* 27 (1977): 59–61.

As the text stands, it says that the guards of the royal complex worked a rotation of one week out of three, with one rotation coming on duty at the beginning of Sabbath, and the previous one going off duty at the end of Sabbath, thus giving a double guard on the Sabbath day. Jehoiada directed that all three rotations be present on this Sabbath. Those who were coming on duty would guard the palace and key entrances and exits.[373] If the reading of *HALOT* for מַסָּח, *massāḥ* as "alternately" is correct (see n. 350 above), then possibly the three parts of that rotation would spell each other at the three locations.[374] The other two rotations, both the one going off duty and the one in reserve were assigned to the temple with responsibility for the safety of the boy-king. Obviously, everything hung on this group. If something should go wrong and some supporter of Athaliah should break through and kill the boy, then all would be lost. So they were to surround him at every moment, weapons drawn, prepared to strike first and ask questions later. In all this the care that had gone into the planning is evident. As much as possible, nothing was left to chance. The differences between these actions and Jehu's somewhat *ad hoc* approach to his coup are fascinating.

10–12 Our unfamiliarity with the details of temple practice continues to hamper us in the interpretation of these verses as well. We know nothing of David's spear or spears[375] being placed in the temple, and while it is said in 2 Sam 8:7 that David had put certain gold objects (הַשְּׁלָטִים, *haššᵉlāṭîm*, the same term used here) belonging to Hadad-ezer in the temple, it is not at all certain that the traditional translation "shields" is correct.[376] Later we are told that the gold shields Solomon had made for the temple were looted by Shishak and replaced with bronze ones by Rehoboam, but there the well-known term for shield (מָגֵן, *māgēn*) is used (1 Kgs 14:26–27). So it is not clear what is taking place here. Presumably these were not actual weapons being passed out to the guards, but perhaps some sort of ceremonial emblems establishing the right of the guards to be where they were stationed.

The interpretation of v. 11 is problematic because it is not clear what the "shoulder" (כָּתֵף, *kāṯēp̄*) of the temple refers to. Perhaps the "shoulders" of

373. There is no other reference to "the Sur gate." Given the meaning of the root סוּר, *sûr* as "to turn aside, depart from," perhaps this was a primary exit. It has been suggested the "the gate behind the guards" was a primary access between the palace and the temple.

374. Provan's recommendation that מַסָּח, *massāḥ* be read as "destruction" and applied to the temple of Baal has not gained much support (222).

375. See n. 351 above on the number of this noun.

376. In Akk. *šalṭu* refers to a quiver or a bowcase. That also seems to be the meaning when the term is used in the DSS "War Scroll." See the lengthy discussion in Hobbs, 141.

the building were the front corners on either side of the central porch.[377] If this is correct, the guards would have formed a semi-circle from the right (south) corner around the altar to the left (north) corner. This would ensure that when the son of the king was brought out (וַיּוֹצִא, *wayyôṣiʾ*) and presented on the porch, no one could break through and get to him.

As with other technical terms in this account, there is not complete agreement among scholars on the meaning of the key terms here translated "crown" (נֵזֶר, *nezer*) and "testimony" (עֵדוּת, *ʿēḏûṯ*). Elsewhere the vb. with the root נזר, *nzr* generally occurs in connection with the priest and his consecration (Lev 21:12) and with the dedication vows of the Nazirite (Num 6). The noun נֵזֶר was an object placed on the turban of the high priest with the words "Holy to Yahweh" inscribed on it. It was a plate with a blue cord attached that would encircle the turban and hold the plate in place (Exod 26:36–38). This suggests that the נֵזֶר of the king may have been a circlet of gold, with or without an inscription, but indicating his consecration to God (2 Sam 1:10; Pss 89:39 [MT 40]; 132:18).[378]

If anything, there is even more uncertainty about עֵדוּת, *ʿēḏûṯ*. The term itself is one of the frequent synonyms for the Torah (Exod 40:20) and refers regularly to the tablets or the scroll that was deposited in the ark of the covenant, but it seems unlikely that an entire torah scroll, much less the stone tablets, would have been presented to the young boy at this time.[379] It is more generally thought that it was copy of the "royal warrant" expressed in Deut 17:14–20. But there is no agreement about the form which this material took. Was it a small parchment scroll, or an inscribed amulet, or even an inscribed metal scroll, like those found at Ketef Hinnom?[380] In any case, this item established the subservience of the king to Yahweh. The king in Israel was no absolute monarch. He ruled at the behest of Yahweh, and under his mandate, with an understanding that he was the shepherd of Yahweh's flock (2 Sam 5:2; 7:7). When these two symbols of dedication and responsibility (see Pss 89:39 [MT 40]; 132:12 where נֵזֶר is paralleled with בְּרִית, *bᵉrîṯ* "covenant") were coupled with the act of anointing with sacred oil, the king's identity was both established and constrained. The anointing represented God's choice, and the people's shouted acclamation, "Long live the King" (יְחִי הַמֶּלֶךְ, *yᵉḥî hammeleḵ*), expressed their acceptance of that choice.[381]

---

377. For a discussion, see Robert D. Haak, "The 'Shoulder' of the Temple," *VT* 33 (1983): 271–78.

378. See *HALOT* (3.684–85).

379. Although see S. A. B. Mercer's long-ago contention to the contrary in "The 'Testimony' of II Kings 11,12," *ATR* 6 (1923): 44–45.

380. Gabriel Barkay, et al., "The Amulets of Ketef Hinnom: A New Edition and Evaluation," *BASOR* 334 (2004): 41–71. For a lengthy discussion of the possibilities, see Gray, 573–74.

381. For other such acclamations, see 2 Sam 16:16; 1 Kgs 1:25, 34, 39.

13–16 There was evidently a good-sized crowd on hand for the event, both ordinary Sabbath worshippers, and those who may have been clandestinely invited, and their approval of what was taking place was vociferous. While the absence of any report of support for Athaliah should not be taken too far, the unalloyed success of the coup suggests that the Queen Mother may have been a very autocratic, if not oppressive, ruler, and that whatever popular support she might have had at one time had long ago been eroded. In any case, the shouting, trumpet-blowing, and general uproar in the temple reached Athaliah's ears and she undoubtedly went as quickly as her dignity allowed to see what was going on.[382] Presumably, the guards at the entrance had been briefed to let her pass.

What she saw (note the repetition of the vb. ראה, *rʾh* from v. 1) was profoundly shocking. (The use of הִנֵּה, *hinnēh*, here translated "there," underlines this sense of shock.) That small boy "standing beside the pillar" (עֹמֵד עַל־הָעַמּוּד, *ʿōmēḏ ʿal-hāʿammûḏ*) in the customary place of coronation, a place where she had probably seen her son stand, had to be a descendant of David. She had failed in her attempt to destroy the dynasty. But maybe all was not lost. With the dramatic act of ripping her royal robe in two and screaming "Treason! Treason!" (קֶשֶׁר קָשֶׁר, *qešer qāšer*). She must have hoped to galvanize some loyal followers who would come to her aid and get her out of this trap. Of course, if there was any treason involved, it was her own six years previously when she, a person with no possible pretense of Davidic ancestry, had usurped the throne, and tried to kill everyone who might have had a rightful claim. But "the people of the land" (עַם הָאָרֶץ, *ʿam hāʾāreṣ*) (v. 14)[383] did not lift a finger to help her; she was alone.

Using language similar to that he had used earlier when he commanded the guards to close ranks around the king, so here Jehoiada commanded the captains to march her out "between the ranks" (אֶל־מִבֵּית לַשְּׂדֵרֹת, *ʾel-mibbêṯ laśśᵊḏērōṯ*). That is, the guards should surround Athaliah and take her out of the temple precincts, not allowing any one to break through to help her,

382. As mentioned above, there seems to have been no bar to her entering the temple precincts at will.

383. This descriptive phrase (עַם הָאָרֶץ) occurs three more times in this passage (vv. 18, 19, 20). Whereas in postexilic and Second Temple periods, the phrase became derogatory, speaking of those who opposed the restoration, here, prior to the exile, that is clearly not the case (21:24; 23:30, 35; 24:14; 25:19; Jer 1:18; 34:19; 37:2). At the same time, there is little agreement as to exactly what was meant by the phrase. Some take it to refer to an elite, land-owning class, while others think it refers to all who worked the land. Still others argue that it was something of a national assembly. In any case, they are people whose voices count and those whose opinions carried weight in the affairs of the nation. See E. W. Nicholson, "The Meaning of the Expression עם הארץ in the Old Testament," *JSS* 10 (1965): 59–66; T. Ishida, "'The People of the Land' and the Political Crises in Judah," *AJBI* 1 (1975): 14–36.

or even to follow her out. Obviously, it would have been less risky to kill her on the spot, but the priest did not want shed blood to defile the house of Yahweh. So the one who had made herself supreme in the nation for six years died in a back alley of the royal complex (דֶּרֶךְ־מְבוֹא הַסּוּסִים, *derek̲-mᵉb̲ôʾ hassûsîm*, ""the place where the horses entered"),[384] and, as far as the text is concerned, no one mourned her passing. At the same time, it must be pointed out that Athaliah alone died. There was no bloodbath destroying everyone who had ever had anything to do with the woman, as had been the case in the north. A different spirit is prevailing here.

17–18 In these verses we encounter some other differences from what had taken place in the north. The most obvious is the renewal of the covenant. There is no mention of such a thing taking place there. But covenant renewal had been a feature of Israel's relationship with Yahweh from the outset. There had been the one after the golden calf episode (Exod 34), then after the successful entry into the land of promise (Josh 9) and then again at the end of Joshua's life (Josh 24). Now at this critical moment when it had looked like Yahweh's covenant with David had failed, and it was found that indeed it had not failed, there was clearly a sense that the covenant of Sinai should be renewed. Gray (579–80) believes that there are three covenant renewals here: (1) the one between Yahweh and the king (Davidic), (2), the one between Yahweh and the people (Sinai), and (3) the one between the king and the people (see David's covenant with the people, 1 Chr 11:3). Others (e.g., Long, 391–92) think there are just two, grouping Gray's first and second into one (Sinai). That seems to be the more natural way to read "between Yahweh and the king and the people to become Yahweh's people" (בֵּין יהוה וּבֵין הַמֶּלֶךְ וּבֵין הָעָם, *bên yhwh ûb̲ên hammelek̲ ûb̲ên hāʿām*). This event is not merely about restoring a Davidide to the throne; it was also about restoring the divine מִשְׁפָּט (*mišpāṭ*), the divine order of things, whereby the king ruled out of his commitment to Yahweh for the sake of Yahweh's people, and the people agreed to accept the rule of the king as an expression of their devotion to Yahweh. Yahweh was their ultimate Sovereign. This complex relationship was then further formalized in the covenant between the king and the people. The only absolute monarch here was Yahweh.[385]

Some commentators (e.g., House, 300) see a causal connection between vv. 17 and 18 although none is formally expressed. But such a relationship is certainly likely. The covenant with Yahweh called for the destruction of all

---

384. Gray believes this location is the Horse Gate, mentioned in Jer 31:40 and Neh 3:28, but that is not specified here (578–79). It seems more likely that it is the first out-of-the-way place the guards reached that was outside of the temple itself.

385. It is unnecessary to see this covenant language as a later insertion by a "Deuteronomist." Even if one were to hold to the outdated idea that the book of Deuteronomy did not exist before 621 BC, the covenant as expressed in Exodus (20–23, 34) is an adequate basis for such covenant thinking.

idols and places of idolatrous worship (Exod 34:10–14). Thus, having just subscribed again to those terms, it is very likely that the people would have put their commitment into action. Once more, note the dramatic difference between what took place here and what had taken place in the north. In both places, the temples of Baal, along with their sacred objects, were destroyed. But in the north the basis for the action was deception (10:18–19), it was carried out by the king's bodyguards (10:25), and it involved a wholesale slaughter (10:24–25). Here it was carried out by the people, probably in expression of their covenant commitments, and although the destruction was carried out *completely,* only one man died: Mattan the priest of Baal. We need not whitewash the Judeans—they were capable of the same kinds of things as had happened in the north; however, it is right for us to notice the differences, and to suggest that while Jehu could justify his actions on the basis of Yahweh's predictions, he did not have the kind of covenantal relationship with Yahweh that would provide any kind of check on the murderous instincts of humans in power.

When it is said (v.18) that Jehoiada "appointed" (פְּקֻדּוֹת, *pᵊquddôṯ*), that word has such a wide range of possible meanings that it is difficult to be certain what is intended. Possibly these are "officers" appointed to protect the temple from any vandalism by enraged Baal worshippers. But it is also possible that these are "overseers" who were to begin the work of repair (see chap. 12:11 [MT 12]) after years of neglect under Jehoram, Ahaziah, and Athaliah. It is also possible that they are a select group of "guards" who are to remain on duty in the temple while the majority go with the king to continue to provide protection for him in the still tenuous situation.

19–21 [MT 12:1] With Athaliah out of the way, and all the popular support swinging to Joash, it was time to take possession of the palace. It must have been something of a mob that passed through "the gate of the guard" (דֶּרֶךְ־שַׁעַר הָרָצִים, *dereḵ-šaʿar hārāṣîm*), evidently the primary access between the temple and the palace. It included the guards and "the people of the land," as well as any priests and Levites who could get free, all continuing to "rejoice" (שׂמח, *śmḥ*). That rejoicing reached its climax when the small boy sat on the great Solomonic throne (1 Kgs 10:18–20) in the "Forest of Lebanon," Solomon's judgment hall (1 Kgs 7:7). Some see a contrast between the rejoicing of "the people of the land" and the "quiet in the city" (וְהָעִיר שָׁקָטָה, *wᵊhāʿîr šāqāṭâ*), taking it that the rural people supported the new king while the urbanites (supporters of Athaliah?) were more restrained. But it is much more likely that the two statements are complementary. There was general approval of the change, and there was not the uproar in the capital city that might have been expected with this kind of sudden change.[386] In

386. Note that שָׁקַט, *šāqaṭ*, "quiet" is used in Josh and Judg to speak of effect of victory over enemies (Josh 11:23; Judg 3:11, 30). When there is victory, there is quiet.

fact, everyone was quite content, that "Athaliah had been killed" (עֲתַלְיָהוּ הֵמִיתוּ, *ʿăṯalyāhû hēmîṯû*).[387]

Although the MT chapter division puts the statement of Joash's[388] age (seven) as the first verse of chapter 12, the Masoretic punctuation has a petuhah (פ), comparable to a hard paragraph break, at the end of that verse. This probably explains why the Vulgate and Syriac, followed by English versions, include this verse with chapter 11. Organized in this way, Athaliah's death is not the key point of the chapter, but Joash's coronation.

Biblical Theology Comments

Obedience to civil authority. The idea of a covenant between Yahweh, king, and people (to be Yahweh's people; 11:17) lies behind Paul's thinking expressed in Romans 13. It is through obedience to earthly expressions of authority that we, the people, express our obedience to God. However, this does not entail blind obedience to these authorities, nor does it grant absolute authority to them, as though they were Yahweh. The authorities are expected to be in covenant with Yahweh, whether they acknowledge that or not. So long as they exercise their authority in a way that is consistent with that covenant and its spirit, they deserve our obedience. Paul is assuming that to be the case. He does not say what we are to do if it is not the case, but he certainly assumes it. Our allegiance is to Yahweh, and he is the one who is to be obeyed, even in defiance of civil authorities if they are acting in defiance of God. This was clearly what impelled Jehoiada's actions. What Paul was dealing with was evidently an attitude among new believers that since they were now set free in Christ, they were set free from all restraints of any kind, including those of civil authority. The apostle was hastening to correct such a false idea.

Application and Devotional Implications

Civil disobedience. There are a number of elements in this account that can give guidance to us should we find ourselves in a situation where the authorities under whom we live are clearly in defiance of God's מִשְׁפָּט, *mišpāṭ*, his revealed order for human life. First, beware of haste. Jehoiada, whether he was in a position to do so or not, did not attempt to remove Athaliah in the first year of her reign. On the other hand, there *are* moments for precipitate action and selfless courage. For Jehosheba to do what she did reveals

---

387. This second reference to the killing of Athaliah has been used to support the hypothesis of two original accounts. However, as Cogan and Tadmor point out, this is merely a resumptive statement closing the account (131).

388. The name is here spelled "Jehoash." Later (12:19 [MT 20]) it appears as "Joash." The same variation is found in the northern king of the same name (13:10, 25). In order to minimize confusion between the two, it is conventional to call the Judean king "Joash" and the Israelite "Jehoash."

a decisiveness and a courage that are the diametric opposite of these same characteristics displayed negatively in Athaliah. When life itself is at stake, delay is not a virtue.

Second, plan in detail and in depth, in part to minimize unintended consequences. When authority is dismantled, the results are typically chaotic, as was the case in Jehu's revolt. That they were not in this case is a testimony to the level of planning that Jehoiada and his compatriots engaged in.

Third, cultivate reliable and committed associates. Jehoiada obviously did not broach his plans to the captains "out of the blue." He knew who they were, and what their commitments were, and whether they would follow him and be loyal to him long before the day when he called them into the temple. He may well have had a hand in the appointment of these particular men. He knew that they would not run amok, and would not let their men do so, but also that they would follow orders.

Fourth, be sure that what you are doing is in the will of Yahweh. Self-interest will corrupt anything it touches, and when the societal restraints are intentionally broken down, that self-interest can justify the most horrible excesses, as the French and Russian revolutions have most graphically illustrated. Be very skeptical of your own motivations.

Selected Bibliography

Branch, R. G. "Athaliah, a Treacherous Queen: A Careful Analysis of Her Story in 2 Kings 11 and 2 Chronicles 22:10–23:21." *In Die Skriflig* 38 (2004): 537–59.

Kuloba, R. W. "Athaliah of Judah (2 Kings 11): A Political Anomaly or an Ideological Victim?" In *Looking through a Glass Bible: Postdisciplinary Biblical Interpretations from the Glasgow School.* Edited by A.K.M. Adam and Samuel Tongue, 139–52. Leiden: Brill, 2014.

Schulte, H. "Die Rettung des Prinzen Joaš: Zur Esegese von II Reg 11,1–3." *ZAW* 109 (1997): 549–56.

The Reign of Joash (12:1–21 [MT 12:2–22])

This account is composed of four parts: the accession report (1–3 [MT 2–4]); repair of the temple (4–16 [MT 5–17]); conflict with Hazael (17–18 [MT 18–19]); and the death report (19–21 [MT 20–22]. On the surface, it seems somewhat strange in this context. Since 1 Kings 17 we have become accustomed to rather dramatic accounts of conflicts between Yahweh and Baal, or between Yahweh and the house of Ahab. Here we have just two elements reported from Joash's forty-year reign, and these are reported in the rather prosaic language we have come to associate with chronicles, whether temple chronicles or royal ones. But in fact, the selection of these particular materials may actually represent the climax of the Elijah/Elisha narratives that began in 1 Kings 17. With the repair of the temple of Yahweh in Jerusalem, the threat that the worship of Baal would displace Yahweh as the God of Israel and Judah was fully erased—that particular crisis was now past. The fact that the phrase "the house of Yahweh" (בֵּית יהוה, *bêṯ yhwh*) is repeated thirteen times between vv. 4 and 17 is an indication of the importance of this idea. The houses of Baal in both Samaria and Jerusalem had been demolished (2 Kgs 10:27; 11:18). But most emphatically, the house of Yahweh did not merely survive, but was rebuilt.[389] What remained was one of the consequences of the apostasy: the depredations of Hazael. Those depredations are detailed in 12:17–18 [MT 18–19]) and in 13:3, 7, 15–19, and 22. Finally, with Hazael's death during the reigns of Amaziah of Judah and Jehoash of Israel (13:24), the work of Elijah and Elisha came to its full end.

The Restoration of the Temple (12:1–16 [MT 12:2–17])

TRANSLATION

1 [**2**] In the seventh year of Jehu, Joash became king. He ruled for forty years in Jerusalem; his mother's name was Zibiah from Beersheba. **2** [**3**] Joash did what was right in Yahweh's sight all his days while Jehoiada the priest was instructing him. **3** [**4**] However, the high places were not removed; the people were still sacrificing and making offerings on the high places. **4** [**5**] Joash said to the priests, "All the dedicated money[390] that is brought to the house of Yahweh, the money that is a man's assessment money, the silver for his life, that is his due, and the silver that a man gives voluntarily to the house of Yahweh, **5** [**6**] the priests shall take, each from his agent,[391] and they shall repair the damage of the house, every place where damage is found. **6** [**7**] Now in the twenty-third year of king Joash the priests had not repaired the damage in the house. **7** [**8**] King Joash called Jehoiada the priest and the priests and said to them, "Why are you not repairing the damage of the house? Do not take any more money from your agents; but put it to the damage of the house." **8** [**9**] The priests agreed not to take money from the people and not to repair the damage of the house. **9** [**10**] Jehoiada the priest

---

389. Brueggemann says that the Jerusalem temple, its building and ultimate demise provides the story line for the books of Kings (419–20). Perhaps we might go a bit farther and say that the interweaving of the house of David and the house of Yahweh is the story line.

390. The actual term here and throughout is כֶּסֶף, *kesep̄* "silver." Coinage is not known in the ANE until the fifth c. BC and later. Pieces of silver valued according to standard weights were used for commerce prior to that time and after it as well. See "Coinage," *ADB* 1:1076–89.

391. There is no agreement either among the ancient versions or among modern commentators as to how this word (מַכָּר, *makkār*) should be translated. Gk. has "their sale"; Vulg. "his rank"; and Syr. "him who has decided to give." The present "agent" reflects the idea that there were temple accountants who received the money and allotted it to the priests on some agreed-upon basis. See the "Commentary."

took a[392] chest and bored a hole in its lid and put it near the altar on the right as one enters the house of Yahweh. The priests who guarded the threshold put into it all the money brought into the house of Yahweh. **10** [**11**] Now when they saw that there was a great deal of money in the box the king's scribe and the high priest went up and tied up and counted the money that was found in the house of Yahweh. **11** [**12**] They gave the counted money into the care[393] of those doing the work, the overseers of the house of Yahweh, and they distributed it to the carpenters and to the builders who were working on the house of Yahweh, **12** [**13**] to the masons and the stonecutters and the buyers of wood and cut stone to the repair the damage to the house of Yahweh, and for all the outlay on the house to repair it. **13** [**14**] However, none of the money that was brought into the house of Yahweh could be used[394] for silver basins, snuffers, bowls, trumpets, or any gold or silver objects for the house of Yahweh. **14** [**15**] They gave it to those doing the work and they repaired the house of Yahweh. **15** [**16**] They did not require an accounting from the men to whom they gave the money to give to those doing the work because they were working faithfully. **16** [**17**] Guilt money and sin money were not brought to the house of Yahweh; it belonged to the priests.

Textual Notes

3a. כָּל־יָמָיו: Gk. and Vulg. "all the days"; Syr. with MT. MT is the harder reading.

4a. הַבָּמוֹת: Gk. Adds "some of"; Vulg. and Syr. with MT.

5a–a. כֶּסֶף עוֹבֵר אִישׁ כֶּסֶף נַפְשׁוֹת עֶרְכּוֹ כָּל־כֶּסֶף: Gk. reads "the assessment money—when a man receives assessment money—all the money whatever"; Vulg. "which is offered for the price of a soul"; Syr. "even the money which every man gives for the salvation of his soul." MT best explains the others.

6a. אֶת־בֶּדֶק: Gk. "*bedek*"; so also throughout.

10a–a. הַמִּזְבֵּחַ בַּיָּמִין בְּבוֹא־אִישׁ בֵּית יְהוָה: Gk "*iamibin* in the house of a man of the house of Yahweh"; Vulg. and Syr. with MT.

11a–a. וַיָּצֻרוּ וַיִּמְנוּ: Vulg. "poured out and counted"; Syr. "counted and bagged"; Gk. with MT. *CTAT* (399–400) MT probable.

12a–a. עֹשֵׂי הַמְּלָאכָה הַפְּקֻדִים בֵּית יְהוָה: Vulg. "those who were over the stonecutters of the house of Yahweh and were over"; Gk. and Syr. with MT.

---

392. The numeral "one" (אֶחָד, *ʾeḥāḏ*) being used as an indef. art. Seven of sixteen occurrences in the OT are found in the books of Kings. See *IBHS* (§15.2.1f) and GKC (§125*b*).

393. *Ketiv* is יַד, *yaḏ*, and *qere* is יְדֵי, *yᵉḏē*, "hand" or "hands of."

394. This (יֵעָשֶׂה, *yēʿāśe*) is an impf. of permissibility or capability. So also in v. 14 [15]. See *IBHS* (§§31.2b, 31.4c). Could also be customary: "would be used."

12b. K הַפְּקֻדִים: Q הַמָּפְקָדִים; both mean "ones who have been appointed." K is a *qal* pass. ptcp.; Q is a *hophal* ptcp., perhaps reflecting the later disappearance of the *qal* passive conjugation.

12c. וְלַבֹּנִים: Vulg. "stonecutters"; Gk. and Syr. with MT.

14a–a. לֹא יֵעָשֶׂה: Gk. "shall not be made"; Vulg. and Syr. past tense. See the "Commentary" below (on 15a–a. also).

15a–a. יִתְּנֻהוּ וְחִזְּקוּ־בוֹ: Gk. "shall give it and shall repair with it"; Vulg. and Syr. past tense.

Commentary

12:1-3 [MT 2–4] As noted above, the MT punctuation has a strong break between the first and second verses of what is now chapter 12 in the Hebrew. As a result, several of the versions, followed by the English versions, count that verse as the final one in chapter 11. For the impact of that action on the reading of chapter 11, see the previous' section "Commentary" above.

If we follow the Hebrew chapter break, the accession formula begins with the age of Joash when he began to reign and is followed by the synchronization with the northern kingdom (12:2 [Eng 1]).[395] On this basis, understanding that Athaliah's reign began in Jehu's first year, which 11:1 would fully support, then Jehu's forty years do not include Athaliah's reign.[396] That Joash's mother Zibiah "came from Beersheba" has suggested to several commentators (e.g., Wiseman, 235; Sweeney, 350) that Ahaziah (or his managers) arranged the marriage as an attempt to strengthen ties with those living on Judah's southern borders.

2 Chronicles 24:7–25 reports in some detail how Joash fell away from Yahweh after the death of Jehoiada. Gray (590) says that Kings knows nothing of "this declension." To be sure, the details are not found in the account here, because that material does not fit into the overall point of the defeat of Baalism that is being made here. However, v. 2 makes it clear that the commendation of Joash that it gives only applied while Jehoiada was alive. Thus, Kings clearly does know what happened after Jehoiada died, even if it does not choose to use the material.

---

395. This same pattern (age of the king when he began to reign, followed by the number of years he reigned, followed by the mother's name) applies in the case of the other Judean kings after the split beginning with Asa (1 Kgs 15:10). However, it is only here that the synchronism (so long as Israel existed) does not precede this statement.

396. According to Thiele's calculations "forty" is a round figure, the actual reign having been thirty-eight years (*The Mysterious Numbers of the Hebrew Kings*, 3rd ed. (Grand Rapids, MI: Zondervan, 1983), 72–73.

As noted above, when the statement about "the high places" (הַבָּמוֹת, *habbāmôṯ*) remaining first appeared in connection with Asa (1 Kgs 15:14), it seems clear that these were understood to be Yahwistic high places, and not places where other gods were worshipped. It is very hard to believe that the final editors who were so deeply committed to Deuteronomistic theology would have allowed it to be said that Asa, Jehoshaphat, and Josah "did right in the sight of Yahweh" (וַיַּעַשׂ הַיָּשָׁר בְּעֵינֵי יהוה, *wayyaʿaś hayyāšār bᵊʿênê yhwh*) had they left pagan shrines standing. Ultimately, it was left to Hezekiah, and ultimately Josiah, to carry out the full Deuteronomic program of centralizing all the worship of Yahweh in one place, namely Jerusalem.

4–5 [MT 5–6] We do not know when Joash gave this command to the priests, except that it was sometime prior to his twenty-third year.[397] Presumably it was not too long before that time in that it can be expected the king would have fairly quickly noticed the failure of the priests to take action.[398] While it is clear that the money being applied to the repairs was to come from the miscellaneous offerings that came into the temple treasury, it is not very clear in these two verses exactly how many different categories of offering are included. As in the previous section, this language seems to be jargon that those in the situation would have understood at once. Hobbs (152) believes there were five different categories involved: (1) money for holy things, (2) money for crossing over (assessment, see Exod 30:13–14); (3) money for temple services (his "life" נַפְשׁוֹת, *napšôṯ*); (4) money voluntarily given, and (5) money from the priest's private income (repointing מַכָּר, here translated "agent"). Cogan and Tadmor (140) see only two categories: assessment money and voluntary money. They understand the opening phrase "dedicated money" (כֶּסֶף הַקֳּדָשִׁים, *kesep̄ haqqŏḏāšîm*) to describe the total, while the phrases "crossing over" (כֶּסֶף עוֹבֵר, *kesep̄ ʿôḇēr*) and lit. "for lives of his provision" (כֶּסֶף נַפְשׁוֹת עֶרְכּוֹ, *kesep̄ napšôṯ ʿerkô*) are two different expressions of the assessment (as is the case in Exod 30:12–13). Provan (225) sees three categories: vows, assessment, voluntary. This latter breakdown seems to fit

397. The account displays numerous similarities with that of the temple repair commanded by Josiah (2 Kgs 22:1–7), and some commentators have proposed the dependency of one on the other. Hobbs argues against dependency, pointing to common authorship and common subject matter (149). So also, Cogan and Tadmor, 141n3. For a full discussion, see Na'aman Nadav, "Notes on the Temple 'Restorations' of Jehoash and Josiah," *VT* 64 (2014): 640–651.

398. For archeological evidence of such practices, see Pierre Bordreuil, Felice Israel and Dennis Pardee, "King's Command and Widow's Plea: Two New Hebrew Ostraca of the Biblical Period," *NEA* 61 (1998): 2–5, 7, 9–13; Victor Hurowitz, "Another Fiscal Practice in the Ancient Near East: 2 Kings 5–17 and a Letter to Esarhaddon (*LAS* 277)," *JNES* 45 (1986): 289–94; Herschel Shanks, "Three Shekels for the Lord: Ancient Inscription Records Gift to Solomon's Temple," *BAR* 23/6 (1997): 28–38; Shanks, "Is It or Isn't It?: King Jehoash Inscription Captivates Archeological World," *BAR* 29/2 (2003): 22.

best what we hear of in the general worship of Israel. (See Lev 27:1–25 for things that may be dedicated and the monetary values involved.)

This money would not normally have come to the priests. Their income was from the offerings given by the people (see Lev 2:3; 6:26; 7:6–10, 28–34). What they could not immediately eat could be sold (thus the reference to the "agents", i.e., "sellers").[399] The only money they would have normally received would have come, as v. 16 [MT 17] says, from that accompanying sin and guilt offerings (Lev 5:15–16). In particular, the assessment money had always been intended for the upkeep of the sanctuary (see Exod 30:16). Likewise, the mention of money given voluntarily is reminiscent of the voluntary offerings that were given for the building of the tabernacle (Exod 35:21) and this suggests again that dedicating such funds to the repair of the temple was not an innovation. No specification is given for the use of money given in payment of a vow of dedication, but there is no indication that this was intended for the priests' personal use. Thus, Joash was not requiring that the priests use their own income to repair the temple, as some have suggested. Rather, he seems to have been giving the priests the responsibility for collecting this money then using it as it was originally intended: for the upkeep of the temple complex.

6–10 [MT 7–11] Whenever the king had given the initial directions for the repair of the temple, it eventually reached his attention that the work was not being done. He would have been thirty years old in his twenty-third year and may have become largely independent of Jehoiada by this time. Wiseman (236) suggests that possibly the aging Jehoiada was not able to keep the priests under control as he should have. While it is possible that the priests were using the money for themselves, it is also possible that since it was of no particular benefit to them, they were just not carefully collecting it.[400] In any case, the king realized that his original plan was not working. As the text has it, after his stern rejoinder, he did not wait for an explanation of what had gone wrong but moved straightaway to take the matter out of the hands of the priests at large, and to centralize it. The task of collecting the money remained in the charge of the priesthood, but now it was a small group who could be more easily supervised, "the keepers of the threshold" (שֹׁמְרֵי הַסַּף,

399. The root is מכר, *mkr*, "to sell." To arrive at the idea of "donor" (NIV) one would have to assume either the same root with a different meaning, or the idea that the one giving the gift had sold something to get the gift money. The variety of translations is surprising; here are a few: "business assessor," "donation administrators," "benefactors," "treasurers," "acquaintances," "purchasers," and "donors." See Logan S. Wright, "MKR in 2 Kings xii 5–17 and Deuteronomy xviii 8," *VT* 39 (1989): 438–48, who argues that it is income from the sale of the priestly portions. If he is correct, then this part of the money would have come from priestly income.

400. 2 Chr 24:4–6, which has the Levites sent out into the countryside to collect the assessment money, makes it explicit that it was a case of neglect, not misappropriation,

šōmᵉrê hassap̄) (v. 9 [MT 10]).[401] Furthermore, their handling of the money was confined to taking it from the worshippers as they came into the temple precincts and putting it into a presumably locked chest which had a hole drilled in the lid. Thus, the possibilities for mishandling, misappropriation, or simple forgetfulness were sharply curtailed.

There has been some disagreement about where this box was located because of the two apparently contradictory statements about that location. On the one hand, it is said it was on the "right [side] of the altar" (אֵצֶל הַמִּזְבֵּחַ בַּיָּמִין, *ʾēṣel hammizbēaḥ bayyāmîn*). But it is also said that it was as "one came into the house" (בְּבוֹא־אִישׁ בֵּית יהוה, *bᵉḇô - ʾîš bêṯ yhwh*) (9 [MT 10]). But the altar was in the center of the court and not at the entrance to the precincts or at the entrance to the temple building itself. For this reason, there has been the long-standing suggestion that מִזְבֵּחַ, *mizbēaḥ* "altar" should be emended to מַצֵּבָה, *maṣṣēḇâ*, "pillar"; taking "pillar" to refer to the pillars on the porch of the temple. However, there is no support for such an emendation in any of the ancient versions. That being so, it has been suggested that there was an altar at the entrance of the temple, a "threshold altar."[402] However, in the absence of any mention of such an installation in the text, it is more probable that the gatekeepers took the money at the entrance and carried it across the court to the chest located beside the altar (so Cogan and Tadmor, 138).

It is significant that those collecting the money were not those counting it. Furthermore, there was not merely one person counting it. There was a representative from the palace, "the king's scribe" (סֹפֵר הַמֶּלֶךְ, *sōp̄ēr hammelek̠*)[403] and a representative from the temple, "the chief priest" (הַכֹּהֵן הַגָּדוֹל, *hakkōhēn haggāḏôl*). The wisdom of such a procedure has been demonstrated again and again through the years. (See the "Application and Devotional Implications" below.)

The presence of the scribe is an indication of the king's interest in the process, but he did not simply take the matter into his hands; the priesthood had a vital interest in what was taking place and needed to be directly involved.[404] Again, we see the marks of wisdom on the part of Joash.

It is not entirely clear what the counting process involved. As said above, these were not coins whose value could be reckoned at sight. Rather, they were pieces of silver of varying sizes and weights. That being so, the order given in the MT: וַיָּצֻרוּ וַיִּמְנוּ, *wayyāṣurû wayyimnû* "tied up and counted (lit. measured)" becomes more understandable. They "tied up," that is, collected,

401. On this position, see 22:4; 25:18; Jer 35:4; Jer 52:24. It is an indication of the importance of the position that the three doorkeepers are specifically identified along with the chief priest and the assistant chief priest, as being chosen for execution by the Babylonians.

402. See William McKane, "A Note on II Kings 12.10 (Evv 12:9)," *ZAW* 71 (1959): 260–65.

403. On this position, see 2 Sam 8:17; 20:25; 1 Kgs 4:3.

404. For a similar pairing of responsibility under Jehoshaphat, see 2 Chr. 19:11.

the silver pieces together (in containers of some sort; "bags"" may be anachronistic) and weighed the containers.[405]

11–16 [MT 12–17] Four points are worthy of note in these verses. One is that the variety of workmen involved (11–12 [MT 12–13]), the same as those involved with the initial building of the complex (1 Kgs 5:15–18), indicates how serious the deterioration had become. The point is underlined by the statement that none of the money could be spent on incidentals such as the various vessels and objects used in temple worship (13 [MT 14]; 2 Chr. 24:14 says that when the repair work was finished, the money left over was put to that purpose). Whatever might have been the case under Asa and Jehoshaphat, it is evident that during the reigns of Jehoram and Ahaziah, not to mention that of Athaliah, the building had been neglected and even vandalized (2 Chr. 24:7) to the extent that now major renovation was required, and every bit of the money available had to be applied to that task.

A second point is less significant, but worth noting. Those "doing the work" (עֹשֵׂי הַמְּלָאכָה, *ʿōśê hammᵉlāʾkâ*) in vv. 11 and 14 were the supervisors of the work. That is made clear by the appositional phrase "the overseers of the house" (הַפְּקֻדִים בֵּית יהוה, *happᵉquḏîm bêṯ yhwh*) in v. 11. A term from the same root (פקד, *pqd*), here translated "overseers" appeared in 11:18, there variously translated "watchmen," "officers," and "guards."[406] Perhaps the use here suggests that in the prior reference the function of those with "oversight" was to prevent further damage. In any case, they were the ones to whom the money was given, and who then distributed it to the individual workers (11–12 [MT 12–13]). They were evidently not from among the priesthood (8 [MT 9]).

The third point is that no accounting was required of these supervisors. Some commentators (e.g., Hobbs, 155) suggest that this is an implied critique of the priests, who supposedly had kept the funds for themselves. That may be the case. However, I suspect that the more important purpose of the statement is to comment on the dedication of those whom the king was able to recruit for this vitally important task. It suggests that for those who know that Yahweh is faithful, their faithfulness in return becomes a point of honor.

Finally, v. 16 [MT 17] makes it clear that the priests were not expected to give up their income for the work of restoration. When it is said that the money associated with the "guilt" (אָשָׁם, *ʾāšām*) and sin (חַטָּאוֹת, *ḥaṭṭāʾôṯ*) offering were not brought into the temple, it is not saying that those monies

405. NIV (as well as Syr.) reverses the order, which would be appropriate for coins. Vulg. reads "poured" for MT "tied up." This has led to the proposal that the original was יָצַר, *yāṣar* (instead of צוּר, *ṣûr*), "to cast, melt" with the idea that the silver was first cast into bars of standard weight and then counted. While it is reasonable to believe that the silver would indeed have been cast into bars before it was distributed to the workmen, the absence of any other support for the Vulg. reading does not argue in favor of that being said here.
406. There the term is a pl. of the fem. noun (פְּקֻדּוֹת) meaning "oversight."

were somehow handled outside the temple precincts. Rather, it is saying that they were not counted as part of what was brought in for the purpose of renovation. Certainly, worshippers who came with those offerings and the money associated with them brought them into the temple.[407] But the doorkeepers would make the distinction.

Biblical Theology Comments

The intertwining of "the house of David" and "the house of Yahweh" in the books of Samuel and Kings (the Books of Kingdoms in the LXX) is the central theme of the books. Beginning with the birth of the "kingmaker" Samuel and proceeding through until the enigmatic note about the survival and elevation of the Davidide Jehoiachin at the very end (2 Kgs 25:27–30), these ideas are inseparable. David's desire, typical for a new king in the ancient world, to build a house for his God is met with the remarkable declaration that God is more interested in building a "house," an enduring dynasty, for David (2 Sam 7). Why is this? It is not, as we might expect, in response to David's single-minded devotion to Yahweh, and his upright walk, which became the formula by which "good" kings of Judah were later identified. It is simply an expression of Yahweh's חֶסֶד (*ḥeseḏ*), the favor shown by a superior to an inferior, especially when undeserved (2 Sam 7:15).

What is happening? Yahweh clearly wants to live in the midst of his people. That is plain in the book of Exodus. He does not want to exist in isolation upon the fiery mountain. Recognizing that, we can go back to the promises to Abraham and recognize that presence among his creatures to be the ultimate purpose of the promises. He wants to "walk" with us, and for us to "walk" with him (Gen 17:1). He wants his presence to be a blessing to the world and not a curse. Thus, he promised that Abraham, his friend, would become a great people, a promise fulfilled by the end of Exodus. He promised that they would have a land, a promise fulfilled by the end of Joshua. But a blessing to the nations? Hardly. Having gotten the first two promises, for which they had lived with a future orientation, the people as described in the book of Judges, have clearly lost their way. Far from being a blessing to the nations, they have become one of the nations, absorbed into them.

That situation comes to its bitter fruition in the opening chapters of 1 Samuel. It is expressed pointedly in the capture of the ark of the covenant, the death of Eli and his sons, and the destruction of the tabernacle (according to Jer 7:12–15). Religious chaos stemmed from those events. It seemed as though all was lost. But with Yahweh it never is. When the people demanded

---

407. Leviticus 5:15 speaks of a "ram…of the proper value in silver" in connection with the guilt offering. A similar mention of "proper value" appears in connection with the sin offering (Lev. 6:6). Otherwise there is no other mention of money. Perhaps worshippers who traveled a long distance would sell the animal sacrifice in their home location, and bring the money to the temple in place of the animal.

a king, Yahweh was perfectly willing to use their less-than-purely motivated demand for his purposes. Saul represented what could go wrong with a king who was not fully surrendered to Yahweh, a king whose devotion to Yahweh was subsumed under his own need to serve himself.

Thus, we arrive at David. How is God to fulfill that third promise, the promise to bless the world through his presence? How can his presence be a blessing and not a curse? He did it through the "house" of David. Was David fallible? Yes. Did his dynasty ultimately fail? Yes. But has God kept his promise? Yes! Psalm 89 poses an apparently insoluble problem. Yahweh's promised steadfast love and faithfulness seem to have failed. The house of David has fallen. Likewise, the house of Yahweh is in ruins. But have the promises failed? That open question is what ends the Books of Kingdoms. The inner story climaxing in this chapter gives reason to think that the question closing the book of 2 Kings may indeed have a different answer than the one that seems obvious. In 1 Kings 17–2 Kings 12, we see that there was a concerted attempt to replace the worship of the transcendent Yahweh with the worship of the forces of the cosmos, as represented by Baal. The houses of Omri and Baal were in the ascendant; the house of David was first subservient and then in danger of extinction, and the house of Yahweh was deteriorating and vandalized. But it was not to be! The house of Omri was extinguished, and the house of David survived; the houses of Baal were demolished, and the house of Yahweh restored.

At the end of 2 Kings, however, we seem to be back at the same point: the temple in Jerusalem is in ruins, and the dynasty of David seems to be at an end. But 1 Kings 17–2 Kings 12 suggests that may not be the end of the story. All seemed lost before, and it was not. At the end of Psalm 89 and 2 Kings the question remains open. Will the promises to David somehow survive, making God's presence among the people of earth truly possible? We wait for the New Testament to see how the question will be answered, but we have reason to believe from this account that somehow, some way, it will be answered positively.

Application and Devotional Implications

In this apparently simple story, there are some very important lessons for the collection and management of funds. First, there is the principle that simply giving instructions to others is not enough. Joash seemed to assume that telling the priests to collect the money and do the work was all that was required. It never is. There must be guidance given as to the successive steps by which the task can be accomplished, and there must be mechanisms by which its achievement may be progressively measured. When that guidance and those mechanisms are not in place, expectations will not be realized.

A second principle is that if everyone is given the responsibility for completing a task, no one will. All the priests were to collect the money, and all were to repair the temple. No one did either. It was only when specific persons were given specific tasks with both the responsibility and the means to carry out the tasks that the work could be completed.

The third principle has to do with the management of money. Humans are fallen creatures. When temptation is placed before us, it is to be expected that we will fail. Thus, the two-step process whereby one group of people collected the funds, put them in a place to which they only had one-way access, and a second group counted and disbursed the funds, is a time-proven way to guard against the ever-present temptation that money poses. It is also significant that on both levels, groups were involved: it was the doorkeepers, not one doorkeeper, who collected the money, and it was the royal scribe *and* the high priest who counted it and disbursed it.

A final principle is more ephemeral, but still very important. There is no system that is foolproof against financial mismanagement. What must be at the bottom of everything is people of demonstrated, unquestionable integrity. It is wrong to put persons in places of responsibility if we have the slightest question about their maturity, their judgment, and their integrity. If we have to insist on an accounting to quiet our fears, then we have put the wrong person in place. It is the person from whom we do not need an accounting who will most likely insist on giving it, not because they think we doubt them, but simply because they are that kind of person under God.

Selected Bibliography

Van Dorp, J. "De Templerestauratic van Joas (2 Konigen 12): Het Gebruik van Een Motief in Het Bock Kiningen." *ACEBT* 9 (1988): 77–89.

Herr, Bertram. "Hat das Alte Testament als Quelle der Geshichte Israels Ausgedienst?: Die Probe auf das Exempel 2 Reg xii 5 – 17." *VT* 51 (2001): 42–54.

Levin, Christoph. "Die Instandsetzung des Tempels unter Joasch ben Ahasja." *VT* 40 (1990): 51–88.

The End of Joash's Reign (12:17–21 [MT 18–22])

Translation

17 [**18**] Hazael, king of Syria, came up and fought against Gath and captured it. Then Hazael set his face to go up against Jerusalem. **18** [**19**] Joash, king of Judah, took all the dedicated things which Jehoshaphat, Jehoram, and Ahaziah, his fathers, had dedicated, and his own dedicated things and all the gold to be found in the treasuries of the house of Yahweh and the house of the king and sent it to Hazael, king of Syria and he went up from Jerusalem. **19** [**20**] The rest of the matters concerning Joash and all that he did, are they not written in the chronicles of the kings of Judah? **20** [**21**] His servants arose and conspired together and struck Joash in Beth Millo on the descent to Sela. **21** [**22**] Jozachar[408] ben Shimat and Jehozabad ben Shomer

408. MT reads יוֹזָבָד, *yôzāḇāḏ* "Jehozabad," but all the versions support the present reading. MT looks like dittography since the same name appears twice, although with different patronymics.

his servants struck him and he died. They buried him with his fathers in the city of David and Amaziah his son succeeded him.

Textual Notes

21a–a. בֵּית מִלֹּא הַיּוֹרֵד סִלָּא: Gk. "in Mallo's house in Galala"; Vulg. "in Mello's house on the descent to Sela"; Syr. "in Bet Millo as he was going down to Sela." MT best explains the others.

22a. וִיהוֹזָבָד: Gk. "Jezichar"; Vulg. "Josachar"; Syr. "Jozachar." "Jozachar" probable, *CTAT* (400). MT seems to be dittography.

Commentary

17–18 [MT 18–19] These verses remind us that choices have consequences and that correcting the choices does not always alter the consequences. The choice to worship Baal that had been made in both Israel and Judah resulted in Yahweh's removing his protections from his people and giving Syria, under the capable leadership of Hazael, permission to punish the people. Thus, the materials detailing the destruction of the house of Ahab and the houses of Baal (8:16–13:21) is enclosed between the announcement of Hazael's appointment (8:7–15) and the description of final relief from Syrian oppression that came during the reign of Hazael's son (13:22–25). Hazael must have been a remarkable leader because he not only ruled for some forty years, he also survived several attacks by Assyria and thoroughly dominated Israel and Judah throughout his reign.

It is an indication of this dominance that Hazael was able to attack and capture Gath. While the identification of this city is not absolutely certain,[409] most commentators (e.g., Gray, 589; Sweeney, 353; Konkel, 514) believe that it is the Philistine city of that name, located at the mouth of the Elah Valley. Part of the reason for this uncertainty is that if it is the Philistine city, that would mean that the Syrian army had unhindered access from Damascus all the way through Israel to reach the coastal plain, and feared no Israelite reprisals in its rear. However, if we take seriously the humiliation of Jehoahaz reported in 13:7 that condition seems to be entirely likely. Furthermore, it seems unlikely that Hazael would have had designs on Jerusalem had he not already been fairly close in Philistia.

Presumably this attack took place sometime between about 830 BC when Assyria was plagued with revolts and 806 BC when the Assyrian Adad-Nirari III attacked Damascus and then campaigned on the coastal plain. Whether Hazael actually believed he could conquer Jerusalem is somewhat moot. The threat was real enough so that he was able to go away enriched without having to expend any of his military capital.

---

409. There is, for instance, Jonah's hometown of Gath-hepher (14:25), that was located, on the basis of Josh 19:13, in the northern territory of Zebulon.

The mention of Jehoshaphat, Jehoram, and Ahaziah is because the "dedicated things" (הַקֳּדָשִׁים, *haqqŏḏāšîm*) had been accumulating in the temple during those reigns after Asa had stripped out the earlier ones to pay the Syrian king Ben-hadad (1 Kgs 15:18). The Syrians seem to have had a ready source of income in the dedicated things of the Jerusalem temple![410] Sweeney (353) holds that the money intended for the repair of the temple was actually lost to Hazael when Joash bought him off. However, this does not seem likely to me because it would mean that since there is no other mention of temple repair until Josiah, the temple would have continued in a state of increasing dilapidation for another century. It seems more likely that the repairs had been completed before Hazael's raid.

19–21 [MT 20–22] Long (400) makes the significant observation that there is no indication that Joash sought the help of Yahweh when he was faced with the Syrian crisis. This would be in keeping with the account in Chronicles of Joash's falling away from Yahweh after the death of Jehoiada. It is also in keeping with the qualified statement here (12:2 [MT 3]) that Joash did right during the lifetime of Jehoiada. It would appear that his religious zeal was more a matter of outside influence than genuine inner conviction. While the text here makes no explicit connection between the attack by the Syrians and Joash's falling away from Yahweh, Chronicles definitely does (2 Chr 24:24). Furthermore, Chronicles links his assassination to his order to have Zechariah, Jehoiada's son, stoned in the temple court (2 Chr 24:25). Again, Kings gives no reason for the assassination, but given that this is evidently not a military coup, and that Joash's son Amaziah was allowed to succeed him, and that his own servants did the act, something of the sort that Chronicles represents seems very plausible.[411]

The location where the assassination took place is uncertain. The versions take it that it occurred in the house of someone named Mallo or Mello. However, it is almost certain that "Millo" (בֵּית מִלֹּא, *bêṯ millōʾ*) refers to the stepped structure that was built at the top of the portion of Jerusalem known as the City of David just below the temple mount.[412] It seems to have been later called "Ophel."[413] It may have provided foundational support for David's palace.[414] It is also evident from the variety of translations that the versions did not know what to make of "the descent to Sela" (הַיּוֹרֵד סִלָּא,

410. See E. Theodore Mullen Jr., "Crime and Punishment: The Sins of the King and the Despoliation of the Treasuries," *CBQ* 54 (1992): 231–48.

411. Kings did not include such information because it is not germane to the main point being made: in spite of the powerful influences to the contrary, the house of David built by Yahweh stood when the house of Ahab associated with Baal had fallen.

412. See 2 Sam 5:9; 1 Kgs 9:15, 24; 11:27; 1 Chr 11:8; 2 Chr 32:5.

413. 2 Chr 27:3; 33:14; Neh 3:26, 27; 11:21.

414. See "Beth-Millo," *ADB* 1:690; "Millo," *ADB* 4:834-35.

hayyôrēḏ sillā ʾ). All in all, it looks as though the event might have occurred on a staircase in what had been David's palace.

Application and Devotional Implications

The experience of Joash, like that of Solomon, should act as a caution for all believers: a good start is no guarantee of a good end. Unless the choices with which one began the journey of life are repeated and confirmed along the way, it is possible that erosion can occur and one will discover oneself making choices at the end of the journey one could never have imagined at the beginning. This is especially true if those early choices were not really one's own, but "inherited," as it were. We may be simply following in the footsteps of parents, or teachers, or friends. But the choices were actually theirs and not ours. We may have thought them ours, but time has proven they were not. Then, when the pressures come, we do not instinctively turn to Yahweh, but to our own resources, and when we do that Yahweh becomes a tool to be used, as in this case, and not the infinite God to be adored.

Selected Bibliography

Mazar. B, "Gath and Gittaim, *IEJ* 4 (1954): 227–35.

Jehoahaz, Jehoash, the Death of Elisha, and the End of Syrian Dominance (13:1–25)

In this chapter we come to the end of the narrative of the downfall of the house of Ahab and of the consequences that stemmed from the attempt to make Baal the God of Israel (and of Judah). That narrative began in chapter 8 with the appointment of Hazael (in fulfillment of the command given to Elijah in 1 Kings 19:15), and here it comes to an end with the announcement that as a result of Yahweh's mercy Jehoash was able to recapture from Hazael's son the towns that Hazael had captured (13:25).

Intrinsic to this account is the final incident involving Elisha (14–21). It was Elisha who set this train of events in motion with Hazael's appointment and now he is the one who symbolically brings it to an end with his prophecy of Jehoash's victories over Ben-hadad. Between the two events, apart from the delegated anointing of Jehu, nothing is heard of him. It is as though once the process was started nothing more was necessary. There was an inexorability about it which had its own violent momentum. Previously, in chapters 3 through 7, when it seemed there might yet be a glimmer of hope for Joram, Ahab's son, Elisha had been the central figure, revealing the character and nature of Yahweh. But once that hope was gone, nothing more remained to be said or done.

Not only does Elisha's appearance here signal the end of this portion of the narrative, but also of the entire Elijah/Elisha narrative that began in 1 Kings 16:29. The importance of the events recorded in these chapters is seen in the amount of material included. They cover only about seventy-five years, but fully twenty chapters, only slightly less than half of the two books, are devoted to this story in which the two prophets are either main characters or in the background. Whatever might lie ahead for the people of God, they could only have a future if Yahweh was the sole God of Israel. Thus, the extreme importance of what is reported to have taken place in these chapters. In contrast, only three chapters are given to the events of the next seventy-five years. Again, there is a certain inexorability in play: yes, Jehu had eliminated any possibility that Baal would replace Yahweh as the God of Israel, but once he showed that he was not going to repent of the sins of Jeroboam, the Assyrian exile became something of a foregone conclusion. There was still hope that the Assyrian exile could be avoided, for Yahweh graciously sent at least the prophets of Hosea and Amos, to call his people back to a worship of him that was not paganized, but given that their faces were set, there was little more to be said.

The chapter includes four segments, and they are marked in the Hebrew text. The first is the account of Jehoahaz's reign (vv. 1–9), the second a summary account of Jehoash's reign (vv. 10–13), the third Elisha's prophecy and death (vv. 14–21), and a final summary (vv. 22–25).

Jehoahaz King of Israel (13:1–9)

Translation

13:1 In the twenty-third year of Joash, son of Ahaziah, king of Judah, Jehoahaz, son of Jehu, became king of Israel in Samaria for seventeen years. **2** He did evil in the eyes of Yahweh and walked after the sins of Jeroboam, son of Nebat who made Israel sin; he did not turn aside from it. **3** Yahweh was angry with Israel and gave them into the hand of Hazael, king of Syria, and into the hand of Ben-hadad, son of Hazael, all the days. **4** Jehoahaz begged mercy from Yahweh and Yahweh heard him because he saw the oppression of Israel, because the king of Syria oppressed them. **5** Yahweh gave Israel a deliverer so that they could get out from under the hand of Syria, and the children of Israel lived in their tents as formerly. **6** However, they did not turn aside from the sins of the house of Jeroboam which he made Israel to sin; Israel walked in it; moreover, the Asherah[415] stood in Samaria. **7** As a result, no army[416] remained to Jehoahaz but fifty horsemen, ten chariots, and ten thousand men on foot, because the king of Syria had destroyed them and made them like dust under foot.[417] **8** The rest of the matters relating to Jehoahaz and all that he did and his might, are they not written in the book of the chronicles of the kings of Israel? **9** Jehoahaz slept with his fathers and they buried him in Samaria, and Jehoash, his son, succeeded him.

---

415. הָאֲשֵׁרָה, *hā ʾăšērâ* perhaps a pillar; Gk. "sacred grove"; Vulg. "grove"; Syr. "idol worship."

416. Heb. has עָם, *ʿām* "people."

417. Gk. χοῦν εἰς καταπάτησιν, *choun eis katapatēsin* and Heb. כֶּעָפָר לָדֻשׁ, *ke ʿāpār lāḏuš* "dust for trampling"; Vulg. "dust on the threshing floor"; Syr. "dust under his feet."

Textual Notes

2a. מִמֶּנָּה: The versions read "from them" agreeing with pl. "sins." Perhaps not so much evidence of textual variations as much as different conventions governing agreement. Gk^{B} has "from it."

6a–a. בָּהּ הָלַךְ: The versions read "they walked in them." Gk^{B} "in it." As in the previous note, the differences may simply reflect differences in conventions of agreement.

Commentary

Jehoahaz is represented in a very contradictory way. One the one hand, he receives the standard condemnation for the northern kings: he did not turn aside from the sins of Jeroboam (v. 2). As a result, he experienced the wrath of Yahweh, and was reduced to a pitiable state by the Syrians under Hazael (vv. 3, 7). On the other hand, he pleaded for mercy from Yahweh, and as a result Israel experienced a measure of peace during his reign (vv. 4–5). In this way, he follows the pattern of Ahab (1 Kgs 21:27–29) and Manasseh (2 Chr 33:12–17, although only in Chronicles, not Kings). That Yahweh would have mercy on these two kings, the worst of their respective kingdoms, is a testimony to his settled intent to bless anyone who would turn to him on whatever pretext. Jehoahaz shares in that blessedness.

1 There appears to be a discrepancy in the figures assigned to Jehoahaz's reign. Here he is said to have begun his reign in the twenty-third year of Joash and to have reigned seventeen years. However, v. 10 says that Jehoash began to reign in the thirty-seventh year of Joash, only fourteen years later. Perhaps the discrepancy is to be explained by a combination of a co-regency and a change in accession-year dating.[418]

2–5 Many commentators (e.g., Cohn, 86) observe that in these verses the pattern established in the book of Judges is replicated. That pattern is: sin—judgment—crying out to God—deliverance. This pattern is especially clear in Judg 3:7–9. The implication of this comparison here is to be found in that the pattern in Judges is repeated in a downward spiral that was only broken in the time of Samuel. The point here is that in the case of Israel the spiral will not be broken and will ultimately issue in the destruction of the nation. Yahweh's patience did have a limit.

Hobbs (166) observes correctly that Israel was not the only nation to conclude that when adversity occurred, it was because their God was angry with them. A classic example is recorded on the Moabite Stone when the

418. Thiele, *Mysterious Numbers of the Hebrew Kings*, 72. He makes the interesting point that whereas Athaliah had moved Judah's accounting to that used in Israel (Egyptian), at this point both kingdoms moved to the one Judah had formerly used (Mesopotamian).

Moabite king attributes Israel's domination of Moab to the anger of their god Chemosh.[419] The difference in Israel is that Yahweh's anger is not an arbitrary matter as it is elsewhere. In Israel, Yahweh's responses are on the basis of the clearly stated terms of the covenant to which Israel had agreed. Jeroboam's sins (1 Kgs 12:25–33), from which no northern king ever deviated, were an explicit rejection of the fundamental basis of that covenant: the exclusive worship of the one God who cannot be identified in any way with his creatures.[420]

The three consonants of the word here (חלה, *ḥlh*) translated "begged mercy" (v. 4) are elsewhere regularly associated with "sickness" or "illness" (חָלָה, *ḥālâ*). BDB argues for two different roots. However, when used with this meaning the word only occurs in the *piel* form and there is no other *piel* form with any other meaning. Thus, *HALOT* (2.316–7) takes it to be a single root with a base idea of "weakness," or "softness," and in the *piel* it has the sense of softening a person's face or God's face. Thus, to translate merely with "to pray" misses some of the flavor of what is being said, since Jehoahaz is attempting to get God to soften his face towards him and his people in the northern kingdom. Provan (231) points out, in connection with 1 Kgs 13:6, that it does not necessarily presume repentance.[421] Yahweh's compassion may be unleashed for a time upon a very slight pretext. He was pained with the pain of this people (cf. Exod 2:23–25). The danger lies in assuming that this will always be the case and that deep and genuine repentance is unnecessary.

As in the book of Judges parallels, God's response to Joash's plea was to send a "deliverer" (מוֹשִׁיעַ, *môšîa* ʿ). Who this deliverer was is left unspecified. Many take it to be Elisha, and appeal to the experience related in 13:10–19. However, it seems very strange that if this were the case, the prophet is not named. Furthermore, the experience just mentioned falls far short of the activities of the deliverers in the book of Judges. The fact that the narrator does not name the deliverer argues strongly that Elisha is not intended. In fact, the lack of specificity suggests that it is not someone whom the community would readily identify as a God-given deliverer, and that the point is not the person's identity, but what they accomplished. Such a person might be the Assyrian Adad-Nirari III who, by decimating Damascus on two different occasions, definitely relieved the Syrian pressure on Israel.[422] But the sense need not be limited to any one person; the point is that Yahweh responded graciously and set in motion a series of events that restored Israel to a previous

---

419. *ANET*, 320.

420. כָּל־הַיָּמִים, *kol-hayyāmîm* "all the days" is thought by some to mean throughout Jehoahaz's entire reign. However, the indefiniteness of the phrase argues that it should be understood as "a long time."

421. See also Exod 32:11; 1 Sam 13:12; Jer 26:19.

422. So Wiseman, 240. See Adad-Nirari's annals in *ANET*, 281–82.

state. The reference to "in their tents" (בְּאָהֳלֵיהֶם, *bᵊʾohŏlêhem*) (v. 5) seems designed to evoke a peaceful past.

6–7 Just as Jehoahaz did not respond to his peaceful accession to the throne of his father (the first of the four promised generations, 10:30) with changed behavior, neither did the people respond to their deliverance from the incessant pressure of Syria with changed behavior. It was like king, like people, or very possibly, like people, like king. Again, the parallel with the book of Judges is clear: as soon as the oppression was relieved, the covenant commitments were soon forgotten. We may ask why this passage in particular contains such clear evocations of the past with its allusions to Exodus and Judges? Perhaps it is because in some senses this is the beginning of a new day, with institutionalized Baalism now expunged. Has Israel learned anything? Are they ready to go back past Jeroboam to a full reaffirmation of their covenant? Evidently not.

The use of the article on Asherah (הָאֲשֵׁרָה, *hā ʾăšērâ*) could suggest that this is the same object (idol, grove, or pole?) that Ahab had erected (1 Kgs 16:33) and that Jehu had not removed it. However, the presence of the article is not definitive for that argument. In any case, it seems likely, in view of the rejection of Baal, that Asherah was considered the consort of Yahweh, and was revered as such (so e.g., Long, 404).

Verse 7 seems intrusive here, and many regard it so. If it is, perhaps the reason for its inclusion is to parallel v. 3.[423] There the oppression of Hazael is seen as the result of Jehoahaz's sin. Here, perhaps the decimation of Israel's armed forces[424] is presented as the result of the people's sin. That decimation, particularly of horsemen (פָּרָשִׁים, *pārāšîm*)[425] and chariots (רֶכֶב, *rekeḇ*), was devastating. Without these mobile forces, the ten thousand footmen[426] (note that the Assyrians claimed more than 100,000 troops, see *ANET*, 280) would have been at the mercy of a fully armed enemy. The only way the peaceful situation described in v. 5 was possible was as a result of Yahweh's mercy. Israel certainly did not have the means to procure it on her own.

---

423. An alternative view is that 4–6 is intrusive. See Dennis J. McCarthy, "2 Kings 13:4–6," *Bib* 54 (1973): 409–10.

424. For the use of עָם, *ʿām* "people" as "armed forces" see Exod 14:6; Num 21:23, 33; 1 Kgs 16:15; 2 Kgs 8:21.

425. It is not clear whether these should be considered as chariot crews or cavalrymen. At this point cavalry was still not a widely-used military weapon, so perhaps Israel did not yet use it (for discussion of cavalry, see Yadin, *The Art of Warfare in Biblical Lands*, 2:286–7, 360, 382–5).

426. If it is pointed out that this is no fewer than Ahab had brought to the battle at Qarqar in 854 BC (*ANET*, 279), it should also be pointed out that this was only his contribution to the larger coalition, and that his total army was almost certainly much larger.

8–9 The standard closing regnal formula. No evidence of the royal tombs has yet been found in Samaria.

Selected Bibliography

Benjamin M. "The Aramean Empire and its Relations with Israel." Pages 151–72 in *The Early Biblical Period: Historical Essays*. Jerusalem: Israel Exploration Society, 1986.

William H. S. "Adad-Nirari III and Jehoash of Israel." *JCS* 30 (1978): 104–9.

Jehoash and the Death of Elisha (13:10–21)

Translation

10 In the thirty-seventh[427] year of Joash, king of Judah, Jehoash son of Jehoahaz reigned over Israel in Samaria for sixteen years. **11** He did evil in the eyes of Yahweh; he did not turn aside from all the sins of Jeroboam, son of Nebat, which he made Israel to sin; he walked in them. **12** The rest of the matters relating to Jehoash and all that he did and all his might with which he fought with Amaziah, king of Judah, are they not written in the chronicles of the kings of Israel? **13** Now Jehoash slept with his fathers and Jeroboam sat upon his throne and Joash was buried in Samaria with the king of Israel.

14 Now Elisha was ill with the illness of which he would die, and Jehoash, king of Israel, went down to him and wept in his presence. He said, "My father, my father, the chariots of Israel and its horsemen." **15** Elisha said to him, "Take a bow and arrows," so he took a bow and arrows. **16** He said to the king of Israel, "Put your hand on the bow," so he put his hand on the bow, and Elisha placed his hands on the king's hands. **17** He said, "Open the window facing east," and he opened it. Elisha said, "Shoot," and he shot. He said, "Yahweh's arrow of victory and the arrow of victory over Syria. You will strike Syria in Aphek completely. **18** He said, "Take arrows," and he took them. He said to the king of Israel, "Strike the earth," and he struck three times and stopped. **19** The man of God was angry with him and said, "By striking five or six times you would have struck Syria completely. But now you will strike Syria three times."

20 Elisha died and they buried him. Now Moabite raiders used to come[428] into the land at the beginning of the year.[429] **21** It happened that they were burying a man, and suddenly saw the raiders, so they threw the

427. A few Gk. MSS read "thirty-ninth year," an evident attempt to resolve the apparent discrepancy between this verse and 13:1. But the rest of the versions agree with MT here, and that problem can be solved in other ways (see the note on 13:1). MT is almost certainly correct, *CTAT* (402).

428. An impf. form (יָבֹאוּ, *yāḇōʾû*) used to express frequent or habitual action. GKC (§107*d*).

429. Cogan and Tadmor say that the phrase as it stands (בָּא שָׁנָה, *bāʾ šānâ*) is meaningless and repoint the first word as בְּבֹא , *bĕbōʾ* (148). This accords with the Gk.

man into the grave of Elisha. When the man touched the bones of Elisha, he revived and stood on his feet!

Textual Notes

10a. שֵׁשׁ עֶשְׂרֵה: Syr. "thirteen"; Gk. and Vulg. with MT. See the footnote on v. 1 above.

11a. בָּהּ: The versions read "in them." See the "Textual Note" 2a.

13a–a. וַיִּקָּבֵר יוֹאָשׁ: Gk. omits; Vulg. and Syr. with MT.

13b. מַלְכֵי יִשְׂרָאֵל: Gk. reads "sons"; Vulg. and Syr. with MT.

15a. קַח: Vulg. "bring" and "brought"; Gk. and Syr. with MT.

16a. יִשְׂרָאֵל: Gk. lacks; Vulg. and Syr. with MT.

17a. עַד־כַּלֵּה: The appearance of an inf. abs. in the genitive case (here as obj. of prep., also v. 19) is rare. *IBHS* (§35.3.3a) suggests it may be a frozen form.

18a. הַחִצִּים: Gk. "bows"; Syr. "an arrow"; Vulg. with MT.

19a. לְהַכּוֹת: The present translation takes the construction to be a ל (*lamed*) of means plus an inf. Const. GKC offers two different explanations: assuming an elided הָיָה preceding it would speak of a compelled or appointed action: "you should have" (§114*k*); the following אָז requires that the construction be understood conditionally: "if you had" (§159*dd*).

21a. וַיְהִי: The combination of הָיָה and הִנֵּה is intended to show that the previous action is simultaneous with the following (see GKC §111*g*).

Commentary

10–13 The regnal summary of Jehoash here is unusual in that the opening formula (10–11) is immediately followed by the closing formula (12–13). It is made more unusual since events relating to Jehoash's reign follow (13:13–14:14) and another closing regnal summary, almost identical to the one here appears in 14:15–16. Most scholars (e.g., Fritz, 311; Cogan and Tadmor, 145) accept that this one is secondary, but there is no agreement as to why it has been included here. Perhaps one version reflects a northern document and the other a southern one, and in combining them the editor(s) was (were) reluctant to alter what they had received (see "Composition" in the Introduction on page 8 of this volume).[430]

---

reading ἐλθόντος τοῦ ἐνιαυτοῦ, *elthontos tou eniautou* "when the year came," but Vulg. and Syr. both read "in that year."

430. Note a similar situation with the opening formula of Joram (2 Kgs 1:17 and 3:1).

There is little worthy of comment in this summary. Jehoash, like all the other northern kings, would not turn off the path laid down by Jeroboam more than one hundred years earlier. In the closing formula, reference is made to his struggle with the Judean Amaziah, events that will be given fuller treatment in chapter 14. The other interesting point is seen in a difference with 14:16; there it is said in the conventional parlance that "Jeroboam his son succeeded him." Here however, we read that "Jeroboam sat upon his throne" (וְיָרָבְעָם יָשַׁב עַל־כִּסְאוֹ, *wᵉyārob̲ʿām yāšab̲ ʿal-kisʾô*). Long (415–6) suggests that this might point to a coregency between Jehoash and Jeroboam, something that Thiele affirms.[431] Wiseman (241), on the other hand, offers the possibility that, on the pattern of Assyrian documents, a takeover was involved. In any case, the differences in the two statements seem to offer further support for the hypothesis that differing sources may be involved.[432]

14–19 Once again, some of the drama that has been characteristic of much of the Elijah/Elisha narrative returns. But also, as in previous accounts, there are a number of questions left unanswered. We do not know why the king visited Elisha; had he heard of "his [Elisha's] illness" (חָלְיוֹ, ḥolyô), as the text implies, or did he seek the prophet's blessing as he prepared for war with Syria (as Cogan and Tadmor [150] wonder)? Where did the encounter take place? Hobbs (169) notes that "and he went down" (וַיֵּרֶד, *wayyēreḏ*) (v. 14) need not connote actual movement downward. In contrast, others (Fritz, 313; Sweeney, 359), especially in the light of the reference to "Moabite raiders" in v. 20, suggest that Elisha may have been in Jericho or Gilgal, favorite haunts of his in the past (2:15; 4:38), nearer Moab, and that the king went down from Samaria to one of those places.

It is also not clear how his exclamation, "the chariots of Israel and its horsemen" (רֶכֶב יִשְׂרָאֵל וּפָרָשָׁיו, *rekeḇ yiśrāʾēl ûpārāšāyw*) should be taken. Is he lamenting the soon-to-come-departure of this man who has been the real defense of Israel through the long years of his life? Or is he lamenting the sad state of Israel's armaments in the light of the Syrian depredations, and asking the prophet what he should do? Or is it possible that he knows the prophetic traditions well enough to know that this is what Elisha had said at the departure of Elijah, and is generously according Elisha parity with his mentor? Although the last is perhaps less likely than the other two, all of them are possible.

Whatever our answers to the questions above might be, it is evident that Elisha wasted no time with niceties, and this points to the probability that he

---

431. Thiele, *Mysterious Numbers,* 82–86.

432. LXX omits "Jehoash was buried" resulting in Ιεροβοαμ ἐκάθισεν ἐπὶ τοῦ θρόνου αὐτοῦ ἐν Σαμαρείᾳ μετὰ τῶν υἱῶν Ισραηλ, *Ieroboam ekathisen epi tou thronou autou en Samareia meta tōn huiōn Israēl*: "Jeroboam sat on his throne in Samaria with the sons of Israel." The other versions support MT. Is Gk. attempting to avoid some of the overlap with 14:16?

understood Jehoash's concern to be for how he would be able to confront the Syrians. He gives Jehoash two symbolic actions as predictions of the victory that Yahweh would give his people over their longtime enemy. But if the significance of the actions is only symbolic, why did the prophet engage in them at all (as he did in much of his ministry)? The answer to that question is found in the unique biblical understanding of the relationship of symbol and reality. In brief, the symbolic action does not cause something to happen in reality; however, by participating in the symbolic activity, the participant is enabled to experience the reality in ways otherwise impossible. For further discussion, see the "Excursus on Symbol and Reality."

Here, three elements should be noticed. First, the simplicity of what takes place. There is nothing of ritual complexity in which connections with the spirit world are solidified. Second, the prophet is at first directly involved. Just as the touch of his body was intrinsic to the resurrection of the Shunammite's son, so here his hands upon the king's hands is important. The involvement of Yahweh's representative is vital.[433] The third element is the necessity of full participation. That seems to be the point of "strike [the arrows] on the ground" (הַךְ־אַרְצָה, *hak̲- ʾarṣâ*). In the first action, the king simply followed instructions, and, to his credit, he followed them very precisely. But in the second, the directions were more open-ended. Elisha did not tell Jehoash how many times he should strike the ground. We know from the outcome that the king was now intended to enter into the activity on his own account, both with energy and commitment. In fact, he did not. "He struck three times and stopped" (וַיַּךְ שָׁלֹשׁ־פְּעָמִים וַיַּעֲמֹד, *wayyak̲ šālōš-pᵊ ʿāmîm wayya ʿămōd̲*). Did he wonder at the foolishness of an old man, and wish to get this bizarre activity over as soon as possible? Had he been simply "going through the motions" to satisfy the whims of a dying man? Given Elisha's anger, this incident may express the attitude of all the northern kings: they wanted Yahweh's blessings without an all-out commitment on their own part. They wanted what Yahweh's prophets could do for them, but they did not want to be Yahweh's men. Would striking five or six times actually *cause* the complete victory that was now denied Jehoash? No, but the kind of passionate commitment to, and faith in, God that such an action would represent would have.

20–21 If Elisha's final act in life was to predict relief for God's people from the oppression that their sin had brought upon them, his final act in death was to bring life back for one who had been dead. These two are fully intertwined in the life and ministry of Elisha. Even though he was the one to bring down final and terrible doom on the house of Ahab, his ministry had again and

433. There is little agreement among commentators concerning the reference to Aphek in v. 17. Noting Ahab's victory at that site reported in 1 Kgs 20:26–30, some take it to be a duplicate account. Others, despite a degree of uncertainty about the exact location, but understanding it to be a site about three miles east of the sea of Galilee, where it would guard the access from Gilead into the valley of Jezreel, take it that this was a place of perennial conflict between Israel and Syria.

again involved deliverance from oppression and death. The two miracles chosen to represent his ministry in chapter 2: the healing of the water and cursing of the young men, illustrate the two aspects of his work. But the beginning and the end have to do with life: just as the water would no more produce death (2:21), so would the touch of his dead "bones" (עַצְמוֹת, *ʿaṣmôṯ*) restore life to a corpse. This is illustrative of what Yahweh intended for Israel. If death for the nation could not in the end be avoided, nevertheless, the Holy One's intention was to bring life out of death, and it may well be that this is the reason the editor(s) included this little story in the account.

While some would take this to be a fanciful tale, the very particular details in it argue for its veracity. It seems likely that a now independent Moab was taking advantage of Israel's Syria induced weakness to raid the country at the "beginning of the year" (בָּא שָׁנָה, *bāʾ šānâ*) when the barley harvest was starting. The pattern of putting bodies on a carved stone shelf in a natural or man-made cave until decay was complete explains what took place. After the flesh was completely consumed, the bones might be put in a separate ossuary ("bone box") or simply piled with others at the back of the cave. In this case, the body was hastily thrown into the cave where it came in contact with Elisha's bones either still on the shelf or piled with others.[434]

Selected Bibliography

Millard, A. R. "Adad-Nirari III, Aram, and Arpad." *PEQ* 105 (173): 161–64.

Relief from Syria (13:22–25)

Translation

22 Hazael, king of Syria, oppressed Israel all the days of Jehoahaz.[435] **23** But Yahweh was gracious to them and had compassion on them and turned to them on account of his covenant with Abraham, Isaac, and Jacob. He was not willing to destroy them and did not banish them from his presence until now. **24** Hazael, king of Syria, died and Ben-hadad, his son, succeeded him. **25** Jehoash, son of Jehoahaz, turned around and took back from the hand of Ben-hadad, son of Hazael, the cities he had taken from the hand of

434. Zakovitch, Yair, "Elisha Died … He Came to Life and Stood Up (2 Kings 13:20–21): A Short 'Short Story' in Exegetical Circles," in *"Shar ʿarei Talmos": Studies in the Bible, Qumran, and the Ancient Near East Presented to Shemaryhu Talmon*, ed. Michael Fishbane et al. (Winona Lake, IN: Eisenbrauns, 1992), 53–62.

435. The Lucianic, or Antiochian, recension of the LXX adds several words to this sentence. Whereas earlier commentators tended to accept the addition as original, more recent ones have been doubtful. See Cogan and Tadmor for a brief resumé (149). See Shuichi Hasegawa, "The Conquests of Hazael in 2 Kings 13:22 in the Antiochian Text," *JBL* 133 (2014): 61–76 for a full discussion, and a proposal that the original Heb. text must be reconstructed.

Jehoahaz, his father, in warfare. Jehoash struck him three times and restored the cities of Israel.

Textual Notes

22a–a. מֶ֫לֶךְ אֲרָ֑ם: Gk. omits; Vulg. and Syr. with MT.

23a–a. וַיָּחָן יְהוָה אֹתָם: Vulg. omits; Gk. and Syr. with MT.

23b. אָבָה: Gk. adds "the Lord"; Vulg. and Syr. with MT.

23c. עַד־עָתָּה: Gk. omits; Vulg. and Syr. with MT. Gk. possibly omits for theological reasons (*CTAT* 402).

25a. וַיָּשָׁב: Vulg. omits; Gk. and Syr. with MT.

Commentary

There is not much agreement among commentators over either the provenance or the character of this paragraph. Some see the reference to "until now" (MT, v. 23) as locating the material in the period before the fall of Israel. Others see that phrase as a reference to the postexilic period and as a result take the account to be a creation of the final editors. Long (408) can call it "one of the more important paragraphs in 2 Kings," while Gray (601) regards it as a pastiche of annalistic references and "secondary redactional" comments. As I have argued above, I see it as an intrinsic part of this final chapter of the Elijah/Elisha narrative. It functions both to report the fulfillment of Elisha's final prophecy, and the conclusion of Hazael's function as the scourge of Baalistic Israel. While Long's judgment may be somewhat overstated, the paragraph is still vitally important as a closing statement on this critical era in Israel's life. The theological interpretation of these events that appears in v. 23 is fundamental to that importance.

22–23 The paragraph begins with the reminder that Hazael had free rein during the rule of Jehoahaz. In view of Jehu's failure to walk in the path of David and to bring about a full restoration of the worship of Yahweh, we might have expected that the Syrian monarch would have been permitted to destroy the northern kingdom. However, that was not to be. But the reason is not, as we might have expected, the promise to Jehu of four generations of descendants on the throne. Instead, it is something much more profound. Yahweh would not let the nation be destroyed because of his "grace" (חנן, *ḥnn*) and "compassion" (רחם, *rḥm*) that had been particularly expressed in his covenant with "Abraham, Isaac, and Jacob." This is the only reference to this covenant in the books of Kings.[436] However, Elijah defined Yahweh as

436. See Sweeney for a vigorous argument against the conclusion that this unique mention necessarily dates the material to the postexilic period, as some have argued (360–61).

"the God of Abraham, Isaac, and Israel" in his prayer on Mt. Carmel (1 Kgs 18:36), and its occurrence there near the beginning of the cycle and here at the end can hardly be coincidental. Yahweh had promised that Abraham would become a great people through whom the world would be blessed. That promise was without conditions.[437] This does not say that discipline, even severe discipline, could not be visited upon Abraham's descendants, but it does say that any such discipline, such as that imposed through the hand of Hazael, would not be allowed to result in the destruction of Yahweh's people.[438] This theological interpretation of history is at the heart of Israel's self-understanding. God had brought them into existence as a people and their continued existence was only as a result of the continuation of the grace that had been extended to their first fathers and mothers. If that was their past and their present, it was the foundation of any hope for the future. As a result, although a Hazael might be permitted to do them great harm because of their sins against Yahweh, he would never be permitted to destroy them. A century later, this same theology would breathe through the work of the prophet Isaiah. Even if Assyria or Babylon were permitted to do great harm, they would not be permitted to wipe out God's people. When all was said and done, Assyria and Babylon would cease to exist, but the people of Israel would still be flourishing.

As mentioned above, a good deal of controversy swirls around the time intended in the phrase "until now" (עַד־עָתָּה, *ʿad- ʿāttâ*). While many commentators (e.g., Sweeney, 361; Wiseman, 243) argue that it must refer to the time before Samaria fell and Israel ceased to be an independent kingdom, others insist that it must date to the final edition of the book in the exilic, or even postexilic, period (e.g. Gray, 601n.b; Montgomery and Gehman, 436; Provan, 232). That conclusion, whichever it may be, is often then directly connected to conclusions about the original date of the material. However, I suggest that while Sweeney (360–61) is likely correct in arguing for the origin of the material during the Jehu dynasty, with the phrase in question referring to a time before 722 BC and the fall of Samaria, the very retention of the phrase in the final edition gives it an important nuance. If earlier hearers and readers might have interpreted "did not banish them from his presence" (וְלֹא־הִשְׁלִיכָם מֵעַל־פָּנָיו, *wᵉlōʾ-hišlîḵām mēʿal-pānāyw*) to mean that God would not allow the political entity "Israel" to be destroyed, later readers would have to know that interpretation was incorrect. They would understand, correctly, I think, that it was the people "Israel" that would continue

437. Wiseman's statement that the reference to the covenant here would have evoked in the hearers the recognition that disobedience would result in exile (242), overlooks the point that the Abrahamic covenant was unconditional.

438. Provan's argument that while it was the Davidic covenant that insured the survival of Judah, it was the Abrahamic one that insured Israel's survival (230), seems strained to me. Both covenants were addressed to the whole people. The tribe of Judah was no less a descendant of Abraham than were the other tribes.

to exist in Yahweh's presence despite the efforts of any force in the world to wipe them out.[439] That thought would have been most poignant during the exile and after.

24–25 During the latter part of Hazael's reign Assyrian attentions had been focused on other parts of the empire with the result that the Syrian monarch had been able to do much as he wished. But just at the time of the accession of his son Ben-hadad the new Assyrian emperor Adad-Nirari III, renewed the perennial push westward. Attacking probably in 806 BC and again in 796, he greatly reduced Syria's strength, defeating them and demanding a large tribute. It was probably in the latter year Jehoash also paid tribute to Adad-Nirari, perhaps in return for what the Assyrian had done or would do to Israel's old enemy.[440] As a result, the punishment that the Syrians had been visiting upon Israel for nearly 40 years was dramatically reduced, and Jehoash was able to enjoy the fulfillment of Elisha's final prophecy: three victories over Syria, enabling the Israelite king to take back cities that Hazael had taken from Jehoahaz. The identity of these cities is uncertain. While it seems likely that Aphek was one (13:17), it is unclear whether there were any others in the Transjordanian area. Amos 6:13 mentions victories over Lo-debar and Karnaim, located in Transjordan, but those could well have been victories Jeroboam II had won, and that later time frame would accord better with that of Amos himself. Several commentators assert that these cities would not have been in the Transjordanian area because this was later captured by Jeroboam (14:25). However, capture of certain cities would not necessarily imply control of the entire area.

Biblical Theology Comments

As I said in the introduction to chapter 13, we come here to the end of the Elijah/Elisha cycle. It is apparent that the editors do not consider this to be two consecutive narratives, but a single continuous one (see especially the comments on chapter 2). The conclusion is further underlined when we recognize that there is a remarkable parallelism between the events in the ministries of the two men. Cohn (91–5), followed by Long (411–13), has identified more than a half dozen of these parallels, including the raising of a boy from the dead, the providing of food and water, etc. While some of the proposed parallels seem somewhat forced, there is still enough evidence to suggest that the narrator is framing the narrations to emphasize the continuity between the two.

At the same time, the two personalities are different: Elijah is represented as being more isolated from society, whereas Elisha is a more social creature. Although Elisha does not regularly consort with kings, he still has contact,

---

439. For further reflection on these themes, see John W. Olley, "2 Kings 13: A Cluster of Hope in God," *JSOT* 36 (2011): 199–218.

440. For a discussion of the sources for this information, see Cogan and Tadmor, 152.

whereas Elijah has to be brought to the kings in unusual ways. These two examples serve to show that Elisha is not merely a literary "clone" of Elijah, an imaginary figure created to somehow duplicate Elijah. What then are we to make of the close connections between the two ministries? I believe the point is to show how from 1 Kings 17 to 2 Kings 13, it is Yahweh who is the "master of ceremonies." From the announcement that there would be no rain until Yahweh said so (1 Kgs 17:1) until as an expression of Yahweh's grace and compassions the cities Hazael had captured were restored to Israel, it is Yahweh who is the Lord of history. Thus, though there are two prophets, there is only one ministry, the one that leaves Baal dethroned and Yahweh alone enthroned, and the one that shows Israel's perennial enemy, Syria, to be nothing more than a tool in Yahweh's hand. When he decrees that Syria will conquer, they will conquer, and when he decrees that Israel has suffered enough, Syria will pass from the scene. So we see one ministry with two prophetic faces.

Finally, the Elijah/Elisha ministry insists that the one great issue facing every living creature on earth—life and death—is only to be resolved in connection with Yahweh. Again, from the announcement of the drought until the corpse's springing to life on contact with Elisha's bones, it is only through Yahweh that life is maintained, and death is defeated. Life-giving rain comes from Yahweh, not Baal. Fertility, whether of earth or womb, is his, not Asherah's. Food is dispensed from his hand, not from that of Shamash, the sun. When Yahweh is trusted, the arrogant oppressor will fail, but when God-given power is used to oppress the weak, Yahweh becomes the enemy, and that is bad news indeed. Throughout, the point is that Yahweh is not to be identified with any of his creatures in an attempt to get the benefit of those creatures for oneself. Rather, our lives are to be solely surrendered to him in trust. When we do that, his creatures will surround us in blessing.

Selected Bibliography

Begg, C. T. "Joash and Elisha in Josephus, Ant 9:117–85." *AbrN* 32 (1994): 28–46.

Amaziah to the Fall of Samaria (14:1–16:20)

Introduction

This sub-division begins with a fairly lengthy discussion of Amaziah's reign (14:1–22), of which a significant part (vv. 8–14) is a description of the warfare between Judah under Amaziah and Israel under Jehoash. For the previous sixty or seventy years, Judah had been a subordinate partner, if not a vassal, of Israel. Now, perhaps because of the way Syria had dominated Israel for the previous twenty-five years or so, Amaziah seems to have thought it would be a good time for Judah not only to break free of Israel, but to defeat her one-time overlord. However, he chose his timing badly. Jehoash was leading Israel in a recovery, and however the nation might have been weakened, they were more than a match for Judah, even capturing Amaziah in the conflict (v. 13), resulting in a coregency with his son Azariah (v. 21).

The rest of chapters 14 and 15 is a fairly straight-forward synchronous report of the next seventy years for the two kingdoms. The two dominant kings, Jeroboam II of Israel and Azariah of Judah (called Uzziah in 2 Chronicles, and also in 2 Kgs 15:13, 30, 32, and 34, all referring to him outside of his regnal account), are given much shorter treatment than we would expect if this were primarily a historical account (Jeroboam: 14:23–29 and Azariah: 15:1–6). But, as we have seen repeatedly above, although the account is not ahistorical, its larger purpose is to show how Yahweh's covenants with Israel and with David, far from failing, explain what happened to the two parts of the nation. Thus, the editors have little interest in satisfying our historical curiosity. As a result, Zechariah, who reigned just six months, receives almost as long a notice (15:8–12) as his father who reigned for forty-one years (14:23–29). But the key point in both cases is that they broke the covenant. Zechariah's murderer, Shallum, who reigned but one month, receives four verses, making the same point (15:13–16)!

From the death of Jeroboam in 753 BC until the destruction of Samaria thirty years later there was a succession of conspiracies and palace coups in Israel that produced six different kings and five different dynasties. This sad story is related in 15:8–31. In Judah, the dynasty of David continued on with just three different kings, two of whom, Azariah and his son Jotham, "did what was right in Yahweh's sight" (15:3, 34), and one of whom, Ahaz, did not (16:2–4). Azariah and Jotham together receive just fourteen verses (15:1–7, 32–38) while chapter 16 is devoted entirely to a report of the sins of Ahaz, especially regarding the worship of Yahweh.

Chapter 17 is given first to a discussion of the sins of Ahaz's contemporary in the north, Hoshea, and the capture of Samaria and the exile (17:1–6), then to an explanation of the ways in which the people of Israel had broken the covenant (vv. 7–23), and finally to the resettling of the region of Samaria and the resulting paganization of worship there (vv. 24–41).

Outline

II. The Divided Monarchy 1 Kings 12:1–2 Kings 17:41
- C. Amaziah to the fall of Samaria 14:1–16:20
  1. Amaziah of Judah 14:1–22
  2. Jeroboam II 14:23–29
  3. Azariah of Judah 15:1–7
  4. Zechariah and Shallum 15:8–16
  5. Menaham and Pekahiah 15:17–26
  6. Pekah 15:27–31
  7. Jotham of Judah 15:32–38
  8. Ahaz of Judah 16:1–20

Amaziah of Judah (14:1–22)

TRANSLATION

14:1 In the second year of Jehoash, son of Jehoahaz, king of Israel, Amaziah, son of Joash, king of Judah, became king. **2** He was twenty-five years old when he began to reign, and he reigned twenty-nine years in Jerusalem. His mother's name was Jehoaddin from Jerusalem. **3** He did right in Yahweh's sight, only not like David his father. As Joash his father had done, so he did. **4** However, they did not remove the high places; the people were still sacrificing and burning incense on the high places. **5** Now after the kingdom was secure in his hand, he struck down his servants who had struck down the king, his father. **6** But he did not kill the children of the killers, as it is written in the book of the law of Moses, where Yahweh commanded, "Fathers shall not be killed on account of their children, nor shall children be killed on account of their fathers. But rather, a man shall be killed for his own sin."
7 He struck Edom in the Valley of Salt, 10,000, and captured Sela in war. He named it Joktheel to this day.

8 Then Amaziah sent messengers to Jehoash, son of Jehoahaz, son of Jehu, king of Israel, saying, "Come, let us look one another in the face."
9 Jehoash, king of Israel, sent to Amaziah, king of Judah, saying, "The thistle that was in Lebanon sent to the cedar that was in Lebanon saying, 'Give your

daughter to my son as wife.' Then a wild animal that was in Lebanon passed by and stepped on the thistle. **10** You really struck down Edom, and your heart has lifted you up. Enjoy your glory and sit in your house. Why should you stir up trouble so that you fall, you, and Judah with you?" **11** But Amaziah would not listen, so Jehoash, king of Israel, went up and they confronted one another, he and Amaziah, in Beth-shemesh that is in Judah. **12** Judah was stricken before Israel and every man fled to his tent. **13** As for Amaziah, king of Judah, son of Joash, son of Amaziah, Jehoash, king of Israel, captured him in Beth-shemesh. Then he came to Jerusalem and broke down the wall of Jerusalem from the Gate of Ephraim to the Gate of the Corner, 400 cubits.[1] **14** He took all the gold and silver and all the utensils found in the house of Yahweh and the treasuries of the house of the king, and hostages and returned to Samaria. **15** The rest of the matters pertaining to Jehoash, what he did and his might and how he fought with Amaziah, king of Judah, are they not written in the chronicles of the kings of Israel? **16** Jehoash slept with his fathers and was buried in Samaria with the kings of Israel, and Jeroboam his son succeeded him.

17 Now Amaziah, son of Joash, king of Judah, lived for fifteen years after the death of Jehoash, king of Israel. **18** The rest of the matters pertaining to Amaziah, are they not written in the chronicles of the kings of Judah? **19** A conspiracy was plotted against him in Jerusalem and he fled to Lachish, but they sent after him to Lachish and they killed him there. **20** They carried him on horses and he was buried in Jerusalem with his fathers in the city of David. **21** All the people of Judah had taken Azariah, when he was sixteen years old, and made him king instead of his father Amaziah. **22** He built Elath and restored it to Judah, after the king slept with his fathers.

Textual Notes

2a. K יְהוֹעַדִּין: Gk. "Joadin" (w. K); Vulg. and Syr. "Joadan" (w. Q [יְהוֹעַדָּן], and 2 Chr 25:1).

4a. סָרוּ: Gk. and Vulg. "he did not remove"; Syr. with MT. Most Eng. versions treat as pass., thus taking it as indef. 3rd pl.

5a. אֶת־הַמֶּלֶךְ: Gk. omits; Syr. "King Joash"; Vulg. with MT.

6a.K יָמוּת: Reading as *hophal* with Q (יוּמָת).

7a. עֲשֶׂרֶת אֲלָפִים: Syr. "20,000"; Gk. and Vulg. with MT.

8a. אֲמַצְיָה: Syr. adds "king of Judah"; Gk and Vulg. with MT.

8b. פָנִים: GKC (§156*c*) suggests this is short for "face to face" (so also v. 11). The versions closely follow MT.

---

1. About 600 feet.

9a. חַיַּת: Gk. and Vulg. pl.; Syr. sing.

11a. יְהוֹאָשׁ: Gk. omits; Vulg. and Syr. with MT.

12a. לְאֹהָלוֹ: Reading with K (לְאֹהָלָיו) "his tent"; Q "his tents."

13a–a. בֶּן־יְהוֹאָשׁ בֶּן־אֲחַזְיָהוּ: Syr. omits; Gk. and Vulg. with MT.

13b. K וַיָּבֹאוּ: Gk. and Syr. with Q (וַיָּבֹא); Vulg. and Gk^{L} "he brought him" with K? (K might also be read "they came.")

14a. וְלָקַח: GKC (§112*pp*) says the *waw* + suffixed form here is the result of Aramaic influence (but [§112*tt*] suggests it is an error). But see *IBHS* (§35.3) for a discussion of the *waw* copulative + suffixed form.

14b. אֶת־כָּל־הַזָּהָב־וְהַכֶּסֶף: Gk. lacks "all"; Vulg. and Syr. with MT.

Commentary

Although the chapter begins with the conventional accession formula for the Judean king, Amaziah, it offers several breaks from convention. One of these is the statement in v. 6 that when Amaziah brought down vengeance on the killers of his father, he did not extend it to their children on account of the command in "the law of Moses" (בְּסֵפֶר תּוֹרַת־מֹשֶׁה, *bᵉsēper tôraṯ-mōšeh*). A second unusual feature is the description of his provocation of war with his northern counterpart Jehoash, a provocation that ended in disaster for him and for Judah (vv. 8–14). What makes the description unusual is its apparent northern origin. Its conclusion with a second death notice for Jehoash (vv. 15–16, the first having appeared in 13:12–13) seems to support this conclusion.[2] Amaziah's own death notice (vv. 17–20) is marked by the reference to his death as a result of a "conspiracy" (קֶשֶׁר, *qešer*). The final oddity is found in vv. 21–22, where we have the unusual description of the coronation of Azariah, Amaziah's son, and an action of his prior to his actual accession announcement (found in 15:1–4). I suggest that one thread that might explain all of these is the unusual circumstances surrounding Amaziah's reign, including his imprisonment by Jehoash, and his coregency with Azariah.[3]

2. Commentators vary widely over the possible reason for the apparent northern orientation of much of the account. Hobbs suggests that Amaziah is presented as a foil for the editor to speak of Yahweh's continued grace to the north in the face of its coming destruction (186). Sweeney argues that it was originally part of a hypothetical history of the Jehu dynasty that was incorporated in the Hezekian (and Josianic) editions to justify the Davidides redressing such wrongs as these done to the south (363–64).

3. Thiele, *Mysterious Numbers*, 84–85 argues cogently that the oddities of the chapter largely reflect the double coregencies (Jehoash–Jeroboam II, and Amaziah–Azariah)

1 "In the second year of Jehoash" introduces the thorny chronological problems of Israel and Judah in the eighth century BC. Simply put, if one only adds up the numbers for the two kingdoms, the sums will be some thirteen years different, and in neither case do the end results square with the corresponding dates of the Assyrian Empire, which are by this time fairly secure. For possible solutions see the "Excursus on Chronology 792–739 BC." In the upshot, it seems likely this year was 796 BC.

3–4 Amaziah is the second in a succession of three Judean kings: Joash, Amaziah, and Uzziah, who are all said to have "done right in the sight of Yahweh" (וַיַּעַשׂ הַיָּשָׁר בְּעֵינֵי יהוה, *wayyaʿaś hayyāšār bᵊʿênê yhwh*) but who do not receive the additional encomium that it was "as David, his father, had done" as did Asa (1 Kgs 15:11), Hezekiah (2 Kgs 18:3), and Josiah (22:2). Rather, all three kings acted as their mentor (Joash), or their father had. In the case of both Amaziah and Azariah, that statement is somewhat ambiguous in that Joash and Amaziah were less-than-perfect examples of covenant faithfulness. But in the case of Amaziah, the point is made even more forcefully: "only not like David his father" (לֹא כְּדָוִד אָבִיו, *lōʾ kᵊḏāwiḏ ʾāḇîw*). Here the lack of conformity to David's pattern is not merely omitted but is explicitly refuted. 2 Chr 25:2 makes the same point in different words when it says that he did not do what was right with a whole heart. Perhaps this negative evaluation, found in both books, relates to his action reported in Chronicles, but not in Kings, of worshipping Edomite gods (2 Chr 25:14–15).

On the failure to remove the high places, something said of every Judean king until Hezekiah, who did remove them (2 Kgs 18:4), see the "Excursus on Worship at High Places ('country shrines')."[4]

5–6 "After the kingdom was secure" (כַּאֲשֶׁר חָזְקָה הַמַּמְלָכָה, *kaʾăšer ḥozqâ hammamlāḵâ*) argues for a time of uncertainty after the assassination of Joash. Just as Solomon had to take certain actions before he could feel secure (cf. 1 Kgs 2:46), so did Amaziah. The fact that he could only strike down his father's killers after he was secure, and that they are described as "his servants" (עֲבָדָיו, *ʿăḇāḏāyw*), or officers, argues that the conspiracy against Joash had come from the highest levels of the court. The suggestion that they may have been supporters of Athaliah or, alternatively, of the Jehu dynasty is purely speculative.

The statement that Amaziah did not kill the children of the conspirators because of the Mosaic law is very significant. He was neither following a

---

that existed between 792 and 782 BC with Amaziah probably imprisoned in Samaria for that period.

4. Sweeney argues that the repeated statement is made to serve the ends of Hezekian editors who wish to promote their king (364). However, the historic fact seems to have been significant from the earliest collection of these materials, given the actions of Solomon and then Rehoboam (1 Kings 11:7; 15:23).

mere instinct for mercy on his own part, nor, on the other hand, the custom of the day which would have argued for doing as Jehu did in wiping out every member of any family that might pose a threat to the king. Here was a man who was sufficiently acquainted with the revelation of God to want to conform his behavior to it; he was committed to doing "what was right in the sight of his God," in accord with God's revealed will (Deut 24:16). But evidently his knowledge of the revelation was somewhat spotty, in that he did not remove the high places (Deut 16:1–8, 20–22), nor did he avoid the worship of the gods of surrounding nations (Deut 13:6–11).

7 The MT punctuation includes this verse as part of the preceding paragraph which we might expect as part of the typical regnal report. In very terse terms it reports one of this king's significant accomplishments. It consisted of a very complete victory over Edom, the region south and east of the Dead Sea which had been a vassal of Judah's from the time of David (2 Sam 8:14) until that of Jehoram (8:22), when they successfully broke away. That breaking away would have constituted a serious economic loss for Judah because it would have meant loss of control of the lucrative Red Sea trade coming up through the port of Elath (see v. 22 below), up the Arabah Valley and out through the Philistine ports of Gaza and Ashkelon. Thus, it makes sense that as soon as any Judean king felt strong enough to retake Edom, he would seek to do it, and that is what Amaziah did. The location of the Valley of Salt, also referred to as the place of David's victory is uncertain. There is a location of that name just south of Arad, but that is in Judean territory. Perhaps it refers in a more generic way to the Arabah, the rift valley that runs south from the Dead Sea to the Gulf of Elath. While the salt flats immediately south of the sea would be a difficult place to maneuver an army, the general area somewhat farther south would be easier. The location of Sela, "the rock," has often been taken as that of Petra, the city cut from rock that became the capitol of Nabataea. However, it does not seem to have been founded until after Amaziah's times, and more recent study has argued that it is to be identified with es-Selaʿ, a short distance north-west of Bozrah, the ancient capital of Edom.[5] Virtually all commentators (e.g., Barnes, 292; Montgomery and Gehman, 440; Wiseman, 244) agree that the number 10,000 is generic.

8–10 With v. 8 the tone of the narration changes from the rather terse and generic typical of regnal accounts to a more anecdotal one. Many commentators (e.g., Cogan and Tadmor, 158; Hobbs, 177) opine that vv. 8–14, and possibly vv. 15–16, are an excerpt from a northern source, especially because it

---

5. See *ABD* 5:1073–74. For the name change from Sela to Joktheel, Cogan and Tadmor, noting that the name has currency elsewhere in Judah (Josh 15:38; 2 Chr 25:12), have suggested it might have been an act of recognition of certain faithful Judean soldiers (155–156).

presents Jehoash as moderate and restrained whereas Amaziah is seen as rash and foolish. For possible reasons why this might have taken place, see below.

The full formal title of Jehoash here, tracing him to his grandfather Jehu, is set against that of Amaziah in v. 13, where he is traced to his grandfather Ahaziah. Cohn (100) is likely correct when he sees this as a framing technique reminding us that it was the powerful and successful Jehu who dispatched the hapless Ahaziah. It was the grandson of Ahaziah who was foolish enough to challenge the grandson of Jehu, and the result was predictable.

While it is possible that "let's look one another in the face" (נִתְרָאֶה פָנִים, *niṯrāʾe p̄ānîm*) was a request for a face-to-face meeting and some sort of negotiation, both Jehoash's response and the repetition of the phrase in v. 11 where the context is military confrontation argues that this was the point from the outset. Fresh from his victory over his smaller foe, Edom, Amaziah felt like taking on his greater foe, and perhaps former overlord, Israel. Some commentators (e.g., Hobbs, 180), given the reference to a marriage alliance in Jehoash's fable, have thought that perhaps this is what Amaziah was proposing. But given no trace of such a suggestion in the text, it seems more likely that the fable, which served the purpose of shaming an unworthy opponent, was already in a fixed form which included the marriage reference.[6]

It is evident, both from the Bible (see Jotham in Judg 9:8–15a) and elsewhere, that the use of fables was fairly common in communications of the day. But this one seems to have a particularly contemptuous tone. It is not merely that the thistle is obviously in no class with the cedar, but the cedar does not even have to respond to the audacious request before a wild animal walking through the forest quite unknowingly flattens the upstart. This was clearly not chosen as a means of calming the ardor of Amaziah. On the other hand, Jehoash's own comment is less inflammatory. He graciously recognizes that Amaziah had secured a real victory over Edom but counsels the Judean king not to make too much of it. He should go back to his palace (בְּבֵיתֶךָ, *bᵉḇêṯeḵā*, "your house") and enjoy the "glory" (הִכָּבֵד, *hikkāḇēḏ*, "be honored/glorified") of that achievement. If he persists in this unwise challenge, the result will be humiliation not only for him but Judah, as well. Interestingly, there is no reference to Yahweh or his will on the part of either one of these monarchs.

11–14 Beth-shemesh, about 17 miles south-west of Jerusalem, guarded the point where the Sorek Valley opens out onto the coastal plain. Specifying that it is in Judah looks like a northern designation to distinguish it from the two Beth-shemeshes that were located in Israel (Josh 19:22, 38). Along with the Ascent of Beth-horon to the north, this was one of the two ways to gain access to Jerusalem from the west. Either one is easier than an approach from

6. On this interaction, see M. R. Eaton, "Some Instances of Flyting in the Hebrew Bible," *JSOT* 19 (1994): 3–14. See also Ann M. Vater Solomon, "Jehoash's Fable of the Thistle and the Cedar," in *Saga, Legend, Tale, Novella, Fable: Narrative Forms in Old Testament Literature*, ed. G. W. Coats (Sheffield: JSOT Press, 1985), 126–132.

the north. Why Jehoash should have chosen the southern of the two is not clear. Perhaps, with the demise of Syrian influence in the area (see 12:17 and comments) he was reasserting himself among the Philistines as well. Once Amaziah was captured (תפשׂ, *tpś*; the same verb used of Amaziah's capture of Sela in v. 7) and his army had fled (cf. 1 Sam 4:10; 2 Sam 18:17; 2 Kgs 8:21 for other examples of "fled to his tent" [וַיָּנֻסוּ אִישׁ לְאֹהָלוֹ, *wayyānusû ʾîš lᵉ ʾāhŏlw*], referring to a rout), there was nothing to prevent Jehoash treating Jerusalem as he wished.[7] Here there was no buying off as there had been with Hazael (12:18). With its king a captive, the city obviously surrendered, Jehoash sacked the temple and palace treasuries of whatever was left after paying off Hazael, and destroyed the fortifications on the north, or Israelite, side of the city. Although the location of neither the Ephraim Gate nor the Corner Gate is given, there is no question that the Ephraim Gate would have been in the northern wall facing toward Ephraim, and with ca. 600 feet between it and the Corner Gate, that argues that this second gate would have been on the north side as well, probably at the north-west corner (see 2 Chr 26:9; Jer 31:38; Zech 14:10). With the national treasury plundered, it would be some time before the ruined wall could be repaired. In the meantime, the city would know that an Israelite army could march in whenever it chose. This would certainly have a dampening effect on the schemes of any Judean king who foolishly contemplated another face-off with Israel. In addition to the treasures, Jehoash also took "hostages" (בְּנֵי הַתַּעֲרֻבוֹת, *bᵉnê hatta ʿărubôṯ*), the word occurring only here and in the parallel passage in 2 Chr 25:24. These may have been other members of the royal family guaranteeing good behavior on the part of the rest of the Judeans.

15–16 The presence of Jehoash's death notice at this point seems to me the clearest confirmation of the northern provenance of vv. 8–16. While some scholars regard these two verses as an insertion,[8] I think it is more likely that they originally appeared at the end of the narrative concerning the defeat of Amaziah, and that the editor included the entire piece of material including the death notice. But this then raises the question why this material was inserted into the Amaziah regnal account. Why is something that makes a southern king look bad and a northern king look good included in a work whose final form was surely Judean? Since no reason is apparent in the text, caution is advised. Before going further, it should be observed that this phenomenon argues strongly against the idea that a thorough-going anti-Israelite, pro-Judean bias controlled the final form of the text, as some scholars (e.g., Gray, 37; Sweeney, 6–7) have asserted. But perhaps the reason

7. The reversed word order (obj. [וְאֵת אֲמַצְיָהוּ מֶלֶךְ־יְהוּדָה, *wᵉ ʾēṯ ʾămaṣyāhû meleḵ-yᵉhûḏâ*] before subj. [יְהוֹאָשׁ מֶלֶךְ־יִשְׂרָאֵל, *yᵉhô ʾāš meleḵ-yiśrā ʾēl*]) in the statement of Amaziah's capture (v. 13) emphasizes the momentous nature of this event.

8. Provan believes it was placed here in order to contrast Jehoash's peaceful end with Amaziah's violent one (236).

is this: the persons doing the compiling of the material after the fall of the northern kingdom during the reign of Hezekiah (see the "Introduction" on the formation of the book) knew of Amaziah's worship of the Edomite gods (as per 2 Chr 25:14, 20), and with the later Chronicler, understood his defeat and capture to be a judgment by means of the northern king. Perhaps they did not discuss Amaziah's behavior because it was an aberration and not a settled deviation from the worship of Yahweh. Nonetheless, it was reprehensible and reaped a result that was best expressed in the northern form of the narrative that was now accessible to them.[9]

It should be noted that the statement "Jeroboam his son succeeded him" (וַיִּמְלֹךְ יָרָבְעָם בְּנוֹ תַּחְתָּיו, *wayyimlōḵ yārob̲ʿām bᵊnô taḥtāyw*) is the normal form for a death notice and differs from the statement in 13:13 where it is said that "Jeroboam sat on his throne." To some scholars, this has suggested a coregency between Jehoash and Jeroboam. See the "Excursus on Chronology (792–739 BC)."

17–18 There is no indication how long Amaziah's imprisonment may have lasted. Suggestions range from an immediate parole once Jehoash had taken his hostages (v. 14) to being held in Samaria until Jehoash's death in 782 BC. What does seem significant is the statement here that "Amaziah lived (חיה, *ḥyh*) (not reigned) after the death of Jehoash ... for fifteen years." This suggests to many that Amaziah was not functioning as king during that period at least. When this statement is coupled with that of v. 21 that "all the people took Azariah ... and made him king at age sixteen," there is a strong suggestion that upon Amaziah's capture (for the probable date see the "Excursus on Chronology [792–739 BC]"), Uzziah became the functioning king, and for however long Amaziah may have been imprisoned, he was king in title only for the rest of his life.

19–20 As in many other instances in this book, our historical curiosity over the circumstances of Amaziah's death is not rewarded. Given the fact that Uzziah did not take action to punish the conspirators, it may be that the old king was becoming meddlesome, wishing to reassert his power, and that Azariah/Uzziah gave tacit approval to the scheme. The matter may have been even more serious, given the fact that Amaziah fled to Lachish. This city, about thirty miles south-west of Jerusalem, was the second city of the kingdom, after Jerusalem. It was the major fortress guarding access from the coastal plain to Jerusalem from the southwest. It alone was still holding out when Sennacherib sent his officer up to Hezekiah at Jerusalem in 701 BC to demand surrender (18:17). Thus, it is not impossible that Amaziah was

9. For further discussion of the way in which earlier northern accounts which were not necessarily negative have been integrated into the final narrative, see Omer Sergi, "The Omride Dynasty and the Reshaping of Judahite Historical Memory," *Bib* 97 (2016): 503–26.

hoping to establish himself in Lachish as a foe of his son in Jerusalem. If that was his hope, it was a failure, because Jerusalem's reach was long enough that the citizens of Lachish permitted the conspirators to carry out their aim in their city. This has suggested to many (e.g., Gray, 613; Provan, 239; Cogan and Tadmor, 159) that the conspiracy had its roots in the highest levels of the Judean government.

Whatever the reasons for the conspiracy, Amaziah had been a king and so his body was brought to Jerusalem on horses, which suggests some sort of official entourage, and he was buried there with his ancestors.

21–22 These verses have created a good deal of controversy among commentators because they are unusual in several respects. Instead of the normal reading "and his son Azariah succeeded him" we are told that "the people of Judah took Azariah … and made him king (וַיַּמְלִכוּ אתו, *wayyamliḵû ʾōṯô*)". Then before Azariah's regular accession formula which appears in 14:1–4, we are told of one of his accomplishments, something that is quite irregular. Finally, we are told that this activity took place after the death of "the king," without any identification of that king. There is some unanimity among commentators that the reference to the people making Azariah king does refer to making him coregent. However, there is less agreement as to why the reference to Elath occurs here, or when that action took place. Several argue that "the king" who died is Jehoash, and Cogan and Tadmor (158) say that the phrase cannot refer to Amaziah. They make this statement because nowhere else does the phrase "slept with his fathers" (שְׁכַב־הַמֶּלֶךְ עִם־אֲבֹתָיו, *šᵉḵaḇ-hammeleḵ ʿim-ʾăḇōṯāyw*) occur with a murdered king. However, it was Amaziah's death that was referred to most recently (v. 20) and he would thus be the most natural referent. While patterning is important, it does not seem wise to me to argue that no exceptions to the pattern can ever occur. Provan (236–38) argues that the latter part of the chapter from verse 8 onward is presenting Jehoash as the dominant figure in both Israel and Judah and is thus "the king" here. While that is possible, I do not find the evidence convincing.

The reason why Azariah is not introduced until this point (if he really became coregent fairly early in Amaziah's reign) is according to the pattern generally followed in these books of letting one series of events, or one reign, play out to its end before introducing a series of events, or a reign, that were concurrent with the previous. The reason he is introduced at all here, before his accession formula, is that he *was* coregent and thus did rule concurrently with his father. But why announce his capture and rebuilding of Elath here? Because in some ways it was the result of joint action with his father. His father had subjugated Edom, which opened the way for the Judeans to travel down the Arabah to its southern extreme where the port of Elath lay. The father started the process and the son completed it. When this happened is answered by answering the question of which "king" is intended in v. 22. Did Azariah accomplish it after his father's death (767 BC), but as a result of what his father had accomplished in life? I think that would be the most logical conclusion from the structure of the narrative. However, the ambiguity of the text leaves open the possibility that the action was taken after the death of Jehoash (782 BC), while Amaziah was still alive.

Biblical Theology Comments

The command quoted from Deut 24:16 that parents are not to be killed for their children's sin, and vice versa, is sometime cited as an advance over Exodus 34:7 where the sins of the fathers are "visited upon" (פֹּקֵד, *pōqēḏ*) (KJV) the children to the third and fourth generations. However, that verb is very significant in the context of what that verse is saying. It is not speaking of the guilt of the ancestors' sins being laid on the children, but of the *consequences*, the impact, of their sins. Free forgiveness is promised in the first part of the verse, but it does not, indeed cannot, promise a blanket release from the consequences of sin. A person should not think that because they can sin, and if truly repentant, be forgiven, there will be no ongoing consequences of their actions. We need only look at the children of alcoholics to know the truth of this statement.

At the same time, it is very easy to use these facts to excuse ourselves. This was clearly the situation that Ezekiel faced in Babylon. The people there were complaining that they were in exile because of what their ancestors had done, that, in the universal sentiments of children of all ages, what had happened to them was "not fair." Ezekiel reiterates in two different places that whatever our ancestors have done, and whatever consequences we may have experienced in our lives, we are still responsible for our own choices (Ezek 18:1–32; 33:12–20; cf. Jer 31:29-30). The claims that "it was their fault" and "I couldn't help it" are dismissed out of hand. This passage in Kings would have served to underline that truth for the exiles.

Application and Devotional Implications

This narrative invites two related applications. The first relates to the statement that Amaziah did what was right, but not as David did (v. 3). As noted above, 2 Chr 25:2 makes the same point in different words, namely that he did right but not with a whole (שָׁלֵם, *šālēm*, "perfect" KJV) heart. That concept speaks to the behavior of the Christian. While it is important to do what is right, the motivation with which we do right is even more important. A "whole heart" means that one's entire personality ("heart") is united around one motivation: the glory and honor of Yahweh. That was what characterized David. It does not mean we are thereby incapable of doing wrong. David certainly demonstrates that (2 Sam 11). But it does mean that we have been delivered from that neurotic self-consciousness that pollutes everything we do. Doing right with a divided heart results in legalism. We are not doing right for the love of God, but for the approval of others, indeed, for self-approval! When our hearts are divided, we are ever open to the lure of idols, as Amaziah was. That is, we believe that the pleasure, the possessions, and the power that this world offers can satisfy our deepest need. They cannot, they never could. Furthermore, a divided heart clouds our judgment. Our need to build up our self-image means that we are tempted to do foolish things because they promise to build up our ego. If we are wholly surrendered to God, then our image is in his hands, not ours, and we can rest secure there.

The second point is closely related to the first. Whether Jesus had Amaziah in mind or not, the Judean king is a perfect example of a king going to war without having considered carefully enough his own resources and the resources of his enemy (Luke 14:28–32). Jesus was referring to the cost of following him as his disciple. The highest price of all is our right to our self. Jesus did not sugarcoat what he asks of his disciples. He does not ask us to do right, although that is certainly included in discipleship to Jesus. What he asks for is the key to our innermost self. If he only gets right behavior, he may very well not get our self. But if he gets our self in the deepest, truest sense, right behavior will follow.

Selected Bibliography

Klein, R. W. "The Chronicler's Theological Rewriting of the Deuteronomistic History: Amaziah, a Test Case." Pages 237–245 in *Raising up a Faithful Exegete: Essays in Honor of Richard D. Nelson*. Edited by K. L. Noll and Brooks Schramm. Winona Lake, IN: Eisenbrauns, 2010.

Jeroboam II (14:23–29)

Translation

23 In the fifteenth year of Amaziah, son of Joash, king of Judah, Jeroboam, son of Jehoash, king of Israel, became king in Samaria and ruled for forty-one years. **24** He did evil in the sight of Yahweh; he did not turn aside from all the sins of Jeroboam, son of Nebat, which he made Israel sin. **25** He restored the border of Israel from the entrance of Hamath to the Dead Sea[10] according to the word of Yahweh, God of Israel, that he spoke through his servant Jonah, son of Amittai, the prophet, who was from Gath-hepher. **26** For Yahweh had seen that the misery of Israel was very bitter,[11] and there was no one, bond or free,[12] no helper for Israel. **27** But Yahweh had not said that he would wipe out the name of Israel from under heaven, so he delivered them by the hand of Jeroboam, son of Jehoash. **28** The rest of the matters pertaining to Jeroboam and all that he did and his might with which he fought and with which he restored Damascus and Hamath to Judah in Israel, are they not

10. יָם הָעֲרָבָה (*yām hā ʿărāḇâ*), "sea of the Arabah."
11. Emending מֹרֶה *mōre,* "rebel" to הַמַּר *hammar,* "the bitter".
12. Cf. Deut 32:36; 1 Kgs 14:10; 21:21; 2 Kgs 9:8. Gk. "and that there were few and in want and abandoned"; Vulg. "and that it was being devoured and closed to the land"; Syr. "there was no one in power."

written in the chronicles of the kings of Israel? **29** Jeroboam slept with his fathers,[13] with the kings of Israel, and Zechariah, his son, ruled after him.

Textual Notes

24a. אֶת־יִשְׂרָאֵל: Syr. adds "and he walked in them"; harmonization? Gk. and Vulg. with MT.

25a. הֵשִׁיב: Gk. "removed"; Vulg. and Syr. with MT. Gk. attempting to deal with the problem of v. 28? See below.

25b. מִגַּת הַחֵפֶר: Vulg. "from Gath which is in Opher"; Gk. "Gethchober"; Syr. "Gath-hepher." The article on חֵפֶר is problematic and the Vulg. may be attempting to represent that. In Josh 19:13 Gath is spelled with a final ה (*he*) = גִּתָּה. Perhaps it has gotten misplaced here.

26a. מֹרֶה: Emending the text to הַמַּר "the bitter" with all the versions. MT "a rebel."

26b–b. וְאֶפֶס עָצוּר וְאֶפֶס עָזוּב: The versions all struggle to translate this phrase, but there is no evidence that the different translations represent differing texts. See the "Translation."

27a. אֶת־שֵׁם: Gk. "seed"; Vulg. and Syr. with MT.

28a–a. הֵשִׁיב אֶת־דַּמֶּשֶׂק וְאֶת־חֲמָת לִיהוּדָה בְּיִשְׂרָאֵל: Gk. reads "how he turned against Damascus and Hamath belonging to Judah in Israel"; Vulg. with MT; Syr. "How he restored Damascus and Hamath to Israel." Both Gk. and Syr. are attempting to deal with the problem the MT presents. *CTAT* (403) asserts that, as the harder reading, MT is probably correct.

29a. אֲבֹתָיו: Syr. and Targ. add "and was buried with his fathers"; G[L] adds "was buried in Samaria." Gk. and Vulg. with MT. MT best explains the rest.

29b–b. וַיִּמְלֹךְ זְכַרְיָה בְנוֹ תַּחְתָּיו: Gk. reads "Azariah, son of Amaziah, ruled after his father," apparently an error by a distracted copyist thinking of 15:1 following; Gk[L] reads with MT, as do Vulg. and Syr.

Commentary

This account is surprising in two different ways. First, it is very brief, only seven verses to cover what is by far the longest reign of any of the northern

---

13. Syr. and Targ. insert "and was buried with his fathers." G[L] inserts "was buried in Samaria." Cogan and Tadmor argue that the Lucianic reading is correct because it adheres to the common pattern of these death notices (162). However, it is not present in Gk. and Vulg. and the principle of the harder reading would support the MT, as would the reading that best explains the rest.

kings: forty-one years, and from all that we can tell, one of the most successful. Second, although Jeroboam is introduced with the same condemnation that Kings applies to all the northern kings: "he did evil in the sight of Yahweh (וַיַּעַשׂ הָרַע בְּעֵינֵי יהוה, *wayya ʿaś hāraʿ bᵉ ʿênê yhwh*); he did not turn aside from the sins of Jeroboam [I]" (לֹא סָר מִכָּל־חַטֹּאות יָרָבְעָם, *lōʾ sār mikkāl-ḥaṭṭōʾwt yārāḇʿām*), yet we are told that Yahweh used him to bring deliverance to Yahweh's people Israel. What should we make of this? I suggest that the two features are closely related. Whatever Jeroboam was able to achieve was the result of Yahweh's grace, a grace that was extended to Israel throughout the Jehu dynasty for the century after the destruction of institutionalized Baalism.[14] So, for the editor's purpose there is no reason to expand on those accomplishments. It is as though Yahweh was offering Israel a special opportunity, in the light of his defeat of Baal, for the nation to turn back to him. This is why this portion of the book emphasizes the direct involvement of the prophets, from Elijah and Elisha to Jonah declaring God's word to the Israelites. In this regard, as Amos and Hosea saw it, it was during Jeroboam's reign that the culmination of the promises to Jehu were realized, but at the same time, in that hour of apparent prosperity and power, Israel had her last opportunity to turn to Yahweh in true covenant obedience. Thus, for Hosea, Jezreel, which had been the great moment of hope for Israel, had become the sign of Israel's condemnation (Hos 1:4–5). From an apparent restoration of all Solomon's glory, it was only twenty years after Jeroboam's death, through five different kings and four different dynasties, until the northern kingdom ceased to exist. Thus, it is that Jeroboam's accomplishments are given little attention. They were soon gone, while it is Yahweh's grace that endures forever.

25–27 The particular comments about Jeroboam's reign are sandwiched between the accession formula in vv. 23–24 and the death notice in vv. 28–29. Verse 25 contains the single report (apart from the repetition in v. 28) of his accomplishments, namely that he "restored the border of Israel from the entrance of Hamath to the sea of the Arabah" (הוּא הֵשִׁיב אֶת־גְּבוּל יִשְׂרָאֵל מִלְּבוֹא חֲמָת עַד־יָם הָעֲרָבָה, *hûʾ hēšîḇ ʾeṯ-gᵉḇûl yiśrāʾēl millᵉḇôʾ ḥămāṯ ʿaḏ-yām hā ʿărāḇâ*). These two extremities defined the ideal Solomonic kingdom from north to south (1 Kgs 8:65).[15] Most commentators (e.g., Hobbs, 182; Sweeney, 386) agree that "the entrance to Hamath" is the city of Lebo-hamath which is to be identified with the modern Lebweh. This site is located at the point where "the Valley" (Arab. *Biqʿa*) between the Lebanon and Anti-Lebanon mountain ranges opens out into the North Syrian plain, about forty-five miles north of Damascus. Although Sweeney (368) takes "the sea of the Arabah" to

14. As I have said above, there is clear evidence, both in the text and in material findings, that the worship of Baal continued in the land. However, it never again threatened to replace or supplant the worship of Yahweh as the God of Israel.

15. Cf. Num 13:21; 34:8; Josh 13:5; Judg 3:3.

be the Red Sea, most others take it to be the Dead Sea. The reference point would be to the northern border of Moab, over which Israel had held dominance until the revolt of Mesha (see the "Commentary" on chapter three). Amos (6:14) used these same reference points to castigate the Israelites for their boasting in their conquests, saying that a nation would soon come to strip it all away.

Thus, Jeroboam was particularly able to break Israel free from some seventy-five years of Israelite "misery" (עֳנִי, *ʿŏnî*) at the hands of the Syrians with their capital at Damascus, and to reestablish control over not only the lands Syria had taken from Israel, but over the Syrian homelands. Part of the reason he was able to do this has become clear from Assyrian records. They tell us of devastating attacks on Damascus under Adad-Nirari III in 806 BC and again under Shalmanezer IV in 783 BC. Then for some fifty years there are few Assyrian records, and what we have points to a serious diminution of Assyrian aggressiveness.[16] While most scholars take the book of Jonah to be a much later composition, Wiseman (249) has argued that this fact may well be explained by the ministry of that prophet in Assyria.[17] In any case, these two factors: (1) weakening of Damascus and (2) reduction of Assyrian pressure, meant that Jeroboam, building on the successes of his father Jehoash (13:25), had something of a free hand to restore "the border of Israel."

Like other prophets, such as Micaiah (1 Kgs 22), Jonah, son of Amittai appears only here in the Kings record.[18] His prophecy, like that of Elisha to Jehoash (13:17), was one of salvation. If Yahweh had brought judgment upon his people, it was not because he wanted to "wipe out the name of Israel" (לִמְחוֹת אֶת־שֵׁם יִשְׂרָאֵל, *limḥôṯ ʾeṯ-šēm yiśrāʾēl*).[19] In fact, he was committed to them, and wished only to bring them to repentance. Undoubtedly, that message would have resonated with the exiles, as they read or heard this material. Brueggemann (445–46) observes importantly that the absence of any reference to Yahweh in the Amaziah account only underlines the importance of the reference here. Although he does not make the point, I suggest that the reason for this fact is precisely in view of the looming presence of the exile of Israel. Judah was not yet facing that threat, but Israel was. It is for the same reason that God gave the prophets Amos and Hosea to Israel at

16. A basic resource on this period is Menahem Haran, "Rise and Decline of Jeroboam Ben Joash," *VT* 17 (1967): 266–97. However, he argued that Jeroboam's accomplishments were achieved late in his reign, because of earlier Assyrian power. More recent research has shown that the Assyrian decline began earlier than Haran allowed.

17. Donald Wiseman, "Jonah's Nineveh," *TynBul* 30 (1979): 29–51.

18. "Gath-hepher" was located in the territory of Zebulon (Josh 19:13). It is identified with the site of al-Meshed, about a mile and a half north of Nazareth.

19. Cogan and Tadmor say that this refers to washing off a sheet of papyrus for its reuse (161).

this time. Some of the Israelites could hear these messages, both positive and negative, and be armed not to lose their faith in the harrowing days that lay ahead. Cohn (104) says that "the prophecy-fulfillment structure transcends the dominant regnal structure in 2 Kings."

Probably the deliverance here attributed to Jeroboam in v. 27 is not the same as that mentioned in 13:5. There it is a deliverance from Syria probably achieved through the Assyrian emperor Adad-Nirari III. Here the deliverance seems to be of a more general nature. The idea that someone like Jeroboam could possibly be the means of Yahweh's deliverance seems incongruous. That Yahweh would use a person who might not be all that God could wish for in terms of moral character is jarring. Yet, if there was no one else "bond or free" (וְאֶפֶס עָצוּר וְאֶפֶס עָזוּב, *wᵊ ʾep̄es ʿāṣûr wᵊ ʾep̄es ʿāzûḇ*)[20] available, he would use the one who was available. The point is that it is Yahweh who is the ruler of history and is working in it to achieve his goals. Jeroboam only accomplished what he did because of God's grace.

28 This verse has presented a major problem with its statement that Jeroboam "restored Damascus and Hamath to Judah in Israel." On the surface, the statement makes no sense. As a result, many emendations of the text have been proposed. The most common proposals have been to eliminate "Judah in,"[21] taking it that "Judah" was inserted by a (confused) Judean editor, or to read "Judah and Israel," assuming that the two countries were effectively united during the reigns of Jeroboam and Azariah. The proposal to read "from Yaudi to Israel," which was dependent on the discovery that the region north of Hamath was sometimes referred to as *y'dy* in Assyrian texts has now largely been rejected on the basis of the usage of the term in those texts.[22] Given the support of Gk. and Vulg. for the MT *CTAT* (403) believes MT to be likely. If that is so, then perhaps the sense is that Jeroboam took for Israel these territories which (from an Israelite perspective) had once belonged to Judah.

Biblical Theology Comments

One of the prevailing themes of the Old Testament is Yahweh's compassion, his tender feeling for his creatures. This first emerges in Exodus 2 where we are told that God saw his people's oppression and heard their cries (Exod 2:24–25). Here is the first intimation of the point made elsewhere: though he has no ears, he hears; though he has no eyes, he sees. He is the living God, not a dead idol. The point is then explicitly expressed in Exodus 34:6, after the golden calf incident. Because he is compassionate, Yahweh is unwilling

---

20. Sweeney says this is a cryptic reference to the repeated promise to wipe out Ahab's house (1 Kgs 21:21; 2 Kgs 9:8) and before that Jeroboam's house (1 Kgs 14:10) (368). But it seems more likely that it is a direct reference to the promise in Deut 32:36 that Yahweh will prove himself when all the false trusts have failed.

21. With Syr.

22. See Cogan and Tadmor, 161–62.

to destroy his covenant-breaking people. Instead, he unilaterally renews the covenant, thereby setting a pattern that he would follow for centuries, all the way up to and beyond the reign of Jeroboam. The thought is expressed most powerfully in the poetry of the Psalms. Psalm 103:8–18 offers a reflection on Exodus 34:6 in the midst of which we read these memorable words:

> "As a father shows compassion to his children,
> so Yahweh shows compassion to those who fear him.
> For he knows our nature; he remembers that we are dust."
> (Ps 103:13–14)

In the New Testament, apart from the several places where we are told that Jesus "had compassion" on crowds of hungry, sick, and harassed people (Matt 9:36; 14:14; 15:32), we also hear of his compassion for suffering individuals (Luke 7:13). But one of the most moving expressions of divine compassion is found in the well-known parable often called "The Prodigal Son" (Luke 15:11–32) but which might be better labeled "The Prodigal Father." The father sees the son who has foolishly lost everything and is coming dragging home in rags, and the father "had compassion" (not rage) on him (Luke 15:20). There we see illustrated the consistent character of Yahweh that is displayed from the time of the exodus (and before) right up to the present.

The idea that Yahweh could use a sinful man like Jeroboam to accomplish his purposes seems intuitively wrong, but it is not so. The point is made with some force in Isaiah 45. There the prophet has asserted that Yahweh would use the Persian emperor Cyrus to deliver his people and rebuild Jerusalem and would reward him for doing so. Verses 9–14 seem to be a response to those who would challenge Yahweh's right to do such a thing. He compares them to pots that are attempting to tell the potter how to do his work, or to a baby chastising his parents for the way he or she is formed. Yahweh asserts the right of the Creator to determine how best to achieve his creative purposes.

This is of course similar to the points made in the books of Job and Habakkuk. We contingent humans are in no position to tell I AM what should be so and not so, or how he can and cannot do his work. We have enough evidence to know that in the end he will be consistent with his own nature, and that that nature is consistently "good," that is, constructive. However, along the way, we who cannot see the future are in no position to determine in what ways this or that divine act is good.

That having been said, when God uses a flawed tool for his purposes, that does not absolve that tool from responsibility. For we are not inanimate objects, but persons who have the capacity for choice. The responses of "I couldn't help it" or "he/she made me do it" will not stand in the final judgment. Neither will "but my actions had a good outcome." The fact that what Joseph's brothers meant for evil, God meant for good (Gen 50:20) does not mean that their actions were good! God used Jeroboam to accomplish deliverance from Syrian oppression, but Jeroboam seems to have done nothing to change the moral direction of the nation that Amos and Hosea, and later Isaiah, so vividly picture, and which would result in the destruction of his nation within a generation of his death.

Selected Bibliography

Lichtert, C. "Perspective Narrative sur un Personage Dit Historique (2 R 14,23–29)." Pages 159–168 in *Écritures et Réécritures*. Edited by Claire Clivaz, Corina Combet-Galland, Jean-Daniel Macchi, and Christophe Nihan. Leuven: Peeters, 2012.

Na'aman, N. "Azariah of Judah and Jeroboam II of Israel." *VT* 43 (1993): 227–34.

Azariah of Judah (15:1–7)

Translation

15:1 In the twenty-seventh year of Jeroboam, king of Israel, Azariah, son of Amaziah, king of Judah, became king. **2** He was sixteen years old when he became king, and he ruled for fifty-two years in Jerusalem. His mother's name was Jecoliah; she was from Jerusalem. **3** He did right in the sight of Yahweh according to all that Amaziah his father did. **4** Only, the high places were not removed; the people were still sacrificing and burning incense on the high places. **5** Yahweh struck the king and he had an infectious skin disease until the day of his death. He lived in a house of seclusion, and Jotham, the king's son, was over the house, governing the people of the land. **6** The rest of the matters pertaining to Azariah and all that he did, are they not written in the chronicles of the kings of Judah? **7** Azariah slept with his fathers and they buried him with his fathers in the city of David and Jotham, his son, ruled in his place.

Textual Notes

4a. לֹא־סָרוּ: Gk. and Syr. "he did not remove"; Vulg. with MT.

5a. וַיֵּשֶׁב: Gk. "he reigned"; Vulg. and Syr. with MT.

5b. הַחָפְשִׁית: Gk. "aphphousoth" (see 2 Chr 26:21); Vulg. "apart"; Syr. "seclusion."

Commentary

As was the case with Jeroboam II in the preceding segment, this narration is surprisingly brief, both in the light of Azariah's unusually long reign and in view of the lengthy treatment found in Chronicles (2 Chr 26:1-23 [where he is consistently called Uzziah]). Apart from the standard opening and closing formulae (vv. 1–4, 6–7) the only particular thing said about him is that Yahweh struck him with leprosy and that his son Jotham "governed" (שֹׁפֵט, *šōpēṭ*) in his place (v. 5). I suggest the reason for this brevity is that the editor was wanting to focus on the precipitate collapse of Israel after the reign of Jeroboam II. In keeping with his pattern of synchronism, he had to identify the king of Judah whose long reign largely corresponded with that of Jeroboam and with at least three of his successors, but he did not want to mitigate the effects of what he was about to convey with what was, to him, a beside-the-point discussion of Azariah's accomplishments. Again, as has been said frequently above, while the book of Kings is based in actual events of history, and reports them faithfully within its purpose, it makes no attempt to be a history as such. Its purpose is to show how Yahweh acted (and spoke) in the historical experience of his people, and how their responses to that revelatory activity affected the outcome of their lives. Thus, in this case, it should not come as a surprise to us that the one event of Azariah's life that the narrator wants to call to our attention is the effects in life of his fateful encounter with Yahweh.

1–2 Earlier it was common to suggest that Azariah was this king's personal name, while Uzziah (see vv. 13, 30, 32, 34, as well as 2 Chr 26) was a throne name. However, more recently it has been argued that the roots *ʿzr* and *ʿzz* are largely synonymous with a meaning of "victory, valor, or strength" (see the proposal of Gershon Brin cited by Cogan and Tadmor, 165–66). "The twenty-seventh year" would be the beginning of Azariah's sole reign in 767 BC. "Sixteen years" would have been his age when he began his coregency with his father Amaziah in 791 BC. Azariah's total reign of fifty-two years not only included that coregency, but also the one with his son Jotham, beginning in 750 BC. On the probable coregencies of this time see the "Excursus on Chronology (739–696 BC)."

3–4 These verses contain the usual approbation of a good king in Judah with the normal *caveat* (until Hezekiah) that the Deuteronomic requirement for centralized worship had not yet been enforced. However, the statement that Azariah "did right (וַיַּעַשׂ הַיָּשָׁר, *wayyaʿaś hayyāšār*) ... according to all that his father Amaziah did (כְּכֹל אֲשֶׁר־עָשָׂה אֲמַצְיָהוּ אָבִיו, *kᵉḵōl ʾăšer-ʿāśâ ʾămaṣyāhû ʾāḇîw*)," given the very equivocal report on Amaziah (14:1–22 and 2 Chr 25:1–28), leaves us with a degree of uncertainty. When we couple this with the explanation of the reason for the skin disease given in 2 Chr 26:16–20 we get a picture of a man who was upright in his behavior and in his dealings with his subjects, but yet without the selfless devotion to God that had characterized David and some of his descendants (i.e., Asa in 1 Kgs 15:11; Hezekiah in 2 Kgs 18:3; Josiah in 2 Kgs 22:2).

5 Given the report of Azariah's successes found in Chronicles, and the evident effectiveness that allowed him a reign of fifty-two years, it is surprising that the only thing the narrator chooses to highlight from that long reign is Azariah's contracting a "skin disease" (מְצֹרָע, *mᵉṣōrāʿ*)[23] that left him confined

---

23. Heb. has only one term for all kinds of skin diseases, probably none of them being the disfiguring Hansen's disease that is commonly called "leprosy" today. See *ABD* 4:277–82.

in "a house of seclusion" (בְּבֵית הַחָפְשִׁית, *bəḇêṯ haḥopšîṯ*).[24] Beyond stating that it was the result of an action by Yahweh, the narrator does not expand on the incident nor does he take the opportunity to give the kind of theological rationale for the event that he could have in light of the Chronicler's comments. As stated above, the brevity of the treatment is probably explained by the intention to focus on the precipitate decline of Israel. But why pick this one item to comment on and then not use it to the extent one could have? Cohn's comment (105) that the mention of fifty-two years emphasizes the stability of the Davidic dynasty as against what was happening in the north gives us an important clue to what is happening here. I suggest the narrator has chosen this incident to show us how differently things were being handled in Judah than in Israel. The king had been struck—by Yahweh—with an illness that made him ritually impure. What an opportunity for a rival faction to dispose of him. That was the kind of thing that was going to happen in Israel over and over again between 752 and 722 BC. But it did not happen in Judah. Here, as the text tells us, Uzziah remained in power behind the scenes while his son carried out the official functions of government. Just as Asa's long reign had provided stability for Judah while the infant Israel was going through four dynastic changes (1 Kgs 15:9–16:34), so here during Israel's final convulsions, the determination to be faithful to Yahweh, as expressed in faithfulness to his promise to David, was holding Judah firm.

6–7 The death notice is unremarkable, except for two matters. The first is the terseness in v. 6. With other kings, especially those who had accomplished anything notable, it is not uncommon to add after "all that he did" (כָּל־אֲשֶׁר עָשָׂה, *kol- ʾăšer ʿāśâ*) something like "and his might" (e.g., Jehu, 2 Kgs 10:32) or "and how he fought with so and so" (e.g., Jeroboam II, 2 Kgs 14:28) but not here. The narrator is not going to allow anything to divert the focus from what was happening in the north.

The second matter relates to the place of Azariah's burial. Kings tell us that he was buried "with his fathers in the city of David" (עִם־אֲבֹתָיו בְּעִיר דָּוִד, *ʿim- ʾăḇōṯāyw bəʿîr dāwiḏ*). But Chronicles has it that he was buried "in the burial field belonging to the kings, because they said, 'He had a skin disease' "

24. There is considerable uncertainty about the precise meaning of the term here translated "seclusion." The term only occurs here and in the parallel passage in 2 Chr 26:21 and is spelled differently in the two places. The root (חָפַשׁ *ḥāp̄aš*) has the basic meaning of "to be free" (*HALOT* 1.341), thus there has been a movement to see the point of this term as "free of obligation" (so REB "he was relieved of all duties and lived in his palace"). However, Vulg. and Syr. agree on the idea of "separation" (Gk. only transliterates the Heb.), and the Chronicler's explanation of the event would certainly make it appear that the king was not merely "set free" but was forced into seclusion, as Lev 13:46 prescribes for this condition. Cogan and Tadmor, having surveyed the various options, suggest leaving the term untranslated (as Gk. did), saying that we really do not know what the word means (166).

(2 Chr 26:23). The implication is that this was not the normal burial place for a king. Josephus make this explicit when he says that he was buried in his garden (*Ant.* 9.10. 4 §227). A stone tablet that might have been the cover of a bone box dating to the first century has been discovered. It is inscribed with the words "Here were brought the bones of Uzziah, king of Judah. Do not open" (Cogan and Tadmor, 167). While some say this supports the idea that he was buried separately, it is hard to say that, especially being removed several centuries.

Selected Bibliography

Theile, E. R. *The Mysterious Numbers of the Hebrew Kings*. Third edition. Grand Rapids, Zondervan, 1983.

Zechariah and Shallum (15:8–16)

Translation

8 In the thirty-eighth year of Azariah, king of Judah, Zechariah, son of
Jeroboam, reigned in Samaria for six months. **9** He did evil in the sight
of Yahweh as his fathers had done. He did not turn aside from the sins of
Jeroboam, son of Nebat, which he made Israel to sin. **10** Shallum, son of
Jabesh, conspired against him and struck him before the people and ruled in
his place. **11** The rest of the matters pertaining to Zechariah, they are written
in the chronicles of the Kings of Israel. **12** This was the word of Yahweh which
he spoke to Jehu, saying, "Sons to the fourth generation will sit for you on
the throne of Israel." And so it was.

13 Shallum, son of Jabesh, became king in the thirty-ninth year of Uzziah,
king of Judah, and he ruled all of one month in Samaria. **14** Then Menahem,
son of Gaddi, came up to Samaria from Tirzah and struck Shallum, son of
Jabesh, in Samaria, and killed him, and ruled in his place. **15** The rest of the
matters pertaining to Shallum and his conspiracy, they are written in the
chronicles of the kings of Israel. **16** Then Menahem struck Tiphsah and all
who were in it and its borders as far as Tirzah; because it would not open,[25]
he struck; he ripped open its pregnant women.

Textual Notes

10a–a. בֶּן־יָבֵשׁ וַיַּכֵּהוּ קָבָל־עָם וַיְמִיתֵהוּ: Gk. reads "and Keblaam and they struck him and killed him and Shallum…". This all stems from transposing the Aramaizing "before the people" (קָבָל־עָם) from after the vb. נכה "struck" to before it, transliterating it as a proper noun ("Keblaam"), changing the number of the vb., and adding the harmonistic "they killed him." Vulg. "publicly"; Syr. "before the people." *CTAT* (403–4) noting the differences in

25. The vb. is masc. (פָּתַח, *pāṯaḥ*) whereas a city (תִּרְצָה, *tirṣâ*) is fem. On disagreement in gender see GKC (§§122*g*, 145*a*). See also RJW (§23).

the masora, does not find any of the readings compelling, including the Lucianic "Ibleam."

13a. לְעֻזִּיָּה: Gk. and Vulg. read "Azariah." Syr. with MT. The variety of treatments in the chap. makes determining the original difficult. Syr. reads "Uzziah" throughout, while Gk. reads "Azariah" throughout. Vulg. reads "Uzziah" with MT in v. 34.

14a–a. וַיִּמְלֹךְ תַּחְתָּיו: Gk. lacks; Vulg. and Syr. with MT.

16a. אֶת־תִּפְסַח: Gk. reads "Thersa" (Tirzah); Gk[L]. reads "Tappuah"; Vulg. and Syr. with MT. See the "Commentary" below.

16b. פָתַח: All versions add "to him."

16c. וַיַּךְ: Gk. and Syr. add "it"; Vulg. lacks the vb. 16b. and c. are addressing the very terse MT. But the Heb. is possible and may be intentionally terse. It is preferred as the harder reading.

16d. הֶהָרוֹתֶיהָ: The article is anomalous and may be the result of dittography.

Commentary

The present unit opens the floodgates of doom on the northern kingdom. After some fifty years of stability and prosperity under the reign of Jeroboam II, there comes a succession of five kings in four different dynasties in a matter of 30 years. Of the five kings, only one dies in his bed. Under the relentless pressure of the rapidly expanding Assyrian Empire, beginning with the reign of Tiglath-pileser III in 745 BC, one king after another is assassinated and replaced by his killer. The grace period granted to Jehu and his descendants (15:10) is over, and the destruction already spoken of in 1 Kgs 14:15 is let loose. Yahweh's patience has come to an end.

8–11 The extreme brevity of the reign of Zechariah suggests that some sort of resentment against Jeroboam and his policies must have been building up for some time. The resentment would have been held in check as long as the old king was still alive. But once he was gone, it boiled up and over. Many commentators (e.g., Hobbs, 195; Konkel, 549) suggest that the designation of Shallum as son of Jabesh (v. 10) is identifying him as being from the clan of Jabesh in Gilead in the Transjordan. Sweeney (372) then proposes that his conspiracy may have been motivated by a wish to undo the alliance with Assyria which Jeroboam had pursued and to align Israel with Syria.

One of the features that shapes the entire narrative from v. 8 through v. 31 is the repetition of the standard format of the regnal formulae. Again and again, we hear the data of the beginning of a reign, and then in all cases except Elah (1 Kgs 16:8) and Shallum, we hear the standard denunciation of the northern kings: "he did evil in the sight of Yahweh (וַיַּעַשׂ הָרַע בְּעֵינֵי יהוה, *wayya ʿaś hāra ʿ bᵊ ʿênê yhwh*); he did not turn aside from the sins of Jeroboam son of Nebat which he caused Israel to commit" (לֹא סָר מֵחַטֹּאות יָרָבְעָם בֶּן־נְבָט אֲשֶׁר הֶחֱטִיא אֶת־יִשְׂרָאֵל, *lō ʾsār mēḥaṭṭō ʾwṯ yārob̲ ʿām ben-nᵊb̲āṭ ʾăšer heḥĕṭî ʾ ʾeṯ-yiśrā ʾēl*) (9, cf. also 18, 24, 28). Finally, we hear that the records of the king's reign (even Shallum's) can be found in the royal chronicles. Like the blows of a hammer, these repeated phrases take the kingdom down to its end. Here there is no word of Yahweh's compassion or forbearance (in contrast to 13:4–5, 23; 14:26–27). Neither kings nor people will turn back to him, and that being so there seems to be no possibility of deliverance.

The Heb. that is translated "before the people" (קָבָל־עָם, *qāb̲āl- ʿām*) (v. 10) is problematic. The preposition קָבָל appears to be of Aramaic origin, and "people" (עָם) should have an article. However, both Vulg. and Syr. support this reading. The Lucianic recension of LXX has "Ibleam," the city in Manasseh referred to in 9:27 near where Jehu killed Ahaziah. Given the rather neat inclusio this would provide (the beginning and the end of the Jehu dynasty in bloodshed) and the relative lateness of this recension, it seems best to remain with the Vulg. and Syr. reading, and to see the Lucianic reading as an attempt to solve a hard reading.[26]

12 This statement, in which the narrator reminds us both of Yahweh's faithfulness to his promises, and of the end of that promise, adds to the sense of doom. For nearly a century, through all the difficulties that had occurred, Yahweh had given his people another chance, as it were, preserving them from their enemies by sheer grace. But Jehu's descendants had not led the people away from the idolatrous worship of Yahweh that inevitably compromised his transcendence and all that it implied.[27] Now nothing more will be heard of Yahweh in these accounts.

13–15 If Shallum's assassination of Zechariah was precipitate, his own assassination was even more so. He had not been on the throne a month before the reaction set in and Menahem killed him. Tirzah, from which Menahem came, was the old capital of the kingdom. Located about 6 miles north of Shechem, it had been fortified by Jeroboam I (1 Kgs 14:17) and had continued as the capital city until Omri had moved the seat of power to Samaria (1 Kgs 16:24). Thus, it may have been the second city of the kingdom, and Menahem may have been its governor. In any case, if he was able to assassinate Shallum in Samaria itself, he must have had a significant number of troops available to him. Whether the action was anything more than a power grab is unclear, but in any case, the later statement that Menahem needed an alliance with Assyria to cement his hold on the kingdom (v. 19) is an indicator of the chaotic conditions that were prevailing.

26. Gk. transliterates the Heb. as though it is a placename: Keblaam (Κεβλααμ).

27. For a comprehensive discussion of the Jehu dynasty, see Walter Brueggemann, "Stereotype and Nuance: the Dynasty of Jehu," *CBQ* 70 (2008): 16–28.

The absence of any religious condemnation of Shallum is interesting and is possibly the result of the very short reign. However, note that Zimri, who only reigned a week, did receive the standard condemnation (1 Kgs 16:19), so caution on this point is advisable. There is no statement of the burial of either Zechariah or Shallum as is typical of northern kings who were assassinated. The situation is different for the royal victims of such treatment in Judah, who are all said to have been buried with their ancestors (see Ahaziah, Joash, and Amaziah in 2 Kgs 9:28; 12:21; 14:20, respectively). Possibly this is the result of the veneration of the Davidic dynasty.

16 Here is another example of the actions of a king being described before the actual regnal summary is given (see 14:22). In this case, it seems plausible that Menahem may have carried out these acts on his way to Samaria. However, that suggestion depends heavily upon the decision made with regard to the identification of Tiphsah. Thus far, the only place known to carry this name is located on the Euphrates River, and it seems highly unlikely that a governor of Tirzah would have had any dealings that far north. Haran has argued that Jeroboam II had controlled Syria that far north, and that perhaps Menahem had been an officer of his and had carried out such an attack to try to maintain control of the territory after Jeroboam's death.[28] However, Lucian reads "Tappuah," which was probably located about 6 miles south of Shechem (Josh 17:7, 8). This would accord better with "its borders as far as Tirzah." Once again, the lack of support for this reading in the other versions makes it somewhat questionable. The viciousness of this attack is another witness to the breakdown of all the restraints as the kingdom reeled its way to destruction. The brutality that was carried out elsewhere and had been inflicted upon them had now become part of their own behavior (8:12; see Amos 1:13; Hos 13:8).[29]

Selected Bibliography

Haran, M. "The Rise and Decline of the Empire of Jeroboam ben Joash." *VT* 17 (1967): 266–97.

Menahem and Pekahiah (15:17–26)

Translation

17 In the thirty-ninth year of Azariah, king of Judah, Menahem, son of Gaddi, became king of Israel and ruled for ten years in Samaria. **18** He did evil in the sight of Yahweh; he did not turn aside from all the sins of Jeroboam, son of

28. M. Haran, "The Rise and Decline of the Empire of Jeroboam ben Joash," *VT* 17 (1967): 284–90.

29. Mordechai Cogan, "'Ripping Open Pregnant Women' in Light of an Assyrian Analogue," *JAOS* 103 (1983): 755–57.

Nebat, which he made Israel sin all his days. **19** Pul, king of Assyria, came up
against the land, and Menahem gave Pul 1,000 talents of silver to become
his ally so as to secure the kingdom in his hand. **20** Menahem brought out
this silver from Israel, from the men of the upper class, to give to the king of
Assyria; fifty shekels of silver per man. So the king of Assyria turned back
and did not stay there in the land. **21** The rest of the matters pertaining to
Menahem and all that he did, are they not written in the chronicles of the
kings of Israel? **22** Menahem slept with his fathers and Pekahiah his son
ruled in his place.

23 In the fiftieth year of Azariah, king of Judah, Pekahiah, son of
Menahem, became king over Israel and he ruled for two years. **24** He did
evil in the sight of Yahweh; he did not turn aside from the sins of Jeroboam,
son of Nebat, which he made Israel sin. **25** Pekah, son of Remaliah, his officer,[30] conspired against him and struck him down in Samaria, in the tower
of the king's house, along with Argob and "the Lion." Fifty men of Gilead
were with him. So he killed him and reigned in his place. **26** The rest of the
matters pertaining to Pekahiah, and all that he did, they are written in the
chronicles of the kings of Israel.

Textual Notes

18a–a. כָּל־יָמָיו: Gk. begins v. 19 here and reads "In his days, ..."; Syr. reads "all his days" after סָר; Vulg. with MT. The phrase is unusual in the typical statement of condemnation (as MT has it) and this may account for the Gk. and Syr. variants.

19a–a. לְהַחֲזִיק הַמַּמְלָכָה בְּיָדוֹ: Gk. omits; Vulg. and Syr. with MT. Gk. haplography with "hand"?

20a. עַל ... עַל: With the *hiphil* of יָצָא, עַל has the sense of "from." "He brought out from... ." See also 12:12.

25a. בְּאַרְמוֹן: Gk. "in front of"; Syr. "in the palace of"; Vulg. "tower."

25b. K מֶלֶךְ ; Q הַמֶּלֶךְ .

25c–c. מִבְּנֵי גִלְעָדִים: Gk. "of the 400"; Vulg. and Syr. with MT.

Commentary

These verses record the rule of the only dynasty, such as it is, to govern Israel between the end of Jehu's dynasty in 752 BC and the two-year reign of Manasseh's son. Apart from the recurring hammer blows of the regnal formulae, and the condemnation rubric, we are told only two things about these twelve years: Menahem became a vassal of Tiglath-pileser III, and Pekahiah, his son, was assassinated by his successor, Pekah. For the narrator,

30. Heb. שָׁלִישׁ, (*šālîš*) "third." See 7:2; 9:25; 10:25 and discussions there.

this information is all we need to know as we slide toward the inevitable crash at the bottom.

19–20 During the reign of Menahem, which began in the same year Jeroboam died (752 BC; Jeroboam's son Zechariah only having ruled for six months, and his murderer, Shallum, only one month), a very momentous event occurred. This was the seizure of the Assyrian throne in 745 BC by a man named Pul, who took the throne-name Tiglath-pileser (III).[31] For some fifty years the Assyrian emperors had been content largely to rest on their laurels while dealing with matters on their northern frontier. With Tiglath-pileser's accession all that was to change. In a series of hammer-blows that persisted all through his eighteen-year reign (745–727 BC), this man drove his way westward, ultimately establishing himself on the coast of the Mediterranean Sea. By the time he died, he had set Assyria up for a century long series of conquests that would leave it standing alone astride the entire Near Eastern world, from Egypt in the west to Elam in the east.

It was this reality that Menahem had to face. It appears that he may have also faced rebellion in his own ranks. It is very probable that the Transjordanian regions of Israel were under the thumb of a warlord named Pekah (see below on v. 27), whose inclinations were to ally with his northern neighbor, Syria, against the Assyrians. As noted above, it is not impossible that Shallum may have had these same inclinations. So Menahem may have already assassinated Shallum because he was committed to maintaining the alliance with Assyria that seems to have been the foreign policy of the descendants of Jehu. Thus, when Tiglath-pileser arrived in the neighborhood, demanding surrender and tribute, it would have been perfectly natural to acquiesce, particularly if the Assyrian would assure him of help against his Syria-oriented Transjordanian rival.

As Hobbs (199) and others point out, the expression "come against" (בָּא ... עַל, *bā ʾ ... ʿal*) does not connote an attack, per se. Rather, it accords with a standard Assyrian practice: arriving in force in an area and offering "an alliance." Unfortunately, that alliance would come at a very high price, as was the case in this instance: 1,000 talents of silver. This would have amounted to about thirty-seven tons of the precious metal; fifty shekels from every man of high social standing in the country.[32,33] Once the tribute was paid,

31. On the early belief that Pul and Tiglath-pileser were two different kings, see Steven Holloway, "The Quest for Sargon, Pul and Tiglath-Pileser in the Nineteenth Century" in *Mesopotamia and the Bible: Comparative Eplorations,* eds. Mark W. Chavalas and K. Lawson Younger, Jr. (Grand Rapids: Baker, 2002), 68–87.

32. This would indicate that unless a significant amount also came from the royal treasury, there were between 60 and 70,000 such noblemen in the country.

33. Hobbs (200), supported by Konkel (551), points out that the term גִּבּוֹרֵי הַחַיִל, *gibbôrê haḥayil* regularly refers to soldiers, men of war, and argues that Menahem was buying the services of mercenaries from Assyria. However, it is apparent that

the Assyrians would withdraw (as v. 20 has it). But, of course, they would be back later with higher demands.

In the Assyrian annals there are mentions of tribute paid by Menahem to Tiglath-pileser, but it is difficult to coordinate these with this instance. However, given the date of the Assyrian's accession, it could not have been earlier than 745 BC. Thus, if the assumptions concerning Pekah's rival status are correct, the conflict may have become severe enough as Menahem's reign went on that he had become fearful for his continued rule, and, despite the high price, welcomed the Assyrian strength on his side.[34] Perhaps it was as a result of that strength that he was able to maintain control until his death and ensure the succession of his son.

25 However, by 740 BC, Pekahiah's second year, Pekah, son of Remaliah was emboldened to take his chances. Perhaps Tiglath-pileser's attention was momentarily diverted elsewhere.[35] The statement that he was an officer (שָׁלִישׁ, *šālîš*) of Pekahiah's may suggest that although Pekah had been ruling Transjordan for a dozen years, it was nominally under the authority of Menahem and then Pekahiah. But if that was the case, Pekah was no longer willing to be an underling. That he carried out his coup in the "tower of the king's house" (בְּאַרְמוֹן בֵּית־מֶלֶךְ, *bᵊ ʾarmôn bêṯ-meleḵ*), probably the innermost section of the palace (see 1 Kgs 16:18), says that Pekah was either trusted to a degree, or that, more likely, Pekahiah was incapable of defending himself. The reference to "fifty men of Gilead" argues for the latter interpretation. Pekah came from his fiefdom with a military company (see 1:9, 11, 13) to enforce his will.[36]

The mention here of "Argob and '"the Lion' " (אֶת־אַרְגֹּב וְאֶת־הָאַרְיֵה, *ʾeṯ-ʾargōḇ wᵊ ʾeṯ-hā ʾaryē*) has been a source of great uncertainty. One position, and perhaps the most obvious one, is that they are two associates of Pekah.

---

the term has a wider reference than merely warfare. These are men of power, and that power is not restricted to military matters. So in Ruth, Boaz is such a person (Ruth 2:1). See also 1 Kgs 11:28; 2 Kgs 5:1; 1 Chr 9:13; 26:31.

34. Hayim Tadmor, *The Inscriptions of Tiglath Pileser III, King of Assyria* (Jerusalem: Israel Academy of Sciences and Humanities, 1994), 69, 107. *ANET,* 283. See also Thiele, *Mysterious Numbers*, 90–117, Oswald Loretz and Werner R. Mayer, "Pulu-Tiglatpileser III und Menahem von Israel nach Assyrischen Quellen und 2 Kön 15,19–20, *UF* 22 (1990): 221–31, and Peter Dubovsky, "Tiglath-Pileser III's Campaigns in 734–732 B.C.: Historical Background of Isa 7; 2 Kgs 15–16 and 2 Chr 27–28," *Bib* 87 (2006): 153–170.

35. There are indications that although Tiglath-pileser had defeated Urartu in the north early in his reign the northern frontier demanded continued attention and that significant segments of the army had to be sent north repeatedly. See H. W. F. Saggs, *The Greatness that was Babylon* (New York: Hawthorne Books, 1962), 108.

36. Cohn points out that these kinds of details in the midst of the repeated formulae impart an unmistakable air of historicity (108).

However, the apparent definite article on the second is problematic for a personal name. That leads to a second possibility, that they are two figures on the gates of the palace: an eagle and a lion.[37] Neither of these require an emendation of the text, but the most popular alternative does. This position takes the two terms to be place names that have been, for some reason, displaced from the list of Tiglath-pileser's conquests in v. 29. The chief support for this idea is that Argob is indeed a place in 1 Kgs 4:13 and Deut 3:4. However, explaining how the displacement occurred is very difficult, especially since the versions are unanimous in reading with the MT. Thus, it seems best to take the first term as a personal name derived from the man's home area and the second as a nickname.

Selected Bibliography

Shea, W. J. "Menahem and Tiglath-Pilezer III." *JNES* 37 (1978): 43–49.

Pekah (15:27–31)

Translation

27 In the fifty-second year of Azariah, king of Judah, Pekah, son of Remaliah
became king and ruled Israel in Samaria for twenty years. **28** He did evil in
the sight of Yahweh; he did not turn aside from the sins of Jeroboam, son of
Nebat, which he caused Israel to sin. **29** In the days of Pekah, king of Israel,
Tiglath-pileser, king of Assyria, came and took Iyyon, Abel Beth Maacah,
Yanoah, Qadesh, and Hazor, and Gilead, and Galilee, all the land of Naphtali,
and exiled them to Assyria. **30** Then Hoshea, son of Elah, conspired against
Pekah, son of Remaliah; he struck him and killed him and reigned in his place
in the twentieth year of Jotham, son of Azariah. **31** The rest of the matters
pertaining to Pekah and all that he did, they are written in the chronicles
of the kings of Israel.

Textual Notes

No significant variants.

Commentary

27 There is a significant conflict here between the statements that "Pekah became king in the fifty-second year of Azaraiah" and that "he reigned in Samaria twenty years." Since Azariah's death is well-established as having occurred in 739 BC, an additional twenty years would place the end of Pekah's reign in 720 or 719 BC. But we know that Samaria fell to the Assyrians in 722 BC. Furthermore, Pekah's successor, Hoshea, is said to have reigned for an additional nine years. The simplest solution to the problem is

37. M. J. Geller, "A New Translation for 2 Kings xv 25," *VT* 26 (1976) 374–77 proposes this on the basis of a Ugaritic parallel.

the one proposed by Thiele: the twenty years of Pekah's reign did not begin in Azariah's final year.[38] His sole reign began then, but he was ruling in the Transjordan for the entire reign of Menahem and Pekahiah. Thus, the twenty years is from 752 to 732 BC.[39] If Menahem was a governor in Tirzah under Jeroboam II (see on v. 14 above), then Pekah may have filled a similar role in Transjordan. With the dissolution of Jeroboam's empire which finally settled out with Menahem on the throne in Samaria, Pekah may well have refused to give up his governorship, a reality which Menahem could only seek to paper over with the formality that Pekah was an officer of his.

The appellation "Pekah, son of Remaliah," is a way of saying that Pekah was not from the royal family and had no legitimate claim to the throne. Isaiah reinforces this point by repeatedly referring to him without his name, but only calling him "the son of Remaliah" (Isa 7:4, 5, 9).

29 It is apparent from Isaiah 7 that unlike Menahem, the Assyrian vassal, Pekah and Rezin, the king of Syria in Damascus, were allied against Assyria. This explains the statements of this verse. Assyrian records indicate that Tiglath-pileser conducted campaigns in the west at least three times during the years 734–732 BC. In these campaigns he not only captured and destroyed Damascus; he also punished Israel by taking from her all the territories north of the Jezreel Valley, as well as Gilead, the northern part of the Transjordan.[40] The cities mentioned were all located north of the sea of Galilee and would have been on or near the great highway which lead from the Euphrates to Egypt. Isaiah seems to have been reflecting on these losses when he prophesied that light would begin to dawn in Galilee (Isa 9:1 [MT 8:23]).

Although it appears that Assyria had practiced exile selectively for many years, it was under Tiglath-pileser that the practice, like so many other areas of Assyrian practice, became regularized and formalized. From this point onward, it was the regular outcome for any who fell afoul of the Assyrians. Here the Israelites seem to have gotten their first taste of it. From the point of view of empire-building, exile made a good deal of sense. Not only did it remove from a country or region those who might conceivably lead revolts; it also served to "homogenize" the empire, breaking down distinctive cultures,

---

38. Thiele, *Mysterious Numbers,* 118–34.

39. Thiele, *Mysterious Numbers,* 118–34. See also Nadav Na'aman, "Historical and Chronological Notes on the Kingdoms of Israel and Judah in the 8th Century B.C.," *VT* 36 (1986): 71–92.

40. Stuart A. Irvine, "The Southern Border of Syria Reconstructed," *CBQ* 56 (1994): 21–41. For a full discussion of these places and their probable locations, see Cogan and Tadmor, 177–78.

religions, and languages as exiles struggled to accommodate themselves to completely unfamiliar situations.[41]

30 Pekah's seven or eight years of sole rule were brought to an end just as he had begun them, in bloodshed. It seems apparent that there were those in Israel who understood where his attempts to stand against Assyrian were leading: destruction. Thus, it appears that a pro-Assyrian party gained enough of a following to push through a successful assassination attempt. At its head was another "nobody," Hosehea, son of Elah. That he was pro-Assyrian is indicated by 17:20 below where it is stated that he became an Assyrian vassal. Tiglath-pileser even claimed to have placed Hoshea on the throne.[42]

The statement that this event occurred "in the twentieth year of Jotham" is another example of the practice mentioned above: length of reign is not determined from the death of the previous king, but includes all the years of a person's reign, including coregencies. So here, if we begin calculating these twenty years at the death of Azariah in 739 BC we end up with discrepancies that cannot be rationalized. However, if we understand that Jotham became coregent with his father in 750 BC, the discrepancies can be explained.[43]

Selected Bibliography

Cook, H. J. "Pekah." *VT* 14 (1964): 121–35.

Dubovsky, P. "Why Did the Northern Kingdom Fall According to 2 Kings 15?" *Bib* 95 (2014): 321–46.

Jotham of Judah (15:32–38)

Translation

32 In the second year of Pekah, son of Remaliah, king of Israel, Jotham, son of Azariah, king of Judah, became king. **33** He was twenty-five years old when he became king and ruled in Jerusalem for sixteen years. His mother's name was Jerusha, daughter of Zadok. **34** He did right in the sight of Yahweh according to all that Uzziah his father had done. **35** Only the high places were not removed;[44] the people were still sacrificing and burning incense on the high places. He built the upper gate of the house of Yahweh. **36** The rest of

41. See Bustenay Oded, *Mass Deportations and Deportees in the Neo-Assyrian Empire* (Wiesbaden: Reichert, 1979). See also K. Lawson Younger, "The Deportation of the Israelites," *JBL* 117 (1998): 201–227.

42. *ANET*, 284.

43. On whether Jotham reigned twenty years or sixteen (as per v. 33), see the "Commentary" on v. 33.

44. The versions all read "he did not remove." MT's indef. 3rd pl. (סָרוּ, *sārû*) yields the virtual passive.

the matters pertaining to Jotham and all[45] that he did, are they not written in the chronicles of the kings of Judah? **37** In those days Yahweh began to send Rezin, king of Damascus, and Pekah, son of Remaliah, against Judah. **38** Jotham slept with his fathers and he was buried with his fathers in the city of David and Ahaz, his son, ruled in his place.

Textual Notes

34a. עֻזִּיָּהוּ: Gk. "Azariah"; Vulg. and Syr. with MT.

35a. סָרוּ: The versions all read "he did not remove."

36a. אֲשֶׁר: All the versions add "and all."

Commentary

Having brought Israel almost to the brink of destruction, the narrator finds it time to circle back and pick up the Judean thread in the skein. Before he takes Israel on the final plunge, he needs to cover the reigns of Jotham and his son Ahaz (16:1–20) who were contemporary with what had taken place and would take place in Israel. Like his father Azariah, Jotham receives very short shrift. But this is in sharp contrast to Ahaz. If I am correct in thinking that the editor has not wanted anything to interfere with the telling of the story of Israel's downfall, what is happening here? I think it is this: neither Azariah nor Jotham particularly participated in what was taking place in Israel, so they are passed over fairly quickly. On the other hand, Ahaz most assuredly did participate; frantically trying to avoid the fate of first Syria, and then Israel. Ahaz refused to cooperate with Syria and Israel, and threw himself *not* into the arms of Yahweh, as Isaiah begged him to do (Isa 7:4–9), but into the arms of Assyria, his ultimate enemy. Thus, prior to the telling of Israel's last act, the editor tells in some detail how Judah began to go down the very same road to destruction that Israel had taken.

32–35 Here we encounter the chronological difficulties mentioned above. In v. 30 we were told that Hoshea came to the throne in Jotham's twentieth year, yet here, in v. 33 it is said that Jotham only reigned sixteen years. Furthermore, v. 32 tells us that Jotham became king in Pekah's second year. This matter is more easily solved. If Pekah began his sole rule in the last year of Azariah's life (15:27, see the "Commentary" there) and Jotham began his sole rule (see the "Commentary" on 15:1–2) the next year, after Azariah's death, that would be during Pekah's second year.

But what about the discrepancy between sixteen and twenty? Here the text gives us few clues, except the one found in v. 37. There it is said that Pekah and Rezin began to come against Judah during Jotham's reign, while 16:5 (and Isaiah 7:1–2) dates this incursion during the reign of Ahaz. Perhaps, then,

45. MT lacks "and all," but all the versions include it.

Jotham, still alive, was virtually removed from office during his sixteenth year, and his son Ahaz was made acting head during the last four years of his father's life. In fact, the Syro-Ephraimite threat may have been the event that gave rise to this extraordinary action. While it has to be said that the evidence for this solution is very thin, it must also be said that if it is allowed, it helps to solve yet further chronological difficulties that will be addressed below.

Jotham's coregency with his father would have begun in 750 BC and his sole reign eleven years later in 739 BC. Then Ahaz would have been forced upon him in 735 BC, so that Jotham would only have ruled alone for four or five years. Nevertheless, the sixteen years between 750 and 735 were years of relative peace and prosperity for Judah, during which Jotham ruled with Yahweh's favor. He receives the standard accolade for a good king at this time with the single exception for all good kings prior to Hezekiah, that he did not centralize the worship of Yahweh in Jerusalem. It is interesting that the note about his repairing "the upper gate of the temple"[46] (בָּנָה אֶת־שַׁעַר בֵּית־יהוה הָעֶלְיוֹן, *bānâ ʾeṯ-šaʿar bêṯ-yhwh hāʿelyôn*), the only specific act of his that is mentioned, is appended immediately following the statement about "the high places" (בָּמוֹת, *bāmôṯ*). Perhaps this is intended to assure us of the sincerity of his worship of Yahweh. Given the fact that Zadok (v. 33) is a common priestly name (1 Kgs 1:8; 2 Chr 6:12, 53), it may be that Jotham's grandfather was a priest. If so, that might further explain the king's solicitude for the temple. In any case, the point is in stark contrast to the four repetitions in the previous verses (vv. 9, 18, 24, 28) that the northern kings had perpetuated the idolatrous worship begun by Jeroboam, son of Nebat. When this one act is compared to the extensive list of his accomplishments in 2 Chronicles 27, it stands out even more. The editor has one thing in mind, contrasting Jotham in the briefest way with the sorry story of sin and intrigue that he has just narrated.

37 As mentioned above, this verse, both in its location and its content may point to a coregency (of sorts) with Jotham's son, Ahaz. The location between the standard announcement of the source of further information (v. 36) and the death notice (v.38) is strange. Typically, these go together (e.g., 14:28–29; 15:6–7; 21–22). If some other information intervenes, as in the case of Amaziah (cf. 14:19–20), it is because an important point is being made about the nature of his death. Here, I suggest that the Syro-Ephraimite incursion came before Jotham died, but after any independent actions of Jotham had been completed and he was effectively shunted aside.

---

46. See Jer 20:2, and Ezek 9:2. These refs. indicate that this upper gate faced north (toward the territory of Benjamin). It is tempting to think that these repairs were necessitated by the damage done by Jehoash (14:13–14). However, this would mean that the gate was in disrepair for more than thirty years, including during the reign of Azariah, an unlikely scenario.

Here, for only the second time in this chapter Yahweh is said to be the cause of some event in history. (The first being Azariah's skin disease, v. 5.) He is conspicuously absent in the conspiracies of the Israelites and the movements of the Assyrians (the latter in sharp contrast to, say, Isaiah). How should we explain this? I suggest that we are intended to think that with the failure of Jeroboam II, God's gracious instrument of deliverance, the last effective king of Jehu's descendants, to bring Israel back to Yahweh, Yahweh had simply withdrawn his hand, and had let the processes of history take their course.[47] But the die was not yet cast for Judah. Perhaps the hand of divine discipline would yet prevent Judah from plunging down a similar road to destruction. Thus, it seems significant that it is said here that "Yahweh began" (הֵחֵל יהוה, *hēḥēl yhwh*). Israel is lost, and so Yahweh's attention is turned to Judah.[48]

Selected Bibliography

Clancy, F. "Jotham and Shallum: A Redactor's Choice." *JSOT* 26 (2012): 289–302.

Ahaz of Judah (16:1–20)

Translation

16:1 In the seventeenth year of Pekah, son of Remaliah, Ahaz, son of Jotham,
king of Judah, became king. **2** He was twenty years old when he became king
and ruled for sixteen years in Jerusalem. He did not do right in the sight of
Yahweh his God like David his father. **3** He walked in the ways of the kings
of Israel. He even made his son pass through the fire, like the abominations
of the nations whom Yahweh drove out before the sons of Israel. **4** He sacrificed and burnt incense on the high places and on the hilltops and under
ever green tree.

5 Then Rezin, king of Syria, and Pekah, son of Remaliah, king of Israel,
came up to fight against Jerusalem. They besieged Ahaz, but they were not
able to prevail. **6** At that time Rezin, king of Syria restored Elath to Syria;
he ejected the Judeans from Elath and the Edomites[49] came to Elath and
dwelt there unto this day. **7** Ahaz sent messengers to Tiglath-pileser, king of
Assyria saying, "I am your servant and your son. Go up and deliver me from
the hand of the king of Syria and from the hand of the king of Israel who
have risen against me." **8** Ahaz took the silver and gold that was found in the

47. The ministries of Amos and Hosea during this time show that Yahweh had not forgotten his people, but the absence of any mention of those ministries here only adds to the sense of inevitability that seems to be the point being made.

48. See Ehud Ben Zvi, "Tracing Prophetic Literature in the Book of King: the Case of II Kings 15:37," *ZAW* 102 (1990): 100–105 for the suggestion that this statement is an excerpt from a prophetic source.

49. Reading with *qere*; *ketiv* has "Arameans" (Syrians). See "Textual Note" on v. 6a.

house of Yahweh and in the treasuries of the king's house and sent a bribe
to the king of Assyria. **9** The king of Assyria listened to him and the king of
Assyria attacked Damascus, captured it, exiled it to Qir, and killed Rezin.
10 King Ahaz went to meet Tiglath-pileser, king of Assyria, at Damascus
and he saw the altar that was in Damascus. King Ahaz sent to Uriah the priest
an illustration of the altar along with all the specifications for its construction.
11 Uriah the priest built the altar according to all that King Ahaz sent from
Damascus. Thus, Uriah the priest did until King Ahaz came from Damascus.
12 The king came from Damascus and the king saw the altar and the king
approached the altar and mounted up on it. **13** He burned his burnt offering
and his grain offering and poured out his libation and splashed the blood of
his peace offering upon the altar. **14** But the bronze altar[50] which was before
Yahweh he moved from in front of the house, from between the altar and
the house of Yahweh and put it on the north side of the altar. **15** King Ahaz
commanded Uriah the priest saying, "On the great altar burn the morning
burnt offering and the evening grain offering, and the burnt offering of the
king and his grain offerings, and the burnt offering of all the people of the
land and their grain offerings and their libations, and all the blood of the
burnt offering and all the blood of sacrifice you shall splash on it. But the
bronze altar shall be for me to inquire by."[51] **16** Uriah the priest did just as
King Ahaz commanded him. **17** King Ahaz cut off the side panels from the
stands and removed the lavers from them. As for the Sea, he took it down
from upon the bronze oxen that were under it and put it on a stone pavement.
18 As for the covered walkway for the Sabbath which was built in the house
and the outer entrance of the king, he turned around the house of Yahweh
on account of the king of Assyria.
19 The rest of the matters pertaining to Ahaz which he did, are they
not written in the chronicles of the kings of Judah? **20** Ahaz slept with his
fathers and he was buried with his fathers in the city of David and Hezekiah,
his son, succeeded him.

Textual Notes

2a. עָשָׂה: Gk. adds "faithfully"; Vulg. and Syr. with MT.

3a. מַלְכֵי יִשְׂרָאֵל: Gk. reads "Jeroboam, son of Nebat, king"; Vulg. and Syr. with MT.

3b. כְּתֹעֲבוֹת: Vulg. "idols"; Syr. "custom"; Gk. with MT.

---

50. Note that the material from which the object is made (הַנְּחֹשֶׁת, *hannᵊḥōšeṯ*) is placed in apposition to the main noun (הַמִּזְבֵּחַ, *hammizbaḥ*). So also 16:17. See *IBHS* (§12.3c).

51. Gk. "for me in the morning"; Vulg. "prepared for my wish"; Syr. "for me for my inquiry."

5a–a. וַיָּצֻרוּ עַל־אָחָז: Syr. lacks; Gk. and Vulg. with MT.

6a. K וַאֲרַמִּים or וַאֲרֹמִים: "Arameans"; Q (ואדמים) "Edomites"; Gk. and Vulg. with Q; Syr. with K. *CTAT* (406) suggests that Q is probable.

7a. הַקּוֹמִים: Unusual form for ptcp. of middle weak vb. (see GKC §72*p*).

8a. וּבְאֹצְרוֹת: Gk. transposes "treasuries" before "house of Yahweh"; Vulg. and Syr. with MT.

8b. אַשּׁוּר: Gk. lacks; Vulg. and Syr. with MT.

9a–a. מֶלֶךְ אַשּׁוּר: Vulg. "he"; Gk. and Syr. with MT.

9b–b. וַיַּגְלֶהָ קִירָה: Gk. "he exiled it"; Vulg. "he carried its people to Cyrenica"; Syr. "he carried its people to Qir." MT best explains the others.

11a–12a. כֵּן עָשָׂה ... וַיָּבֹא הַמֶּלֶךְ מִדַּמֶּשֶׂק: Gk. lacks; Vulg. and Syr. with MT. Gk. omission the result of homoioteleuton.

12b–b. וַיִּקְרַב הַמֶּלֶךְ עַל־הַמִּזְבֵּחַ: Gk. lacks; Vulg. "he worshipped at it"; Syr. with MT. Gk. homoioteleuton.

13a. וַיַּסֵּךְ: Gk. lacks; Vulg. and Syr. with MT. Vulg. begins v. 13 here.

14a–a. מִבֵּין הַמִּזְבֵּחַ וּמִבֵּין: Gk. "from the one between the altar and from the one between"; Vulg. "and the place of the altar and the place of"; Syr. with MT. MT is the harder reading.

15a–a. יִהְיֶה־לִּי לְבַקֵּר: Gk. "shall be for me in the morning"; Vulg. "shall be prepared for my pleasure"; Syr. "shall be mine for my inquiry." See the "Commentary" below.

18a–a. וְאֶת־מֵיסַךְ הַשַּׁבָּת אֲשֶׁר־בָּנוּ: Gk. "He built the foundation of the seat"; Vulg. "The *musach* for the Sabbath which he had built"; Syr. with MT. Gk. probably reads מיסד for MT מיסך. Vulg. supports Q מוּסַךְ.

18b. מִפְּנֵי: Syr. "for fear of"; Gk. and Vulg. with MT.

19a–a. עָשָׂה הֲלֹא־הֵם כְּתוּבִים: Syr. (with Gk.[L]) "and all that he did, behold, they are"; Gk. and Vulg. with MT.

20a. עִם־אֲבֹתָיו: Gk. lacks; Vulg. "with them"; Syr. with MT.

Commentary

Commentators vary widely in their estimate of Ahaz of Judah's character. Brueggemann (463) has no hesitation in labeling him the second most wicked king of Judah after his grandson Manasseh. Fritz (340–41), on the other hand, thinks that Ahaz was slandered by later Deuteronomistic theologians.

Between these two poles almost every opinion can be found, including that of Wiseman (260), that he was perhaps more weak than wicked, or Sweeney (379–81) that the text glosses over the hard political realities that Ahaz faced. However, if we take the text at face value, there seems little doubt that Ahaz is seen as the Judean king who started Judah down the same road that was just about to bring the kingdom of Israel to an end. In part this is seen when we compare the amount of attention given to his reign with that given to his father, Jotham. Jotham, not contributing materially to the decline of Judah, receives just eight verses (15:32–38), whereas Ahaz, who ruled for sixteen years, just as his father did, receives twenty verses. The reason for this discrepancy is very clear. Ahaz *did* contribute materially to the decline of Judah that was to lead to the same result for Judah that Israel had now come to.

It is certainly true that Ahaz faced a very serious political crisis. If we understand that he was coregent with his father Jotham between 735 and 730 BC (see the "Excursus on Chronology 739–696 BC"), then he was on the throne when Tiglath-pileser III was renewing his thrust to the west. By 738 BC the Assyrian had established himself on the outskirts of Damascus. Then for four years events elsewhere occupied his attention. But by 734 BC he was ready to renew his drive toward the ultimate goal: Egypt. In that year he forced his way down the Mediterranean coast all the way to Gaza. In 733 BC he swept through northern Galilee and the Transjordan (15:29). Finally, in 732 BC he took Damascus itself (16:9). Early in this period (probably 735 BC) Pekah of Israel and Rezin of Syria attacked Judah (15:37; 16:5). The reason for this attack is not specified in the text, but most commentators (e.g., Cogan and Tadmor, 190–91; Sweeney, 379) agree that the Syro-Ephraimite coalition had probably called for Judah to join them and others in an attempt to block the Assyrian advance that they saw coming, and that Ahaz had refused. After Ahaz's refusal, the coalition was now trying to force the issue by attacking Jerusalem. Clearly, Ahaz had some hard decisions to make; he was caught between the anvil of Assyria and the hammer of Syria-Israel. What could he do? What he could do was the one thing that the text makes clear he would not do: trust Yahweh (see Isa 7:2–17). Is this weakness or wickedness? As far as the text is concerned, it is a weakness borne out of wickedness. Because Ahaz had fostered a paganized Yahwism, just as the kings of the north had done (16:3–4), he had lost the capacity for the kind of daring faith that was called for in this crisis.

The discussion of Ahaz falls into three obvious parts. First, there is the opening regnal summary, verses 1–4. Third, there is the closing summary, verses 19–20. Between these is the two-part discussion of Ahaz's response to the political situation during his reign (vv. 5–9), and the fallout from that response as regards the temple (vv. 10–18).

1–4 On the surface, the pattern of this opening regnal summary largely follows the pattern of all that we have seen so far: a synchronism, the total years of reign, the nature of the reign from Yahweh's point of view and in relation to the king's ancestors, and a comment about the high places. However, after the opening names and dates, the content of these segments is frankly shocking: Ahaz "did not do right in the sight of Yahweh" (וְלֹא־עָשָׂה הַיָּשָׁר בְּעֵינֵי יהוה, *wᵉlō ʾ- ʿāśâ hayyāšār bᵊ ʿênê yhwh*); he did not "walk in the way of David his father," but rather in "the way of the kings of Israel," and not only that, but "like the abominations of the nations" (כְּתֹעֲבוֹת הַגּוֹיִם, *kᵉt̲ō ʿăb̲ôt̲ haggôyim*). Furthermore, whereas up to this point it was the people who worshipped on "the high places," now it was the king himself who did so, and furthermore, he did it everywhere, "on the hilltops and under every green tree" (וְעַל־הַגְּבָעוֹת וְתַחַת כָּל־עֵץ רַעֲנָן, *wᵊ ʿal-haggᵊb̲ā ʿôt̲ wᵉt̲aḥat̲ kol- ʿēṣ ra ʿănān*).[52] To this point, the only kings of Judah who have received this kind of condemnation have been Jehoram (8:16–24) and Ahaziah (8:25–29), and even they have not been so thoroughly excoriated. Clearly, the editors see this reign as some kind of a turning-point in the history of Judah. Furthermore, it is clear that we are intended to read the rest of this account in the light of this introduction.

1 Ahaz is short for Jehoahaz, a name he shared with his northern counterpart from seventy-five years earlier (13:1–8) and with his descendant a century later (23:31–34). We know this on the basis of one of Tiglath-pileser's inscriptions where he claims to have received tribute from Jehoahaz (*Ia-u-ḫa-zi*) of Judah.[53] Unfortunately, this inscription is not dated so we cannot place the time when this tribute was given.

The "seventeenth year of Pekah" would be 735 BC, and this supports the supposition that Ahaz was coregent (or even acting king) with his father Jotham, who was nominally king until his death in 731 or 730 BC (see above on 15:32–35, and the "Excursus on Chronology [739–696 BC]").

2 There are two striking features about this verse. First, the only other Judean king whose mother is not named is Jehoram (8:17). It is tempting to wonder if it was their mothers who influenced their sons in the direction of apostasy and are thus left unnamed. That is only speculation, but the remarkable omissions beg for some rationale. The second striking feature of this verse is that Ahaz is compared negatively not merely to Jotham, his immediate father, but rather to David, his ultimate father. It is said of Solomon and Abijah (1 Kgs 11:4; 15:3) that their hearts were not wholly for Yahweh as David's was, and Amaziah is said to have "done right" but not on the same scale as David (2 Kgs 14:3), but of Ahaz it is simply said that "he did not do right in the sight of Yahweh like David his father" (וְלֹא־עָשָׂה הַיָּשָׁר בְּעֵינֵי יהוה אֱלֹהָיו כְּדָוִד אָבִיו, *wᵉlō ʾ- ʿāśâ hayyāšār bᵊ ʿênê yhw ʾĕlōhāyw kᵉd̲āwid̲ ʾāb̲îw*). If we

52. This seems to be a convention to speak of times when idolatrous worship had become ubiquitous. See Deut 12:2; 1 Kgs 14:23; 2 Kgs 17:10, Jer 2:20; 3:6; 17:12. See Susan Ackerman, *Under Every Green Tree,* HSM (Atlanta: Scholars Press, 1992).

53. *ANET,* 282.

think of the other three kings as being on something of a downward slide in regard to David, this is the nadir.

3 Whereas Jehoram at least had an excuse for following the northern kings in paganizing the worship of Yahweh, in that he had been married into their family (8:18), Ahaz had no such excuse. He simply chose to go that way. But he went even farther: "he even made his son pass through the fire," in the manner that the Canaanites had done with their gods (תֹּעֲבוֹת, *tōʿăḇôṯ*; "abominations"). So the narrator is saying that Ahaz had gone a step farther back into evil than even the kings of the northern kingdom had gone: he had not merely made Yahweh into an idol who could be manipulated to provide for our needs; he had reverted to the despicable use of God's best gifts for that manipulation.[54] Gray (632), citing Eissfeldt, suggests that Ahaz's action might have been an act of desperation, like that of the Moabite king, Mesha, in an effort to avoid defeat (see 2 Kgs 3:27). The reference to the driving out of the Canaanites is ominous. If those people had been driven out of the land for such practices, what was to prevent that same thing from happening to Judah?

5–6 Little is known of Rezin beyond what is said here, in Isaiah, and in the fragmentary inscriptions of Tiglath-pileser. He first appears paying tribute to the Assyrian emperor in 738 BC. He was evidently a strong ruler in that he was able to maintain some degree of independence from the Assyrians until his final defeat in 732 BC. The statement (v. 6) that he was able to wrest the port of Elath on the Gulf of Elath on the Red Sea from Judah's control is another testimony to that strength. However, since Elath is more than 140 miles from Damascus, the claim has seemed unlikely to some, and they have proposed that all the references to Aram (Syria) be emended to Edom.[55] On the surface this is very plausible since Elath is in the territory of Edom, and since the *qere* reading for the final term is "Edomites" (see the "Translation Note" on v.6a). However, not only would the national name have to be changed, but so also Rezin would have to be excised. Then, if we are talking

54. There is continuing discussion about how widespread this practice was. The many child burials at Carthage, a Phoenician colony, have been used to substantiate the practice among the Phoenicians, who were Canaanites, but the meaning of that evidence is still debated. The Bible relates the practice to the worship of Baal, also called Molech, which may be a pejorative spelling of the word for "king." Thus, this might have been a cult of the so-called king of the gods. For the Biblical prohibitions and condemnations, see Deut 18:10; Jer 7:31; 19:5; 32:35; Ezek 23:37, 39. See also 2 Kgs 21:6; 23:10.

55. In Heb. the consonants *d* and *r* are very similar. See NRSV; but see John H. Hayes, "Historical Reconstruction, Textual Emendation, and Biblical Translation: Some Examples from the RSV," *PRSt* 14 (1987) 7–8 for an argument against the emendation.

about activities of the king of Edom, it becomes difficult to understand why v. 6 is interposed between vv. 5 and 7. When it is further noted that none of the versions support the emendations, it seems best to retain the MT and to believe that in the attack of Rezin and Pekah on Judah, the Syrian king took the opportunity to secure the entire length of the King's Highway, and to deprive Judah of the lucrative asset of Elath at the southern end of that highway. Losing the asset would make Ahaz's condition that much more precarious. If the *qere* reading is correct, it is very likely that after Rezin had once gotten Elath away from Judah, he then would have permitted the Edomites to settle there as his allies. It is unlikely that, given the Assyrian threat on his northern border, Rezin would have weakened his forces by leaving an occupying force there. With Elath in their hands, the Edomites may well have been emboldened to carry out the attack that 2 Chr 28:17 reports.[56]

The statement in v. 5 that the Syria-Israelite attack failed is probably in reference to the final goal of capturing Jerusalem and, as Isaiah tells us, unseating Ahaz. 2 Chr 28:5–8 reports that the Judean army had suffered a devastating defeat, but such a defeat still would not guarantee the success of a siege, especially if the city was well-defended, as Jerusalem was. Nevertheless, such a defeat could well explain why "the hearts of Ahaz and his people were shaken as the trees of the forest are shaken by the wind" (Isa 7:2). If the siege were to succeed, the Davidic dynasty would be brought to an end with the Syria-Israelite nominee Tabeel put on the throne (Isa 7:5).

7–9 We do not know the precise timing and circumstances of Ahaz's appeal to Tiglath-pileser. Sweeney (380) thinks that Ahaz would have already become an Assyrian vassal, and that the appeal would have been for the help which an overlord typically promised to a vassal. However, it does not seem likely that someone who was already a vassal (and had already therefore paid tribute) would need to add an additional payment to get his overlord to fulfill the terms of their covenant.[57] It is rather an indication of Ahaz's desperation that without any prior commitment he throws himself at the feet of his worst enemy, paying him a great deal of money (which the text bluntly calls a "bribe" [שֹׁחַד, *šōḥad*])[58] to do what the Assyrian no doubt was already planning to do. The terrible irony is that none of it was necessary. As Isaiah tried to get his king to realize, Yahweh is the Lord of history, and within a

---

56. Cogan and Tadmor note that the three occurrences of "to this day" (8:22; 14:7; 16:6) are all with reference to Edom and they believe that this dates these comments to the time of Josiah (193–94).

57. However, see Saggs, *Greatness*, 109.

58. For the negative connotations of the term (שֹׁחַד, *šōḥad*), see Exod 23:8; Deut 10:17; 16:19; 27:25; Prov 17:23; Isa 5:23. The only other occ. in these books is in the similar instance in which Asa sent a "bribe" to Ben-hadad to attack Baasha (1 Kgs 15:19). The use of the term in Asa's "buying" an alliance with Ben-hadad suggests that a similar thing was taking place here.

very short time, three years at a maximum, the two kings Ahaz was so terrified of would be gone (Isa 7:4–7; 8:4). This is, of course, precisely what happened. In the series of devastating raids during the years 734–732 BC Tiglath-pileser completely changed the political face of the northern part of the Levant. He subjugated all of Syria,[59] incorporating it into the provincial structure of the empire, reduced Israel to barely more than a "county" surrounding Samaria and brought much of the southeastern coast of the Mediterranean under his control. So, in the end, as Isaiah had foretold, Ahaz's looting of the temple and of the palace "treasuries" (אֹצְרוֹת, *ʾōṣᵊrôṯ*) was unnecessary and, in fact, only accelerated the devastation of Judah that was sure to follow. Three mice had been fighting and one of them had hired the cat.[60]

10–18 As there is much disagreement about Ahaz's character, so there is much disagreement about the significance of the lengthy description in these verses. Was Ahaz importing Assyrian religion into the temple in Jerusalem? Or was Ahaz merely "updating" the temple in line with new fashions? Was Ahaz altering Yahwistic religion? Or was he simply furthering the practices of his predecessors? All these opinions, and others besides have been expressed.[61]

The starting point for our understanding of what was happening here has to be vv. 1–4. There the narrator has clearly signaled what he thinks of Ahaz's commitments to Yahweh, and by including vv. 10–18 under that rubric, he is clearly intending that we, the readers should understand what is said here in that light. If it should be pointed out, as Hobbs (216) does, that the narrator does not pass judgment on the behaviors described here, it should also be pointed out that neither does the narrator of the book of Judges pass judgement on most of the behaviors narrated there. I suggest that in both cases the narrators want to leave it to the readers to draw the appropriate conclusions. Here, whatever Ahaz was doing, he was not motivated by anything approaching orthodox Yahwism. Whatever was motivating him, it was not an innocent desire to promote more contemporary worship of Yahweh. The second factor here is the length of this chapter. Clearly, the reason for the length of this chapter on Ahaz is because of Ahaz's significance in setting Judah on the path of a paganized Yahwism, a path that

---

59. The enigmatic statement וַיַּגְלֶהָ קִירָה, *wayyaḡlehā qîrâ* "he exiled (it) to Qir" reflects another practice that was the result of the Tiglath-pileser's organizational genius. Although exile had been practiced occasionally by the Assyrians and others for many years, it was under Tiglath-pileser that it became a regular policy that was carried out in careful detail, especially involving movements both out of and into captured territories. The location of Qir is uncertain. Amos (9:7) refers to it as the homeland of the Arameans (Syrians), while Isa 22:6 refers to it in parallel with Elam.

60. For further discussion, see Hayim Tadmor and Mordechai Cogan, "Ahaz and Tiglath-Pilezer," *Bib* 60 (1979): 491–508.

61. For a variety of points of view on the passage see the "Selected Bibliography" below.

despite the best efforts of Hezekiah and Josiah, Judah would never fully forsake. Thus, just as Jeroboam, seeking to preserve his kingdom made a "few, small" changes in Israel's religion (1 Kgs 12:28–33), so Ahaz is depicted here as making "small" changes, changes which, like those in Israel two centuries earlier, had no divine warrant whatsoever.[62] Finally, the references to Tiglath-pileser at the beginning (v. 10) and at the end (v. 18) of the segment must be taken into account.

As Hobbs (216) points out, the deliberate and repetitive tone point to some official document that the narrator has abstracted for his specific purpose in this context. The repeated references to "the king" and "King Ahaz" makes Ahaz's responsibility in all this very clear.

10 Ahaz's journey to Damascus was probably to confirm the vassal status into which he had pledged himself. It cannot be incidental that it was in that context that he got the idea for a grand new altar. This is not to say that such a thing was imposed upon him as part of the requirements for being an Assyrian vassal. This does not seem to have been a characteristic Assyrian practice.[63] On the other hand, it is difficult to believe that Ahaz would have been impressed by a merely Syrian altar when Damascus, the Syrian capital, had just fallen to the Assyrians. Cogan and Tadmor (193) seem to be most nearly correct when they see this as the first act in acculturation to an empire which was increasingly fascinated with all things Aramean. The Assyrians would adopt the Aramaic language as the imperial lingua franca, and they would incorporate other features of Aramean life as well. Thus, it may well be that Ahaz was attracted to that style of altar precisely because he perceived that Tiglath-pileser was as well.

In any case, Ahaz was clearly eager to get this innovation into place immediately. He could not wait for work to begin on it only after he arrived back from Damascus. (His return could well be delayed indefinitely by the whims of his new master.) Clearly, he wanted it ready for use as soon as he returned. Brueggemann (469) describes these as the actions of an enthusiastic, new convert. So he sent some sort of an "illustration" (דְּמוּת, *dᵊmûṯ*)[64] of the altar as well as fully detailed "specifications" (תַּבְנִית, *taḇnîṯ*, "pattern") of it. Unlike the patterns for the tabernacle given by Yahweh (Exod 25:9), this pattern came from the altar of a foreign god.

62. For a similar point of view regarding the editor's intent, see Klaus A. D. Smelik, "The New Altar of King Ahaz (2 Kings 16): Deuteronomic Re-interpretation of a Cult Reform" in *Deuteronomy and Deuteronomic Literature: Festschrift C. H. W. Brekelmans,* ed. Marc Vervenne and Johan Lust, BETL 133 (Louvain: Leuven University Press, 1997), 263–78.

63. See esp., Mordecai Cogan, *Imperial Religion: Assyria, Judah, and Israel in the Eighth and Seventh Centuries BC,* SBLMS 19 (Missoula: Scholars Press, 1974).

64. "model," the translation that appears in several Eng. versions, is somewhat anachronistic.

11 Uriah the priest is probably the same Uriah whom Isaiah recruited to be a witness for the naming of his son (Isa 8:2). That he is there described as being reliable certainly conforms to the description given of him here and in the following verses. He could be depended on to do as he was told. Whether this also implies faithfulness to Yahweh is left as an open question. That he registers no protest, or even question, to the royal prerogative to treat the temple as the king wished suggests that he saw his first loyalty as being to the king.

12–13 The succession of verbs here with Ahaz as the subject is striking. It tends to confirm Brueggemann's judgment. The impression is that as soon as the king got back, he rushed to see his new altar, and immediately went to it and "the king mounted up on the altar" (וַיִּקְרַב הַמֶּלֶךְ עַל־הַמִּזְבֵּחַ, *wayyiqraḇ hammeleḵ ʿal-hammizbēḥ*) and made *his* offerings. That is, he took over the role of priest. Several commentators point out that this is nothing other than what David (2 Sam 6:17–18) and Solomon (1 Kgs 8:63) did. But in fact, it is not what they did. They did not go up onto the altar. To be sure they "offered sacrifices" but there is no indication that they actually officiated in the offering. Here, the statement that Ahaz mounted the altar and offered his offerings points very clearly in that direction. This is very reminiscent of Jeroboam I whom the text says was "standing upon the altar to offer sacrifices" (עֹמֵד עַל־הַמִּזְבֵּחַ לְהַקְטִיר, *ʿōmēḏ ʿal-hammizbēaḥ lᵉhaqṭîr*) when the man of God denounced him (1 Kgs 13:1). To be sure, there is no denunciation from Uriah the priest here, as there had been from the priests when Uzziah attempted to offer incense in the temple (2 Chr 26:16). In addition, it might be asked why, if the scenario I have described is correct, Yahweh did not take action, as he did with Uzziah. I suggest that Ahaz was a very different man than Uzziah and would have removed any priest who opposed him, and who was well beyond any corrective action from Yahweh. In any case, there is no reference to serving Yahweh, or seeking his guidance throughout the entire segment.

14–16 In these three verses the key is to be found in the contrast between Ahaz's new "great altar" (הַמִּזְבֵּחַ הַגָּדוֹל, *hammizbēaḥ haggāḏôl*) and the "bronze altar which was before Yahweh" (הַמִּזְבַּח הַנְּחֹשֶׁת אֲשֶׁר לִפְנֵי יהוה, *hammizbaḥ hannᵊḥōšeṯ ʾăšer lip̄nê yhwh*). No longer was Solomon's bronze altar in its prominent place between the gate and the porch. Ahaz's Aramaean altar was there now, with the bronze altar moved off to the north side of it, out of the line of sight. To be sure, all the orthodox offerings: "the morning burnt offering and the evening grain offering," both for people and king, were continued, along with "their libations" and "the splashed blood of the burnt offerings and sacrifices"—but to what purpose?[65] That altar whose antecedents went

65. For the daily sacrifices, see Exod 29:38–42 and Num 28:2–8. In these treatments both animals and grain are to be offered in the morning and the evening. Two classic studies of biblical sacrifices are: Roland de Vaux, *Studies in Old Testament Sacrifices*

back to Sinai as a place where the redeeming grace of God was made available to his people (Exod 27:1–8; Lev 1:1-17) was now Ahaz's personal possession, to be used for his purposes alone. Exactly what those purposes were is not clear. The verb in v.15, בָּקַר (*bāqar*) (which only occurs seven times in the OT) is used in Lev 13:36 when a priest "examines" a person who had had a skin disease, and in Lev 27:33 in the prohibition of "distinguishing" between good and bad animals when the tithe animal is selected. So, it is to be used for the king's selection or examination? As the "Translation Note" above indicates, the versions do not agree on the translation. Most English versions follow the Syriac "to inquire by," that is, for divination, as we do here. But in any case, the altar that was "before Yahweh" representing the people's redemption and their communion with their covenant Lord is now reserved for the king's use. A small change? Yes, but a real change.

17 The text does not supply a reason for the actions described in this verse, but many commentators (e.g., Brueggemann, 470; Wiseman, 262) believe that it was to supply bronze for the annual tribute to Tiglath-pileser (cf. 2 Chr 28:21). These bronze elements might have been thought the most expendable and least important. Fritz (345) says that it is the removal of figurative decorations, but it is hard to see why that would be considered necessary unless it was thought that they were too Phoenician, and thus offensive to Mesopotamian eyes.

18 As mentioned above on v. 10, the fact that this collection of things that Ahaz did in the temple begins and ends with reference to Tiglath-pileser does not seem coincidental. All that "King Ahaz" did was done with an eye on the man who knew himself to be the real "King." The difficulty for us is that we do not always know how the vassal relationship caused these behaviors. So here, while the reason for these changes in the temple structure is "on account of the king of Assyria" (מִפְּנֵי מֶלֶךְ אַשּׁוּר, *mippᵉnê meleḵ ʾaššûr*), no specific explanation is offered. Are we to think that the Assyrian emperor sent emissaries to Jerusalem and that they demanded the changes? Or was it rather that it was feared that these structures might offend the overlord if he came to know of them, and that the changes were proactive? Either seems possible. The phrase "the outer entrance of the king" (וְאֶת־מְבוֹא הַמֶּלֶךְ הַחִיצוֹנָה, *wᵉʾeṯ-mᵉḇôʾ hammeleḵ haḥîṣônâ*) is thought to provide a clue. Perhaps these structural features of the temple seemed to give special privilege to the Davidic king and would thus arouse the anger of the Assyrian monarch. So, the מֵיסַךְ, *mêsaḵ* ("covered way"?) of the Sabbath (הַשַּׁבָּת, *haššabbāṯ*) may have been a special procession way leading to a private entrance to the temple. Jeremiah 17:19 may refer to this when it speaks of a gate "through which the

(Cardiff: University of Wales, 1964), esp. 27–90, and Rolf Rendtorff, *Studien zur Geschichte des Opfers im Alten Israel,* WMANT 24 (Vluyn: Neukirchener, 1967), esp. 45–50.

kings of Judah go in and out." See also 2 Kgs 11:5–7 and the "Commentary" there. Verhaug has argued that Ps 24:7–10 might have been used in connection with such a procession.[66]

19–20 After the full and repetitive comments preceding, this terse death notice is like a closing door.[67] With brisk finality the story is brought to its close. What is done is done, with a long shadow extending out over the future.

Biblical Theology Comments

While issues of faith and trust are in the background in this account, they are brought to the foreground in the corresponding report in Isaiah chapters seven through nine. For Ahaz the overriding reality was the threat of a devastating siege by the combined forces of Israel and Syria with the certain prospect that if the siege was successful, he would be killed and the Davidic dynasty brought to an end. That being so, a flight into the arms of Assyria seemed a wise course of action. If we are correct in thinking that the date of these events was 735 BC, the great danger from Assyria was not yet apparent. Tiglath-pileser had not been active in the area since 738 and Ahaz and others may well have thought that he had reached as far west as he would. With that short-sightedness, he could only see the "conspiracy" (קֶשֶׁר, *qešer*) (Isa 8:12) of Syria and Israel ranged against him.

Isaiah called on Ahaz to look to the true reality: Yahweh, the Holy One of Israel, the Lord of Heaven's Armies, the true Lord of History. If Ahaz would rest securely in Yahweh, then Yahweh would make him truly secure (Isa 7:9, expressed through a wordplay on אָמַן, *ʾāman* "to be firm"). To Ahaz, such advice must have seemed pure folly. What could Yahweh do? But Ahaz could not see the future. He could not see how quickly Assyria would become the major threat and how quickly Pekah and Rezin would be rushing back home to shore up their own crumbling fortunes. When Isaiah challenged him to ask Yahweh for some sign that what he was saying about Assyria, Syria, and Israel was true (7:11), Ahaz fled from the challenge into a false piety. He would not think of putting Yahweh to the test in such a way (7:12). This corresponds well with the Ahaz depicted here in 2 Kings: a man with a gift for mixing apparent orthodoxy in Jerusalem with paganism in the countryside.

---

66. Jorn Verhaug, "Psalm 24:7-10 as a Cult Liturgy and 2 Kings 16:18" in *"My Spirit at Rest in the North Country" (Zechariah 6.8): Collected Communications to the Xxth Congress of the International Organization for the Study of the Old Testament, Helsinki, 2010* (Frankfort am Main: Peter Lang, 2011) 165–72. See also Martin Jan Mulder, "Was war die am Tempel Gebaute 'Sabbathalle' in 2 Koen 16:18?" in *Von Kanaan bis Kerala*, ed W. C. Delsman (Vluyn: Neukirchener Press, 1982) 161–72.

67. 2 Chr 28:27 says that Ahaz was not buried with the kings of Judah (Israel), but there is no indication of that here.

Thus, Ahaz chose to trust his worst enemy, Assyria, before he would trust the Holy One of Israel. He chose apparent reality over true reality. The result, as Isaiah predicted, was that within thirty years, Assyria was knocking on Jerusalem's gates, with every prospect of Judah's disappearing into the Assyrian empire, just as Israel had. But it was not to be. Someone had learned the lessons that are encompassed in Isaiah 7–35, lessons in which Yahweh, through his prophet, showed the folly of trusting humanity in place of Yahweh. That person was no less than Hezekiah, Ahaz's son. In the face of, not Syria or Israel, but Assyria herself, Hezekiah dared to trust Yahweh, and Judah was miraculously delivered and continued to exist as an entity in its own right for another 115 years. Yahweh can be trusted.

Application and Devotional Implications

Psalm 34 makes a powerful statement: "he delivered me from all my fears" (Ps 34:4 [MT 5]). How is such a thing possible? Could it have been possible for Ahaz? When we look deeper into the psalm, we see this statement, "Fear Yahweh, his holy people, for those who fear him lack nothing" (v. 9 [MT 10]). What is the psalmist saying? He is saying that those who fear Yahweh, that is, those who conduct their lives in the determination to please the awesome God of eternity at all costs, need fear nothing else. Whatever it is that they most truly need will be provided for them. In short, if we fear Yahweh, we need fear nothing else. This is what the apostle Paul meant when, having given a long list of very real calamities he said that we are more than conquerors (Rom 8:37). If we fear Yahweh, we need fear nothing else.

On the other hand, if we, like Ahaz, refuse to live in ways that recognize his awesome power, his lordship of history, and our responsibility to live lives that reflect Yahweh's life, in short, to fear him, we will become, like Ahaz, slave to every fear that comes our way. Like Ahaz, unable to trust Yahweh, we will be inclined to trust anything else that appears to be able to calm those fears, and in doing so will deliver ourselves over to yet greater calamities. For the truth is: like Assyria, whatever we trust in place of Yahweh will ultimately turn on us and destroy us. If we will not fear Yahweh, then we will become prey to fears of everything.

In Ahaz's case what seem to be small and insignificant changes in the temple furnishings and structure are indicators of much deeper issues. He was more concerned over the favor of Tiglath-pileser than he was the favor of Yahweh. It can be the same in our lives. An acquaintance who had been part of a small group of conservative Christian graduate students at a major university told me, "Whenever one of our number began to smoke a pipe, we knew his doctrine of Scripture was changing." Is there a necessary connection between pipe-smoking and one's doctrine of Scripture? Of course not. Can one smoke a pipe and have a high view of Scripture? Of course. But the point is still valid. If, because of one's view of Scripture, one has maintained a certain lifestyle, and then one changes the lifestyle, what is the reason? Surely, it may be because one's *interpretation* of Scripture has changed, in which case the change may be entirely justified. But it is also possible that the change is the result of a lessening of one's *reverence* for Scripture and, more importantly, for the God of Scripture. In this case, the small change is diagnostic of a far deeper, and more important, change. The love of God is being pushed aside by the love of what the apostles call "the world" (2 Tim 4:10; 1 John 2:15–17). That was what happened to Ahaz.

Selected Bibliography

Ackroyd, P. R. "The Biblical Interpretation of the Reigns of Ahaz and Hezekiah." Pages 247–59 in *In the Shelter of Elyon: Essays on Ancient Palestinian Life and Literature in Honor of G. W. Ahlstrom*. Edited by W. Boyd Barrick and John R. Spencer. Sheffield; JSOT Press, 1984.

Axskjöld, "C.-J. "Ataret från Damaskus: En Ideologisk Förståelse." *SEÅ* 67 (2002): 19–25.

Bustenay, O. "The Historical Background of the Syro-Ephraimite War Reconsidered." *CBQ* 34 (1972): 153–65.

Irvine, S. A. *Isaiah, Ahaz, and the Syro-Ephraimitic War*. SBLDS 123. Atlanta: SBL Press, 1992.

Na'aman, N. "Royal Inscriptions and the Histories of Joash and Ahaz, Kings of Judah." *VT* 48 (1998): 333–49.

Nelson, R. D. "The Altar of Ahaz: A Revisionist View." *HAR* 10 (1986): 267–76.

Smelik, K. A. D. "The Representation of King Ahaz in 2 Kings 16 and 2 Chronicles 28." Pages 143–85 in *Intertextuality in Ugarit and Israel: Papers Read at the Tenth Joint Meeting of the Society for Old Testament Study and Het Oudtestamentisch Werkgeselschap in Nederland en Belgie held at Oxford, 1997*. Edited by Johannes C. de Moor. Leiden: Brill, 1998.

Zwickel, W. "Die Kultreform des Ahas (2 Kön 16,10–18)." *SJOT* 7 (1993): 250–62.

The Fall of Samaria (17:1–41)

Introduction

This pivotal chapter is composed of four parts: the reign of Hosea concluding with the fall of Samaria (vv. 1–6); the narrator's comment on the reasons for that fall (vv. 7–23); data about the resettlement of Samaria (vv. 24–33); the narrator's comment on the spiritual conditions in Samaria after the resettlement (vv. 34–41). While there is general agreement on this division, there is no agreement as to the sources that may have been used in composing the materials. Some would still adhere to Martin Noth's hypothesis that the comments in vv. 7–23; 34–41 were the work of the Deuteronomist, writing during the exile (Gray, 645). Others would relate the comments to Josianic times (Sweeney, 391–92). Still others would see the chapter as a pastiche of literary pieces from a wide variety of sources, all put together during postexilic times.[1]

In any case, the chapter is of great importance as it closes the book on what has arguably been the central focus of the narrative since 1 Kings 12: the sad tale of the northern kingdom's demise. The northern kingdom began shakily until stabilized under Omri (1 Kgs 13–16), encountered the threat of institutionalized Baalism (1 Kgs 17–2 Kgs 8); recovered from that threat (2 Kgs 9–10), but failed in its fidelity to Yahweh (2 Kgs 11–16). Chapter 17:7–23 summarizes the story powerfully, recapping all the ways in which Israel had repeatedly broken its covenant with God, and ominously mentioning that Judah was not markedly different (v. 19). Verses 21–23 provide something of a summary of the summary, formally charging Jeroboam I as the one who sent Israel down this track.

The latter half of the chapter takes the story forward, showing that if anything, Samaria's spiritual condition became worse after other peoples were brought in to replace the exiled Israelite leaders. Whereas previously it was a paganized Yahwism that had been practiced, now the worship was a thorough admixture of Yahwism and the religions of the other peoples. The

1. On the structure of the chapter, see Burke O. Long, "Framing Repetition in Biblical Historiography," *JBL* 106 (1987): 385–99, and Pauline A. Viviano, "2 King 17: A Rhetorical and Form-Critical Analysis," *CBQ* 49 (1987); 548–59.

syncretism seems to put the narrator into a quandary. He says on the one hand that they did worship Yahweh (17: 32, 33, 41), and on the other that they did not (v. 34). The point is surely that their worship of Yahweh was so corrupted that it was not worship of him at all. In the light of the reference to children and children's children (v. 41) the repeated "to this day" (עַד הַיּוֹם הַזֶּה, *'aḏ hayyôm hazzeh*) (vv. 34, 41) probably points to a recension that was produced during Josianic times.

Outline

II. The Divided Monarchy 1 Kings 12:1–2 Kings 17:41
  D. The fall of Samaria 17:1–41
    1. Hoshea 17:1–6
    2. Reasons for the exile 17:7–23
    3. Samaria resettled 17:24–33
    4. A reflection on religious conditions in resettled Samaria 17:34–41

Hoshea (17:1–6)

Translation

17:1 In the twelfth year of Ahaz, king of Judah, Hoshea, son of Elah became king in Samaria and ruled over Israel nine years. **2** He did evil in the sight of Yahweh, but not like the kings of Israel who preceded him. **3** It was against him that Shalmaneser, king of Assyria, had come up. Hoshea had become his servant and paid him tribute, **4** but the king of Assyria found conspiracy in him in that he sent messengers to So, king of Egypt, and did not pay the annual tribute.[2] So the king of Assyria shut him up and bound him in prison. **5** The king of Assyria came up into all the land and attacked Samaria and besieged it for three years. **6** In Hoshea's ninth year[3] the king of Assyria captured Samaria and exiled Israel to Assyria, settling them in Halah, on the Habor, the river of Gozan, and in all the cities of the Medes.

Textual Notes

No significant variants.

Commentary

1–2 After picking up the threads of the story on the Judean side, the narrator goes back to the Israelite side that he left at 15:31. There is some narrative

---

2. The versions translate Heb. (כְּשָׁנָה בְשָׁנָה, *kᵉšānâ ḇᵉšānâ*) "according to a year in a year" variously. GKC (§118*u*) suggest "as in former years."

3. On the use of the ordinal with a const. (בִּשְׁנַת הַתְּשִׁיעִית, *bišnaṯ hattᵉšî'îṯ*), see GKC (§134*p*).

skill involved because the more slow-paced Judean reports interrupted the account of the precipitate decline of the north that had been narrated in 15:8–31. There the events of twenty years with five different kings and four different dynasties were recounted in rapid-fire succession, and we were prepared for the final dénouement. Instead, the narrator made us wait through the accounts of Jotham and Ahaz. Now comes the climax. We return to Hoshea, assassin of Pekah (15:30), vassal of Tiglath-pileser (*ANET*, 284), last of Israel's kings. He came to the throne in 732 BC, here called the twelfth year of Ahaz. That is not possible (see the "Excursus on Chronology [739–696 BC]"). Although there is no textual support for it, it still seems that Gray's (641n.a) recommendation to emend "twelfth" to "second" which would correspond correctly with a coregency between Jotham and Ahaz beginning in 735 BC, is a very feasible solution to the problem (always taking into account the matter of accession-year, and non-accession year datings).

The regnal summary is interesting for two reasons. First, we are told that Hoshea, though "evil" (הָרַע, *hāra'*), was not as evil as his predecessors, and second, the typical refrain concerning the sin of Jeroboam is missing. Lacking any explanation of these facts, we can only speculate on their significance. Brueggemann and others suggest that perhaps the narrator considers Hoshea's abortive attempt at independence a commendable thing. However, there is no indication that this was an expression of faith in Yahweh, so it seems unlikely. I suspect it is more likely that the intent is ironic. How far had Israel's sin, the sin of Jeroboam, gone? Far enough that small steps in the other direction were too little and too late.

3–6 While no one questions the essential accuracy of the facts given here, there is some question about their order, especially when coupled with the extensive, but somewhat fragmentary Assyrian records. This much is clear: Shalmaneser V succeeded his father Tiglath-pileser in 727 BC and reigned for five years until 722 BC. In his last year Samaria fell to him. He was succeeded by his brother (?) Sargon II, who seems to have been a usurper. Sargon reigned until 705 BC. He claims no less than eight different times to have captured Samaria (*ANET*, 284–5). The most recent reading of these data is that the city fell just at the time Shalmaneser was dying. The army withdrew to the homeland during the upheavals associated with Sargon's takeover, so that two years later in 720 BC, he had to come back and finish the task, including exiling the Israelite leadership to the Assyrian homeland.[4] The account here has condensed these two parts into one.

Another issue here is whether these verses should be read sequentially or not. If they are read sequentially the upshot is that Hoshea must have been called to Assyria and imprisoned there before Shalmaneser began to besiege the city (so Cogan and Tadmor, 198–201). But there is no record of this.

4. See K. Lawson Younger, Jr., "The Fall of Samaria in the Light of Recent Research," *CBQ* 61 (1999): 461–82 and the bibliography contained therein.

Thus, Hobbs (226), following Snaith, has made the attractive suggestion that vv. 5 and 6 should be read in parallel with vv. 3 and 4, and not in sequence. In short, they are describing the same events first as they apply to Hoshea, and second as they apply to the land and people. On this reading, Hoshea, having been an Assyrian vassal from the beginning of his reign, and having renewed his vows with Shalmaneser upon Tiglath-pileser's death (v. 3), had decided to break those vows, probably with the encouragement of one of the three reigning kings of Egypt[5] (a "conspiracy" [קֶשֶׁר, *qešer*] in the Assyrian king's eyes), shown especially by his refusing to pay the "annual tribute" (מִנְחָה, *minḥâ*).[6] As a result, the Assyrians mounted a siege that, among other things, resulted in Hoshea's capture, imprisonment, and disappearance from the stage of history (v. 4).

Verses 5 and 6 then describe the siege on a more expanded basis. It involved isolating Samaria by capturing "all the land" (בְּכָל־הָאָרֶץ, *bᵊḵol-hā ʾāreṣ*) around Samaria, and it required three years before the city which Omri and Ahab had built so well could be brought down. Then just at the moment of collapse, perhaps when the work of destruction had begun, the word came from Nineveh that the king was dead. That must have seemed like a reprieve, but it was not to be. Two years later the new king came with his army and swiftly finished the task, in particular sending the leadership off into exile.

Unlike the later Judean exile, where the entire party seems to have been settled in one area (Ezek 1:1, etc.), the Israelites were settled in several areas, all far from home. *Halah* was north-west of Nineveh, whereas *Gozan* was north-east of that city. Others were settled yet farther east, in *Media* in the Zagros Mts. These may have been persons who were conscripted into the army, as Sargon reports (*ANET* 285), since he was attempting to subdue the Medes at this time.

---

5. There is a large literature devoted to attempting to explain סוֹא מֶלֶךְ־מִצְרַיִם, *sôʾ meleḵ-miṣrayim* ("So, the king of Egypt") since no such person is known in Egyptian records. Several of the earlier suggestions have now been shown to be impossible, but no consensus has been reached. Of the three kings reigning in Egypt at this time, perhaps the most likely candidate is Tefnakt, ruling at Sais, but there is no way that "So" can be made to apply to him without emending the text and making the term into some form of the placename Sais. The other alternative is that it is a shortening of the name Osorkon of Zoan, one of the other two kings. For the latest treatment, see Seung Il Kang, "A Philological Approach to the Problem of King So," *VT* 60 (2010): 241–48, who supports the latter alternative.

6. Isaiah is eloquent in his contempt for any reliance on Egypt (Isa 19:11, 13, 16; 20:5; 30:3–5; 31:3).

Selected Bibliography

Becking, Bob. *The Fall of Samaria: An Historical and Archaelogial Study*. SHANE 2 Leiden: Brill, 1992.

Galil, Gershon. "Israelite Exiles in Media: A New Look at ND 2443+." *VT* 59 (2009) 71–9.

Kelle, Brad E. "Hoshea, Sargon, and the Final Destruction of Samaria: A Response to M. Christine Tetley with a View toward Method." *SJOT* 17 (2003) 226–44.

Reasons for the Exile (17:7–23)

Translation

7 Now it was because the people of Israel sinned against Yahweh their God who brought them out from the land of Egypt from under the hand of Pharaoh, king of Egypt, and feared other gods, **8** and walked in the statutes of the nations whom Yahweh had dispossessed before the people of Israel and the kings of Israel which they did. **9** The people of Israel ascribed[7] to Yahweh things that were not right and built for themselves high places in all their cities, from watchtower to fortified city. **10** They erected for themselves pillars and Asherah groves on every high hill and under every green tree. **11** They burned incense there on all the high places like the nations whom Yahweh removed before them, and they did evil things to provoke Yahweh. **12** They served filthy idols of whom Yahweh had said to them, "Do not do this thing." **13** Yahweh warned Israel and Judah by the hand of every prophet and every seer[8] saying, "Repent of your evil deeds and keep my commands, my statutes, according to all the torah that I commanded your fathers and which I sent to you by the hand of my servants the prophets." **14** But they would not listen and stiffened their neck like the neck of their fathers who did not keep faith with Yahweh their God. **15** They rejected his laws and his covenant which he cut with their fathers and his warnings by which he warned them and they went after worthless idols and became worthless, and after the nations who were around them of whom Yahweh commanded them not to do what they did. **16** They abandoned all the commands of Yahweh their God and

7. Heb. חפא, *ḥp'* is a *hapax legomenon*. The meaning "to do secretly" is derived from the assumed synonym חפה, but this idea is not found elsewhere in Kings. An Akk. cognate meaning "to utter" has been cited, but that is disputed (see Cogan and Tadmor, 205). "Ascribe things" reflects the statements in Jeremiah that child sacrifice had never even occurred to Yahweh (Jer 32:35). Note the Vulg. "offended ... with words," and Syr. "spoken ... words."

8. MT בְּיַד כָּל־נְבִיאוֹ כָּל־חֹזֶה, *bᵊyad kāl-nᵊḇî'ô kāl-ḥōze* ("every prophet of his, every seer"). Here understanding that an original *waw* conjunction on "every seer" had accidentally gotten attached to the preceding "prophet" where it was taken to be a 3ms suffix. A few medieval MSS, and Vulg. and Syr. also read as here.

made for themselves two cast idols of calves and they made an Asherah pole and worshipped all the host of heaven and served Baal. **17** They made their sons and daughters pass through the fire and they consulted omens and sold themselves to do evil in the eyes of Yahweh to provoke him. **18** So Yahweh was very angry with Israel and removed them from his presence, so that none remained except only the tribe of Judah. **19** But even Judah did not keep the commands of Yahweh their God. They walked in the statutes of Israel which they did. **20** So Yahweh rejected all the descendants of Israel; he afflicted them and gave them into the hand of the plunderers until he had sent them from his presence. **21** When he had torn Israel from the house of David, they made Jeroboam, son of Nebat, king, and Jeroboam drove[9] Israel away from Yahweh and made them sin a great sin. **22** The people of Israel walked in all the sins of Jeroboam which he did; they did not turn away from them,[10] **23** until Yahweh removed them from his presence as he had said by the hand of all his servants the prophets. So Israel was exiled from their land to Assyria as it is to this day.

Textual Notes

8a–a. וּמַלְכֵי יִשְׂרָאֵל אֲשֶׁר עָשׂוּ: Gk. "Both the kings of Israel, as many as did it, and [connecting to v. 9]"; Vulg. "and the kings of Israel, who did likewise"; Syr. omits. MT best explains the others, but it is very difficult. See "Commentary" below.

9a–a. וַיְחַפְּאוּ בְנֵי־יִשְׂרָאֵל דְּבָרִים אֲשֶׁר לֹא־כֵן עַל־יְהוָה אֱלֹהֵיהֶם: Gk. "the people of Israel, as many as clothed themselves with words, not just against Yahweh their God"; Vulg. "The people of Israel offended Yahweh their God with words that were not right;" Syr. "The people of Israel had spoken against Yahweh their God with words that were not right." All three versions are struggling with the correct meaning of חָפָא 'whereas Gk. seems to be emending the sentence to couple it with the end of v. 8. Vulg. and Syr. both support MT.

11a. דְּבָרִים: Gk. "partners"; Vulg. and Syr. with MT. Hobbs (223) suggests Gk. mistakenly read חברים for דברים.

12a. הַזֶּה: Gk. adds "to Yahweh"; Vulg. and Syr. with MT.

13a–a. K כָּל־חֹזֶה כָּל־נְבִיאוֹ: "every prophet of his"; Q "all the prophets of" (נְבִיאֵי); Gk. "all his prophets, every seer"; Vulg. "all the prophets and seers"; Syr. "all his servants the prophets and by all the seers." Perhaps the best solution is to understand that the ו (*waw*) was originally attached to the

---

9. Reading with Q *hiphil* of נָדַח, *nāḏaḥ.*

10. MT (מִמֶּנָּה, *mimmennâ*) and Gk. (αὐτῆς, *autēs*) "it"; Vulg. and Syr. "them." The sing. might have "the great sin" (חֲטָאָה גְדוֹלָה, *ḥăṭāʾâ gᵊḏôlâ*) of v. 21 as its referent.

following כָל and became displaced [so *BHS*], thus yielding "every prophet *and* every seer."

13b. בְּכָל־הַתּוֹרָה: Gk. "and all"; Vulg. and Syr. with MT.

14a. כְּעֹרֶף: Gk. "more than the neck"; Vulg. and Syr. with MT. An emendation in Gk. necessitated by the homoioteleuton following, *CTAT* (409).

14b–15a. אֲשֶׁר לֹא ... אֶת־אֲבוֹתָם: Gk. omits (homoioteleuton with "fathers"); Vulg. and Syr. with MT.

15b. וְאֵת: Gk. adds "They did not heed"; Vulg. and Syr. with MT. Another emendation necessitated by the homoioteleuton.

15c–c. אֲשֶׁר סְבִיבֹתָם: Syriac omits; Gk. and Vulg. with MT.

17a. וַיִּתְמַכְּרוּ: Gk. "they were sold"; Syr. "they purposed"; Vulg. with MT.

19a. בְּחֻקּוֹת: Vulg. "errors"; Gk. and Syr. with MT.

19b–b. אֲשֶׁר עָשׂוּ: Syr. "who had done that which is evil in the sight of Yahweh and provoked him to anger all the days" [harm.]; Gk. and Vulg. with MT.

20a–a. וַיִּמְאַס יְהוָה בְּכָל־זֶרַע: Gk. "They rejected Yahweh from among the seed"; Vulg. and Syr. with MT.

20b. וַיְעַנֵּם: Gk. "he shook"; Syr. "he despised"; Vulg. with MT.

21a–a. כִּי־קָרַע יִשְׂרָאֵל מֵעַל: Gk. "for only Israel was away from"; Syr. "For Israel had seceded from"; Vulg. with MT.

21b. K וַיַּדֵּא: Q וַיַּדַּח, *hiph.* of נָדַח "to scatter, turn away from." נדא' *is* a *hapax legomenon.*

22a. חַטֹּאות: Gk. sing.; Vulg. and Syr. with MT.

22b. מִמֶּנָּה: Vulg. and Syr. pl.; Gk with MT.

23a. דִּבֶּר: Gk. adds "the Lord"; Vulg. and Syr. with MT.

Commentary

This passage, often called a sermon, is pivotal in the books of Kings, in that it summarizes the material from 1 Kings 11 to 2 Kings 17:6, and at the same time, with verses 18–20, points to what lies ahead in 17:24–25:30. It tells us in the clearest of terms why Israel fell to Assyria, and prepares us to hear that in spite of the reforms of Hezekiah and Josiah, the evil seed has been sown, and will eventually bear its fruit in Judah as well. The narrator's purpose is very clear: it is not the happenstance of geo-politics that has determined Israel's fate. Assyria was not the cause of the disaster; Assyria, as Isaiah says so graphically in Isaiah 10:5–34, was only a tool in Yahweh's hand, working out his purposes. Israel fell because they persistently broke their covenant with Yahweh. This is made very clear by the preponderance of Deuteronomic language that is found in the unit. Almost every verse can be linked to the book of Deuteronomy, which is clearly cast as a covenant document.

While there is broad agreement that the unit is composed of two parts: vv. 7–17, and vv. 18–23, there is little agreement as to the relationship between the two segments. Many scholars (see the discussions in Cogan and Tadmor, 206–07; Fritz, 349–52; Gray; 645–52) take v. 18 and vv. 21–23, as original, later supplemented by vv. 7–17; later still, after Judah's fall, verses 19–20 were added. But these views are shaped by assumptions about the history of the text that, by and large, cannot be demonstrated to be correct. If we take the text as it stands, verses 7–20 can be read together, with v. 20 forming the conclusion. Then vv. 21–23 provide a summarizing conclusion to the whole.[11]

This extended theological reflection by the narrator comes as something of a surprise after the rather sparse editorial comments in the preceding material. It seems very likely that it was necessitated by the terrible shock of the northern kingdom's fall, something that modern readers do not pay enough attention to. Israel and Judah were not two separate countries, as were, say, Israel and Syria. They were two parts of a whole, as many indicators show (e.g., Amos, a man from Judah, called to prophesy to Israel). Thus, the disaster which struck fully three-fourths of the "the children of Israel" must have raised great questions not only in the minds of the Israelites, but in minds of the Judeans, as well.[12] Thus, we can imagine these reflections, perhaps in a somewhat earlier form than the final canonical one, functioning as a conclusion to the book as it had developed thus far already in the time of Hezekiah. (For further discussion on the possible composition of the book, see the "Introduction.")

7–8 Several commentators (e.g., Cogan and Tadmor, 206) call attention to the fact that until this point, the narrator has focused attention on the (sinful) activities of the kings of Israel, but now shifts attention to the people of Israel. Some go so far as to make this a reason for doubting the originality of the material (e.g., Fritz, 351). But surely this is to go too far. There is no indication in the previous chapters that the people wanted to go in any other

---

11. For further discussion of the organization of the unit 17:7–23, see Bob Becking, "From Apostasy to Destruction: A Josianic View on the Fall of Samaria (2 Kings 17, 21–23)" in *Deuteronomy and Deuteronomic Literature: Festschrift C. H. W. Brekelmans,* eds. M. Vervenne and J. Lust (Leuven: Peeters, 1997), 279–97. For the suggestion that there are five parts: 7–12, 13–18a, 18b–20, 21–22, 23, see Marc Zvi Brettler, "Ideology, History, and Theology in 2 Kings 17:7–23," *VT* 39 (1989): 268–82.
12. On the possible impact of the fall of Israel on the formation of the book of Isaiah, see John Oswalt, "Who Were the Addressees of Isaiah 40–66?" *BSac* 169 (2012): 33–47.

direction than that in which their kings were taking them. That connection between kings and people is made explicit in v. 8 and again in v. 22. The point is that Israel did not fall because of wicked kings, while the people were piously following Yahweh. Israel fell because the people were all too eager to walk "in the statutes" (בְּחֻקּוֹת, *bᵊḥuqqôṯ*) of the neighboring nations, following the leadership of their own kings.[13]

These two verses set the stage very clearly. Yahweh, their God had delivered them from Egypt, and had dispossessed other nations before them. That is, even without covenant obligations Israel ought to give exclusive allegiance to Yahweh because of his gracious acts and gifts on their behalf, bringing them into existence as a nation. But they would not do that. Instead of fearing Yahweh, that is, conducting their lives ("walking") in ways consistent with his power and his grace, they chose to fear "other gods" (אֱלֹהִים אֲחֵרִים, *ʾĕlōhîm ʾăḥērîm*). And instead of following Yahweh's patterns for life (statutes, v. 13), they followed the "statutes" of the very nations God had driven out for them.

9–12 What Yahweh called for—exclusive allegiance—was a major problem for Israel. Given his transcendent nature, it was not possible to manipulate him through this world. One could only surrender to him and trust him (see below on v. 14). That was terrifying. The alternative was not to abandon Yahweh—he seemed to be unwilling to let go of them—but rather to paganize him, to make him one of the gods. It was to ascribe to him "things that were not right" (דְּבָרִים אֲשֶׁר לֹא־כֵן עַל־יהוה, *dᵊḇārîm ʾăšer lōʾ-ḵēn ʿal-yhwh*), according to his nature.[14] These included the typical behaviors (statutes) of the surrounding nations, among which were worshipping him in a variety of places (i.e., "high places" [בָּמוֹת, *bāmôṯ*], resulting in the localizing of him in space), representing him with standing stones ("pillars" [מַצֵּבוֹת, *maṣṣēḇôṯ*]), which were not quite idols, but the next thing to it,[15] and associating him with the fertility goddess Asherah, and her sacred groves.[16] Verses 11 and 12

---

13. The final clause in v. 8 וּמַלְכֵי יִשְׂרָאֵל אֲשֶׁר עָשׂוּ, *ûmalḵê yiśrāʾēl ʾăšer ʿāśû* ("and the kings of Israel which they did") seems somewhat awkward, as Hobbs notes (223). Gray wishes to omit it on the basis of Syr. (although both Gk. and Vulg. include it) (645n.b). But notice that "which they did" is a common concluding clause, see vv. 19, 22, particularly in the context of following the behavior of someone else. Here is it is to follow the other nations as well as what their own kings did. As Hobbs points out, the very awkwardness argues against it being a later addition.

14. On this phrase see Ronnie Goldstein, "A Suggestion Regarding the Meaning of 2 Kings 17:9 and the Composition of 2 Kings 17:7–23," *VT* 63 (2013): 393–407.

15. For a recent discussion of standing stones, see Richard S. Hess, *Israelite Religions: An Archaeological and Biblical Survey* (Grand Rapids: Baker Academic, 2007), 198–200, 206.

16. "Asherah" (אֲשֵׁירָה, *ʾăšērâ*) (v. 16) is not used as a proper noun in the OT. It refers to an object of some sort. The versions typically use a word for "pole" or "grove." Verbs describing its destruction include "cut down" (Deut 7:5) or "uproot" (Mic

suggest that not only did they worship Yahweh on the high places (see the "Excursus on Worship at High Places ('country shrines')," they also worshipped other gods ("filthy idols")[17] there as well, just as the other nations did. Elsewhere, these practices are specifically ascribed to the Judeans under Rehoboam (1 Kgs 14:23) and Ahaz (2 Kgs 16:3–4). Later, they would be revived by Manasseh (2 Kgs 21:2–3). As vv. 19 and 20 make plain here, these sins were by no means limited to Israel.

13–15 Whereas vv. 7–12 speak of obedience to Yahweh as what might be expected in view of what he had done for them, these verses emphasize that what Israel had done was a violation of their express covenant with him. The use of עוּד, *ʿûḏ* "to bear testimony to, or against" (here "to warn") is significant since one of the synonyms for the covenant stipulations is "the testimony" (עֵדוּת, *ʿēḏûṯ*). The particular task of the prophets, as defined here, was to testify against the people for their abandonment of their covenant, the testimony of Yahweh. Not only had they "abandoned" (עזב, *ʿzb*) (v.16) it; they had "rejected" (מאס, *mʾs*) (v. 15) it, and when the prophets called them to "repent" (שֻׁבוּ, *šuḇû*), they had only "stiffened their necks" (וַיַּקְשׁוּ אֶת־עָרְפָּם, *wayyaqšû ʾeṯ-ʿorpām*). This metaphor pictures an animal that refuses to be led, instead digging in its hoofs and holding its neck stiff against the halter. In this way, they were behaving just as their ancestors had (v. 14). In other words, these people were only replicating the practices of generation upon generation. Yahweh was not visiting upon them merely the sins of a generation or two, like some short-tempered tyrant. This sort of covenant violation had been going on for centuries. It was a failure to "keep faith" (v. 14), that is, "to be true to." The basic sense of the root ʿis אמן, *ʾmn* "to be reliable." When it occurs in the *hiphil,* the sense is "to make something reliable," "to rely upon it," "to trust it." Israel had been called upon to put their entire trust in Yahweh, to give up all the pagan attempts to manipulate the forces of the cosmos for their own benefit. But that was too frightening, so they had broken faith. Refusing to trust God, they had become untrustworthy. As Gray (647) points out, the frantic political activity in Israel during the last 30 years of its existence is a testimony to this complete lack of trust in Yahweh, and it is this kind of trust to which Isaiah unsuccessfully called Ahaz (Isa 7). Israelites and Judeans alike had made gods in their own image: empty, "worthless things" (הֶבֶל,

---

5:14). For discussion of the possibility of Asherah as a consort of Yahweh, see Saul M. Olyan, *Asherah and the Cult of Yahweh in Israel,* SBLMS 34 (Atlanta: Scholars Press, 1988).

17. The term is הַגִּלֻּלִים, *haggillulîm* , a favorite of Ezekiel's, and occurring elsewhere in these books in 1 Kgs 15:12; 21:26; 2 Kgs 21:11, 21; 23:24. The precise meaning is not clear. It is evidently based on a root meaning "round." Some say it is an idol carved in the round. However, it is often associated with terms for abomination, and this has suggested to some that it means "animal droppings." In any case, it is an extremely derogatory term, as seen in its association with Ahab and Manasseh in Kings.

hebel), and in so doing, made themselves *worthless* (v. 15). This is a profound thought, echoed elsewhere in Scripture.[18] If we reduce God to our own level, thus making ourselves the most significant beings in the universe, we end up making ourselves of no value whatsoever. If we are ultimate, nothing is ultimate, for we are merely a breath, soon to be gone. On the other hand, if we make Yahweh, the transcendent One, supreme, then we, his creatures, come to share his ultimate worth.

16–18 This further catalog of Israel's sins may have in mind the more particular ones into which Ahab led his people. The joint references to Asherah and Baal (cf. 1 Kgs 16:31–33) might point in that direction. Cogan and Tadmor (205) also point out that the use of *cast idols* (מַסֵּכָה, *massēkâ*) with reference to the golden calves in Hosea 13:2 might be an oblique reference to Ahab. The statement that "they sold themselves to do evil" (וַיִּתְמַכְּרוּ לַעֲשׂוֹת הָרַע, *wayyiṯmakkᵊrû la ʿăśôṯ hāraʿ*) (v. 17) only elsewhere appears in connection with Ahab (1 Kings 21:20, 25). The worship of "the host of heaven" (צְבָא הַשָּׁמַיִם, *ṣᵊḇāʾ haššāmayim*) is not specifically associated with Ahab, nor is child sacrifice, nor "divination" (קְסָמִים, *qᵊsāmîm*). This combination is only found elsewhere with reference to Manasseh (2 Kgs 21:3–6). The similarities between that passage and this suggest strongly that the connection is intentional with the narrator making the point that the Judean monarch was leading his people into the very same sins that brought Israel down. The reference to divination is significant in relation to the earlier mention of the prophets. Having rejected the God-ordained method by which they might receive guidance for living, the Israelites had to resort to the manipulative methods of guidance that were based on the very worldview that the Bible rejects (cf. Isa 8:16–22). Divination presumes a connection between the realms of humanity, nature and deity whereby what takes place in one realm will in some way be replicated in the others. The Bible everywhere rejects such an idea.[19] Yahweh reveals his will through speech. This is why the other ancient cultures have many volumes of omen texts, while Israel has none, and why Israel has large collections of prophetic speech, and the surrounding cultures have nearly none.[20] It is for these reasons that divination is firmly prohibited in Israel (Deut 18:10; notice that as here, divination and child sacrifice are treated together).

At the end of v. 17, and in preparation for v. 18 we have the reiteration of the point made above in v. 11: these sins provoked Yahweh to anger. Yahweh is not an angry God; that is, anger does not define his character. In fact, the opposite is true: he is slow to get angry (Exod 34:6; repeated no less than

18. Ps 115:8; Isa 2:17–22; 44:14–20; Jer 2:5; Hos 9:10.

19. On the conflict in worldviews, see John Oswalt, *The Bible Among the Myths* (Grand Rapids: Zondervan, 2009), 47–84.

20. See John Oswalt, "Is there Anything Unique in the Israelite Prophets," *BSac* 172 (2015): 67–84.

nine times in the OT).[21] But unlike the Greek concepts of transcendence, namely, of an immutable, passion-less force, Yahweh is personal. That is, he is capable of emotion. To be sure, his emotions are not like the petty storms that sweep the human psyche, but ours are of the same order as his. He loves, and he can be provoked to anger. It took several hundred years for that anger to be stoked to the point where he could no longer look at his people ("he drove them away from his presence [lit. 'face' "] [וַיְסִרֵם מֵעַל פָּנָיו, *waysirēm mē ʿal pānāyw*]), but the day did come. It was in the end their persistent idolatry that was the provocation.[22]

19–20 It is apparent that as the text stands now, these verses cannot be separated from v. 18 which ends with the statement that "only the tribe of Judah" (רַק שֵׁבֶט יְהוּדָה, *raq šēḇeṭ yᵉhûḏâ*) remained. Without the following verses, the reader might think that Judah was spared because that nation did not participate in such sins as the Israelites had committed. In fact, that was not the case at all, for Judah was following in the footsteps of Israel, whom Ezekiel was to style as Judah's older sister (Ezek 23). Although we are not told it here, the clear implication of the book is that if Ahaz of Judah had been directly followed by a Manasseh, Judah's destruction would have followed hard on the heels of Israel's. In any case, even the reigns of the righteous Hezekiah and Josiah could only defer it.

As Provan (249) says, "all the descendants of Israel" ([בְּ]כָל־זֶרַע יִשְׂרָאֵל, *ḵol-zera ʿyiśrā ʾēl*) is somewhat ambiguous. It could be a way of reverting again to the northern kingdom. However, following v. 19 as it does, and differing somewhat in tone from v. 21, and given the broad sense of "seed," it seems more likely that the reference is to the entire nation. No one, neither Israel nor Judah, would escape the "plunderers" (שֹׁסִים, *šōsîm*) whom Yahweh would permit to take his people out of his sight. This latter statement recaps the point of the entire passage: Yahweh is the Lord of history; the Assyrias, the Babylonias, even the Romes, that might sweep across the stage are only his tools to accomplish his ultimate purposes.

21–23 These verses provide a brief, but comprehensive summary of what has been said above. In doing so they provide a remarkably nuanced view of the historical process, one that is as far from a deterministic one as could be imagined. While it was "Yahweh who tore Israel from the house of David" (קָרַע יִשְׂרָאֵל מֵעַל בֵּית דָּוִד, *qāra ʿyiśrā ʾēl mē ʿal bêṯ dāwiḏ*), it was the people who "made Jeroboam ... king," and it was Jeroboam who "drove Israel away from Yahweh,"[23] and it was "the people who walked in all the sins of Jeroboam ...

---

21. Either in direct quotations of Exod 34:6 or in allusions to it: Num 14:18; Neh 9:17; Joel 2:13; Jon 4:2; Nah 1:3; Ps 86:15; 103:8; 145:8.

22. 1 Kgs 14:9, 15; 15:30; 16:2, 7, 13, 26, 33; 21:22; 22:53; 2 Kgs 21:6, 15; 23:19.

23. חֲטָאָה גְדוֹלָה, *ḥăṭā ʾâ gᵉḏôlâ* ("the great sin") referred to in v. 21 harkens back to the description of the golden calf in Exod 32:21, 30, 31. See also 1 Kgs 12:30 and 13:34.

and did not turn from them." Through "his servants, the prophets," Yahweh had warned the people of the historical consequences of these historical choices, but they would not listen, and as a result "he exiled Israel" (וַיֶּגֶל יִשְׂרָאֵל, *wayyiḡel yiśrāʾēl*). Although Yahweh was the initiator of the process, and was directly involved from beginning to end, there is no sense in which he was the direct cause of anything that happened. It was humans who made choices in respect of Yahweh's revealed will, choosing to behave ("walk") in certain ways, and while the results were carried out in history, they were not merely historical, but were an expression of a theological reality: Yahweh drove them away from his presence.[24]

Biblical Theology Comments

The concept of Yahweh as Lord of history was of vital importance if Israel (including Judah) was to survive the exile. The common idea in the rest of the world that when nations fought their gods were fighting, and that the victor nation had the victor god, would have meant the end for Israel, and even for Yahweh. But that was not how those who represented the core of Israel's faith thought. They had been taught to think differently by the prophetic tradition that extended back to Moses. Yahweh, who cannot be identified with natural forces or with nations, stands outside the circle of time, and as such has an overarching progressive purpose in time. That purpose is nothing less than the blessing of all peoples. Thus, human experience is a process toward an ultimate goal, one in which Yahweh is intimately involved. Human experience is not a collection of disparate, unrelated events.

But at the same time, Yahweh is not merely the "stage director" moving the characters in his drama this way and that to serve his purposes. He is motivated by love (חֶסֶד, *ḥeseḏ*) and that precludes determinism. He must grant his creatures freedom to make choices, even to reject him if that is what they determine is in their best interests. But he must not fail to make the results of those choices clear, as he did at Sinai, and then through his prophets' continual reversion to those instructions (תּוֹרָה, *tôrâ*). Thus, human historical experience, which has served, and will serve Yahweh's ultimate purposes, is yet the arena in which human choices determine the intermediate directions that the drama will take.

So, there were Judeans, in particular, who would understand that Yahweh had not been defeated in their exile, that neither Assyria nor Babylonia had done anything in defiance of his will, that, in fact, the exile of God's people

24. עַד הַיּוֹם הַזֶּה, *ʿaḏ hayyôm hazze* ("until this day") has evoked a variety of opinions. Obviously, it dates the writing to sometime after the exile of Israel. Some would date it to the final recension during the exile, while others, believing that there were earlier more or less complete recensions, such as Hezekian or Josianic, would locate it to one of those. Of the two, the Josianic, as being farther from the events discussed here seems more likely.

had been *of their own making*. The conquerors were simply the tools the Creator was using to accomplish his larger purposes in his people and in the world. While it is not in evidence in this chapter, it was that sense of the unified purpose of Yahweh in history that enabled some of the people to believe the incredible promises that Yahweh was not through with them and would not abandon them to their exile. He was not destroying them, but disciplining them, and would one day deliver them back to their land so that they could continue to participate in the fulfillment of his great historical purpose. Thus, at least some of them stubbornly retained their sense of identity in the face of all the pressures to accommodate themselves to the imperial culture and religion, and when the unthinkable happened: permission, even encouragement, to return home, they, and no one else that we know of, were intact and ready to go. It was their belief in Yahweh's lordship of history that made it all possible.

Application and Devotional Implications

Trust is at the very heart of any relation with Yahweh. There is no other basis for relationship with him. That is because of his nature. He is not a part of his creation; he is utterly other than anything that he has spoken into existence. That means he is utterly beyond human control. We have no power over him whatsoever. So, we must believe that he is good, and believing that cast ourselves upon him. If we will not do that, there is nothing he can do for us.

But, as I said above, that alternative is frightening. It means we surrender the supply of our needs into his hands, not knowing if he will supply them or not. Even worse, it means that we will surrender the direction of our lives into his hands, not knowing if he may lead us into a dead end. Now in fact, if we will listen to the testimony of those who have gone before us, he *is* good, and he *is* reliable ("true") (Ps 100). They tell us that he does supply our needs (if not always our desires), and that he leads his people to places of rest, refreshment, and restoration (Ps 23). He can be trusted.

As we do trust, and discover that Yahweh is trustworthy, it becomes easier to put down our weight on him and trust him. But the sense of risk is never taken away. Will he be there this time? This is why idolatry is always hovering on the fringes of our lives. Idolatry is the attempt to avoid the necessity of trust. We believe that we can manipulate the forces of this cosmos to make ourselves secure, comfortable, and powerful, and *not have to trust*. But this is exactly why idolatry, ancient or modern, is so reprehensible. It puts us "in the driver's seat," in control—the place we were never meant to be. Only the I AM, the basis of existence, can be there, and any attempt by creatures, dying creatures, to sit there can only result in disaster (Isa 14:4–21).

One manifestation of that disaster is what happens to those who refuse to trust Yahweh. They become untrustworthy! If I am God in my life, which is what idolatry is truly about, if I am the supplier of my needs, then anything necessary to that supply is justifiable. If it is necessary to break a promise, then the promise must be broken. Certainly I cannot be expected to keep a promise if doing so is not in my best interest. This is what the text means when it says that those who worship what is worthless become themselves worthless. There is nothing of permanent worth in this ever-changing cosmos, and certainly not in humans themselves. Neither are security, comfort, or power of any permanent worth. If we make these things ultimate, we testify, as modern philosophy has, that nothing is of ultimate worth. So, in that mode, what is a person's word worth? Nothing. Refusing to trust Yahweh, they cannot be trusted.

On the other hand, those who have committed their lives, their needs, their life-direction into Yahweh's hands have the luxury of becoming increasingly trustworthy. They know that their worth is not in themselves, but in what Yahweh thinks of them ("My son!" My daughter!"). They know that they can leave their needs in his hands, that they do not have to manipulate people or forces to fulfill them. This is not passivity; those who trust God will often work harder than anyone else. But they can work at peace, knowing that the outcome is not in their hands. These people would rather be in need than to break a promise, because they know that as God has been true to them, they must be true to others.

Selected Bibliography

Rösel, H. N. "Why 2 Kings 17 Does Not Constitute a Chapter of Reflection in the 'Deuteronomic History.' " *JBL* 128 (2009): 85–90.

Viviano, P. A. "2 Kings 17: A Rhetorical and Form-Critical Analysis." *CBQ* 49 (1987): 548–59.

———. "Exhortation and Admonition in Deuteronomic Terms: A Comparison of Second Kings 17:7–18, 34–41, Second Kings 21:2–16, and Jeremiah 7:1–8:3." *BR* 56 (2011) 35–54.

Samaria Resettled (17:24–33)

Translation

24 The king of Assyria brought people from Babylon, from Cutha, from Avva, from Hamath, and from Sepharvaim, and settled them in the towns of Samaria in place of the people of Israel and they possessed Samaria and dwelt in its towns. **25** Now when they began to live there, they did not revere[25] Yahweh, and Yahweh sent lions among them and they were killing them. **26** So they said to the king of Assyria, saying, "The nations that you deported and made to live in the towns of Samaria do not know the

25. לֹא יָֽרְאוּ, *lō ʾyor ʾû* ("they did not fear"); often translated by the versions as "worship." However, the vb. implies more that merely liturgical behavior.

customary requirements[26] of the god of the land. He has sent lions among them and, look, they are killing them." **27** The king of Assyria commanded, "Send there one of the priests whom you deported and let him go and live there and teach them the customary requirements of the god of the land. **28** So one of the priests they had deported from Samaria came and lived in Bethel. He was teaching them how they should revere Yahweh. **29** Now each nation had made its own gods and deposited them in the temples on the high places[27] the Samarians had made, each nation in their towns where they were living. **30** The people of Babylon made Sukkoth-Benoth; the people of Cuth made Nergal; the men of Hamath made Ashima; **31** the Avvites made Nibhaz and Tartaq; the Sepharvites were burning their children in the fire to Adrammelek and Anammelek, the gods of Sepharvaim. **32** So they revered Yahweh and they made priests for themselves from all sorts of their people, and they were working for them in the temples on the high places. **33** It was Yahweh they were revering and their god they were serving following the customs of the nations from which they had been deported.[28]

Textual Notes

24a. מִבָּבֶ֜ל: Gk. adds "the people" and omits the conjunction on "from Cutha"; Vulg. and Syr. with MT.

24b. וַיֹּ֫שֶׁב: The versions all supply "them," which MT does not.

27a–a. הֹלִיכוּ שָׁמָּה אֶחָד מֵהַכֹּהֲנִים אֲשֶׁר הִגְלִיתֶם מִשָּׁם וְיֵלְכוּ וְיֵשְׁבוּ שָׁם וְיֹרֵם: Gk. reads "Bring from there, and let them go and live there, and they shall teach"; Vulg. and Syr. with MT except that they have sings., e.g., "he will go and he will live there." Perhaps the final ו (*waw*) on הלךְ is a dittograph of the following conj., and then ישב was made pl. to conform.

28a. וַיָּבֹא: Gk. "they brought"; Vulg. and Syr. with MT.

29a–a. אֲשֶׁר עָשׂוּ הַשֹּׁמְרֹנִים: Syr. "which had been made in Samaria"; Gk. and Vulg. with MT.

31a. נִבְחַז: Gk. "Eblazer"; Vulg. "Nebahaz"; Syr. "Jebzah."

---

26. מִשְׁפָּט, *mišpāṭ* "judgment, regulation, custom, pattern." Translated in a variety of ways by the versions, including "judgment," "ceremony," "rite," "requirement," and "religion."
27. בְּבֵית הַבָּמוֹת, *bᵉḇêṯ habbāmôṯ*, see GKC (§124*r*) for other examples where the first member of a const. though sing. in form is understood to be pl. because of the plurality of the second member.
28. הִגְלוּ, *hiḡlû*; indef. 3rd pl. functioning as a virtual passive.

32a–a. וַיִּהְיוּ יְרֵאִים אֶת־יְהוָה: Vulg. makes the clause the conclusion of the previous sentence; Gk. runs the two verses together as a single sentence; Syr. with MT.

32b. וַיַּעֲשׂוּ: Gk. inserts here "their abominations dwell in the houses of the high places that they had made in Samaria, each nation in the city where they dwelt, and they were fearing the Lord and they made." Most of this is a dittograph of v. 29. It is difficult to explain what may have prompted it. Vulg. and Syr. with MT but see 32c. below.

32c. מִקְצוֹתָם: Gk. omits; Vulg. "new"; Syr. "some of them." MT explains the others. See the "Commentary."

32d–d. וַיִּהְיוּ עֹשִׂים לָהֶם: Gk. "they acted for them"; Vulg. "they placed them"; Syr. "who served them."

33a–a. אֲשֶׁר־הִגְלוּ אֹתָם מִשָּׁם: Syr. "So the children of Israel were carried away out of their land"; Gk. and Vulg. with MT.

Commentary

Just as vv. 1–23 included a report (vv. 1–6) followed by a commentary, so does the second part of the chapter (vv. 24–41). Here the report is found in vv. 24–33. It describes the situation in Samaria after the exile had taken place. Like the language of 1–7, and indeed, of most of the book, the language here is straightforward and noncommittal. Although it describes a situation which cannot help but be appalling to the narrator, he recounts it without comment, reserving that comment for vv. 34–41. As has been seen throughout the book, the skill of the narration is that we the readers are able to get the point without having to be told what the point is. But that being so, why the commentary? Commentators differ on the reason, but it seems most likely to me that the writer wishes to make clear the results of Israel's failure, and how difficult the situation was that first Hezekiah and then Josiah would face when they attempted to re-exert the influence of Jerusalem over the former Israelite area. Some scholars believe that the purpose is to explain and justify the later proscription of the Samaritans, but an equal number doubt that, as I do. The primary reason for that doubt is that the Samaritans were anything but syncretistic, as the people here are described as being. (For more discussion on this question, see the "Selected Bibliography" after 17:34–41.)

24 It appears that Sargon II instituted the program of double deportation. At least he is the first to speak of having done it (on the resettlement of Samaria, see *ANET*, 284). The fact that the Assyrian king is not named would accord with the probability that the process of deportation and resettlement may have extended over several years and through several different reigns (see Ezra 4:2, 10). The mention of Babylon supports this idea since Babylon did not fall during Sargon's reign, but only during Esarhaddon's. Cutha is probably to be identified with tell Ibrahim located some twenty miles northeast of Babylon. Hamath, an important Syrian city, was located on the Orontes River north of Damascus, while Avva is possibly Kefer Ayya, also on the Orontes. Many suggestions have been made for the identity of Sepharvaim, but all remain highly tentative.

One of the key elements in this verse is the statement that the people from these nations "possessed" (ירשׁ, *yrš*) the land. The irony of the statement is unmistakable; seventy-one times, extending from 1:8 to 33:23, Deuteronomy speaks of Yahweh's promise that Israel would possess the land of Canaan.[29] It was Yahweh's land that he was graciously allowing his people to possess. Now that had come to an end. Because of their sins the land had "spewed them out" (Lev 18:28; 20:22), and it was possessed by foreigners.

25–26 But even if the land had rejected them, it still belonged to Yahweh, and if the newcomers did not recognize that, the results would be bad. Lions were fairly common throughout the ANE and remained so through the Middle Ages. Very probably with the dead from Assyrian destruction having littered the land, and with some degree of depopulation, wild animals of all sorts would have increased. As pointed out elsewhere in this commentary, we should not drive a wedge between "natural" causation and divine causation.[30] This is Yahweh's world, and nothing happens apart from his will, whether permissive or directive. In this case, someone made the correct deduction that these depredations were the result of the displeasure of "the god of the land" (אֱלֹהֵי הָאָרֶץ, *ʾĕlōhê hāʾāreṣ*) and informed the Assyrian emperor, further adding that the people could not appease this god because they did not know how he required to be served, his מִשְׁפָּט, *mišpāṭ*. As noted above in the translation, this Hebrew term has a wide range of connotations, and it is a mistake to make "judgment" or "justice" (as per LXX) the default translation. Here it refers to "an expected pattern of behavior."[31] The speaker thinks that if the people can simply figure out how this God expects to be served, all will be well.

27–28 As we know from Assyrian documents, the emperor was quite willing to address the problem.[32] He had sent persons to Dur-Sharrukin to educate deportees in the customs of the local gods. So, he directed that a "priest"

29. E.g., 8:1; 10:11; 12:1; 19:2; 31:13.

30. On Yahweh's use of lions to do his bidding, see 1 Kgs 13:24–32; 20:36. See also Amos 3:12.

31. See, "שׁפט," *TLOT* 3:1392–99.

32. Shalom M. Paul, "Sargon's Administrative Diction in 2 Kings 17:27," *JBL* 88 (1969): 73–4.

(כֹּהֲנִים, *kōhănîm*)[33] be selected from the Israelite deportees and sent back to Israel to "teach them the customary requirements of the god of the land" (וְיֹרֵם אֶת־מִשְׁפַּט אֱלֹהֵי הָאָרֶץ, *wᵉyōrēm ʾet-mišpaṭ ʾĕlōhê hā ʾāreṣ*). When we learn that this priest settled in Bethel, the irony of the whole undertaking becomes clear. What is it this god wants? Will he be satisfied to be one among many, just so long as his religious customs are included with all the others? Far from it! He expects to be treated as the only God, and that in a completely iconic way. Is it likely that this Israelite priest (who may not have even been a Levite, see 1 Kgs 12:31), living at Bethel, the headquarters of Yahwistic idol worship, would teach these foreign peoples, steeped in polytheistic idolatry anything about the genuine מִשְׁפָּטִים, *mišpāṭîm* of Yahweh? Probably not. He could give them the forms of Israelite religious practices that they could incorporate into their own practices and gain the feeling that they had appeased him, but he would never be able, or willing, to teach them about the God that Amos knew. The "fear" (ירא, *yrʾ*) or "reverence" of Yahweh (v.28), that the priest would teach would fall far short of what Deuteronomy 10:12–13 instructs.

29–31 These verses, introduced by the narrative element וַיִּהְיוּ, *wayyihyû*, tell us just how far from the fear of Yahweh these people were. They "made" (עָשׂוּ, *ʿāśû*) their own gods, an act of consummate folly as far as the biblical writers were concerned.[34] Despite a great deal of scholarly attention, the exact identity of almost all these gods still escapes us.[35] "Nergal," the god of Cuth, is known to be the consort of Ereshkigal, the goddess of the underworld. Thus, he is a god of massacre and pestilence. But apart from him, the rest are unknown. It is possible that some of them are pejorative; perhaps "Ashima of Hamath" is a rewriting of Asherah into the "Guilty One" (see Amos 8:14). "Sukkoth" may be the same as "Sakkuth" referred to in Amos 5:26. Fritz (356) thinks the writer has made up the names to serve his polemical purposes. But it may well be that the uncertainty about the identities is a mark of the authenticity of the text. Because of the multiplicity of gods, each locality had its own special minor deities who did not appear in the catalogs of the great deities that we know from the important literary documents that have been recovered. So the presence of these gods that are unknown to us may be evidence that the writer had an intimate familiarity with the situation

33. Gray considers that one priest would not be enough for the task and proposes to emend the text to read "certain priests" (652). While this proposal gains some support from the two (out of three) pl. vbs. following, the emendation itself has no support in the versions. The emperor may well have thought that one would be more than enough to pass on the forms of worship required by this strange foreign god.
34. For a sample of the Bible's scorn, see Judg 18:24; 1 Kgs 14:9; Ps 96:5; Isa 2:8; 31:7; Jer 2:28; Dan 3:15; Amos 5:26. Yahweh has made us; how could we think that we could "make" a god?
35. See Cogan and Tadmor for a concise, yet full, summary (212). See also the relevant articles on these gods in *DDD*.

that was prevailing in the Samarian province during the end of the eighth century BC and the beginning of the seventh.[36]

The picture of the syncretistic worship that characterized the new Assyrian province of Samaria is further developed when we hear where the manufactured gods were placed. They were placed in the "temples on the high places that the Samarians had made" (בְּבֵית הַבָּמוֹת אֲשֶׁר עָשׂוּ הַשֹּׁמְרֹנִים, *bᵊḇêṯ habbāmôṯ ʾăšer ʿāśû haššōmᵊrōnîm*). In other words, the Israelites, with their paganized Yahwism, had already prepared the worship centers into which the fully pagan worship could move. So they were "revering" Yahweh, while making idols of foreign gods, and placing them in ready-made Israelite temples. This is, of course, exactly what the Assyrian policy of exile was designed to achieve: a "homogenization" of all the different cultures, religions, and languages in the empire into one amorphous mass.

32–33 These two verses, again introduced with וַיִּהְיוּ, *wayyihyû*, amplify and summarize the absorption of Yahwism into the generally syncretistic atmosphere. The narrator does not need to raise his eyebrows or put his tongue in his cheek when he tells us twice that "they were revering Yahweh" (אֶת־יהוה הָיוּ יְרֵאִים, *ʾeṯ-yhwh hāyû yᵊrēʾîm*). He does not need to do these because in each case what he adds after that statement clearly makes a mockery of it. How could they truly revere Yahweh when they made their own priests to serve the gods they had made "in the temples of the high places?" How could they revere Yahweh when they were "serving their gods in accordance with the customs of the nations" (וְאֶת־אֱלֹהֵיהֶם הָיוּ עֹבְדִים כְּמִשְׁפַּט הַגּוֹיִם, *wᵊʾeṯ- ʾĕlōhêhem hāyû ʿōḇᵊḏîm kᵊmišpaṭ haggôyim*), something Deuteronomy forbade in the strongest of terms.[37]

The incompatibility of the two sets of behaviors is highlighted in v. 33 with the reversed structure of the first two clauses (compared to typical Hebrew sentence structure), and then with the breaking up of the pair-words "revered" (יְרֵאִים) and "served" (עֹבְדִים). The reversed word order places the direct object at the head of the clause in both cases. One could even translate "It was Yahweh they revered, but it was their gods that they served." Yahweh has been reduced merely to a member of the pantheon, the local representative, as it were, who needed to be nodded to while one's own gods, the ones with whom one was comfortable, were truly served. Yahweh had been humiliated during the years of the Israelite kingdom, and this was the full flowering of that humiliation. This was what the Israelites had brought him to.

Selected Bibliography

Cogan, M. "'For We, Like You, Worship Your God': Three Biblical Portrayals of Samaritan Origins." *Birkat Shalom* (2008): 135–41.

36. Unlike the euphemistic (?) references to the Israelites causing their children to "pass through the fire" (2 Kgs 16:3; 21:6), here it is specifically said that the people of Sepharvaim "burned" (שֹׂרְפִים, *śōrᵊpîm*) their children for their god.

37. Deut 12:2, 30; 18:9, 14; 29:18.

A Reflection on Religious Conditions in Resettled Samaria (17:34–41)

Translation

34 Until this day, they are acting according to their former practices. No
one fears Yahweh and no one is acting according to their statutes, their
regulations, the instruction and the command which Yahweh commanded
the descendants of Jacob, whom he gave the name Israel. **35** Yahweh cut
a covenant with them and commanded them, saying, "Do not fear other
gods and do not worship them; do not serve them and do not sacrifice to
them. **36** Rather, Yahweh, who brought you up from the land of Egypt with
great power and an outstretched arm, him you shall fear, and him you shall
worship and to him you shall sacrifice. **37** The statutes, the regulations, the
instructions, and the commandment he wrote for you perform carefully all
the days, and do not fear other gods. **38** The covenant that I cut with you
do not forget, and do not fear other gods. **39** Rather, it is Yahweh your God
whom you shall fear, and he will deliver you from the hand of all your enemies." **40** But they did not listen; instead, it was according to their former
practices that they were acting. **41** Now these nations were fearing Yahweh,
but it was their carved images that they were serving. Moreover, their children and grandchildren have been doing what their parents did right up to
the present day.

Textual Notes

34a–a. כַּמִּשְׁפָּטִים הָרִאשֹׁנִים: Gk. "their judgment"; Vulg. and Syr. with MT.

34b. אֵינָם: Gk. omits; Vulg. and Syr. with MT.

38a. כָּרַתִּי: Gk. and Vulg. "he cut"; Syr. with MT.

40a–a. כִּי אִם־כְּמִשְׁפָּטָם הָרִאשׁוֹן הֵם עֹשִׂים: Gk. "to their judgment that they practice."; Vulg. and Syr. with MT.

41a. יְרֵאִים: Syr. adds "also who dwelt in Samaria"; Gk. and Vulg. with MT.

Commentary

Commentators are divided over who is being addressed in this section, and even what its purpose is. Some would suggest that its purpose, along with vv. 24–33, it to paint the later Samaritans in an unfavorable light (Fritz, 356). But Cogan and Tadmor (213–14) rightly dispute this, showing that the description of the behaviors here do not really fit the historic Samaritans. Others suggest that it is describing the Israelite exiles, constituting a further call for their repentance.[38] Still others (e.g., Sweeney, 396) believe it

38. For further discussion on this point, see Gary N. Knoppers, "Cutheans or Children of Jacob?: The Issue of Samaritan Origins in 2 Kings 17" in *Reflection and Refraction: Studies in Biblical Historiography in Honour of A. Graeme Auld*, ed.

is speaking of the newcomers in Israel, either showing that they can never become members of the covenant community or demanding that they do become obedient to the covenant. I want to offer a further suggestion. I suggest that it reflects the appeals of both Hezekiah and Josiah to the people in the new Assyrian province of Samaria, both native (left behind when the leaders were deported) and non-native, to become once again, or for a first time, full participants in the covenant of Yahweh (2 Chr 30:1–12; 34:6–9). One can almost hear a prophet dispatched from Jerusalem speaking the words of vv. 35–39. That sort of setting could explain the sudden shift from the prevailing third person references to Yahweh to first person in v. 38, a kind of shift that is not uncommon in prophetic speech. But the narrator, probably speaking from the time of Josiah, reflects on the overall failure of these efforts (perhaps in the hopes that his Judean audience would not take the same path). The references to "to this day" (עַד הַיּוֹם הַזֶּה, *ʿaḏ hayyôm hazze*) and "former practices" (הֵם עֹשִׂים כַּמִּשְׁפָּטִים הָרִאשֹׁנִים, *hēm ʿōśîm kammišpāṭîm hāriʾšōnîm,*) in vv. 34 and 40–41 form an inclusio that defines the unit, and also tell us what was the final outcome: the people (both old and new) preferred their former מִשְׁפָּטִים, *mišpāṭîm* ("practices") to the מִשְׁפָּטִים ("regulations") of Yahweh. The word play makes the point forcefully: they did not want their lives to be constricted by any exclusive loyalty to Israel's God. They wanted to follow old, familiar practices of their own, whether Israelites or newcomers. They did not want to allow this uncontrollable God to be able to tell them what to do.

34 More so even than vv. 7–23 this unit stresses the terms of the covenant: "according to their statutes, regulations, instruction, and commandment" (כְּחֻקֹּתָם וּכְמִשְׁפָּטָם וְכַתּוֹרָה וְכַמִּצְוָה, *kᵊḥuqqōṯām ûḵᵊmišpāṭām wᵊḵattôrâ wᵊḵammiṣwâ*) (again in v. 37). It is hardly accidental that while these terms all appear in Deuteronomy (5:31; 6:1; etc.), this particular combination of them first appears in David's charge to Solomon in 1 Kings 2:3, and not again until here. Then they are found again in Neh 9:13 and 10:29, which seem to be a conscious reflection on this passage, asserting that the returned exiles have finally gotten the point and are ready to obey.

35–36 Here the meaning of "fearing" (ירא, *yrʾ*) a deity is made very clear.[39] It is much more than merely worshipping or admitting the existence of. It is to allow this deity's wishes, intents, and directions to shape one's life. Given the unique nature of Yahweh, to fear him has an exclusive quality that precludes

---

Robert Rezetko, Timothy H. Lim and W. Brian Aucker (Leiden: Brill, 2006) 223–39.

39. Shawn Z. Aster maintains on the basis of Akkadian usage that "fear" has two somewhat differing connotations: worship of a deity and exclusive allegiance. He sees the first usage in vv. 25–33, and the second here. "'They Feared God'/'They Did Not Fear God': On the Use of *Yērēʾ* and *Yārēʾ et YHWH* in 2 Kings 17:24–41," *Birkat Shalom* (2008): 135–41.

allowing the wishes of any other so-called god from such life-shaping. Here, it is the particular involvement of Yahweh with people in history that gives his claims their exclusive power. He is the one who picked out their ancestor Jacob and gave him the name Israel. Then he "brought them up" (הֶעֱלָה, *he ʿělâ*) from Egypt with an unmistakable demonstration of his power. The remaining Israelites should know this, and the new non-Israelites, like the "mixed multitude" (עֵרֶב רַב, *ʿēreḇ raḇ*) of Exodus 12:38, are invited to become part of this unique family, and to demonstrate it by living out his covenant requirements.

Throughout the segment terms are "fronted" to give them emphasis. So here "Yahweh" (אֶת־יהוה, *ʾeṯ-yhwh*), the object, precedes a long descriptive clause, then to be resumed in "him you shall fear" (אֹתוֹ תִירָאוּ, *ʾōṯô ṯîrāʾû*). He is the one to whom you should "prostrate yourself (i.e., worship)" (תִשְׁתַּחֲווּ, *ṯišᵉttaḥăwû*) and "bring sacrifice" (תִזְבְּחוּ, *ṯizbāḥû*), not some foreign god. That prohibition is repeated three times (vv. 35, 37, 38). Clearly, the Israelites remaining in the land, already conditioned to an idolatrous worship of Yahweh on all the high places, with a touch of Baalism thrown in, would be very prone to fall into the practices of all these newcomers with their exotic new deities. The appeal was that they refuse those deities, and that the newcomers recognize that this land was Yahweh's, not Nergal's or Ashima's or whoever's, and choose to live in the fear of him.

39 As Long (458) points out, the final promise of this verse, that Yahweh would protect his "fearers" from "all your enemies" (כָּל־אֹיְבֵיכֶם, *kol-ʾōyᵉḇêḵem*), would have had relevance for multiple audiences. The terribly insecure people, native and nonnative, in the new province of Samaria could have heard it. The people of Judah, watching Assyria crumble under the blows of the Medo-Babylonian alliance, and wondering what it could mean for them, could have heard it. The exiles in Babylon could have heard it. The returnees, facing enemies north, south, and east could have heard it.

40 Sadly, the people in Samaria, would not hear it. As has been said elsewhere above, to "listen" (שׁמע, *šmʿ*) in the biblical setting is to obey. That was not something they were willing to do. The Israelites kept on with their former practices, and the newcomers did as well (2 Chr 30:10). Neither group was willing to leave the comfortable confines of a manipulative religion and launch out into the frightening waters of an exclusive trust of Yahweh.

41 This is not to say that either group ignored Yahweh. Obviously, that would be a dangerous thing to do—they remembered the lions. But give him exclusive rights to oneself? Why would one do that? The irony of the situation is expressed in this verse through the sentence structure. The first clause is in normal order: "Now these nations were fearing Yahweh" (וַיִּהְיוּ הַגּוֹיִם הָאֵלֶּה יְרֵאִים אֶת־יהוה, *wayyihyû haggôyim hāʾēlle yᵉrēʾîm ʾeṯ-yhwh*) but the second is reversed: "but their carved images they were serving" (וְאֶת־פְּסִילֵיהֶם הָיוּ עֹבְדִים,

wᵉ ʾeṯ-pᵉsîlêhem hāyû ʿōḇᵉḏîm). We might paraphrase it in this way: "They appeared to be fearing Yahweh, but it was actually their idols that they were serving." So it was in the years immediately following Israel's defeat, and so it continued for generations thereafter.

Application and Devotional Implications

The temptation to superficial religion is a perennial one. It is far too easy to claim adherence to God, while living in ways that say we do not adhere to him at all. This was the continual concern of the prophets, and it is no less a concern today. Unless our relationship to God affects our bank accounts, our diversions, our entertainment, and the way we treat others, especially our family, observers have every right to question whether we have any relationship with him at all. Dietrich Bonhoeffer spoke of "cheap grace" in his classic book *The Cost of Discipleship*.[40] He meant that believing we could have Christ's gracious forgiveness without a corresponding giving of ourselves to him for remaking and for service was to misunderstand why Christ came in the first place. This is the point that the apostle Paul is making in Romans 6: to receive Christ is to die with him, to die to a life of self-serving and self-aggrandizement, and to rise with him to a life of self-denying, self-giving love. It is impossible to fear Yahweh and to serve idols. It will not work.

Selected Bibliography

Amit, Y. "The Samaritans: Biblical Considerations in the Solution of a Political Problem." Pages 192–203 in *Secularism and Biblical Studies*. Edited by Roland Boer. London: Equinox, 2010.

House, P. R. "Examining the Narratives of Old Testament Narrative: An Exploration in Biblical Theology." *WTJ* 67 (2005): 229–45.

Jobling, D. "The Salvation of Israel in 'The Book of the Divided Kingdoms': Or, Was There any 'Fall of the Northern Kingdom'?" Pages 50–61 in *Redirected Travel: Alternative Journeys and Places in Biblical Studies*. JSOTSup 382. Edited by Edgar W. Conrad and Roland Boer. London: T&T Clark, 2003.

Kartveit, M. "The Date of II Reg 17,24–41." *ZAW* 126 (2014): 31–44.

Knoppers, G. N. *Jews and Samaritans: The Origins and History of Their Early Relations*. Oxford: Oxford University Press, 2013.

40. Dietrich Bonhoeffer, *The Cost of Discipleship* (New York: Scribner, 1963), 3.

Judah Alone
(18:1–25:30)

The final division of the book(s) of Kings is given over to a treatment of the last 150 years of the Israelite people's existence as an independent nation, in the form of the kingdom of Judah. Although Judah had eight different kings during that period the lion's share of attention is given to just two of them: Hezekiah and Josiah. Clearly the author/editor(s) is of the opinion that these two did more to shape the ultimate destiny of the Israelite people than all the rest put together. Hezekiah receives three chapters and Josiah two while the other five altogether receive only three. Perhaps the reasoning behind this treatment was that because of Hezekiah's trust in Yahweh, Judah was spared from succumbing to Assyria at the same time the northern kingdom of Israel did. Likewise, because of Josiah's thoroughgoing purging of idolatrous worship, some of those who went into captivity after Zedekiah's calamitous reign were prepared to survive the captivity with their faith intact.

This final section of the book(s) of Kings completes the story of the monarchy that began with the accession of David's son Solomon and ends with the deliverance of David's descendant Jehoiachin from a Babylonian prison. The primary focus of attention after the report of the division of the kingdom in 1 Kings chapter twelve has been on events in the northern kingdom of Israel, with particular attention given to the dual ministry of Elijah and Elisha, and the struggle to prevent Baalism from replacing Yahwism in Israel (1 Kgs 17:1–2 Kgs 13:25). This is not to say that Judah has been ignored, but by and large it has been discussed against the backdrop of what was taking place in the north. But now Israel is gone, a province of Assyria, and the storyline is limited to the southern kingdom.

It would be pleasant to be able to say that the Judeans had observed what took place in the north and learned from it. To be sure, there were two moments, Hezekiah's twenty-nine years and Josiah's thirty-one, when it seemed that might have been the case. But in fact, these were anomalies in an inexorably downward course, arguably set by Hezekiah's father Ahaz, and confirmed by Hezekiah's son Manasseh, that followed the same track

Israel had laid out already. It is worth noting that there is no concluding statement concerning Judah's sins as there was for Israel in 2 Kings 17. It is as though what was said there looking backward over Israel's behavior is understood also to point forward to the same behavior in Judah that would result in the same fate.[1]

1. As noted above, on 17:16–17, some of the sins described, particularly child sacrifice, are more typical of Judah than of Israel (16:3–4; 21:5–6). This gives further credence to the likelihood that chapter 17 is fulfilling a dual function. It must also be considered that an earlier form of the book might have ended with chap. 17 and that chaps. 18–25 are a postscript. See the "Introduction."

Hezekiah (18:1–20:21)

Introduction

The text of Hezekiah's reign is composed of his regnal account (18:1–12; 20:20–21) and two narratives which have been inserted into that account. The first of these details the attack of the Assyrian King Sennacherib on Jerusalem in 701 BC (18:13–19:37), while the second reports the events surrounding an illness of Hezekiah's (20:1–19). In the main, these accounts are duplicated in Isaiah 36–39, and the relationship between that material and this is a matter of some question. (See the "Excursus on 2 Kings 18:13–20:21 in Comparison to Isaiah 36:1–39:8.") Here the inserted accounts serve to illustrate the statements of 18:5–8 that Hezekiah was remarkably faithful to Yahweh and that Yahweh reciprocated by caring for Hezekiah in special ways.

Outline

- III. JUDAH ALONE 18:1–25:30
  - A. Hezekiah 18:1–20:21
    - 1. Hezekiah's opening regnal account 18:1–12
    - 2. Hezekiah versus Sennacherib 18:13–19:37
      - a. Hezekiah's attempt to pay Sennacherib to withdraw 18:13–16
      - b. Sennacherib's messenger 18:17–37
        - i. The Rab-shaqeh's first address 18:17–25
        - ii. The Israelite party's request 18:26
        - iii. The Rab-shaqeh's second address 18:27–37
      - c. Hezekiah's anguish and Yahweh's response 19:1–7
      - d. Sennacherib's letter and Hezekiah's prayer 19:8–19
      - e. Yahweh's response 19:20–34
      - f. The destruction of the Assyrian army 19:35–37
    - 3. Hezekiah's illness and recovery 20:1–11
    - 4. The embassy from Babylon 20:12–21

Hezekiah's Opening Regnal Account (18:1–12)

Translation

18:1 It was in the third year of Hoshea, son of Elah, king of Israel, that Hezekiah, son of Ahaz, king of Judah, became king. **2** He was twenty-five years old when he began to reign and was king for twenty-nine years in Jerusalem; his mother's name was Abi, daughter of Zechariah. **3** He did right in the sight of Yahweh according to all his father David did. **4** He took away the high places, broke the standing stones, cut down the Asherah pole, and broke in pieces the bronze serpent Moses made, because until that time the people of Israel had burned incense to it. He called it Nehushtan. **5** It was in Yahweh, God of Israel, that he trusted, and after him there was none like him among all the kings of Judah, nor those who were before him. **6** He clung to Yahweh and he did not turn aside from after him and he carefully kept his commandments which Yahweh had commanded Moses. **7** Yahweh was with him; every place he went he was successful. He rebelled against the king of Assyria and would not serve him. **8** He struck the Philistines as far as Gaza and its borders, from watchtower to fortified city.

9 It was in the fourth year of King Hezekiah, that is, the seventh year of Hoshea, son of Elah, king of Israel, that Shalmaneser, king of Assyria, went up against Samaria and besieged it. **10** At the end of three years he captured it;[1] in the sixth year of Hezekiah, that is, in the ninth year of Hoshea, king of Israel, Samaria was captured. **11** The king of Assyria deported Israel to Assyria and settled them[2] in Halah, on the Habor, the river of Gozan, and in the cities of Medea. **12** It was because they would not listen to the voice of Yahweh their God; they transgressed his covenant, all that Moses, the servant of Yahweh, commanded. They did not listen nor do.

Textual Notes

4a. וְכִתַּת: Gk. omits; Vulg. and Syr. with MT.

4b. עַד־הַיָּמִים: Syr. adds "the children of Israel had gone astray after it and"; Gk. and Vulg. with MT.

10a. וַיִּלְכְּדֻהָ: All the versions "he [sg.] captured it."

Commentary

This account consists of three parts: the first part is found in verses 1–4 and corresponds with the opening statements for most Judean kings up to this point: a synchronism with the northern kingdom for the beginning of the reign; the king's age at his accession; the total years of his reign; his mother's

1. "he captured it" with the versions (see "Textual Note" 10a). Perhaps omitted in MT as redundant with the final verb.

2. Reading the vb. וַיַּנְחֵם, *wayyanḥēm* as a *hiphil* with the versions.

name; and an evaluation of his behavior. The second part is found in verses 5–8 and is an expansion of the evaluation. The third part (vv. 9–12) expands on the synchronism with Israel, calling attention to the capture of Samaria as the final act in the destruction of the kingdom of Israel. All of this information is preparing us for the report of one particular event in Hezekiah's reign, which extends from 18:13 through 21:27. The account deals with Sennacherib's response to Hezekiah's rebellion against him, and why Judah did not suffer the same fate that Israel had suffered just twenty years earlier.

1 There is disagreement over Hezekiah's dates because of what appears to be a discrepancy in the biblical data. The third year of Hoshea would be 726 BC, and the narrative clearly supports Hezekiah being on the throne before Samaria fell in 722 BC. But this was not a sole rule; it was a coregency with his father Ahaz, whose rule did not end until 717/16 BC. The problem arises in 8:13 which states that Sennacherib came against Judah in Hezekiah's fourteenth year. If we take 727/26 BC as the beginning of Hezekiah's reign and count his regnal years from that date as the Bible typically does, the Assyrian attack would have occurred in 712/11 BC, a clear impossibility given the secure Assyrian chronology.[3] The attack occurred in 701 BC. It seems most likely to me that in 8:13 the Bible, against its normal pattern, is dating the Assyrian attack from the beginning of Hezekiah's sole rule.[4,5] If we accept this explanation, it is not necessary to go through the rather elaborate process that Thiele does to explain how the Bible got Hezekiah's opening dates wrong and then creates an imaginary narrative of his reigning during Israel's final years.[6]

2 This verse poses chronological problems for a coregency with Ahaz, in that Hezekiah could not have been twenty-five years old in 726 BC, as this would have had Ahaz engendering Hezekiah when Ahaz was five years old! Once

3. See William R. Gallagher, *Sennacherib's Campaign to Judah: New Studies*, SHCANE 18 (Leiden: Brill, 1999).

4. For a recent review of the issues and the suggestion that 18:13a was originally the heading for the account of Hezekiah's illness (and was correctly referring to 712 or 711 BC), see David Miano, "What Happened in the Fourteenth Year of Hezekiah?: A Historical Analysis of 2 Kings 18–20 in the Light of New Textual Considerations," in *Milk and Honey: Essays on Ancient Israel and the Bible in Appreciation of the Judaic Studies Program at the University of California, San Diego*, ed. Sarah Melana and David Miano (Winona Lake, IN: Eisenbrauns, 2007), 113–32.

5. Montgomery and Gehman made the suggestion that "fourteenth" is an error for "twenty-fourth," an easy change in Hebrew (483). But there is no textual support for the variant.

6. Thiele, *Mysterious Numbers*, 139–59; Galil, on the other hand, argues concisely and convincingly for the chronology outlined above (*The Chronology of the Kings of Israel and Judah*, 98–104). So also Cogan and Tadmor, 216. See Long for a helpful review of the various alternatives (461–63).

again, it appears that this was Hezekiah's age when he began his sole reign, but that the total years of his reign were counted from the beginning of his coregency.[7] With this understanding, Hezekiah would have been about 15 years old when an anti-Assyrian group in the Judean hierarchy would have forced him upon his father as coregent. Perhaps we can hypothesize a revolt against Ahaz's Assyrian alliance as being the cause of such an action.

3 The direct comparison with David is only found elsewhere, and not unexpectedly, with Asa (1 Kgs 15:11) and Josiah (2 Kgs 22:2). These three were the kings who in the eyes of the editor(s) met the qualifications of a Davidic monarch; he does not merely do right "as his father(s) did" (1 Kgs 22:43; 2 Kgs 15:3, 34), but in the manner of the man David who had a heart for God. These were men whose hearts were wholly for God (1 Kgs 15:14; 2 Kgs 20:3; 23:3).

4–6 The description of Hezekiah's actions given in v. 4 is very terse compared to what is said of Josiah (23:4–20). Rosenbaum suggests that the report here may have been condensed to highlight Josiah's actions.[8] Whatever the explanation might be, it is still very significant that this is the first Judean king to effectively reverse what took place during Rehoboam's reign (1 Kgs 14:23). The parallel language of that verse and this ("high places [הַבָּמוֹת, *habbāmôṯ*], standing stones [הַמַּצֵּבֹת, *hammaṣṣēḇōṯ*], Asherah pole [הָאֲשֵׁרָה, *hāʾăšērâ*]"[9]) makes it look as though there is an intentional connection between that event and this.[10] Hezekiah had restored Judah (and Israel?) to a state unlike any since the best days of Solomon. In fact, it was better than Solomon's day because Hezekiah destroyed "the bronze snake Moses had made" (נְחַשׁ הַנְּחֹשֶׁת אֲשֶׁר־עָשָׂה מֹשֶׁה, *nᵊḥaš hannᵊḥōšeṯ ʾăšer-ʿāśâ mōše*) (Num 21:4–9).[11] Commentators debate whether the object may have had Egyptian overtones that were now offensive to Mesopotamian powers, but that is to engage in speculations which are quite foreign to what the text is attempting to communicate.[12] As Cogan and Tadmor (220) rightly say, there is every reason to think that Hezekiah had learned the lessons of the fall of the northern kingdom, that it was the worship of false gods that had precipitated the tragic event, and that he was determined, so far as he was able, to turn Judah

---

7. So also Gray, 670.

8. J. Rosenbaum, "Hezekiah's Reform and the Deuteronomic Tradition," *HTR* 72 (1979): 41–3.

9. Provan, noting the sg. in MT, suggests this may have been an Asherah pole which Ahaz had erected (254).

10. Interestingly 2 Chr 31:1 makes this the work of the people in a frenzy of enthusiasm at the completion of the Festival of Unleavened Bread, one unlike any since the days of Solomon.

11. Note the word play involved in the name given the bronze snake: "bronze" is נְחֹשֶׁת, *nᵊḥōšeṯ*, while "snake" is נָחָשׁ, *nāḥāš*.

12. Hershel Shanks, "The Mystery of the Nechushtan," *BAR* 33/2 (2007): 58–63.

away from such a fate. Evidently Hezekiah's actions were so complete and widespread that they even attracted the attention of the Assyrians (18:22).[13] As far as the text is concerned, there was one motivation for the actions: trust *in Yahweh, the God of Israel* (v. 5). The Assyrian officer understood this, but to him, not understanding Israel's covenant with Yahweh, the destruction of the high places was counterintuitive. To an idolater, it would seem that more worship centers, not less, would be advisable. The idea that there is only one God, not many, was unthinkable.[14]

The statement that "there was no one like him among all the kings of Judah …" (לֹא־הָיָה כָמֹהוּ בְּכֹל מַלְכֵי יְהוּדָה, *lō ʾ-hāyâ kāmōhû bᵉkōl malkê yᵉhûdâ*) seems contradicted by the same statement made of both Solomon (1 Kgs 10:23) and Josiah (2 Kgs 23:25). Knoppers suggests that each of the three excelled in different ways: Solomon in riches and wisdom; Hezekiah in trust in Yahweh, and Josiah in rooting out paganism.[15] Sweeney (403–4) believes rather that the discrepancy reflects a Hezekian recension whose statement was not corrected when the Josianic recension was completed. While this is certainly not impossible, it would reflect an inconsistency in the editing process that is hard to explain. Knoppers' reading seems more likely.[16]

The use of Deuteronomic language is v. 6 is very marked. "And he clung to" (וַיִּדְבַּק, *wayyidbaq*), "did not turn aside from it" (לֹא־סָר מֵאַחֲרָיו, *lō ʾ-sār mē ʾaḥărāyw*), and "and he carefully kept" (וַיִּשְׁמֹר, *wayyišmōr*) are all expressions that occur frequently in that book. Their appearance here underscores the argument that Hezekiah's actions were shaped by a renewed commitment to the Mosaic covenant, growing out of his observation of what had happened to the northern kingdom. In particular, "clung to" is notable. It occurs

---

13. Evidence of Hezekiah's actions is found at Beersheba, where a horned altar was dismantled at this time and pieces of it were incorporated in a nearby wall. See Yohanon Araroni, "The Horned-Altar of Beer-Sheba," *BA* 37 (1974): 2–6."

14. The absence of conclusive archeological evidence for these actions has spawned a considerable literature. Some of these are: Oded Borowski, "Hezekiah's Reforms and the Revolt Against Assyria," *BA* 58 (1995): 148–55; Diane Edelmann, "Hezekiah's Alleged Cultic Centralization," *JSOT* 32 (2008): 395–434; Nadav Na ʾaman, "The Debated Historicity of Hezekiah's Reform in the Light of Historical and Archeological Research, *ZAW* 107 (1995): 179–95.

As with the activity of Jehu in the north a century earlier, the actions of the king do not necessarily translate into a true reformation of the people and their sentiments. That Manasseh was so quickly able to reverse all that Hezekiah had done is an indication that the reform had not touched the hearts of many people.

15. Gary N. Knoppers, "'There Was None Like Him': Incomparability in the Books of Kings," *CBQ* 54 (1992): 411–431. Long shares this way of understanding what the text says (466).

16. So also, Hobbs, 252.

with reference to Yahweh five times in Deuteronomy,[17] twice in Joshua (22:5; 23:8), in Psalm 63:8 [MT 9] and here. The other 46 occurrences are not used in this way. All this supports Hezekiah's plea in 20:3 that he had followed God with his whole heart.

7–8 In these verses we are given two examples of Yahweh's response to Hezekiah's devotion: because Hezekiah "clung to" Yahweh, "Yahweh was with him (וְהָיָה יהוה עִמּוֹ, *wᵉhāyâ yhwh ʿimmô*) ... he was successful (יַשְׂכִּיל, *yaśkîl*)." Because of the divine presence, Hezekiah was able to rebel successfully against Assyria and was able to reassert Judean control over the Philistine coastal cities for the first time since that of David. This latter action was a specific expression of his rebellion against Assyria since Sargon II had captured Gaza only a few years earlier. No chronological data is given here since these two elements are only presented as evidence of Yahweh's power being extended on Hezekiah's behalf.

9–12 Wiseman (273) argues that the reason for the inclusion of this report of Israel's fall in these verses is to highlight the contrast with Hezekiah and Judah. Israel fell, but Judah did not. Why? The explanation of Israel's fall is given in v. 12. It happened because the Israelites had persistently broken their covenant with Yahweh. The Assyrians under Sennacherib were no less devastating than those under Shalmaneser V, but the difference was that Yahweh was with Hezekiah, and he was not with Hoshea.

9–10 Cogan and Tadmor (196, 199, 216) have argued that Hoshea had been removed at the beginning of the siege and that there was actually no king in Israel during the time of the siege. If that were correct, then the datings given in vv. 9–10 would be artificially constructed. Galil agrees that Hoshea was imprisoned at the beginning of the siege, but dates that event in 722 BC, and that thus the biblical synchronisms are correct.[18]

It is perhaps significant that it is not said who the Assyrian emperor was when Samaria fell (Heb. "and "they took it," [וַיִּלְכְּדֻהָ, *wayyilkᵉḏuhā*] thus NIV "the Assyrians took it"). Shalmaneser's successor, Sargon II, claims in several different places (cf. *ANET*, 284, 285, 286) that he was the one who captured Samaria and exiled its inhabitants. Possibly Shalmaneser began the siege but died just as it was ending.[19]

12 "They did not listen to the voice of Yahweh their God" (לֹא־שָׁמְעוּ בְּקוֹל יהוה אֱלֹהֵיהֶם, *lōʾ-šomʿû bᵉqôl yhwh ʾĕlōhêhem*) is conventionally translated "they did not obey Yahweh their God." That is certainly not incorrect, but it misses some of the relational flavor of the Hebrew. The central characteristic of the

---

17. 4:4; 10:20; 11:22; 13:4 [MT 5]; 30:20.

18. Galil, *The Chronology of the Kings of Israel and Judah*, 86–94.

19. See the "Commentary" above on 17:3–6 for further discussion.

God of the Bible is that he speaks, not merely indirectly through possessed persons whose mutterings must be interpreted, but in a whole variety of ways. He speaks because he wants intimate relationships with human beings. Thus, to listen to him is not merely to do what he wants, but to hear his heart. Because they did not listen, they did not merely break their covenant with him, but they violated it, they "transgressed" (עבר, *ʿbr*) it. This is very different behavior from that of Hezekiah, who trusted Yahweh (v. 5), clung to him, did not turn aside from after him, and carefully kept the commands Moses gave (v. 6).

Selected Bibliography

Jonker, L. C. "The Disappearing Neḥushtan: The Chronicler's Reinterpretation of Hezekiah's Reformation Measures." Pages 116–40 in *"From Ebla to Stellenbosch": Syro-Palestinian Religions and the Hebrew Bible*. Edited by Izak Cornelius and Louis Jonker. Wiesbaden: Harrassowitz, 2008.

Tadmor, H. "The Campaigns of Sargon II of Assur: A Chronological-Historical Study." *JCS* 12 (1958): 22–40, 77–100.

Vera Chamaza, G. W. "Literarkritische Beoabachtung zu 2 Kön 18:1–12." *BZ* 33 (1989): 222–33.

Weinfeld, M. "Cult Centralization in Israel in the Light of a Neo-Babylonian Analogy." *JNES* 23 (1964): 202–12.

Hezekiah versus Sennacherib (18:13–19:37)[20]

It seems probable that Hezekiah attempted to put together a coalition of the small states located in the southern Levant to oppose Sennacherib. The clearest evidence of this is the statement that he had captured and imprisoned the king of the Philistine city, Ekron (*ANET*, 287b). The probable reason for this is that Padi refused to join the coalition (just as Ahaz had refused to join the coalition sponsored by Pekah and Rezin [Isa 7:1]). This meant that Hezekiah was "enemy number one" on Sennacherib's list. This was a very dangerous position in which to be, for by 701 BC, Sennacherib had

20. Ever since the work of B. Stade, "Anmerkungen zu 2 Kö 15–21," *ZAW* 6 (1886): 172–186, it has been customary to see the material between 18:13 and 19:37 as being composed of two accounts of the same experience (called the A account and the B account). The A account (18:13–16) is taken to be factual, whereas the B account (18:17 – 19:37) is made up of two prophetic narratives (B1 and B2) which are two differing depictions of Sennacherib's attack on Judah. See Cogan and Tadmor for a fairly standard exposition of this view (241–244). Sweeney, without holding that the material as it now stands reflects a factual account, nevertheless, rejects the thesis presented by Stade, saying that it is built upon an outmoded 19th century understanding of the creation of literature, and argues for looking at the account as a whole from the point of more modern understandings of that creation (411–414).

dispatched all the other contenders for the throne, had defeated enemies in Urartu to the north and Babylon to the south and was in a position to enforce his will anywhere he chose.

If Hezekiah had succeeded in forging a coalition, it fell apart the instant the Assyrian army appeared on the scene, and Judah was left alone to face the full wrath of the Assyrian emperor. This passage records the details of that encounter and its surprising denouement.

Hezekiah's Attempt to Pay Sennacherib to Withdraw (18:13–16)

Translation

13 In the fourteenth year of King Hezekiah Sennacherib, king of Assyria, came up against all the fortified cities of Judah and captured them. **14** Hezekiah, king of Judah, sent to the king of Assyria at Lachish, saying, "I have sinned; turn back from against me. Whatever you impose on me, I will bear." The king of Assyria imposed on Hezekiah, king of Judah, 300 talents of silver and thirty talents of gold. **15** Hezekiah gave all the silver that could be found in the house of God and in the treasuries of the house of the king. **16** At that time Hezekiah stripped the gold from the doors of the temple of Yahweh and the doorposts that Hezekiah had overlaid and gave it to the king of Assyria.

Textual Notes

14a. מֶלֶךְ־יְהוּדָה: Gk. adds "messengers"; Vulg. and Syr. with MT.

15a. בֵּית: Vulg. omits: Gk. and Syr. with MT. Vulg. result of homoioarchton with preceding word?

16a. קִצַּץ: Syr. reads "stripped the gold from"; Gk. and Vulg. with MT.

16b–b. וְאֶת־הָאֹמְנוֹת אֲשֶׁר צִפָּה חִזְקִיָּה מֶלֶךְ יְהוּדָה: Vulg. reads "and the gold plates he had affixed"; Gk. and Syr. "and the doorposts which Hezekiah, king of Judah had gilded." אֹמנוֹת' only occurs here.

Commentary

13–16 Those who believe that Isaiah 36–39 are copied from the original in 2 Kings,[21] often take it that the author of the Isaiah passage intentionally left out this material because it reflects badly on Hezekiah. However, as argued in the "Excursus on 2 Kings 18:13–20:21 in Comparison to Isaiah 36:1–39:8," there is good reason to believe that Isaiah 36–39 is original to Isaiah, and that the editors of Kings have used that material, edited for their purposes, and have supplemented it with this short excerpt from a Judahite chronicle (so

21. See e.g., Dana N. Fewell, "Sennacherib's Defeat: Words at War in 2 Kings 18.13–19.37," *JSOT* 34 (1986): 79–90.

Cogan and Tadmor, 240–41). Its position here prior to the material shared with Isaiah supports that conclusion.[22]

13–14 This campaign of Sennacherib, besides furthering the long-time Assyrian goal of reaching and subduing Egypt, was also an attempt to put down the various revolts that had occurred after the death of Sargon II, while Sennacherib was establishing himself as king. One of these revolts was in Babylon, and that was the first one that had to be seen to. With that out of the way, it was time to go to the west, where the Judean King Hezekiah had persuaded several of his neighboring nations, sometimes by force, to join him in rebelling against Assyria.[23] Judah was unable to withstand the Assyrian forces which seem to have ranged freely throughout the Judean countryside. Sennacherib reports that he took forty-six cities.[24] That must certainly have included every village that had any kind of fortification. Ultimately, only the great cities of Lachish and Jerusalem remained. Lachish was holding out, but it appeared to be only a question of time before it fell.[25] Faced with that probability, Hezekiah tried to buy off the Assyrian. The biblical report agrees with the Assyrian one as regards the amount of gold ("thirty talents") that Sennacherib demanded, but the Assyrian report has 800 talents of silver. The biblical account (18:14) has 300 talents of silver, which seems more realistic.

---

22. 18:13 is paralleled by Isaiah 36:1, but it is as easy to imagine the Kings material (18:14–16) as having been inserted into the original Isaiah material, as to imagine that Isaiah deleted it.

23. John Bright in his influential *History of Israel* (Philadelphia: Westminster, 1981), 298–309 argued forcefully for the theory that the Bible has conflated two campaigns against Judah into one. At various points this theory has surfaced again. See e.g., William Shea, "Sennacherib's Second Palestinian Campaign," *JBL* 104 (1985): 401–18. Paul S. Evans has argued that it is in fact the theory of two sources behind the biblical Sennacherib narrative that requires two campaigns, and that if the material is read as a literary unity, as is most natural, no second campaign needs to be posited (*The Invasion of Sennacherib in the Book of Kings: A Source-critical and Rhetorical Study of 2 Kings 18–19* VTSup 125 [Leiden: Brill, 2009], 198). Cogan and Tadmor point out that the Assyrian annals do not require such a reading either (246–51), as does also Murray Adamthwaite, "Sennacherib After Jerusalem," *RTR* 76 (2017): 1–22.

24. *ANET*, 288.

25. Sennacherib commemorated the capture of Lachish with several large reliefs in his palace at Nineveh. They show the fall of the city in graphic detail. Archeological excavations at Lachish confirm a massive destruction at this time. See David Usshiskin, *The Conquest of Lachish by Sennacherib* (Tel Aviv: Tel Aviv University, the Institute of Archeology, 1982). It is to be wondered whether Sennacherib's lavish self-congratulation over the fall of Lachish was a consolation prize for his failure to take Jerusalem.

While it is tempting to read into Hezekiah's words to Sennacherib ("I have sinned" [חָטָאתִי, *ḥāṭā ʾtiy*]) as an admission of failure to consult Yahweh prior to his actions, it seems more likely in the context that he is referring to the breaking of the vows of loyalty that Ahaz had made to Tiglath-pileser III many years earlier when he had paid the Assyrian to attack Syria and Israel (2 Kgs 16:7–10). It is a measure of Hezekiah's desperation that he would make such a huge payment (one ton of gold and eleven tons of silver) with no assurance whatsoever that Sennacherib would do what Hezekiah was asking. Any anxiety he may have had on that point would have been very warranted since the Assyrian king took all the money and stayed where he had been. In fact, if the material is in chronological order, his next step was to send his top officers to demand surrender.[26] One wonders what Isaiah had to say about Hezekiah's effort. Provan (255) calls it a regrettable lapse before Hezekiah's finest hour.

15–16 Once more Yahweh's temple and the king's treasuries are stripped to pay tribute to an enemy king. This had happened with boring frequency during the previous two centuries. It had been done by Rehoboam (1 Kgs 14:26); and by Asa (1 Kgs 15:18); Joash (2 Kgs 12:18), Amaziah (2 Kgs 14:14) and Ahaz (2 Kgs 16:8–9). Now it was Hezekiah's turn. Hobbs (248) makes the interesting observation that very often this stripping of the temple and the treasuries happened shortly after a great deal of money had been put into them. Perhaps Jesus' words "Do not lay up treasure on earth" (Matt 6:19) are appropriate in this setting.

It should be observed that "gold" in v. 16 is only implied, not actually stated. The text says that Hezekiah cut off the doors and doorposts which he had overlaid and gave them to the king of Assyria. However, it is highly unlikely that he would give the doors and doorposts themselves to Sennacherib. Thus, given the statement that Hezekiah had overlaid (צפה, *ṣph*) these objects, the implication (with virtually all English translations) seems probable (see p. 328, n16a and 16b–b).

Selected Bibliography

Cogan, M. "Sennacherib's Siege of Jerusalem: Once or Twice?" *BAR* 27/1 (2001): 40.

Kim, Y.-K. "In Search of a Narrator's Voice: A Discourse Analysis of 2 Kings 18:13–16." *JBL* 127 (2008): 477–89.

---

26. Evans, *Invasion*, 149–50, noting that v. 15 only reports that Hezekiah paid the silver, posits that Sennacherib remained (and sent his messengers demanding surrender) because he only received partial payment. While this is an intriguing theory, it must be pointed out, as Evans does to his credit, that Sennacherib claimed in his annals to have received the full amount of gold and silver he demanded (*ANET*, 288).

Sennacherib's Messenger (18:17–37)

The address quoted here is a masterpiece of psychological warfare. It is not logically arranged, and some of what is said in this first speech is contradicted in the second, but its impact is not intended to be rational. Rather, it is simply a series of hammer-blows designed for effect, that effect being the undermining of any will to resist the Assyrian demands. In particular, it is an attempt to demonstrate that there is absolutely nothing that can be trusted to deliver Judah from Assyria; not Egypt, not military strength, not Yahweh, and certainly not Hezekiah. The two parts of the message (18:19-25, and 18:27-35) are separated by the Israelite party asking the Rab-shaqeh to speak to them in Aramaic, not the Hebrew language of the listening crowd.

The word בָּטַח, *bāṭaḥ*, "trust" occurs no less than six times in vv. 19–24. As noted above, this emphasis fits very well in the context of Isaiah chapters seven to thirty-nine, where the central theme is trust in Yahweh or in human nations. There, this address serves to introduce the climax of that entire discussion.[27] Here, while the emphasis on trust is not inappropriate, it has not been central to the previous discussion as it is in Isaiah.

The Rab-shaqeh's First Address (18:17–25)

Translation

17 The king of Assyria sent the Tartan, the Rab-saris, and the Rab-shaqeh with a strong force from Lachish to Jerusalem. They went up and came to Jerusalem. They went up and came and stood by the aqueduct of the upper pool which in on the highway to the fuller's field. **18** They summoned the king, and Eliakim, son of Hilkiah, who was over the house, Shebna, the scribe, and Joah, son of Asaph, the recorder, went out to him. **19** The Rab-shaqeh said to them, "Say to Hezekiah, 'Thus says, the Great King, the King of Assyria, "What is this trust of yours in which you trust? **20** You have said, 'Mere words of the lips are counsel and strength for war.' Now in whom do you trust that you have rebelled against me? **21** Now look, you have entrusted yourself to the staff of broken reed, to Egypt, which when a man leans on it,

27. In Isaiah, chapters 36–39 function with chapters 7–12 as an inclusio. The latter chapters are certainly not a "historical appendix" as some Isaiah commentaries label them. Ahaz had refused to trust Yahweh, and Isaiah had therefore predicted the Assyrian "flood" that now engulfed Judah (7:12; 8:6–8). Now Hezekiah, Ahaz's son, is faced once more with the challenge to trust Yahweh. Formerly, it was Isaiah standing on "the highway to the fuller's field" (7:3) with the invitation to trust Yahweh. Now it is the Assyrian officer, standing on the same spot (36:2), who dares Hezekiah to trust Yahweh. The intervening chapters, 13–35, are a collection of materials designed to teach the folly of trusting the nations instead of Yahweh. We are intended to believe that Hezekiah had, in the end, learned the lesson those chapters are teaching.

it will go into his palm and pierce it. This is the pharaoh, king of Egypt, to all
those who trust in him. **22** But if you say to me, 'It is in Yahweh our God that
we are trusting,' was he not the one whose high places and altars Hezekiah
removed and said to Judah and Jerusalem, 'Before this altar you shall prostrate
yourselves in Jerusalem'?" **23** So now make a bargain with my lord, the King
of Assyria: I will give you 2,000 horses if you are able to put riders on them.
24 How can you withstand one officer of the least of my master's servants
when you put your trust in Egypt for chariots and horsemen? **25** Now is it
without Yahweh that I have come up against this place to destroy it? Yahweh
said to me, "Go up against this land and destroy it." ' "

Textual Notes

17a–a. וַיַּעֲלוּ וַיָּבֹאוּ: Lacking in Gk. and Vulg.; Syr. "and when they had come up." *CTAT* (410) considers MT likely in view of Kings' typical style.

18a–a. וַיִּקְרְאוּ אֶל־הַמֶּלֶךְ: Does not appear in Isa 36:3. Gray (675n.e) thinks the Isaiah reading is original.

20a–a. אָמַרְתָּ אַךְ־דְּבַר־שְׂפָתַיִם עֵצָה וּגְבוּרָה לַמִּלְחָמָה: Gk. "You said, 'Mere words of the lips are strategy and power for war' "; Vulg. "Perhaps you are taking counsel and preparing yourself for war"; Syr. "You have said that you are a good speaker and that you have counsel and strength for war." The differences in the versions seem to affirm the MT but testify to the uncertainty of its meaning. See the "Commentary" below.

21a. בָטַחְתָּ: Vulg. treats this sentence as a question; Gk. and Syr. with MT.

22a. אֱלֹהֵינוּ: Gk. omits "our"; Vulg. and Syr. with MT.

22b. בִּירוּשָׁלָםִ: Does not appear in Isa 36:7.

Commentary

17 The three Assyrian officers are the army commander (תַּרְתָּן, *T̲artān*, Isa 20:1), the "chief eunuch" (רַב־סָרִיס, *Rab̲-sārîs*, Jer 39:3, 13), and perhaps, the "chief cupbearer" (רַב־שָׁקֵה, *Rab̲-šāqēh*).[28] The last two almost certainly were historical terms that by this time no longer actually reflected the realities of their situation. Rather, they would have been, respectively, the king's official representative and his chief advisor. Why his chief advisor would have been selected for this task is unclear. It has been speculated that it may have been because he knew the Judean dialect (v. 28), but the text gives no explanation. Isaiah does not mention the first two officers. If Isaiah is the original text, then the editor(s) of Kings has probably included them for purposes of historical completeness.

---

28. In Neh 1:11 "cupbearer" is מַשְׁקֶה, *mašqeh,* which suggests the reading here.

Although Sennacherib claimed to have "shut up Hezekiah like a bird in a cage" (*COS* 2:203), that need not mean that he ever actually besieged Jerusalem. The "strong force" (בְּחֵיל כָּבֵד, *bəḥêl kāḇēḏ*) (v. 17) that accompanied the officers from Lachish was not the main Assyrian army. If it had been, Sennacherib would have come with them. This was an attempt to provoke a surrender and avoid the trouble and expense of having to move the army up to Jerusalem after the fall of Lachish and maintain it there for however long a siege might last, at the same time leaving Egypt free to attack his rear.

As has been noted above (p. 331n27), the location from which the Rab-shaqeh spoke, "the highway to the fuller's field" (בִּמְסִלַּת שְׂדֵה כוֹבֵס, *bimsillaṯ śəḏē kôḇēs*), is entirely appropriate to Isaiah, being the spot where Isaiah had challenged Ahaz to trust Yahweh thirty-five years earlier. There is no agreement as to where this site was located. Since the Gihon Spring, Jerusalem's main water source, was in the Kidron Valley, east of the city, it is tempting to think that it was located there. This would also be just below the structure thought to support the palace and might be a place for people to sit on the walls to observe the proceedings (vv. 26, 27). On the other hand, this narrow valley would not be a good place in which to arrange an army. For that reason, a site north of the city, perhaps at the head of the Tyropean Valley on the west side, has been suggested.

18 "They summoned the king" (וַיִּקְרְאוּ אֶל־הַמֶּלֶךְ, *wayyiqrəʾû ʾel-hammeleḵ*) does not appear in Isaiah. Again, it is likely that this is an addition to the Isaianic original, filling in the narrative with a likely historical detail which the original narrator had not felt it necessary to include. Hezekiah's three representatives were Eliakim, "who was over the house" (אֲשֶׁר עַל־הַבָּיִת, *ʾăšer ʿal-habbāyiṯ*), Shebna, "the scribe" (הַסֹּפֵר, *hassōp̄ēr*), and Joah, "the recorder" (הַמַּזְכִּיר, *hammazkîr*). As Isaiah had predicted in Isa 22:19–20, Shebna, who had been "over the house," had been demoted, and Eliakim had been put in his place. The position, which might be translated "king's steward" was almost certainly equivalent to "prime minister" (see the the "Commentary" above on 10:5). Although Shebna had been demoted, the position of official scribe was still very important. Writing would still have been an uncommon skill, and the production of official documents would have been vital. It is not clear exactly what the duties of the recorder were. Some believe that he was the chief accountant. However, it is also tempting to think that he may have been the official historian. The three positions are mentioned along with others in 1 Kings 4:1–6.

19–20 There is general agreement that the Rab-shaqeh's opening words are a calculated demeaning of Hezekiah. He calls the Judean by his personal name and gives him no title while he gives Sennacherib the formal title of "Great King, the King of Assyria" (הַמֶּלֶךְ הַגָּדוֹל מֶלֶךְ אַשּׁוּר, *hammeleḵ haggāḏôl meleḵ ʾaššûr*) without the individualizing personal name. Clearly, these two figures are not comparable in any way. Little Hezekiah has opposed himself to the mightiest figure in the world. Of course, the Bible will put the contest on the exact opposite footing. Little Sennacherib has opposed himself to I AM, the Lord of the universe.

If there were any question what this speech is about, it is dramatically answered in the Assyrian's first words, "What is this trust in which you are trusting?" (מָה הַבִּטָּחוֹן הַזֶּה אֲשֶׁר בָּטָחְתָּ, *mâ habbiṭṭāḥôn hazze ʾăšer bāṭāḥᵉttā*). Two sentences later, he states the issue even more pointedly: "In whom do you trust that you have rebelled against me?" (עַל־מִי בָטַחְתָּ כִּי מָרַדְתָּ בִּי, *ʿal-mî ḇāṭaḥtā kî māraḏtā bî*). What is it that could possibly make Hezekiah believe that he could successfully defy the mightiest man in the world? If we understand the intervening sentence correctly (the variety of translations in the versions is a testimony to the difficulty of the Heb.), the officer is saying that Hezekiah seems to have accepted the promises of Egypt (and also, perhaps, the promises of Isaiah?) and is trusting them. But they are only words, and as such, are worthless. Again, there is a very subtle undertone here. If the man's hearers wish to include the words of Yahweh in this category of worthlessness, they certainly may. It is not promises that count in "counsel and strength for war" (עֵצָה וּגְבוּרָה לַמִּלְחָמָה, *ʿēṣâ ûgᵉḇûrâ lammilḥāmâ*); it is military power on the ground.

21 Is Egypt likely to provide that military power? Hardly! Egypt is no more than one of the reeds that grow beside the Nile, and one that has already been bent at that. Try to lean on it and it will break and stab your hand. Ezekiel uses the same metaphor of Egypt many years later (Ezek 29:6), perhaps indicating a knowledge of this passage on his part.

22 As quickly as he moved to decimate Jerusalem's trust in Egypt, the messenger now moves to their trust in Yahweh. Here he shows the effectiveness of the Assyrian intelligence system. Whether from Judean sources or elsewhere, he knows about Judah's internal affairs, although his understanding of Hezekiah's religion is somewhat faulty. He knows that Hezekiah has destroyed all the shrines around the countryside where Yahweh was worshipped. To someone nurtured in the understanding that deity and nature (and humanity) are all one with each other, such an act would be senseless. The more places the divine can be placated and ritually served, the happier the divine is. The idea that Yahweh is *not* continuous with this world, and that ritual is not about caring for him was simply unthinkable. But it seems highly likely that there were plenty of Judeans who thought like the Rabshaqeh did and for whom this argument would have made a good deal of sense: Yahweh is not for you, because you have offended him by getting rid of his shrines. In fact, the exact opposite was the case; to the extent that Hezekiah had obeyed Yahweh's command, given through Moses hundreds of years earlier at the very beginning of the covenant stipulations (Deut 12:1–7), Yahweh was pleased.

23–24 Again, without pausing to elaborate on the previous hammer-blow, the Assyrian delivers another, this one dripping with sarcasm. Can Egypt supply the military equipment ("of chariots and of horsemen" [לְרֶכֶב וּלְפָרָשִׁים, *lᵉreḵeḇ ûlᵉpārāšîm*]) with which Judah can contend with Assyria? Suppose they could; does Judah have the trained soldiers to accompany them and make use of the equipment? Of course not! If it is equipment they need, why "make a bargain" (הִתְעָרֶב, *hiṯʿāreḇ*) with Egypt;[29] Assyria offers a better one. The reference to "horses" here may be to cavalry, a devastating new tactic being utilized by Assyria at this time, and one that Judah would have been ill-prepared to make use of. The point is that even with the latest military equipment, Judah would be unable to take advantage of it and would be hopelessly outclassed.

25 One more hammer blow falls. The Rab-shaqeh declares that Yahweh is not going to deliver them; in fact, Assyria has been sent by him "to destroy it" (לְהַשְׁחִתוֹ, *lᵉhašḥiṯô*). The text gives no reason to believe that this is connected to the statement in v. 22. It is simply one more devastating argument. It is possible that this is another intelligence coup: the Assyrian has been informed of Isaiah's and Micah's words to this effect (Isa 10:5–6; Mic 2:3–5).[30] However, it was not uncommon for the Assyrians to make such claims when they attacked a nation: "Your gods are angry with you and have sent us to destroy you," so that may the case here.[31] Nevertheless, it is indicative of careful preparation that the personal name of Judah's God, Yahweh, is used both here and in v. 22.

The Israelite Party's Request (18:26)

Translation

26 Then Eliakim, son of Kilkiah, and Shebna, and Joah said to the Rab-shaqeh, "Please speak to your servants in Aramaic because we understand it. Do not speak Judean with us in the ears of the people on the wall."

Textual Notes

26a. בֶּן־חִלְקִיָּהוּ: Lacking in Isa 36:11.

26b. בְּאָזְנֵי: Gk. adds "Why do you speak"; Vulg. and Syr. with MT.

Commentary

26 Cohn (131) makes the plausible suggestion that it was the claim that Yahweh had sent the Assyrians to destroy Jerusalem that prompted the

---

29. This is the only occurrence of this root in the *hithpael*. The sense is apparently reciprocal.

30. But if he knew of those words, did he also know of the judgments on Assyria that both prophets announced in the name of Yahweh (Isa 10:12–19; Mic 5:5–6)?

31. See Mordechai Cogan, *Imperialism and Religion: Assyria, Judah and Israel in the Eighth and Seventh Centuries B.C.E.*, SBLMS 19 (Missoula, MT: Scholars Press, 1974), 9–21, 111.

request that the Rab-shaqeh should put anything more he had to say in the common diplomatic language of the empire: Aramaic (אֲרָמִית, *ʾărāmîṯ*). This was the Semitic language of Syria. It is not known exactly why the Assyrians had adopted it as their diplomatic language. Since Syria was more or less in the center of the empire and the language was related to Akkadian, the Assyrians spoke it as well as all of the other Northwest Semitic languages, so it does seem to have been a good candidate.[32] If the Assyrian was going to enlist Yahweh on his side, it may well be that the ambassadors did not want the people thronging the tops of the walls to hear more of that.

Selected Bibliography

Bowman, R. A. "Arameans, Aramaic, and the Bible." *JNES* 7 (1948): 65–90.

The Rab-shaqeh's Second Address (18:27–37)

Translation

27 The Rab-shaqeh said, "Did my master send me to speak these words to your lord and to you? Is it not to the men sitting on the wall who will eat their own dung and drink their own urine with you?" **28** Then the Rab-shaqeh stood forth and called out in a loud voice in Judean and he spoke[33] and said, "Hear the word of the Great King, the king of Assyria: **29** Thus says the King, 'Do not let Hezekiah mislead you, because he is not able to deliver you from my[34] hand. **30** And do not let Hezekiah make you trust in Yahweh, saying, "Yahweh will surely deliver us, and this city will not be given into the hand of the king of Assyria."' **31** Do not listen to Hezekiah because thus says the king of Assyria, 'Do yourselves a favor,[35] and come out to me. Each man will eat from his vine and his fig tree and drink water from his own cistern, **32** until I come and take you to a land like your land, a land of grain and new wine, a land of bread and vineyards, a land of olives, olive oil, and

32. See Hayim Tadmor, "The Aramaization of Assyria," in *Mesopotamien un seine Nachbarn: Politische und kulturelle Wechselbziehungen im alten Vorderasien vom 4. bis 1. Jahrtausend v. Chr.,* ed. H-J. Nissen and J. Renger, BBVT 1 (Berlin: Reimer, 1983), 449–70.

33. This word (וַיְדַבֵּר, *waydabbēr*) does not occur in Isa 36:13 nor in the Vulg. Cogan and Tadmor take it to be a copyist's error, perhaps the result of the following דבר המלך *dbr hmlk* (232).

34. מִיָּדוֹ, *miyyāḏô* "his hand." All the versions "my hand."

35. Tg. reads "Make peace" and as that is what would be expected, it is followed by many translations. But MT has "Make a blessing" (עֲשׂוּ־אִתִּי בְרָכָה, *ʿăśû- ʾittî bᵉrāḵâ*), which is very unusual in this context. Cogan and Tadmor suggest "Bring a gift" and cite Josh 15:19; 1 Sam 30:26; 2 Kgs 5:15 (232). The present reading understands the "blessing" as being for themselves.

honey; live and do not die.[36] Do not listen to Hezekiah because he misleads you saying, "Yahweh will deliver us." **33** Has any god of the nations delivered his land from the hand of the king of Assyria? **34** Where are the gods of Hamath or Arpad? Where are the gods of Sepharvaim, Hena, or Ivvah, that they delivered Samaria from my hand? **35** Who is it among all the gods of the lands who delivered their land from my hand that Yahweh should deliver Jerusalem from my hand?' " **36** The people were silent and did not answer him a word because it was the command of the king, saying, "Do not answer him." **37** Eliakim, son of Hilkiah, who was over the house, Shebna the scribe, and Joah the recorder, went to Hezekiah with their clothes torn and informed him of the words of the Rab-shaqeh.

Textual Notes

27a–a. הַעַל אֲדֹנֶיךָ וְאֵלֶיךָ שְׁלָחַנִי אֲדֹנִי לְדַבֵּר אֶת־הַדְּבָרִים הָאֵלֶּה הֲלֹא: Syr. "It was not to you and your master that my master sent me to speak these words, but to"; Gk. and Vulg. with MT.

27b. הֲלֹא: Gk. "and not"; Vulg. with MT.

28a. בְקוֹל־גָּדוֹל: Lacking in Isa 36:13.

28b. וַיְדַבֵּר: Lacking in Vulg.; Gk. and Syr. with MT.

28c. מֶלֶךְ: Lacking in Gk.; Vulg. and Syr. with MT.

29a. חִזְקִיָּהוּ: Gk. adds "with words"; Vulg. and Syr. with MT.

29b. מִיָּדוֹ: Lacking in Isa 36:14. The versions (except Vaticanus, which agrees with MT) read "my hand."

31a–a. וְאִכְלוּ אִישׁ־גַּפְנוֹ וְאִישׁ תְּאֵנָתוֹ: Gk. "each man drink from his vine and eat from his fig tree"; Vulg. and Syr. with MT.

32a–a. אֶרֶץ דָּגָן וְתִירוֹשׁ: Vulg. "a fruitful land, and fruitful vines"; Syr. "a land of many kinds of fruit trees" Gk. with MT.

34a–a. הֵנַע וְעִוָּה: Lacking in Isa 36:19 and in Gk.; Vulg. and Syr. with MT, except Syr. reads "Na" for "Hena"; *CTAT* (411) considers MT possibly correct.

36a. הָעָם: Gk. lacks, thus reading "They were silent"; Vulg. and Syr. with MT.

---

36. Most Eng. versions follow the lead of the KJV and translate "that you may live and not die." But the Heb. is very terse (וִחְיוּ וְלֹא תָמֻתוּ, *wiḥyû wᵊlōʾ tāmuṯû*), simply giving two imperatives, as shown in the "Translation" above.

Commentary

27 But the Rab-shaqeh would have none of it. His purpose in coming was to intimidate the Judeans into surrender, and he was not going to limit that effort in any way. It was precisely those common people on the tops of the walls that he wanted his appeal to reach. Ambassadors could only have so much influence on "my lord" (אֲדֹנִי, *ʾădōnî*), but if he could incite a mob panic, that would nullify anything the king could do. He could speak in the "Judean" (יְהוּדִית, *yᵉhûḏîṯ*) dialect of Hebrew and he was not going to squander that opportunity. Doing so, he made his appeal as blunt as he could. These people needed to know what a prolonged siege would mean for them. They would be reduced to nearly unthinkable depths and he was going to express it as brutally as he could (see 2 Kgs 6:25 and the "Commentary" there).

28–30 Once again the Assyrian emissary returns to his technique of hammer-blows without any necessary concern for logical connections. He says that Hezekiah, whom he continues to denigrate by refusing to give the title of king, is "misleading" (נשׁא, *nšʾ*) them (the word has some of the overtones of seduction or enticement). He has no ability to "deliver" (נָצַל *nāṣal*) them, and neither does Yahweh in whom Hezekiah is deceitfully encouraging them to trust. The man makes the point with devastating power. There is nothing and no one who can deliver anyone from Assyrian power. "Deliver" occurs in this second part of the speech no less than nine times.[37] No one, neither king nor god, can do it, and the people had better make their decisions in that searing light. He declares his message directly from the king with the same "messenger formula" that a prophet would use: "Hear the word of the Great King, the king of Assyria: Thus says the King." This sets up the confrontation that is coming: does the Rab-shaqeh speak the truth, or does the prophet Isaiah? Who is the "Great King"? Is it Sennacherib, or is it Yahweh?

31–32 They should not listen to helpless Hezekiah because he is unable to make good on his promises. On the other hand, Sennacherib's promises are quite reliable. All the people have to do is surrender and they will not need to undergo a siege. Instead of eating "dung" (חֲרָאִים, *ḥărāʾîm*) and drinking "urine" (שַׁיִן, *šayin*), they will be able to eat their own grapes and figs, and drink water from their own cisterns.[38] What a pleasant prospect! Then after a short while (during which Sennacherib will be finishing the destruction of Lachish) he will take them to another place at least as good as their own. This is certainly to put the very best interpretation on what was nothing other than a brutal uprooting of whole peoples. Here, Sennacherib is presenting himself as Lord of the Earth, who can dispense land as he wishes. This is of course diametrically opposite to the truth: Yahweh, the Creator, owns the

37. Vv. 29, 30, 32, 33, 34, 35.

38. See Deut 8:7–9; Mic 4:4; Zech 3:10. This language may have been in the nature of a proverb known widely.

earth and he alone can give it as he chooses.[39] The confrontation continues to sharpen.

33–35 In these verses "the gloves come off" and the fight is down to bare knuckles. Hobbs (259) rightly says that this is the core of the Deuteronomic History's theological contentions: who is God? The shocking thing in this presentation is that this is not a confrontation between the gods of Assyria and Yahweh, the God of Judah. This is a confrontation between Sennacherib and Yahweh! Here is humanity, couched in the most cynical terms, ranged against deity. As has been said previously, this way of framing the issues fits very well into the larger context of the book of Isaiah, but it has not been so characteristic of the books of Kings.

We have now come to the point: the Assyrian kings have the power to do whatever they want, and there is nothing that can deliver anyone from that power. There is no king, no nation, no military power, and at bottom, no god that can stand against them. On the surface, the logic was quite impeccable. "Has any god of the nations delivered his land from the hand of the king of Assyria?" (הַהַצֵּל הִצִּילוּ אֱלֹהֵי הַגּוֹיִם אִישׁ אֶת־אַרְצוֹ מִיַּד מֶלֶךְ אַשּׁוּר, *hahaṣṣēl hiṣṣîlû ʾĕlōhê haggôyim ʾîš ʾet- ʾarṣô miyyaḏ meleḵ ʾaššûr*). The answer was quite clearly "no." The cities listed were those located in northern Syria and had been conquered by Sennacherib's predecessors. Hena and Ivvah are otherwise unknown, but if the reading is correct,[40] they were probably located in the same area. Presumably the fates of these cities were known to the listeners, and the conclusions inescapable. When the argument then reached Samaria, capital of their sister kingdom, which had fallen only some twenty years earlier, it became even more frightening.[41] In the end Yahweh was only one more of these helpless deities in the Assyrian's mind, and that made the thought "that Yahweh should deliver Jerusalem from my hand" (כִּי־יַצִּיל יהוה אֶת־יְרוּשָׁלַם מִיָּדִי, *kî-yaṣṣîl yhwh ʾeṯ-yᵉrûšālam miyyāḏî*) simply nonsensical. There was no reason to think that anything different from what had happened everywhere else would happen here. What he was simply unprepared to believe was that there was a God who was not part of this world, was not bound by its endless cycles, and was therefore able to do something that had not happened before or elsewhere.

36–37 Greek here (ἐκώφευσαν, *ekōpheusan*), as well as Isaiah 36:21, reads only "They remained silent." This seems more likely than "The people remained

39. See Josh 1:2–3; 2:9, etc.

40. They are lacking in Gk. and Isa 36:19.

41. It is unnecessary to emend the text of v. 34 by adding "Where are the gods of Samaria" as some commentators propose on the basis of GL (see Hobbs, 245, and Montgomery and Gehman, 490). The question is simply asking whether any gods whatsoever had delivered Samaria. In some ways the contempt for the gods is made even stronger by this indeterminacy.

silent" (וְהֶחֱרִישׁוּ הָעָם, *wᵊheḥĕrîšû hā ʿām*) as MT (along with Vulg. and Syr.) has it. It is doubtful that the people would have known of "the command of the king" (מִצְוַת הַמֶּלֶךְ, *miṣwaṯ hammeleḵ*) and even if they had it is hard to believe that there would not have been a few who could not resist making some kind of remark. Rather, it is the emissaries who received and obeyed the king's command that they not enter into anything that might smack of negotiations, a position from which they could not recover.

But Eliakim, Shebna, and Joah probably did not need the royal command to silence. Their behavior indicates how deeply the Assyrian's words had affected them. While "garments torn" (קְרוּעֵי בְגָדִים, *qᵊrû ʿê ḇᵊḡāḏîm*) is often an expression of mourning (2 Sam 1:2), it is not restricted to that. More broadly, it is an expression of deep emotional distress (e.g., 2 Kgs 5:7; 6:30), and that is certainly the case here. The Rab-shaqeh's hammer had struck them down. If ever a situation had appeared hopeless, this was it. They were as convinced as the Assyrian was that Jerusalem had only two options, neither of them good: surrender or be decimated. They did not really believe in Yahweh's promises (2 Kgs 20:6) any more than the enemy did.

Biblical Theological Comments

Trust is at the heart of all personal relationships, for with the complexity of persons nothing can ever be guaranteed. If one person promises to do something for another, and the second person accepts the promise, trust is fundamental. Of course, there can be evidence from the past that the promise-maker is trustworthy, but the one receiving the promise must still take the risk of faith, especially if the promise is of something he or she needs. Marriage relationships rest on trust, as do family relations, and business relations as well.

All of this is pointedly illustrated in this passage. When Hezekiah promises to deliver his people from the Assyrian threat, can he really be trusted to do that? Does he have the military power in Judah itself or in his alliance with Egypt? Can Egypt be trusted to provide help when faced with all the power of Assyria? But most of all, can Yahweh be trusted? He has promised to deliver Jerusalem (2 Kgs 20:6), but can he? Is he really any different from all the gods whose countries now lie in ruins, and whose peoples are in captivity? The question is especially poignant given the nature of Yahweh. If the divine is an integral element in the cosmos, then there is at least an illusion of control. We can perform rituals which, if done correctly, will, we believe, infallibly produce the desired results in the divine realm and then in the realm of nature. The trust factor is minimized. We are not dealing with persons so much as forces, forces wearing human-like masks, but forces just the same.

But what if the Divine is not an integral element of the cosmos? What if the Force we are trying to control cannot be manipulated through manipulation of the cosmos? What then? What if he is not a Force, but a multi-faceted person? How can we get him to do what we want? Are we going to have to surrender our wants to him, and *trust* that he actually cares about our wants, and that he wants to meet our wants, and beyond even that, is able to do something about them? In short, is this cosmos and the manipulation of it not the ultimate issue in existence? Such an idea was totally beyond the capacity of Sennacherib and his Rab-shaqeh to conceive. This cosmos is ultimate; there is nothing beyond it, and they had it by the throat. Thus, trust in any other power, human or divine, was not merely foolish, it was unthinkable. If there was a power, a person, outside of the cosmos, it would be beyond human control, and that thought did not bear considering.[42]

But of course it is true; I AM is not part of this cosmos. He interpenetrates it at every point, but is not constrained by it in any way. There *is* only one way to relate to him, and that is in trust and surrender, surrender above all of our need to control him. This is where the human problem all began: in the question of trust and surrender. Genesis 3 makes this point in a disarmingly simple, but deeply profound way. The serpent's strategy was to undermine Eve's trust in God. In his outrageous suggestion that Yahweh had forbidden every tree, he got her to doubt Yahweh's generosity: why is he in the business of prohibition, anyway? In his subtle lie about death, he got her to doubt Yahweh's honesty. In his blatant lie about the reasons for the prohibition, he got her to doubt Yahweh's character. Clearly, if a person cannot be trusted, it is not in our best interests to do what they say. Thus, the path was chosen, the path of distrust, that has dogged the footsteps of Eve and Adam's descendants ever since.

Here is where biblical faith rises or falls: can Yahweh be entrusted with our earthly life and our eternal destiny? Or are the Rab-shaqehs of the world correct? Is Sennacherib, the human, the only power in the cosmos, and all the gods, including Yahweh, simply a projection of humanity on an empty sky? That being so, must we abandon our dreams of worth, and bow under the lash of the latest tyrant who has learned how, for a short time, to lay hold of the reins of power? Or is the Creator of the Universe full of undeserved favor for his creatures; right and just and good and true, in whom we can trust forever?

Selected Bibliography

Ussishkin, D. "The 'Camp of the Assyrians' in Jerusalem." *IEJ* 29 (1979): 137–42.

42. These questions are at the very heart of all of Isaiah 7–39: do we dare place our trust in Yahweh, in his desire and his ability to deliver us from the threats of life, or should we rather put our trust in humanity and the gods which we have made in our own image with our own hands. The issue of trust only comes into Kings in a major way here. This is one of the reasons I argue that Isa 36-39 have priority and that the editor(s) of Kings have made use of the Isaianic original. (See "Excursus on 2 Kings 18:13–20:21 in Comparison to Isaiah 36:1–39:8.")

Hezekiah's Anguish and Yahweh's Response (19:1–7)

Translation

1 Now when King Hezekiah heard, he tore his clothes and covered himself with burlap and went to the house of Yahweh. **2** He sent Eliakim, who was over the house, and Shebna, the scribe, and the elders of the priests to Isaiah, the prophet, son of Amoz. **3** They said to him, "Thus says Hezekiah, 'This day is a day of distress, rebuke, and contempt. For children have come to birth and there is no strength to deliver them. **4** Perhaps Yahweh, your God, hears[43] all the words of the Rab-shaqeh, whom his lord has sent to mock the living God and he will rebuke the words that Yahweh your God has heard. So pray for the remnant that remains.' " **5** So the servants of King Hezekiah came to Isaiah. **6** Isaiah said to them, "Thus you shall say to your lord, 'Thus says Yahweh, "Do not be afraid on account of the words you have heard with which the lads of the king of Assyria have blasphemed me. **7** Look, I am about to put a spirit in him, and he will hear a report and return to his land; I will make him fall by the sword in his land." ' "

Textual Notes

3a. לֵדָה: Gk. "she who gives birth"; Vulg. with MT; Syr. (confl.) "there is no strength in the mother to deliver."

4a. אֱלֹהִים חַי: Gk. "a living god"; Vulg. and Syr. "the living God."

4b–b. וְהוֹכִיחַ בַּדְּבָרִים: Gk. "to blaspheme with words"; Vulg. and Syr. with MT.

Commentary

1–2 Hezekiah was in no doubt about the dreadful implications of the message he received from his emissaries. Sennacherib was not going to turn around and go home in view of Hezekiah's tribute. He was going to keep the money and still destroy Jerusalem, along with its rebel king. Hezekiah's response was, like that of his servants (18:37) to tear his clothes in anguish, but then he did two very significant things: (1) he went to the temple, and (2) he sent a message to the prophet Isaiah. These actions are significant because they are so contrary to those of his father who had faced a somewhat similar crisis thirty-five years earlier (2 Kgs 16:5–6; Isa 7:1–12). Ahaz had looked to his water supply and sent messengers to the Assyrian emperor Tiglath-pileser III. In the end Isaiah had to seek out Ahaz with Yahweh's message of hope. If it is true that Hezekiah was *in extremis,* having earlier tried to use human means, whether Egyptian alliances (cf. Isa 29:15; 30:1–2; 31:1), or defense works (cf. Isa 22:8–11), to defend himself, it is still true that in the end he turned to the only source of hope: Yahweh.

---

43. Heb. impf. (יִשְׁמַע, *yišmaʿ*) used in a modal sense relating to possibility; see *IBHS* (§31.4).

Gray (684) suggests that Hezekiah's actions (including substituting the "elders of the priests" [זִקְנֵי הַכֹּהֲנִים, *ziqnê hakkōhănîm*] for Joah, the recorder) were intended to institute a national fast. However, there is nothing in the text to suggest such a thing, and Sweeney (416) points out that it was usual to involve priests in a request for an oracle from a prophet (Exod 4:10–17; 2 Kgs 22:11–20). Furthermore, it seems likely that the recorder would have been included with the original group because of the event's political significance, something that was not the case in the visit to Isaiah.

3 Hezekiah's use of this particular metaphor, possibly a proverb (see Hosea 13:13), to describe the situation in which Judah found itself would have been particularly poignant. Everyone would have known of an instance where a pregnant mother had labored herself to exhaustion and death in her inability to force her baby through a pelvic opening that was too small.[44] This was where Judah found itself. They had labored and labored to free themselves from the oppressive grip of the Assyrians, and now it looked as though it was all coming to nothing. It was indeed a "day of distress, rebuke, and contempt" (יוֹם־צָרָה וְתוֹכֵחָה וּנְאָצָה, *yôm-ṣārâ wᵉṯôḵēḥâ ûnᵉʾāṣâ*). They had made big plans, had taken deep risks, and now all that was about to be proven a foolish and deadly error.

4 But it is not Judah's reputation and fate that is Hezekiah's first concern. Nor does he seem especially concerned about the Rab-shaqeh's other arguments. Rather, it is Yahweh's character and reputation that concerns the Judean king. As Long points out, the language that he uses is very suggestive. Hezekiah says that the king of Assyria has "mocked," or "ridiculed" (חָרַף, *ḥārap̄*) "the living God" (אֱלֹהִים חַי, *ʾĕlōhîm ḥay*). This is the same language that David used in speaking of Goliath (1 Sam 17:26). The verb חָרַף, *ḥārap̄* only occurs thirteen times in Deuteronomy–2 Kings, and "living God" only six times (ten in the entire OT). These facts argue for an intentional allusion to David here. It is the honor of Yahweh that is at stake, and Hezekiah, the current Davidic monarch is motivated by the same concern that motivated the founder of the dynasty: the honor of Yahweh. To mock this one is, as Brueggemann (506) says, to fly in the face of reality. Yahweh is not a lifeless piece of wood or lump of stone, but the "living God"!

Provan (261) points out that the verb שָׁאַר, *šᵉʾār,* "to remain" occurs several times in 1 and 2 Kings; however, the term "remnant" (שְׁאֵרִית, *šᵉʾēriṯ*) occurs only here and in 19:31 and 21:14.[45] In the latter (not a duplicate with Isaiah) Yahweh speaks of forsaking the remnant. In contrast, "remnant" (either שְׁאָר' or שְׁאֵרִית') occurs sixteen times in Isaiah chapters six through

44. The childbirth metaphor is used elsewhere in Isaiah: e.g., 26:17–18; 66:7–9.

45. Long (479) says forms of the root שׁאר, *šʾr* occur in 24 times in Kings. However, virtually all of these are the vb. form occurring in settings that have no particular theological significance.

thirty-seven. The appearance of this term, a favorite of Isaiah's, here is another indication of the priority of the Isaiah passage (see the "Excursus on 2 Kings 18:13–20:21 in Comparison to Isaiah 36:1–39:8"). Isaiah, and Hezekiah, were facing the reality that only Judah was now remaining from Solomon's once mighty nation, and after the depredations of Sennacherib, little remained of Judah.[46] Thus "prayer for the remnant that remains" (תְּפִלָּה בְּעַד הַשְּׁאֵרִית, *ṯᵊpillâ bᵊ ʿaḏ haššᵊ ʾērîṯ*) was not only appropriate, it was absolutely necessary. It is a mark of the function of the Hebrew prophet that he is not expected to search for an omen, nor to perform a set of rituals, but only to take advantage of personal intimacy with Yahweh to pray for Yahweh's action on behalf of his people. This was the case of Elijah on Mt. Carmel and it is again the case of Isaiah in Jerusalem.

6–7 The Rab-shaqeh began his message with the portentous "Thus says the Great King, the King of Assyria" (18:19). But now it is the King of the universe, the eternal I AM, whom Isaiah introduces with "Thus says the Lord Yahweh" (כֹּה אָמַר אֲדֹנָי יהוה, *kō ʾāmar ʾăḏōnāy yhwh*). Although it is the authoritative word, yet it is couched is perfectly plain speech, from the God who speaks. He has been "reviled" (גדף, *gdp*), not by great and consequential men, but by "lads" (נְעָרִים, *nᵊ ʿārîm*), mere lackeys, and Isaiah need not be bowled over by them. Then with the attention-getting "Look" (הִנְנִי, *hinnî*), Yahweh announces in clipped terms what he is about to do.[47] The use of "spirit" (רוּחַ, *rûaḥ*) and "report" (שְׁמוּעָה, *šəmû ʿâ*) seem combined to express an air of indeterminacy.[48] Sennacherib was used to being a man of action, decisive and self-directed. Yahweh is going to unsettle him and make him prey to fears and speculations. That was certainly to be the case in the upshot. What was he to make of the loss of much of his army in a single night? Should he stay with the remainder and try to bull on through with what might still have been a formidable force, or should he cut his losses and run, accepting the terrible loss of face that would involve? Yahweh was going to cut out from under Sennacherib all the self-assured foundation that had shone through the entirety of the Rab-shaqeh's tirade.

---

46. Isaiah's son, who accompanied him when he first encountered Ahaz, was named Shear-jashub (שְׁאָר יָשׁוּב), "Only a remnant will return" (Isa 7:3).

47. נֹתֵן, *nōṯēn* is a ptcp. of incipient action.

48. Long compares the spirit here to the "lying spirit" of 1 Kgs 22:22 (480; see also Esther J. Hamori, "The Spirit of Falsehood," *CBQ* 72 [2010]: 15–30). However, there is nothing in the text itself to support such a comparison. More apt comparisons would be Judg 7:21; 1 Sam 14:15; 16:14–16 wherein Yahweh produces panic in the enemy. Wiseman's suggestion that the report was of Tirhaqah's approach (279) does not seem to fit what is claimed, especially when it is coupled, as it is, with Sennacherib's departure from the land. Sweeney's suggestion that it had to do with a threat of Merodak-Baladan's approach seems even more tenuous (413).

But that was not all. The Sennacherib who had not deigned to mention an Assyrian god throughout his entire pronouncement would die at Yahweh's command "in his own land" (בְּאַרְצוֹ, *bᵊ ʾarṣô*). The Assyrian who had been so certain that he could defeat Yahweh in Yahweh's land was going to find out that Yahweh could take Sennacherib's life in Sennacherib's land. Furthermore, as the Assyrian records tell us (*COS* 1:467), confirmed by 2 Kings 19:37, the Assyrian died in the temple of one of his gods. Nothing, neither distance nor religion, could protect him from Yahweh, the living God of Israel, the God whom Sennacherib had mocked by foolishly comparing him to the lifeless idols of the nations.

Selected Bibliography

Lambert, W. G. "Destiny and Divine Intervention in Babylon and Israel." *OTS* 17 (1972): 65–72.

Sennacherib's Letter and Hezekiah's Prayer (19:8–19)

Translation

8 The Rab-shaqeh returned and found the king of Assyria fighting against
Libnah because he had heard that he had left Libnah. **9** Then he heard
concerning Tirhaqah, king of Ethiopia, saying, "Look, he has come out to
fight with you." So he went back[49] and sent messengers to Hezekiah saying,
10 "Thus you shall say Hezekiah, king of Judah, saying, 'Do not let the god in
whom you are trusting deceive you, saying, "Jerusalem will not be given into
the hand of the king of Assyria." **11** Look, you yourself have heard what the
kings of Assyria have done to all the lands, completely destroying them,[50] and
will you be delivered? **12** Did the gods of the nations which my ancestors
devastated deliver them – Gozan, Haran, Reseph, and Bene-Eden which is
in Telassar? **13** Where is the king of Hamath, or the king of Arpad, or the
king of the city[51] of Sepharvaim, Henah, and Ivvah?' "

14 Hezekiah took the letters from the hand of the messengers and read
them. Then he went up to the house of Yahweh and spread it before Yahweh.
15 They he prayed before Yahweh and said, "O Yahweh, God of Israel, who is
enthroned with respect to the cherubim,[52] you are God alone of all the kingdoms of the earth; it is you who made the heavens and the earth. **16** Incline

---

49. There is considerable disagreement among the versions as to how שׁוּב, *šûḇ* should be understood here: Gk. "And he returned and sent …"; Vulg. "and he went against him and sent …"; Syr. "again he sent … ."

50. חָרַם, *ḥāram*, often used of dedicating something to God by totally destroying it (cf. Josh 6:17).

51. Possibly a place name. There was a city of La ʿir in northern Babylonia.

52. There is no preposition attached to "the cherubim" (הַכְּרֻבִים, *hakkᵊruḇîm*) which one would expect if the expression simply meant "enthroned upon the cherubim," which is a frequent translation. Instead, "the cherubim" is probably in the acc. and is

your ear, O Yahweh, and hear; open your eyes, O Yahweh, and see. Hear the words of Sennacherib which he sent to mock the living God. **17** Truly, O Yahweh, the kings of Assyria have destroyed the nations and their lands. **18** They did put their gods into the fire, because they are not gods, but rather the works of human hands, wood and stone, so they destroyed them. **19** But now, O Yahweh, our God, deliver us please, from his hand so that all the kingdoms of the earth may know that you, Yahweh, are God alone."

Textual Notes

9a. וַיָּשָׁב: Isa 37:9 "and "he heard" (וַיִּשְׁמַע), Gk. and IQIs[a] include both שָׁמַע and שׁוּב. The versions here all seem to be interpreting שׁוּב. See the note on the translation below.

10a–a. כֹּה תֹאמְרוּן אֶל־חִזְקִיָּהוּ מֶלֶךְ־יְהוּדָה לֵאמֹר: Gk. lacks; Vulg. and Syr. with MT.

11a. אֲשֶׁר: Gk. adds "all"; Vulg. and Syr. with MT.

12a. הַגּוֹיִם: Vulg. sing.; Gk. and Syr. with MT.

13a–a. וּמֶלֶךְ לָעִיר: Gk. "and where is"; Syr. "the king of"; Vulg. with MT.

14a. וַיִּקְרָאֵם: Isa 37:14 "and he read it" (וַיִּקְרָאֵהוּ).

15a–a. וַיִּתְפַּלֵּל חִזְקִיָּהוּ אֶל־יְהוָה לֵאמֹר: Gk. "And he said"; Vulg. "And he prayed before him"; Syr. with MT.

15b. יְהוָה: Isa 37:16 adds "of heaven's armies" (יהוה צְבָאוֹת).

15c–c. לְכֹל: Vulg. "of the kings of all the earth"; Gk. and Syr. with MT.

16a. יְהוָה: Vulg. omits; Gk. and Syr. with MT.

16b. דִּבְרֵי: Vulg. and Syr. (with Isa 37:16) adds "all" (לְכֹל); Gk. with MT.

16c. אֱלֹהִים חָי: Vulg. "our living God"; Gk. and Syr. with MT.

17a. וְאֶת־אַרְצָם: Gk. omits, reading only "the nations"; Vulg. and Syr. with MT. Isa 37:18 reads "all the lands and their land" (כָּל־הָאֲרָצוֹת וְאֶת־אַרְצָם), whereas 1QIs[a] reads "all the lands." It appears that the final ארצם was the source of considerable textual confusion.

19a. וְעַתָּה: Vulg. and Syr. add "therefore"; Gk. with MT.

---

intended to be taken adverbially. The text seems to be seeking to avoid simply making the ark of the covenant a throne for Yahweh. See further in the "Commentary" below.

Commentary

The careful reader will observe a number of similarities between this material and that found in 18:17–19:7. In several cases these go beyond similarities to duplication (e.g., Hezekiah going to the house of Yahweh [19:1, 14]). This resulted in the hypothesis that these are duplicate reports of a single event. For a discussion of this hypothesis, see the "Excursus on the Composition of 2 Kings 18:13–19:37." As the text stands, the two events serve to focus the issue: it is finally between Yahweh the Creator and Sennacherib the creature, the creature who represents all creatures who dare to make God in their own image.

8 It is not entirely clear what Sennacherib's "fighting against Libnah" (נִלְחָם עַל־לִבְנָה, *nilḥām ʿal-libnâ*) indicates. Did the Assyrians temporarily withdraw from besieging Lachish to attack this other location, or did they complete the siege and then move to Libnah? The answer to the question is made somewhat more uncertain because of the uncertainty over the location of that city. Hobbs (276) says it is Tell el Beida which is east of Lachish. In this case, Lachish having fallen, the Assyrian army is moving toward Jerusalem and reducing a potential trouble spot in the way. But Gray (663) says it is Tell aṣ Ṣafi, which is at the mouth of the Elah Valley, some ten miles north, northwest of Lachish. Nevertheless, Wiseman (280) identifies Libnah with Tell Bornat, about halfway between Lachish and Tell aṣ Ṣafi. If either of the latter two are correct, then perhaps this action had some relation to the anticipated northward thrust by the Egyptians, and thus the Assyrians were attempting to block them from reaching Jerusalem by way of the Elah Valley in the one case or the Ajalon Valley in the other.[53]

9 "Tirhaqah" (eg., Taharka) was a member of the Ethiopian twenty-fifth dynasty of Egypt. Because his reign has been dated as beginning in 690 BC it has become customary to presume that his mention here is anachronistic. However, it has been argued by Kitchen and Hoffmeier that Tirhaqah was acting as a lieutenant for Shebitku, the Egyptian king in 701 BC, and that calling him "king" in this instance reflects the fact that this was his title when this recension was compiled (after Sennacherib's death in 681 BC, 19:37).[54]

10–13 Clearly, Sennacherib wanted to keep the pressure on Hezekiah, not wanting a hope of Egyptian intervention to somehow reenergize the Judean king and diminish the impact of the Rab-shaqeh's verbal tour de force. Here

---

53. On the location of Libnah see *ABD* 4:323, which prefers the current site of Tell Bornat.

54. Kenneth A. Kitchen, *On the Reliability of the Old Testament* (Grand Rapids: Eerdmans, 2003), 16; James K. Hoffmeier, "Egypt's Role in the Events of 701 B.C. in Jerusalem," in *Jerusalem in Bible and Archeology: The First Temple Period*, ed. Andrew G. Vaughn and Ann E. Killebrew (Leiden: Brill, 2003), 219–34.

the message, in the form of a letter (v. 14), goes directly to the heart of the matter. The Assyrian king does not even address the issues of Judean strength or Egyptian support, but rather goes straight to Yahweh. The Rab-shaqeh called on the people not to let Hezekiah deceive them, but here, speaking directly to Hezekiah, Sennacherib says not to let Yahweh be the deceiver. It is to be wondered whether the word of Yahweh's promise through Isaiah (19:6–7) had reached Sennacherib and he was reacting to that, or if he was responding to an earlier promise (20:6; on the probable date of this event, see the "Commentary" below). In any case, he has no understanding at all that Yahweh was any different from the idol-gods of all the nations. In his defense, it has to be said that the experiences which he and his ancestors had had would indeed lead to the conclusions he drew: no gods of northern Mesopotamia or northern Syria (the locations mentioned)[55] had delivered their lands from the Assyrian depredations. The Assyrian monarchs had taken down everyone, so why would Hezekiah think that his god was any different? But this was exactly the point: Yahweh is not one of the gods, and Hezekiah knew it.

14 The messengers from Sennacherib would have had a written copy of the message, and it was this that Hezekiah "spread" (וַיִּפְרְשֵׂהוּ, *wayyip̄rᵉśēhû*) before Yahweh (see 5:4–6). Some commentators (e.g., Konkel, 602) believe that given the reference to the cherubim in v. 15, he had been given emergency access to the Holy of Holies, but the text gives no hint of that, and the reference does not require it.

15–19 Hezekiah's prayer here is one of the greatest of the Bible. It reveals a deep and fundamental trust in Yahweh at a moment when it would have been very easy to cast that trust aside. Perhaps all the evidence that Sennacherib had marshalled was correct. Perhaps Yahweh was just one more of the gods. After all, he had not been able to deliver Samaria, as the Assyrian had pointed out in his earlier message (18:34). But Hezekiah did not fall for any of that. He dared to believe the evidence that Yahweh himself had given in the history of the people of Israel. The language he uses betrays a clear apprehension of that history and all that it portends. One of the features of the language is its directness. Hezekiah speaks directly and intimately with Yahweh; the king understands that unlike the gods, which are forces with human-like personas, Yahweh is a full-orbed person, who, though utterly transcendent, is yet fully immanent. From Abraham onward, and especially with Moses, Yahweh is to be known face to face.

---

55. Telassar is probably Tell Aššuri, a site probably located in the Zagros Mountains to which the people of Adin (Eden) were transported. Cogan and Tadmor point out that the Israelite deportees were resettled in Gozan and Haran (17:6), while people from Hamath and Sepharvaim were resettled in Israel (17:24) (235). Thus, these sites would have had special interest for the Judeans.

In the parallel passage in Isaiah (37:16) Hezekiah addresses Yahweh as "Yahweh of Heaven's Armies (יהוה צְבָאוֹת, *yhwh ṣᵉḇāʾôṯ*), God of Israel." Cogan and Tadmor, noting the association of the title with the ark of the covenant in 1 Samuel 4:4 and 2 Samuel 6:2, conclude that Isaiah is probably more original. See also 2 Samuel 7:27. In the combination ("Yahweh of Heaven's Armies"), much like Isaiah's "Holy One of Israel" the transcendence and immanence of Yahweh are masterfully combined: He has all of heaven's power at his behest, but he had graciously given himself to the descendants of Jacob. The reference to his presence among the "cherubim" (הַכְּרֻבִים, *hakkᵉruḇîm*) is laden with implications. Above all is his aniconic nature. He is *not* an idol! This point cannot be emphasized enough. He is present in his temple, but not in any form made by human hands. The second implication is the covenant context. This God is not to be related to through sympathetic magic, but through obedience to the covenant that he so graciously offered to his people. Furthermore, he has proven himself true to his covenant promises to his people again and again.[56]

From these aspects of his uniqueness, it is a small step to the understanding that there is no supposed divine being who is on a par with Yahweh. He is "God alone of all the kingdoms" (הָאֱלֹהִים לְבַדְּךָ לְכֹל מַמְלְכוֹת, *hā ʾĕlōhîm lᵉḇaddəḵā lᵉḵōl mamlᵉḵôṯ*). If the Assyrians have destroyed the nations, it is not because their gods could not prevent it, but because Yahweh has permitted it! Isaiah makes that point powerfully in Isaiah 10:5–19. Assyria is only a tool in Yahweh's hand. But Hezekiah takes a further step. Yahweh is God of the nations because the whole cosmos—"heaven and earth" (אֶת־הַשָּׁמַיִם וְאֶת־הָאָרֶץ, *ʾeṯ-haššāmayim wᵉ ʾeṯ-hā ʾāreṣ*)—was made by him. This is another point that is especially characteristic of Isaiah: Yahweh is the Maker of the earth.[57]

16 One of the diatribes against the idols is that although they have eyes, they cannot see, and although they have ears, they cannot hear (Pss 115:5–7; 135:16–17). Paradoxically, although Yahweh has no eyes, he sees perfectly, and although he has no ears, he can hear the faintest cry. In Genesis 29:31, Yahweh "saw that Leah was hated." In Exodus 2:24 he "heard their groaning." Finally, in Daniel 9:18, which well may be an allusion to this verse, Daniel calls on Yahweh to "hear" and "see" the desolation of Jerusalem. Both Hezekiah's and Daniel's words have common ground with Solomon's prayer dedicating the temple. There, as he reached his conclusion and envisioned a time when the nation's sin might have brought it into exile and despair, he prayed that Yahweh might "see" and "hear" their pleas (1 Kings 8:52). In this context, the words of David concerning Goliath are again appropriate (19:4; 1 Sam 17:26.) This is not a dead idol who can do nothing for his people; this is "the living God" (אֱלֹהִים חַי, *ʾĕlōhîm ḥāy*), and to declare that he is merely one

56. Ps 80 is a similar entreaty, and like this one begins with an appeal to the One who is present in reference to the cherubim.

57. Isa 17:7; 22:11; 45:9, 11; 51:13; 54:5.

more of the gods who is helpless to protect his people is indeed "to mock" (לְחָרֵף, *lᵊḥārēp̄*) him.

17–18 Hezekiah admits that what Sennacherib had claimed for himself and his ancestors was correct. They had indeed conquered "nations and their lands," and none of the gods had been able to prevent it. He goes farther and says that they even burned the gods, something Sennacherib had not mentioned. But at this point he parts ways with the Assyrian monarch. Sennacherib had drawn the wrong conclusion. He had concluded that the reason for the Assyrian successes was that the Assyrian kings were superior to other nations' gods. That was the wrong conclusion; the reason the gods could not deliver their nations was that they, and the religious philosophy they represented, were human creations. The idols were helpless because they were "works of human hands, wood and stone" (מַעֲשֵׂה יְדֵי־אָדָם עֵץ וָאֶבֶן, *maʿăśē yᵊḏê-ʾāḏām ʿēṣ wāʾeḇen*). They were personified natural forces, and as part of the world such forces cannot transcend the world and cannot save it from itself. Isaiah makes this point again and again, especially in chapters forty-one through forty-six. The Assyrian successes were not because of superior Assyrian power, but because the gods the people were trusting were human creations.

19 Here in this final petition Hezekiah shines the brightest. How easy it would have been for him to ask for deliverance because the Judeans were righteous people, or because they were the elect people. In short, he could have constructed some fabric of deserving. But that was not what he did at all. Rather, he asked Yahweh for deliverance "so that all the dominions of the earth might know that you, Yahweh, are God alone" (וְיֵדְעוּ כָּל־מַמְלְכוֹת הָאָרֶץ כִּי אַתָּה יהוה אֱלֹהִים לְבַדֶּךָ, *wᵊyēḏᵊʿû kol-mamlᵊḵôṯ hāʾāreṣ kî ʾattâ yhwh ʾĕlōhîm lᵊḇaddeḵā*). Hezekiah knew, as David had (1 Sam 17:46), and as Elijah had (1 Kgs 18:37) that the survival of a people was not the most crucial issue. What the world needed, and needs, is to know that there is one God who is not this world, but who made the world, and thus can break into it at any point and transform it.

Biblical Theology Comments

Hezekiah's prayer is focused on the uniqueness of Yahweh among the gods of the ancient Near East. It is a view that modern scholarship is increasingly unwilling to credit. The reason for this unwillingness is that such a view requires divine revelation, something that is contrary to the secularism that is coming to dominate biblical studies. That is, modern biblical scholars are entirely unwilling to accept the Bible's own explanation for its ideas. Chief among these is the idea that there is a single transcendent Being who has entered into human history, revealing his nature, character, and purposes in the process. Rather, it appears that these scholars are determined to find explanations for the rise of Yahwism that are consistent with the evolutionary development of religion elsewhere in the world, particularly in the ancient Near East.[58] The fact that such evolutionary development led everywhere else to an understanding of deity that was remarkably uniform, and directly contradictory to what the Old Testament teaches about deity has not deterred them from their self-confident quest. But the ideas presented in this brief prayer cannot be gainsaid. There is one God, not many; God cannot be represented by any natural object, especially one made by humans; God is not the world, nor any part of it; rather, he made the world (from nothing). God is transcendent, yet profoundly immanent, a person, not a persona. To suggest, in defiance of what the Bible claims, that Israelite religion developed exactly like its neighboring religions, beginning with the same starting points and following the same paths, yet ending up at a radically different place, is to strain credulity beyond the breaking point.

Selected Bibliography

Barnes, W. H. *Studies in the Chronology of the Divided Monarchy of Israel*. HSM 48. Atlanta: Scholars Press, 1991.

Cloete, W. T. W. "Distinguishing Prose and Verse in 2 Ki 19:14–19." Pages 31–40 in *Verse in Ancient Near Eastern Prose*. Edited by J.C. de Moor and W.G.E. Watson. AOAT 42 Kevelaer: Neukirchener Verlag, 1993.

Holloway, S. W. "Harran: Cultic Geography in the Neo-Assyrian Empire and its Implications for Sennacherib's 'Letter to Hezekiah' in 2 Kings." Pages 276–314 in *Pitcher is Broken: Memorial Essays for Gösta W. Ahlström*. Edited by Lowell K. Handy and Steven W. Holloway. JSOTSup 190. Sheffield: Sheffield Academic, 1995.

Kahn, D. "The Inscription of Sargon II at Tang-I Var and the Chronology of Dynasty 25." *Or* 70 (2001): 1–18.

Kitchen, K. A. *The Third Intermediate Period in Egypt (1100–650 B.C.)*. Second Edition. Oxford: Aris & Phillips, 1996.

Redford, D. B. *Egypt, Canaan, and Israel in Ancient Times*. Princeton: Princeton University Press, 1992.

Yun, I. A. "Different Readings of the Taharqa Passage in 2 Kings 19 and the Chronology of the 25th Egyptian Dynasty." Pages 169–81 in *From Babel to Babylon: Essays on Biblical History and Literature in Honour of Brian Peckham*. Edited by Joyce Rilett Wood, John E. Harvey, and Mark Leuchter. New York: T&T Clark, 2006.

58. While skepticism about the biblical claims for the character and nature of Yahweh has been present in scholarship at least since the beginnings of the enlightenment in the sixteenth century (AD), the particular attempt to explain Yahwism as one element of the common evolution of West Semitic religion is more recent. See, for example, Mark Smith, *The Origins of Biblical Monotheism: Israel's Polytheistic Background and the Ugaritic Texts* (New York: Oxford, 2001) and a succession of similar books since that time.

Yahweh's Response (19:20–34)

Translation

20 Isaiah, son of Amoz, sent to Hezekiah, saying, "This is what Yahweh,
God of Israel, says, 'What you prayed to me concerning Sennacherib, king
of Assyria I have heard.' **21** This is the word which Yahweh spoke concerning
him,

'She despises you, she mocks you, the virgin daughter Zion.
The daughter Jerusalem wags her head at you.[59]
22 Whom did you reproach and revile;
against whom did you raise the voice[60]
and lift your eyes haughtily?
It was the Holy One of Israel!
23 By the hand of your messengers you have reproached the Sovereign[61]
and said, "With the multitude of my chariots
I myself ascended the heights of the mountains, the slopes[62] of Lebanon.
I cut down the tallest of its cedars,
the choicest of its cypresses.
I went into its farthest coverts, its densest forest.
24 I myself dug and drank foreign waters;
with the soles of my feet I dried up the rivers of Egypt."
25 Have you not heard from long ago? This is my doing!
From ancient days, I formed it and now I bring it to pass,
that you should cause fortified cities to crash into heaps of ruins,
26 and their inhabitants weak, dismayed, and ashamed,
like grass in the field, green grass,
grass on the roofs, blasted before it is grown.
27 Your sitting down, your going out, and your coming in I know,
and your raging against me.
28 Because you have raged against me
and your self-confidence[63] has come up into my ears,
I will put my hook in your nose and my bit between your lips,
and I will make you return by the way you came.'

---

59. *IBHS* (§11.21) argue that the prep. אַחַר, *ʾaḥar* is used here in the sense of interest, advantage or disadvantage. Thus "at."
60. קוֹל, *qôl*, the versions all read "your voice."
61. Not the divine name, but אֲדֹנָי, *ʾădōnāy,* "lord."
62. יַרְכְּתֵי לְבָנוֹן, *yarkᵊṯê lᵊḇānôn*, Lit. "sides," so Syr. Gk. reads "thighs"; Vulg. "heights."
63. This word, שַׁאֲנָן, *šaʾănān*, occurs only here in Kings (five times in Isa). Evidently it was not familiar to the ancient translators. Thus, Gk. "wantonness"; Vulg. "arrogance"; Syr. "blasphemy." For the sense of "self-confidence," see Job 12:5; Ps 123:4.

29 This will be a sign to you: eating this[64] year what grows by itself,
and the second year what comes up from that.[65] But in the third year, sow
and reap, plant vineyards, and eat the produce. **30** The remnant that sur-
vives from the house of Judah will again take root downwards and bear fruit
upwards. **31** For a remnant will go out from Jerusalem and survivors from the
hill of Zion; the zeal of Yahweh of Heaven's Armies[66] will accomplish this.
32 Therefore, thus says Yahweh concerning[67] the King of Assyria, 'He will
not enter this city, nor shoot an arrow there, nor confront it with a shield,
nor pour out soil for a siege ramp against it. **33** On the same way he came,
he will return, but he will not enter this city,' says Yahweh. **34** 'I will defend
this city in order to deliver it, both for my own sake and for the sake of my
servant David.'

Textual Notes

22a. קוֹל: All the versions add "your."

23a. מַלְאָכֶיךָ: Vulg. (and Isa 37:24; עֲבָדֶיךָ) "your "servants"; Gk. and Syr. with MT.

23b. K בְּרֶכֶב: Q reads ברב and this is followed by all the versions. K appears to be the result of the accidental insertion of a כ (*kaph*) under the influence of the following word.

23c–c. מְלוֹן קִצֹּה: Gk. "*mᵊlon* [translit.] of its end"; Vulg. "as far as its limits"; Syr. "extreme limits." MT best explains the others.

23d–d. יַעַר כַּרְמִלּוֹ: The versions all take כַּרְמִלּוֹ as a place name. *HALOT* (499) "tree plantation."

24a–a. אֲנִי קַרְתִּי: Vulg. reads these two words with the previous phrase: "the forest of his Carmel I cut down"; Gk. "I sought the cool air"; Syr. with MT.

24b. זָרִים: Lacking in Isa 37:25.

24c. מָצוֹר: None of the ancient versions understand this as Egypt (although all mod. versions do) because the term normally appears in a dual form מִצְרַיִם. So Gk. "the rivers of enclosure"; Vulg. "the enclosed waters"; Syr.

64. The article (הַ) being used as a demonst., *IBHS* (§13.5.2).

65. סָחִישׁ, *sāḥîš* only occurs here and in the parallel in Isa. It seems to be a synonym of סָפִיחַ, *sāp̄îaḥ* "what grows by itself" (Lev. 25:5, 11) and thus the translation "what comes up from that."

66. *Ketiv* lacks צְבָאוֹת, *ṣᵉḇāʾôṯ* ("of heaven's armies") but *qere* supplies it and it is found in all the versions, as also in the *ketiv* in Isa 37:32.

67. The Heb. prep. is אֶל, *ʾel* which would normally be translated "to." However, this prep. is often interchanged with עַל, *ʿal* which has the sense of "concerning."

"great rivers." But note that Egypt is referred to as *muṣur* in the Assyrian annals, which are clearly in view here (cf. *ANET,* 292, 5, 6)

25a–a. הֲלֹא־שָׁמַעְתָּ לְמֵרָחוֹק אֹתָהּ עָשִׂיתִי לְמִימֵי קֶדֶם: Gk. omits; Vulg. and Syr. with MT.

25b. וִיצַרְתִּיהָ: The versions treat this vb. as past tense (*waw* conjunc.?).

25c. וּתְהִי: The versions treat this vb. as past tense (*waw* conjunc.?). Many commentators recommend emending MT to conform to the versions (the previous vb. as well). However, the Heb. impf. form may be used in these cases to reflect modality rather than time of action, (see *IBHS* §31:1, 4).

25d. לַהְשׁוֹת: The א' (*aleph*) (retained in Isa 37:26) has been dropped, (see GKC §§23*f*, 75*qq*).

25e–e. לַהְשׁוֹת גַּלִּים נִצִּים: Gk. "and it [the enclosure?] turned into warlike colonies"; Vulg. and Syr. with MT although both are somewhat paraphrastic.

26a–a. וּשְׁדֵפָה לִפְנֵי קָמָה: Gk. "trodden opposite him who stands"; Vulg. and Syr. with MT. The textual situation here is very complex. Isa 37:27 has שְׁדֵמָה "field" instead of שְׁדֵפָה "blasted." This looks very much like a confusion between the labials מ (*m*) and פ (*p*). IQIs[a] confuses the matter still further with its *nšdp lpny qdym qwmkh* which would read "blasted before the east wind. Your rising..." Proposals to emend the text of Isaiah in the directions now attested by 1QIs[a] were made already by Wellhausen in the 19th century. What Heb. lies behind Gk. πάτημα, "trodden" is a matter of dispute. For a full discussion of these issues, (see *CTAT* 412–13).

29a. הָאוֹת: Vulg. adds "Hezekiah"; Gk. and Syr. with MT.

29b. אָכוֹל: On the inf. abs. functioning as an emphatic impf, (see GKC §113*ee*).

29c. זִרְעוּ: '*IBHS* (§34.4c)argues that the imps. here are an example of heterosis, the exchange of one vb. form for another. By utilizing the imps. instead of impf. forms, the promise is given greater emphasis and vividness.

31a. K ׃ Q צְבָאוֹת "armies"; all the versions agree.

32a. לָכֵן: Gk. "Not so!"; Vulg. and Syr. with MT.

34a. וְגַנּוֹתִי: Gk. "I will hold a shield over"; Vulg. and Syr. with MT.

34b. לְהוֹשִׁיעָהּ: Gk. omits; Vulg. and Syr. with MT.

Commentary

Many scholars see two oracles here: the first in vv. 20–31 and the second (and supposedly the more original) in vv. 32–34. However, Hobbs (279) is more accurate when he identifies three responses: vv. 20–28; 29–31; and 32–34. The first and the third are judgment speeches addressed to Sennacherib, while the second is a salvation oracle addressed to the people of Jerusalem. Again, as Hobbs says (279), supported by Sweeney (418), there is much throughout that breathes the air of Isaiah. When the three parts are viewed together, there is first a longer address to Sennacherib, rebuking him for his arrogance and blasphemy, then a word of encouragement to the people, and finally a brief statement of conclusion, announcing that Sennacherib will not be able to do anything to Jerusalem. Seen in this way, the three parts fit together to form a unity.

Here Yahweh asserts in a climactic way that while the Assyrian may congratulate himself on all his glorious achievements, mocking Yahweh as one more god to be destroyed in his triumphant progress, that is not true. Far from being one of the gods whom an all-powerful Sennacherib can trample under his feet, Yahweh is the very One who has planned all this in advance and has made it possible for Sennacherib to do whatever he has done. The truth is that the Assyrian has things exactly backwards: he cannot, in his independent power, dispatch Yahweh. It is Yahweh who is empowering him and will shortly dispatch him back the same way he came (vv. 28, 33).

20 In his prayer Hezekiah had invoked the living God, the One who unlike the idols, can truly see and hear. Now Isaiah assures Hezekiah that Yahweh has heard, not only Hezekiah's prayer, but also the taunts of the Assyrian monarch. The content of the following oracle of judgment gives ample evidence of that. If the Rab-shaqeh had prepared for his speech by familiarizing himself to some degree with Judean life and thought, Isaiah has done no less with regard to the Assyrian boasts. The quotations of Sennacherib in vv. 23 and 24 ring with the authenticity of the Assyrian annals.[68] These are indeed the kinds of things the Assyrian emperors claimed. Yahweh has indeed heard.

21–28 This poem, much like Isaiah 14:4–21, contains elements of the lament form. Several of the cola show the 3:2 meter that is typical of that form. But like Isaiah 14, it is a parody of a lament. Weak, delicate "daughter Jerusalem" (בַּת יְרוּשָׁלָם, *baṯ yᵉrûšālām*), whom Sennacherib had confidently expected to rape, sticks her tongue out at the conqueror, and offers him mock condolences

68. While some see this as evidence of the lateness of the material, arguing that such knowledge could have only been gained by someone who had been exiled to Mesopotamia, that is hardly necessary. It is very likely that this kind of boasting was not limited to the walls of the Assyrian palaces and temples, where we have found the Annals. It is probable that the Annals are only the final "publication" of proclamations that had been made orally wherever the Assyrian kings had gone long before the words were finally chiseled in stone. For examples of such boasting as seen in the Assyrian annals, see *ANET,* 274–301. Yet, the clearest parallels are found in Sargon's Annals as reproduced in *ARAB* II:142–144.

for the disgrace and shame he is about to suffer (v. 21). He did not realize with whom he was contending when he mocked Yahweh (v. 22). He did not realize that he had only been able to accomplish all the "extreme" things he had (vv. 23–24) because he was fulfilling Yahweh's plans (vv. 25–26). He had not accomplished anything without Yahweh's prior knowledge (v. 27). Now, because he had arrogated to himself what was actually the work of Yahweh, he would go slinking back to Assyria, in the same direction as all the exiles he had dispatched and had expected to dispatch.

21 To "wag [the] head" (רֹאשׁ הֵנִיעָה, *rōʾš hēnîʿâ*) from side to side while looking at someone is an almost universal gesture of contempt and mockery.[69] Here the coupling of this gesture with the figurative description of Jerusalem as "virgin daughter" (בְּתוּלַת בַּת, *bᵊtûlat bat*) makes the contempt more pointed. Jerusalem is defenseless and helpless before the might of Assyria. Or so it would seem. But, in fact, Jerusalem has all the power of the universe on her side. It is as though a man is threatening a thirteen-year old girl (cf. Isa 10:32) when her father, seven feet tall and three hundred and fifty pounds, arrives on the scene. Peeking out from behind her father's back, the little girl sticks out her tongue at the aggressor.[70]

22 The thought continues as Yahweh, the seven-foot-tall father, points out to Sennacherib that Sennacherib did not know who he was provoking when he picked this particular fight. He is "the Holy One of Israel" (קְדוֹשׁ יִשְׂרָאֵל, *qᵊdôš yiśrāʾēl*). This distinctly Isaianic phrase is one more indication of the priority of the Isaianic material here.[71] Sennacherib unthinkingly had imagined that Yahweh was simply one more of the human created gods that he had so easily smashed. That was not the case at all. This is the Holy One, the one truly transcendent being in the universe, not made with human hands and minds, but the Maker of all things. But there is more. This transcendent

69. See Job 16:4; Pss 22:7; 109:25. Cogan and Tadmor argue that there is also an element of commiseration in the term (237). However, the examples they cite are of the somewhat synonymous נוּד, *nûd*. The occs. of נוּעַ, *nûaʿ* the vb. here, do not, in my judgment, show that connotation.

70. Most of the twenty-five occurrences of בַּת־צִיּוֹן, *bat-ṣiyyôn* "daughter (of) Zion" (six in Isa; eight in Lam) emphasize weakness and vulnerability. "Daughter (of) Jerusalem" (בַּת יְרוּשָׁלָםִ, *bat yᵊrûšālām*) is much less frequent, occurring only five times other than here and in the parallel in Isaiah ("daughters of Jerusalem" occurs only in Song, while "daughters of Zion" occurs only once in Song, and in Isa 3:16, 17; 4:4). For the same combination of the two phrases as here, see Lam 2:13.

71. The phrase occurs twenty-five times (twenty-six if the single occurrence of "Holy One of Jacob" [Isa 29:23] is counted) in Isaiah. Apart from this parallel passage in Kings there are only five other occurrences in the rest of the OT: Pss 71:22; 78:41; 89:18; Jer 50:29; 51:5. Interestingly, three of these, Ps 78:41, and both Jer passages, speak of the foolishness of defying the "Holy One of Israel."

One has chosen to give himself especially to one of his created peoples: Israel. This is the One with whom Sennacherib has foolishly chosen to pick a fight.

23–24 As mentioned above, the language in these two verses, presented as an example of Sennacherib's boasting, sounds as though it could have been taken straight from an Assyrian proclamation that later ended up on the temple walls in Nineveh. The prophet is making it clear that his claims about the Assyrian's "raised voice" and "lifted eyes" (v. 21) are not something falsely attributed to Sennacherib, but have come straight from his mouth, or at least from the mouths of Assyrian monarchs. These kinds of claims to have subdued the most difficult "mountains" (הָרִים, *hārîm*), the thickest "forest[s]," (יַעַר, *ya ʿar*) and the deepest "rivers" (יְאֹרִים, *yᵊ ʾōrîm*) are typical of the Assyrian annals.[72] It is a way of asserting that these men, and this nation, are superior to anything on earth or in heaven.[73] It should be noted that first-person pronouns occur six times in the two verses, with two of those in emphatic positions. This is a man who considers himself to be the apex of the universe.

25–28 But Sennacherib has it all wrong. Nothing he has done has been on his own initiative, and nothing of the outcome will be of his doing. It has all been a carrying out of the plans and purposes of the One who is indeed the apex of the universe. The six first-person pronouns of vv. 23–24 are now countered by ten such pronouns in these verses, all referring to Yahweh. Sennacherib is not the first cause of anything, Yahweh is. This is another theme that is particularly characteristic of Isaiah's thought, and is especially applied to Assyria, Babylon, and Cyrus (Isa 10:5–15; 14:24–26; 19:17; 22:11; 41:2; 44:28, etc.). These mighty powers of the world were doing nothing other than fulfilling the purposes and plans of the Maker of the world.

25–26 In the same vein as Isaiah 10:5–15, Yahweh declares that all the accomplishments about which Sennacherib and the other Assyrian monarchs had boasted were simply the carrying out of Yahweh's plans. It is he who has made it possible for the Assyrians to turn "fortified cities into heaps of ruins," (לַהְשׁוֹת גַּלִּים נִצִּים עָרִים בְּצֻרוֹת, *lahšôṯ gallîm niṣṣîm ʿārîm bᵊṣurôṯ*) and to reduce

72. The ref. to Egypt (here מָצוֹר, *māṣôr* normally מִצְרַיִם, *miṣrayim*) is taken by some to be anachronistic, since Sennacherib did not conquer Egypt. But Gray, noting that וְאַחְרִב, *wᵊ ʾaḥriḇ* shows a conjunctive *waw,* suggests that the comment is prospective since Egypt is the goal of the Assyrian aggression (691). It seems more likely that none of this is intended to be historical but is simply propaganda (cf. Provan, 262).

73. Provan (262) points out that reference to the "heights," מְרוֹם, *mᵊrôm* (22, 23), is reminiscent of Isa 14:13–15 where the king of Babylon thought he could mount up into heaven and usurp the place of God.

the inhabitants of those cities to quivering helplessness, with no more power or endurance than a few blades of grass.[74, 75]

27–28 In language similar to that of Psalm 139:1–3, Yahweh makes it clear to Sennacherib that nothing he does is hidden from Yahweh, in particular his "raging" (רגז, *rgz*) against Yahweh. In the light of what had just been said, this raging was particularly foolish. Sennacherib was only Yahweh's agent, and as Sennacherib had undoubtedly had occasion to point out to his subordinates, it was very unwise to offend one's master, as he had most certainly done. As a result, Sennacherib, like an animal out of control, will be subdued with a "hook in your nose" (חַחִי בְּאַפֶּךָ, *ḥaḥî bᵊ ʾappeḵā*), and "a bit in your mouth" (מִתְגִּי בִּשְׂפָתֶיךָ, *miṯgiy biśpāṯêḵā*). The sense of חַח, *ḥāḥ*, "hook" is not entirely clear. Ezekiel 29:4 speaks of it as a fishhook, but elsewhere in Ezekiel (19:4; 38:4) it seems, as here, to be a ring put in a bull's nose to which a halter rope could be attached. The same language appears in Ashurbanipal's annals (*ANET,* 300), speaking of the humiliation of an enemy king (as was done to Manasseh, 2 Chr 33:11). In that Sennacherib is being sent back to his homeland, the direction in which exiles would go, it seems likely that there is an allusion here to the treatment of exiles (cf. *ANEP,* 447). What he had intended to do to others would be done to him.

29–31 This second oracle, an oracle of salvation, is addressed to Hezekiah and the survivors in Jerusalem. It contains the same sort of "sign" (אוֹת, *ʾôṯ*)

---

74. For a similar use of the figure of "grass," see Isa 40:6–8. Grass would grow on the flat roofs of houses that were plastered with mud. However, it had little rootage and would swiftly dry up under the direct sun.

75. The concluding word of verse 26 (קָמָה, *qāmâ*), paralleled in Isa 37:27, seems questionable. It is קָמָה, a third feminine singular perfect form of קוּם, *qûm*, "to arise." It has been interpreted as here: "blasted before it can grow up" (שְׁדֵפָה לִפְנֵי קָמָה, *šᵊḏēpâ lip̄nê qāmâ*). However, there is nothing actually representing "before." Both the Vulgate and the Syriac support this understanding, while the LXX reads "trodden opposite him who stands." Although this latter is a different interpretation, it still clearly reflects the present Heb. text. A century and a half ago it was proposed (by Wellhausen, cited by Hobbs, 268) that the original text was לפני קמך (*lpny qmk*) (see v. 27). "Others have favored a reading of לפני קדתם (*lpny qdtm*) 'before the east wind.' (27) Your rising and your sitting... ." Thus, the present text would have been the result of conflation of two similar and adjacent words into the one word: קמה, *qmh.* This is a very attractive suggestion in part because the emended text would provide another example of the conventional pairing of rising and sitting (Deut 6:7; Ps 139:2; Lam 3:63; however, note Deut 11:19 where sitting is not paired with rising). This proposal has now actually been confirmed in Isaiah by 1QIsa. This is a strong argument for its adoption, both in Isaiah and here. However, given the uniform witness of the versions in both places, the thought must still be entertained that perhaps both ancient and modern interpreters arrived at the same solution for a knotty problem.

as was given to Moses (Exod 3:12), and is, in fact, typical of Hebrew prophecy. Something is promised for the future precisely so that when it does occur, the people will know that its occurrence was not accidental, but a part of the providence of God (cf. Isa 48:5). In this case, it is the promise that within three years, the Assyrian threat would be gone.[76] As House (370) says, Hezekiah did not think he had three months, and here Isaiah is promising three years. However, that seems a rather long time to survive on only grain that comes up by itself. Probably what is intended is parts of three years. Presumably the Assyrians had devastated the farmlands when they had conquered the rest of the land (18:13) (see the claims of Tiglath-pileser to such destruction; *ARAB* 1:792, 96). That devastation would have taken place in the summer and destroyed the harvest of that year (year 1). It would also have prevented fall planting (year 2). But by time for the fall planting of year three, the Assyrians would be gone. Thus, we are speaking of fourteen or fifteen months on the calendar.

But that situation: a devastated land, and survival through scavenging the fields for a few plants that might have come up from the grain that had been slashed down, would have certainly made the Rab-shaqeh's glowing promises (18:31–32) attractive. Isaiah's words spoke to that situation: wait (trust) through apparently hopeless days and you will again plant, harvest, "and eat the fruit" (וְאִכְלוּ פִּרְיָם, *wᵊʾiklû piryām*) right here in your own land.

30–31 The situation described in v. 29 provided Isaiah with a perfect set of images to describe the regrowth of Judah/Israel. Somehow from God's people, like plants that had been cut down, seeds would be scattered that would take "root downward and bear fruit upward" (שֹׁרֶשׁ לְמָטָּה וְעָשָׂה פְרִי לְמָעְלָה, *šōreš lᵊmāṭṭâ wᵊʿāśâ pᵊrî lᵊmāʿᵊlâ*). This promise of "the remnant" (הַנִּשְׁאָרָה, *hanniš ʾārâ*) that would survive the coming judgment is found throughout the book of Isaiah, encapsulated in the name of his son Shear-jashub, "A Remnant Will Return" (Isa 7:3), but emerging again and again (e.g., 4:2–6; 10:20–23; 11:1–16; 14:1–2). Having experienced the recent destruction of the northern kingdom and the consequent exile of its leadership, this promise that a remnant would survive "from the hill of Zion" (מֵהַר צִיּוֹן, *mēhar ṣiyyôn*) to bear fruit in the world would have been a wonderful encouragement to the embattled citizens of Jerusalem. The guarantee of the promise was the passionate attachment ("the zeal" [קִנְאָה, *qin ʾâ*]) that Yahweh bore for his people. Nowhere else in the world than in Israel did this conceptuality exist: absolute transcendence coupled with passionate attachment. Elsewhere (e.g., Plato or Aristotle) you might find the germ of divine transcendence, but it was, of logical necessity, utterly without passion. Among the gods, you might find passion. But only in Yahweh can transcendence and passion be found in inseparable unity. In many ways, this is best captured in Isaiah's phrase: The Holy One of Israel.

76. The pattern of threes is typical of the book of Isaiah: 8:4; 16:14; 20:3.

32–34 For those who understand these verses to be independent of the preceding ones, the "Therefore" (לָכֵן, *lāḵēn*) which begins v. 32 is introducing the announcement of judgment in a prophetic judgment speech. In that case the messenger formulation and the accusation are missing. However, it is possible to understand this material in a less stereotyped way. In that case, "therefore" is simply introducing the conclusion—the effect—of the two preceding parts, the statements of the causes. Because Sennacherib has defied the living God, claiming for himself what Yahweh alone had made possible, and in the process derogating the very source of his accomplishments, and because of Yahweh's passionate attachment to his people, the ones whom Sennacherib believes he is free to destroy, "therefore," not only will Sennacherib not be able to do what he intends to Jerusalem, but he is going to go straight "back the way he came" (בַּדֶּרֶךְ אֲשֶׁר־יָבֹא בָּהּ יָשׁוּב, *badderek ʾăšer-yābōʾ bāh yāšûb*).[77]

Some commentators (see Hobbs, 272–73), noting Sennacherib's claim (*ANET*, 288) to have besieged the city, question the authenticity of the words here. Wiseman (283) responds by arguing that Sennacherib did not actually make such a claim, that the Akkadian word which has been translated "earthworks" is better translated "watchtowers" or something of the sort. But even with that helpful observation, it ought still to be pointed out that the Assyrian annals are full of hyperbole, and that Yahweh's statement through Isaiah has at least as much right to be taken at face-value as Sennacherib's. The fact is, Sennacherib did not capture Jerusalem and left the central figure of a regional revolt unpunished and alive. It seems very unlikely that Hezekiah's large tribute, or a sally by the Babylonians under Merodach-baladan (for whom the date is wrong in any case) could account for this action on the Assyrian emperor's part. It seems most probable that such an action would require events of much greater significance, events that the text is just about to reveal.

34 This final statement of the reason for Yahweh's defense of Jerusalem is very interesting. Two reasons are given: "for my [Yahweh's] sake and for the sake of my servant David" (לְמַעֲנִי וּלְמַעַן דָּוִד עַבְדִּי, *lᵉmaʿănî ûlᵉmaʿan dāwid ʿabdî*). In the context, the first is entirely understandable. Sennacherib had belittled Yahweh, arguing that he was no different from any of the other gods, and would be just as helpless as they had been before the might of Assyria. Clearly, Yahweh was on his mettle; was Sennacherib correct or not? If he was not, then Yahweh had to prove it by preventing the Assyrian from doing what he intended to Yahweh's city, the place where Yahweh had placed his name (Deut 12:11; 26:2; 1 Kgs 11:36; 14:21).

But the second reason is not, at first glance, so transparent. Why is the city defended for David's sake, and not, say, for the sake of God's people?

---

77. Brueggemann notes that in contrast to the claimed accomplishments with their first-person pronouns in vv. 23 and 24, here we have a succession of "nots" (512–13). As the true Cause, Yahweh, details what Sennacherib will *not* be permitted to do.

I believe the answer is to be found in the close intertwining of the Davidic dynasty and the name of Yahweh. In what is almost David's first appearance in the narrative, we find him answering the Philistine giant's taunts with the words, "I come to you in the name of Yahweh of Heaven's Armies, the God of the armies of Israel, whom you have defied" (2 Sam 17:45). Then we find him wishing to build a temple for Yahweh's name, and being given the promise that his son will build it (2 Sam 7:13), a point that his son, Solomon, reiterates (1 Kgs 5:5). Furthermore, it is in the context of the division of the kingdom that it is explicitly said that Jerusalem was where Yahweh had chosen to place his name (1 Kgs 11:36; 14:21). Jerusalem had to be retained for David because Yahweh's name was inseparably associated with David and with David's city.

Thus, we may argue that "Yahweh's sake" and "David's sake" are inseparable. Sennacherib, like Goliath, had defied Yahweh, profaning his name. It was because of David's passion for Yahweh's name that he had been anointed and given the promise of an enduring "house." Hezekiah, the most recent representative of that house, had displayed the same passion as his ancestor for Yahweh's name. He had not prayed that Yahweh would deliver Jerusalem because of his people's good behavior, but in order that the world might know Yahweh. Thus, Yahweh's name had been in the beginning, and was still in this moment, inseparable from "David's" commitment to Yahweh and Yahweh's commitment to "David."[78]

Biblical Theology Comments

The expression of faith in Yahweh's unique superiority that is displayed here is little short of breathtaking. After twenty centuries of Christian faith in the West it is easy to become blasé about Yahweh's uniqueness. But in the context in which Isaiah was declaring it the claim is nothing short of stunning. As Hezekiah had said, Sennacherib and his predecessors had done all they claimed to, and had done so, by that time, for some two hundred years. Furthermore, the world was full of great gods who, in spite of what Assyria may or may not have done, were still going to hold sway over hundreds of thousands of people. The people of Damascus were not going to give up their allegiance to Hadad, their version of the storm god, just because the Assyrians may have violated his temple and carried off his idols. Yet, here is Isaiah, who can declare with absolute assurance that Yahweh is not one more of the gods, and that everything the Assyrians had done was not the result of the activities of their gods, but of his preexistent plans and purposes. Again, this is an unheard of claim. It is not that Yahweh is chief of the gods, or that he is more powerful than the other gods, it is, as Isaiah says elsewhere (cf. 45:5), that there are no other gods. The world functions at his direction alone.

---

78. This is one of the reasons that Provan argues that the first recension of Kings was a Hezekian one, with Hezekiah being portrayed as the ideal Davidic king. Iain W. Provan, *Hezekiah and the Books of Kings* (Berlin: de Gruyter, 1988).

It is maintained by many that this understanding of Yahweh is exilic or even postexilic, but it is here presented, although not as explicitly as elsewhere, as having been fully present already in 701 BC. Of course, if we take the Bible as it wishes to be taken, that Moses was the author of Deuteronomy, the thought existed long before Isaiah (Deut 4:35, 39; 32:39). In fact, it seems that it must have been well established before the exile so that it could enable the Israelite people to survive the exile with their faith intact. To believe that they had no real concept of Yahweh's uniqueness before the exile, only to conceive of such a thing after the Assyrians and the Babylonians had decimated them, clearly having defeated Yahweh on every hand, is to ask too much. On the other hand, if the idea had been birthed at Sinai, and nourished ever since by the prophets, then confirmed in such a way as this in Hezekiah's day, it is still revolutionary, but not without grounds, which it is, if we suggest that the experiences of the exile gave rise to it.

Sennacherib clearly illustrates the human problem as the Bible defines it: it is not so much that we are inveterate idol-makers, but rather that each of us, like Sennacherib, imagines ourselves to be the center of existence. It might be protested that this is to overstate the issue. How many of us would actually state such a conviction? That may be so, but that is the way humans typically function. Our own pleasure, comfort, position, and power dominate our motivations and goals. In fact, this is the motive of idol-making: an attempt to enlist the power of the spirit world in the achievement of our goals.

The Bible calls us to realize that we are not the center of our world, let alone *the* world. It is Yahweh alone who is I AM, self-existing. This was the realization that Daniel reports Nebuchadnezzar came to, if only fleetingly. Nebuchadnezzar was not the maker of kingdoms, Yahweh is (Dan 4:25, 34–37), and anyone who denies that reality, denies reality itself. It is also the truth that permeated the ministry of Jesus. We hear him saying things like, "If anyone wants to follow me, he must deny himself, and pick up the cross" (Matt 16:24), or "it is easier for a camel to go through the eye of a needle than it is for a rich person to enter the kingdom of heaven" (Luke 18:25), or "whoever is least among you is the greatest" (Luke 9:48).

It is not that the Bible denies the fact of human psychology that each of us can only perceive the world through our own senses and from within ourselves. None of us can become someone else. But what it does call for is that we will no longer live for ourselves and unto ourselves. We must, as the Holy Spirit enables us, live for others. So the apostle Paul says that we should not look to our own interests, but to the interests of others (Phil 2:4). This is what it is to be genuinely Christlike. Paul goes on to describe Timothy and Epaphroditus as being examples if such persons. They are unlike those who look only to their own interests (Phil 2:21). He makes a similar point in Romans chapter twelve where he describes the Christian life which results from what God has done for us in Christ and through the Holy Spirit. Such a life is characterized by self-denying, self-giving love (Rom 12:1–13:10).

Selected Bibliography

Clements, R. E. "The Prophecies of Isaiah to Hezekiah Concerning Sennacherib, 2 Kings 19.21–34//Isa 37.22–35." Pages 65–78 in *Prophetie und Geschichtliche Wirklichkeit im Alten Israel: Festschrift für Siegfried Herrmann zum 65 Geburtstag.* Edited by Rüdiger Liwak and Siegfried Wagner. Stuttgart: W. Kohlhammer, 1991.

Evans, P. S. *The Invasion of Sennacherib in the Book of Kings: A Source-Critical and Rhetorical Study of 2 Kings 18–19.* Leiden: Brill, 2009.

The Destruction of the Assyrian Army (19:35–37)

Translation

35 It happened that night that the Angel of Yahweh went out and struck 185,000 in the Assyrian camp. When they arose early in the morning, there they were, all of them dead corpses. **36** Sennacherib, king of Assyria, departed and went and returned and stayed in Nineveh. **37** Now he was worshipping in the house of Nisroch, his god, and his sons, Adrammelech and Sharezer, struck him with the sword, and fled to Ararat, and his son Esarhaddon reigned in his place.

Textual Notes

35a. בַּלַּ֫יְלָה הַהוּא: Gk. has "while it was night"; Vulg. and Syr. with MT. The phrase does not appear in Isa 37:36.

35b–36b. וַיִּסַּע וַיֵּלֶךְ וַיַּשְׁכִּימוּ בַבֹּקֶר וְהִנֵּה כֻלָּם פְּגָרִים מֵתִים: Vulg. "when he saw ... he departed and went. [36] Sennacherib, king of Assyria, returned... ."; Syr. and Gk. with MT. Vulg. is perhaps troubled by the indef. 3rd person subj. of "they rose early," as are some mod. versions (ESV "When the people rose...").

37a. K ֯; Q בָּנָיו; all the versions agree with Q. Isa 37:38 has "sons" (בָּנָיו) in K.

Commentary

The reader cannot help but be struck by the terseness of this report. After the lengthy buildup in chapters eighteen and nineteen, these brief words seem almost anticlimactic. We see a somewhat similar example in Exodus 3–4. In those chapters we have a lengthy dialogue between Yahweh and Moses over whether Moses will go to Egypt or not. In the end we are simply told that Moses returned to Jethro and announced that he was going to Egypt (Exod 4:18). The point in both cases seems to be that in the end, the issue is whether action will be taken or not. If it will, then no lengthy discussion is necessary. Will Moses submit? Yes. Can Yahweh deliver? Yes.

35 It seems likely that the reference to "the Angel of the Lord" (מַלְאַךְ יהוה, *mal'ak̲ yhwh*) is intentional. Sennacherib had sent his messengers to belittle Hezekiah and to mock Yahweh, insisting that Yahweh would be as helpless before the Assyrians as all the other gods had been. Now Yahweh sends his messenger, and it is the Assyrians who are helpless before him.

Commentators have offered numerous solutions to what seems an excessive number of Assyrian victims. These range from 185 men (the letter א 'having stood for אִישׁ', *'îš* ["man"], as discussed in Cogan and Tadmor, 239) to 185 units (אֶלֶף', *'ālep̄* [""chiefs"] having been intended; Wiseman, 284). One of the issues relates to the size of the Assyrian army at this time. Shalmaneser III claims to have had 120,000 men at Qarqar in 854 BC so perhaps it is not out of the question that Sennacherib might have had double that amount one hundred fifty years later. But it is clear that the Israelites did not use numbers as we do with a strict limitation to quantity. They used them in a broader, more hyperbolic way to express quality as well. Thus, without demanding numerical precision, we can say that Sennacherib suffered a devastating loss, one that crippled his army, making a further stay on the Philistine plains decidedly unwise.[79]

Commentators who do not accept the possibility of divine miraculous intervention in human affairs struggle to explain Sennacherib's withdrawal without capturing and killing the rebel leader, Hezekiah.[80] Many assert that the Assyrian accepted Hezekiah's tribute (18:14) and withdrew (so Fritz, 376). This assertion depends upon the hypothesis of two different accounts of what took place, since the biblical account records that Sennacherib's demands for surrender came after the tribute was given and taken. Furthermore, it is difficult in the circumstances to see why Sennacherib would leave Hezekiah on the throne, tribute or not.[81]

It is equally unlikely that Sennacherib would have withdrawn because of the threat of Merodach-baladan, as Sweeney (413) suggests. Surely the Babylonian rebel would not be able to mount anything like a serious threat to the Assyrian grand army so far from the Babylonian rebel base. Neither is there credible evidence for a strong Egyptian thrust northward at this time.

All in all, the most likely explanation for the Assyrian withdrawal is the one the Bible gives: a sudden catastrophe of some sort overwhelming the army to the extent that they could not continue the campaign and had to surrender the ground hurriedly or risk military defeat. It is a matter of no small import that as far as Assyrian records go, Sennacherib did not attempt any more campaigns in the west during his ensuing nineteen years on the throne. It was only his successor Esarhaddon who renewed the long-held goal of conquering Egypt.

36 Here is the final occurrence of the theme of "return" (שׁוּב, *šûḇ*) that recurs throughout this narrative (19:7, 8, 28, 33). Yahweh had said that Sennacherib

79. Note the several predictions elsewhere in Isaiah of the Assyrian defeat: 10:12; 14:25; 30:31; 31:8.

80. For Sennacherib's report of the events see *ANET*, 287–88.

81. See A. R. Millard, "Sennacherib's Attack on Hezekiah," *TynBul* 36 (1985): 61–77, which is a rejoinder to R. E. Clements, *Isaiah and the Deliverance of Jerusalem*, JSOTSup 13 (Sheffield: University of Sheffield, 1980).

would turn back on the same way that he had come, and so it occurred. Sennacherib could claim in his annals that he concluded his campaign in victory and returned home in triumph. But the plain fact is that he did not succeed in his main purpose, destroying the head and the headquarters of the western rebellion. He turned back from his goal and putting the best light on his failure could not make it anything less than that.[82] The other important statement is that "he stayed in Nineveh" (וַיֵּשֶׁב בְּנִינְוֵה, *wayyēšeḇ bᵊnînᵊwē*). He did not return to attack Jerusalem again. At one time, it was common to assert that there were two attacks on Jerusalem: the one in 701 BC and another perhaps as late as 686 BC. This hypothesis was felt necessary because of discrepancies connected with the supposed two accounts found in chapters eighteen and nineteen. However, even those who continue to argue for the two accounts now dismiss two attacks (e.g., Cogan and Tadmor, 248–51).

37 The author/editor(s) complete the story by reporting the somewhat ignominious death of Sennacherib.[83] This man, who insisted that Hezekiah's god could not deliver Hezekiah from the Assyrian armies, and learned to his dismay that indeed Yahweh could deliver, now found his own god helpless to deliver him from his own sons. The author/editor(s) clearly feel no need to comment on this obvious irony, but it is a most fitting end to the story.

Mesopotamian records confirm that Sennacherib, having designated his youngest son Esarhaddon as his successor, was murdered by his son Arda-mulissi,[84] and that the murderer fled to Urartu, the biblical Ararat (*COS* 1:467). Although these records mention only one son, Esarhaddon's annals, while not mentioning Sennacherib's murder, speak of his brothers' (pl.) hatred of him and their attempt to usurp the throne.[85] As Cogan and Tadmor (244) say, there is every reason to take the statement that two brothers were involved as factual.

It is highly likely that "Nisroch" is a pejorative renaming of some Assyrian god, perhaps Ninurta. This practice is common in the Bible. See for instance שִׁקּוּץ שֹׁמֵם, *šiqqûṣ šōmēm*, ("abomination of desolation") for Baal Shamayim, "lord of the heavens" (Dan 12:11).

Selected Bibliography

Caesar, S. W. "The Annihilation of Sennacherib's Army: A Case of Septicemic Plague?" *JBQ* 45 (2017): 222–28.

82. In his annals, Esarhaddon insisted that he never turned back (*ANET*, 289) and it is likely Sennacherib did as well. But Yahweh decreed that he would, and he did.

83. Cogan and Tadmor point out that the simple, factual nature of the report suggests it might have been copied from a chronicle (244). It is not impossible that it was done so when the book was in its final stages in Babylon.

84. Although it is not apparent, the reading Adram-melek (2 Kgs 17:31) is fairly easily explained from this original.

85. *ANET*, 289.

Grabbe, L. L. "Of Mice and Dead Men: Herodotus 2.141 and Sennacherib's Campaign in 701 BCE." Pages 119–40 in *'Like a Bird in a Cage': 'The Invasion of Sennacherib in 701 BCE.* Edited by Lester L. Grabbe. London: Sheffield Academic, 2003.

Lettinga, J. P. "A Note on 2 Kings 19:37." *VT* 7 (1957): 105–06.

Parpola, S. "The Murderer of Sennacherib." Pages 171–82 in *Death in Mesopotamia: Papers Read at the XXVIue Rencontre Assyrologique Internationale.* Edited by Bendt Alster. Copenhagen: Akademisk Vorlag, 1980.

Hezekiah's Illness and Recovery (20:1–11)

Translation

20:1 In those days Hezekiah became ill enough to die[86] and Isaiah the prophet, son of Amos, came to him and said to him, "Thus says Yahweh, 'Instruct your house because you are going to die and will not live.' " **2** He turned his face to the wall and prayed to Yahweh, saying, **3** "O Yahweh, please remember how I have walked before you in truth and with an undivided heart and have done what is good in your eyes," and he wept out loud. **4** Now Isaiah had not gone out of the middle court when the word of Yahweh came to him, saying **5** "Return and say to Hezekiah, the leader of my people, 'Thus says Yahweh, the God of David your father, "I have heard your prayer and I have seen your tears, so now I am going to heal you; on the third day you will go up to the house of the Lord. **6** I will add fifteen years to your days and I will deliver you and this city from the hand of the King of Assyria; I will defend this city for my sake and the sake of David my servant." ' " **7** Isaiah had said, "Take a cake of figs, take it and put it on the boil," and he lived.[87] **8** Hezekiah said to Isaiah, "What is the sign that Yahweh will heal me and I will go up to the house of Yahweh on the third day?" **9** Isaiah said, "This will be the sign to you from Yahweh, that Yahweh will do the thing which he said: the shadow has gone down[88] ten steps; shall it return ten steps?" **10** Hezekiah said, "It is an easy thing for the shadow to stretch up ten steps; rather let the shadow turn backward ten steps." **11** Isaiah the prophet called to Yahweh,

86. For this rendering of simultaneous verbal action, see RJW (§235).

87. וַיֶּחִי, *wayyeḥî*: Heb. *waw* consec. Plus impf. Gk. and Syr. translate with a future tense ("he will live"). Isa 38:21 has it as a jussive (וְיֶחִי, *wᵉyeḥî* ["that he may live"]).

88. The vb. is a pf. (הָלַךְ הַצֵּל, *hālak̲ haṣṣēl*) Montgomery suggests repointing it as an inf. abs. being used interrogatively. The versions all understand this to be a question, which might suggest an original הֲיֵלֵךְ, *hăyēlēk̲*. Isaiah omits the alternative entirely, simply having Yahweh say through Isaiah, "I am going to make the shadow go back… ." *CTAT* (414) suggests the alternative "The shadow has gone down… , shall it go back… ?" So also Provan ("the shadow has gone forward … shall it go back…"; 265) and Cogan and Tadmor (255).

and he caused the shadow which had gone down[89] the steps of Ahaz to go back ten steps.

Textual Notes

MT1a. יְהוָה: Vulg. adds "God"; Gk. and Syr. with MT.

2a. וַיַּסֵּב: Gk. and Syr. add "Hezekiah" as does Isa 38:2; Vulg. with MT.

4a–a. וַיְהִי יְשַׁעְיָהוּ לֹא יָצָא הָעִיר הַתִּיכֹנָה: Gk. "Isaiah was in the middle court when"; Vulg. and Syr. "Before Isaiah had gone out of the middle court"; Isa 38:4 omits, reading "the word of Yahweh came to Isaiah"

MT4b. K הָעִיר "the city": Q חָצֵר , "court." All the versions with Q.

5a. שׁוּב: Isa 38:5 הָלוֹךְ, "go," which Hobbs (286) calls "a normal use of the inf. abs."

5b–b. נְגִיד־עַמִּי: Isa 38:5 omits.

5c–c. הִנְנִי רֹפֵא לָךְ בַּיּוֹם הַשְּׁלִישִׁי תַּעֲלֶה בֵּית יְהוָה: Isa 38:5 omits.

6a–a. וְגַנּוֹתִי עַל־הָעִיר הַזֹּאת לְמַעֲנִי וּלְמַעַן דָּוִד עַבְדִּי: Isa 38:6 omits. But the phrase does appear in 1QIsa.

7a. וַיֹּאמֶר: Vv. 7 and 8 do not appear here in Isaiah, but at the end of the chapter as Isa 38:21–22.

9a–11a. Appear in altered form in Isa 38:7–8.

10a. מַעֲלוֹת: Vulg. adds "I do not wish that." Gk. and Syr. with MT.

11a–a. וַיָּשֶׁב אֶת־הַצֵּל בַּמַּעֲלוֹת אֲשֶׁר יָרְדָה בְּמַעֲלוֹת אָחָז אֲחֹרַנִּית: Gk. "the shadow on the stairs returned"; Vulg. and Syr. with MT.

Commentary

As I have argued elsewhere, it seems likely that the two incidents reported here took place at least ten years prior to 701 BC when the events of chapters eighteen and nineteen occurred. This is probable, both because of the dates of Hezekiah and the dates of Merodach-baladan. If Hezekiah's reign began in 727/26 BC (as a coregency with his father Ahaz, see the "Commentary" above on 18:1) then he died in 696 BC, and the additional fifteen years (v. 6)

89. There is a problem of agreement between "the shadow" (הַצֵּל, *haṣṣēl*; masc.) and "had gone down" (יָרְדָה, *yārḏâ*; fem.). In Isa 38:8, it is the sun (f.) which has "gone down," and perhaps the sun is to be understood here. So *CTAT* (414-15).

would have been given about 711 BC, a date that accords well with Merodach-baladan's rule over Babylon that ended in 709 BC.[90]

A further piece of support for this conclusion is found in v. 6 where Yahweh promises to "deliver you and this city from the hand of the king of Assyria" (מִכַּף מֶלֶךְ־אַשּׁוּר אַצִּילְךָ וְאֵת הָעִיר הַזֹּאת, *mikkap̄ melek̲- ʾaššûr ʾaṣṣîlᵊk̲ā wᵊ ʾēt̲ hā ʿîr hazzō ʾt̲*). If he had already done so, this promise is redundant. On the other hand, if the promise were made before the events, then it could well explain the quotation of such a promise in Sennacherib's message in 19:10.[91]

There is no explanation for this misarrangement, chronologically speaking, in Kings. But there is a very good explanation in Isaiah. There, the prophet, or his disciples, have arranged the materials now constituting Isaiah 36–39 with a very clear theological purpose. The ruling theme of everything in Isaiah 7–39 is the establishment of Yahweh's trustworthiness. Hezekiah's trust in Yahweh in the face of Sennacherib's threats, and Yahweh's deliverance from those threats, have clearly validated that trustworthiness. This act of trust might lead the reader to believe that Hezekiah is the child of Isaiah 9, or the Messiah of Isaiah 11. But that is not the case. For that person, we must look elsewhere. Isaiah thirty-eight and thirty-nine make that point with devastating poignancy. Fifteen more years or not, Hezekiah is very mortal, as the oddly sober psalm of Hezekiah in Isaiah 38:9–19 makes clear.[92] Nor is he infallible, as his response to the Babylonian envoys demonstrates. Given an opportunity to give glory to Yahweh for his healing, he instead parades his wealth and armaments. In short, the arrangement of Isaiah 36–39 is intended to bring chapters seven through thirty-five to a close and prepare the reader for the revelations that will follow in chapters forty to sixty-six.[93]

---

90. He regained control in Babylon in 703 BC, but was ousted by Sennacherib and fled, making it very unlikely that he would have been anywhere near Sennacherib in 701 BC.

91. Cogan and Tadmor, while they argue that in their present form the two accounts in chapter 20 are presented as taking place in connection with the events of 701 BC, nevertheless agree that the healing and the Babylonian embassy must have occurred before that time (260–63).

92. That psalm is omitted here in Kings because the editors of Kings have no use for it. All this testifies that just as the editors incorporated the narratives of Elijah and Elisha into their work, so they also incorporated the materials from Isaiah, adapting them to their own historical and didactic purposes.

93. While there are some textual differences between Isa 36–37 and 2 Kgs 18:17–19:37, most of them additions in Kings, there are many more differences between 2 Kgs 20:1-11 and Isa 38:1–22, the account of the illness. (Interestingly, there are only four minor differences between 2 Kgs 20:12–21 and Isa 39:1–8, the account of the envoys). The Kings account of the illness and recovery is considerably longer. Sweeney (421), arguing with the majority for the priority of Kings, says the shorter version in Isaiah is the result of the Isaianic editors removing materials from the

So, while the arrangement of these materials is easily explicable in Isaiah, it is not at all clear how it serves the particular purpose of Kings. What happened was that the Kings editors, having at hand in Isaiah a useful source for historical information about the good king Hezekiah, a man who fulfilled their vision of the ideal Deuteronomic king, availed themselves of that material, and in typical manner, took it over as it was without making any attempt to reorganize it. They only added some information here and there for the benefit of their readers.[94]

1 While "In those days" (בַּיָּמִים הָהֵם, *bayyāmîm hāhēm*) could link this narrative to the preceding one, that is not necessarily the case, as the phrase can be simply an indeterminate temporal marker for past time (cf. *IBHS* [§17.1]). In the three other cases where a king was deathly "ill" (חָלָה, *ḥālâ*) (Jeroboam I, 1 Kgs 14; Ahaziah, 2 Kgs 1; and Ben-hadad, 2 Kgs 8), the king requested some prophetic word. Here the word comes at Yahweh's initiative. Isaiah, son of Amoz, is not a functionary of Hezekiah, but a messenger of Yahweh. Given the imminence of his death, the king needs to give instructions to his household concerning his final wishes in order to secure an orderly transition. David had given such instructions (1 Chr 22), but there was evidently a long interval between that time and what finally appeared to be his last hours and Adonijah had tried to take advantage of the resulting uncertainty (1 Kgs 1:5–10).

2–3 Hezekiah, a relatively young man at the time, in his early thirties, was not willing to accept that this verdict was unalterable. Here is one of the remarkable characteristics of Hebrew prophecy. Whereas attempts to divine the future elsewhere in the ancient world operated on the premise that future events had been determined in advance, and it was the province of the prophet or diviner to discover what those were, Israelite prophecy saw the future as remarkably open, its happenings a factor of the relations between Yahweh and his people.[95] If that relationship was exclusive and if the people's ethical treatment of one another betrayed a deep congruency between their character and Yahweh's, in short, if the covenant was intact, then the future

---

Kings account to stress Hezekiah's piety. In fact, that is not at all clear, as will be shown at various points below. An equally strong case can be made that the Kings editors have added historical details to the Isaiah account for their own historical purposes. The entire account, from 2 Kgs 18:7 onward, looks like an insert into Kings from another source and where else but Isaiah. Note, in particular, the single occurrence in Kings of "the Holy One of Israel" in this section (2 Kings 19:22), a phrase that occurs in Isaiah no less than twenty-five times.

94. It seems probable that the Kings editor(s) did much the same thing with the prophetic narratives of Elijah and Elisha.

95. On these issues, see my "Is There Anything Unique in the Israelite Prophets?" *BibSac* 172 (2015): 67–84.

was bright. If for any reason this was not the case, the future took on a very different cast (cf. Ezek 18:5–17). Hezekiah clearly understood this, so he was unwilling to accept that Isaiah's, and indeed Yahweh's, announcement was necessarily unchangeable.

Commentators differ over what Hezekiah's actions tell us about his character. In 1 Kgs 21:4 Ahab's act of turning his face (to the wall) is a sign of petulance, and when that act is here accompanied by weeping out loud ("a great weeping," [בְּכִי גָדוֹל, *bᵊḵî gāḏôl*]), some believe that Hezekiah too is responding in an unworthy manner (Hobbs, 290). However, Hezekiah does what Ahab did not do: he prays. Much in the manner of the psalms of lament he poured out his case directly to Yahweh, and this is surely the mark of the man.[96] Just as he turned to God's man, Isaiah, in the first instance (19:2) and directly to God in the second (19:14–19), so again in a desperate hour Hezekiah's instinct is to turn to God. So, whatever Hezekiah's emotional state may have been, all his instincts were correct. He does not simply rail against an unfair fate (so Brueggemann, 521–22).

What Hezekiah says is profoundly important. He calls on Yahweh to "remember" (זְכָר־נָא, *zᵊḵor-nāʾ*). This God is not one for whom there is no past and no future. He has entered into human-historical experience and has revealed himself in that context. He is a God who has made promises, and he is faithful to keep his promises in the present and the future. It is frequently pointed out (e.g., Cohn, 141; Long, 487) that Hezekiah is speaking in Deuteronomic language. But it is more than that. It goes straight back to Genesis and the earliest expressions of what living in the covenant entails. Thirteen years after the birth of Ishmael with all its tragic implications, Yahweh came to Abram (Abraham) and renewed all the promises (Gen 17:1–8). In that context he gave the very significant instruction to Abraham (17:1) as to what Abraham's part in the arrangement was to be: "Walk (*hithpael*; הִתְהַלֵּךְ, *hiṯhallēḵ*) before me and be perfect ("whole", [תָמִים, *ṯāmîm*])." We have already noted the connections between Hezekiah and David, and here the connection goes farther back still. Hezekiah has fulfilled the most basic covenant requirement: walking (*hithpael*; הִתְהַלַּכְתִּי, *hiṯhallaḵtî*), conducting all one's life, in exclusive commitment ("with a perfect ['whole'; שָׁלֵם, *šālēm*] heart") to Yahweh. This was the character of David (1 Kgs 15:3), replicated by Asa (1 Kgs 15:14), but it did not begin with David. David was only walking in the footsteps of the father of the faithful, Abraham. He had an exclusive commitment to Yahweh, and his behavior was what the Creator of the universe has decreed is good. In short, Hezekiah believed he

96. The typical features of the lament are: direct address, complaint, petition, and vow of praise. The first two are explicit here, while the petition for recovery is certainly implicit, and one wonders if the assurance that he will go up to the temple implies the presence of the vow.

had fulfilled the requirements to be entitled to the blessings of the covenant: long life (Ps 91:16) and children (Ps 37:26–28).[97]

4–6 Clearly, Yahweh agreed with Hezekiah's claims, for he responded immediately, while Isaiah was still in the "middle court"[98] between the palace and the temple. He also responded generously: not only did he heal Hezekiah, but he guaranteed him fifteen more years,[99] and promised to "deliver" (נצל, *nṣl*) the city from the king of Assyria. This latter was no small thing, given that Samaria had fallen only a few years previously and the Assyrian emperor, Sargon, seemed at the peak of his powers. How could little Judah hope to avoid Israel's fate? The answer was straightforward: Judah could survive if they, like their king, kept the covenant.

Cohn (142) points out the prominence of Yahweh's activity here: "I have heard (שָׁמַעְתִּי, *šāma ʿtî*) … and seen (רָאִיתִי, *rā ʾîṯî*); I have healed (רֹפֵא, *rōpē ʾ*);[100] [and] I will add (וְהֹסַפְתִּי, *wᵉhôsapṯî*); I will deliver (אַצִּילְךָ, *ʾaṣṣîlᵉḵā*); [and] I will defend (וְגַנּוֹתִי, *wᵉgannôṯii*)." The Yahweh whom Sennacherib would mock as helpless was far from such. He is sensitive to his creatures' concerns, he desires to act on their behalf, and nothing but their sin can prevent him from so acting.

The references to David here (vv. 5, 6) underline what was said above about Yahweh's faithfulness and his power. He is a God of the future, and his promises bear witness to that. He is not interested in the static present. He looks forward to a better day not only for his people, but for all the people of the world—David's dynasty is crucial to that better day. But he not only makes promises; he is faithful enough and powerful enough to keep them. Since Hezekiah is a true son of David, and Jerusalem is the locus of the Davidic promise, Yahweh will deliver.[101] When Jeroboam I's son was

---

97. If the dating proposed here is correct, Manasseh had not been born at this time.

98. K has הָעִיר, *hā ʿîr* "the city," but Q and all the versions have חָצֵר, "court," which entails only a two consonant difference. This reference is lacking in Isa 38:4. There is no explanation why Isaiah would have omitted it if Kings is the original. It does nothing to establish Hezekiah's piety as Sweeny (413) suggests such omissions would do. On the other hand, Kings could have added it for its historical interest.

99. In Isa 38:5, the promise of fifteen more years is given, but the verb "to heal" (רָפָא, *rāpā ʾ*) does not appear. It is of course assumed, but the Kings editors want to make it explicit. There is no reason to believe the Isaiah editors would have intentionally omitted it if the Kings version is original.

100. Modern versions tend to follow the ancient ones, with the exception of the Vulg. and translate this vb. with the future tense. The Heb. form suggests present or imminent action.

101. The phrase "leader of my people" (נְגִיד־עַמִּי, *nᵉgîḏ- ʿammî*) seems to be used to assert the continuity of Hezekiah with the beginnings of the monarchy. It is elsewhere used of Saul (1 Sam 9:16; 10:1); David (2 Sam 5:2; 6:21; 7:8); and Solomon (1 Kgs 1:35).

sick unto death, the prophetic word was that he would die and so would his dynasty because he did not follow David (1 Kgs 14:7–10). Hezekiah, on the other hand, did follow David and so the word to him is one of life and hope.

As noted above, the promise that Hezekiah will shortly ("three days" is probably not to be taken literally since "the third day" refers to the near future, see Luke 13:32) go up to the temple may indicate that there was an implied vow of praise in Hezekiah's prayer. Alternatively, it may refer to ritual cleansing after his being healed from what was apparently a deadly skin disease (see Num 19:12).

7–11 The verses pose a conundrum for many commentators (e.g., Cohn, 143; Gray, 699–700) because they seem to contain logical problems. Hezekiah is healed, but now after the fact, we are told that a device was employed to bring about his healing. Then we find Hezekiah asking for a sign that he will shortly go to the temple (i.e., will be healed). I suggest that the difficulty is the result of the editors' attempt to correct what they saw as a problem in their Isaiah source. In the account as it stands in Isaiah 38:1–8 there is no mention of either the cake of figs, or of Hezekiah's asking for a sign. These elements only appear in two separate statements at the very end of the chapter in vv. 21 and 22, even after Hezekiah's psalm. Most commentators (e. g. Cogan and Tadmor, 263; Fritz, 382; Gray, 699) have taken this as evidence that the Kings account is original and that a later editor of Isaiah, having found that the first copyist left out these details, tacked them on the end rather than disturb the Isaiah account as he then found it. While that is possible, the logical problems in the Kings account, as mentioned above, suggest another alternative. Perhaps the Kings editors, using the Isaiah account, felt the need to bring those details up from the appendix, as it were, and try to get them into the flow of the narrative. Unfortunately, they were unable to weave them in very well, given the contours of the narrative as they received it from Isaiah. This scenario has as much to commend it as the priority of the Kings account does.[102]

7 The idea that Isaiah would utilize "a cake of figs" (דְּבֶלֶת תְּאֵנִים, *dᵊḇeleṯ tᵊʾēnîm*) as a device to promote healing causes some commentators (e.g., Gray, 699) consternation, with them saying that this is more like Elijah or Elisha than the austere declarer of oracles that we know Isaiah to be. In fact, this glimpse into Isaiah's life should not be surprising at all. The consternation is, in fact, the result of our drawing an artificial line between the so-called writing prophets and the non-writing prophets. Elijah and Elisha could have declared beautiful theologically profound oracles as well as Isaiah could have,

102. This does not explain the appearance of the two verses at the end of Isaiah 38. Perhaps we need to think of an original in which the details were well integrated, then of the Isaiah version, where for brevity and clarity they were left out, only to be inserted at the end by a later hand, and then the Kings version.

and Isaiah could work with the folk medicine of the day just as well as either of his non-writing predecessors. Notice that we are told that Isaiah walked "naked and barefoot for three years" (Isa 20:3). That is hardly the austere declarer of oracles. The biblical depictions of Jeremiah and Ezekiel give a more complete picture of the life and activity of a biblical prophet.

As with many Hebrew terms, "boil" (שְׁחִין, *šᵉḥîn*) seems to cover a wide variety of skin eruptions, from the plague in Egypt (Exod 9:9–11) to the skin diseases of Leviticus (13:18–20) to the "diseases of Egypt" (Deut 28:35) to the affliction of Job (2:7).[103] In any case, healing, whether through some medicine, or by direct divine intervention, is the work of God.

8 Long (488) suggests that there is an intentional contrast between Hezekiah's requesting a "sign" (אוֹת, *ʾôṯ*) and Ahaz's rejection of an offered sign (Isa 7:12). However, that seems to ask too much. In fact, the request for a sign could be seen as a certain lack of faith on the part of Hezekiah, as it seems to have been in the case of Gideon (Judg 6:36–40). Hezekiah is nowhere, either in Kings or Isaiah, presented as infallible.

9–11 This account of the conversation between Isaiah and Hezekiah does not appear in Isaiah 38:7–8. In the book bearing his name, Isaiah simply announces that Yahweh's sign will be to make the shadow go backward down " the steps" (הַמַּעֲלוֹת, *hammaʿălôṯ*). The editor(s) of Kings, as above, have added explanatory material in the interest of historical completeness. There has been some difference among scholars over whether the steps referred to were part of a kind of sun dial or were just a staircase to an upper chamber of the palace on which the sun cast a "shadow" (צֵל, *ṣēl*).[104] The discussion is further complicated by the reference to "the steps of Ahaz" (מַעֲלוֹת אָחָז, *maʿălôṯ ʾāḥāz*) in v. 11. Some have suggested that Ahaz had built some sort of a structure for the worship of the Sun (see his projects mentioned in 2 Kgs 16:10–18). But it is nowhere said that he actually did such a thing. Most recent opinion seems to be tending toward some sort of a construction for measuring time.[105]

Hezekiah's comment about it being easier for the shadow to go up the steps than come down has suggested to many that he is also thinking that it is easier for time to pass than it is for time to go backward. Many years

---

103. See Margaret Barker, "Hezekiah's Boil," *JSOT* 26 (2001): 31–42 for the suggestion that this was a manifestation of bubonic plague, a disease that also killed the Assyrian army.

104. 1QIsa has עֲלִיַּת, *ʿăliyyaṯ* "upper chamber" (of Ahaz) instead of "steps" in Isa 38:8 (as does Gk. at that point). Here Gk. uses steps and omits any reference to Ahaz.

105. See Jaap van Dorp, "The Prayer of Isaiah and the Sundial of Ahaz (2 Kgs 20:11)," in *Psalms and Prayers: Papers Read to the Joint Meeting of the Society of Old Testament Study and Het Oudtestamentische Werkgezelschap in Nederland en België*, ed. Bob Becking and Eric Peels (Leiden: Brill, 2007), 253–65. Cf. Vulg. *horologio Achaz.*

ago, G. A. Smith, commenting on Isaiah, pictured an ill Hezekiah watching the sun's shadow climbing inexorably up the steps and thinking of his own impending death, and then hearing the prophet promising fifteen more years. Could time indeed be turned back?[106] But for the Author of time, that is not a problem. Again, we see a picture of the God of the impossible at work.

Speculation about what actually happened to make the shadow go backwards is fruitless. We need not doubt that it did so, but whether it was the result of some astronomical anomaly or a refraction of the light or what is beside the point. The point of a miracle is never "how," but always "why": Why at that precise moment, and in response to that particular prayer? The God of the universe has no difficulty whatsoever with "how."

Biblical Theology Comments

The abrupt change in Yahweh's declarations may be troubling to some. First, he says something will happen, and then he turns right around and says it won't happen. We cannot help but remember such a statement as "He is not a mortal that he should change his mind" (1 Sam 15:29). But that seems to be the very thing he has done here and elsewhere (see 1 Sam 15:11, 35). It is exactly what Jonah was afraid would happen when he was sent to Nineveh (Jonah 4:2). Is Yahweh fickle? No, he is not. The point of the Samuel passage is that he will not change his mind without good cause. The implication in that passage is that Saul is not in a position to give such good cause. By this point in his life, any genuine repentance, any real change in his attitudes and behavior, is not really possible. If there was good cause, the evidence is that Yahweh would have gladly changed the doom that was pronounced on Saul and his house. After all, he forgave Nineveh!

But this situation is not exactly the same. The pronouncement here is not in respect of any need for repentance, as was the case with Saul and Nineveh, and Hezekiah does not repent. So what explains the change in Yahweh's mind here? I suggest that there *was* no change of mind. Note that the initial announcement from Yahweh is not a divine decree, but simply a statement of fact. Yahweh does not say that Hezekiah *must* die, but simply, given the nature of Hezekiah's present illness, that he *will* die. Given that fact, Yahweh wants to be certain that Hezekiah does not leave the question of his succession in doubt. But there may be more than this going on; perhaps Yahweh wants to give Hezekiah an opportunity to exercise faith and trust. The blunt announcement could be met with despair and hopelessness, or perhaps with prayer and hope. If this second suggestion is the case, then Hezekiah once again passed the test, as he was later to pass the one posed by Sennacherib, with flying colors. In either case, Yahweh did not change his mind. Rather, he was moved to intervene in the natural course of events

106. G. A. Smith, *The Book of Isaiah,* 2 vols. rev. ed. (London: Hodder and Stoughton, 1927) 2:246.

by the claim that the kind of life Hezekiah had lived to this point, a life of covenant faithfulness, deserved more of the covenant blessings than it had yet received. Yahweh did not change his mind, but he did change the course of Hezekiah's life, not only giving him fifteen more years, but through him giving Judah 150 more years, outliving even Assyria itself.

Selected Bibliography

Fullerton, K. "The Original Text of 2 K. 7–11=Isa. 38:7, 8, 21f." *JBL* 44 (1925): 44–62.

Kasher, R. "The Sitz im Buch of the Story of Hezekiah's Illness and Cure (II Reg 20,1–11; Isa 38,1–22." *ZAW* 113 (2001): 41–55.

Williamson, H. G. M. "Hezekiah and the Temple. Pages 47–52 in *Texts, Temples, and Traditions: A Tribute to Menahem Haran.* Edited by Michael Fox. Winona Lake, IN: Eisenbrauns, 1996.

The Embassy from Babylon (20:12–21)

Translation

12 At that time Merodach-baladan, son of Baladan, king of Babylon sent letters and a gift to Hezekiah because he heard that he had been ill. **13** Hezekiah rejoiced[107] over them and showed them his entire treasure house: the silver, the gold, the spices, the fine oil, and the house of his armor,[108] and all that was to be found among his treasures. There was nothing that Hezekiah did not show them in his house and in all his dominion. **14** Isaiah the prophet came to King Hezekiah and said to him, "What did these men say and where did they come from to you?" Hezekiah said, "They came from a distant land, from Babylon." **15** He said, "What did they see in your house?" Hezekiah said, "It was everything in my house that they saw.[109] There was not a thing I did not show them among my treasures." **16** Isaiah said to Hezekiah, "Hear the word of Yahweh. **17** Look, the days are coming when everything in your house and what your fathers stored up until now will be taken up to Babylon. Not one thing will remain. **18** Some[110] of your sons who will come forth from you, whom you will engender, will be taken, and they will be eunuchs in the palace of the king of Babylon." **19** Hezekiah said to Isaiah, "The word of Yahweh which you have spoken is good." He said, "Will there not be peace and security in my days?"

107. Reading with Isa 39:2 (וַיִּשְׂמַח, *wayyiśmaḥ*) and all the versions.

108. כְּלִי, *kᵊlî* "utensils, instruments," but in the context here, surely weapons. See 2 Kgs 7:15 where the same word is used with probably the same sense.

109. The Heb. word order lays emphasis on the predicate: כָּל־אֲשֶׁר בְּבֵיתִי רָאוּ, *kol-ʾăšer bᵊbêṯiy rāʾû.*

110. Partitive use of the prep. מִן, *min.*

20 The rest of the matters relating to Hezekiah and all his might, how he made the pool and the conduit and brought water into the city, are they not written in the book of the chronicles of the kings of Judah? **21** Hezekiah slept with his fathers and Manasseh his son, succeeded him.

Textual Notes

12a. בְּרֹאדַךְ: Gk. and Syr. "Merodach"; Vulg. with MT. According to ancient sources, the letter/sound "M" is correct. Vulg. and MT are possibly the result of a confusion of labial consonants or duplication of the first consonant of the father's name.

13a. וַיִּשְׁמַע: Isa 39:2 has וַיִּשְׂמַח, "rejoiced." All the versions, including the Tg., read some form of "rejoiced" here. *CTAT* (416) considers MT somewhat more probable, but *BHS* does not. In view of the possibility that there was confusion with the שָׁמַע three words earlier, "rejoiced" is preferable.

13b. נְכֹתֹה: Gk. Transliterates; Vulg. "spices"; Syr. "treasures." Possibly a loan from Akk.: *bit nakkamti*, "house of treasure."

13c. שֶׁמֶן: GKC (§126*x*) explains the absence of an article, by understanding the phrase as a construct.

14a. בָּאוּ: All the versions add "to me," as does Isa 39:3 (אֵלַי).

15a. בְּאֹצְרֹתָי: Gk. inserts "but also what is"; Vulg. and Syr. with MT.

17a–a. לֹא־יִוָּתֵר דָּבָר אָמַר יְהוָה: Gk. "not one word which the Lord has said will fall"; Vulg. and Syr. with MT, although Syr. adds "for you" after "remain."

18a. יִקָּח: K "He will take away" foll. by Gk; Q "they will take away" foll by Syr or "they will be taken way" (*pual*) foll. by Vulg. and Eng. translations.

19a–a. הֲלוֹא אִם־שָׁלוֹם וֶאֱמֶת יִהְיֶה בְיָמָי: Gk. "Let there be peace in my days"; Syr. "But would that there be peace and truth in my days"; Vulg. with MT.

Commentary

12 The phrase "at that time" (בַּיָּמִים הָהֵם, *bayyāmîm hāhēm*) signals that this account follows directly on the previous one, as does the statement that "he heard that Hezekiah had been ill" (שָׁמַע כִּי חָלָה חִזְקִיָּהוּ, *šāmaʿ kî ḥālâ ḥizqiyyāhû*). This means that the time frame of the two events is the same. As Cogan and Tadmor (261, so also Gray, 701) point out, it does not seem likely that Merodach-baladan would have had much interest in faraway Judah during the nine months or so in 704–3 BC when he was trying to survive a siege from Assyria.[111] It is much more likely that this event would

111. At the present time, no "Baladan" is known. Wiseman suggests that it is a form of the common Babylonian name "Bel-iddin" (288)."

have occurred sometime during the period when he was undisputed king of Babylon (722–709 BC).[112] Few commentators are willing to take the text at face value, that it was the illness and recovery that provoked the visit. Rather, they supply a reason that the text does not give: the Babylonian ruler was seeking some sort of alliance (e.g., Hobbs, 294; Sweeney, 423). On the surface, this is hardly likely. What kind of support could tiny Judah supply to Babylon, arguably one of the richest, most powerful cities of the world? This is a part of the irony of Hezekiah's displaying his wealth and armaments to Merodach's emissaries (v. 13). What Hezekiah perhaps did have, in view of his remarkable recovery, was some access to divine power. That was something the Babylonian monarch could definitely use. Wealth and armaments he had plenty of. But one can never have enough of divine miracle-working power. Did Hezekiah know something about such power that he would be willing to share? That was the reason for the embassy.

13 Those who are argue (e.g., Hobbs, 294) that both events of this chapter occurred following the attack of Sennacherib are forced to argue that Hezekiah was able to amass wealth and armaments quickly after Sennacherib's departure, since he had so much to display to the Babylonians. That seems very unlikely given the devastation that Sennacherib would have visited on the land. It is better to understand that these events took place prior to Sennacherib's arrival, and prior to the ruinous tribute that Hezekiah paid him.

In Isaiah 39:2 the phrase describing Hezekiah's response to the Babylonians' arrival is "and "he rejoiced over them" (וַיִּשְׂמַח עֲלֵיהֶם, *wayyiśmaḥ ʿălêhem*). Here in Kings it is "he listened over them" (וַיִּשְׁמַע עֲלֵיהֶם, *wayyišmaʿ ʿălêhem*). The versions here all contain some form of "rejoiced." Almost certainly the MT is an error, perhaps caused by the following *ʿayin* in עֲלֵיהֶם. Hezekiah was delighted that mighty Babylon would pay attention to him.[113] His error was to believe they were coming to see him rather than to discover the cause of his recovery. Whatever polishes our self-esteem is dangerous to us.

112. Since Cogan and Tadmor believe that the illness and recovery occurred in connection with Sennacherib's attack in 701 BC they are forced to create a fairly elaborate theory (261–63) to explain why a later editor has put the two accounts together. It is much better, as argued above, to believe that the two events did occur together, about 711 BC, and that it was Isaiah who reversed the chronology of the siege and the illness/visit for his theological purposes, and that the Kings editors utilized the Isaiah original as they found it.

113. For the opposite point of view, see Christopher Begg, "The Reading at 2 Kings 20:13," *VT* 36 (1986): 339–41.

Hobbs notes the prevalence of the personal pronoun in this verse: "his entire treasure house" (כָּל־בֵּית נְכֹתֹה, *k̲ol-bêt̲ nᵊk̲ōt̲ō*),[114] "the house of his armor" (בֵּית כֵּלָיו, *bêt̲ kēlāyw*),[115] "his treasures" (אוֹצְרֹתָיו, *ʾôṣᵊrōt̲āyw*), "his house" (בְּבֵיתוֹ, *bᵊb̲êt̲ô*), "his dominion" (מֶמְשַׁלְתּוֹ, *memšaltô*). One cannot avoid comparison with Solomon in the visit of the queen of Sheba (1 Kgs 10), a passage that ends in the devastating judgments of 10:23–11:11, with their clear hearkening back to Deuteronomy 17:16–17, with their prohibition of the accumulation of wealth and armaments. See below in the "Biblical Theology Comments" for a discussion of the Bible's ambivalence concerning wealth.

Here we see again the way in which Isaiah, followed by Kings, is demonstrating that for all of Hezekiah's goodness and faithfulness, for all that he had demonstrated how trustworthy Yahweh is and will be, Hezekiah is not infallible. He is not the promised Messiah. If there is ultimate hope for the people of God, they must look somewhere far beyond the all-too-human Hezekiah. Attempts to analyze the biblical text on the basis of an imposed unity (such and such a text would have only presented Hezekiah as a paragon; therefore, if we find critical comments about him, that must be another author/editor's work) display far too low an estimate of these persons' subtlety and insight.

One must look to the Isaianic setting of this material to fully understand the great tragedy taking place here. Isaiah had said, in concert with Micah, that all the nations would come to Jerusalem to learn to walk in the ways of Yahweh (Isa 2:2–4; Micah 4:1–3). Now that very thing had happened: the nations had heard of Yahweh's mighty acts and come to learn more of him. But instead of declaring the glory of Yahweh, Hezekiah had sought to display his own glory. As noted above, such actions were pitiable. What wealth or armaments could the Judean king have possessed that would have impressed the Babylonians in the slightest degree? It is as though a group of New Yorkers visit a small town in Kansas, and the mayor tries to impress them with all the amenities of his town. Hezekiah showed these emissaries what could not possibly impress them and failed to show them the one asset he had that they did not have.[116]

14–15 "Isaiah the prophet" poses some questions that on the surface seem disarmingly simple. We have the feeling that he already knows the answers. He simply asks where these men came from and what was said and what Hezekiah has shown them. However, Hezekiah could not help but know of Isaiah's extreme suspicion of any kind of alliance with foreign powers (Isa 30:1–7; 31:1–3). Isaiah was by no means alone in this suspicion. It can

---

114. It seems likely that this term, occurring only here, is loaned from Akk. *bit nakkamti*, "house of treasure." There is no good explanation why it is employed here unless it was a special type of structure, copied from similar Mesopotamian structures.

115. 1 Kgs 10:16–17 suggests the armory may have been in the "Forest of Lebanon" in the palace.

116. Note that there is no mention of the Temple of Yahweh.

be found in many of the prophets, who often compared it to adultery and prostitution (Jer 22:20–22; Ezek 16:33–37; Hosea 8:9). Reliance on other nations could all too often be a way of avoiding reliance on Yahweh.

Perhaps it was because Hezekiah suspected that Isaiah's questions were not as mild as they seemed that he answered as he did. First, he seems to suggest that the emissaries were really no problem since they came from so far away, "from a distant land, from Babylon" (מֵאֶרֶץ רְחוֹקָה בָּאוּ מִבָּבֶל, *mēʾereṣ rᵉḥôqâ bāʾû mibbābel*). But then he seems to decide to take a hard stand. If Isaiah is slightly concerned, well, Hezekiah will give the prophet cause to be highly concerned: "There was not a thing I did not show them among my treasures" (לֹא־הָיָה דָבָר אֲשֶׁר לֹא־הִרְאִיתִם בְּאֹצְרֹתָי, *lōʾ-hāyâ dābār ʾăšer lōʾ-hirʾîtim bᵉʾōṣᵉrōtāy*). Here we note the first-person pronouns.

16–18 Here is the judgment speech that Hezekiah may have suspected was coming. But it is hard to believe that the king could have imagined what the content of the judgment would be. Everything, everything, that the king had shown the Babylonians would one day be theirs. Echoing Hezekiah's own words, "not one thing will remain" (לֹא־יִוָּתֵר דָּבָר, *lōʾ-yiwwātēr dābār*). But the judgment will not stop there. A more devastating word is coming: Hezekiah's descendants, the scions of the Davidic dynasty, the dynasty upon which Hezekiah had brought such glory, and whose endurance Hezekiah's faithfulness had done so much to ensure, would be "eunuchs[117] in the palace of the king of Babylon" (סָרִיסִים בְּהֵיכַל מֶלֶךְ בָּבֶל, *sārîsîm bᵉhêkal melek bābel*).

This all seems too much. Simply for showing off his wealth to the Babylonians, the Babylonians would possess it all, and the dynasty itself would come to an apparent end? And why Babylon? Assyria was the problem; Babylon was simply a thorn in the Assyrians' side, which the Assyrians periodically, and brutally, subdued. Many commentators (e.g., Brueggemann, 526; Fritz, 385; Montgomery and Gehman, 510) argue that Isaiah himself never said such things, that they have been put into Isaiah's mouth by later editors who know "how things turned out." This is of course to deny the whole genius of biblical prophecy. For further comments see below under "Biblical Theology Comments." Here, two points should be made. First, note that there is no causal statement in what Isaiah says. It is not directly because of what Hezekiah has done that this judgment will come. Second, for all that Hezekiah had done to demonstrate the validity of the Davidic dynasty, the hope for the world did not lay in even the best of David's sons, humanly speaking.

117. While there is reasonably good evidence to say that the term "eunuch" can often connote simply a royal official without his necessarily being physically mutilated, it is also true that the basic sense of the term does involve such mutilation. It is hard to avoid the conclusion that in this context Isaiah used the term with its basic sense. Given the emphasis upon Hezekiah's having engendered these men, their inability to do so in turn seems apparent.

Yet, once more, it is necessary to see all of this in the larger Isaianic context. Without that context Isaiah's words make little sense. Hezekiah was not the cause of the Babylonian exile, but as the account is structured in Isaiah, he was an example of what it would be in Judah that would bring about that exile. Hezekiah had demonstrated that if Yahweh is trusted, he *will* fulfill all his promises (Isa 36–37; 2 Kgs 18–19). The pattern of: challenge—prayer—deliverance was established. The pattern was further demonstrated in the case of Hezekiah's illness: challenge—prayer—deliverance (Isa 38:1–8; 2 Kgs 20:1–11).[118] But in the third case what happened? The challenge was not to be swept away by the amazing honor of having Babylonian emissaries come all this way to meet me, Hezekiah! Probably Hezekiah did not even recognize the challenge. He certainly did not turn to Yahweh in prayer to see how he should meet it. The end result was far from deliverance.

What was Isaiah establishing? He was establishing that trust is not a "one-off" kind of thing. It is a settled way of life in which intimacy with Yahweh, and a concern that his glory may indeed fill the earth. Because that would not be the settled response of Judah over the next 150 years, the day would come when, having been delivered from Assyria, they would not be delivered from Babylon. What Isaiah predicted was not a judgment upon Hezekiah, per se, but a judgment upon the way of life of which Hezekiah was an example. In the context of the book of Isaiah all this raises the question: now that we know Yahweh can be trusted, what will motivate us to make trust a way of life and not just an emergency measure? It will not be Hezekiah, mortal and fallible as he is. What will it be? The answer appears in Isaiah chapters forty to fifty-five. Kings does not have that theological agenda, but apart from dropping the lament over mortality (Isa 38:9–20), the editor(s) see no compelling reason to tamper with the order Isaiah has presented them with in chapters thirty-six through thirty-nine of his book.

19 It is hard to see this verse as doing anything other than establishing that Hezekiah is not the Messiah.[119] Although his first words may simply indicate a quiet acceptance of God's will (cf. Eli, 1 Sam 3:18), it is difficult to put a positive interpretation upon his second statement, especially if we take Isaiah's

---

118. The relatively shorter version in Isaiah is because Isaiah is simply using it to state the second example of the pattern, and then to lead into the psalm in which Hezekiah laments his mortality. The editor(s) of kings, who did not have that concern, left out the psalm and expanded the account somewhat to fit with their historical (as opposed to theological) concerns.

119. Here is another argument for the priority of Isaiah. The concern about the M(m)essiah is not an issue in Kings, whereas it is a major issue in Isaiah. The editor(s) of Kings has simply taken over the Isaiah material.

reading as original as Cogan and Tadmor do (260).[120] The Isaiah 39:8 reading is "because there will be peace…" (כִּי יִהְיֶה שָׁלוֹם, *kî yihye šālôm*). This is instead of "Will there not be peace… ." In other words, Isaiah has him saying, "God's will is good because everything will be all right for me." But Kings is not far different. Here we understand, "God's will is good. Won't everything be fine for me?" (paraphrase of הֲלוֹא אִם־שָׁלוֹם, *hălô ʾim-šālôm*). In either case, the lack of sensitivity to what the prophet's words mean for his people and his dynasty is rather shocking. This man has indeed demonstrated that he is a true son of David, a man of faith and good works, exclusively devoted to Yahweh, but the point is still clear: he is not the Messiah, passionately concerned for his people's peace and security at whatever cost to himself.

20–21 Here the editor(s) of Kings revert to their standard closing regnal formula. They have finished with the excerpts from other sources that they have used to fill out their account of Hezekiah. The first of those excerpts (2 Kgs 18:13–16) came from two different official sources, and the second (2 Kgs 18:17–20:19) came from the book of Isaiah. The formula fits the standard pattern, pointing the reader to the royal chronicles for any further information he or she may desire, but including one or two key facts that can be investigated further in those chronicles.[121] Here the editor(s) wishes to call attention to the waterworks for which Hezekiah has become famous, the tunnel of Siloam running from the spring of Gihon on the east side of the old city under that city to a pool at the south end. While there is ongoing scholarly discussion as to exactly what was accomplished during Hezekiah's reign, it is difficult to gainsay the inscription in the tunnel itself which seems to confirm the work as his.[122]

Biblical Theology Comments

On the Bible's ambivalence about wealth see the "Biblical Theology Comments" above on 1 Kings 10:14–29.

It has become something of a mantra over the last two centuries to say that biblical prophecy is not so much about foretelling as it is about forthtelling. The saying could not have attained so much currency unless it had a grain of truth in it. If we think of prophecy as nothing else but prediction and then approach virtually all of the writing prophets, we will be surprised. The prophets are moral preachers who speak as Yahweh's ambassadors to call the

120. Sweeney's statement that Isaiah has changed the Kings original to make it appear that peace and security are certain for Hezekiah misses the point of the statement (423). It does not make Hezekiah look better, but worse.

121. Cf. 1 Kgs 15:23–24; 22:39–40; 2 Kgs 12:20–21; 14:15.

122. For a recent thorough treatment, see Mary Katherine Hom, "Where Art Thou, O Hezekiah's Tunnel?: A Biblical Scholar Considers the Archaeological and Biblical Evidence Concerning the Waterworks in 2 Chronicles 32:3–4 and 2 Kings 20:20," *JBL* 135 (2016): 493–503.

people of Israel and Judah back to their covenant with Yahweh. That much is true, but it also true that this call is inseparable from statements about the future implications of the responses the people make to the call. To suggest that the predictive element can be stripped from the prophets, or that all the supposed predictions be explained by having future editors after the event put the prediction in the mouth of the earlier prophets is to do irreparable harm to the prophetic message.

This is nowhere clearer than in Isaiah 41–46. There again and again Yahweh asserts that his having predicted both the exile and the deliverance from exile, including the naming of the deliver, was the inescapable proof that he alone is God. Long ago he had specifically predicted what was taking place at that time, including the naming of the deliverer Cyrus. The Babylonian so-called gods were simply the forces of this world with masks on. They could not explain where they had come from nor why they existed. Furthermore, they could not explain why the world existed nor what its destiny was. But the transcendent Yahweh, sitting "above the circle of the earth" (Isa 40:22) can do all these things. He can see the end from the beginning and can reveal it all to his prophets (44:24–28).

When biblical scholars, such as those cited above (vv. 16–18), say that predictive prophecy is an impossibility, they nullify this argument and make Yahweh indistinguishable from the gods. If he is who the Bible claims him to be then we must grant the possibility of predictive prophecy, something that Jesus Christ, as well as all the gospel writers, surely believed in quite firmly. Could Isaiah predict the Babylonian captivity with certainty 150 years in advance? Humanly speaking? Of course not. But what if we grant the biblical claim that God, the sole, transcendent, creator God, was speaking to and through the prophet? Must we not grant the possibility that God could convey such information? If we will not grant it, what are we saying about the Bible's claims to reveal God? It is not possible to have it two ways at once. Either these men and women could foretell the future, or they were liars. They were not great moral teachers, they were deluded, people whose prognostications were doctored later to make them appear validated when in fact they were not. We cannot have it otherwise.

Selected Bibliography

Ackroyd, P. R. "Interpretation of the Babylonian Exile: A Study of 2 Kings 20, Isaiah 38–39." *SJT* 27 (1974): 329–52.

Begg, C. "2 Kings 20:12–19 as an Element of the Deuteronomistic History." *CBQ* 48 (1986): 27–38.

Ridge, G. "The Curious Diplomacy of a Babylonian King: 2 Kings 20:12–19." *Conversations With the Biblical World* 36 (2016): 46–58.

The Reign of Manasseh (21:1–18)

Introduction

The tragedy of Manasseh's reign can hardly be overstated. Hezekiah had set Judah on a trajectory of faithfulness. Had the nation followed that trajectory, who can imagine the positive results for the nation's future? But it was not to be. Manasseh's extreme youth at his accession raises the possibility that other sons of Hezekiah were passed over and that he was placed on the throne by a clique that was opposed to what Hezekiah stood for. So perhaps they put the child on the throne with the expectation that they could manipulate the boy in favor of a more pagan direction. If that is the case, it was certainly successful.

Outline

III. JUDAH ALONE 18:1–25:30
B. The reign of Manasseh 21:1–18

TRANSLATION

21:1 When Manasseh began to reign, he was twelve years old. He reigned
fifty-five years in Jerusalem. His mother's name was Hephzibah. **2** He did
evil in Yahweh's sight, like the abominations of the nations that Yahweh
had driven out before the descendants of Israel. **3** He rebuilt the high places
which Hezekiah his father destroyed. He erected altars to Baal and made an
Asherah like Ahab, king of Israel, and he worshipped all the host of heaven
and served them. **4** He built altars in the house of Yahweh where Yahweh
had said, "In Jerusalem I will place my name." **5** He built altars for all the
host of heaven in the two courts of the house of Yahweh. **6** He made his
son pass through the fire and used divination and omens and dealt with
mediums and necromancers; he multiplied the doing of evil in Yahweh's
sight so as to provoke him.[1] **7** He put a carved image of Asherah which he

1. Supplying "him" after לְהַכְעִיס, *lᵉhak̲ʿîs*. Heb. *waw* possibly lost through haplography with the *waw* beginning the next word.

made in the house of which Yahweh had said to David and his son Solomon,
"In this house and in Jerusalem which I have chosen out of all the tribes of
Israel I will place my name forever. **8** And I will not make Israel's foot to stray
from the soil I have given to the fathers; that is, if they are careful to do all
that I command them and all the *Torah* that Moses my servant commanded
them. **9** But they did not listen and Manasseh led them astray to do more
evil than the nations which Yahweh destroyed before the descendants of
Israel." **10** Yahweh spoke by the hand of the servants the prophets, saying,
11 "Because Manasseh, king of Judah, did these abominations (he has done
more evil than all the Amorites that were before him), and has made even
Judah sin with his filthy idols, **12** therefore, thus says Yahweh, the God of
Israel, 'Look, I am bringing calamity on Jerusalem and Judah which will
make both the ears of all who hear ring. **13** I will stretch over Judah the line of
Samaria and the plumb-bob of the house of Ahab. I will wipe Jerusalem just as
a person might wipe a dish, wiping it and turning it on its face.[2] **14** I will forsake
the remnant of my special possession and I will give them into the hand of their
enemies, **15** because they have done evil in my sight, and have been provoking
me from the day their fathers came out of Egypt until today. **16** Moreover,
Manasseh has poured out a great deal of innocent blood until Jerusalem is
filled from one end to the other, apart from his sin[3] that he made Judah sin,
to do evil in the sight of Yahweh.' " **17** The rest of the matters pertaining to
Manasseh and all that he did and his sin that he sinned, are they not written
in the chronicles of the kings of Judah? **18** Manasseh slept with his fathers,
and was buried in the garden of his house, in the garden of Uzzah, and his
son Amon succeeded him.

Textual Notes

2a. כְּתוֹעֲבֹת: Vulg. "idols"; Gk. and Syr. with MT.

3a. מִזְבְּחֹת: Gk. sing. (so also in vv. 4, 5). Vulg. and Syr. pl. with MT.

3b. אֲשֵׁרָה: Gk. "sacred groves"; Vulg. "groves"; Syr. "idols."

6a. אֶת־בְּנוֹ: Gk. "sons"; Vulg. And Syr. With MT.

6b–b. הִרְבָּה לַעֲשׂוֹת הָרַע: Vulg. "he did evil"; Gk. and Syr. with MT.

7a. הָאֲשֵׁרָה: Gk. "sacred grove"; Vulg. "grove"; Syr. "false god."

7b–b. אֲשֶׁר עָשָׂה: Gk. omits; Vulg. and Syr. with MT.

8a. וּלְכָל: Gk. "every commandment"; Vulg. and Syr. "all the laws."

---

2. Reading מָחָה, *māḥâ* and הָפַךְ, *hāpak̲* as infs. abs.
3. All the vss. read this (מֵחַטָּאתוֹ, *mēḥaṭṭāʾt̲ô*) as pl. Perhaps it is a collective.

11a–a. הַתֹּעֵבוֹת הָאֵלֶּה הֵרַע: Gk. "these abominations, evil things"; Vulg. and Syr. with MT.

11b. בְּגִלּוּלָיו: Vulg. "with their uncleannesses"; Gk. "with their idols"; Syr. "with his idols."

12a. לָכֵן: Gk. "Not so"; Vulg. and Syr. "Therefore."

12b. K שֹׁמְעָיו: Reading with Q שֹׁמְעָהּ (fem. suff. to agree with רַע).

12c. תְּצַלֶּנָה: For this formation see GKC)§67*g*(.

13a–a. וּמָחִיתִי אֶת־יְרוּשָׁלַםִ כַּאֲשֶׁר־יִמְחֶה אֶת־הַצַּלַּחַת מָחָה וְהָפַךְ עַל־פָּנֶיהָ: Gk. "I will wipe Jerusalem like an alabaster jar is wiped, when it is wiped and turned on its face"; Vulg. "I will destroy Jerusalem just as a person might destroy a used tablet and destroy, turn over, and drag a stylus across its face"; Syr. "I will smite Jerusalem and destroy it because of all the abominations that Manasseh has committed in Judah." MT best explains the others. GKC (§113*hn.*2) suggests the final two vbs. should be understood as infs. abs., as virtually all modern Eng. versions do, (on the vocalization, see §29*u*).

14a–a. וְהָיוּ לְבַז: Vulg. "they will become a waste"; Gk. and Syr. "they will become prey."

16a. מֵחַטָּאתוֹ: All the versions "sins."

Commentary

Coming as it does between the accounts of Hezekiah and Josiah, this chapter with its extensive treatment of the sins of Manasseh (1–18) and his son Amon (19–26) strikes a distinctly discordant note. In spite of the good work of both those kings, was Judah's fate sealed by this one man (with the brief concurrence of his son)?[4] A careful reading of the description of Manasseh's actions here will reveal that in fact, it is Hezekiah's and Josiah's reforms that were the anomalies, whereas what Manasseh did reflected the settled pattern of the Israelite people for hundreds of years.[5] Those two periods of revival and reform meant that there were faithful people who could carry the faith

4. Sweeney highlights the differences between this account and that in 2 Chr 33:1–20, arguing that they are two different attempts to make sense of the destruction of Judah and Jerusalem. I suggest that the difference is in the audiences to which the two accounts are addressed. Kings is addressed to the exiles, explaining why the promises to Israel were not kept, whereas Chronicles is addressed to those who have returned from exile, explaining that if repentance is done, there is hope for anyone. Neither account is more "historical" than the other, but each has utilized historical material to serve its point.

5. Ezekiel (23:3, 19–21) traces their idolatry all the way back to Egypt.

into the exile and beyond, but in neither case was there true national revival. Manasseh's actions were by no means his own. He was able to carry them out only because the bulk of his people were quite comfortable with them.

Verses 1–18 are carefully structured. Between the opening and concluding regnal formulas (v. 1 and vv. 17–18) we have charges (vv. 2–9), an indictment (vv. 10–11), a sentence (vv. 12–15), and a further charge (v. 16). The charges in vv. 2–9, nicely enclosed by the statement that the things done were those practiced by the inhabitants of the land, are cultic in nature, whereas the charge in v. 16 is social. Throughout, the point is made that although Manasseh was the leader in the sins committed, it was the people's actions, actions which reflected long years of misbehavior that precipitated Yahweh's judgment.

1 The statement that Manasseh ruled for fifty-five years causes difficulties if we believe with Thiele and others that Hezekiah was alive until 687 BC.[6] It is clear from comparison with Assyrian and Babylonian chronologies that Manasseh must have died in 642/1 BC and that means he must have begun his reign in 697/6 BC. That would then demand a ten-year coregency with Hezekiah. As noted above, such coregencies are a feature of Judean and Israelite history, so such a thing is certainly possible here, but it is unnecessary if we recognize that 697 was actually the year of Hezekiah's death, having begun his reign in 726 BC.[7]

Since "Manasseh was twelve years old" when he began to reign, Hezekiah must have been forty-two when Manasseh was born. This suggests that Manasseh was not the firstborn son. It is to be wondered if older sons were passed over in order to put this boy on the throne. Perhaps a pro-Assyrian faction in the government was responsible for the accession. If that were the case, and he were under the thumb of people who had no love for the anti-Assyrian Hezekiah, this might explain some of Manasseh's evident antipathy to his father's policies.

The name of Manasseh's mother, Hephzibah, (חֶפְצִי־בָהּ, *ḥep̄ṣî-ḇāh*) "my delight is in her" appears in Isaiah 62:4. Perhaps this was a favorite term of the prophet, one that came to be applied to women of his era.

Two factors relating to Manasseh's long reign deserve comment. The first has to do with the complete lack of any report here of his accomplishments or activities during such a long time. This underlines the point I have made repeatedly that the editor's purpose is not to write a history. Rather it is to use historical data to demonstrate that if the people of Israel had adhered to the Deuteronomic ideals, then the covenant promises would have been regularly and fully carried out. This is not to say that the editor had no concern for the way he used the data; Yahweh is true and is known through his interactions with humans in history, so one does not have the luxury of

6. Thiele, *Mysterious Numbers*, 132–40, 148–61.

7. See the "Commentary" above on 18:1. See also G. Galil, *Chronology*, 98–104.

rewriting history. But the purpose here is to draw theological inferences, not to produce a history.[8]

The second factor has to do with why, if Manasseh was so wicked according to covenant standards, he was allowed to live such a long life, since typically a long life is seen as a reward for faithfulness (e.g., Ps 91:14–16). More specifically, Deuteronomy 17:20 promises a long reign to faithful kings. First, this is evidence for the accuracy with which historical data was employed. Just because the data did not fit a stereotype did not give the editor(s) *carte blanche* to make the data say what he wanted it to say. But second, perhaps it had to do with Manasseh's repentance, as reported in 2 Chronicles. Just as Ahab was spared destruction because of his repentance (1 Kgs 21:29), with the judgment being visited on his son, the same might have been true of Manasseh, although the kinds of sources being used here might not have made the observation about the effect of the repentance that the Elijah/Elisha source did.

2 This verse introduces the charges against Manasseh and Judah/Jerusalem. It makes two significant statements. The first is that "he did evil in Yahweh's sight" (וַיַּעַשׂ הָרַע בְּעֵינֵי יהוה, *wayyaʿaś hāraʿ bᵉʿênê yhwh*), an assertion that is common enough in regards to the kings of Israel, but only made of three earlier Judean kings: Solomon (1 Kgs 11:6), Jehoram, son-in-law of Ahab (2 Kgs 8:18), and Ahaz (2 Kgs 16:2 "he did not do what was right"). The connection with Ahaz, only two generations earlier, raises the ominous possibility that the behavior that had characterized the northern kings was now coming to be a feature in Judah as well. Indeed, that was to be the case, with Amon (21:20), Jehoahaz (23:32), Jehoiakim (23:37), Jehoiachin (24:9), and Zedekiah (24:19). What had been an aberration had become the norm. Judah's fate was not determined by one man's sin. Rather, this man's sin was to inaugurate the pattern that would determine Judah's fate.

The second significant statement that appears in v. 2 is the startling one that Manasseh jumped back across seven hundred years of Israel's experience with Yahweh in the promised land to "the abominations of the nations which Yahweh drove out" (תוֹעֲבֹת הַגּוֹיִם אֲשֶׁר הוֹרִישׁ יהוה, *tôʿăḇōṯ haggôyim ʾăšer hôrîš yhwh*). It is as though in one moment all that history has been wiped out. But in fact, the infection had been there all along. Given that Solomon had opened the door, the people under Rehoboam were acting in these ways (1 Kgs 14:24), and under Ahaz, there they were again (2 Kings 16:3). Deuteronomy had been very clear in calling for the destruction of these practices (12:31; 18:9). An "abomination" (תוֹעֵבָה, *tôʿēḇâ*) was something

8. 2 Chronicles tells us a bit more, and the Assyrian records tell us that he was a faithful vassal supplying troops (*ANET*, 294) and materials (*ANET*, 291) during the reigns of Esarhaddon and Ashurbanipal, as required to do so. Some commentators insist that he could not have been so bad as the editor paints him (e.g., Fritz, 389), but they do so without any supporting evidence.

contrary to God's creation order and plan. Thus, an idol was an abomination, but so also were all the practices associated with idolatry, up to and including child sacrifice. It was because the people had not fully obeyed Moses' (and Yahweh's) instructions to utterly destroy them that these practices were always lurking, ready to spring up again, like weeds in a garden.

It is important that this idea of "the abominations of the nations" forms an inclusio around the charges (vv. 2, 9). They frame the rest of the actions, putting them in their proper perspective, showing that indeed what Manasseh was promoting, and the people were willingly participating in, was not some recent innovation, a sudden departure from a long-held practice of exclusive commitment to Yahweh. Rather, they were one more manifestation of a persistent tendency to fall away from what they had once committed themselves to in blood. The statement in v. 15, that these things had been endemic among them since Egypt, while perhaps somewhat hyperbolic, still fits the overall point being made all too well. As stated above, Manasseh was not the anomaly; Hezekiah and Josiah were.

3–6 These verses list in devastating detail what Manasseh led his people into, in effect giving them permission to engage in everything that Hezekiah had tried to deprive them of. The opening statement about "the high places" (הַבָּמוֹת, *habbāmôṯ*) sets that tone. What Hezekiah had destroyed his son rebuilt.[9] It is likely that there were people who had disliked Hezekiah's attempt to centralize worship of Yahweh, who welcomed the reinauguration of the local shrines. Never mind all their pagan overtones. Instead of emulating his father Manasseh chose to emulate Ahab, worshipping Baal and Asherah and the various astral deities (cf. 1 Kgs 16:31–33).[10] All these deities with their powerful imagery and comforting illusions of control of natural forces would have been much more attractive than the austere, aniconic worship of Yahweh in his one central sanctuary in Jerusalem.

But it was not enough to repopulate the land with the ancient gods. Yahweh's temple in Jerusalem was not to escape (vv. 4–7). The very house of Yahweh himself would be polluted. This building was to have been the place where the transcendent character and nature of Yahweh, his "name" (שֵׁם, *šēm*) (vv. 4, 7), was to be displayed and illustrated.[11] It was the place Yahweh had particularly "chosen" (בָּחַר, *bāḥar*), the place he had appointed his covenant partner "David and his son Solomon" to build, there to memorialize "forever" (לְעוֹלָם, *lᵉʿôlām*) exclusive devotion to him (v. 7). But it was in that

9. וַיָּשָׁב וַיִּבֶן, *wayyāšoḇ wayyiḇen* ("returned and built") is a hendiadys expressing the single idea "rebuilt."

10. Since only one court is clearly identified for Solomon's temple (1 Kgs 7:9), the "two courts" of v. 5 has raised questions. Perhaps "the middle court" of 2 Kgs 20:4 is one of the two. It was apparently constructed to connect the palace and the temple. Note that Jer 36:10 speaks of an "upper courtyard" (Fritz, 390).

11. On the שֵׁם, *šēm* "name," see Deut 12:11–13; 2 Sam 7:13; 1 Kgs 8:16; 11:36; 14:21.

place that Manasseh put "altars for all the host of heaven" (מִזְבְּחוֹת לְכָל־צְבָא הַשָּׁמָיִם, *mizbᵉḥôṯ lᵉḵol-ṣᵉḇāʾ haššāmāyim*) (v. 5), and even "a carved image of Asherah" (פֶּסֶל הָאֲשֵׁרָה, *pesel hāʾăšērâ*) (v. 7), suggesting that Yahweh, having a consort, was one more of the sexualized forces of this world.[12]

6 Not only was Manasseh sponsoring idolatry of several sorts, he was also engaging in other "abominations" that Deuteronomy specifically forbade (Deut 18:9–14). These involved child sacrifice, sorcery, divination, spiritism, and necromancy. Although this passage does not directly reproduce the list as it appears in Deuteronomy, all the features are there. These are the typical practices of a culture that believes there is direct continuity between this world and the spirits that inhabit it. Those who believe that Yahweh is not this world and cannot be manipulated through it are forbidden to engage in any of these things. You cannot buy his favor by sacrificing your most precious possession, your children, to him.[13] You may not attempt to get him or anyone else to do your will through imitative magic. You may not attempt to divine the future through the observance of objects, whether lots or birds or stars or sheep livers.[14] You may not attempt to raise the dead in order to gain knowledge through them.

The language of provocation (see also v. 15) is significant. It is relational language. We do something to someone else and provoke a response. Yahweh's response is not mechanical or even legal. It is personal. When we

---

12. It has been suggested that whereas the usual representation of the fertility goddess was a pole or a grove of poplars (the versions regularly translate אֲשֵׁרָה, *ʾăšērâ* with "grove" or "groves"), the use of "image" (פֶּסֶל, *pesel*) says that an actual idol was used. This may be "the idol that provokes jealousy" referred to in Ezek 8:3, 5. In any case, to get some sense of the "abominations" being practiced in the temple, see Ezek 8:3–18. On Asherah, see Judith M. Hadley, "Yahweh and 'His Asherah': Archaeological and Textual Evidence for the Cult of the Goddess," in *Ein Gott allein? JHWH-Verehrung und biblischer Monotheismus im Kontext der israelitischen und altorientalischen Religionsgeschichte,* ed. Walter Dietrich, Martin A. Klopfenstein, OBO 139 (Göttingen: Vandenhoeck & Rupprecht, 1994), 235–68; Ziony Zevit, *The Religions of Ancient Israel: A Synthesis of Parallactic Approaches* (London: Continuum, 2001), 359–405.

13. Exactly what is meant by "passing [his son's] through the fire" (וְהֶעֱבִיר אֶת־בְּנוֹ בָּאֵשׁ, *wᵉheʿĕḇîr ʾeṯ-bᵉnô bāʾēš*) (see also 2 Kgs 16:3) is disputed. It has been recently argued that Israel did not practice child sacrifice and that this phrase involved burning the bodies of children who died. However, it is difficult to understand why a practice like that would be judged as harshly as this is. Cogan and Tadmor discuss it at length and conclude that probably child sacrifice is intended (266–67). For an unambiguous example, see 2 Kgs 3:27. See Zevit, *Religions,* 550–52.

14. There are two somewhat similar examples in early Israel: the ephod (Judg 8:27; 18:14) and the Urim and Thummim (1 Sam 14:41). The use of both seems to have been limited fairly early as having too many overtones of the occult.

choose to treat him as an object, and indeed one among many objects that we can manipulate at will for our own supposed benefit, he is "provoked to anger" (לְהַכְעִיס, *lᵉhaḵʿîs*). That was his settled response to the idolatrous Yahwism of the northern kingdom, but it had not been the case so much with Judah.[15] We can think of the rather plaintively hopeful words of Hosea 4:15, "Do not let Judah become guilty." Unfortunately, they were not to be fulfilled (see 2 Kgs 23:26).

7–8 In these verses the dependable and yet conditional nature of the blessings of God is made very clear. Yahweh will place his name on his house in Jerusalem forever. He will never again "cause Israel's feet to wander" (וְלֹא אֹסִיף לְהָנִיד רֶגֶל יִשְׂרָאֵל, *wᵉlōʾ ʾôsîp̄ lᵉhānîḏ reḡel yiśrāʾēl*) in a barren wilderness. He had given them rest (a roost for their feet, Deut 3:20; 12:9–10; Josh 21:44). Those are unconditional promises from God's side and can be counted on. These words must have been an encouragement to Josiah to believe there was still hope. But the promises are conditional upon human participation (see the "Biblical Theology Comments" above on 20:1–11). History is not pre-determined. This is why divination is forbidden. It presumes that you can tap into knowledge of a future that is simply fixed in the endless cycles of existence.

But that is not true. The future is conditional. What are the conditions? They are profoundly ethical. The Israelites must keep the terms of the covenant, the Torah ("instructions," [הַתּוֹרָה, *hattôrâ*]) of Moses. These are not arbitrary "commands" (from צָוָה, *ṣāwâ*) of a heavenly tyrant who wishes to limit human freedom and creativity. They are the instructions of the Creator as to how the world is made to work. Live within those patterns ("be careful to do" [תִּשְׁמֹר וְעָשִׂיתָ, *tišmōr wᵉ ʿāśîṯā*], an oft repeated injunction, e.g., Deut 23:23 [MT24]; Josh 1:8; 2 Kgs 17:37) and all the promises of God are ours. Insist on rewriting them to serve our own demand for autonomy, and the results are predictable: disaster. But even here, the results are not merely mechanical. They are relational. We have provoked our Father to anger.

9 "But they did not listen" (וְלֹא שָׁמֵעוּ, *wᵉlōʾ šāmēʿû*). As Brueggemann (533) points out, listening is "defining for the covenant theology of Deuteronomy." It is to admit that life is found in the address of that One who alone calls all existence into being. It is also important to point out that in Hebrew to truly hear someone is inseparable from doing what they say. If you do not respond appropriately, you did not hear. So, whatever the Judeans might have said about their cognition, their behavior shows they did not hear. They are no different from the Canaanites around them.

---

15. See 1 Kgs 14:9, 15; 15:30; 16:2, 7, 13, 26, 33; 21:22; 22:53; 2 Kings 17:11, 17; 22:17; 23:19, 26.

10 We do not know who these "prophets" were since they are not named, and the only canonical prophet between Micah/Isaiah in the late 700's and early 600's and Zephaniah, presumably about the time of Josiah (620 BC?) is Nahum, dated about 650 BC. However, we need not doubt that there were such persons whose names are not known to us, as there were in the time of Ahab (1 Kgs 18:4) and far earlier (Judg 6:8). As Yahweh had sent Hosea and Amos to the northern kingdom in its last, desperate hours, so he sent his prophets to Judah as it approached the precipice.

11–15 Once again the indictment and sentence are framed by references to the enduring nature of the sins of Manasseh and his people. In verse eleven, it is that the sins of Manasseh are worse than those of "the Amorites who were before him" (הָאֱמֹרִי אֲשֶׁר לְפָנָיו, *hā ʾĕmōrî ʾăšer lᵉpānāyw*). Then in verse fifteen, the people have been provoking[16] Yahweh since "their fathers came out of Egypt" (יָצְאוּ אֲבוֹתָם מִמִּצְרַיִם, *yoṣ ʾû ʾăḇôṯām mimmiṣrayim*). That is, of course, literally true. Not only is there the incident of the golden calf, barely five weeks after the most solemn covenant oaths not to do such a thing, but one can only read the book of Numbers with shaking one's head. This is not to say that no Israelites adhered to the covenant faithfully. Obviously, there were many who did. That is why the faith survived. But there is a persistent thread of refusing to "listen" that runs through the history of Israel. Moses, after forty years of experience with these people in the wilderness, could see the future all too plainly unless there occurred radical changes (Deut 31:15–29).

11 On the term גִּלּוּלִים, *gillûlîm,* "filthy idols," see the "Commentary" above on 1 Kgs 15:12. Almost certainly a pejorative term, it is a favorite of Ezekiel. It occurs only six times in Kings, all in significant places: what Asa removed (1 Kgs 15:12), what Ahab served (21:26, note association with Amorites), what Israel served in defiance of Yahweh (2 Kgs 17:12), what Manasseh and his son worshipped (21:11, 21), what Josiah destroyed along with other "abominations" (23:24). These are not just idols, harmless images; they are "nasty" things that lead one to death and decay.

The association of Manasseh with the northern kings is reinforced with the use of the *hiphil* form of the verb "sin": "He caused even Judah to sin" (וַיַּחֲטִא גַם־אֶת־יְהוּדָה, *wayyaḥăṭi ʾgām- ʾeṯ-yᵉhûḏâ*) (also v. 16). This is what is said of most of the kings of Israel, there almost always associated with Jeroboam's idolatrous actions.[17] As Jeroboam had made idols of Yahweh, it is to be wondered if Manasseh did as well.

12–15 The sentence, introduced by "Therefore," flows straight out of the indictment in verse eleven. Because of the "evil" (רַע, *ra ʿ*) that Manasseh

16. מַכְעִסִים, *maḵ ʿisîm* is a ptcp. denoting characteristic behavior.

17. 1 Kgs 14:16; 15:26, 30, 34; 16:26; 21:22; 22:52; 2 Kgs 10:29, 31; 13:2, 6, 11; 14:24; 15:9, 18, 24, 28; 23:15.

had done and the sin into which he had led Judah, Yahweh was going to bring "calamity" (רָעָה, *rā ʿâ*) on Jerusalem and Judah. The one leads inevitability to the other. The disaster will be so resounding that it will make the ears of anyone who hears it "ring" (צלל, *ṣll*).[18] Hobbs (307) says trenchantly that Judah's "fame" (19:19) will turn to "shame." Jerusalem will have come a long way from the days of the queen of Sheba (1 Kgs 10:6–7). Jeremiah and Ezekiel speak of the destruction being so horrific that Jerusalem will become a "byword" (מָשָׁל, *māšāl*) among the nations (Jer 24:9; Ezek 23:10).

13 Under Manasseh's guidance Jerusalem and Judah have become as corrupt as Israel (see Ezek 23) therefore they will be judged by the same standards. Normally the "[measuring] line" (קָו, *qāw*) and the "plumb-bob" (מִשְׁקֹלֶת, *mišqōleṯ*) would be tools of construction, but now (as in Amos 7:8 and Isa 34:11) they are used to demonstrate that the structure has leant so far out of "true" that there is nothing to do but push it on over. It is beyond any possibility of being straightened up again. As the irony of "evil" and "calamity," so there is the sad irony here, that what is meant to be used for good can only be used for demolition.

The second metaphor in the verse is equally telling. Jerusalem is like a moldy dish, and the only thing to do with it is to "wipe" (מָחָה, *māḥâ*) every scrap out of it. In this context, the point is not to wash it clean, but to scrape it bare and turn it upside down.[19]

14 If the land of Canaan was Israel's "special possession" (נַחֲלָה, *naḥălâ*), Israel was "his [Yahweh's] special possession" (נַחֲלָתוֹ, *naḥălāṯô*) (Deut 32:9–11). But Israel forsook (נָטַשׁ, *nāṭaš*) Yahweh, so now Yahweh would "forsake" (נָטַשׁ, *nāṭaš*) them (Deut 32:15; Ps 78:60; Jer 12:7). The "remnant" (שְׁאֵרִית, *šᵊʾērîṯ*) that he had lovingly protected during Hezekiah's day (2 Kgs 19:30–31) would now be turned over to their enemies. But it is important to remember that if God's promises are conditional, so are his threats. These words, spoken some time before 642 BC, did not dictate the future. God would have been happy to rescind these words, if genuine national repentance had ever taken place. That is clear from both Jeremiah's and Ezekiel's calls to repentance (Jer 36:3–4; Ezek 14:6; 18:30) when the Babylonians were already at the door. There was no such repentance, so the train of events that Manasseh had set in motion was not turned aside (2 Kgs 23:26). But it could have been.

---

18. There is disagreement among commentators as to the exact meaning of this word. "Tingle" has a long history, but perhaps "roaring" or "quivering" (Provan, 268, notes the parallel with "shaking" in Hab 3:16) might be possible as well. See 1 Sam 3:11; Jer 19:3.

19. The Vulg. changes the metaphor to a used wax tablet, that has to be scraped with a stylus. Syr. abandons the metaphor completely and says Jerusalem must be destroyed because of the abominations that are in it.

16 Manasseh's sins were not merely cultic; they were also social. "Apart from his sin" (לְבַד מֵחַטָּאתוֹ, *lᵉḇaḏ mēḥaṭṭāʾṯô*) (perhaps to be understood collectively) of leading Judah away from exclusive devotion to Yahweh and back into idolatry, he was also guilty of bloodshed. This can be understood both literally and figuratively. Given his close comparison to Ahab (v. 3), it is not at all out of the question that Manasseh too persecuted and killed the prophets who opposed him, as Ahab and Jezebel had done (1 Kgs 18:4; cf. Jer 26:15). Furthermore, there are the indications of child sacrifice in v. 6 (cf. Ezek 23:36–39). But this phrase is regularly associated closely with acts of violence and oppression, and this suggests that it may sometimes be used figuratively to define this behavior for what it really is.[20] Perhaps the reason why the Bible so regularly couples idol worship with social injustice is that it sees such worship as an exercise in manipulation in order to gain power. That being so, oppression of the weak follows naturally.

17–18 The concluding regnal formula follows the standard pattern but two points require comment. The first occurs in verse seventeen where the formula typically highlights something of significance in the king's reign (for Hezekiah, it was his waterworks, 20:20). Here uniquely among all the kings in the books, it is Manasseh's sin! Not even Ahab is treated in this way. This speaks something of the editor's anger over what he/they sees as Manasseh's responsibility in the coming disaster.

The second unusual feature is the mention of Manasseh's burial place. Up to this point, if a burial place is listed, it is with the ancestors in the city of David (e.g., Ahaz, 2 Kgs 16:20; no place of burial is given for Hezekiah). But Manasseh (and Amon as well, 21:26) is said to have been buried "in the garden of his house, in the garden of Uzzah" (בְּגַן־בֵּיתוֹ בְּגַן־עֻזָּא, *bᵉgan-bêṯô bᵉgan-ʿuzzāʾ*). This has provoked two sets of comments, both of which are necessarily indeterminate. First, why are these two not buried with their ancestors? Two different answers are proposed. The first is that because they were apostates, they were denied burial in hallowed ground. The second is that the royal burial chamber was full, and that since these were the bones of kings, no one wanted to remove them to make room for Manasseh and Amon. Most commentators opt for the latter (e.g., Cogan and Tadmor, 269–70; Wiseman, 293).

The second question relates to the identity of Uzzah. There are four main suggestions: this is Uzzah, the man who was killed in touching the ark (2 Sam 6:6–7; Provan, 269); this is a shortening of the name of the leprous king Uzziah, who is said to buried "near" his ancestors (2 Kgs 15:9; Cogan and Tadmor, 270); it is a palace official whose name was known to his contemporaries (Cohn, 149); it is the place where Venus (Canaanite "Attarmelek," Arabic "Uzzah") was worshipped (Gray, 710). Each of these has its proponents, but none of them can be demonstrated to be correct. I can

20. Jer 7:6; 22:3, 17; Ezek 22:6–7; 27; Mic 3:9–11.

think of no reason why Uzzah would have been buried on the grounds of the royal palace. Neither can I think why the name of Uzziah (which is little used in Kings) would have been shortened to Uzzah. The final alternative is somewhat attractive, given Manasseh's proclivities, but it is strange that the Arabic name of the goddess would be used. All in all, it seems that the third option has the least problems.[21]

Biblical Theology Comments

While the line and plumb-bob (or plumbline) by which Samaria and then Jerusalem were judged may be no more than a figure of speech in the editor's mind, the figure does align very well with what he had said earlier. Why was judgment coming? It was coming because neither Israel nor Judah had "listened" to what Yahweh was saying to them through their Torah. Judged by its standards their ways of living had come up far short. The Word of God is the standard by which life is to be measured.

This is certainly what the fathers had in mind when they came to call the received scriptures "the canon," that is, "the measuring stick." The community of believers, whether Jewish earlier, or Christian later, understood itself to be defined by their scriptures. It is surely no accident that Muslims referred to the Jews as people of "the Book." This from a people who would certainly revere their Qur᾽an. Yet they recognized another, higher level of devotion in the Jewish people. God, the sole Creator, has spoken in the Bible, we believe, and has made known his will for human life. If that is so, then every aspect of our lives can be measured, evaluated, by what it says. We may feel that the structure is perfectly solid and upright, but it is not our perceptions that determine the truth. Just as the plumbline stands apart from our individual perceptions, so the Bible stands over against them, as well. If the plumbline says the wall is not vertical, the wall is not vertical, no matter how it may look to me.

To be sure, the Bible must be interpreted. We must determine how what it said to Bedouin herders four millennia ago, or Roman citizens two millennia ago, relates to people of the twenty-first century. That is not an easy task, but, on the other hand, it is by no means as hard as some would make it out to be. For instance, the summary of the torah, the so-called Ten Commandments, comes right across the ages with stunning clarity. As Dallas Willard said, "Even a fairly general practice of them would lead to a solution of almost every problem of meaning and order now facing Western

21. Bob Becking, "The Enigmatic Garden of Uzzah: A Religio-Historical Footnote to 2 Kings 21:18, 26," in *BerührungspunkteStudien zur Sozial- und Religionsgeschichte Israels und seiner Umwelt: Festschrift für Rainer Albertz zu seinem 65. Geburtstag*, ed. Ingo Kottsieper, Rüdiger Schmitt, Jakob Wöhrle (Münster: Ugarit-Verlag, 2008), 383–91. Nadav Na᾽aman, "Death Formulae and the Burial Place of the Kings of the House of David," *Bib* 85 (2004): 245–54.

societies."[22] It is largely because we humans wish to submit to no authority at all that we say the Bible is unclear. Surely there are interpretive difficulties, but there is more than enough that is crystal clear, and it judges our society today just as surely as it judged ancient Samaria and Jerusalem.

Selected Bibliography

Abadie, P. "From the Impious Manasseh (2 Kings 21) to the Convert Manasseh (2 Chronicles 33): Theological Rewriting by the Chronicler." Pages 89–104 in *Chronicler as Theologian: Essays in Honor of Ralph W. Klein.* Edited by M. Patrick Graham, Steven L. McKenzie, Gary N. Knoppers. London: T&T Clark, 2003.

Eynikel, E. "The Portrait of Manasseh and the Deuteronomic History." Pages 233–61 in *Deuteronomy and the Deuteronomic Literature: Festschrift C. H. W. Brekelmans.* Leuven: Leuven University Press; Uitgeverij Peeters, 1997.

Hulbert, W. G. "Good King and Bad King: Traditions about Manasseh in the Bible and Late Second Temple Judaism." *Stone-Campbell Journal* 11 (2008): 71–81.

Kelly, B. E. "Manasseh in the Books of Kings and Chronicles (2 Kings 21:1–18; 2 Chron 33:1–20)." Pages 131–146 in *Windows into Old Testament History: Evidence, Argument, and the Crisis of 'Biblical Israel.'* Edited by V. Philips Long, David W. Baker, Gordon J. Wenham. Grand Rapids: Eerdmans, 2002.

Lasine, S. "Manasseh as Villain and Scapegoat." Pages 163–83 in *New Literary Criticism and the Hebrew Bible.* JSOTSup 143. Edited by David J. A. Clines, J. Cheryl Exum. Sheffield: Sheffield Academic, 1993.

McKay, J. W. *Religion in Judah Under the Assyrians 732–609 B. C.* Naperville, IL: Allenson, 1973.

Ohm, A. T. "Manasseh and the Punishment Narrative." *TB* 61 (2010): 237–54.

Schmid, K. "Manasse und der Untergang Judas: 'Golaorientierte' Theologie in den Königsbüchern?" *Bib* 78 (1997): 87–99.

Schniedewind, W. "History and Interpretation: The Religion of Ahab and Manasseh." *CBQ* 55 (1995): 649–61.

22. Dallas Willard, *The Divine Conspiracy: Discovering Our Hidden Life in God* (New York: Harper, 1998) 56–57.

The Reign of Amon (21:19–26)

Introduction

The brevity of Amon's reign ending in assassination raises several questions. Is it possible that his evidently hearty embrace of his father's paganization of Israel's religion was just a little too much for some powerful persons in the court? Is it possible that Amon's rejection of his father's late attempt at correction (cf. 2 Chr 33:13-16) offended these persons who were trying to rein in the process? If so, they must have been shocked at how far in the opposite direction their chosen replacement was to go.

Outline

III. JUDAH ALONE 18:1–25:30
C. The reign of Amon 21:19–26

TRANSLATION

19 Amon was twenty-two years old when he became king and he reigned for two years in Jerusalem. His mother's name was Meshullemet, the daughter of Haruts, from Yotbah. **20** He did evil in Yahweh's sight as Manasseh his father had done. **21** He walked in all the way[s] his father had walked and he served the filthy idols[1] that his father had served and he worshipped them. **22** He abandoned Yahweh, the God of his fathers and did not walk in the way of Yahweh. **23** Amon's servants conspired against him and they killed the king in his house. **24** Then the people of the land struck down all the conspirators against King Amon and the people of the land made Josiah, his son, king in his place. **25** The rest of the matters pertaining to Amon, which he did, are they not written in the chronicles of the kings of Judah? **26** He was buried in his tomb in the garden of Uzzah and Josiah his son reigned in his place.

1. הַגִּלֻּלִים, *haggillulîm*. Vulg. "unclean things." See the "Commentary" above on 2 Kgs 21:11.

Textual Notes

23a. אֶת־הַמֶּלֶךְ: Syr. (as well as Gk^{L}) "him"; Gk. and Vulg. with MT.

24a. עַם־הָאָרֶץ: Gk. and Vulg. add "all"; Syr. with MT.

24b. עַם־הָאָרֶץ: Vulg. omits; Gk. and Syr. with MT.

26a. וַיִּקְבֹּר: All the versions pl. GKC (§144*dn.*2) recommends emendation. Perhaps the sing. is meant to convey the passive. However, this is not common.

Commentary

The reign of Manasseh's son, Amon, is treated as almost a postscript to Manasseh's, as indeed it was, lasting only two years or less (depending on whether antedating or postdating was in effect at the time). Apart from the regnal formulas in verses nineteen and twenty-five and twenty-six, only two things are said about him: he did not deviate from his father's practices (vv. 20–22), and he was assassinated (vv. 23–24).

19 If Amon was twenty-two years old at the beginning of his reign, it is very unlikely that he was Manasseh's first-born, having been born when his father was forty-four. Perhaps older brothers had been sacrificed to the gods, or perhaps Amon was selected over them for some reason.

The home of his mother Meshullemet has excited some scholarly interest because it is not known for certain where it was located. There was a Yotbah on the Sinai Peninsula, about thirty miles north of Elat (Num 33:33; Deut 10:7), and thus the name of her father is found on some Sinai inscriptions. However, Josephus mentions a place called Yatapata in Galilee, and the Assyrian, Tiglath-pileser III, also mentions a place of that name in Galilee.[2] In neither case is it a locality in Judea. If the former is correct, it might point to efforts by Manasseh to further his claims to Edom. On the other hand, it might be the result of efforts to exert Judean influence over parts of the former Israelite kingdom.

20–22 Although the list of Amon's sins is by no means as exhaustive as his father's, it is no less devastating, especially as it asserts no less than three times that he did what his *father* did. He did evil as his father had;[3] he behaved ("walked" [הָלַךְ, *hālak̲*]) as his father had; and he worshipped the same "filthy idols" (הַגִּלֻּלִים, *haggillulîm*) his father had. But to all this, something more is

2. Cited in Cogan and Tadmor, 275.

3. Barnes asks somewhat humorously how much evil a man can do in a reign as short as this (355). But Wiseman points out that in view of what Manasseh tried to do of a corrective nature late in his life (as per 2 Chr 33), Amon must have immediately set out to undo that (293). He chose to follow the young Manasseh and not the elder, wiser one.

said, something that is not even said of Manasseh: "he abandoned Yahweh the God of his fathers" (וַיַּעֲזֹב אֶת־יהוה אֱלֹהֵי אֲבֹתָיו, *wayya ʿăzōḇ ʾeṯ-yhwh ʾĕlōhê ʾăḇōṯāyw*). "Abandoned" (עזב) is the same verb that can be translated "divorced" in a marital context and given the nuptial overtones of covenant relationship between Yahweh and his people, those connotations should not be overlooked here. Deuteronomy 33:16 and 17 paint the picture graphically. If the people forsake Yahweh, then Yahweh will forsake them. Amon has not only embraced other lovers, but to do it he has forsaken the only One who ever truly loved him.

23 The fact that no reason is given for the conspiracy against Amon has occasioned a good deal of speculation on the part of commentators. The suggestions generally fall into three groups. The first and probably most likely is that the assassination was the work of an anti-Assyrian group among Amon's officials (Gray, 712). Assyria's iron grip upon its vassals was beginning to slip. Although she was able to put down serious rebellions in Babylon and Elam, she was wearing down. In that context, it is possible that some persons saw an opportunity if the king could be put out of the way. In that case, Josiah could have been put on the throne by a pro-Assyrian group anxious to mollify the still-dangerous Assyria. The second possibility is that there may have been passed-over elder brothers who hoped to usurp the throne. The third is that there may have been priests who were angry at what was being done to corrupt the Jerusalem Temple. But as Cogan and Tadmor (276) point out, there really is no way of adjudicating among these. We only know that violence begets violence, and it appears that the violence that Manasseh had practiced (v. 16) was bearing its bitter fruit.

24 Once again "the people of the land" (עַם־הָאָרֶץ, *ʿam-hā ʾāreṣ*), as earlier in the case of Joash (see 2 Kgs 11:14–18), step in to ensure that the Davidic dynasty will survive. The fact that they killed the conspirators suggests the possibility that the conspirators may have been planning to put a non-Davidide on the throne. For a discussion of the identity of these "people of the land" see the "Commentary" above on 2 Kings 11:18, 20. It is possible that these were people who would on the one hand, freely acquiesce to the burgeoning paganism of Manasseh and Amon, but on the other hand, had a visceral love for their royal traditions. The connection between the Davidic covenant and Yahweh may have had less of a hold on them than merely ancient political custom. It is interesting how often theological truth can be left to fall to the side, but traditions are fought for to the death.

Since Amon was only twenty-four at his death, it is probable that Josiah was his firstborn son and that the people had no choice but to put the eight-year-old on the throne. It is also possible that those who did so were happy to have a child in place whom they might feel they could manipulate to their own advantage. But whatever the reasons might have been, God had other plans. He planned that even if there was no national turning to God and the sins of Manasseh and Amon would come to full fruition in destruction and exile, there would yet be those whose faith had been renewed and grounded. That renewed and grounded faith would survive the exile and become the foundation for the ultimate fulfillment of Yahweh's promises.

25–26 On the identity of Uzzah, see the "Commentary" on 2 Kgs 21:18.

Selected Bibliography

Holloway, S. W. "Smart Mobs, Bad Crowds, Godly People and Dead Priests: Crowd Symbols in the Josianic Narrative and some Mesopotamian Parallel." *BR* 51 (2006): 25–52.

Oded, B. "The Reigns of Manasseh and Amon." Pages 452–58 in *Israelite and Judean History*. Edited by John H. Hayes, J. Maxwell Miller. London: SCM Press, 1977.

Rudman, D. "A Note on the Personal Name Amon (2 Kings 21,19–26 // 2 Chr 33,21–25)." *Bib* 81 (2000): 403–5.

The Reign of Josiah (22:1–23:30)

Introduction

In these two chapters we come to the climax of the book(s) of Kings. Here we have the picture of how it was supposed to have been. Josiah is the fulfillment of the promise to David; he is the one Davidic king of whom nothing bad is said. He is the one who models all that exclusive devotion to Yahweh should mean, in its hatred of idolatry in all its forms, in its determination that no defilement of any sort should touch Yahweh's holy precincts, in its devotion to the ancient Torah of Moses. The line between him and David is direct, as he even surpasses Solomon, destroying the pagan shrines Solomon had built (23:13). He is the one king who is named in prophecy (1 Kgs 13:2). Thus, as Cohn (151) says, a trajectory is established reaching all the way from the beginning of the divided monarchy to its end. But it all comes too late. One has the feeling that if a Josiah had succeeded Hezekiah, Judah might have genuinely turned back to its covenant Lord and the exile might have been averted. But it was not to be. Manasseh and Amon had cemented the ancient Canaanite ways in place too deeply for a mere smashing of idols to root them out and Josiah only serves to demonstrate what might have been.[1]

The book of Chronicles (2 Chr 34) gives a somewhat expanded version of Josiah's story, both at the beginning and the end of that story. In the beginning, we are told that Josiah began at age sixteen to "seek the God of David his father" (34:3). Then when he was twenty, he began to cleanse Judah of her idolatry (34:3–7). When he was twenty-six, he set out to repair the temple. In other words, whereas Kings would make Josiah's rooting out of idolatry

1. Some (e.g., Sweeney, 15–20) have argued that a major (perhaps the first) recension of the book was created to celebrate Josiah's accomplishments in the faith that he had indeed averted the exile. On this way of thinking the cast of the book in general would have been more optimistic. It was only after the Babylonian exile had become a reality, that another (final?) recension was created in which there was overall a much darker tone, with a more negative attitude toward the monarchy, and an explanation of how it was that the exile had ever occurred. See "Composition of the Book" in the "Introduction."

more the result of the discovery of the covenant, Chronicles has him doing that before the discovery. Kings makes relatively more of that rooting out, whereas Chronicles makes more of the worship surrounding the Passover celebration. The differences correspond well to the differing purposes of the two books: Kings emphasizing the covenant, and covenant obedience, and Chronicles emphasizing the power of faithful worship in the temple. As to when the destruction of idolatry took place, I suspect it is not a case of "either-or," but "both-and." The ancient narratives and covenant traditions of Israel were still a fundamental part of certain segments of the society, and those could account for Josiah's early piety and interest in reform. But it was the rediscovery of "the Book" with its explicit statement of the covenant obligations that would give wings to the reform.

The end of Josiah's story is somewhat different in the two accounts: in Kings it is briefly presented as an unfortunate fact of history (2 Kgs 23:29), whereas in Chronicles it is the result of Josiah's refusal to obey God's speaking through the Egyptian King Neco (2 Chr 35:20–34). Chronicles clearly wishes to make this a teaching moment on the necessity of continued obedience to the voice of God if we wish to have his blessing, no matter where that voice came from. On the probable point of view of Kings see the "Commentary" on 23:29–30 below.

Despite these differences in detail, the two accounts are in full agreement in their assessment of Josiah's remarkable reign: with Israel gone and Judah about to be exiled, this man effected Yahweh's absolute lordship over the whole land in ways no other king since David had. It was too late to avert the tragedy, but when Josiah finished there was no question that the land of Israel belonged to Yahweh, the transcendent One, alone.

It is possible to date Josiah's reign with a good deal of precision because of the various Mesopotamian annals and chronicles that are available by this time. He reigned between 640 and 609 BC. These were years of tumult in the ancient Near East. After almost 300 years of dominance the Assyrian empire was brought to an end with surprising suddenness. The last significant emperor, Ashurbanipal, died ca. 628 BC, and Babylon almost immediately revolted and was not recovered. From that victory the Babylonian King Nabopolassar went on the offensive and with the help of the Medes from the Zagros Mountains east of Mesopotamia brought Assyria to its knees within twenty years. First Asshur fell (614 BC) then Nineveh itself (612 BC), and when the remnants fled westward and attempted to establish themselves at Haran, they suffered a crushing defeat in 609 BC. The final blow was delivered at Carchemish by Nabopolassar's son, Nebuchadnezzar, in 605 BC.[2]

The Bible does not report any of this except in Josiah's death notice (2 Kgs 23:29) where we are told that the Egyptian pharaoh, Neco, was going

2. For a full discussion of Assyria's fall, see Amélie Kuhrt, *The Ancient Near East, c. 3000 – 300 BC*, 2 vols (New York: Routledge, 1995) 2:544–46.

[in 609 BC] to "the Euphrates River to help the king of Assyria." But it does explain how it is that Josiah might have had the freedom to undertake the kinds of things he did: Assyria had pressing business elsewhere, and former vassals could enjoy a reduction of pressure, for a while, at least.

Leithart (268) has argued that this Josiah material, leaving out the death notice, is arranged in a chiastic form, as follows:

A. Opening: Josiah does not turn to the right or the left (22:1–2)
 B. Book of the Torah found (22:3–20)
  C. Renews covenant according to "The Book of the Covenant" (23:1–3)
   D. Reforms (23:4–20)
  C'. Passover according to "The Book of the Covenant" (23:21–23)
 B'. All the words of the Torah (23:24)
A'. Closing: Josiah turns to Yahweh with heart, soul, and strength (23:25)

While this is very attractive, it is not without some difficulties, one of which is not including the death notice. Another is the imbalance between the B and B' segments (eighteen verses paralleled by one verse). These factors and others argue that the form is more a result of scholarly ingenuity than of editorial intent.

Outline

III. JUDAH ALONE 18:1–25:30
 D. The reign of Josiah 22:1–23:30
  1. Josiah's accession 22:1–2
  2. The discovery of the book of the Torah 22:3–20
  3. Josiah's reforms 23:1–27
  4. Josiah's death 23:28–30

Josiah's Accession (22:1–2)

Translation

22:1 Josiah was eight years old when he became king and he reigned in Jerusalem for thirty-one years. His mother's name was Jedidah, daughter of Adia, from Bozkath. **2** He did what was right in Yahweh's sight. He walked in all the way of David, his father: he did not turn to the right or to the left.

Textual Notes

There are no textual variants.

Commentary

By this point in the book, the pattern of the opening regnal formula is unmistakable: age at accession, number of years in the reign, mother's name, mother's hometown, a comment about the general relationship to Yahweh, and a comment about the king's general manner of life. That is what we have here, and only two matters deserve some comment. The first is the hometown of his mother, Jedidah ("Beloved," a fem. form [יְדִידָה, *yᵉḏîḏâ*] of the personal name of Solomon, 2 Sam 12:25). She was from Bozkath, which on the basis of Joshua 15:39, was located in the Shephelah, the hilly country between Judah and Philistia, southwest of Lachish. Without making too much of this, it may suggest that Assyria had given control of this fertile area to its faithful vassal Manasseh. It is worth mentioning that one of Josiah's wives, Hamutal, was from the same region (2 Kgs 23:31).

The second matter to note here is the fulsome praise that is given to Josiah as a man of virtue and rectitude. Unlike Manasseh and Amon, and indeed, all his successors, Josiah "did what was right in Yahweh's sight" (וַיַּעַשׂ הַיָּשָׁר בְּעֵינֵי יהוה, *wayya ʿaś hayyāšār bᵊ ʿênê yhwh*). What that right was is defined, as was true with every good Judean king, by the statement that in the conduct of his life (his "walk") he emulated David. As Jeroboam I set the pattern for all the succeeding kings of the north, particularly in the matter of idolatry, so David set the pattern for the three key kings of Judah: Asa (1 Kgs 15:11), Hezekiah (2 Kgs 18:3), and now Josiah.[3] The statement that "he did not turn to the right or the left" (וְלֹא־סָר יָמִין וּשְׂמאוֹל, *wᵊlō ʾ-sār yāmîn ûśᵊmō ʾwl*) corresponds to the "perfect heart" ascribed to Asa (1 Kgs 15:14) and Hezekiah (2 Kgs 20:3). That is, there was never any question where the loyalties of these men lay: they belonged to Yahweh alone with never a question about it.[4] And because of their faithfulness at key moments the faith was able to survive even though the consequent disasters on disobedience in the populace could not be averted.

The Discovery of the Book of the Torah (22:3–20)

Translation

3 Now in the eighteenth year of King Josiah, the king sent Shaphan, son of Azaliah, son of Meshullam, the scribe, to the house of Yahweh, saying, **4** "Go

3. Jehoshaphat (1 Kgs 22:43) and Joash (2 Kgs 12:2) are also said to have "done right in Yahweh's sight," but it is not explicitly connected with David.

4. Note especially the command to the king in Deut 17:20. Note also the qualifier in Deut 28:14: not "following other gods or serving them." None of these kings performed perfectly, but none of them deviated from exclusive devotion to Yahweh. But Josiah is the only one who receives the accolade "he did not turn to the right or to the left."

up to Hilkiah, the high priest, and have him gather up[5] the silver brought into
the house of Yahweh which the doorkeepers collected from the people. **5** Let
them give it into the hand of the workers who have been put in charge of the
house of Yahweh. Let them give it to the workers in the house of Yahweh to
repair the defects in the house, **6** to the carpenters, builders, and masons, to
buy wood and dressed stones to repair the house. **7** However, they do not
need to account for the silver that is given them; they are honest workers."
8 Hilkiah, the high priest, said to Shaphan, "The book of the Torah, I have
found in the house of Yahweh."[6] Hilkiah gave it to Shaphan and he read it. **9**
Shaphan the scribe went to the king and brought back a report[7] to the king.
He said, "Your servants have poured out[8] the silver found in the house and
gave it into the hand of the workers who have been put in charge of the house
of Yahweh. **10** Shaphan, the scribe, told the king, "Here is a book Hilkiah the
priest gave me." Shaphan read it to the king. **11** Now when the king heard the
words of the book of the Torah he tore his clothes. **12** The king commanded
Hilkiah, the priest, and Ahikam, son of Shaphan, and Akbor, son of Micaiah,
and Shaphan, the scribe, and Asaiah, servant of the king, saying, **13** "Go,
inquire of Yahweh on my behalf, and on behalf of the people, and on behalf
of the land of Judah concerning the words of this book that has been found,
because a great wrath of Yahweh is kindled against us because our ancestors
did not listen to the words of this book to do all that has been written to
us." **14** Hilkiah, the priest, Ahikam, Akbor, Shaphan, and Asaiah went to
Huldah the prophetess, the wife of Shallum, son of Tikvah, son of Harhas,
keeper of the wardrobe. She was living in Jerusalem in the second quarter,
and they spoke to her. **15** She said to them, "Thus says Yahweh, the God of
Israel, 'Say to the man who sent you to me, **16** thus says Yahweh, "Look, I am
about to bring calamity on this place and on its inhabitants: all the words of
the book that the king of Judah has read. **17** Because they have forsaken me
and burned incense to other gods so as to provoke me with all the work of
their hands, my wrath will be kindled against this place and it will never be
quenched." **18** But to the king of Judah who sent you to inquire of Yahweh,
thus say to him, "Thus says Yahweh, the God of Israel, concerning the words
that you have heard, **19** 'Because your heart was tender and you humbled

---

5. The sense of the vb. יַתֵּם, *yattēm* is "to be whole, complete." Here a *hiphil.*
6. The obj. of the vb. has been put in the emphatic position: הַסֵּפֶר סֵפֶר הַתּוֹרָה מָצָאתִי, *hassōpēr sēpēr hattôrâ māṣā ʾṯî*. GKC (§142*f*) So also v. 10.
7. Lit. וַיָּשֶׁב אֶת־הַמֶּלֶךְ דָּבָר, *wayyāšeḇ ʾeṯ-hammeleḵ dāḇār* ("returned the king a word"). Some commentators feel this is awkward, but that is more a perception than an actual grammatical difficulty.
8. This vb. (נתך, *ntk*) can mean "to melt" and this is how Gk. and Vulg. take it here. Perhaps it is the idea of melting down the bits of silver collected and casting it into official ingots. But it might also mean pouring the silver pieces out of whatever vessel they were collected in. See the "Commentary" below.

yourself before Yahweh when you heard what I said concerning this place and its inhabitants, that it would become a waste and a curse, and you tore your clothes and you wept before me, I myself[9] have also heard you,' " says Yahweh. "Therefore, look here, I will gather you to your fathers and you will be gathered to your grave in peace; your eyes will not see all the calamity that I am going to bring upon this place." ' " So, they brought the word back to the king.

Textual Notes

3a. יֹאשִׁיָּהוּ: Gk. adds "in the eighth month"; Vulg. and Syr. with MT.

3b. הַסֹּפֵר: Gk. and Vulg. "scribe of the house"; Syr. "to the house." MT is not a construct phrase, but also lacks any prep. Perhaps "house of Yahweh" is an adverbial acc. of direction, (cf. Hobbs, 314).

4a. וְיַתֵּם: Gk. "seal" which suggests a mistaken reading חֲתֹם. Vulg. "pour out" which appears to be an assimilation to the vb. in v. 9. Syr. has "deliver." The MT vb. תַּם "to be whole" suggests that Hilkiah was to gather the silver together. See *CTAT* (417) in support of MT, which best explains the other readings.

5a. K וְיִתְּנֹה: K "let him give it"; Q וְיִתְּנֻהוּ "let them give it." Gk. "And he gave"; Vulg. and Syr. with MT Q.

5b. בֶּדֶק: Gk. transliterates; Vulg. "restorations"; Syr. "breaches." See also 12:7.

6a. אֶת־הַבָּיִת: Gk. inserts βεδεκ (see 5b.); Vulg. and Syr. with MT.

9a–a. וַיָּבֹא שָׁפָן הַסֹּפֵר: Gk. "He brought it in"; Vulg. and Syr. with MT.

9b. הִתִּיכוּ: Syr. "delivered" (probably assimilating to the translation in v. 4. See 4a.); Gk. and Vulg. with MT.

13a. אֲשֶׁר־הִיא: GKC (§138*b*) points out the unusual occ. of the indep. pron. here. Perhaps the vb. is being construed as a ptcp.

14a. בַּמִּשְׁנֶה: Gk. transliterates; Vulg. *secundum*; Syr. "second quarter."

17a–a. תַּחַת אֲשֶׁר: The combination introduces a causal clause, (RJW §353).

17b. לְמַעַן: Rarely this prep. can introduce a result clause; *IBHS* (§38.3n25) and RJW (§198).

17c–c. וְלֹא תִכְבֶּה: Syr. "and I will destroy you"; Vulg. and Syr. with MT.

---

9. The subj. (אָנֹכִי, *ʾānōḵî*) is emphasized.

18a. הַדְּבָרִים: Gk. adds "As for"; Vulg. "In view of the fact that"; Syr. with MT. Perhaps an עַל has been lost here because of the two letters preceding.

20a. וַיָּשִׁיבוּ: Vulg. begins chap. 23 here. Gk. and Syr. with MT.

Commentary

In this section we have the report of the discovery of the "book of the Torah" in the context of repair work begun on the temple.[10] The speech of Josiah recorded in verses four through six in which he directed this work to begin contains much of the same language and vocabulary as that found in somewhat fuller form in the report of the repairs that took place under Joash (2 Kgs 12:4–12). This has suggested to some (e.g., Hobbs, 320–21) that this is the language of the temple archives and that this was the way one spoke of temple repairs. Here the much shorter statement makes it clear that the main point of the account is not the repairs, but the startling discovery of the "book" and its authentication, events that led to the intensive reforms reported in chapter 23.

3 "In the eighteenth year" Josiah would have been twenty-six years old, an age when he would no longer be under the control of those who had managed him during his childhood and could now take independent action. As noted above, the reports in 2 Chronicles about his seeking "the God of his father David" at age sixteen and beginning reforms at age twenty (2 Chr 34:3) need not be considered contradictory of the report here.[11] Kings wishes to emphasize the importance of "the book" to what Josiah eventually undertook. Chronicles is demonstrating that while "the book" did have a profound impact upon him, it only brought to fruition what was already underway in his life. Somehow, perhaps as in the case of Joash where a regent had a profound impact on the child and young man, that situation prevailed again. Whatever the cause, after nearly sixty years of apostasy, God had another man "after his own heart."

"Shaphan" (שָׁפָן, *šāpān*; ""rock-badger") was almost certainly not merely "the scribe" (הַסֹּפֵר, *hassōpēr*), but the royal scribe whose position was identified in 1 Kgs 4:3. Thus, he is here the king's official representative to the

10. I prefer to use "Torah" rather than "law" because of the negative connotations of "law" in the modern context. It seems to me that the connotations of "instruction" carried by Torah are more accurate. Note that Cogan and Tadmor translate סֵפֶר הַתּוֹרָה, *sēper hattôrâ* as "the book of teaching" (277).

11. This would be evidence that even if the Torah scroll, as a scroll, was not in anyone's consciousness, people did recall the stipulations of the covenant and the faith that surrounded those stipulations. While some might say that it was Hezekiah's innovative idea of trying to centralize worship in Jerusalem that gave rise to the Deuteronomic stipulations, it is equally likely that it was Hezekiah's awareness of those stipulations that explains his actions.

high priest. Perhaps in the naming of both father and grandfather (Azaliyah and Meshullam, respectively) the scribe is making a point about the significance of this family line. Shaphan had two sons (Ahikam [Jer 26:24], and Gemariah [Jer 36:12, 25]) and two grandsons (Micaiah [Jer 36:11]; Gedaliah [Jer 40:5]) who were not only important officials in Judah's government, but more importantly, men of faith and integrity.

4 Probably the temple and everything associated with it had been allowed to fall into disrepair during the reigns of Manasseh and Amon, (as with Ahaziah and Athaliah). Now, Josiah wants to put both the collection and the building itself back on a more secure foundation. It seems very likely that he had no inkling of the upheaval this step was going to unleash.

While Hilkiah was also the name of Jeremiah's father (Jer 1:1), it is unlikely that the two are the same. The high priest would likely reside in Jerusalem and not in the village of Anathoth (cf. Jer 1:1; 32:7). Although this title, frequent after the exile, only appears here in Kings, there seems little reason to late-date this material on that basis. There was undoubtedly a chief priest before the exile.[12]

5–7 The high priest was to give the money to the workers who were "in charge" (הַמֻּפְקָדִים, *hammupqādîm*), and they in turn were to give it to the workers, that is, the craftsmen, who would actually make the repairs. That no accounting was required is a powerful testimony to the integrity of these men.[13]

8 This verse comes with sudden abruptness. There is no report of the progress of the work, or even of the circumstance of the finding of "the book of the torah" (סֵפֶר הַתּוֹרָה, *sēper hattôrâ*). We have a picture of Shaphan arriving at the site to check up on things, and Hilkiah bursting out of a door carrying a scroll and shouting, "The book of the Torah! I've found it!" From this point on in the narrative, everything takes a backseat to this discovery. Hilkiah gives Shaphan the scroll (the text giving no information about where the scroll was found) and the first thing he does is to "read it" (וַיִּקְרָאֵהוּ, *wayyiqrāʾēhû*). We have the impression that Shaphan has heard about this book before and is eager to see what it actually says. Hilkiah seems to have read it is as well,

12. As Cogan and Tadmor point out, the very variety of translations of the action Hilkiah was to perform in verse 4 argues that the unique occurrence of תָּמַם, *tāmam* "to be whole" here with the sense of "to gather up in one place" best explains all the rest (281).

13. This focus on the Jerusalem temple and the money involved to maintain it has suggested to Eugene Claburn that a possible motive behind this entire reform movement was money. By moving all worship to Jerusalem, the king would be taking a collection of funds out of the hands of a myriad of local priests: "Fiscal Basis of Josiah's Reforms," *JBL* 92 (1973): 11–22.

because he knows what it is. This is not some dusty old scroll of accounts, or even of priestly traditions. This book was the defining document of their existence as a people, and here it was. Many commentators (e.g., Hobbs, 325) correctly point out that a part of the power of the narrative is that we, the readers, don't actually know what it says yet. Hilkiah evidently does, and that may explain a part of his excitement. Now Shaphan knows, but we still don't.

9–10 These verses are a testimony to the narrative skill of the editor. After the terse excitement of verse eight, when we are left wondering what the book says, we are given a long wordy report from Shaphan concerning the building. The suspense builds until finally, almost in an off-handed way, the scribe tells the king, "And by the way, there is a book here Hilkiah gave me," and proceeds to "read it to the king" (וַיִּקְרָאֵהוּ שָׁפָן לִפְנֵי הַמֶּלֶךְ, *wayyiqrāʾēhû šāpān lipnê hammelek*). He does not ask permission, nor does the king ask what the book is; Shaphan simply unrolls the scroll and reads it. We have the feeling that he has been bursting to do so. Now there are three people who know what it says, but we readers still do not.

11–12 Now the action picks up speed again. Josiah's immediate reaction, upon hearing "the words of the book of the Torah" (דִּבְרֵי סֵפֶר הַתּוֹרָה, *dibrê sēper hattôrâ*), is to do two things: (1) to rip his royal robes in two, and (2) to commission a very significant group of people to attempt to discover what are the immediate implications of this document. What does it say? We still do not know, but evidently whatever it is, it is of terrible import.

We sometimes use the phrase "blue-ribbon commission" to describe a group of very significant people delegated to look into some matter. This was definitely a "blue-ribbon commission," made up of the chief priest (Hilkiah), the royal scribe (Shaphan), the scribe's son, (Ahikam), apparently already a prominent official in his own right, another prominent man (Achbor),[14] and the king's personal representative (Asaiah). Why not simply send Shaphan, someone whom the king obviously trusts? It was because this is a matter of cataclysmic importance. If what Josiah expects is true *is* true, then the very fate of the nation hangs in the balance. This has to come in the mouth of not just one or two, but several, witnesses. But we still do not know what the book actually says!

13 Once again, the narrator slows the pace with a long statement from the king that now begins to reveal a bit of what was on the scroll. It expressed "the wrath of Yahweh" (חֲמַת יהוה, *ḥămat yhwh*) that was the result of "our ancestors not listening to [i.e., 'obeying'] the words of this book to do all that was written to us" (לֹא־שָׁמְעוּ אֲבֹתֵינוּ עַל־דִּבְרֵי הַסֵּפֶר הַזֶּה לַעֲשׂוֹת כְּכָל־הַכָּתוּב עָלֵינוּ,

---

14. Since Achbor (עַכְבּוֹר, *ʿakbôr*; "mouse") is said to be the father of Elnathan, an important official in Jehoiakim's court (Jer 26:22; 36:12, 25) it may be inferred that Achbor too was prominent in the court of Jehoiakim's father, Josiah.

lōʾ-šomʿû ʾăḇōṯênû ʿal-diḇrēy hassēp̄er hazze laʿăśôṯ kᵊḵol-hakkāṯûḇ ʿālênû).[15] So why was Josiah sending the commission to the prophet? Why did he want to "inquire of Yahweh" (דִּרְשׁוּ אֶת־יהוה, *ḏiršû ʾeṯ-yhwh*)?[16] He did not want to know whether this book was authentic or not. His action in tearing his robe shows there was no question about that in his mind. Neither did he want to know its identity. Like Hilkiah, he knew what it was; it was the Torah, something he had undoubtedly heard about; it was what defined Israel's existence. The fact that its content did not surprise him in any way shows that he knew of such a document's existence. What he wanted to know from the living Word of God in the mouth of the prophet was how what the written Word was saying might impinge on him, on his people, and on his nation ("all Judah"). Could this wrath be propitiated? Could it be deferred? These were the kinds of questions that Josiah hoped to get an answer to, and for which he appointed such a high ranking group. His concern for his people and his country here seems to cast him in a better light than Hezekiah, who seems to have been mostly concerned over what would immediately befall him (20:19). On the identity of this book and the circumstances surrounding its appearance, see the "Excursus on The Finding of the Book of the Torah."

14 There is no explanation why the group chose to go to Huldah the prophetess. Some commentators (e.g., Fritz, 400) say that it was because she was the official court prophetess, as Nathan was to David (2 Sam 7). However, there is no indication of that, and the lengthy list of identifying factors given to her argues against it. Rabbinic literature says that it was because the men thought a woman might give a more merciful response (b. Meg. 14b; Qimḥi cited in Cogan and Tadmor, 283). That is attractive, but without any biblical basis. Others (see the discussion in Cogan and Tadmor, 295) say she was Josiah's choice, but there is no indication of that. The question is also asked why they did not consult Jeremiah, or Zephaniah, both of whom were active at this time. The answer is that we do not know. It may have been as simple as that this woman was well accredited and was easily accessible. What the event does point to is the historical veracity of the account. If this were simply a fictional narrative created to serve some politico/theological point, it is hard

15. In Ezekiel's day there were those who claimed that it was unfair that they should be punished for their ancestors' sins. Ezekiel responded that no one is punished for someone else's sins (17:1–32). How does that compare to what is said here? Is punishment going to come on them even if they repent and change their behavior? No. These are not good and righteous people who are suffering solely because of something someone did in the past. These are people who are fully participating in the very same sins their ancestors committed. If there had been genuine repentance (like that of Josiah, v. 19), then the punishment would not have happened, or would have at least been mitigated. The evidence that there was no such repentance is seen in the situation after Josiah's death that Jeremiah described throughout his book.
16. On the meaning of this phrase see the "Commentary" on 1 Kgs 22:5 above.

to imagine this set of "quirky" details having gotten into it. Although there are not many female prophets mentioned in the Bible, those who are form a distinguished list. Among them are Miriam and Deborah (Exod 15:20; Judg 4:4). On the debit side is Noadiah (Neh 6:14) who was allied with a group of prophets attempting to discourage Nehemiah. It is also possible that Isaiah's wife may have been a prophet in her own right since she is identified as a "prophetess" (Isa 8:3).[17] It is not clear why the position of Huldah's husband is identified. Apparently, he was in charge of the ceremonial garments in the temple (cf. 10:22). Some suggest (see Hobbs, 327) that the purpose of this information was to give Huldah some social status. But such status does not seem to have been important to most of the prophets. Almost all commentators agree that the "second quarter" or "new quarter" (מִשְׁנֶה, *mišneh*) refers to the expanded area of the city on the so-called "western hill," west of the temple mount (e.g., Sweeney, 445). Archeological evidence seems to confirm that Hezekiah enclosed this area within the city walls and that residences were built there during his time.[18]

15–20 Whatever Huldah's position may have been, she shows no trace of hesitancy before the august group that confronts her. The text records no greeting of them, nor question about their mission. She seems to know who they are and why they have come, and speaks with the full authority of Yahweh, "Thus says Yahweh, the God of Israel..." (כֹּה־אָמַר יהוה אֱלֹהֵי יִשְׂרָאֵל, *kō- ʾāmar yhwh ʾĕlōhê yiśrāʾēl*) (vv. 15, 18), and "Thus says Yahweh..." (כֹּה אָמַר יהוה, *kō ʾāmar yhwh*) (v. 16). The presence of the two rubrics in verses fifteen and eighteen certainly divide the oracle into two parts, but it is not clear to me as it seems to be to some, that there are two separate oracles here. Neither is it clear to me that the oracle(s) have been "heavily redacted" (Gray, 727). That judgment is based on theories about the creation and development of the so-called "Deuteronomic History" which are often in serious conflict with one another. As it stands, the message is very clear: there will be no mitigation of the prescribed punishment for breaking the covenant, except that the repentant king will be spared from seeing that punishment carried out.

15–17 The language employed here carries a tone of distance and severity; it is a formal sentence. "Say to the man who sent you" (אִמְרוּ לָאִישׁ אֲשֶׁר־שָׁלַח אֶתְכֶם, *ʾimrû lāʾîš ʾăšer-šālaḥ ʾeṯkem*)—not "King Josiah," or even "king." His royal position is of no consequence here.[19] He was simply the agent of their coming. So also "this place" (הַמָּקוֹם הַזֶּה, *hammāqôm hazze*)—not "Jerusalem," or even "this city." It no longer has any special claim on Yahweh, it is just a place on

17. From this limited information it is difficult to assess how important female prophets may have been in Israel. There may have been many more than we know.
18. Amihai Mazar, *Archaeology of the Land of the Bible, 10,000–586 B.C.E.* (New York: Doubleday, 1990), 417–24.
19. Cf. 2 Kgs 5:7.

which judgment must fall. This is similar to the identification of Israel as "this people" in the prophets. There is a note of contempt, even disgust.[20] Because they had done evil (רַע, *ra ʿ*), Yahweh is going to bring *calamity* (רָעָה, *ra ʿâ*). The one leads to the other. When "calamity" is associated with "all the words of the book" (כָּל־דִּבְרֵי הַסֵּפֶר, *kol-dibrê hassēper*) this suggests that whatever else was on the scroll, it must have included something like the curses found in Deuteronomy 27–28.

17 The reason why the curses are coming on these people is simply that they have broken their covenant with Yahweh, a covenant in which they swore—on pain of death—exclusive commitment to the God who had made them and delivered them from Egypt. This transcendent God cannot be manipulated by any activity on earth. He can only be surrendered to, trusted, and obeyed (i.e., his directions listened to). This is frankly terrifying. We want comfortable little gods, "the work of our hands" (metaphorically as well as literally) whom we can manipulate with our rituals, gods who will do what we want. This was the sin of the Israelites: they had substituted their vision of reality for actual reality, and now they were about to crash into actual reality.

18–20 The tone in this second part of the oracle is markedly more personal. Now Josiah is recognized as "the king of Judah" who in his official capacity had sent men "to inquire (לִדְרֹשׁ, *lidrōš*) of Yahweh" (unlike, say, Ahaziah who had sent emissaries to inquire of Baal-zebub, 2 Kgs 1:1). He is addressed directly throughout as "you." The oracle of judgment for the nation is coupled to an oracle of salvation for the nation's king. Because Josiah "heard the words" (הַדְּבָרִים אֲשֶׁר שָׁמָעְתָּ, *haddᵊbārîm ʾăšer šāmāʿttā*) (vv. 18, 19) of the scroll, and showed that he truly "heard" them by his response, a "tender heart[21] and a humbled self" (רַךְ־לְבָבְךָ וַתִּכָּנַע, *rak-lᵊbobkā wattikkāna ʿ*), Yahweh himself has "heard" Josiah (בְּשָׁמְעֲךָ, *bᵊšomʿăkā*; lit: "when hearing you") (v. 19). The relational aspects here are important. Josiah is responsive to Yahweh and Yahweh is responsive to Josiah. Human persons are made in the image of a personal Creator. Josiah's instant response to what he knew to be God's word was impressive to Yahweh. Such a response is remarkable to anyone who has read through the book from Solomon to this point. We have seen in Judah's and Israel's kings equivocation and questioning, delaying and refusing, but rarely have we seen the kind of response Josiah shows. He needed no prophetess to tell him this was God's word. He recognized it at once and acted at once. The "humbling" element is important. This word only appears one other place in Kings when Ahab, of all people, humbled himself before Yahweh (1 Kgs 21:29). That is, these two men, arguably the best and the worst, did the one

20. Isa 8:6; 28:11, 14; Jer 5:14, 23; 11:14; Micah 2:11.

21. See also Deut 20:3; 2 Chr 13:7; Isa 7:4; Jer 51:46 where רַךְ לֵבָב, *rak lēbāb* is paralleled with expressions for fear and timidity. This is the opposite of the stony heart of which Ezekiel speaks (36:26).

thing requisite of all humans. They recognized they are not God and acted appropriately upon that knowledge. Ahab was sorry for his own sin, while Josiah was sorry for the sin of the group of which he was an inescapable part. But both recognized that there is a God to whom we are all accountable and that there are tragic consequences when we fail that accountability.

For "a waste" (שַׁמָּה, *šammâ*), see Deuteronomy 28:22–23 and for "a curse" (קְלָלָה, *qᵉlālâ*) see Deuteronomy 28:37.

20 Some commentators (e.g., Cogan and Tadmor, 284; Sweeney, 446) find this verse troubling because they take it that "be gathered to your grave in peace" (וְנֶאֱסַפְתָּ אֶל־קִבְרֹתֶיךָ בְּשָׁלוֹם, *wᵉne ʾĕsap̄tā ʾel-qiḇrōṯêḵā bᵉšālôm*) can only be understood to be a prediction that Josiah will die in a peaceful manner, something that was, in fact, not to be the case (23:29). To resolve the apparent problem, they posit that this oracle must have been recorded before Josiah's death and, inexplicably, not corrected afterwards.[22] But the phrase, which only occurs here and in 2 Chronicles 34:28 need not be understood in this way. In fact, the statement that indicates a king died a normal death is "he slept with his fathers."[23] That one does not occur here. I suggest the point of Huldah's words is to say that Josiah will not die in some conflagration when all Jerusalem's and Judah's sins are being visited upon them. He will die before that happens while his country is still in a state of peace. "Your eyes will not see all the calamity" (וְלֹא־תִרְאֶינָה עֵינֶיךָ בְּכֹל הָרָעָה, *wᵉlōʾ-ṯir ʾênâ ʿênêḵā bᵉḵōl hārāʿâ*) Yahweh is going to bring. That is the point, and not the manner of his death, about which Huldah does not intend to say anything.[24]

Biblical Theological Comments

Living Word and written Word: this combination is vital to biblical faith from end to end. Together they combine the objective and subjective elements of biblical faith. We see this in two ways. The first is seen in the priority of the living word. Yahweh "spoke" to Abram (Gen 12:1). This simple statement is astounding. Where else does a god speak directly to a person? There is no suggestion of an intermediary. This, of course, is why Abraham is called a prophet (Gen 20:7). A prophet is someone God speaks to. What did this involve? Was there an audible voice or was it an interior one? We cannot know. But the unusual fact is that rational content was conveyed.

---

22. If this understanding of the phrase is correct, it is even more surprising that it was allowed to stand in 2Chr 34:28, when that book clearly has Josiah's death the result of disobedience to God's word as expressed through the pharaoh.

23. 1 Kgs 2:10, and 24 others in 1 and 2 Kgs. Never of a king who died a violent death.

24. See P. S. F. van Keulen, "The Meaning of the Phrase *wnʾspt ʾl-qbrtyk bšlm* in 2 Kings XXII,20," *VT* 46 (1996): 256–60.

This was not a mystical encounter with the *mysterium tremendum*.[25] This was God, the God the Israelites were to come to know as Yahweh, speaking as one person with another. Here was the living Word communicating himself to his creature.

That experience continued throughout the life of Abraham, and Jacob, and reached something of a climax with Moses. Again, there is no religious functionary mediating any of this communication; it is a direct, intimate, and personal communion. This is clearly what Yahweh wants with all of his people. In some unusual cases, as with these men, it will involve much more content than it does with the majority of people; but across the centuries this sense of being spoken to intimately and directly by God has been a hallmark of biblical faith.

However, it is very easy for most persons to become confused about what exactly God is saying to us. It is all too easy for us to hear what we want to hear, what is comfortable and nondemanding. Here is where the written Word comes in. The priority of the living Word is well-established between Genesis 12 and Exodus 19. But at that point, things begin to change. What does it mean to live with the speaking God? What is he like? What does relationship with him entail? These are questions the covenant was designed to answer. It was time to write down for all God's people the revelations that God spoke "mouth to mouth" to Moses. Here comes the objective check upon the subjective sense of divine reality. Whatever God may be speaking to us, it will always be subject to the check of his written Word. At the same time, the written Word is a "dead letter" unless it is touched by the reality of the living God.

So here, in Judah in 621 BC, what the written Word was saying was crystal clear. But what was not clear were the present implications of that Word for Josiah, his people, and his nation. What was needed was the living Word, to confirm, explain, and apply that truth, and Josiah knew that.

The second way the living Word and the written Word conjoin is really what should be understood as the foundational reality of which the first is the expression. This is the incarnation. Here the Word becomes not merely personal, but a person. Jesus did not come to do away with the written Word, but to fulfill it (Matt 5:17–20). In him is the perfect union of living and written Word. In him the two become one, in the same way that in him, his humanity and his deity are one. Here we find the culmination of Yahweh's passionate desire to be known, to communicate himself to us, to explain how the world is supposed to function. He does not come to supersede the written Word, but to ensure that it will not be merely a lifeless document, communicating ideas and concepts, but never bringing us to an encounter

25. The phrase is that of Rudolf Otto in his *The Idea of the Holy* (London, Oxford, 1926), 12, etc. It speaks of God's holiness as a "terrible mystery" that makes him beyond comprehension.

with the Author that will change every way we think and act. Who is Christ? He is the Yahweh of the Old Testament. What is the Bible? It is that which provides the basis for understanding who Christ is and what he came to do. Who is Christ? The embodiment of the biblical revelation.

One of the perennial objections to the revelatory character of the Old Testament *vis a vis* the New Testament is the supposed prominence of God's furious anger ("the wrath of God") in the Old Testament. Thus, it is often said that whereas the New Testament God is a God of love, the Old Testament God is a God of wrath. Of course, the immediate counter to such an idea is the prevalence of God's undeserved loyalty and love in the Old Testament (cf. the almost 250 occurrences of the word חֶסֶד, *ḥesed*, "love, grace, mercy, steadfast love, unfailing love, etc." [cf. Gen 24:12, 27; Exod 34:6–7; 1 Kgs 3:6; Ps 100:5]).

But given the point that the God of the Old Testament is indeed a God of love (and equally that the God of the New Testament is a God of wrath [ὀργὴν, *orgēn*], cf. Rom 9:22, and the eleven occurrences in Rev), it still must be admitted that, as here, the anger of God is a prominent feature of the Old Testament, and not as prominent in the New Testament. How shall we explain this? The most basic explanation lies in the complementary nature of the two testaments. The Old Testament is explaining the basic nature of reality and expressing the questions which that reality raises. The New Testament is assuming what the Old Testament affirms and is moving ahead to provide the answers to the questions raised. Thus, here the New Testament does not need to reaffirm the fact that we are all living under the wrath of God. That is a fact which it does not deny in any way. What it is doing is answering the question: Is there any way of avoiding that wrath? In providing that answer, it reaffirms and intensifies the truth of the Old Testament, namely, that while he *gets* angry, he *is* love.

But why does he get angry, and why so often, as it seems? Here we are dealing with one of the basic elements of reality that the Old Testament is seeking to teach us. If Yahweh is not an immutable, implacable Force (as Star Wars theology would have it), but is indeed the Person, then we cannot only have him be love. For love is necessarily a two-way street, in personal terms. It cares deeply about the object of its love, and longs passionately for the return of its love. A person cannot love without another person, and if that love is not reciprocated by the other, there is both incompleteness and loss. If we truly say that it is a matter of no consequence whether the other reciprocates, then what we are expressing is not love. We humans are Yahweh's other, and we have taken all the tokens of his love, squandered them on ourselves and asked why there is not more.

But is unrequited love a sufficient cause for furious anger? No, it is not. However, it lays a groundwork for our understanding. For the fact is, one cannot have mere disinterested love. There really is no such thing among persons. For love to be what love must be, it must be reciprocal. But God's love is the love of the Creator for his precious creatures, whom he sees cheerfully destroying themselves and each other as they defy the ways in which they were made to live. Deeper than that, he sees his own chosen people, people who symbolically married him at Sinai, using the marriage jewelry he gave them in an attempt to buy the favors of other lovers. How should he respond to this? With disinterested amusement? Or with tongue-clicking dismissal? How could he? No, he responds with rage. Not only has his constructive love been rejected, but it has been responded to with self-destructive defiance. How could a deeply caring Creator respond otherwise?

The point just made needs to be underlined here. This is not the self-oriented rage of an offended tyrant. For such a person, the only satisfaction can be the utter destruction of the offender. That is not the case with Yahweh. This is the anger of brokenhearted Creator-Husband. He is not concerned for his position, or his rights, or his image. He is enraged at what his spouse is doing to herself by rejecting his love. So we hear him crying "How can I give you up?" (Hos 11:8). This is, of course, what simple cause and effect reality dictates. She must be allowed to experience the necessary results of her choices. The offended tyrant would be delighted with that outcome. But no, Yahweh's anger is not the end of the story, which is precisely what the New Testament is asserting. His anger is for a moment, but his favor is for a lifetime (Ps 30:5 [MT 6]). The Creator/Husband, the Father, will find a way so that his anger will not be the end of the story (cf. Hos 2:13–15 [MT 15–17]).

Selected Bibliography

On Huldah

Auld, A. G. "Prophets Shared—But Recycled." Pages 19–28 in *The Future of the Deuteronomic History*. Edited by Thoms Römer. BETL 147. Louvain: Peeters, 2000.

Edelman, D. "Huldah the Prophet – of Yahweh or Asherah." Pages 231–50 in *Feminist Companion to Samuel and Kings.* Vol. 5 of The Feminist Companion to the Bible. Edited By Karla G. Shargent, Athalya Brenner. Sheffield: Sheffield Academic, 1994.

Hamori, E. J. "The Prophet and the Necromancer: Women's Divination for Kings." *JBL* 132 (2013): 827–43.

Handy, L. K. "Reading Huldah as being a Woman." *BR* 55 (2010): 5–44.

Pietsch, M. "Prophetess of Doom: Hermeneutical Reflections in the Huldah Oracle (2 Kings 22)." Pages 71–80 in *Soundings in Kings: Perspectives and Methods in Contemporary Scholarship.* Edited by Mark Leuchter, Klaus-Peter Adam. Minneapolis: Fortress, 2010.

On the Identity of the Book of the Torah

Ben-Dov, Jonathan. "Writing as Oracle and as Law: New Contexts for the Book-find of King Josiah." *JBL* 127 (2008): 223–39.

Droge, A. J. "'The Lying Pen of the Scribes': Of Holy Books and Pious Frauds." *MTSR* 15 (2003): 117–47.

Glatt-Gilad, D. A. "Revealed and Concealed: The Status of the Law (Book) of Moses Within the Deuteronomistic History." Pages 185–99 in *Mishneh Todah: Studies in Deuteronomy and Its Cultural Environment in Honor of Jeffrey H. Tigay*. Edited by Nili Sacher Fox, David A. Gilat-Gilad, Michael Williams. Winona Lake, IN: Eisenbrauns, 2009.
Henige, D. "Found but Not Lost: A Skeptical Note on the Document Discovered in the Temple under Josiah." *JHS* 7 (2007): 1–17.
Na'aman, N. "The 'Discovered Book' and the Legitimation of Josiah's Reform." *JBL* 130 (2011): 47–62.
Paul, M. J. "Hilkiah and the Law (2 Kings 22) in the 17th and 18th Centuries: Some Influences on W. M. L. de Wette." Pages 9–12 in *Deuteronomium: Entstehung Gestalt und Botschaft*. Edited by Norbert Lohfink. Leuven: Leuven University Press, 1985.
Stott, Katherine. "Finding the Lost Book of the Law: Re-reading the Story of 'The Book of the Law' (Deuteronomy–2 Kings) in Light of Classical Literature." *JSOT* 30 (2005): 153–69.
Sweeney, M. A. *King Josiah of Judah: The Lost Messiah of Israel*. Oxford: Oxford University Press, 2001.

Josiah's Reforms (23:1–27)

Translation

1 The king sent and they gathered to him all the elders of Judah and Jerusalem
2 The king went up to the house of Yahweh along with every man of Judah
and all the inhabitants of Jerusalem with him and the priests and the prophets
and all the people from small to great. He read in their ears all the words of
the book of the covenant that was found in the house of Yahweh. **3** The king
stood beside the column and made the covenant before Yahweh to walk after
Yahweh and keep his commands and his testimonies and his statutes with all
the heart and with all the mind and to establish the words of this covenant
written in this book, and all the people stood in the covenant. **4** The king
commanded Hilkiah, the chief priest, and the priests of the second order
and the keepers of the doors to bring out from the temple of Yahweh all the
objects made for Baal and the Asherah and for all the host of heaven; and
he burned them outside of Jerusalem on the terraces[26] of the Kidron and
carried their ashes to Bethel. **5** He did away with the idol-priests the kings
of Judah had put in place to burn incense on the high places in the cities
of Judah and the surroundings of Jerusalem and those offering to Baal and

26. The word שְׁדֵמוֹת, *šᵉdēmôṯ* would normally be translated "fields." But that seems strange in reference to the relatively narrow, steep-sided Kidron Valley. The word appears in connection with vines in Isa 16:8, and this has led to the suggestion that perhaps "terraces" is intended.

to the sun, the moon, the constellations,[27] and all the host of heaven. **6** He brought the Asherah from the house of Yahweh outside of Jerusalem to the Kidron Valley and burned it in the Kidron Valley, smashing it to dust, and scattered the dust among the tombs of the common people. **7** He tore down the quarters of the male cult prostitutes that were in the house of Yahweh, where the women were weaving hangings for the Asherah. **8** He brought all the priests from the cities of Judah and defiled the high places where the priests burned incense from Geba to Beersheba. He broke down the high places of the gates that were at the entrance of the gate of Joshua, officer of the city, which was on the left of the gate of the city. **9** However, the priests of the high places did not come up to the altar of Yahweh in Jerusalem but rather, they ate unleavened bread along with their brothers. **10** He defiled the Tophet that is the Ben-Hinnom Valley so that no one could make his son or his daughter pass through the fire to Molech. **11** He did away with the horses the kings of Judah had put in place for the sun at the entrance of the house of Yahweh by the chamber of Nathan-melech, the eunuch, which was in the precincts and he burned the chariots of the sun with fire. **12** As for the altars on the roof of the upper chamber of Ahaz which the kings of Judah had made, and the altars which Manasseh had made in the two courts of the house of Yahweh, the king tore them down and crushed them and scattered their dust in the Kidron Valley. **13** As for the high places which were east of Jerusalem, south of the Mount of Corruption, that Solomon, king of Israel, had built for Ashtaroth, vile thing of the Sidonians, and Chemosh, vile thing of Moab, and Milcom, abomination of the sons of Ammon, the king defiled them. **14** He smashed the pillars and cut down the Asherahs and filled their places with human bones. **15** Moreover, the altar that was in Bethel, the high place that Jeroboam, son of Nebat, made, who made Israel sin—moreover, that altar and high place he tore down and burned the high place, smashing[28] it to dust, and he burned the Asherah. **16** Josiah turned and saw the tombs which were there on the mountain. He sent and took the bones from the tombs and burned them on the altar and defiled it according to the word of Yahweh that the man of God spoke[29] when he foretold these events. **17** He said, "What is the monument that I see?" The men of the city said to him, "The tomb of the man of God who came from Judah and revealed these things that you have done to the altar of Bethel." **18** He said, "Let him rest; let no one disturb his bones." So, they let his bones go, along with the bones of the prophet who came from Samaria. **19** Furthermore, all the shrines of the high places that were in the cities of Samaria that the kings of Israel had

27. Vulg. "the Zodiac."

28. Taking the vb. as inf. abs. *ḥādēq*.

29. LXX has a long addition here which many believe to have been original (see NRSV and NLT).

made for provocation,[30] Josiah removed and did to them the same things he had done in Bethel. **20** He sacrificed all the priests of the high places which were there upon the altars and he burned human bones on them and returned to Jerusalem.

21 The king commanded all the people, saying, "Make a Passover to Yahweh your God as is written in this book of the covenant." **22** For no Passover like this had been made since the days of the judges when they judged Israel and all the days of the kings of Israel and Judah. **23** But in the eighteenth year of King Josiah this Passover was kept in Jerusalem.

24 Moreover, the necromancers, the mediums, the household gods, the filthy idols, and all the vile things that were seen in the land of Judah and Jerusalem Josiah burned in order to confirm the words of the Torah that were written in the book that Hilkiah the priest found in the house of Yahweh. **25** There was no king before him like him who turned to Yahweh with all his heart and all his soul and all his strength according to all the Torah of Moses, and after him none arose like him.

26 However, Yahweh did not turn from his great anger with which he was enraged against Judah on account of all the provocation with which Manasseh provoked him. **27** Yahweh said, "Indeed, Judah I will remove from in front of me, just as I removed Israel; I will reject this city that I have chosen, Jerusalem, and this house of which I said, 'My name will be there.' "

Textual Notes

1a. וַיַּאַסְפוּ: Gk. "he gathered"; Vulg. "they were gathered"; Syr. with MT.

2a. בְאָזְנֵיהֶם: Gk. "in their hearing"; Vulg. "and they all heard"; Syr. "in their presence." MT best explains.

3a. עַל־הָעַמּוּד: Vulg. "on the steps"; Gk. and Syr. with MT.

4a. וְלָאֲשֵׁרָה: Here and throughout Gk. "sacred grove"; Vulg. "grove"; Syr. "idol" or "idols."

4b. בְּשַׁדְמוֹת: Gk. transliterates; Vulg. "valley"; Syr. with MT. See the "Commentary" below.

5a. וְהִשְׁבִּית: Here and in at least two other places (vv. 8 and 14) in this passage *waw* + pf. seems to be used as a past narrative tense where normally a *wayyiqtol* form would be expected. Perhaps the influence of Aramaic where no *wayyiqtol* form exists? (See GKC §112*pp*).

30. By this point in the narrative, the writer no longer needs to tell the reader who it was whom the kings of Israel provoked. It was Yahweh, of course. The versions feel the need to fill in that piece of information, but there is no reason to emend the Heb. text.

5b. וַיְקַטֵּר: Gk. "they were burning"; Vulg. and Syr. "to burn." The latter seems to be the most probable reading. So *BHS*.

7a. בָתִּים: Gk. "chettin"; Vulg. "for the chapels"; Syr. "garments." Montgomery (539), citing Šanda and Driver, proposes an Arabic root *batt* "robes."

8a. שָׁמָּה: On this form see RJW (§185).

8b. אֶת־בָּמוֹת: Gk. "house"; Vulg. "entrance"; Syr. with MT. Most Eng. versions follow MT.

10a. K בְנֵי: Q בֶן. Q is preferred (w. the vss.). י(*yodh*) of K possibly result of י at end of prev. word.

10b. לְבִלְתִּי: Gk. omits; Vulg. and Syr. with MT. Gk. possibly the result of homoarchton with foll. wd.

11a–a. נְתַן־מֶלֶךְ הַסָּרִיס: Gk. and Syr. "Nathan, the king's eunuch"; Vulg. with MT.

11b. בַּפַּרְוָרִים: Gk. and Vulg. transliterate; Syr. "suburbs."

12a. וַיָּרָץ: Gk. "pulled down from there"; Syr. "broke them down"; Vulg. "ran from there" (w. MT). Montgomery (540), citing Kimchi, (so also *BHS*) suggests וַיְרַצֵּם שָׁם "he crushed them there."

15a–a. וַיִּשְׂרֹף אֶת־הַבָּמָה: Gk. omits; Vulg. and Syr. with MT.

15b. הֵדַק: Gk. adds "them"; Vulg. and Syr. with MT.

16a. בָּהָר: Gk. "in the city"; Vulg. and Syr. with MT.

16b. קָרָא: Gk. inserts "when Jeroboam stood in the feast by the altar. And turning, he lifted his eyes on the tomb of the man of God who had spoken"; Vulg. and Syr. with MT. This variant is very attractive since MT could have arisen by homoteleuton (from "spoke" to "spoke"), but the lack of support elsewhere makes it questionable.

17a. הַקֶּבֶר: For a discussion of the appearance of the art. on a first member construct (see GKC §127*g*).

19a. לְהַכְעִיס: All the versions add something: Gk. and Syr. "the Lord to anger"; Vulg. "the Lord." So *BHS* suggests an original אֶת־יְהוָה has dropped out. But the text may have simply been elliptical.

20a. אָדָם: See GKC (§117*d*) on the apparent indefiniteness of the object.

22a. לֹא נַעֲשָׂה כַּפֶּסַח הַזֶּה: Gk. "this Passover had not taken place"; Vulg. and Syr. with MT.

24a. בִּעֵר: Gk. "removed"; Syr. "put away"; Vulg. with MT. Gk. and Syr. attempting to soften Josiah's actions?

COMMENTARY

In spite of Huldah's two words, one of certain judgment for the nation and the other of his own death before that judgment would come, Josiah sprang into action. He did three things: he committed himself to covenant obedience (2 Kgs 23:1–3); he radically cleansed the country of anything that was not consistent with exclusive commitment to Yahweh as defined in the "Book of the Covenant" (23:4–20); and he led the people in a national celebration of the Passover (23:21–23). Several commentators argue (e.g., Cogan and Tadmor, 296; Konkel, 638) that the second action is intrusive because the Passover celebration is the expected conclusion of the reaffirmation of the covenant. As a matter of fact, that is not so. It is not the case in Exodus, Joshua, or Nehemiah, the three places where the affirmation or reaffirmation of the covenant is mentioned. In Exodus, the Passover celebration precedes the giving of the covenant by three months, and the covenant meal that is described in Exodus 24:9–12 has nothing to do with Passover. In Joshua (24:1–28) there is no mention of Passover, as there is none in Ezra chapters eight through ten, where the festival is the Festival of Shelters (8:13–18).

That having been said, there is no reason why the cultic cleansing described in 2 Kgs 23:4–20 could not be a topical treatment of all Josiah's actions for that purpose during his reign. The actions may have all followed his affirmation of the covenant, but some may well have preceded that event as 2 Chronicles 34:3–7 has it.[31] If the latter is the case, the editor has grouped all of the actions together here to make it clear that all Josiah did during his reign was shaped by covenant obedience, whether in response to the discovery of the book or not.

We may ask why Josiah did these three things if he knew that the outcome was already fixed (as 23:26–27 confirms). Many propose that he hoped to change God's mind by sparking a national revival. But that is nowhere said, or even implied. Furthermore, notice that all the action verbs here have Josiah as the subject. Even the description of the Passover says nothing about the people's actual involvement (in sharp contrast to 2 Chr 35:1–19). In short, as far as this book is concerned there was no national revival. Undoubtedly, there were people who were encouraged by Josiah's radical obedience and

31. Some commentators (e.g., Gray, 724) argue that the author(s) of Chronicles wish(es) to make Josiah's actions less "book" driven. This seems odd given the growing prominence of the Scriptures in the exile and after. One would think the opposite would be the case if something of that sort was the motive behind the Chronicler's organization of the materials. For an overall comparison of the Kings and Chronicles accounts, see David L. Washburn, "Perspective and Purpose: Understanding the Josiah Story," *TJ* 12 (1991): 59–78.

were themselves motivated to the same kind of obedience, but as far as the nation was concerned, it was only the king who was revived. This suggests that Josiah's motives were genuinely pure. Why did he do these things? Simply because they were what his God, the eternal Yahweh, wanted. If Yahweh wanted Josiah's whole heart and whole being, then that is exactly what Josiah was prepared to give. If Yahweh, the transcendent One, was the sole God, and if worship of all of the forces of the cosmos was a denial of that truth, then Josiah was prepared to carry out every one of Yahweh's commands in that respect. He was not doing these things for any other reason. Truly, this was a man who was in the tradition of his ancestor David, "a man after God's own heart" (1 Sam 13:14).

1–3 Although representatives of the entire nation ("every man of Judah"), and much, if not all, of the population of Jerusalem ("all the inhabitants ... from small to great") was present for this event, as it is described it falls well short of the national reaffirmation of the covenant that many commentators glowingly describe. The king standing in his place of authority "beside the column" (עַל־הָעַמּוּד, *ʿal-hā ʿammûḏ*) (see the coronation of Joash, 2 Kgs 11:12–14) "read...the book of the covenant" (v. 2) and "he made the covenant before Yahweh (וַיִּכְרֹת אֶת־הַבְּרִית לִפְנֵי יהוה, *wayyiḵrōṯ ʾeṯ-habbᵉrîṯ lip̄nê yhwh*) ... and all the people stood in the covenant (וַיַּעֲמֹד כָּל־הָעָם בַּבְּרִית, *wayyaʿămōḏ kol-hā ʿām babbᵉrîṯ*)" (v. 3). It was Josiah who made the covenant while the people "stood" in it.[32] Many argue (e.g., Fritz, 402; Hobbs, 328; Provan, 272) that "stood" here implies agreement or acceptance (NIV "pledged themselves," ESV and NRSV "joined in"). But even if we grant this not very obvious interpretation, note what is not said. There is no trace of conviction or repentance among the people. When Josiah had first heard these words, he had torn his clothes and hurried to obtain some prophetic word on what they might mean for him and his people. Not so here among these people. When Ezra read the Torah to the people at the Water Gate there were cries of anguish (Neh 8:9) followed by sackcloth and ashes (9:1). Not so here. It is also interesting that, unlike Joshua, who had earnestly sought to disabuse his people of their compromised attitudes toward following God (Josh 24:19–24) no one here, not Josiah, or Hilkiah, or anyone else does so. Some commentators (e.g., Seow, 286) ask why Yahweh did not respond to the people's repentance but stubbornly hung onto the sins of Manasseh as a reason to destroy the nation. But there is no indication of any national repentance. Chronicles says the people kept the covenant as long as Josiah lived (2 Chr 34:33), but it, like Kings, gives no indication of national repentance.[33] The suggestion is that they were willing to do what the king wanted as long

32. This is the only place in the Bible where this phrase occurs.

33. 2 Chronicles 34:32, 33 tellingly says that Josiah *made* the people join in the covenant and *made* them serve the Lord (both verbs are in the *hiphil*). Again, this is well short of a voluntary national repentance.

as he was alive, but it was not what they wanted, and the instant he was gone, they slid right back into the old ways, which was what they really wanted.

4–20 Josiah's actions (not the people's) in response to the stipulations of the covenant as expressed in the book of Deuteronomy fall into five categories (the commentary following will be organized according to these categories): (1) cleansing the temple in Jerusalem (vv. 4, 6–7, 11–12); (2), removing both idolatrous priests, and those priests who had served Yahweh at the various high places throughout the land, and destroying those high places (vv. 5, 8–9); (3), cleansing Jerusalem and its surroundings (vv. 8[?], 10, 13–14); (4), destroying the high place at Bethel (vv. 15–18); (5), destroying the high places and priesthood in Samaria (vv. 19-20).[34] The goal was not merely destruction, as burning, crushing, doing away with, etc. clearly convey, but also desecration, as the association with death shows (vv. 6, 14, 16, 20; see also vv. 8, 10, 13 where the word "defiled" [*hiphil* of טָמֵא, *ṭāmēʾ*; "to be unclean"] is used). These objects, which were burned, crushed, and pounded to dust where possible, were never going to be used for supposedly holy purposes again. The intermingling of the reports of the first three actions perhaps shows that they were all a piece of: (1) cleansing the temple, (2) removing the high places and their priests, and (3) cleansing Jerusalem.

Cleansing the Temple

4, 6 It was not merely centralization of worship in Jerusalem that was on Josiah's mind. All the centralization in the world would not serve Yahweh if what took place in the building was hopelessly corrupt. Clearly, it was that. *Baal and Asherah*, the Canaanite fertility pair, were being worshipped there, and not merely clandestinely, but with all the accoutrements ("the objects," [הַכֵּלִים, *hakkēlîm*]). One wonders how involved Hilkiah, the priest of the second order, and the keepers of the doors were in all that pagan worship. Or perhaps they had been troubled by it all and were glad to get rid of it. In any case, they were the ones the king charged "to bring out" (לְהוֹצִיא, *lᵉhôṣîʾ*) the wretched things. Even if the idols were metal plated, they would have probably had wooden cores that could be burned. In the case of "the Asherah" (v. 6), this seems usually to have been a wooden pole and it would have been very susceptible to burning. The Kidron Valley was just to the east of the temple, so it would have been easy to take the idols directly there. It was not only a place of "tomb[s]" (קֶבֶר, *qeḇer*) (v. 6), but also of general rubbish

34. On the existence of such practices as are described here, see W. G. Dever, "The Silence of the Text: An Archaeological Commentary on 2 Kings 23," in *Scripture and Other Artifacts: Essays on the Bible and Archaeology in Honor of Philip J. King*, ed. Michael D. Coogan, J. Cheryl Exum, and Lawrence E. Stager (Louisville: Westminster John Knox, 1994), 143–158. See Zeph 1:1–5 for a catalog of sins very similar to those described here.

(Jer 31:40), so it was a very appropriate destination for what was to be both destroyed and desecrated. We know that the worship of Baal and Asherah, as well as that of the "host of heaven" (צְבָא הַשָּׁמָיִם, *ṣᵉḇāʾ haššāmāyim*), had been introduced into the temple by Manasseh (21:3–5). Second Chronicles 33:15–16 reports that he removed them at the end of his life, but that his son Amon restored them (33:22).

7 We do not know any details of the worship of Asherah (and Baal), although their association with fertility along with certain descriptions of the worship at Ugarit gives the impression that sexual activity was involved. Sexuality was far too important to life for its practice to be left outside the realm of religion. The tradition that the הַקְּדֵשִׁים, *haqqᵉḏēšîm* (lit. "holy ones, dedicated ones") were cult prostitutes is firmly rooted in the ancient versions. While the form here is masculine, the term may be a collective covering both males and females (in Deut 23:17 [MT 18] the genders are clearly differentiated). The problem was a long-standing one, as Asa is said to have removed these same kinds of people (1 Kgs 15:12). In addition to whatever else the people dedicated to Asherah were doing, the women were weaving "hangings" (בָּתִּים, *bottîm*) for the idol. The term translated "hangings" is problematic. The root word seems to be "houses" (בָּתִּים, *bāttîm*), but that makes no sense. Syriac reads "garments" (*ldḥlt*ʾ) but that looks like a guess on the basis of context.[35]

11–12 These actions relate to the outside of the house of Yahweh, at the "entrance" (מִבֹּא, *mibbōʾ*) (v. 11) and "on the roof" (עַל־הַגָּג, *ʿal-haggāḡ*) (v. 12). In both verses, the objects being destroyed are put at the beginning of the sentences in an emphatic position. The worship of the sun was common all over the ancient Near East, from Egypt to Mesopotamia, so it is not surprising that it would appear here in Jerusalem. The connection with "horses" and "chariots" is intuitive, as we can imagine the sun as a flaming chariot being driven across the sky. There is some archaeological evidence in support such as the discovery of horses with a sun-disc on their foreheads (Wiseman). It is not clear what the exact connotation of "and he did away with" (lit. "stopped," [וַיַּשְׁבֵּת, *wayyašbēṯ*] also in v. 5). Translations range from "exterminated" to "deposed" to "removed." The chariots were definitely "burned" (שָׂרַף, *śārap̄*), but the horses may have simply been taken away and put to other uses. Ezekiel mentions sun-worship at the entrance of the temple (8:16).[36] Although we do not know anything else about "Nathan-melech" (נְתַן־מֶלֶךְ, *nᵉṯan-meleḵ*), the presence of the name here adds a note of immediacy and authenticity to the

---

35. Montgomery and Gehman (539), citing Driver, propose that an Arabic root *batt*, "having to do with vestments" is involved.

36. See Mark S. Smith, "The Near Eastern Background of Solar Language for Yahweh," *JBL* 109 (1990): 29–39. See also Glen Taylor, *Yahweh and the Sun: Biblical and Archaeological Evidence for Sun Worship in Ancient Israel*, JSOTSup 111 (Sheffield: Sheffield Academic, 1993).

narrative. "Eunuch" must mean merely "official" here, because a physically mutilated man would not have been allowed into the temple.[37]

Worship on rooftops (v. 12) is known from Ugaritic literature, where, in one text, the hero (KRT) receives a revelation from El while worshipping there (*ANET,* 143). The "upper chamber of Ahaz" (עֲלִיַּת אָחָז, *ʿăliyyaṯ ʾāḥāz*) reminds us of "the steps of Ahaz" (20:11) and the two may well be related. Manasseh's placing of his altars in the two courts (21:5) is reminiscent of Ahaz's creation of a new altar and pushing Solomon's altar to one side (16:10–16). What God might want was irrelevant; it was what the king wanted that was the point. But for Josiah, the opposite was true. In the house of Yahweh, inside and out, Yahweh's instructions were everything.

Destroying the high places and removing their priests

5, 8–9 The term translated "idol-priests" (כְּמָרִים, *kᵊmārîm*; v. 5) gains this connotation from its regular association, as here, with pagan worship (see also Hos 10:5 and Zeph 1:4–5). Again, notice the ambiguous "did away with" (הִשְׁבִּית, *hišbîṯ*). The evident distinction from the "priests" described in vv. 8 and 9 suggests that there were two different "high places" (הַבָּמוֹת, *habbāmôṯ*) in operation at this time: those where the Canaanite gods and goddesses (including the heavenly constellations in v. 5)[38] were worshipped, and those where Yahweh was worshipped. The priests of the latter were brought to Jerusalem and permitted to share in the offerings received at the temple but were not permitted to serve in the temple (v. 9). This treatment is often compared to that specified for disabled priests in Leviticus 21:22–23. Although the priests referred to here had been worshipping Yahweh, they had been doing it in ways not prescribed in the Torah, and they were thus "disabled."[39]

In both cases, pagan and Yahwistic, the high places (see the "Excursus on Worship at High Places ['country shrines']") were thoroughly "defiled" (טמא, *ṭmʾ*) (v. 8). Elsewhere this involved putting human bones on them (v. 14) or even burning human bones on them (v. 20). This association with death would render them permanently unclean (cf. Lev. 21:1; Num 5:2; Deut 26:14). The statement that this was done "from Geba to Beersheba" (v. 8) expresses the geographic extent of Judah from north to south. Geba is

---

37. The term here translated "precincts" (פַּרְבָּר, *parbār*) occurs only here and is a major problem. It is often said to be a Persian loan word and its presence here taken as evidence for a late date for this part of the composition. However, that derivation is far from certain. For a wide-ranging discussion, see Donna Runnals, "The *Parwār*: A Place of Ritual Separation," *VT* 41 (1991): 324–31.

38. A loan word from Akk. *manzaltu.* Wiseman says the zodiac is not attested at this time (320–321), but certainly the idea is there in germ, if not even more established.

39. Provan seems correct in his insistence, contra some other commentators, that the prescriptions of Deut 18:6–8 concerning Levites who move to Jerusalem do not apply to this situation at all (275–76).

either Tell el-Ful, Saul's ancestral home in the territory of Benjamin (1 Sam 10:26), or Jifnah (Gophna in Maccabean times), also in Benjamin. Both are about seven miles from Jerusalem, the first north and the second northwest. Both would be in the border area between Judah and what had been Israel. Beersheba had always been the designator of the southern border of "the promised land" (Judg 20:1).

As noted in the "Excursus on Worship at High Places ('country shrines')," while "high places" were so-called because they had originally been on hilltops, most were simply altar mounds. That is clearly demonstrated by the reference to "the high places of the gates" (בָּמוֹת הַשְּׁעָרִים, *bāmôṯ haššᵉʿārîm*) in v. 8. The city gate (a complex with as many as four sets of doors)[40] was a very important location where legal, commercial, and social activities took place. It would thus not be surprising for religious activities to take place there. Since there is no "gate of Joshua" known for Jerusalem, it has been suggested that the reference is to the just-named Beersheba, where an altar was found near a gate (see Cogan and Tadmor, 287, for references). In any case, these high places are "broken down" (נָתַץ, *wᵉnāṯaṣ*) like all the rest.[41]

Cleansing Jerusalem and its Environs

10, 13–14 The reference to the "gates" in v. 8 leads directly to the treatment of "the Tophet" (הַתֹּפֶת, *hattōp̄eṯ*) in v. 10. Almost certainly the term for the device was תָּפֶת, "*tāphet*" meaning "fireplace" or "cookstove" (*HALOT*, 4.1781), in which the vowels for בֹּשֶׁת, *bōšeṯ*, "shame" have been inserted for derogatory purposes.[42] Probably the same thing has occurred with "Molech" (מֹלֶךְ, *mōlek̠*), where the original might have been Melech, i.e., "king." There is increasing controversy over what "passing through the fire" (לְהַעֲבִיר אִישׁ, *lᵉhaʿăḇîr ʾîš*) means, ranging from Fritz (407), who says flatly that there was no child sacrifice in Israel, to Long (512–13) who offers arguments that child sacrifice is the only thing that can be meant by the phrase (so also Barnes, 364–65). The reference to "burning their sons and daughters with fire" (לִשְׂרֹף אֶת־בְּנֵיהֶם וְאֶת־בְּנֹתֵיהֶם בָּאֵשׁ, *liśrōp̄ ʾeṯ-bᵉnêhem wᵉ ʾeṯ-bᵉnōṯêhem bāʾēš*) in Jeremiah 7:31 leaves no room for ambiguity, and while Ezekiel 23:37 is not quite so explicit, its statement of giving one's children to the idols for food is clear enough. On the theme of defilement through death, Jeremiah 19 repeats again and again that the "Tophet" will be nothing but a burial ground.

40. See Yadin, *Art of Warfare*, 2:370–74.

41. For discussions of shrines at city gates, see John A. Emerton, "'The High Places of the Gates' in 2 Kings XXIII 8," *VT* 44 (1994): 455–67; and Dale W. Manor, "Gates and Gods: High Places in the Gates," *S-CJ* 2 (1999): 235–53.

42. הַמַּשְׁחִית, *hammašḥîṯ* "corruption" for הַמִּשְׁחָה, *hammašḥâ* "ointment." The vb. הַשְׁחִית, *hašḥîṯ* (*hiphil* inf. cst. of שחת, *šḥt*) is often used to speak of "corrupting or departing from" God's way (Deut 4:16, 25; 31:29; Judg 2:19; 2 Chr 27:2; Isa 1:4).

13–14 These verses contain the climactic statement on the cleansing of Jerusalem. Here the root of the problem is traced back to its origins in Solomon, who built shrines for the gods of his wives on "the Mount of Corruption" (הַר־הַמַּשְׁחִית, *šlhar-hammašḥîṯ*), a derogatory wordplay on the Mount of Olives. Here, three hundred years after the fact, a son of David has finally destroyed the violations of the covenant that the first son of David had put in place. It is as though, with destruction for covenant breaking now inescapable, at least the circle is closed. The offense that began the whole downward spiral has at last been expunged. The narrator's contempt is expressed in his unwillingness to refer to the pagan deities in anything but derogatory terms: they are "vile things" (שִׁקּוּץ, *šiqqûṣ*) and "abominations" (תֹּעֵבָה, *tō ʿēḇâʾ*). They are not alternatives to Yahweh, but offenses against the very order of reality, and Solomon himself established them, no, not in Yahweh's city itself, but as close as possible. Now Josiah has "smashed" (שִׁבַּר, *šibbar*) "and cut down" (וַיִּכְרֹת, *wayyiḵrōṯ*) "and filled their places with human bones" (וַיְמַלֵּא אֶת־מְקוֹמָם עַצְמוֹת אָדָם, *waymallēʾ ʾeṯ-mᵉqômām ʿaṣmôṯ ʾāḏām*).

Destroying the High Place at Bethel

15–18 Having disposed of the corruption that Solomon had brought to Jerusalem, Josiah then turned to deal with the corruption that Solomon's planned successor, Jeroboam I, had brought upon the secessionist state of Israel.[43] Fearful that his people would go back to the enemy capital to worship, he had constructed gold bull idols of Yahweh, and placed one immediately on the border with Judah in Bethel, the ancient site that was hallowed by the memories of Jacob's encounter with Yahweh there (1 Kgs 12:26–30). His nerve in so doing is almost breathtaking. But he was committed, as seen in his refusal to alter anything even when a Judean prophet had condemned the entire complex and predicted that a man named Josiah would one day destroy it all (1 Kgs 13:1–8).

Now that day had come, and Josiah brought the ashes of the burned idols of Jerusalem to mingle with the ashes at Bethel (v.1 4). There is an issue with "and he burned the high place" (וַיִּשְׂרֹף אֶת־הַבָּמָה, *wayyiśrōp̄ ʾeṯ-habbāmâ*) (v.15). How does one burn a mound of earth? But presumably the "high place" involved an entire complex of buildings and related structures that were indeed torn down, burned, and made into dust. Although there is no reference to the gold bull statue (it had almost certainly been taken off to Assyria as loot in the 700's BC) the language used here is reminiscent of Moses' treatment of the golden calf (Exod 32:20). He burned it and ground it to dust. In so doing he established a clear trajectory for how to deal with pagan things, and Josiah was following that trajectory most faithfully.[44]

---

43. The connection between the two actions is conveyed by the particle גַּם, *gam*.

44. Hobbs notes that some commentators say this material is secondary because it contains so many similarities to the account of Jehu's purge (2 Kgs 10:25–27) (320). But, as he says, that is exactly the point. This purge of Jerusalem and Bethel is

16 Once again the goal was not merely destruction, but also desecration. Whatever other places there might be where worship of false gods might take place, this place was never going to be so used again. Looking around, Josiah saw some "tombs" (קְבָרִים, *qᵊḇārîm*), and commanded that the bones (typically piled in the back of the tomb) should be taken out and burned with the rest of the conflagration there. It is not specified whether he knew those were the bones of the priests that had served there, as per the prophet's prediction three hundred years earlier, but a moment's reflection would have suggested that. In any case, as the text says, Josiah's actions were in direct fulfillment of those words spoken so many years earlier.[45]

17–18 One of the tombs apparently had a special marker or marking that caught Josiah's attention, and he asked about it.[46] It was the tomb of the man whose prediction Josiah was fulfilling. This underlines further the reality of predictive prophecy. Not only did his bones escape from being burned, but so did those of the old trickster who seduced the prophet into sin (1 Kgs 13:11–22). Clearly the old man's sons had carried out his command and buried him with the prophet (1 Kgs 13:31). In the original account the old prophet was said to have come from Bethel, but here he said to be from "Samaria." Two possible explanations present themselves: first the Assyrian province was called Samaria, and that general term might be used. But a second possibility is attractive: the one prophet was from Judah and the other from Samaria. Perhaps the hope of Samaria is to be found in the deliverance of Judah.

Cleansing Samaria

19–20 It is unclear from these statements just how widespread Josiah's activities were. It does not appear that he took action against any worship centers that the resettled peoples from other nations may have set up (17:29–33), but only those which had been set up by "the kings of Israel." This phrase, coupled with the repeated "the kings of Judah" (vv. 11, 12) and "Solomon, king of Israel" (v. 13) leaves no question where the responsibility for the nation's declension lies. The top leadership of the country carries that responsibility. Here, on the other hand, was one king who took it upon himself to reverse all that. They had provoked Yahweh's anger; Josiah, whatever the outcome, would do what pleased Yahweh. Chronicles has Josiah taking action as far north as Naphtali, which encompassed the Sea of Galilee (2 Chr 34:6). The Assyrian province of Samaria, which seems to be intended here, did not extend that far north. That Josiah could have taken such actions was made

---

intended to be seen as something similar, but better, because Josiah did not deviate, as Jehu did.

45. Barrick W. Boyd, "Burning Bones at Bethel: A Closer Look at 2 Kings 23,16a," *JSOT* 14 (2000): 3–16.

46. See: Jer 31:21, a road sign; Ezek 39:15, a marker for unburied bones.

possible by the rapid Assyrian decline after Ashurbanipal's death in 627 BC (Josiah's twelfth year).

The sacrifice (an intentional use of the word זָבַח, *zāḇaḥ*) of the priests on their altars arouses a shocked feeling in us. Two things should be borne in mind. First, this kind of violence was a part of those times. As Cogan and Tadmor (290) point out, the Assyrians were notable for such behavior. Second, Josiah may have felt that this kind of radical action was necessary to prevent the reinvention of this paganized Yahwism as soon as he and his troops were gone from the country. There is no indication that he was in any position to leave occupying forces, much less settlers, behind.[47, 48]

21–23 As noted above, there is no necessary connection between this Passover celebration and Josiah's reaffirmation of the covenant. It is presented here as one more evidence of Josiah's devotion to Yahweh. Exactly what is meant by the statement "that no Passover like this had been made since the days of the judges" (כִּי לֹא נַעֲשָׂה כַּפֶּסַח הַזֶּה מִימֵי הַשֹּׁפְטִים, *kî lōʾ naʿăśāh kappesaḥ hazze mîmēy haššōp̄ṭîm*) is not clear. In the first place, (setting aside for the moment the Passover celebrated by Hezekiah, as reported by Chronicles [2 Chr 30:1–31:1]), the last Passover reported by the Bible occurred during Joshua's lifetime (Josh 5:10–11). None is reported during the judges period (including, as 2 Chr 35:18 has it, the time of Samuel). In the second, what is to be made of Hezekiah's Passover, which is said to have surpassed anything since Solomon (2 Chr 30:26)? No truly satisfactory answer is forthcoming for the latter question.[49] But perhaps the answer to the former question is that there has been no celebration of a truly national Passover since the time of Samuel. Perhaps this refers to the increasing separation of Judah and Israel that was occurring then and that was never truly healed in the united kingdom under David and Solomon (see the "Commentary" on 1 Kgs 4:7–19). Now, perhaps even more than in the time of Hezekiah, with the destruction of the bull altar at Bethel, the writer is saying that Yahweh is again purely worshipped throughout the entire nation.

A related question arises about the celebration of the Passover. Are we to believe that the Passover had not been celebrated at all during the years between the time of the judges and that of Josiah? A possible answer is that it had continued through those years as an essentially family-oriented

47. See Deut 13:5–11; 18:20; 1 Kgs 18:40.

48. Mordechai Cogan, "A Slip of the Pen? On Josiah's Actions in Samaria (2 Kings 23:15–20)" in *Sefer Moshethe Moshe Weinfeld Jubilee Volume: Studies in the Bible and the Ancient Near East, Qumran, and Post-Biblical Judaism*, ed. Chaim Cohen, Avi Hurvits, Shalom M. Paul (Winona Lake, IN: Eisenbrauns, 2004), 3–8.

49. It is especially puzzling in Chronicles, which reports both events within five chapters (30–35), and gives the same encomium to Josiah's Passover as is found in Kings, with the exception that the previous Passover event is specified as being that of Samuel (2 Chr 35:18).

celebration, but that here (following the lead of Hezekiah?) had been made a truly national celebration sponsored by the king.

As far as the biblical account in Joshua through Kings goes, we see two Passover celebrations forming an inclusio around the entire history. The first occurs after the first foothold on the land has been obtained. It is celebrated at Gilgal (Josh 5:10–11). The second is here, as the land, as Moses had foretold, is about to spit them out (Lev 18:28; 20:22). There is, of course, a terrible irony here, but there is also a glimmer of hope. God had brought them into the land by grace, and he had sustained them in the land in spite of generations of refusing to listen to him. Perhaps, as the death angel had been frustrated through the blood before, he could be frustrated again, and the apparent death of the exile would not be death at all.

24–25 These two verses function to summarize both Josiah's accomplishments and his character that lay behind those accomplishments. Here there is added to the destruction of "the filthy idols" (הַגִּלֻּלִים, *haggillulîm*) and "the vile things" (הַשִּׁקֻּצִים, *haššiqquṣîm*), that is, all the idol worship that had been common in the land, the occult spirituality that went with it (see Deut 18:9–14), including the attempts to inquire of the dead ("necromancers" [אֹבוֹת, *ʾōḇôṯ*], "mediums" [יִדְּעֹנִים, *yiddᵊʿōnîm*]), and devices for divination ("teraphim" [תְּרָפִים, *tᵊrāp̄îm*]).[50]

Where did the radical activity that the king undertook spring from? It sprang from a devotion to Yahweh largely unparalleled in the Judean kings (exceptions are Asa, Jehoshaphat, the young Joash, the young Azariah, and Hezekiah), and never paralleled in the Israelite kings. As mentioned above (see on 18:5), Knoppers sees Hezekiah unparalleled in his trust, whereas Josiah was unparalleled in the way he rooted out paganism.[51] But those actions sprang from the core of his being: "heart, soul, and strength" (בְּכָל־לְבָבוֹ וּבְכָל־נַפְשׁוֹ וּבְכָל־מְאֹדוֹ, *bᵊḵol-lᵊḇāḇô ûḇᵊḵol-napšô ûḇᵊḵol-mᵊʾōḏô*), just as Deut 6:4 and 5 had directed. Brueggemann (559), citing Deuteronomy 34:10–12, goes so far as to argue that the closest comparison is to Moses himself. Whether that is the author's intention or not, the point is very clear: this man was such a king as Yahweh intended for his people. Sadly, he was unique, particularly so in that none of his three sons, or his grandson, who succeeded him were "like him" (כָּמֹהוּ, *kāmōhû*).

26–27 These two verses come as a surprise to most readers who, schooled correctly, believe that God's "property is always to have mercy," as one of the rituals of the church says. This is particularly so when there has been evidence of sincere repentance as has been shown here. Thus, we are prepared for Yahweh to forgive the sin of his people once more and offer deliverance from

50. On teraphim and their uses see Gen 31:19–35; Judg 17:5; 18:14–20; 1 Sam 15:23; 19:13; Ezek 21:21; Hos 3:4–5; Zech 10:2.

51. Knoppers, "None Like Him," 411–31.

coming destruction. Instead, these verses give a picture of divine implacability. Regardless of what Josiah and his people may have done, no mercy will be extended. Manasseh was one wicked king too many; he had "provoked" (כעס, *k ʿs*) Yahweh beyond the limits of his patience. Rejection will trump chosenness. Thus, readers must wrestle with the apparent inconsistency of Yahweh.

I have suggested above that to read the passage (concluded by these two verses) in this way is incorrect. The passage only seems to depict one man's repentance, not that of the people as a whole, and I believe the narrator has given us enough literary clues that he thinks he does not have to belabor the point. Did the people acquiesce in what Josiah wanted to do, and did do? Yes. Did they feel any godly sorrow for what they had done (and would do again)? There is no evidence of it. It was Josiah who committed himself to the covenant while they woodenly agreed. It was Josiah who burned and crushed the idols while they stood by. It was Josiah who turned to Yahweh with all his heart, soul, and strength, not they. We do not have a God who refuses to forgive; we have a people who refuse to repent. Is there a limit to Yahweh's patience? Absolutely, and they have reached it. But they have not reached it in spite of turning back to him. They have reached it because even the best king they ever had could not inspire them to radical, inter-generational change of behavior. Their settled choices were so ingrained in the culture that it sucked in even Josiah's own sons and grandson.

Biblical Theology Comments

Radical Treatment of Sin

It is tempting to see the kind of radical action that Josiah took here as being distinctively "Old Testament" behavior. Surely this immoderate burning, crushing, smashing, and even killing, was indicative of a brutal, immoderate kind of culture that "Old Testament" ethics lead one to. Without denying that the behavior was expressive of other cultural norms than those which the teachings of the New Testament have produced in the West, I would like to point out that Jesus Christ displays a remarkably similar attitude toward sin as did Josiah. It was Jesus who said: "If your right eye causes you to stumble, gouge it out and throw it away. It is better for you to lose one part of your body than for your whole body to be thrown into hell. And if your right hand causes you to stumble, cut it off and throw it away. It is better for you to lose one part of your body than for your whole body to go into hell." (Matt 5:29–30 NIV). It was also he who said, ""Things that cause people to stumble are bound to come, but woe to anyone through whom they come. It would be better for them to be thrown into the sea with a millstone tied around their neck than to cause one of these little ones to stumble" (Luke 17:1–2 NIV).

In fact, the Bible is quite consistent in its insistence that sin is not a little peccadillo, a "slip-up," a "mistake," that can be glossed over and forgotten. Sin is an offense against the very nature of reality, a cancer that will grow aggressively unless the most radical action is taken to root it out. While we do not have a theocratic society in which the "king" has the duty to destroy everything that is not in keeping with the covenant of God, we as churches, and believers within churches, must look at sin in our midst, and particularly in ourselves, with the most serious concern. We dare not coddle it, nor try to explain it away, or worst of all, try to justify it. We must root it out, and the operative word is "root." Not a root of the sin must be left in place. It is deadly, and like the sin of idolatry in Israel and Judah, contaminates everything it touches.

The Importance of Predictive Prophecy

Many commentators gloss over the explicit statement about the fulfillment of the prediction found in this passage. Unquestionably, it is very stark in what it says. Can we possibly believe that a man in tenth century BC could predict what another man, even to the extent of naming that man, would do three hundred years later? Certainly, we cannot if ordinary human rationality is our only standard. If that is the standard then we must say that someone, wanting to convince the reader that Josiah's actions were divinely inspired, created the account of the prophet as a way of justifying what the Judean king did. But the question is: *was* Josiah divinely inspired? For those without a belief in God the answer is very simple: of course not. Josiah's motives were self-serving and political in nature. But what if we have a belief in God? Then the issue begins to get complicated. The responses are often self-contradictory. Yes, there is a God; yes, he did reveal himself to the Israelites; yes, Josiah was motivated by love of God (as he thought he knew what God wanted), but no, God cannot (or perhaps, does not) foretell the future. We must say that the person who inserted the bits about fulfilled prophecy was well intended, but unfortunately misguided. Or perhaps naïve persons heard these kinds of folktales and took them for fact.

But the inescapable question remains, if the argument from fulfilled prophecy is rejected, what other arguments must be rejected as well? It will not do to appeal to the faith argument (just accept the truth of God by faith), because the Bible will not allow us to do that. It tells us in no uncertain terms that we ought to accept its vision of Yahweh on the basis of what he did in time and space. Fulfilled prophecy, culminating in the coming of Jesus Christ, is one of the inseparable features of what it is claimed God both revealed and completed. In particular, see the claims of Isaiah 41–55, where Yahweh's ability to predict the future and explain the course of history is made proof positive that he is not like the gods, a prisoner of this cosmos, but is the transcendent One who stands outside of history and sees it in its entirety. In short, we do not have the luxury of saying that the Bible reveals the transcendent God who has spoken to his people while at the same time saying that what the Bible purports to have him saying is impossible. It is the Bible itself which will not allow this.

Selected Bibliography

Eynikel, E. "The Reform of King Josiah: 2 Kings 23:1–24." Pages 394–425 in *Septuaginta – Texte, Contexte, Lebenswelten: international Fachtagung veranstaltet von Septuaginta Deutsch (LXX. D), Wuppertal 20.-23. Juli 2006.* WUNT 219. Edited by Martin Karrer, Wolfgang Kraus. Tübingen: Mohr Siebeck, 2008.

Fried, L. S. "The High Places (*Bāmôt*) and the Reforms of Hezekiah and Josiah: An Archeological Investigation." *JAOS* 122 (2002): 437–65.

McConville, J. G. "Narrative and Meaning in the Books of Kings." *Bib* 70 (1989): 31–49.

Na᾿aman, N. "The Distribution of Messages in the Kingdom of Judah in Light of the Lachish Ostraca." *VT* 53 (2003): 169–80.

Paul, M. J. "King Josiah's Renewal of the Covenant (2 Kings 22 –23)." Pages 269–76 in *Pentateuchal and Deuteronomistic Studies: Papers Read at the Thirteenth IOSOT Congress, Leuven, 1989.* Edited by Christianus Brekelmans and Johan Lust. BETL 94. Louvain: Leuven University Press, 1990.

Josiah's Death (23:28–30)

Translation

28 The rest of the matters pertaining to Josiah and all that he did, are they not written in the chronicles of the kings of Judah? **29** In his days Pharaoh Neco, king of Egypt went up to the king of Assyria on the river Euphrates, and King Josiah went up to meet him, and he killed him there when he saw him. **30** His servants carried him dying from Megiddo and brought him to Jerusalem and buried him in his tomb. The people of the land took Jehoahaz, son of Josiah, and anointed him and made him king in place of his father.

Textual Notes

29a. עַל־מֶלֶךְ: The versions all read "against," the normal rendering of this preposition. However, it is known that Egypt was an ally of Assyria at this time. So, many commentators recommend reading the preposition as "to," recognizing that עַל and אֶל are often interchangeable. RJW (§§ 295, 300), notes that both can mean "on behalf of."

29b. וַיְמִיתֵהוּ: Syr. adds "to fight with him, and Pharaoh said to him, 'I have not come against you, turn aside from me.' But Josiah would not listen, so Pharaoh"; Gk. and Vulg. with MT. Syr. seems to be an attempt to reconcile this passage with the parallel in 2 Chr 35:20–24.

30a. וַיִּקְבְּרֻהוּ: Gk. adds "in the city of David"; Vulg. and Syr. with MT.

COMMENTARY

This concluding regnal summary is noteworthy for two reasons. The first is the account of Josiah's death in verse twenty-nine, and the second is the unusual wording regarding Josiah's successor, Jehoahaz. Many commentators (see above on 22:20), assuming that Josiah's violent death invalidates Huldah's prediction that Josiah would be buried in peace (22:20), posit some later redaction to explain this account. But the strange thing about redactors, as has been repeatedly observed, is that they are so inconsistent. If a redactor felt that it was important to include this report, why did he not redact Huldah's prophecy at the same time. Why leave these supposedly contradictory statements staring at each other across less than two chapters?

The answer to this question is that the writer did not believe them to be contradictory. As pointed out in the comments above on 22:20, it is only necessary to understand that "buried in peace" does not say anything about the manner of death, but merely that Josiah would not live to see the kingdom of Judah in mortal turmoil. Isaiah's comment about the death of the righteous being a blessing because they are delivered from evil (57:1–2) is very apropos here (see also Wiseman, 299).

A more difficult question is why Josiah apparently attempted to stop Neco in his drive north (the text as it stands—"to meet" [לִקְרָאתוֹ, *liqrā ʾṯô*]—is quite ambiguous about Josiah's purposes). Given the historical fact that the pharaoh's intent was to help the Assyrians (which requires rendering the preposition עַל, *ʿal* as "to" in the sense of advantage)[52] Josiah may have been hoping to keep a weak Assyria between himself and the emerging Babylonian power. It is also possible that he simply wanted to thwart growing Egyptian power. Or, as some (e.g., Barnes, 370) suggest, he may have been summoned to meet Neco and submit to him. In any case it turned out to be a bad choice, even a tragic one. We can only wonder whether if he had lived longer his reforms would have reached deeper into his people's hearts. Chronicles, seeking to explain Josiah's tragic death, has him rejecting the word of God as spoken by Neco (2 Chr 35:21). This idea that, the word of God could be delivered through an unbeliever, is a very remarkable development. The Chronicles account also specifies that Josiah died in Jerusalem whereas this account seems to have him either dead at Megiddo or dying on the way to

52. RJW (§§295, 300). But see J. Richard Coggins, "2 Kings 23,29: A Problem of Method in Translation," in *Pentateuchal and Deuteronomistic Studies: Papers Read at the 13th IOSOT Conference, Leuven, 1989,* ed. Christianus Brekelmans and Johan Lust, BETL 94 (Louvain, Leuven University Press, 1990), 277–81, who believes the writer was not aware of the actual historical facts, a point Cogan and Tadmor deny (301).

Jerusalem.[53] For discussions of the motives and methods of the Chronicler, readers should consult those commentaries.

As with many other instances in these accounts, we are left wishing for more details. This is especially true in the closing regnal accounts. So, in 1 Kings 22:39, we should like to know much more about Ahab's "ivory house" and about "the cities that he built." But we are not given any more information because in the writers' minds, such information is not relevant to the main point regarding Ahab's relationship to Yahweh. The same is true here. We need to know why and how Josiah died, but we don't need to know more than the bare bones because this information does not bear upon the main points being made in the account. The points are these: it was possible for any son of David to walk in the shoes of his great father if he so chose, but that it is also possible for a people to be so far gone in the sins of the fathers that even the best example possible cannot alter the destiny resulting from the choices of another generation that they have made their own. Jesus' words to Judas are very apropos here: "For the Son of Man goes as it is written of him, but woe to that man by whom the Son of Man is betrayed!" (Mark 14:21 ESV). Jesus had to be betrayed, but that did not absolve Judas of personal responsibility. So here, the sins of Manasseh had to be judged, but these people were not innocent.

30 Megiddo is the ancient city which guarded the pass of Arauna where the great international highway penetrated the Carmel ridge line, either coming north from the coast, or south from the Jezreel Valley. This has been a choke point through the centuries and it appears that it was in the control of the Egyptians at this time (so Wiseman, 324–25). So, it is possible that Josiah was attempting to capture it. But he cannot have had an army large enough to challenge the Egyptian one, so that does not seem very likely. But perhaps he simply wanted to block the pass and prevent any more northward movement of the Egyptians. It is also possible in view of the language here that he simply wanted a parley. In any case, the result was disaster. That he could get there from Jerusalem is a testimony to the complete absence of any Assyrian forces in the former kingdom of Israel by this time.

The description of the way in which Jehoahaz became king is more developed than the usual statement found in the closing regnal summaries, which typically say "and x his son reigned in his place" (see 33:20). The lengthier description here suggests that something other than the normal succession was taking place. When we note that Jehoahaz was twenty-three years old when he began to reign (23:31) and that his brother Jehoiakim who succeeded him after only three months was twenty-five at his accession, it appears that Jehoiakim was actually the firstborn and that for some reason the people of the land (see the "Commentary" on 11:14–20 above) preferred his younger brother to him. Gray (748), in a ringing phrase, suggests that Jehoiakim was

53. The Heb. ptcp. מֵת, *mēṯ*, here rendered "dying," admits of both understandings.

"an unprincipled political adventurer," a judgment that later descriptions of his activities seem to support. Brueggemann (568), noting that Jehoahaz and Zedekiah had the same mother, wonders if there was a palace clique at work. Most others suggest that Jehoahaz may have been anti-Egyptian, on which see Commentary below (v. 31).

Biblical Theology Comments

Some scholars explain the terseness of the statements about Josiah's death here as an attempt by the author to avoid a painful discussion of an event that contradicts his simplistic theology of divine retribution: nothing but material blessing for obedience and nothing but deprivation and loss for disobedience (see, Brueggemann, 560–61 and the "Selected Bibliography" below). I suggest this is not the case at all. From Job to Habakkuk to Jesus (John 9:1–5) the Bible develops the truth that not everything that happens in the world is the result of divine retribution. For modern scholars to insist that biblical writers always held such a simplistic understanding is to favor a doctrine of the evolution of theological thought much more than it deserves. It is also to assume a theological naivete for the Old Testament thinkers that has more to do with modern pride than with clear evidence.

Selected Bibliography

Avioz, M. "Josiah's Death in the Book of Kings: A New Solution to an Old Theological Conundrum." *ETL* 83 (2007): 359–66.

Delamarter, S. "The Death of Josiah in Scripture and Tradition: Wrestling with the Problem of Evil?" *VT* 54 (2004): 29–60.

Frost, S. B. "The Death of Josiah: A Conspiracy of Silence." *JBL* 87 (1968): 369–82.

Judah's Final Days (23:31–25:30)

Introduction

With the failure of Josiah's reformation, Judah's fate was fixed – or was it? Suppose the three sons, and one grandson of Josiah had chosen to walk in their father's and grandfather's footsteps? Could it have been that Judah's destiny could yet have been altered? There is no reason to think otherwise. Some commentators think there is such a reason, that Manasseh's sin was such that nothing could alter Yahweh's free decision not to be placated by anything including Josiah's righteous behavior. They find in this freedom to judge a parallel freedom to dispense grace (e.g., Brueggemann, 559–60). But as I have argued above, there is good reason not to take that line of reasoning: that Yahweh was free to decree that in spite of the people's repentance, he was going to punish them for Manasseh's sins anyway. But the people did not repent; Josiah did, but they did not. They only acquiesced in his, and that is never enough, then or now. The consistently evil behavior of Josiah's descendants, and the evident participation of the people in this behavior, makes it plain that no national repentance had occurred, and that the trajectory firmly established by Manasseh, continued undisturbed in spite of Josiah's brief interlude.

Outline

- III. JUDAH ALONE 18:1–25:30
  - E. Judah's final days 23:21–25:30
    1. Jehoahaz 23:21–35
    2. Jehoiakim 23:36–24:7
    3. Jehoiachin 24:8–17
    4. Zedekiah 24:18–25:7
    5. The destruction of Jerusalem and Judah 25:8–21
    6. The death of Gedaliah 25:22–26
    7. Favor shown to Jehoiakim 25:27–30

Jehoahaz (23:31–35)

Translation

31 Jehoahaz was twenty-three years old when he began to reign, and he reigned three months in Jerusalem. The name of his mother was Hamutal, daughter of Jeremiah from Libnah. **32** He did evil in the sight of Yahweh as his fathers had done. **33** Pharaoh Neco imprisoned him in Riblah in the land of Hamath from being king in Jerusalem, and he put a tribute on the land of one hundred talents of silver and a talent of gold. **34** Pharaoh Neco made Eliakim, son of Josiah, king in place of Josiah his father, and he changed his name to Jehoiakim; as for Jehoahaz, he took him and brought him[1] to Egypt, and he died there. **35** As for the silver and the gold, Jehoiakim gave it to the pharaoh. However, he taxed the land to give the money that the pharaoh demanded. He took the silver and the gold from the people of the land to give it to Pharaoh Neco.

Textual Notes

32a–a. אֲשֶׁר־עָשׂוּ אֲבֹתָיו: Syr. "just as Manasseh had done"; Gk. and Vulg. with MT.

33a–a. וַיַּאַסְרֵהוּ פַרְעֹה נְכֹה בְרִבְלָה: Gk. "he removed him … to Diblath; Syr "he bound him … in Diblah"; Vulg. with MT.

33b. K בִּמְלֹךְ: Q מִמְּלֹךְ "from being king." In Ugaritic the prep. ב can also carry the function of "from."

33c. וְכִכַּר: Gk. reads "one hundred talents"; Syr. "ten talents"; Vulg. with MT.

34a. וַיָּבֹא: All the versions "and he brought him," evidently taking the vb. as a *hiphil* with a 3ms suff.

35a. אֶת־עַם: Gk. "together with" (taking אֶת as a prep.); Vulg. and Syr. "from." See the "Commentary" below.

Commentary

31 It seems likely, both from the circumstances of his reign, and from his birth order, that Jehoahaz was put on the throne by an anti-Egyptian faction in the government. According to 1 Chronicles 3:15, he was not the firstborn son of Josiah, but was actually fourth, while Jehoiakim was second.[2] This argues that

---

1. MT: לָקַח וַיָּבֹא, *lāqāḥ wayyāḇōʾ* ("he took and he came"). The versions all read "he took him and brought him" (לקחו ובאהו *lqḥw wbʾhw*).

2. The fact that Jehoahaz's mother was from Libnah, a border town between Judah and Philistia, might suggest that the marriage had a political motive. It is interesting, though probably not vitally important, that she was also the mother of the final king: Mattaniah/Zedekiah (2 Kgs 24:17–18).

the hostility to Egypt was strong enough (surely in part because of the killing of Josiah) that the powerbrokers among the "people of the land" (עַם־הָאָרֶץ, *ʿam-hāʾāreṣ*) (v. 30) were willing to go to some lengths to find a scion amenable to their goals. Neco's treatment of Jehoahaz supports that hypothesis. As soon as he had gained a secure base in Syria (v. 33, Riblah, located on the Litani river about eighteen miles south of Hamath), the Egyptian king summoned Jehoahaz (who apparently could not refuse),[3] deposed him[4] and sent him to captivity in Egypt, where he spent the rest of his life (v. 34).

32 While commentators wonder how much "evil" (הָרַע, *hāraʿ*) Jehoahaz could have done in a short, three-month reign, the point must be that as a new king, he immediately telegraphed that he had no intention of following in his father's footsteps. In his first one hundred days in office, Franklin D. Roosevelt made it clear with a sweeping set of actions what the focus of his presidency would be. That was very possibly the case with Jehoahaz. He demonstrated that his father had not established a new norm but was in fact only an aberration.[5]

33–35 Neco's actions followed the well-established pattern of domination in the Near East at that time: the conqueror deposed the present king, laid tribute on the nation, and installed a king of his own choosing. Hobbs (341) notes that the tribute here ("one hundred talents of silver and one talent of gold") was not excessive by the standards of the time (note Sennacherib's demand for three hundred talents of silver and thirty of gold, 2 Kgs 18:14) and might reflect the fact that Neco had gained control over Judah in a somewhat "accidental" way. In any case Jehoiakim, whom Neco appointed in place of Jehoahaz (not the firstborn Johanan), paid the tribute, but not by stripping the temple and palace, as previous kings had done,[6] but by taxing "the people of the land." While it is possible that there was nothing left in the treasuries, it looks very much as though this was in reprisal for their choosing Jehoahaz (v. 30).

While it was not uncommon for a king to choose a throne name different from his personal name, when the conqueror did it, as here (Eliakim to Jehoiakim, v. 34; see also 24:17), it was a sign of subjection. Jehoiakim seems to have accepted this subjection without qualms, but at the same time it must be said that he really had little choice. The statement that "and he made him

---

3. Fritz suggests that Jehoahaz might have been making an official visit (412). But if he was actually backed by an anti-Egyptian faction, it does not seem very likely that he would have visited willingly.

4. Privative use of the preposition מִן, *min*; see RJW (§321).

5. Fritz suggests that the people of the land may have selected him in the hope that he would follow his father's reform, but this summary judgment suggests that would not have been the case (412).

6. See 1 Kgs 14:26; 15:18; 2 Kgs 12:18; 16:8; 18:15–16.

king (וַיַּמְלֵךְ, *wayyamlēḵ*) in place of Josiah his father" says that in the pharaoh's mind Jehoahaz had never been king at all. Legitimacy was his alone to give. Long gone were the days when Yahweh chose the offspring who would sit on David's throne (2 Sam 7:12).

Selected Bibliography

Malamat, A. "The Twilight of Judah in the Egyptian-Babylonian Maelstrom." Pages 123–45 in *Congress Volume: Edinburgh 1974*. Edited by J.A. Emerton. VTSup 28. Leiden: Brill, 1975.

Jehoiakim (23:36–24:7)

Translation

36 Jehoiakim was twenty-five years old when he began to reign, and he
reigned eleven years in Jerusalem. His mother's name was Zebudah,[7] the
daughter of Pediah from Rumah. **37** He did evil in the sight of Yahweh
according to all his fathers had done. **24:1** In his days Nebuchadnezzar, king
of Babylon attacked Jerusalem and Jehoiakim became his servant for three
years; then he turned and rebelled against him. **2** Yahweh sent against him
bands of Chaldeans, Arameans, Moabites, and Ammonites; he sent them
against Judah to destroy it according to the word of Yahweh that he spoke
through his servants the prophets. **3** Surely, this came about in Judah at the
command of Yahweh to remove Judah from his presence on account of the
sin of Manasseh according to all that he had done. **4** Moreover, the blood of
the innocent that he poured out and filled Jerusalem with innocent blood,
Yahweh was unwilling to forgive. **5** The rest of the matters pertaining to
Jehoiakim and all that he did, are they not written in the chronicles of the
kings of Judah? **6** Jehoiakim slept with his fathers and Jehoiachin, his son,
ruled in his place. **7** The king of Egypt did not come out from Egypt anymore,
because the king of Babylon had taken all that had belonged to the king of
Egypt from the wadi of Egypt to the Euphrates River.

Textual Notes

23:36a.K זְבִידָה: Q זְבוּדָה ; Gk. "Yeldalph"; Vulg. and Syr. with MT, Vulg. and Syr. "Zebidah" with K.24:2a. יְהוָה: Gk. omits; Vulg. and Syr. with MT.

3a. עַל־פִּי: Gk. and Syr. "wrath" (MT אַף); Vulg. with MT. *CTAT* (422) is only marginally in favor of MT.

Commentary

36 The home of Zebudah, Jehoiakim's mother, has aroused a good deal of interest. Rumah is often associated with Tel er-Rumman which is in the

7. Reading with Q (זְבוּדָה). See "Textual Note" 23:36a.

Huleh Valley north of the Sea of Galilee. If that identification is correct, it lends support to claims that Josiah had extended his rule far north into the lands of the former Israel. However, the reference to Arumah in Judges 9:41 should also be noted. This site was evidently located in the vicinity of Shechem in the territory of Manasseh. This might be a bit more likely, as the Bible explicitly refers to Josiah's actions in that area (2 Kgs 23:19).

37 Given the detailed descriptions of Jehoiakim, his attitudes and behavior, in the book of Jeremiah (see Jer 22:13–19; 36:20–26), the comments here seem rather bland. However, as far as the editor(s) here are concerned, this is enough. If a man "has done evil in the sight of Yahweh" (וַיַּעַשׂ הָרַע בְּעֵינֵי יהוה, *wayya ʿaś hāra ʿ bᵊ ʿênê yhwh*) that is really all that needs to be said, especially at this point in Judah's history, when the nation's fate, unless a radical revival should take place, is already set. The nation would not be destroyed because of Jehoiakim's sins, but because of the sins of his ancestors, particularly those of Manasseh, in which he fully participated.

24:1–4 In 605 BC the Babylonian army dealt the final blow to any hope Egypt may have had of filling the vacuum left in the Levant by Assyria's collapse. Led by Nabopolassar's son Nebuchadnezzar, the Babylonians defeated the Egyptians in a devastating manner in a battle fought at Carchemish on the Euphrates in northern Syria. The Egyptian collapse was complete, as indicated by v. 7. However, the process was not immediate because Nabopolassar died that same year and it was necessary for Nebuchadnezzar to return to Babylon to claim the throne. Thus, it was probably in 604 that Nebuchadnezzar returned to Syro-Palestine to claim the spoils of his victory. It would have been in that year that Jehoiakim, apparently with as few qualms as those with which he had accepted Egyptian vassalship, became a Babylonian vassal. But that only lasted three years before he broke his covenant with Babylon and revolted. [8] Verse two suggests that Nebuchadnezzar had other matters to attend to and did not immediately send his army to besiege the city. In fact, he had suffered a serious defeat at the border of Egypt in 601 BC, and apparently retired to Babylon to rebuild his army.[9] It may have been that event that precipitated Jehoiakim's revolt. Thus, it is possible that the "bands" (גְּדוּדֵי, *gᵊḏûḏê*) referred to in verse two reflect a chaotic situation where roving bands were loose in the countryside molesting whomever they could. It is not clear whether or not they might have been acting in response to some nominal Babylonian direction; the reference to the "Chaldeans" (כַּשְׂדִּים, *k̲aśdîm*) suggests they might have been. Once again, however, the author's view of history is apparent in that he does not see

8. It would have been at this time that Daniel and his companions would have been taken into exile as hostages.

9. Hobbs observes that although Neco repulsed Nebuchadnezzar, he no longer had the resources to recover whereas Nebuchadnezzar did (351).

these "bands" either as having been sent by Nebuchadnezzar, or as being simply opportunistic. It was Yahweh who sent them (... וַיְשַׁלַּח יהוה, *wayšallaḥ yhwh* ...). Judah's downfall was not a matter of chance, nor was it the result of geopolitical developments. It was the predicted outcome of a refusal to keep the covenant that the one transcendent God had made with them centuries earlier (see 2 Kgs 21:14–15.)

3–4 Here, the particular sin of Manasseh that is used to characterize and sum up all his sins is that of shedding "innocent blood" (דָּם נָקִי, *dām nāqî*). As noted above (see the "Commentary" on 21:16), while this charge does certainly relate to actual acts of bloodshed, it also seems to be something of a shorthand for injustice of all sorts, especially toward the poor and helpless. Their lives are trampled underfoot, and their lifeblood is poured out on the altar of injustice. This is the particular mark of covenant keeping, along with exclusive worship of Yahweh: reflecting his holy character in the treatment of others, especially those who cannot repay those who care for them. In the absence of any real repentance for this behavior on the part of the people, there was no basis upon which God could "forgive" (סלח, *slḥ*).[10]

5–6 Although there is a final reference to "the chronicles of the kings of Judah" in regard to Jehoiakim in verse six, the data must have been sketchy since the manner of Jehoiakim's death and his replacement by Jehoiachin is left unclear. 2 Chronicles 36:6 has him captured and taken to Babylon in chains. Kings, on the other hand, says only that "he slept with his fathers," usually a reference to a normal, peaceful death. However, the fact that he was only thirty-six years old when he died does not suggest a normal death. Thus, some believe that he was assassinated when the siege became too severe in the hope that his son would do what he in fact did, surrender.[11] Others suggest that he may have died from one of the diseases rampant in a besieged city. In any case, Jehoiakim seems to have died un-mourned; the closing regnal account is about as uninformative as it is possible to be while still conforming to the established pattern.

7 Although it is apparent that Neco defeated Nebuchadnezzar when the latter attempted to complete his triumphal tour by taking Egypt in 601–600 BC, it is also apparent, as Hobbs trenchantly observes, that Nebuchadnezzar had the resources to recover from that defeat, whereas Neco had no resources

---

10. Brueggemann points out that the only other places where סלח, *slḥ* as "forgive" appears in this book are in the repeated petitions in Solomon's prayer (1 Kgs 8:30, 34, 36, 39, 50) (572). Thus, a sad kind of inclusio is produced.

11. Cogan and Tadmor, citing Bright, *History*, 3rd ed., 327 (307). For an argument that he died a natural death, see O. Lipschitz, "'Jehoiakim Slept with His Fathers' (II Kings 24:6): Did He?," *JHS* 4 (2002): 1–33. For a description of the horrors of a siege, see Deut 28:47–57.

to capitalize on his victory, with the result that the Egyptian was unable to recover from Babylon the lands of the Levant that had been taken from him.

Selected Bibliography

Oded, B. "When Did the Kingdom of Judah Become Subjected to Babylonian Rule?" *Tarbiz* 65 (1965): 103–7.

Jehoiachin (24:8–17)

Translation

8 Jehoiachin was eighteen years old when he began to reign and he reigned three months in Jerusalem. His mother's name was Nehushta, daughter of Elnathan from Jerusalem. **9** He did evil in the sight of Yahweh according to all that his father had done. **10** At that time the servants of Nebuchadnezzar, the king of Babylon, had attacked Jerusalem, and the city had come under siege. **11** Nebuchadnezzar, king of Babylon, came to[12] the city while his servants were besieging it. **12** Jehoiachin, king of Judah went out to[13] the king of Babylon, he and his mother and his servants and his officers and his eunuchs, and the king of Babylon took him in the eighth year of his reign. **13** He took out from there all the treasures of the house of Yahweh and all the treasures of the house of the king. He cut into pieces all the gold objects that Solomon, king of Israel, had made for the temple of Yahweh, as Yahweh had said. **14** He exiled all of Jerusalem and all the officers and all the military men, 10,000 exiles, and all the craftsmen and smiths so that none remained except the poor of the people of the land. **15** He exiled Jehoiachin to the land of Babylon and the king's mother, and the king's wives, and his eunuchs, and the leaders of the land, he exiled from Jerusalem to Babylon. **16** All the mighty men, 7,000, the craftsmen and smiths, 1,000, all the soldiers, warriors, the king of Babylon brought them as exiles to Babylon. **17** The king of Babylon made Mattaniah, his uncle, king in his place, and he changed his name to Zedekiah.

Textual Notes

10a. K עָלָה: Gk. Syr. have 3ms עָלָה "he went up"; Q עָלוּ 3mp "they went up." See the following "Textual Note."

12. Normally the construction here "come against" (with עַל, *ʿal*) means "to attack," but that seems redundant here. Syr. has "come against," but Gk. has "entered into" and Vulg. "came to," perhaps understanding that עַל and אֶל ("to") are often used interchangeably. See *IBHS* (§11.2.13).

13. Gk. has ἐξῆλθεν … ἐπὶ, *exēlthen … epi* "went out against," while Vulg. and Syr. have "went out to." Gk. seems to be reversing the interchangeability mentioned in the previous note.

10b. עַבְדֵי: Gk. omits "the servants of" (reflecting K?); Vulg. and Syr. with MT. See the previous "Textual Note."

11a. וַעֲבָדָיו: Vulg. inserts "with"; Gk. and Syr. with MT.

12a–a. וְאִמּוֹ וַעֲבָדָיו: Gk. "his servants and his mother"; Vulg. and Syr. with MT.

14a. וְהִגְלָה: Evidently a *waw* conjunctive and not *waw* consecutive.

14b. אֶת־כָּל־יְרוּשָׁלַםִ: Gk. lacks "all"; Vulg. and Syr. with MT.

14c. גּוֹלֶה: G(L) and the rest of the versions correct the spelling to גּוֹלָה ("the captivity, the exiles, etc.").

14d. עַם־הָאָרֶץ: Gk. lacks "the people of"; Vulg. and Syr. with MT.

15a. K אֱוִלֵי "fools": Q אֵילֵי "leaders." Read with Q.

17a. דֹדוֹ: Gk. "his son"; Vulg. and Syr. with MT.

Commentary

8 As noted above, Jehoiakim's relative youth at his death and Jehoiachin's[14] extreme youth at his accession (eighteen years) suggest that Jehoiakim's death was not a natural one but was somehow associated with the siege. It is possible that "El-nathan" (אֶלְנָתָן, *ʾelnāṯān*) here is the same person referred to in Jer 26:22, and 36:12, 25, an official in Jehoiakim's court.

9 Although three months does not seem to be a very long time in which to do "evil in the sight of Yahweh" (וַיַּעַשׂ הָרַע בְּעֵינֵי יהוה, *wayyaʿaś hāraʿ bᵊʿênê yhwh*), it was long enough to make it clear that no changes from the behavior of his father would be effected (see likewise 2 Kgs 15:8–9).

10–12 The arrival of Nebuchanezzar during the closing days of the siege (598 BC) seems to lend support to the hypothesis offered above (see "Commentary" on vv. 2–4 above) that Nebuchadnezzar spent some time in Babylon reorganizing his armies after his defeat at the border of Egypt in 601 BC. Now, having received word that Jerusalem is ready to capitulate, he makes an appearance to gather up the spoils. Those spoils first included the royal family as well as the high officialdom of the kingdom of Judah. Because Jehoiachin surrendered ("went out [יצא, *yṣʾ*] to [עַל, *ʿal*]"), the horrific things that were to happen to Zedekiah and his family eleven years later (25:6–7) were not visited upon Jehoiachin and his family. As Hobbs (352) points out, this event is a fulfillment of Isaiah's prophecy of some one hundred years earlier (as reported in 20:16–19).

---

14. Also called Jeconiah (Jer 24:1) and Coniah (Jer 22:24).

13 The spoils also included the "treasures" (אוֹצְרוֹת, *ʾôṣᵉrôṯ*) of the temple and the palace. The reference to Solomon is probably intentional on the part of the author, calling the reader to reflect on this sad story that began so stunningly with the abundance of gold in the temple (cf. 1 Kgs 6:19–22) reflecting the blessing of God. At the same time this reference represents the beginning of the fulfillment of the warnings that were already present in the Solomonic account regarding the infallible consequences of disobedience (1 Kgs 9:6–9).[15]

14–16 The numbers given here seem very large. Wiseman (310) notes that "10,000" is not to be taken literally but is simply a way of designating a very large number. Possibly it reflects a total including the 7,000 and 1,000 of v. 16. Brettler argues that these are actually the numbers of the final exile in 586 BC.[16] But it is not clear why such a dislocation would have taken place, or having taken place, would have been allowed to stand. On the other hand, removing the leadership, the military, and the "craftsmen and smiths" (הֶחָרָשׁ וְהַמַּסְגֵּר, *heḥārāš wᵉhammasgēr*) (confirmed in Jer 24:1) after a surrender might well represent an attempt by Nebuchadnezzar to prevent the kind of future revolt that did, in fact, take place eleven years later. If that is what Nebuchadnezzar did, then the revolt under Zedekiah speaks to a kind of fanaticism in the impoverished kingdom that denied the realities of their situation.[17]

17 In placing Mattaniah/Zedekiah on the throne of Judah Nebuchadnezzar was following the standard practice of the Assyrians before him in his treatment of a surrendered city and land. That is, he allowed a native king, but it was the conqueror's choice who that native king would be. Assigning the throne name of that king was another way of asserting that king's subservience to the great king. For more on possible reasons for the choice see below on 2 Kgs 24:18.

---

15. It is interesting that there is no mention of the ark of the covenant here. If the Babylonians had captured it or destroyed it, it seems likely some comment would have been made on the significance of such an event (as in the extended treatment in 1 Sam 4:11–7:2). It does not appear again in any ensuing narrative. The last reference to it is in 2 Chr 35:3 in the reign of Josiah. Note Jer 3:16 which refers to a future day when there will be no ark and no interest in it.

16. Marc Zvi Brettler, "2 Kings 24:13–14 as History," *CBQ* 53 (1991): 541–552.

17. On "the poorest people of the land" (דַּלַּת עַם־הָאָרֶץ, *dallaṯ ʿam-hāʾāreṣ*) see 25:12 "the poorest of the land" and Jer 52:15 "the poorest of the people." Cogan and Tadmor regard the phrase here as a conflation of the other two (312). While that seems possible, it is hardly necessary. For further discussion, see Roger S. Nam, "'The Poorest of the Land': Perception and Identity of the Remnant in 2 Kings and Jeremiah," JRSSupp 10 (2014): 61–69.

Biblical Theology Comments

As Long (530) notes, the persons exiled at this time, among whom was Ezekiel, were the "good figs" of whom Jeremiah spoke in his vision report (Jer 24:1–10). These were the ones who were to keep the faith alive, who were to be refined in the fires of exile. On the other hand, those who congratulated themselves on having escaped exile because of their righteousness, and who condemned the exiles for having committed some sins that must have made them worthy of such punishment, were the ones who would be utterly destroyed (Ezek 24:3–6). This is reminiscent of the Pharisee and the tax-collector of whom Jesus spoke (Luke 18:10–14). It speaks to the biblical principle that those who exalt themselves will be humbled, while those who humble themselves will be exalted.[18]

Selected Bibliography

Larrson, G. "When Did the Babylonian Captivity Begin?" *JTS* 18 (1967): 417-23.

Zedekiah (24:18–25:7)

Translation

18 Zedekiah was twenty-one years old when he began to reign and he reigned eleven years in Jerusalem. His mother's name was Hamutal, daughter of Jeremiah of Libna. **19** He did evil in the sight of Yahweh according to all that Jehoiakim did. **20** Indeed, it was on account of the anger of Yahweh which was against Jerusalem and Judah to the point that he sent them away from his presence; Zedekiah rebelled against the king of Babylon. **25:1** It was in the ninth year of his reign in the tenth month on the tenth of the month that Nebuchadnezzar came, he and all his army, against Jerusalem and encamped against it and built siege fortifications all around it. **2** The city was under siege until the eleventh year of Zedekiah. **3** By the ninth day of the month[19] the famine had become so severe in the city that there was no food for the people of the land. **4** The city was breached, and all the men of war fled[20] by night by way of the gate between the two walls by the king's garden. While the Chaldeans were still surrounding the city, he went on the way to the Arabah plain. **5** The Chaldean army pursued the king and overtook him in the plains of Jericho, and all his army was scattered from him. **6** They captured the king and took him to the king of Babylon at Riblah and he passed judgment on him. **7** Zedekiah's sons they slaughtered in front

18. Job 5:11; Matt 23:12; Luke 1:52; Jas 4:10; 1 Pet 5:6.

19. Jer 52:6 "ninth day of the fourth month."

20. The versions all supply a vb., either "went out" (Gk.) or "fled" (Vulg. and Syr.). Apparently, it was accidentally dropped from MT. "Fled" seems most likely on the basis of the parallel in Jer 52:7.

of him; then Zedekiah's eyes he put out. He bound him in chains and took him to Babylon.

Textual Notes

18a. K חֲמִיטַל: Q חֲמוּטַל; see 23:31.

18b. מִלִּבְנָה: Gk. omits; Vulg. and Syr. with MT.

25:1a–a. בֶּעָשׂוֹר לַחֹדֶשׁ: Gk. omits; Vulg. and Syr. with MT.

3a. בְּתִשְׁעָה: Syr. adds "In the eleventh year"; Gk. and Vulg. with MT.

3b. לַחֹדֶשׁ: Syr. adds "of the fifth"; Gk. and Vulg. with MT.

4a. הַלַּיְלָה: Gk. Adds "they went out"; Vulg. and Syr. add "they fled." See Jer. 52:7. MT seems to have lost the vb. See *CTAT* (423-24) for a lengthy, but somewhat indef. discussion.

4b. וַיֵּלֶךְ: Vulg. "Zedekiah went"; Syr. "they went"; Gk. with MT.

7a. שָׁחֲטוּ: Gk. and Vulg. "he slaughtered"; Syr. "the king of Babylon slaughtered." Since the rest of the vbs. in the sentence are sing. with the king of Babylon apparently the subj. it appears the versions are bringing this vb. into conformity with those. But there is no need to do so; the indef. 3rd pl. functions as a virtual passive. Many Eng. versions take the conformity the other direction and make all the vbs. pl.

Commentary

18 It seems significant that Zedekiah was the full brother of Jehoahaz (2 Kgs 23:31; see "Commentary" there) whom the Egyptians had deposed and carried off to Egypt. This suggests that the maternal line of these two men was at least anti-Egyptian if not positively pro-Babylonian, and that this accounts for Nebuchadnezzar's choice. If so, he did not take into account Zedekiah's extreme pliability before public opinion.

19–20 Here we have the third son of Josiah who did not follow in his father's footsteps. No hint is given us why this was the case. Perhaps it reflects the influence of the surrounding culture on the two mothers and upon those in charge of the royal nursery and schoolrooms (see the "Commentary" above on 23:1–3). It might also speak of a father obsessed with attempting to reform a nation but paying insufficient attention to his own family. In any case, Zedekiah made no attempt to divert the nation from its downward path. The man we see in Jeremiah seems to have no convictions at all but is completely subject to the whims of his officials and his people.

The syntax of verse 20 is difficult, but it appears to say that it was precisely because of Yahweh's determination to "send them away from his presence" (הִשְׁלִכוֹ אֹתָם מֵעַל פָּנָיו, *hišlikô ʾōtām mēʿal pānāyw*) that Zedekiah rebelled.[21] Once more we see the Old Testament writers walking a very fine line between determinism and freewill. Zedekiah did nothing to turn his people from the evil path they were following and, as a result, went with them into an insane rebellion. Why did he and they make such a foolish choice? It was because God had come to the end of his patience. Does that mean God caused the disaster? From one side of the coin, yes. But from the other side of the coin, it was the sum total of their sin, as seen so graphically in the books of Jeremiah and Ezekiel, that caused them to make a foolish choice. We dare not absolutize either side of the equation.

25:1–2 The siege began "In the ninth year," that is, 588 BC, "in the tenth month, on the tenth day," that is, January 15. It was to last for two and a half years, "until the eleventh year" (586 BC), "on the ninth day of the fourth month" (July 18). It seems possible that the siege that had ended with Jehoiachin's surrender had lasted for the better part of three years, from 601 BC until 598 BC.[22] When we recall that Nineveh fell in only three months,[23] these lengthy periods seem to testify to the defensibility of Jerusalem. In any case the text makes it clear that this siege was a no-nonsense affair, with the full battery of techniques, including expensive "siege fortifications" (דָּיֵק, *dāyēq*). Twice in ten years was too much for the Babylonian monarch.

3–5 Zedekiah's end is rather sordid. When food had run out, instead of remaining in the city and enduring the end with his people, he led the remaining troops, evidently not many, in an attempted escape. It is not clear whether "the city was breached" (וַתִּבָּקַע הָעִיר, *wattibbāqa ʿ hā ʿîr*) by the Babylonians, or by the escapees. It seems as if the Babylonians had done it, there would be no escape, but perhaps the Babylonians were coming in one side of the city and the escapees were going out on the other. It is not clear where "the two walls" (הַחֹמֹתַיִם, *haḥōmōṯayim*) were located. Many years ago, an argument was put forward that the flight was down the Tyropean Valley and that there was a wall on the west side of that valley as well as the old city wall on the east side.[24] To date this theory has been neither proven nor disproven. The statement, "While the Babylonians were still surrounding the city" (וְכַשְׂדִּים עַל־הָעִיר סָבִיב, *wᵉkaśdîm ʿal-hā ʿîr sāḇîḇ*) seems to be the subtle comment of

---

21. Thus, Theophile Meek, "Translation Problems in the Old Testament," *JQR* 50 (1959): 45–54. Another way to express the sequence of thought would be "... from his presence; so Zedekiah rebelled ..." (מֵעַל פָּנָיו וַיִּמְרֹד צִדְקִיָּהוּ, *mē ʿal pānāyw wayyimrōḏ ṣiḏqiyyāhû*).

22. However, it should be pointed out that the exact duration of the first siege is not specified, and that it may have been of a shorter duration (see "Commentary" on 2 Kgs 24:2–3).

23. Kuhrt, *The Ancient Near East*, 545.

24. Lewis B. Paton, "The Meaning of the Expression 'Between the Two Walls,' " *JBL* 25 (1906): 1–13.

the editor(s) on the futility of the flight. The final blow was that when the Babylonians caught up with Zedekiah, his troops all fled. How far this last Davidide was from the first; David's troops were fanatically loyal to him, but there seems to have been nothing about Zedekiah to inspire loyalty.

6–7 Nevertheless, despite all of Zedekiah's shortcomings, no one could wish for him the fate that he had to endure. Nebuchadnezzar, apparently managing several projects at once, not merely the siege of Jerusalem, was located in Riblah, in northern Syria. Ironically, it was the same place to which Jehoahaz, Zedekiah's brother, had been taken more than thirty years earlier, there to be deposed by Neco and taken from there into captivity in Egypt (23:33). Unfortunately for Zedekiah, the disposal of his case was not to be so relatively easy. He had broken a vassal covenant, which Jehoahaz had not. The Babylonian tyrant would not let that pass. So, the last thing that Zedekiah was ever to see before his eyes "were put out" (עִוֵּר, *ʿiwwēr*) and he was taken in chains to Babylon was the sight of sons being "slaughtered" (שָׁחֲטוּ, *šāḥăṭû*), with all that term portends. One of the things this atrocity ensured was that there would be no successors to the throne of Jerusalem through the line of Zedekiah.

Selected Bibliography

Bakon, S. "Zedekiah: Last King of Judah." *JBQ* 36 (2008): 93–101.

Begg, C. T. "Zedekiah and the Servant." *ETL* 62 (1986): 393–98.

Derby, J. "The Tragic King." *JBQ* 20 (2001): 180–85.

Pakkala, J. "Zedekiah's Fate and the Dynastic Succession." *JBL* 125 (2006): 443–52.

Person, R. F. "II Kings 24,18–25,30 and Jeremiah 52: A Text-Critical Study in the Redaction History of the Deuteronomic History." *ZAW* 105 (1993): 174–205.

Salibi, K. S. "The 'Flight' from Jerusalem." *TR* 11 (1990): 76–84.

The Destruction of Jerusalem and Judah (25:8–21)

Translation

8 On the seventh day of the fifth month in the nineteenth year of King Nebuchadnezzar, king of Babylon, Nebuzaradan, chief of the guard, servant of the king of Babylon, came to Jerusalem. **9** He burned the house of Yahweh and the house of the king and all the houses of Jerusalem; every great house he burned with fire. **10** As for the walls of Jerusalem all around, all the Chaldean army that was with[25] the chief of the guard tore them down.[26]

25. "with" (אֵת, *ʾet̲*) is omitted in MT. Cf. Jer 52:14.

26. Beginning with this sentence and continuing through v. 16, the objects of the sentences are put first in the emphatic position.

11 The remnant of the people remaining in the city and the deserters who
had deserted to the king of Babylon and the rest of the masses Nebuzaradan,
chief of the guard, carried off. **12** But some of the poorest of the land the
chief of the guard left behind for vintners and farmers. **13** As for the bronze
pillars of the house of Yahweh, and the stands, and the bronze sea that was
in the house of Yahweh, the Chaldeans broke them in pieces and carried the
bronze to Babylon. **14** The pots, the shovels, the snuffers, the dishes, and all
the bronze utensils with which they had served[27] they took away, **15** and the
censors and bowls, which were of pure gold and pure silver, the chief of the
guard took away. **16** As for the two pillars, the one sea and the dishes which
Solomon had made for the house of Yahweh, the bronze of all these objects
was beyond weighing. **17** The one pillar was twenty-seven feet tall and the
bronze capital on it was four and a half feet tall and the latticework and the
pomegranates encircling the capital were all of bronze, and the second had
the same features, including the latticework. **18** The chief of the guard took
Seraiah, the chief priest, and Zephaniah, the second priest, and the three
door-keepers, **19** and from the city he took a eunuch who had been inspector
general of the men of war and five of the king's close advisors who were found
in the city and the scribe who was chief of the army, who mustered the people
of the land and sixty men from the people of the land who were found in the
city. **20** Nebuzaradan, chief of the guard, took them and brought them to
the king of Babylon at Riblah. **21** The king of Babylon struck them and killed
them in Riblah in the land of Hamath and Judah was carried off from its soil.

Textual Notes

8a. עֶבֶד: Gk. "since he stood before"; Vulg. and Syr. with MT. Perhaps the Gk. is the result of confusion of the labials מ (*m*) and ב (*b*). But see Jer 52:12 which agrees with Gk. here.

9a. וְאֶת־כָּל־בֵּית: Gk. and Vulg. "every house"; Syr. "the houses of the princes." GKC (§117*d*) says the phrase is corrupt since it has the def. direct object marker with an indef. object. But *IBHS* (§14.3.3b) describes it as an adj. functioning as a gen. after a const. noun. Hobbs (358–59) says destruction of the houses of the elite fits Babylonian policy. See Jer 52:13 which contains the def. art. *CTAT* (424–25) gives weak support to MT.

9b. בָּאֵשׁ: Gk. omits; Vulg. and Syr. with MT.

10a. וְאֶת־חוֹמֹת: Gk. omits the verse; Vulg. and Syr. with MT.

10b. רַב־טַבָּחִים: All the versions supply אֶת־ "with" as does Jer 52:14.

13a. אֶת־נְחֻשְׁתָּם: Vulg. and Syr. "all the bronze"; Gk. with MT.

27. The so-called "frequentive" use of the impf. (יְשָׁרְתוּ, *yᵉšārᵉṯû*). See GKC (§107*e*).

14a. וְאֶת־הַכַּפּוֹת: Vulg. and Syr. have six items in this list. The added item seems to be "small pots," but it is not possible to reconstruct what Heb. term this might have translated. Gk. with MT.

15a–a. אֲשֶׁר זָהָב זָהָב וַאֲשֶׁר־כֶּסֶף כָּסֶף: Gk. "gold and silver saucers"; Vulg. "what was gold, gold, and what was silver, silver"; Syr. "the gold and silver braziers and the cups." MT seems to explain the others best, (GKC §123*d* supports). Jer 52:19 supports the Vulg. reading.

18a. כֹּהֵן הָרֹאשׁ: GKC (§131*b*) suggests this may be an appositional phrase defining genus and species: "a priest, the chief one."

18b–b. כֹּהֵן מִשְׁנֶה: Gk. "son of the second order"; Vulg. and Syr. with MT.

19a. הַסֹּפֵר: Vulg. treats as a proper noun; Gk. and Syr. with MT.

20a. רִבְלָתָה: Here, as in v. 21 and elsewhere, Gk. and Syr. confuse the similar letters ר and ד rendering "Diblatha."

Commentary

8–10 "On the fifth day of the fifth month," August 14, after Zedekiah had been dispensed with, "Nebuzaradan, chief of the guard, an officer of Nebuchadnezzar," brought not warriors, but dismantlers and destroyers.[28] His mandate was to loot what was worth looting and to destroy the rest. Jerusalem was not going to be a seat of insurrection again for a very long time. So, he took down the palace, the temple, the major buildings, and the biggest houses, burning them to the ground. Then he turned all his men to, and they systematically "tore down" (נָתְצוּ, *nāṯṣû*) the walls. Some sense of the anguish this all caused those remaining in Jerusalem can be gained by reading the book of Lamentations.

11–12 The use of the word "remnant" (הַנִּשְׁאָרִים, *hanniš ʾārîm*) gives us the sense that by this time there were not many left to be exiled. This seems to accord with the suggestion that the majority of those who went to Babylon were taken in 598 BC (see the "Commentary" above on 24:14–16). The reference to "the masses" (הֶהָמוֹן, *hehāmôn*) suggests also that many of the upper classes had already been taken or had died as a result of the famine. Perhaps those "who had deserted to the king of Babylon" (נָפְלוּ עַל־הַמֶּלֶךְ בָּבֶל, *nop̄lû ʿal-hammelek̲ bāḇel*) had expected favored treatment, but they were taken

28. Jer 52:12 offers a slightly different date, namely August 17. Perhaps one is the date of Nebuzaradan's arrival and the other is the date of the burning of the temple. See Michael Avioz, "When was the First Temple Destroyed, According to the Bible?," *Bib* 84 (2003): 563–65. Arthur J. Nevins, "When was Solomon's Temple Burned Down? Reassessing the Evidence," *JOTS* 31 (2006): 3–25 places it after the murder of Gedaliah on the basis of Jer 41:4–7.

too. Conquerors have little respect for traitors. Obviously, for conquered territory to produce some value for the conqueror there had to be some people left behind to make the land produce: "[to be] vintners and farmers" (לְכֹרְמִים וּלְיֹגְבִים, *lᵊkōrᵊmîm ûlᵊyōgᵊḇîm*). "The poorest of the land" (דַּלַּת הָאָרֶץ, *dallaṯ hā ʾāreṣ*) (see also 24:14; and Jer 52:16), struggling just to survive, were the least likely to cause trouble for the new masters of the land.[29]

13–17 The cataloging of the various items which the Babylonians took from the temple, as well as the detailed descriptions of them is clearly meant to remind the reader of the lengthy descriptions of these same items in 1 Kings 6 and 7.[30] All the care and expense that had gone into the design and construction of these features is finally rendered in vain (cf. 1 Kgs 9:6–9). God had never had a particular interest in a building as a building, as he had said to David in the beginning (2 Sam 7:5–7). He was then, and is now, much more interested in people. If the Davidic king was himself demonstrating a heart wholly devoted to God and was leading his people to be similarly devoted, then Yahweh would be pleased to have a glorious temple symbolizing that love and devotion and demonstrating his unique character, i.e., his name.[31] But if no such love and devotion existed, as manifested in covenant obedience, then he had no interest at all in a pile of gold, silver, and bronze. If his name was not being demonstrated in human lives, a building meant nothing at all to him. If there were any doubt about the intent of the editor(s), the words in verse 16 lays that to rest: "which Solomon had made for the house of Yahweh" (אֲשֶׁר־עָשָׂה שְׁלֹמֹה לְבֵית יהוה, *ʾăšer- ʿāśâ šᵊlōmō lᵊḇêṯ yhwh*). The journey that began in the early chapters of 1 Kings has now come to its full end.[32]

29. J. Nigel Graham, "'Vinedressers and Plowmen': 2 Kings 25:12 and Jeremiah 52:16," *BA* 47/1 (1984): 55–8.

30. The lack of any reference to the gold in the temple building itself (1 Kgs 6:19–22) may suggest that whatever was left of it by 598 BC had been stripped away at that time (24:13).

31. 1 Kgs 5:5; 8:16, 18, 19, 29; 9:3, 7; 11:36; 2 Kgs 21:4, 7; 23:27.

32. The theory of the Deuteronomic History, i.e., that the Babylonian exile was a terrible shock and that a brilliant person seeking to explain this event reworked the various bits of quasi-history writing that existed previously into a powerful interpretation of events extending from Moses to Jehoiachin, rests on two very precarious premises: one, that predictive prophecy did not exist, and two, that people needed to be convinced that it does exist. That is, Moses, if he existed, did not predict the exile. Neither did a prophet predict to Solomon that if he and his descendants did not honor the name of Yahweh, his glorious temple would be destroyed, etc. In short, the exile had never been predicted until the time of Josiah, when it was not prediction at all, but simply the recognition of a clear coming event. Yet, the people needed to believe that this had all been within God's providential plans and purposes, so the "Deuteronomist" created these fictional predictions and masterfully interwove them into his work, giving the false impression that the exile, which was just one of

18–21 It is unclear whether we are to see the events of the final chapter of 2 Kings as being in chronological order or not. Jeremiah 52 follows this same order, but Jer 52:10 says that in addition to slaughtering Zedekiah's sons (as per 2 Kgs 25:7), Nebuchadnezzar "also slaughtered all the officials of Judah" (וְגַם אֶת־כָּל־שָׂרֵי יְהוּדָה שָׁחַט, *wᵉgam ʾet-kol-śārê yᵉhûdâ šāḥaṭ*). There are two ways of looking at the discrepancy. First, the officials were indeed killed after the destruction of the city, and Jeremiah is simply making it clear at the earlier point that Zedekiah's sons were not the only ones slaughtered. The second possibility is that the officials were actually killed at the same time as Zedekiah's sons, and both accounts then place the actual report of their deaths after the destruction of the city for some reason not clear. I prefer the first explanation.

When their "places of business": temple, chancellery, and armory, had been destroyed there was no place left for remaining leaders to hide, and Nebuzaradan rooted them out with ruthless efficiency. This included the five most important officials of the temple (v. 18), five members of the royal council, the two top army administrators (presumably the field commanders had been captured with Zedekiah, or made good their escape [25:5, 23]) (v. 19), and "sixty men from the people of the land" (שִׁשִּׁים אִישׁ מֵעַם הָאָרֶץ, *wᵉšiššîm ʾîš mēʿam hāʾāreṣ*), that is, landed citizens (v. 19) (on "people of the land" see the "Commentary" above on 2 Kgs 11:14–18). These leaders die at Riblah and the final sad coda is pronounced: "Judah was carried off from its soil" (וַיִּגֶל יְהוּדָה מֵעַל אַדְמָתוֹ, *wayyigel yᵉhûdâ mēʿal ʾadmātô*) (v. 21). This last term seems significant. It is not the more general, אֶרֶץ, *ʾereṣ* ("land,") but the more redolent, אֲדָמָה, *ʾădāmâ* which connotes "earth." They are taken from the soil, the earth, that had year by year nourished them and thus, they are truly bereft.

Selected Bibliography

Malamat, A. "The Twilight of Judah in the Egyptian-Babylonian Maelstrom." *VT* Sup 28 (1975): 123–45.

The Death of Gedaliah (25:22–26)

Translation

22 As for the people who remained in the land of Judah, whom Nebuchadnezzar had left behind, he appointed over them Gedaliah, son of Ahikam, son of Shaphan. **23** When all the captains of the forces, they and their men, heard that the king of Babylon had appointed Gedaliah they came to Gedaliah at Mizpah. Ishmael, son of Nethaniah, Johanan, son of Kareah, Seriah, son of Thanhumeth, the Netophathiite, and Jaazaniah, son of the

---

the random events of human experience, was actually the result of divine-human interaction in time and space over the span of a thousand years. A masterwork indeed. See further in the "Introduction."

Maachathite, they and their men. **24** Gedaliah swore to them and to their men and said to them, "Do not be afraid of the Chaldean officials; live in the land, and serve the king of Babylon, and it will be well with you." **25** However, in the seventh month Ishmael, son of Nethaniah, son of Elishama, from the royal family, struck Gedaliah, and he died, as well as the Judeans and Chaldeans that were with him in Mizpah. **26** All the people from small to great, and the captains of the forces got up and went to Egypt because they were afraid of the Chaldeans.

Textual Notes

23a. וְהָאֲנָשִׁים: All the versions "their men." MT probably lost the ה of the 3mp suff. See the final word in the sentence (וְאַנְשֵׁיהֶם).

23b. הַמַּעֲכָתִי: Vulg. and Syr. omit the article and take this as a proper noun and not a gentilic. Gk. with MT.

23c–c. הֵמָּה וְאַנְשֵׁיהֶם: Gk. omits; Vulg. and Syr. with MT, but Vulg. has "allies" instead of "men" (as also in v. 24).

24a. מֵעַבְדֵי: Gk. "passing" (reading the Heb. as מֵעֲבֹר?); Vulg. and Syr. with MT.

Commentary

22 Once more, Nebuchadnezzar was following the pattern laid down by the Assyrians: when a principality had revolted a second time and had consequently been reduced to rubble, a military governor was appointed to rule it. Here the governor is a native Judean, which was not always the case. Gedaliah son of Ahikam son of Shaphan came from a remarkable family. Gedaliah's great-great-grandfather had been a court secretary (2 Kgs 22:3), and his grandfather Shaphan had been the one Josiah sent to inquire of Yahweh through the prophetess Huldah. His father Ahikam had protected Jeremiah from being handed over to the mob (Jer 26:24). His uncle, Gemariah, and cousin, Micaiah, reported, apparently favorably, upon Jeremiah's words in his scroll that Baruch read (Jer 36:10–11). We are given no explanation why Gedaliah was chosen. One might think that given the high positions his family members had held in the palace and the temple (Gemariah's chamber was in the temple; Jer 36:10) he would have been targeted for death rather than given this position. Perhaps the family, supporters of Jeremiah, were thought to be pro-Babylonian. The intelligence system of the Babylonians was obviously very efficient: they knew who Jeremiah was and were prepared to give him favorable treatment (Jer 39:9–14), so they evidently knew whom they thought they could trust.[33]

---

33. See John Ritzema, "After Zedekiah: Who and What was Gedaliah Ben Ahikam?," *JSOT* 42 (2017): 73–91.

23 Presumably the "captains of the forces" (שָׂרֵי הַחֲיָלִים, *śārê haḥăyālîm*) are the remnant of those that abandoned Zedekiah and fled (2 Kgs 25:5). The fact that those who would be the assassins are named in such detail says that the author had direct access to records at Mizpah. Evidently Jerusalem was so thoroughly destroyed that the seat of government had to be moved elsewhere. But it is also possible that the Babylonians insisted it be moved to minimize likelihood of any further insurrection. Mizpah was located about seven miles north of Jerusalem, at the modern site of Tel en-Nazbeh. Netophah may have been located at Khirbet Bedd Faluf about two miles southeast of Bethlehem. Other biblical references to Maacah place the region far to the north in the region now known as the heights of Golan. While not impossible, it seems unlikely that Jaazaniah's father was from that far-away area, so perhaps this Maacah is to be located somewhere in Judah.

24–25 Gedaliah's advice was clearly wise. The Babylonians had gone to considerable time and expense to pacify Judah. They clearly had no interest in investing any more time and money in this place. If the inhabitants would simply accept the situation, cultivate the land, and pay the annual tribute, the Babylonians would leave them alone. But clearly emotions were far too inflamed for wisdom to have any effect. Archeological work around the city of Jerusalem has given evidence of the ferocity of the Babylonian attack, and the memory of starvation, mutilation, and death was obviously far too strong. Gedaliah was undoubtedly a marked man from the moment that he accepted his assignment from the hated enemy. It is perhaps surprising that he survived as long as two months, until sometime about the end of October, 586 BC. The depth of the rage against Babylon is indicated by the fact that not only was Gedaliah killed, but so was everyone with him, Judeans and Babylonians ("Chaldeans") alike. The statement that Ishmael was "from the royal family" (מִזֶּרַע הַמְּלוּכָה, *mizzera ʿ hammᵊlûḵâ*) is also significant. This family, and all its royal prerogatives, maintained for some 450 years, was now for all practical purposes destroyed, and its place heartlessly taken over by a minor court official. That shame had to be expunged. Again, the book has come full circle: from the triumph of the Davidic son, Solomon, to a minor member of the Davidic dynasty treacherously murdering one thought to be a usurper, and then running to escape the consequences of his act.

26 But this account is not merely about the revenge killing of the Babylonian appointee, it is even more about the totality of Judah's expulsion from the land. Not only had they been driven out by Babylon but many of those who were left for whatever reason expelled themselves in their own futile rage. "Great and small" (מִקָּטֹן וְעַד־גָּדוֹל, *miqqāṭōn wᵊ ʿad-gāḏôl*), they went to Egypt because they "were afraid of the Chaldeans" (כִּי יָרְאוּ מִפְּנֵי כַשְׂדִּים, *kî yor ʾû mippᵊnê ḵaśdîm*). As if the exile itself were not enough, the Judeans themselves finished the task. The accumulated sins of the centuries, the pursuing of other gods, the breaking of the covenant, had indeed had their effect, and the land of milk and honey, the sanctuary of Yahweh (Exod 15:13) had finally spewed them out, just as it spewed out the Canaanites before them (Lev 18:25, 28; 20:22).[34] Ironically, they need not have fled to Egypt, as Jeremiah tried to tell them (Jer 42), but their refusal to trust Yahweh was so ingrown by this time that they could only listen to the counsel of their fears. We are reminded of Kadesh-barnea (Num 13–14): when God said for them to go up into the land and he would be with him, they would not go. Then, when he said they should go back into the wilderness, they decided to go up even though Moses told them Yahweh would not be with them. Here God told them to repent or be exiled by the Babylonians, but they would not repent, and the exile occurred. Then he told the remnant that he would protect them from the king of Babylon, but they refused to believe it. Like that first generation out of Egypt, this generation too seemed determined to destroy itself.

Selected Bibliography

Albright, W. F. "The Site of Mispah in Benjamin." *JPOS* 3 (1923): 110–21.

Favor Shown to Jehoiachin (25:27–30)

Translation

27 Now in the thirty-seventh year of the exile of Jehoiachin, in the twelfth month, on the twenty-seventh day of the month, Evil-merodach, king of Babylon, in the year of his coronation, freed[35] Jehoiachin from confinement. **28** He spoke kindly to him and placed his seat above the seats of the other kings who were with him in Babylon. **29** He changed his prison garments and as long as he lived ate regularly in his presence. **30** As for his allowance,[36] a regular daily allowance was given him by the king, as long as he lived.

Textual Notes

27a. יְהוֹיָכִין: Gk. "Joakim" (so also 24:8); Vulg. and Syr. with MT.

27b. מִבֵּית: Gk. and Syr. add "and brought him out"; Vulg. with MT.

---

34. It is important to remember Semitic hyperbole when reading statements like these. This is not to say that *every* person left the country. As is the case everywhere, the poorest often have little interest in "current affairs." They are too busy trying to survive, and the great events simply sweep over them. So here they would have remained behind, lacking any means to make the trek anyway. The author is simply making the point that Judah's destruction was utterly thorough, not merely because of Babylonian power, but as a result of their own choices.

35. נָשָׂא ... אֶת־רֹאשׁ, *nāśāʾ ... ʾet-rōʾš* ("lifted the head of").

36. See Ronnie Goldstein, "Administrative Terminology and Its Influence in Biblical Literature: Hebrew ארחה," in *Literature as Politics, Politics as Literature: Essays on the Ancient Near East in Honor of Peter Machinist,* ed. D. S. Vanderhooft and A. Wintzer (Winona Lake, IN: Eisenbrauns, 2013) 137–49 for an argument that this word is an Akkadian loan word meaning something like "left-overs."

Commentary

On one hand, these words are quite unexpected. Except for the Josianic interlude, the trend of the book has been utterly negative since the account of the reign of Manasseh recorded in chapter twenty-one. Yahweh, finding no serious repentance on the part of a people who seem determined to replicate all of Manasseh's sins, intends to carry out the full destruction prescribed in the curses of the covenant. Furthermore, as reported in the previous segment, the people seem determined to make a complete end of themselves in case Yahweh might have overlooked anyone. Yet, here, almost unaccountably, we read of an isolated incident that seems vaguely hopeful. Its full implications are left tantalizingly unspecified, yet the survival of the last legitimate Davidic king opens a most interesting door to the future.

But if from one perspective this event seems surprising, when viewed from another its appearance is not surprising at all. It is not surprising when we remember that Yahweh's intended last word is never destruction. We may go back as far as the Noachic flood for a witness to the truth of this statement (Gen 6–9). Whereas the gods, in the parallel tale of Utnapishtim, provoked by Enlil, fully intended to destroy the human race with their flood (see *ANET*, 93–95), that was never the intention of Yahweh. Then we may come up to Yahweh's representative in the prophet Hosea, who by every right should have rejected his prostitute bride when she persisted in her prostitution. Yet, he bought her back (Hos 3:1–3). It should not be surprising then that this God, faithfully true, who had made an eternal promise to David, would, in the fulfillment of his just punishment, yet find a way to keep that promise and find a way for that promise to be carried on to its ultimate fulfilment in the salvation of the world.

27 The thirty-seventh year of the exile of Jehoiachin would be 561 BC. Evil-Merodach (Awil-Marduk) succeeded his father Nebuchadnezzar in 562 BC.[37] Perhaps this action involved some general amnesty that the new king instituted at the beginning of his reign. It may also have been an attempt by a somewhat uncertain new king to gain the favor and support of the many captive rulers in his prisons. To "lift the head of" speaks of a deliverance from humiliation and is more expressive than a simple "delivered from" would be. It implies a return of status and a recognition of that status.

28 Not only was Jehoiachin given a certain status, it was a higher status than that given to the other kings. No explanation is given for this, and no obvious one comes to mind. Judah was hardly one of the more important principalities in the Babylonian empire, and Jehoiachin could hardly add luster to

---

37. The precise dates given here correspond with the precise dating throughout chapter 25, and argue against the position that these four verses are an epilogue added at some time long after the book's completion (with 25:26) in an effort to soften the determinedly negative tone of the ending of the book.

the Babylonian monarch's rule. But perhaps some personal relationship had grown up between Nebuchadnezzar's son and the young Judean monarch over the thirty-seven years.

29 Eating "regularly" (תָּמִיד, *tāmîḏ*) in the king's presence is reminiscent of the treatment given to Mephibosheth by David (2 Sam 9) and suggests that we are intended to read the two accounts in tandem.[38] Doing so suggests a way of reading this passage that explains some of its ambiguity. In the 2 Samuel passage, there is no question that Saul's kingship is ended, yet there is hope for his family itself; the name of Saul will not die out. So here this passage may be double-edged. On the one hand, there will be no renewal of the kingship of David; it has come to its end. However, the Davidic family has not come to an end; there is hope, whatever that might be, for its continuation.[39]

The repetition of "as long as he lived" (כֹּל יְמֵי חַיָּו, *kōl yᵉmê ḥayyāw*) suggests something of duration. The man was going to live out his life and be cared for to the end of it. So too, the nation was going to endure and there would be provision for it. The prophets who had been vilified for saying that exile would come, from Micah and Isaiah to Jeremiah and Ezekiel, had also insisted that this exile would not achieve its intended purpose: absorption of the people into a homogenous imperial culture and consequent disappearance. No, just as Jehoiachin was going to endure to the end as "the king of Judah," so the people would endure to their appointed end as the people of Yahweh.

Selected Bibliography

Becking, B. "Jehoiachin's Amnesty, Salvation for Israel? Notes on 2 Kings 25,27–30." Pages 283–293 in *Pentateuchal and Deuteronomistic Studies: Papers Read at the 13th IOSOT Congress, Leuven, 1989*. Edited by C. Brekelmans and J. Lust. BETL 94. Leuven: Leuven University Press, 1990.

Begg, C. T. "The Significance of Jehoiachin's Release: A New Proposal." *JSOT* 11 (1986): 49–56.

38. See Jan Jaynes Granowski, "Jehoiachin at the King's Table: A Reading of the Ending of the Second Book of Kings" in *Reading between Texts: Intertextuality and the Hebrew Bible*, ed. Dana N. Fewell (Louisville, KY: Westminster John Knox, 1992) 173–88; Donald F. Murray, "Of All the Years the Hopes—or Fears?: Jehoiachin in Babylon (2 Kings 25:27–30)," *JBL* 120 (2001): 245–65; Jeremy Schipper, "'Significant Resonances' with Mephibosheth in 2 Kings 25:27–30: A Response to Donald F. Murray," *JBL* 124 (2005): 521–29.

39. Another reading is provided by a comparison between Joseph and Jehoiachin: the release points to a new exodus. See Michael J. Chan, "Joseph and Jehoiachin: On the Edge of the Exodus," *ZAW* 125 (2013): 566–77; and Ian Douglas Wilson, "Joseph, Jehoiachin, and Cyrus: On Book Endings, Exoduses and Exiles, and Yehudite/Judean Social Remembering," *ZAW* 126 (2014): 521–34. I find this less compelling than the association with Mephibosheth.

Janzen, D. "An Ambiguous Ending: Dynastic Punishment in Kings, and the Fate of the Davidides in 2 Kings 25.27–30." *JSOT* 33 (2008): 39–58.

Markl, D. "No Future without Moses: The Disastrous End of 2 Kings 22–25 and the Chance of the Moab Covenant (Deuteronomy 29-30)." *JBL* 133 (2014): 711–28.

Pietsch, M. "Zwischen Restauration und Resignation: Die Amnestie Joachins (II Reg 25, 27–30) als Deuteronomistischer Programmtext?" *ZAW* 129 (2017): 390–410.

Excurses

Excursus on Worship at High Places ("country shrines")

Why were the people, and Solomon, worshipping at the high places, country shrines,[1] particularly when Deuteronomy had been so explicit in forbidding it (12:1–14)? One answer that OT scholarship has taught widely is that Deuteronomy did not exist at this time, that its teachings, stemming only from the seventh century BC, have been written back into this material at a later date. Thus, the worship at the country shrines was simply part of the supposed evolution of Hebrew religion. This is, of course, not at all what the author wants us to believe. He wants us to believe that, for some reason, the practices of the people have fallen below what their own existing documents would have been calling for. If we are to take this view seriously, as we must, then what explanation can be given for such behavior? It is most likely that it is the result of two things: (1) the general decline in faithfulness to the covenant depicted in the book of Judges, and (2) the religious chaos that ensued from the capture of the ark and the destruction of the Mosaic Tabernacle at Shiloh by the Philistines (1 Sam 4:11; Jer 7:12–15).

Whatever may have been the religious situation in Israel before these events, it was surely complete chaos afterward. First, the ark was not even brought to the replacement tabernacle at Nob (1 Sam 7:2; 21:1–6); there seems to have been at least one competing tabernacle at Gibeon (1 Sam 9:11–13; 1 Chr 16:39, although it is possible that the tabernacle was moved from Nob to Gibeon after the disaster there). Second, the priesthood was decimated not once but twice: first by the Philistines (1 Sam 4:17–22), and then by Saul (22:17–23), so that Samuel ends up acting as both prophet and priest (13:8–10). If the result of all this was that whatever unity in religious observance there might have been at the end of the conquest period

1. "High places" is the conventional translation for בָּמוֹת (*bāmôṯ*). However, these were not necessarily hilltops as the term might suggest. It may have been used originally because the gods were thought to live on mountains. Thus, wherever the god or goddess was worshipped was a "high place." They were shrines, either open or closed, which might be built on an elevated platform or not. See D. L. Petter, "High Places," in *IVPDOTHB*, 413–18.

(Josh 22:10–29) was fractured and that the people drifted back to the diverse forms of worship that Moses had been so concerned about, it is at least quite understandable.

Excursus on Miracles

Because the narratives of Elijah and Elisha that occur between 1 Kgs 17 and 2 Kgs 8 record a large number of miracles, many commentators label them "legends" (see e.g., Gray, 371-377). The unspoken, although sometimes spoken, assumption behind this label is that miracles are impossible—they cannot occur. Thus, any literature in which the miraculous is found is by definition fiction. However, the assumption that miracles, defined as any deviation from so-called natural laws, cannot occur is based on the conclusion that either there is no supernatural God, or that if there is, he/she cannot or will not intervene to affect natural causation. But that is of course what the entire biblical narrative is concerned to profess. There *is* a transcendent God who can and does intervene to affect natural causation. The miraculous is inseparable from the theology that the entire Bible is insisting upon. It seems equally plausible to allow the existence of miracles as it is to deny them unless one has prejudged the biblical theology to be false from beginning to end. If that were so, the enduring existence of the Jewish and Christian communities with their unique convictions becomes inexplicable. In short, unless one denies biblical theology *in toto*, there is every reason to consider the reports of the miracles of Elijah and Elisha to be historically reliable.

At the same time, it should be noticed, as C. S. Lewis has pointed out, that miracles do not occur everywhere, and haphazardly, throughout the Bible.[2] Rather, they typically occur in groups at significant points in the process of revelation. So, there is a collection of miracles surrounding the exodus and the conquest, there is another here in the climactic battle with Canaanite religion, and there is another in the ministry of Jesus and the founding of the Christian Church. Thus, we may say that miracles are the sparks that fly up when the steel of revelation strikes the turning wheel of time.[3]

Excursus on Symbol and Reality

As mentioned above, the Bible sees a connection between symbol and reality. It is not a causal connection, but what might be called a participative connection. It is a way in which God enables us humans to recognize that the physical and the spiritual worlds are equally real. It is not that the invisible

2. C. S. Lewis, *Miracles* (London: Collins, 1960), 171.

3. For a recent defense of the plausibility of miracles, see Craig Keener, *Miracles: The Credibility of the New Testament Accounts*, 2 vols. (Grand Rapids: Baker Academic, 2011).

world is the real one, and the visible merely a dim reflection of that one, nor is it that the material world is real and the immaterial merely a mental abstraction. The two worlds are equally real, and participation in symbolic actions helps to undergird and reinforce that truth.

Whether these kinds of actions were only symbolic or were expressions of sympathetic magic intended to cause the desired results has engaged the attention of commentators over the last century or more. In the early years of the twentieth century there was a tendency to assume that Israel's religion was largely indistinguishable from that of its neighbors, and thus that such actions as these, and those of other prophets (esp. Jeremiah and Ezekiel) were indeed sympathetic magic. In the middle years of the century when there was more of a tendency to see differences between the religions, the pendulum swung more toward symbolic. Now the pendulum is swinging back again.[4] However, it must be clear that adherents of Deuteronomic and prophetic theology would have eschewed anything understood to involve ritual magic. The presupposition of Yahweh's complete transcendence, and the resulting impossibility of influencing him through ritual is the governing principle in that thought.[5]

Excursus on Chronology (792–739 BC)

If we begin with the fairly secure date of 841 BC for the beginning of Jehu's reign and add up the regnal years of his successors until the death of Pekahiah, who died in the same year as Azariah/Uzziah, the result is 114 years and seven months. If we do the same thing with the Davidides in Judah, the result is 128 years. So, there is a discrepancy of a little more than thirteen years. But in either case, the number is too large. From Assyrian records, it is clear that these reigns only covered about a century. The conclusion is that we must either disregard the number of regnal years and simply attempt to fit the reigns in as we can, or that there were several coregencies. The latter is what Thiele has proposed, and it is followed by Galil, although with somewhat differing combinations.[6] The following is taken from Thiele's proposal (73–89, 135) because it both fits the data and does not mutilate it to do so; thus it is the most likely solution. As Thiele says it (87), the editors do not reflect these coregencies when they report the synchronisms, but they do

4. See for instance Rüdiger Schmitt, "War Rituals in the Old Testament: Prophets, Kings, and the Ritual Preparation for War" in *Warfare, Ritual, and Symbol in Biblical and Modern Contexts*, ed. Brad E. Kelle, Frank R. Ames, Jacob L. Wright (Atlanta: SBL Press, 2014), 149–61. See also W. Boyd Barrick, "Elisha and the Magic Bow: A Note on 2 Kings 13:15–17," *VT* 35 (1985): 355–363.

5. See my *The Bible Among the Myths* (Grand Rapids: Zondervan, 2009), 63–84.

6. Thiele, *Mysterious Numbers*, 73–89, 135; Gershon Galil, *The Chronology of the Kings of Israel and Judah* (Leiden: Brill, 1996), 46–82.

when they report the total years of reigns. When coregencies are considered, both sets of numbers work.

First, there was a coregency between Jehoash of Israel and his son Jeroboam II during the years 792 BC until Jehoash's death in 782 BC. Second, there was a coregency between Amaziah and his son Azariah from 791 BC until Amaziah's death in 767 BC. Third, there was a coregency between Azariah and his son Jotham from 750 BC until Azariah's death in 739 BC. The coregencies of Azariah with Amaziah (beginning with Amaziah's capture) and then with Jotham (see below on 15:5) seem to have the clearest data in support, whereas that of Jehoash and Jeroboam is less evident, apart from the different wording concerning Jeroboam's succession in 13:13 and 14:16. Thiele (83–84) notes that such a coregency would have begun in the year of the battle between Jehoash and Amaziah, and that Jehoash must have prudently placed his son on the throne with him before going off to this battle.

Excursus on Chronology (739–696 BC)

This forty-five-year period was one of calamity after calamity for the small countries of what is now called Palestine. It saw one after another of these countries falling into the maw of voracious Assyria. Under the lash of that terrible pressure, the leadership of the countries flailed back and forth frantically in vain attempts to stem the tide. This goes far to explain many of what for long were thought to be intractable chronological problems here in 2 Kings. It appears that in Judah especially, there was one coregency after another, as the leadership vacillated back and forth between either pro- or anti-Assyrian inclinations, depending on which way the political winds seemed to be blowing at the moment.

Ahaz seems to have been the de facto king during the last five years of his father Jotham's reign (735–730 BC). It seems very likely that this was so because a pro-Assyrian party forced him on his father. However, after the crushing successes of Tiglath-pileser from 734 BC onward, it appears that anti-Assyrian forces gained the upper hand in the Judean government and forced Ahaz to associate his young son Hezekiah with him on the throne about 726 BC. Up until this point the biblical system of reckoning seems to have been quite consistent: the synchronisms between Judah's and Israel's kings record when a king began to rule, regardless of whether he had been a coregent or not, but the total number of years that a king ruled always included the years of any coregency that may have existed. However, at this point the system begins to break down. In the case of Jotham there is a discrepancy between the statements of 2 Kgs 15:33 (sixteen years total) and 15:30 (Hoshea began to reign in Jotham's twentieth year). It appears, as noted above, that while Jotham was nominally king after 735 BC, it was truly in name only, with Ahaz effectively ruling.

Another discrepancy emerges in 2 Kgs 17:1 where we read that Hoshea began to reign in Ahaz's twelfth year. If Hoshea's reign began in 732 BC, as seems likely, this would place the beginning of Ahaz's reign somewhere around 744 BC, frankly an impossibility since it would either make Uzziah, Jotham, and Ahaz coregents or would throw off a whole host of other synchronisms. A possible solution is that the *conclusion* of Hoshea's reign was in Ahaz's twelfth year, and that the scribe recording the regnal data got the figures confused. Another possibility is that twelve is an error for two.[7]

The situation becomes even more complicated with Hezekiah. Both the synchronisms (2 Kgs 18:1, 9, 10) and the narrative have him on the throne in 727 or 726 BC prior to the fall of the northern kingdom. Thus, when v. 2 says that his total rule was twenty-nine years, we would conclude that he died about 696 BC (given discrepancies in counting accession years). However, the report in 2 Kgs 18:13 dates the attack of Sennacherib in Hezekiah's fourteenth year. That should be about 712 BC, if he began to reign in 726 BC. But we know from Assyrian records that this attack took place in 701 BC. This makes it look as though in this case Hezekiah's years are being counted from the beginning of his sole reign in 715 BC and not from the beginning of any coregency. Thiele accepts this dating and concludes that the apparent coregency and its supporting narrative have been created after the fact by a later editor who did not understand the facts.[8] It seems much more likely (and much less complex) to conclude that the error is in 2 Kgs 18:13 and that the total should indeed be counted from 726 BC.[9] The error may have been in the text from the outset as a result of the confused situation at the court, with the northern kingdom falling and Judah's existence being threatened, and as political forces raged back and forth. Ultimately, the only real significance of the debate is to raise a question about the date of Hezekiah's death. Was it twenty-nine years after 726 BC (thus about 696 BC) or twenty-nine years after 715 BC (about 685 BC)? If it was the latter, then his son Manasseh ruled with him from 696 BC onward. See the "Commentary" on 2 Kgs 21:1 for further discussion.

---

7. See Rodger C. Young, "When was Samaria Captured: The Need for Precision in Biblical Chronologies," *JETS* 47 (2004) 588–92, and Gray, 641.

8. See Thiele, *Mysterious Numbers*, 138–140.

9. For a similar conclusion see Galil, *The Chronology of the Kings of Israel and Judah*, 98–106. See also Leslie McFall, "Did Thiele Overlook Hezekiah's Coregency, *BibSac* 146 (1989): 393–404, and Andrew E. Steinmann, "The Chronology of 2 Kings 15 – 18," *JETS* 30 (1987): 391–97. For further discussion, see the "Commentary" below on 20:1–6.

Excursus on 2 Kings 18:13–20:21 in Comparison to Isaiah 36:1–39:8

The materials in these two sections of these two books are largely identical.[10] Many commentators conclude that the material in Kings is original and that the compiler(s) of the book of Isaiah reused the material, editing it to fit his/their purposes, in particular deleting what is now 2 Kings 18:13–16, as well as certain other statements because they supposedly reflect negatively on Hezekiah. Let us address this latter point first. In fact, the book of Isaiah is more negative toward Hezekiah than is this account in 2 Kings. In particular, the representation of him in Isaiah 28–31, while not naming the king directly, is very critical of what must have been his royal policies toward Egypt. Thus, the idea that the differences in the Isaiah version can be explained as an attempt to present Hezekiah in a more favorable light is not tenable. Examination of the two texts shows that in almost all cases Isaiah is the shorter version, with many of the additions in Kings looking like editorial expansions.

In fact, it is more likely that the material now appearing as 2 Kings 18:17–20:21 is original to Isaiah and has been supplemented with 2 Kings 18:13–16. There are four reasons for taking this position: (1) The first one is the most compelling in my mind. The material now found in 2 Kings 18:17–20:21 is very odd in the overall content of the books of Kings. Why pick this particular way of illustrating Hezekiah's trust in Yahweh and his ultimate fallibility? And why spend so much time and space on this single incident in a very eventful twenty-nine-year reign? This is not typical of the way in which the books of Kings have approached other kings' records.

(2) On the other hand, this material suits the book of Isaiah very well. The entire thrust of that book from 7:1 onward through 39:8 is to explore the question of trust in Yahweh versus trust in the nations. Ahaz refused to trust Yahweh and Isaiah then predicted not only the conquest and exile of Israel, but he foresaw that of Judah as well. Chapters thirteen through thirty-five all are focused on the folly of putting one's trust in the nations. Then in chapters thirty-six through thirty-nine Ahaz's son, Hezekiah, is forced to face the issue in a much more dire situation. The prolixity of the account in chapters thirty-six and thirty-seven fits this purpose very well. Will Hezekiah trust? What will Yahweh's response be? That prolixity does not serve any particular purpose in Kings.

(3) Furthermore, the positioning of Hezekiah's illness and the response to his recovery works very well in Isaiah whereas it seems to serve no purpose

10. Unique elements are 2 Kings 18:13–16: Hezekiah's attempt to pay Sennacherib to withdraw, and Isaiah 38:9–22: Isaiah's reflections upon his recovery. The only other major difference is in the placement of Isaiah 38:21–22/2 Kings 20:7–8 (see the discussion below). Otherwise, there are a number of plusses in 2 Kings, many of which appear to be glosses.

in Kings. If we accept that Hezekiah reigned twenty-nine years, and that he began his reign in 726 BC *and* that he lived for fifteen years after the illness described in 2 Kings 20 and Isaiah 38, then the illness occurred about 711 BC, ten years before the events described in 2 Kings 18–19 and Isaiah 36–37. Why is the material out of chronological order? It makes no sense to do so in 2 Kings, but it makes good sense to do so in Isaiah.

(4) In Isaiah 36–37, it has finally been established conclusively that Yahweh can be trusted. It has been established through Ahaz's son Hezekiah. Assyria had been soundly defeated by Yahweh and Sennacherib would not campaign in the west again. On that basis, it might seem obvious that Hezekiah is the "child" of Isaiah 9:6 [MT 5], and the "shoot" of 11:1. Surely, he is the one who will bring the Israelite exiles home, and because of his faithful trust Judah would never suffer exile. Not so. Chapters thirty-eight and thirty-nine demonstrate that Hezekiah is both mortal and fallible. Trust must be a way of life and not merely a one-time event. No, Hezekiah is not the promised Messiah, and the struggle of God's people is only beginning. In the context of the book of Isaiah the reversal of the chronology makes perfect sense. It does not in 2 Kings; in fact, it is difficult to see what purpose the account even serves there.

Further reasons to believe the account was original to Isaiah are found in certain details.

Compare Isaiah 7:3 with 36:2. It is on the very same spot where Isaiah challenged Ahaz to trust Yahweh that the Assyrian officer dared Hezekiah to trust Yahweh. The detail is fundamental to the point Isaiah is making. Yet, we find that detail reported in 2 Kings 18:17 where it is superfluous. Why is it found there? Only because it was in the material to which the Kings editor was referring.

Another detail occurs in the report of Hezekiah's illness. At the end of the report in Isaiah, there are two strange footnotes: "Isaiah had said, 'Let them take a cake of figs and rub it on the boil so that he might live.' And Hezekiah had said, 'What is the sign that I will go up to the house of God?' " (Isa 38:21–22). In the Kings account, these details are integrated into the report and fit very smoothly. It does not seem likely that Kings contains the original version, and that a later clumsy editor, copying the account for Isaiah, accidentally left out these details, and then decided to add them on at the end. It seems more likely that a rougher original has been smoothed out in the second version. The fact that the notes appear in Isaiah after Hezekiah's reflections make it even more difficult to believe that someone has appended them after comparison with Kings. It seems more likely that they would have been added after the report of the incident in that case. Admittedly, it is difficult to explain why an original would have had this arrangement, but neither is it easy to explain the Isaianic arrangement if it is not original.

A final detail is small but telling. The phrase "The Holy One of Israel" occurs only six times in the Bible outside of Isaiah, where it occurs twenty-five times. Three occurrences are in the Psalms (71:22; 78:41; 89:18) and two are in close proximity in Jeremiah (50:29; 51:5). The sixth occurrence is found here in 2 Kings 19:22, where it duplicates Isaiah 37:23. Are we to believe, on the other hand, that Isaiah is at this place duplicating this one occurrence in 2 Kings? Surely not.

In summary, it appears that the editor(s) of Kings, wishing to report the encounter between Hezekiah and Sennacherib, began with a typically brief report of Hezekiah's attempt to pay Sennacherib to withdraw (2 Kgs 18:13–16).[11] Then, because the Isaianic account was in existence he decided to incorporate it (just as he had with the Elijah/Elisha accounts at various points between 1 Kings 17 and 2 Kings 13) instead of continuing with his usual terse reporting style. Even though that account was much fuller than would normally be the case for him, it still served his purpose of showing how a monarch who adhered to the Deuteronomic ideals was protected by Yahweh.

Excursus on the Composition of 2 Kings 18:13–19:37

Since Bernard Stade's *ZAW* article in 1886,[12] it has been the general position of scholars and commentators that there are two accounts of Sennacherib's attack on Judah in Kings and Isaiah, with the second one appearing in two versions. Thus 18:13–16 has been labeled account A, 18:17– 9:9a and 36–37 account B[1] and 19:9b–35 B[2]. In 1967 Brevard Childs undertook a thorough review of the theory particularly from a form-critical viewpoint.[13] He concluded that the theory was correct, and his work has remained the standard treatment ever since. On this reading, account A is the most factual report of the events, including Sennacherib's devastation of Judah, Hezekiah's payment of tribute, and Sennacherib's consequent withdrawal. Both of the B accounts, on Child's reading, have been shaped by later theological concerns, with B[1] being closer to the facts, and B[2] reflecting more of the so-called "Deuteronomic" theology. Despite the widespread acceptance of these conclusions, it is important to remind ourselves that there is no manuscript evidence in support of it.

One of the issues this theory raises is why both Kings and Isaiah share the same structure of the material. It seems reasonable to suppose that if these traditions had the lengthy period of development and transmission, that form critical theory assumes, there would have been alternate versions which either Kings or Isaiah would show. But that is not the case. Apart from the relatively minor textual differences noted at various places above, the two

11. This was not deleted from the account in Isaiah; it was never part of that account. See Christopher R. Seitz, "Account A and the Annals of Sennacherib: A Reassessment," *JSOT* 18 (1993): 47–57.

12. Bernard Stade, "Anmerkungen zu 2 Kö 15–21," *ZAW* 6 (1886): 156–89.

13. Brevard S. Childs, *Isaiah and the Assyrian Crisis,* SBT Second Series 3 (London: SCM Press, 1967).

accounts are duplicates. Thus, if the Kings material is taken from Isaiah, as I maintain, whatever development there was had been fully finalized before the Kings editors reused the account. Whatever theory one takes of the composition of Isaiah, this is asking a great deal. In many ways, the problem becomes even more difficult if Kings is the original.

In support of the argument that 19:9–35 is only a differing account of the same events first reported in 18:17–19:8, frequent appeals have been made to supposed "awkwardness" in the way this "more legendary" account has developed. Hobbs (268–74) has examined these arguments in detail and shows how they are often the result of circular reasoning (since this is a duplicate account it is awkward to make such and such a statement) or of special pleading. More recently Evans has developed a number of arguments pointing to the literary unity of 2 Kings 18 and 19. He attributes this unity to the so-called Deuteronomic Historian, but it is not necessary to grant this claim to recognize the validity of his arguments.[14]

Excursus on The Finding of the Book of the Torah

As early as Jerome, it was argued that the book that was found in the temple in Josiah's day was the book of Deuteronomy (so Gray, 715). The material that is referred to in 2 Kings 22 seems to be Deuteronomic, and Jeremiah is full of quotations and allusions to Deuteronomy, whereas prophets before his time have very few statements that can be clearly attributed to Deuteronomy. These latter facts were some of those that led W. M. L. de Wette in 1809 to argue that in fact, the book was written at that time and placed in the temple to be "found" there during the repairs.[15] This theory ultimately became the linchpin in Wellhausen's Documentary Hypothesis[16], making it possible to date the various biblical materials either earlier or later than 621 BC by their supposed relation, or lack of relation, to Deuteronomy.

This theory raised serious problems for those with a high view of scriptural inspiration, since Deuteronomy makes the clear statement that it was written by Moses (Deut 31:24). Two important arguments that supporters of de Wette put forward were that: (1) writing had not been invented in Moses' time, and (2) the clear predictions of the exile were quite impossible six or seven hundred years in advance of the fact. The latter of these is based on an assumption that genuine predictive prophecy is an impossibility, an assumption which if held true would undercut one of the Bible's strongest arguments for its inspiration by God. But it is an assumption, one which

14. Paul S. Evans, *The Invasion of Sennacherib in the Book of Kings: A Source-Critical and Rhetorical Study of 2 Kings 18-19*, VTSup 125 (Leiden: Brill, 2009).

15. *Beitraege zur Einleitung in das Alte Testament* (2 vols., 1806–07).

16. Julius Wellhausen, *Prolegomena zur Geschichte Israels* (Berlin: Druck und verlag von G. Reimer, 1833).

grows out of Enlightenment thinking, and one that should only be accepted with a very careful examination of all its consequences.

The other support for the theory was severely undercut by the discoveries that the Sumerians and the Egyptians were writing nearly 2,000 years before Moses was born. Moreover, the Canaanites were writing letters to the Egyptian pharaoh at roughly the same time as Moses and the Hebrews were leaving Egypt. By 1,000 BC the people of Tyre and Sidon were writing in an alphabetic consonantal script. However, it has recently been argued that writing was the province of a scribal culture supported by a royal court. Thus, the argument against Moses' ability to write has resurfaced. This is not the place to pursue that discussion, except to say that if we take at all seriously the description of Moses in the Bible, there is every reason to believe that a man raised in the courts of the pharaoh knew how to write and/or that he had persons in his retinue who could do so.

A further point that needs to be made here is that one of the requirements of a covenant was that it be written and that it be deposited in the sanctuary of the chief deity of the subject people. Both of those provisions are specifically addressed in Exodus 24 and 25. There we are told that Moses wrote the covenant (24:4) and that the written covenant on the stone tablets (the "ten words") "were to be kept in a "covenant box" (הָאָרֹן אֵת הָעֵדֻת, *hā ʾārōn ʾēṯ hā ʿēḏuṯ*) in the sanctuary (25:16). When Moses rewrote the covenant in the Deuteronomic form, he stipulated that this document was to be kept by the covenant box (Deut 31:26), and that when they had a king he was to make a new copy for himself, keeping it with him and reading it (Deut 17:18–19).

If we grant any credence to the above claims, we must ask if it is within the realm of possibility that the Torah of Moses, such a vitally important document, *could* be lost. I would argue that it does not stretch the limits of credulity to think so. First, there is the judges period, with all of the religious decline instigated by that period, the regular reading of the covenant that may have occurred during Joshua's lifetime stopped. Then the chaos that occurred after the ark was captured (and the tabernacle destroyed [cf. Jer 7:12–14]?) would only have contributed further to the document's being relegated to tradition and memory. If it was recovered and given some sort of position in the Solomonic temple, it would not have had the kind of iconic status that it would have had if all the previous events had not taken place. It would have been revered and honored but rarely, if ever, consulted; reference to the covenant being a matter of traditional memory rather than a firm connection to a book. Then with the reigns of Manasseh and Amon, the book could have been truly lost, taken from its place by the ark and lodged in some dusty storeroom, there to be happened upon by a workman.[17]

---

17. This is not to say that every word of the present book was necessarily written by Moses. It is evident that while these documents were treasured as foundational, they were also living documents and capable of judicious updating. That being said, the

Today the theory grows more convoluted with the suggestion that nothing was found, that the entire account of the find is a literary fiction. When the argument is made that some sort of discovery is necessary to justify the Josianic reform, it is retorted that there was no reform, that this too is a fiction, created in the fertile mind of an exilic, or postexilic literary creator. The net result is to make de Wette and his followers look conservative.

---

evidence for a thirteenth century date for the original, rather than a seventh century one continues to be compelling. See Kenneth A. Kitchen, *On the Reliability of the Old Testament* (Grand Rapids: Eerdmans, 2003), 299–304.

Bibliography

Monographs and Essays/Articles (Book as a Whole)

Ackroyd, Peter R. "Goddesses, Women and Jezebel." Pages 245–59 in *Images of Women in Antiquity*. Edited by Averil Cameron and Amélie Kuhrt. Detroit, MI: Wayne State University Press, 1983.

Ahlström, Gosta W. *Royal Administration and National Religion in Ancient Palestine*. SHANE 1. Leiden: Brill, 1982.

Alt, Albrecht. *Essays on Old Testament History and Religion*. Oxford: Blackwell, 1966.

Alter, Robert. *The Art of Biblical Narrative*. New York: Basic Books, 1981.

Aquila of Pontus. *Fragments of the Books of Kings According to the Translation of Aquila, from A MS. formerly in the Geniza at Cairo Now in the Possession of C. Taylor D.D. Master of St John's College and S. Schechter D. Litt. University Reader in Talmudic Literature*. Edited by F. Crawford Burkitt, Charles Taylor, S. Schechter. Cambridge: University Press, 1897.

Arbeli, Shoshana. "The Removal of the Tawananna from Her Position." Pages 79–85 in *Society and Economy in the Eastern Mediterranean (C 1500–1000 BC)*. Edited by M. Heltzer and E. Lipinski. OLA 23. Louvain: Peeters, 1988.

Ash, Paul S. *David, Solomon and Egypt: A Reassessment*. JSOTSup 297. Sheffield: Sheffield Academic, 1999.

Auld, A. Graeme. *Kings Without Privilege: David and Moses in the Story of the Bible's Kings*. Edinburgh: T&T Clark, 1994.

———. *Life in Kings: Reshaping the Royal Story in the Hebrew Bible*. Ancient Israel and Its Literature 30. Atlanta: SBL Press, 2017.

———. "Prophets Shared—But Recycled." Pages 19–28 in *Future of the Deuteronomistic History*. Edited by Thomas Römer. BETL 147. Leuven-Louvain: Peeters, 2000.

Aurelius, Erik. *Zukunft jenseits des Gerichts: Eine Redaktionsgeschichtliche Studie zum Enneateuch*. BZAW 319. Berlin: De Gruyter, 2003.

Avishur, Yitshak, and Michael Heltzer. *Studies on the Royal Administration in Ancient Israel in the Light of Epigraphic Sources*. Tel Aviv-Jaffa: Archaeological Center Publication, 2000.

Bach, Alice. *Women in the Hebrew Bible: A Reader*. New York: Routledge, 1999.

Balentine, Samuel E. *Prayer in the Hebrew Bible: The Drama of Divine-Human Dialogue*. OBT. Minneapolis, MN: Fortress, 1993.

Baltzer, Klaus. "Moses Servant of God and the Servants: Text and Tradition in the Prayer of Nehemiah (Neh 1:5–11)." Pages 121–30 in *The Future of Early Christianity: Essays in Honor of Helmut Koester*. Edited by Birger Albert Pearson, A. Thomas Kraabel, George W. E. Nickelsburg, and Norman R. Petersen. Minneapolis, MN: Fortress, 1991.

Barber, Cyril J. *The Books of Kings: The Righteousness of God Illustrated in the Lives of the People of Israel and Judah*. 2 vols. Eugene, OR: Wipf & Stock Publishers, 2004.

Barkay, Gabriel. "The Iron Age II–III." Pages 302–73 in *Archaeology of Ancient Israel*. Edited by Amnon Ben-Tor. Translated by R. Greenberg. New Haven: Yale University Press; Tel-Aviv: Open University of Israel, 1992.

Barr, James. "Revelation Through History in the Old Testament and in Modern Theology," Pages 60–74 in *New Theology No. 1*. Edited by Martin E. Marty and Dean G. Peerman. New York: Macmillan, 1964.

Becking, Bob. *The Fall of Samaria: An Historical and Archaeological Study*. SHANE 2. Leiden: Brill, 1992.

———. "No More Grapes from the Vineyard? A Plea for a Historical Critical Approach in the Study of the Old Testament." Pages 123–41 in *Congress Volume Oslo 1998: Oslo 1998*. Edited by M. Saebo and Andre Lemaire. VTSup 80. Leiden: Brill, 2000.

Beitzel, Barry J. *The Moody Atlas of Bible Lands*. Chicago: Moody Press, 1985.

Bird, Phyllis A. "The End of the Male Cult Prostitute: A Literary-Historical and Sociological Analysis of Hebrew Qādēš-Qĕdēšîm." Pages 37–80 in *Congress Volume Cambridge 1995*. Edited by John Adney Emerton. VTSup 66. Leiden: Brill, 1997.

Blenkinsopp, Joseph. *David Remembered: Kingship and National Identity in Ancient Israel*. Grand Rapids: Eerdmans, 2013.

———. *A History of Prophecy in Israel*. Louisville, KY: Westminster John Knox, 1996.

Block, Daniel I. "What Has Delphi to Do with Samaria? Ambiguity and Delusion in Israelite Prophecy." Pages 189–216 in *Writing and Ancient Near Eastern Society: Essays in Honor of Alan Millard*. Edited by Elizabeth Slater, Christopher Mee, and Piotr Bienkowski. LHBOTS 426. London: T&T Clark International, 2005.

Bodner, Keith. *The Theology of the Book of Kings*. Old Testament Theology. Cambridge: Cambridge University Press, 2019.

Bonhoeffer, Dietrich. *The Cost of Discipleship*. New York: Scribner 1963.

Boyd-Taylor, Cameron. "Robbers, Pirates and Licentious Women: Echoes of an Anti-Dionysiac Polemic in the Septuagint." Pages 559–71 in *Die Septuaginta—Texte, Kontexte, Lebenswelten: Internationale Fachtagung veranstaltet von Septuaginta Deutsch (LXX. D.), Wuppertal 20–23 Juli*

2006. Edited by Martin Karrer and Wolfgang Kraus. WUNT 219. Tübingen: Mohr Siebeck, 2008.

———. "Who's Afraid of Verlegenheitsübersetzungen?" Pages 197–210 in *Translating a Translation: The LXX and Its Modern Translations in the Context of Early Judaism*. Edited by Hans Ausloos. BETL 213. Leuven: Peeters, 2008.

Braulik, Georg. "Zur deuteronomistischen Konzeption von Freiheit Und Frieden." Pages 29–39 in *Congress Volume: Salamanca, 1983*. Edited by John Adney Emerton. VTSup 36. Leiden: Brill, 1985.

Brettler, Marc Zvi. "Interpretation and Prayer: Notes on the Composition of 1 Kings 8:15–53." Pages 17–35 in *Minhah Le-Nahum: Biblical and Other Studies Presented to Nahum H. Sarna in Honour of His Seventieth Birthday*. Edited by Marc Zvi Brettler and Michael Fishbane. JSOTSup 154. Sheffield: JSOT Press, 1993.

Brichto, Herbert Chanan. *Toward A Grammar of Biblical Poetics: Tales of the Prophets*. New York: Oxford University Press, 1992.

Briend, Jacques. "Le Dieu d'Israël Reconnu par des Étrangers: Signe de l'Universalisme du Salut." Pages 65–76 in *Ouvrir Les Écritures: Melanges offerts A Paul Beauchamp A l'Occasion De Ses Soixante-Dix Ans*. Edited by Pietro Bovati and Roland Meynet. LD 162. Paris: Cerf, 1995.

———. "Théologie et Récit: 1 R 12,1–19." Pagese 27–36 in *Penser la Foi: Recherches en théologie aujourd'hui: Mélanges offerts à Joseph Moingt*. Edited by Joseph Doré and Christoph Theobald. Paris: Cerf, 1993.

Bright, John. *A History of Israel*. 3rd ed. Philadelphia: Westminster, 1981.

Brodie, Thomas L. *The Crucial Bridge: The Elijah-Elisha Narrative As an Interpretive Synthesis of Genesis-Kings and A Literary Model for the Gospels*. Collegeville, MN: Liturgical Press, 2000.

Bronner, Leah. *The Stories of Elijah and Elisha as Polemics Against Baal Worship*. Pretoria Oriental Series 6. Leiden: Brill, 1968.

Brueggemann, Walter. *Testimony to Otherwise: The Witness of Elijah and Elisha*. St. Louis, MO: Chalice Press, 2001.

Campbell, Antony F. *Of Prophets and Kings: A Late Ninth Century Document (1 Samuel 1-2 Kings 10)*. CBQMS 17. Washington, DC: Catholic Biblical Association of America, 1986.

Carr, David Mclain. "Empirische Perspekitven auf das deuteronomistische Geschichtswerk." Pages 1–17 in *Deuteronomistischen Geschichtswerke*. Edited by Jan Christian Gertz, Doris Prechel, Konrad Schmid, and Markus Witte. BZAW 365. Berlin: Walter De Gruyter, 2006.

Clements, R. E. *In Spirit and In Truth: Insights from Biblical Prayers*. Atlanta: John Knox, 1985.

Coote, Robert B. *In Defense of Revolution: The Elohist History*. Minneapolis, MN: Fortress, 1991.

Coutts, John J. *Prophets & Kings of Israel: A History of Israel from the Institution of the Monarchy to the Fall of Samaria*. London: Longmans, 1969.

Crenshaw, James L. *Prophetic Conflict: Its Effect Upon Israelite Religion.* BZAW 124. Berlin: De Gruyter, 1971.

Cross, Frank. "The Themes of the Books of Kings and the Structure of the Deuteronomistic History." Pages 274–89 in *Canaanite Myth and Hebrew Epic.* Cambridge, MA: Harvard University Press, 1973.

Dailey, Anne C. "The Judgment of Women." Pages 142–49 in *Out of the Garden: Women Writers on the Bible.* Edited by Christina Büchmann and Celina Spiegel. New York: Fawcett Columbine, 1994.

Deurloo, Karel A. "The King's Wisdom in Judgement: Narration As Example." Pages 11–21 in *New Avenues in the Study of the Old Testament.* Edited by A. S. Van Der Woude. OtSt 25. Leiden: Brill, 1989.

DeVries, Simon J. "The Scheme of Dynastic Endangerment in Chronicles." *Proceedings, Eastern Great Lakes and Midwest Biblical Societies* 7 (1987): 59–77.

Dozeman, Thomas B. "The Composition of Ex 32 within the Context of the Enneateuch." Pages 175–89 in *Auf dem Weg zur Endgestalt von Genesis bis II Regum: On the Way to the Final Form from Genesis to II Kings. Festschrift for Hans-Christoph Schmitt on his 65th Birthday.* Edited by Martin Beck and Ulrike Schorn. BZAW 37. Berlin: Walter De Gruyter, 2006.

Dray, Carol A. *Studies on Translation and Interpretation in the Targum to the Books of Kings.* Studies in the Aramaic Interpretation of Scripture 5. Leiden: Brill, 2006.

Elgavish, David. "Inquiring of God Before Ratifying A Treaty." Pages 73–84 in *Thinking Towards New Horizons: Collected Communications to the XIXth Congress of the Internatiional Organization for the Study of the Old Testament, Ljubljana 2007.* Edited by Hermann Michael Niemann and Matthias Augustin. BEATAJ 55. Frankfurt: Peter Lang, 2008.

Ellis, Peter F. *The Books of Kings.* Old Testament Reading Guide 7. Collegeville, MN: Liturgical Press, 1966.

Eslinger, Lyle M. *Into the Hands of the Living God.* BLS 24. Sheffield: Almond, 1989.

Evans, Carl D. "Cult Images, Royal Policies and the Origins of Aniconism." Pages 192–212 in *The Pitcher Is Broken: Memorial Essays for Gösta W. Ahlström.* Edited by Steven W. Holloway and Lowell K. Handy. JSOTSup 190. Sheffield: Sheffield Academic, 1995.

Eynikel, Erik. "Prophecy and Fulfillment in the Deuteronomistic History (1 Kgs 13; 2 Kgs 23,16-18)." Pages 227–37 in *Pentateuchal and Deuteronomistic Studies: Papers Read at the XIIIth IOSOT Congress, Leuven 1989.* Edited by C. Brekelmans and J. Lust. BETL 94. Louvain: Leuven University Press, 1990. 227–37.

Fernández Marcos, Natalio. *Scribes and Translators: Septuagint and Old Latin in the Books of Kings.* VTSup 54. Leiden: Brill, 1994.

———. "La Vetus Latina de Reyes: Vorlage Distinta o Actividad Creadora?" Pages 64–73 in *Philologia Sacra: Biblische und patristische Studien für Hermann J. Frede und Walter Thiele zu ihrem siebzigsten Geburtstag, Band 1: Altes und Neues Testament.* Edited by Roger Gryson. Vetus

Latina: Aus der Geschichte der lateinishchen Bibel 24/1. Freiburg: Herder, 1993.

Fishbane, Michael A. *Biblical Interpretation in Ancient Israel.* Oxford: Clarendon, 1985.

Fokkelman, J. P. *King David (II Sam. 9–20 & I Kings 1–2).* Vol. 1 of *Narrative Art and Poetry in the Books of Samuel.* SSN 20. Assen: Van Gorcum, 1981.

Freedman, David Noel. *The Unity of the Hebrew Bible.* Distinguished Senior Faculty Lecture Series. Ann Arbor: University of Michigan Press, 1991.

Galil, Gershon. *The Chronology of the Kings of Israel and Judah.* SHCANE 9. Leiden: Brill, 1996.

Geyer, John B. "Where and What?" Pages 95–111 in *"He Unfurrowed His Brow and Laughed": Essays in Honour of Professor Nicolas Wyatt.* Edited by Wilfred G. E. Watson. AOAT 299. Münster: Ugarit-Verlag, 2007.

Gooding, D. W. *Relics of Ancient Exegesis: A Study of the Miscellanies in 3 Reigns 2.* SOTSMS 2. Cambridge: Cambridge University Press, 1976.

Gordon, Cyrus Herzl. *Before the Bible: The Common Backgrounds of Greek and Hebrew Civilization.* New York: Harper & Row, 1962.

Gottwald, Norman K. *The Hebrew Bible—A Socio-Literary Introduction.* · Philadelphia: Fortress, 1985.

Grabbe, Lester L. *1 & 2 Kings: History and Story in Ancient Israel.* T&T Clark Study Guides to the Old Testament. London: T&T Clark, 2017.

Gressmann, Hugo. "The Oldest History Writing in Israel." Pages 9–58 in *Narrative and Novella in Samuel: Studies by Hugo Gressmann and Other Scholars 1906–1923.* Edited by Hugo Gressmann and D. M. Gunn. JSOTSup 116. Sheffield: Almond Press, 1991.

Gros Louis, Kenneth R. R. "Elijah and Elisha." Pages 177–90 in *Literary Interpretations of Biblical Narratives.* Edited by Kenneth R. R. Gros Louis, James S. Ackerman, and Thayer S. Warshaw. Nashville, TN: Abingdon, 1974.

Hagan, G. Michael. "First and Second Kings." Pages 182–92 in *Complete Literary Guide to the Bible.* Edited by Leland Ryken and Tremper Longman III. Grand Rapids: Zondervan, 1993.

Halpern, Baruch. "The State of Israelite History." Pages 540–65 in *Reconsidering Israel and Judah: Recent Studies on the Deuteronomistic History.* Edited by Gary N. Knoppers and J. G. McConville. Sources for Biblical and Theological Study 8. Winona Lake, IN: Eisenbrauns, 2000.

———, and André Lemaire. "The Composition of Kings." Pages 123–54 in the *Books of Kings: Sources, Composition, Historiography and Reception.* Edited by André Lemaire, Baruch Halpern, and Matthew J. Adams. VTSup 129. Leiden: Brill, 2010.

Handy, Lowell K. *The Age of Solomon: Scholarship at the Turn of the Millennium.* SHCANE 11. Leiden: Brill, 1997.

Hanhart, Robert. "The Translation of the Septuagint in Light of Earlier Tradition and Subsequent Influences." Pages 339–79 in *Septuagint, Scrolls, and Cognate Writings: Papers Presented to the International Symposium on the Septuagint and Its Relations to the Dead Sea Scrolls and Other*

Writings (Manchester, 1990). Edited by George J. Brooke and Barnabas Lindars. SCS 33. Atlanta: Scholars Press, 1992.

Hanson, Paul D. *The People Called: The Growth of Community in the Bible: With a New Introduction*. Louisville, KY: Westminster John Knox, 2001.

Hayes, Christine Elizabeth. "Golden Calf Stories: The Relationship of Exodus 32 and Deuteronomy 9–10." Pages 45–93 in *The Idea of Biblical Interpretation: Essays in Honor of James L. Kugel*. Edited by Hindy Najman and Judith H. Newman. Supplements to the Journal for the Study of Judaism 83. Leiden: Brill, 2004.

Heaton, Eric William. *Solomon's New Men: The Emergence of Ancient Israel as a National State*. Currents in the History of Culture and Ideals. London: Thames and Hudson, 1974.

Helms, Randel. "Fiction in the Gospels." Pages 135–42 in *Jesus in History and Myth*, edited by R. Joseph Hoffmann and Gerald A. Larue. Buffalo, NY: Prometheus Books, 1986.

Hoffman, Yair. "Patterns of Religious Response to National Crisis in the Hebrew Bible and Some Methodological Reflections." Pages 18–35 in *Religious Responses to Political Crisis*. Edited by Henning Reventlow and Yair Hoffman. LHBOTS 444. New York: T&T Clark, 2008.

Holladay, John S., Jr. "The Kingdoms of Israel and Judah: Political and Economic Centralization in the Iron IIA-B (Ca. 1000-750 BCE)." Pages 368–98 in *Archaeology of Society in the Holy Land*. Edited by Thomas E. Levy. New Approaches in Anthropological Archaeology. London: Leicester University Press, 1995.

Hurowitz, Victor. *I Have Built You an Exalted House: Temple Building in the Bible in the Light of Mesopotamian and North-West Semitic Writings*. JSOTSup 115. Sheffield: JSOT Press, 1992.

Ishida, Tomoo. *The Royal Dynasties in Ancient Israel: A Study on the Formation and Development of Royal-Dynastic Ideology*. BZAW 142. Berlin: W. De Gruyter, 1977.

Janowski, Bernd. "'Ich Will in Eurer Mitte Wohnen": Struktur und Genese der exilischen Schekina-Theologie." Pages 165–93 in *Der Eine Gott der Beiden Testamente*. Edited by Yehoshua Amir. Jahrbuch für Biblische Theologie 2. Neukirchen-Vluyn: Neukirchener Verlag, 1987.

Jobling, David. "'Old and New Wisdom Mix Admirably': Bertolt Brecht's The Caucasian Chalk Circle." Pages 70–97 in *Marxist Feminist Criticism of the Bible*. Edited by Roland Boer and Jorunn Økland. Bible in the Modern World 14. Sheffield: Sheffield Phoenix, 2008.

———. *The Sense of Biblical Narrative: Structural Analyses in the Hebrew Bible, I*. JSOTSup 7. Sheffield: JSOT Press, 1986.

Kaltner, John, and Louis Stulman, eds. *Inspired Speech: Prophecy in the Ancient Near East, Essays in Honor of Herbert B. Huffmon*. JSOTSup 378. London: T&T Clark International, 2004.

Kaufmann, Yehezkel. *The Religion of Israel: From Its Beginnings to the Babylonian Exile*. Chicago: University of Chicago Press, 1960.

Kelly, Brian E. *Retribution and Eschatology in Chronicles*. JSOTSup 211. Sheffield: Sheffield Academic, 1996.
Kissling, Paul J. *Reliable Characters in the Primary History: Profiles of Moses, Joshua, Elijah, and Elisha*. JSOTSup 224. Sheffield: Sheffield Academic, 1996.
Kitchen, Kenneth A. *On the Reliability of the Old Testament*. Grand Rapids: Eerdmans, 2003.
Klaus, Nathan. *Pivot Patterns in the Former Prophets*. JSOTSup 247. Sheffield: Sheffield University Press, 1999.
Kletter, Raz. *Economic Keystones: The Weight System of the Kingdom of Judah*. JSOTSup 276. Sheffield: Sheffield Academic, 1998.
Knauf, Ernst Axel. "Kinneret and Naftali." Pages 219–33 in *Congress Volume: Oslo 1998*. Edited by André Lemaire and Magne Sæbø. International Organization for the Study of the Old Testament. Leiden: Brill, 2000.
Knoppers, Gary N. "Sex, Religion, and Politics: The Deuteronomist on Intermarriage." *HAR* 14 (1994): 121–41.
———. "Theories of the Redaction(s) of Kings." Pages 69–88 in *The Books of Kings: Sources, Composition, Historiography and Reception*. Edited by Baruch Halpern and André Lemaire. VTSup 129. Leiden: Brill, 2010.
———. *Two Nations Under God: The Deuteronomistic History of Solomon and the Dual Monarchies*. 2 vols. HSM 52, 54. Atlanta: Scholars Press, 1993.
———, and J. G. McConville. *Reconsidering Israel and Judah: Recent Studies on the Deuteronomistic History*. Sources for Biblical and Theological Study 8. Winona Lake, IN: Eisenbrauns, 2000.
Kooij, A. van der. "David, 'Het Licht van Israel.' " Pages 49–57 in *Vruchten van de Uithof: Studies Opgedragen aan Dr. H. A. Brongers ter Gelegenheid van Zijn Afscheid (16 Mei 1974)*. Utrecht: Theologisch Institut, 1974.
Kramer, Susan R. "'We Speak to God with Our Thoughts': Abelard and the Implications of Private Communication with God." *Church History: Studies in Christianity and Culture* 69 (2009): 18–40.
Kratz, Reinhard Gregor. *The Composition of the Narrative Books of the Old Testament*. London: T&T Clark, 2005.
Lamb, David T. *Righteous Jehu and His Evil Heirs: The Deuteronomist's Negative Perspective on Dynastic Succession*. Oxford Theological Monographs. Oxford: Oxford University Press, 2007.
Lang, Bernhard. "No God But Yahweh: The Origin and Character of Biblical Monotheism." Pages 41–49 in *Monotheism*. Edited by Claude Geffre and Jean-Pierre Jossua. Concilium 177. Edinburgh: T&T Clark, 1985.
Lefebvre, Philippe. "Mystìre et Disparition de Dan: De la Septante á l'Apocalypse." Pages 279–307 in *IX Congress of the International Organization for Septuagint and Cognate Studies, Cambridge, 1995*. Edited by Bernard A. Taylor. SCS 51. Atlanta: Scholars Press, 1997.
Lehmann, Karl Cardinal. "Gott und Macht: Ein religionsphilosophischer Versuch." Pages 264–90 in *Vorsehung, Schicksal und Göttliche Macht:*

Antike Stimmen zu einem Aktuellen Thema. Edited by Reinhard G. Kratz and Hermann Spieckermann. Tübingen: Mohr Siebeck, 2008.

Lemaire, André, ed. *Prophètes et Rois: Bible et Proche-Orient.* LD, Hors Série. Paris: Les Éditions Du Cerf, 2001.

———. "Towards a Redactional History of the Book of Kings." Pages 446–61 in *Reconsidering Israel and Judah: Recent Studies on the Deuteronomic History.* Edited by Gary N. Knoppers and J. Gordon McConville. SBT 8. Winona Lake, IN: Eisenbrauns, 2000.

———, Baruch Halpern, and Matthew J. Adams, eds. *The Books of Kings: Sources, Composition, Historiography and Reception.* VTSup 129. Leiden: Brill, 2010.

Leuchter, Mark, and Klaus-Peter Adam, eds. *Soundings in Kings: Perspectives and Methods in Contemporary Scholarship.* Minneapolis, MN: Fortress, 2010.

Lindars, B. "Elijah, Elisha, and the Gospel Miracles." Pages 63–79 in *Miracles: Cambridge Studies in Their Philosophy and History*. Edited by C. F. D. Moule. London: A. R. Mowbray, 1965.

Linville, James Richard. *Israel in the Book of Kings: The Past as A Project of Social Identity.* JSOTSup 272. Sheffield: Sheffield Academic, 1998.

Lowery, R. H. *The Reforming Kings: Cults and Society in First Temple Judah.* JSOTSup 120. Sheffield: JSOT Press, 1991.

Marinatos, Nanno. "The Role of the Queen in Minoan Prophecy Rituals." Pages 86–94 in *Images and Prophecy in the Ancient Eastern Mediterranean.* Edited by Martti Nissinen and Charles E. Carter. FRLANT 233. Göttingen: Vandenhoeck & Ruprecht, 2009.

Marshall, I. Howard. *The Books of Kings and Chronicles.* Scripture Union Bible Study Books. Grand Rapids: Eerdmans, 1968.

Matthews, Victor Harold, and Don C. Benjamin. *Social World of Ancient Israel, 1250-587 BCE.* Peabody, MA: Hendrickson, 1993.

McConville, J. Gordon. *Grace in the End: A Study in Deuteronomic Theology.* Carlisle, PA: Paternoster, 1993.

———. "Narrative and Meaning in the Books of Kings." *Bib* 70, no. 1 (1989): 31–49.

———. "The Old Testament Historical Books in Modern Scholarship." *Them* 22, no. 3 (1997): 3–13.

McKenzie, Steven L. "The Books of Kings in the Deuteronomistic History." 281–307 in *The History of Israel's Traditions: The Heritage of Martin Noth.* Edited by Steven L. McKenzie and M. Patrick Graham. JSOTSup 182. Sheffield: Sheffield Academic, 1991.

———. *The Trouble with Kings: The Composition of the Book of Kings in the Deuteronomistic History*. VTSup 42. Leiden: Brill, 1991.

———, and Matt Patrick Graham. *The History of Israel's Traditions: The Heritage of Martin Noth.* JSOTSup 182. Sheffield: Sheffield Academic, 1994.

Mettinger, Tryggve N. D. *King and Messiah: The Civil and Sacral Legitimation of the Israelite Kings.* ConBOT 8. Lund: Liberläromedel/Gleerup, 1976.

Miller, Patrick D. *They Cried to the Lord: The Form and Theology of Biblical Prayer*. Minneapolis, MN: Fortress Press, 1994.

Miller, Patrick D., Paul D. Hanson, and S. Dean McBride, eds. *Ancient Israelite Religion: Essays in Honor of Frank Moore Cross*. Philadelphia: Fortress Press, 1987.

de Moor, Johannes Cornelis, and H. F. Van Rooy, eds. *Past, Present, Future: The Deuteronomistic History and the Prophets*. OtSt 44. Leiden: Brill, 2000.

Na'aman, Nadav. "Sources and Composition in the Biblical History of Edom." Pages 313–20 in *Sefer Moshe: The Moshe Weinfeld Jubilee Volume*. Edited by Chaim Cohen, Avi Hurvitz, Shalom M. Paul, and Moshe Weinfeld. Winona Lake, IN: Eisenbrauns, 2004.

———. "Was an Early Edition of the Book of Kings Composed during Hezekiah's Reign?" *JSOT* 31, no. 1 (2017): 80–91.

Nelson, Richard. D. *The Double Redaction of the Deuteronomic History: The Case Is Still Compelling*. LHBOTS 18. Sheffield: JSOT Press, 1981.

———. *The Historical Books*. Nashville, TN: Abingdon, 1998.

Newman, Judith H. "The Scripturalization of Prayer in Exilic and Second Temple Judaism." Pages 7–24 in *Prayers That Cite Scripture: Biblical Quotation in Jewish Prayers from Antiquity through the Middle Ages*. Edited by James L. Kugel. Cambridge, MA: Harvard University Press, 2006.

Niditch, Susan. *Ancient Israelite Religion*. New York: Oxford University Press, 1997.

Nielsen, Kirsten. "Hvad er Ansvarlig Eksegese I Dag?" Pages 11–19 in *Vad, Hur Och Varför?: Reflektioner om Bibelvetenskap. Festskrift Till Lnger Ljung*. Edited by Lars Hartman. Uppsala Studies in Faiths and Ideologies 17. Uppsala: Uppsala University, 2006.

———. "Intertextuality and Hebrew Bible." Pages 17–31 in *Congress Volume, Oslo 1998*. Edited by A. Lemaire and M. Sæbø. VTSup 80. Leiden: Brill, 2000.

Noort, Edward. "Child Sacrifice in Ancient Israel: The Status Quaestionis." Pages 103–25 in *Strange World of Human Sacrifice*. Edited by J. N. Bremmer. Dudley, MA: Peeters, 2007.

Noth, Martin. *The Deuteronomic History*. JSOTSup 15. Sheffield: JSOT Press, 1981.

Novak, David. "Is There A Concept of Individual Rights in Jewish Law." Pages 129–52 in *Jewish Law Association Studies VII*. Edited by M. Finley and S. M. Passamaneck. Papers and Proceedings of Jewish Law Association. Atlanta: Scholars Press, 1994.

O'Connor, Michael Patrick. "The Pseudosorites: A Type of Paradox in the Hebrew Verse." Pages 161–72 in *Directions in Biblical Hebrew Poetry*. Edited by Elaine R. Follis. JSOTSup 40. Sheffield: JSOT Press, 1987.

———. "War and Rebel Chants in the Former Prophets." Pagaes 322–37 in *Fortunate The Eyes That See*. Edited by Astrid B. Beck, Andrew H. Bartelt, Paul R. Raabe, and Chris A. Franke. Grand Rapids: Eerdmans, 1995.

Oswalt, John N. *The Bible Among the Myths*. Grand Rapids: Zondervan, 2009.

———. "Is There Anything Unique in the Hebrew Prophets?" *BSac* 172 (January-March 2015): 67–84.

Overholt, Thomas W. "Elijah and Elisha in the Context of Israelite Religion." Pages 94–111 in *Prophets and Paradigms: Essays in Honor of Gene M. Tucker*. Edited by Gene M. Tucker and Stephen Breck Reid. JSOTSup 229. Sheffield: Sheffield Academic, 1996.

Parker, Simon B. "Death and Devotion: The Composition and Theme of Aqht." Pages 71–83 in *Love & Death in the Ancient Near East: Essays in Honor of Marvin H. Pope*. Edited by John H. Marks and Robert McClive Good. Guilford, CT: Four Quarters Pub. Co., 1987.

Peterson, Brian Neil. *The Authors of the Deuteronomic History: Locating a Tradition in Ancient Israel.* Minneapolis, MN: Fortress Press, 2014.

Pitard, Wayne Thomas. *Ancient Damascus: A Historical Study of the Syrian City-State from Earliest Times Until Its Fall to the Assyrians in 732 B.C.E.* Winona Lake, IN: Eisenbrauns, 1987.

Polak, Frank H. "The Septuagint Account of Solomon's Reign: Revision and Ancient Recension." Pages 139–64 in *X Congress of the international Organization for Septuagint and Cognate Studies, Oslo, 1998*. Edited by Bernard A. Taylor. SCS 51. Atlanta: Society of Biblical Literature, 2001.

Porter, J. R. "Old Testament Historiography." Pages 125–62 in *Tradition and Interpretation*. Edited by George Wishart Anderson. Society for Old Testament Study. Oxford: Oxford University Press, 1979.

Provan, Iain W. *Hezekiah and the Books of Kings: A Contribution to the Debate About the Composition of the Deuteronomistic History*. BZAW 172. Berlin: W. De Gruyter, 1988.

Pury, Albert De, and Thomas Römer, eds. *Die Sogenannte Thronfolgegeschichte Davids: Neue Einsichten und Anfragen*. OBO 176. Freiburg: Universitätsverlag, 2000.

Rad, Gerhard Von. *The Problem of the Hexateuch, and Other Essays.* Edinburgh: Oliver & Boyd, 1966.

Rainey, Anson F. "Tel Gerisa and the Danite Inheritance." Pages 59–72 in *Avitsur Book*. Tel-Aviv: Eretz Israel Museum, 1990.

Ramos-Lissón, Domingo. "El Exemplum de la Viuda de Sarepta en el Tratado de Viduis de San Ambrosio." Pages 177–91 in *Chartae Caritatis: Études de Patristique et d'Antiquité Tardive en Hommage á Yves-Marie Duval.* Edited by Benoît Gain, Pierre Jay, and Gérard Nauroy. Collection Des Études Augustiniennes. Série Antiquité 173. Paris: Institut D'études Augustiniennes, 2004.

Reimer, David J. "Stories of Forgiveness: Narrative Ethics and the Old Testament." Pages 359–78 in *Reflection and Refraction: Studies in Biblical Historiography in Honour of A. Graeme Auld*. Edited by Robert Rezetko, Timothy H. Lim, and W. Brian Aucker. VTSup 113. Leiden: Brill, 2006.

Renteria, Tamis Hoover. "The Elijah/Elisha Stories: A Socio-Cultural Analysis of Prophets and People in Ninth-Century BCE Israel." Pages 75–126 in

Elijah and Elisha in Socioliterary Perspective. Edited by Robert B. Coote. SemeiaSt 22. Atlanta: Scholars Press, 1992.

Revell, E. J. "Gentilics and Geography." Pages 113–23 in *Studies in Hebrew and Jewish Languages Presented to Shelomo Morag*. Edited by Mosheh Bar-Asher. Jerusalem: Hebrew University of Jerusalem, 1996.

Rieger, Joerg. "God and Power, Prophets, and Native Lands." Pages 58–71 in *Theology That Matters: Ecology, Economy, and God*. Edited by Darby Kathleen Ray. Minneapolis, MN: Fortress, 2006.

Riley, William. *King and Cultus in Chronicles: Worship and the Reinterpretation of History*. JSOTSup 160. Sheffield: JSOT Press, 1993.

Roberts, J. J. M. "Does God Lie: Divine Deceit as a Theological Problem in Israelite Prophetic Literature." Pages 211–20 in *Congress Volume: Jerusalem 1986*. Edited by J. A. Emerton. VTSup 40. Leiden: Brill, 1988.

Römer, Thomas. *The Future of the Deuteronomistic History*. BETL 147. Leuven-Louvain: Leuven University Press, 2000.

———. *The So-Called Deuteronomic History: A Sociological, Historical, and Literary Introduction*. London: T&T Clark, 2005.

———, and Albert De Pury. "Deuteronomistic Historiography (DH): History of Research and Debated Issues." Pages 24–141 in *Israel Constructs Its History: Deuteronomistic Historiography in Recent Research*. Edited by Albert De Pury, Thomas Römer, and Jean-Daniel Macchi. JSOTSup 306. Sheffield: Sheffield Academic, 2000.

Savran, George. "1 and 2 Kings." Pages 146–64 in *Literary Guide to the Bible*. Edited by Robert Alter and Frank Kermode. Cambridge, MA: Belknap Press of Harvard University Press, 1987.

Sawyer, John F. A., and David J. A. Clines. *Midian, Moab, and Edom: The History and Archaeology of Late Bronze and Iron Age Jordan and North-West Arabia*. JSOTSup 24. Sheffield: JSOT Press, 1983.

Scharbert, Josef. "Die Fürbitte im Alten Testament." Pages 91–109 in *"Diener in Eurer Mitte": Festsschrift für Dr. Antonius Hofmann, Bischof von Passau. zum 75. Geburtstag*. Edited by Rainer Beer. Schriften der Universität Passau: Reihe Katholische Theologie. Passau: Passavia Universitätsverlag, 1984.

Schmidt, Johann Michael. "Biblische Vorstellungen von 'Bund ' als Grundlage und Orientierung für das Jüdisch-Christliche Gespräch." Pages 153–68 in *"Wenn Nicht Jetzt, Wann Dann": Aufsätze für Hans Joachim Kraus zum 65. Gerburtstag*. Edited by Hans Georg Geyer. Neukirchen-Vluyn: Neukirchener Verlag, 1983.

Schulman, Alan R. "The Curious Case of Hadad the Edomite." Pages 122–35 in *Egyptological Studies in Honor of Richard A Parker: Presented on the Occasion of His 78th Birthday*. Edited by Leonard H. Lesko. Hanover, NH: University Press of New England, 1986.

Shenkel, James D. *Chronology and Recensional Development in the Greek Text of Kings*. HSM 1. Cambridge, MA: Harvard University Press, 1968.

Shupak, Nili. "Some Idioms Connected with the Concept of 'Heart' in Egypt and the Bible." Pages 202–12 in *Pharaonic Egypt: The Bible and Christianity*. Edited by Sarah Israelit-Groll. Jerusalem: Magnes Press, 1985.

Sicre, José Luis. "Diversas Reacciones ante el Latifundismo en el Antiguo Israel." Pages 393–412 in *Simposio Biblico Español*. Edited by Fernandez Marcos, J. Trebolle Barrera, and Fernandez Vallina. Madrid: Universidad Complutense, 1984.

Siebert-Hommes, Jopie. "The Widow of Zarephath and the Great Woman of Shunem: A Comparative Analysis of Two Stories." Pages 231–50 in *On Reading Prophetic Texts: Gender-Specific and Related Studies in Memory of Fokkelien Van Dijk-Hemmes*. Edited by Bob Becking and Meindert Dijkstra. *BibInt* 18. Leiden: Brill, 1996.

Slagboom, D. "Eerst het Altaar Geheeld (Meditatie)." Pages 16–21 in *Dominee in de Politiek*. The Hague: Staatkundig Gereformeerde Partij, 1982.

Smith, Carol. "'Queenship' in Israel? The Cases of Bathsheba, Jezebel and Athaliah." Pages 142–62 in *King and Messiah in Israel and the Ancient Near East: Proceedings of the Oxford Old Testament Seminar*. Edited by John Day. JSOTSup 270. Sheffield: Sheffield Academic, 1998.

Spohn, William C. "The Use of Scripture in Moral Theology." *TS* 47, no. 1 (1986): 88–102.

Sweeney, Marvin A. *King Josiah of Judah: The Lost Messiah of Israel*. Oxford: Oxford University Press, 2001.

Talstra, Eep. "Biblical Hebrew Clause Types and Clause Hierarchy." Pages 180–93 in *Studies in Hebrew and Aramaic Syntax: Presented to Professor J. Hoftijzer on the Occasion of his Sixty-fifth Birthday*. Edited by Karel Jongeling, Heleen Murre-van den Berg, and van Rompay. Studies in Semitic Languages and Linguistics 17. Leiden: Brill, 1991.

———. "From the 'Eclipse' to the 'Art' of Biblical Narrative: Reflections on Methods of Biblical Exegesis." Pages 1–41in *Perspectives in the Study of the Old Testament and Early Judaism*. Edited by Ed Noort and Florentino García Martínez. VTSup 73. Leiden: Brill, 1998.

———. "The Name in Kings and Chronicles." Pages 55–70 in *Revelation of the Name YHWH to Moses*. Edited by George H. van Kooten. Themes in Biblical Narrative 9. Leiden: Brill, 2006.

Terrien, Samuel L. *The Elusive Presence: Toward a New Biblical Theology*. Religious Perspectives 26. San Francisco: Harper & Row, 1978.

Tetley, M. Christine. *The Reconstructed Chronology of the Divided Kingdom*. Winona Lake, IN: Eisenbrauns, 2005.

Thiel, Winfried. "Die Erkenntnisaussage in den Elia- und Elisa-Überlieferungen." Pages 255–69 in *Von Gott Reden: Beiträge zur Theologie und Exegese des Alten Testaments: Festschrift für Siegfried Wagner zum 65 Geburtstag*. Edited by Dieter Vieweger and Ernst-Joachim Waschke. Neukirchen-Vluyn: Neukirchener, 1995.

Thiele, Edwin Richard. *The Mysterious Numbers of the Hebrew Kings: A Reconstruction of the Chronology of the Kingdoms of Israel and Judah*. 3rd ed. Grand Rapids: Zondervan, 1983.

Thomas, Benjamin D. *Hezekiah and the Compositional History of the Book of Kings*. FAT 2. Reihe 63. Tübingen: Mohr Siebeck, 2014.

Thon, Johannes. "Das Grab des 'Lügenpropheten' im Dienste der Wahrheit (1 Kön 13,11–32; 2 Kön 23,15–18)." Pages 467–75 in *Die unwiderstehliche Wahrheit: Studien zur alttestamentlichen Prophetie: Festschrift für Arndt Meinhold*. Edited by Ruediger Lux. Arbeiten zur Bibel und ihrer Geschichte 23. Leipzig: Evangelische Verlagsanstalt, 2006.

Trebolle Barrera, Julio C. "Light from 4QJudga and 4QKgs on the Text of Judges and Kings." Pages 315–24 in *The Dead Sea Scrolls: Forty Years of Research*. Edited by Uriel Rappaport and Devorah Dimant. STDJ 10. Leiden: Brill, 1992.

———. "A Preliminary Edition of 4QKings (4Q54)." Pages 229–46 in the *Madrid Qumran Congress: Proceedings of the International Congress on the Dead Sea Scrolls, Madrid, 18-21 March, 1991*. Edited by Julio C. Trebolle Barrera and Luis Vegas Montaner. STDJ 11. Leiden: Brill, 1992.

Van Seters, John. "The Deuteronomistic History: Can It Avoid Death by Redaction?" Pages 213–22 in *Future of the Deuteronomistic History*. Edited by Thomas Romer. BETL 147. Louvain: Peeters, 2000.

Vaughn, A. G., and A. E. Killebrew. *Jerusalem in Bible and Archaeology: The First Temple Period*. SBL Symposium 18. Atlanta: Society of Biblical Literature, 2003.

Vaux, Roland De. *Ancient Israel: Its Life and Institutions*. New York: McGraw-Hill, 1961.

Vieweger, Dieter. "'… Und Führte euch Heraus aus dem Eisenschemlzofen Aus Ägypten …': *Bwr Hbrzl* als Metapher für die Knechtschaft in Ägypten (Dtn 4,20; 1 Kön 8,51 und Jer 11,4)." Pages 265–76 in *Gottes Recht als Lebensraum: Festschrift für Hans Jochen Boecker*. Edited by Peter Mommer, Werner H. Schmidt, and Hans Strauss. Neukirchen-Vluyn: Neukirchener Verlag, 1993.

Wallace, Ronald S. *Elijah and Elisha: Expositions from the Book of Kings*. Edinburgh: Oliver and Boyd, 1957.

Wardle, W. L., H. Wheeler Robinson, and Harold H. Rowley. "The History of Israel." Pages 110–86 in *Record and Revelation: Essays on the Old Testament by Members of the Society for Old Testament Study*. Edited by H. Wheeler Robinson. Society for Old Testament Study. Oxford: Clarendon Press, 1938.

Weinfeld, Moshe. *Deuteronomy and the Deuteronomic School*. Oxford: Clarendon Press, 1972.

Weisman, Ze'ev. *Political Satire in the Bible*. SemeiaSt 32. Atlanta: Scholars Press, 1998.

Weitzman, Steven. *Song and Story in Biblical Narrative: The History of a Literary Convention in Ancient Israel.* Indiana Studies in Biblical Literature. Bloomington: Indiana University Press, 1997.

Wénin, André. "Personnages Humains et Anthropologie dans le Récit Biblique." Pages 43–71 in *Analyse Narrative et Bible: Deuxiéme Colloque International du RRENAB*. Edited by C. Focant. BETL 191. Leuven: Peeters, 2005.

Wevers, John William. *A Study in the Hebrew Variants in the Books of Kings and Their Relationship To the Old Greek and Other Greek Recensions, Dedicated to Professor Henry S. Gehman on the Occasion of His 60th Birthday*. Berlin: A. Töpelmann, 1948.

White, Marsha C. *The Elijah Legends and Jehu's Coup.* BJS 311. Atlanta: Scholars Press, 1997.

Whybray, Norman. *The Succession Narrative: A Study of II Samuel 9–20, I Kings 1 and 2*. SBT II/9. Napierville, IL: A. R. Allenson, 1968.

Wilcox, Max. "'Silence in Heaven' (Rev 8:1) and Early Jewish Thought." Pages 241–44 in *Mogilany 1989: Papers on the Dead Sea Scrolls offered in Memory of Jean Carmignac*. Edited by Zdzislaw Jan Kapera. Kraków: Enigma Press, 1991.

Willard, Dallas. *The Divine Conspiracy: Discovering Our Hidden Life in God*. New York: Harper, 1998.

Wilson, Robert R. *Prophecy and Society in Ancient Israel.* Philadelphia: Fortress Press, 1980.

Wind, Renate. "Widerstand ist Möglich—Fünf Frauengeschichten aus der Bibel." Pages 173–84 in *Wer Ist Unser Gott?: Beiträge zu Einer Befreiungstheologie im Kontext der "Ersten" Welt*. Edited by Luise Schottroff and Willy Schottroff. München: Chr Kaiser Verlag, 1986.

Wood, Bryant G. *The Sociology of Pottery in Ancient Palestine: The Ceramic Industry and the Diffusion of Ceramic Style in the Bronze and Iron Ages.* JSOTSup 103. Sheffield: JSOT Press, 1990.

Yadin, Yigael. *The Art of Warfare in Biblical Lands: In the Light of Archeological Discovery*. Translated by M. Pearlman. 2 vols. New York; McGraw-Hill, 1963.

Zakovitch, Yair. "Assimilation in Biblical Narratives." Pages 175–96 in *Empirical Models for Biblical Criticism*. Edited by Jeffrey H. Tigay. Philadelphia: University of Pennsylvania Press, 1985.

Monographs and Essays (2 Kings)

Abadie, Philippe. "From the Impious Manasseh (2 Kings 21) to the Convert Manasseh (2 Chronicles 33): Theological Rewriting by the Chronicler." Pages 89–104 in *Chronicler as Theologian: Essays in Honor of Ralph W. Klein*, edited by Patrick M. Graham. JSOTSup 371. London: T&T Clark, 2003.

———. "Personnages Bibliques et 'formation' Éthique des Lecteurs." Pages 73–94 in *Analyse Narrative et Bible: Deuxieme Colloque International Du RRENAB, Louvain-La-Neuve, Avril 2004*. Edited by C. Focant. BETL 191. Leuven: Peeters, 2005.

Ackroyd, Peter R. "The Biblical Interpretation of the Reigns of Ahaz and Hezekiah." Pages 247–59 in *In the Shelter of Elyon: Essays on Ancient Palestinian Life and Literature in Honor of G. W. Ahlström*. Edited by W. Boyd Barrick and John R. Spencer. JSOTSup 31. Sheffield: JSOT Press, 1984.

Ahlström, Gösta W. "The Battle at Ramoth-Gilead in 841 BC." Pages 157–66 in *Wünschet Jerusalem Frieden: Collected Communications to the XIIIth Congress of the International Organization for the Study of the Old Testament, Jerusalem 1986*. Edited by Matthias Augustin and Klaus-Dietrich Schunck. Beiträge zur Erforschung des Alten Testaments und des antiken Judentums 13. Frankfurt: Peter Lang, 1988.

Akoto, Dorothy B. E. A. "Women and Health in Ghana and The Trokosi Practice: An Issue of Women's and Children's Rights in 2 Kings 4:1–7." Pages 96–110 in *African Women, Religion, and Health: Essays in Honor of Mercy Amba Ewudzi Oduyoye (Women from the Margins)*. Edited by Isabel Apawo Phiri, Sarojini Nadar, and Mercy Amba Oduyoye. Maryknoll, NY: Orbis Books, 2006.

Aster, Shawn Zelig. "'They Feared God'/'They Did Not Fear God': On the Use of Yĕrēʾ and Yārēʾ ʾet YHWH in 2 Kings 17:24–41." Pages 135–41 in *Birkat Shalom Studies in The Bible, Ancient Near Eastern Literature, and Postbiblical Judaism: Presented to Shalom M. Paul on The Occasion of His Seventieth Birthday*. Edited by Chaim Cohen. Winona Lake, IN: Eisenbrauns, 2008.

Aucker, W. Brian. "A Prophet in King's Clothes: Kingly and Divine Re-presentation in 2 Kings 4 and 5." Pages 1–25 in *Reflection and Refraction: Studies in Biblical Historiography in Honour of A. Graeme Auld*. Edited by Robert Rezetko, Timothy H. Lim, and W. Brian Aucker. VTSup 113. Leiden: Brill, 2006.

Auld, A. Graeme. "Jeremiah-Manasseh-Samuel: Significant Triangle? Or Vicious Circle?" Pages 1–9 in *Prophecy in the Book of Jeremiah*. Edited by Hans M. Barstad and Reinhard G. Kratz. BZAW 388. Berlin: Walter De Gruyter, 2009.

Barré, Lloyd M. *The Rhetoric of Political Persuasion: The Narrative Artistry and Political Intentions of 2 Kings 9–11*. CBQMS 20. Washington, DC: Catholic Biblical Association of America, 1988.

Barrick, W. Boyd. *The King and the Cemeteries: Toward a New Understanding of Josiah's Reform*. VTSup 88. Leiden: Brill, 2002.

Bartlett, John R. "The 'United' Campaign Against Moab in 2 Kings 3:4–27." Pages 135–46 in *Midian, Moab and Edom: The History and Archaeology of Late Bronze and Iron Age Jordan and North-West Arabia*. Edited by John F. A. Sawyer and David J. A. Clines. JSOTSup 24. Sheffield: JSOT Press, 1983.

Baumgart, Norbert Clemens. "Gottes Gegenwart in Krieg: Zum Zusammenhang zwischen den Erzählungen 2 Kön 6,8–23 und 6,24–7,20." Pages 57–76 in *Das Manna Fällt auch Heute Noch: Beiträge zur Geschichte und Theologie des Alten, Ersten Testaments: Festschrift für Erich Zenger.* Edited by Frank-Lothar Hossfeld and Ludg Schwienhorst-Schönberger. Herders biblische Studien 44. Freiburg: Herder, 2004.

Beach, Eleanor Ferris. "Transforming Goddess Iconography in Hebrew Narrative." Pages 239–63 in *Women and Goddess Traditions: in Antiquity and Today*. Edited by Karen L. King. Studies in Antiquity and Christianity. Minneapolis, MN: Fortress Press, 1997.

Beauchamp, Paul. "La Lettre à la Divinité ou le Psaume comme Ex-Voto: Des 'Sefârîm' de Is 37,14 (2 R 19,14) au 'Miketâv' de Is 38,9." Pages 105–20 in *Lettres dans la Bible et Dans la Littérature: Actes du Colloque de Lyon, 3–5 Juillet 1996*. Edited by Louis Panier. LD 181. Paris: Cerf, 1999.

Becking, Bob. "The Enigmatic Garden of Uzza: A Religio-Historical Footnote to 2 Kings 21:18,26." Pages 383–91 in *Berührungspunkte: Studien zur Sozial- und Religionsgeschichte Israels und seiner Umwelt: Festschrift für Rainer Albertz zu seinem 65. Geburtstag*. Edited by R. Schmitt, J. Wöhrle, and I. Kottsieper. AOAT 350. Münster: Ugarit-Verlag, 2008.

———. *The Fall of Samaria: An Historical and Archaeological Study.* SHANE 2. Leiden: Brill, 1992.

———. "From Apostasy to Destruction: A Josianic View on the Fall of Samaria (2 Kings 17,21–23)." Pages 263–78 in *Deuteronomy and Deuteronomic Literature: Festschrift C.H.W. Brekelmans*. Edited by M. Vervenne and J. Lust. BETL 133. Louvain: Leuven University Press, 1997.

———. "From Exodus to Exile: 2 Kgs 17,7–20 in the Context of Its Co-Text." Pages 215–31 in *Studies in Historical Geography and Biblical Historiography: Presented to Zechariah Kallai*. Edited by Gershon Galil and Moshe Weinfeld. VTSup 81. Leiden: Brill, 2000.

———. "Jehojachin's Amnesty, Salvation for Israel? Notes on 2 Kings 25,27–30." Pages 283–93 in *Pentateuchal and Deuteronomistic Studies: Papers Read at the XIIIth IOSOT Congress, Leuven 1989*. Edited by C. Brekelmans and J. Lust. BETL 94. Louvain: Leuven University Press, 1990.

Begg, Christopher T. "Joash of Judah According to Josephus." Pages 301–20 in *Chronicler as Theologian: Essays in Honor of Ralph W. Klein*. Edited by Patrick M. Graham. JSOTSup 371. London: T&T Clark, 2003.

Ben-Barak, Zafrira. "The Case of Naboth the Jezreelite in the Light of Documents from Mesopotamia—A New Perspective." Pages 15–20 in *Proceedings of the Ninth World Congress of Jewish Studies. Division A: The Period of the Bible*. Edited by Raphael Giveon and Dawid 'Asaf. Jerusalem: World Union of Jewish Studies, 1986.

Ben Zvi, Ehud. "Imagining Josiah's Book and the Implications of Imagining It in Early Persian Yehud." Pages 193–212 in *Berührungspunkte. Studien zur Sozial- Und Religionsgeschichte Israels und seiner Umwelt. Festschrift für Rainer Albertz zu seinem 65. Geburtstag*. Edited by R. Schmitt, I. Kottsieper, and J. Wöhrle. AOAT 350. Münster: Ugarit-Verlag, 2008.

———. "Malleability and Its Limits: Sennacherib's Campaign Against Judah as a Case-Study." Pages 73–105 in *'Like a Bird in a Cage': The Invasion of Sennacherib in 701 BCE*. Edited by Lester L. Grabbe. JSOTSup 363. London: Sheffield Academic, 2003.

Bergen, Wesley J. "The Prophetic Alternative: Elisha and the Israelite Monarchy." Pages 127–37 in *Elijah and Elisha in Socioliterary Perspective*. Edited by Robert B. Coote. SemeiaSt 22. Atlanta: Scholars Press, 1992.

Boogaart, Thomas Arthur. "Drama and the Sacred: Recovering the Dramatic Tradition in Scripture and Worship." Pages 35–61 in *Touching the Altar: The Old Testament for Christian Worship*. Edited by Carol M. Bechtel. Grand Rapids: William B Eerdmans Publishing, 2008.

Bordreuil, Pierre. "A Propos de l'inscription de Mesha ͑ Deux Notes." Pages 158–67 in *Studies in Language and Literature in Honour of Paul-Eugène Dion. Vol. 3 of World of the Aramaeans*. Edited by P. M. Michèle Daviau, Michael Weigl, and John W. Wevers. 3 vols. JSOTSup 326. Sheffield: Sheffield Academic, 2001.

Bostok, David. "The Theme of Faith in the Hezekiah Narratives." PhD dissertation, University of Durham, 2003.

Braulik, Georg. "'Die Weisung und das Gebot' im Enneateuch." Pages 115–40 in *Das Manna Fällt auch Heute Noch: Beiträge zur Geschichte und Theologie des Alten, Ersten Testaments: Festschrift für Erich Zenger*. Edited by Frank-Lothar Hossfeld and Ludg Schwienhorst-Schönberger. Herders biblische Studien 44. Freiburg: Herder, 2004.

Camp, Claudia V. "Female Voice, Written Word: Women and Authority in Hebrew Scripture." Pages 97–113 in *Embodied Love: Sensuality and Relationship as Feminist Values*. Edited by Paula M. Cooey, Sharon A. Farmer, and Mary Ellen Ross. San Francisco: Harper and Row, 1987.

Carroll, Robert P. "Textual Strategies and Ideology in the Second Temple Period." Pages 108–24 in *Second Temple Studies: 1. Persian Period*. Edited by Philip R. Davies. JSOTSup 117. Sheffield: Sheffield Academic, 1991.

Childs, Brevard S. *Isaiah and the Assyrian Crisis*. Studies in Biblical Theory 3. London: S.C.M., 1967.

Clements, Ronald E. "The Prophecies of Isaiah to Hezekiah Concerning Sennacherib 2 Kings 19.21–34//Isa 37.22–35."Pages 65–78 in *Prophetie und Geschichtliche Wirklichkeit im Alten Israel: Festschrift für Siegfried Herrmann zum 65. Geburtstag*. Edited by Rüdiger Liwak and Siegfried Wagner. Stuttgart: Kohlhammer, 1991.

———. "A Royal Privilege: Dining in the Presence of the Great King (2 Kings 25.27–30)." Pages 49–66 in *Reflection and Refraction: Studies in Biblical Historiography in Honour of A. Graeme Auld*. Edited by Robert Rezetko, Timothy H. Lim, and W. Brian Aucker. VTSup 113. Leiden: Brill, 2006.

Cloete, Walter Theophilus Woldemar. "Distinguishing Prose and Verse in 2 Ki 19:14–19." Pages 31–40 in *Verse in Ancient Near Eastern Prose*. Edited by Johannes C. De Moor and Wilfred G. E. Watson. AOAT 42. Neukirchen-Vluyn: Neukirchener Verlag, 1993.

Cogan, Mordechai. "The Chronicler's Use of Chronology as Illuminated by Neo-Assyrian Royal Inscriptions." Pages 197–20 in *Empirical Models for Biblical Criticism*. Edited by Jeffrey H. Tigay and Richard Elliott Friedman. Philadelphia: University of Pennsylvania Press, 1985.

———. "A Slip of the Pen? on Josiah's Actions in Samaria (2 Kings 23:15–20)." Pages 3–8 in *Sefer Moshe: The Moshe Weinfeld Jubilee Volume: Studies in the Bible and the Ancient Near East, Qumran, and Post-Biblical Judaism*. Edited by Chaim Cohen, Avi Hurvitz, Shalom M. Paul, and Moshe Weinfeld. Winona Lake, IN: Eisenbrauns, 2004.

Coggins, Richard J. "2 Kings 23,29: A Problem of Method in Translation." Pages 277–81 in *Pentateuchal and Deuteronomistic Studies: Papers Read at the XIIIth IOSOT Congress, Leuven 1989*. Edited by C. Brekelmans and J. Lust. Ephemeridum Theologicarum Lovaniensium 94. Louvain: Leuven University Press, 1990.

Conrad, Joachim. "2 Kön 2,1–18 Als Elija-Geschichte." Pages 263–71 in *"Wünschet Jerusalem Frieden": Collected Communications to the XIIIth Congress of the International Organization for The Study of the Old Testament, Jerusalem 1986*. Edited by Matthias Augustin and Klaus-Dietrich Schunck. Beiträge zur Erforschung des Alten Testaments und des antiken Judentums 13. Frankfurt: Peter Lang, 1988.

Conroy, Charles. "Methodological Reflections on Recent Studies of the Naaman Pericope (2 Kings 5): Some Backgrounds to Luke 4:27." Pages 32–47 in *Luke and Acts*. Edited by G. O'Collins and G. Marconi. New York: Paulist, 1992.

———. "Reflections on the Exegetical Task: Apropos of Recent Studies on 2 Kings 22–23." Pages 255–68 in *Pentateuchal and Deuteronomistic Studies: Papers Read at the XIIIth IOSOT Congress, Leuven 1989*. Edited by C. Brekelmans and J. Lust. BETL 94. Leuven: Leuven University Press, 1990.

Cooley, Robert. "Gathered to His People: A Study of a Dothan Family Tomb." Pages 47–58 in *Living and Active Word of God: Studies in Honor of Samuel J. Schultz*. Edited by Morris A. Inch and Ronald Youngblood. Winona Lake, IN: Eisenbrauns, 1983.

Coote, Robert B., ed. *Elijah and Elisha in Socioliterary Perspective*. SemeiaSt 22. Atlanta: Scholars Press, 1992.

———. "Yahweh Recalls Elijah." Pages 115–20 in *Traditions in Transformation: Turning Points in Biblical Faith*. Edited by Baruch Halpern and Jon D. Levenson. Winona Lake, IN: Eisenbrauns, 1981.

Delamarter, Steve. "The Vilification of Jehoiakim (A.K.A. Eliakim and Joiakim) in Early Judaism." Pages 190–204 in *Function of Scripture in Early Jewish and Christian Tradition*. Edited by A. Evans and James Sanders. Library of New Testament Studies 154. Sheffield: Sheffield Academic, 1998.

Delcor, M. "La Divinité Ashima de Samarie En 2R 17,30 et ses Survivances." Pages 33–48 in *Proceedings of the First International Congress of the Société d'Études Samaritaines, Tel-Aviv, April 11-13, 1988*. Edited by A. Tal and M. Florentin. Tel-Aviv: Chaim Rosenberg School for Jewish Studies, 1991.

Dever, William G. "The Silence of the Text: An Archaeological Commentary on 2 Kings 23." Pages 143–68 in *Scripture and Other Artifacts: Essays on the Bible and Archaeology in Honor of Philip J. King*. Edited by Michael D. Coogan, J. Cheryl Exum, and Lawrence E. Stager. Louisville, KY: Westminster John Knox Press, 1994.

Dijk-Hemmes, Fokkelien Van. "The Great Woman of Shunem and the Man of God: A Dual Interpretation of 2 Kings 4:8–37." Pages 218–30 in *Feminist Companion to Samuel and Kings*. Edited by Athalya Brenner. FCB 5. Sheffield: Sheffield Academic, 1994.

Dorn, Christopher. "The Ways of God in the World: The Drama of 2 Kings 6:8–23." Pages 9–20 in *Probing the Frontiers of Biblical Studies*. Edited by J. Harold Ellens and John T. Greene. Eugene, OR: Pickwick Publications, 2009.

Dorp, Jaap Van. "The Prayer of Isaiah and the Sundial of Ahaz (2 Kgs 20:11)." Pages 253–65 in *Psalms and Prayers: Apeldoorn August 2006*. Edited by Bob Becking and Eric Peels. OtSt 55. Leiden: Brill, 2007.

Driscoll, Jeremy. "Exegetical Procedures in the Desert Monk Poemen." Pages 155–78 in *Steps to Spiritual Perfection: Studies on Spiritual Progress in Evagrius Ponticus*. Edited by Jeremy Driscoll. Mahwah, NJ: Paulist Press, 1995.

Dutcher-Walls, Patricia. *Narrative Art, Political Rhetoric: The Case of Athaliah and Joash*. JSOTSup 209. Sheffield: JSOT Press, 1996.

Edelman, Diana. "Huldah the Prophet—of Yahweh or Asherah." Pages 231–50 in *Feminist Companion to Samuel and Kings*. Edited by Athalya Brenner. FCB 5. Sheffield: Sheffield Academic, 2000.

Evans, Carl D. "Naram-Sin and Jeroboam: The Archetypal *Unheilsherrscher* in Mesopotamia and Biblical Historiography." Pages 97–125 in *Scripture in Context II: More Essays on the Comparative Method*. Edited by William W. Hallo, James C. Moyer, and Leo G. Perdue. Winona Lake, IN: Eisenbrauns, 1983.

Evans, Paul S. "Sennacherib's 701 Invasion into Judah: What Saith the Scriptures?" Pages 57–77 in *Function of Ancient Historiography in Biblical and Cognate Studies*. Edited by Patricia G. Kirkpatrick and Timothy D. Goltz. JSOTSup 489. New York: T&T Clark, 2008.

Eynkiel, Erik. "The Portrait of Manasseh and the Deuteronomistic History." Pages 233–61 in *Deuteronomy and Deuteronomic Literature: Festschrift C.H.W. Brekelmans*. Edited by M. Vervenne and J. Lust. BETL 133. Leuven: Leuven University Press, 1997.

———. *The Reform of King Josiah and the Composition of the Deuteronomistic History*. OtSt 33. Leiden: Brill, 1996.

———. "The Reform of King Josiah: 2 Kings 23:1–24." Pages 394–425 in *Die Septuaginta—Texte, Kontexte, Lebenswelten: Internationale Fachtagung veranstaltet von Septuaginta Deutsch (LXX. D.), Wuppertal 20–23 Juli*

2006. Edited by Martin Karrer and Wolfgang Kraus. WUNT 219. Tübingen: Mohr Siebeck, 2008.

Fernández Marcos, Natalio. "On Double Readings, Pseudo-Variants and Ghost-Names in the Historical Books." Pages 591–604 in *Emanuel: Studies in Hebrew Bible, Septuagint, and Dead Sea Scrolls in Honor of Emanuel Tov*. Edited by Shalom M. Paul, Robert A. Kraft, Lawrence H. Schiffman, and Weston W. Fields. VTSup 94. Leiden: Brill, 2003.

———. "La Reanimación del Hijo de la Sunamita en el Texto Antioqueno." Pages 119–28 in ΚΑΤΑ ΤΟΥΣ Ο': *Selon les Septante: Trente Études sur la Bible Grecque des Septante: en Hommage à Marguerite Harl*. Edited by Gilles Dorival and Olivier Munnich. Paris: Cerf, 1995.

———. "La Vetus Latina de Reyes: ¿Vorlage Distinta o Actividad Creadora?" Pages 64–73 in *Philologia Sacra: Biblische und patristische Studien für Hermann J. Frede und Walter Thiele zu Ihrem siebzigsten Geburtstag, Band 1: Altes und Neues Testament*. Edited by Roger Gryson. Vetus Latina: Aus der Geschichte der lateinishchen Bibel 24/1. Freiburg: Herder, 1993.

Fewell, Danna Nolan. "The Gift: World Alteration and Obligation in 2 Kings 4:8–37." Pages 109–24 in *Wise and Discerning Mind: Essays in Honor of Burke O. Long*. Edited by Saul M. Olyan and Robert C. Culley. Providence, RI: Brown Judaic Studies, 2020.

Fontinoy, Charles. "Les Noms du Diable et Leur Étymologie." Pages 157–70 in *Orientalia: J. Duchesne-Guillemin Emerito Oblata*. Edited by Charles Fontinoy. Acta Iranica, Deuxième série: Hommages et Opera Minora. Leiden: Brill, 1984.

Fox, Everett. "The Translation of Elijah: Issues and Challenges." Pages 156–69 in *Bible Translation on the Threshold of the Twenty-First Century: Authority, Reception, Culture and Religion*. Edited by Athalya Brenner and Jan Willem Van Henten. JSOTSup 353. London: Sheffield Academic, 2009.

Ghantous, Hadi. *The Elisha—Hazael Paradigm and the Kingdom of Israel: The Politics of God in Ancient Syria-Palestine*. Bible World. Durham: Acumen, 2013.

Gonçalvìs, Francolino J. "2 Rois 18,13–20,19 par Isaïe 36–39: Encore Une Fois, Lequel des Deux Livres fut le Premier?" Pages 27–55 in *Lectures et Relectures de la Bible: Festschrift P.-M. Bogaert*. Edited by J.-M. Auwers and A. Wenin. BETL 144. Louvain: Leuven University Press, 1999.

Grabbe, Lester L., ed. *"Like A Bird in A Cage": The Invasion of Sennacherib in 701 BCE*. JSOTSup 363. London: Sheffield Academic, 2003.

———. "Of Mice and Dead Men: Herodotus 2.141 and Sennacherib's Campaign in 701 BCE." Pages 119–40 in *"Like a Bird in a Cage": The Invasion of Sennacherib in 701 BCE*. Edited by Lester L. Grabbe. JSOTSup 363. London: Sheffield Academic, 2003.

———. "Omri and Son, Incorporated: The Business of History." Pages 61–83 in *Congress Volume Helsinki 2010*. Edited by Marti Nissinen. VTSup 148. Leiden: Brill, 2012.

Granowski, Jan Jaynes. "Jehoiachin at the King's Table: A Reading of the Ending of the Second Book of Kings." Pages 173–88 in *Reading Between Texts: Intertexuality and the Hebrew Bible*. Edited by Danna Nolan Fewell. Louisville, KY: Westminster John Knox, 1992.

Greenfield, Jonas C. "Doves' Dung and the Price of Food: The Topoi of 2 Kings 6:24–7:2." Pages 121–26 in *Storia e Tradizioni di Israele: Scritti in onore di J. Alberto Soggin*. Edited by Daniele Garrone and Felice Israel. Brescia: Paideia Editrice, 1991.

Halpern, Baruch. "The Taking of Nothing: 2 Kings 14.25, Amos 6.14 and the Geography of the Deuteronomistic History." Pages 186–204 in *Biblical Studies in Honour of Paul-Eugène Dion. Vol. 1 of World of the Aramaeans*. Edited by P.M. Michle Daviau, Michael Weigl, and John W. Wevers. 3 vols. JSOTSup 324. Sheffield: Sheffield Academic, 2001.

Handy, Lowell K. "Historical Probability and the Narrative of Josiah's Reform in 2 Kings." Pages 252–75 in the *Pitcher Is Broken: Memorial Essays for Gösta W. Ahlström*. Edited by Steven W. Holloway and Lowell K. Handy. JSOTSup 190. Sheffield: Sheffield Academic, 1995.

Hardmeier, Christof. "King Josiah in the Climax of the Deuteronomic History (2 Kings 22–23) and the Pre-Deuteronomic Document of a Cult Reform at the Place of Residence (23.4–15): Criticism of Sources, Reconstruction of Literary Pre-Stages and the Theology of History in 2 Kings 22–23." Pages 123–63 in *Good Kings and Bad Kings: The Kingdom of Judah in the Seventh Century BCE*. Edited by Lester L. Grabbe. LHBOTS 393. London: T&T Clark International, 2005.

Heckl, Raik. "Die Errettung des Königs durch seinen Gott: Die literarische Quelle der Gebete Hiskijas im Kontext von 2 Kön 19f (Par) und ihre Rolle bei der Ausformulierung des Monotheismusbekenntnisses." Pages 157–70 in *Mensch und König: Studien zur Anthropologie des Alten Testaments: Rüdiger Lux zum 60. Geburtstag*. Edited by Angelika Berlejung and Raik Heckl. Herders Biblische Studien 53. Freiburg: Herder, 2008.

Hentschel, Georg. "Elija und der Kult des Baal." Pages 54–90 in *Gott, der Einzige: zur Entstehung des Monotheismus in Israel*. Edited by Georg Braulik and Ernst Haag. Quaestiones Disputatae 104. Freiburg: Herder, 1985.

Hoffmeier, James K. "Egypt's Role in the Events of 701 B.C. in Jerusalem." Pages 219–34 in *Jerusalem in Bible and Archaeology: The First Temple Period*. Edited by Andrew G. Vaughn and Ann E. Killebrew. Society of Biblical Literature Symposium Series 18. Atlanta: Society of Biblical Literature, 2003.

Holloway, Steven W. "Harran: Cultic Geography in the Neo-Assyrian Empire and Its Implications for Sennacherib's 'Letter to Hezekiah' in 2 Kings." Pages 276–314 in *The Pitcher Is Broken: Memorial Essays for Gösta*

W. Ahlström. Edited by Steven W. Holloway and Lowell K. Handy. JSOTSup 190. Sheffield: Sheffield Academic, 2009.

———. "The Quest for Sargon, Pul and Tiglath-Pileser in the Nineteenth Century." Pages 68–87 in *Mesopotamia and the Bible: Comparative Explorations*. Edited by Mark W. Chavalas and K. Lawson Younger, Jr. JSOTSup 341. Sheffield: Sheffield Academic, 2002.

Horst, Pieter W. van der. "Anti-Samaritan Propaganda in Early Judaism." Pages 25–44 in *Persuasion and Dissuasion in Early Christianity, Ancient Judaism, and Hellenism*. Edited by M. J. J. Menken and P. W. Van Der Horst. Contributions to Biblical Exegesis and Theology 33. Leuven: Peeters, 2003.

Hutter, Manfred. "Widerspiegelungen religiöser Vorstellungen der Luwier im Alten Testament." Pages 425–42 in *Aussenwirkung des späthethitischen Kulturraumes. Güteraustausch—Kulturkontakt—Kulturtransfer*. Edited by Mirko Novák, Friedhelm Prayon, and Anne-Maria Wittke. AOAT 323. Münster: Ugarit-Verlag, 2004.

Irizarry-Fernández, Aida. "See-Judge-Act: A Different Approach to Bible Study." Pages 47–80 in *Engaging the Bible: Critical Readings from Contemporary Women*. Edited by Choi Hee An and Katheryn Pfisterer Darr. Minneapolis, MN: Fortress, 2006.

Jobling, David. "A Bettered Woman: Elisha and the Shunammite in the Deuteronomic Work." Pages 177–92 in *Labour of Reading: Desire, Alienation, and Biblical Interpretation*. Edited by Fiona C. Black, Roland Boer, and Erin Runions. SemeiaSt 36. Atlanta: Society of Biblical Literature, 1999.

Jonker, Louis C. "Textual Identities in the Books of Chronicles: The Case of Jehoram's History." Pages 197–217 in *Community Identity in Judean Historiography: Biblical and Comparative Perspectives*. Edited by Gary N. Knoppers and Kenneth Ristau. Winona Lake, IN: Eisenbrauns, 2009.

Kaltner, John. "What Did Elijah Do to His Mantle? The Hebrew Root GLM." Pages 225–30 in *Inspired Speech: Prophecy in the Ancient Near East, Essays in Honor of Herbert B. Huffmon*. Edited by John Kaltner and Louis Stulman. JSOTSup 378. London: T&T Clark, 2004.

Kelly, Brian E. "Manasseh in the Books of Kings and Chronicles (2 Kings 21:1–18; 2 Chron 33:1–20)." Pages 131–46 in *Windows into Old Testament History: Evidence, Argument, and the Crisis of "Biblical Israel."* Edited by V. Philips Long, David W. Baker, and Gordon J. Wenham. Grand Rapids: Eerdmans, 2002.

Kim, Uriah Yong-Hwang. *Decolonizing Josiah: Toward a Postcolonial Reading of the Deuteronomistic History*. The Bible in the Modern World 5. Sheffield: Sheffield Phoenix Press, 2005.

Klein, Ralph W. "The Ironic End of Joash in Chronicles." Pages 116–27 in *For a Later Generation: The Transformation of Tradition in Israel, Early Judaism, and Early Christianity*. Edited by Randal A. Argall, Beverly

Bow, Rodney Alan Werline, and George W. E. Nickelsburg. Harrisburg, PA: Trinity Press International, 2000.

Knoppers, Gary N. "Cutheans or Children of Jacob? The Issue of Samaritan Origins in 2 Kings 17." Pages 223–39 in *Reflection and Refraction: Studies in Biblical Historiography in Honour of A. Graeme Auld*. Edited by Robert Rezetko, Timothy H. Lim, and W. Brian Aucker. VTSup 113. Leiden: Brill, 2006.

———. "In Search of Post-Exilic Israel: Samaria After the Fall of the Northern Kingdom." Pages 150–80 in *In Search of Pre-Exilic Israel*. Edited by John Day. JSOTSup 406. London: T&T Clark, 2004.

Köckert, Matthias. "'Gibt es kein Gott in Israel?': Zum Literarischen, Historischen und religionsgeschichtlichen Ort von II Reg 1." Pages 253–71 in *Auf dem Weg zur Endgestalt von Genesis bis II Regum: Festschrift Hans-Christoph Schmitt zum 65 Geburtstag*. Edited by Martin Beck and Ulrike Schorn. BZAW 370. Berlin: Walter De Gruyter, 2006.

Kooij, A. van der. "David, 'Het Licht van Israel.' " Pages 49–57 in *Vruchten van de Uithof: Studies Opgedragen aan Dr. H.A. Brongers ter Gelegenheid van zijn Afscheid*. Edited by A. R. Hulst. Utrecht: Theologisch Institut, 1974.

———. "The Story of Hezekiah and Sennacherib (2 Kings 18–19): A Sample of Ancient Historiography." Pages 107–19 in *Past, Present, Future: The Deuteronomistic History and the Prophets*. Edited by Johannes C. De Moor and H. F. Van Rooy. OtSt 44. Leiden: Brill, 2000.

Kratz, Reinhard Gregor, and John Bowden. "Chemosh's Wrath and Yahweh's No: Ideas of Divine Wrath in Moab and Israel." Pages 92–121 in *Divine Wrath and Divine Mercy in the World of Antiquity*. Edited by Reinhard G. Kratz and Hermann Spieckermann. FAT 2. Reihe 33. Tübingen: Mohr Siebeck, 2008.

Laato, Antti. "Immanuel—Who Is With Us?—Hezekiah or Messiah?" Pages 313–22 in *"Wunschet Jerusalem Frieden": Collected Communications to XIIIth Congress of International Organization for Study of the Old Testament, Jerusalem, 1986*. Edited by Matthias Augustin and Klaus D. Schunck. Beiträge zur Erforschung des Alten Testaments und des antiken Judentums 13. Frankfurt: Peter Lang, 1988.

Lang, Bernhard. "No God but Yahweh: The Origin and Character of Biblical Monotheism." Pages 41–49 in *Monotheism*. Edited by Claude Geffre and Jean-Pierre Jossua. Concilium 177. Edinburgh: T&T Clark, 1985.

Lasine, Stuart. "Manasseh as Villain and Scapegoat." Pages 163–83 in *The New Literary Criticism and the Hebrew Bible*. Edited by J. Cheryl Exum and David J. A. Clines. JSOTSup 143. Sheffield: JSOT Press, 1993.

Liverani, Mario. "Kilamuwa 7–8 E 2 Re 7." Pages 177–84 in *Storia e Tradizioni di Israele: Scritti in onore di J. Alberto Soggin*. Edited by Daniele Garrone and Felice Israel. Brescia: Paideia Editrice, 1991.

Lohfink, Norbert. "The Cult Reform of Josiah of Judah: 2 Kings 22–23." Pages 459–75 in *Ancient Israelite Religion: Essays in Honor of Frank Moore*

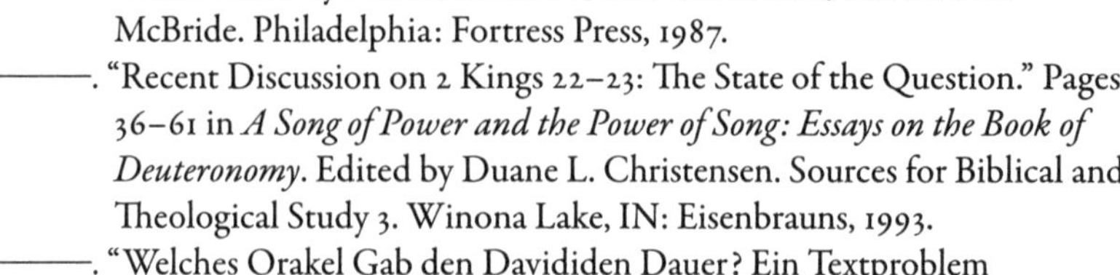

Cross. Edited by Patrick D. Miller, Paul D. Hanson, and S. Dean McBride. Philadelphia: Fortress Press, 1987.

———. "Recent Discussion on 2 Kings 22–23: The State of the Question." Pages 36–61 in *A Song of Power and the Power of Song: Essays on the Book of Deuteronomy*. Edited by Duane L. Christensen. Sources for Biblical and Theological Study 3. Winona Lake, IN: Eisenbrauns, 1993.

———. "Welches Orakel Gab den Davididen Dauer? Ein Textproblem in 2 Kön 8,19 und das Funktionieren der dynastischen Orakel im deuteronomistischen Geschichtswerk." Pages 349–70 in *Lingering Over Words: Studies in Ancient Near Eastern Literature in Honor of William L. Moran*. Edited by Tzvi Abusch, John Huehnergard, and Piotr Steinkeller. Harvard Semitic Studies 37. Atlanta: Scholars Press, 1990.

Long, Burke O. "A Figure at the Gate: Readers, Reading, and Biblical Theologians." Pages 166–86 in *Canon, Theology, and Old Testament Interpretation: Essays in Honor of Brevard S. Childs*. Edited by Gene M. Tucker, David L. Petersen, and Robert R. Wilson. Philadelphia: Fortress Press, 1988.

———. "Letting Rival Gods Be Rivals: Biblical Theology in a Postmodern Age." Pages 222–33 in *Problems in Biblical Theology: Essays in Honor of Rolf Knierim*. Edited by Henry Sun, Keith L. Eades, James M. Robinson, and Garth I. Moller. Grand Rapids: Eerdmans, 1997.

———. "Sacred Geography as Narrative Structure in 2 Kings 11." Pages 231–38 in *Pomegranates and Golden Bells: Studies in Biblical, Jewish, and Near Eastern Ritual, Law, and Literature in Honor of Jacob Milgrom*. Edited by David P. Wright, David Noel Freedman, and Avi Hurvitz. Winona Lake, IN: Eisenbrauns, 1995.

Long, Jesse C., Jr., and Mark Sneed. "'Yahweh Has Given These Three Kings into the Hand of Moab': A Socio-Literary Reading of 2 Kings 3." Pages 253–75 in *Inspired Speech: Prophecy in the Ancient Near East Essays in Honor of Herbert B. Huffmon*. Edited by John Kaltner and Louis Stulman. JSOTSup 378. London: T&T Clark, 2004.

Marinkovic, Peter. "'Geh in Frieden' (2 Kön 5,19): Sonderformen legitimer Jhwhverehrung durch 'Heiden' in 'heidnischer' Mitwelt." Pages 3–21 in *Die Heiden: Juden, Christen und das Problem des Fremden*. Edited by Reinhard Feldmeier, Ulrich Heckel, and Martin Hengel. WUNT 70. Tübingen: Mohr, 1994.

Massmann, Ludwig. "Sanheribs Politik in Juda: Beobachtungen und Erwägungen zum Ausgang der Konfrontation Hiskias mit den Assyrern." Pages 167–80 in *Kein Land für sich Allein: Studien zum Kulturkontakt in Kanaan, Israel/Palästina und Ebirari für Manfred Weippert zum 65. Geburtstag*. Edited by Ulrich Hübner and Ernst Axel Knauf. OBO 186. Göttingen: Vandenhoeck & Ruprecht, 2002.

Mayer, Walter. "Sennacherib's Attack on Hezekiah."Pages 168–200 in *"Like a Bird in a Cage": The Invasion of Sennacherib in 701 BCE*. Edited by Lester L. Grabbe. JSOTSup 363. London: Sheffield Academic, 2003.

Menn, Esther. "Child Characters in Biblical Narratives: The Young David (1 Samuel 16–17) and the Little Israelite Servant Girl (2 Kings 5:1–19)." Pages 324–52 in *The Child in the Bible*. Edited by Marcia J. Bunge, Terence E. Fretheim, and Beverly Roberts Gaventa. Grand Rapids: Eerdmans, 2008.

Moore, Rick Dale. *God Saves: Lessons from the Elisha Stories.* JSOTSup 95. Sheffield: JSOT Press, 1990.

Morrison, Craig E. "Handing on the Mantle: The Transmission of the Elijah Cycle in the Biblical Versions." Pages 109–29 in *Master of the Sacred Page: Essays in Honor of Roland E. Murphy, O. Carm., on the Occasion of His Eightieth Birthday*. Edited by Roland Edmund Murphy, Keith J. Egan, and Craig E. Morrison. Washington, DC: Carmelite Institute, 1997.

Nakanose, Shigeyuki. *Josiah's Passover: Sociology and the Liberating Bible.* Bible and Liberation. Maryknoll, NY: Orbis Books, 1993.

Nobile, Marco. "Les Quatre Pâques dans le Cadre de la Rédaction Finale de Gen-2 Rois." Pages 191–96 in *Pentateuchal and Deuteronomistic Studies: Papers Read at the XIIIth IOSOT Congress, Leuven 1989*. Edited by C. Brekelmans and J. Lust. BETL 94. Louvain: Leuven University Press, 1990.

Nzimande, Makhosazana K. "Reconfiguring Jezebel: A Postcolonial Imbokodo Reading of the Story of Naboth's Vineyard (1 Kings 21:1–16)." Pages 223–25 in *African and European Readers of the Bible in Dialogue: In Quest of a Shared Meaning*. Edited by Hans de Wit and Gerald O. West. Studies on Religion in Africa 32. Leiden: Brill, 2008.

Oberhänsli-Widmer, Gabrielle. "Elijah als Pate des Bundes, oder die Dynamik rabbinischer Rezeption." Pages 126–37 in *Text, Ethik, Judentum und Christentum, Gesellschaft Ekkehard W. Stegemann zum 60. Geburtstag*. Edited by Gabriella Gelardini. Kontexte der Schrift 1. Stuttgart: W. Kohlhammer, 2005.

Ockinga, Boyo. "Hiskias 'Prahlerei': Ein Beitrag zur Interpretation von 2 Könige 20:12–19 und Jesaja 39,1–8." Pages 342–46 in *Fontes Atque Pontes: Eine Festgabe für Hellmut Brunner*. Edited by Manfred Görg. Aegypten und Altes Testament 5. Wiesbaden: Otto Harrassowitz, 1983.

O'Connor, M. "War and Rebel Chants in the Former Prophets." Pages 322–37 in *Fortunate the Eyes that See: Essays in Honor of David Noel Freedman in Celebration of His Seventieth Birthday*. Edited by Astrid B. Beck, Andrew H. Bartelt, Paul R. Raabe, and Chris A. Franke. Grand Rapids: Eerdmans, 1995.

Overholt, Thomas W. "Elijah and Elisha in the Context of Israelite Religion." Pages 94–111 in *Prophets and Paradigms: Essays in Honor of Gene M. Tucker*. Edited by Gene M. Tucker and Stephen Breck Reid. JSOTSup 229. Sheffield: Sheffield Academic, 1996.

Parker, Julie Faith. "You Are a Bible Child: Exploring the Lives of Children and Mothers Through the Elisha Cycle." Pages 59–69 in *Women in the*

Biblical World: A Survey of Old and New Testament Perspectives. Edited by Elizabeth A. Mccabe. Lanham, MD: University Press of America, 2011.

Parpola, Simo. "The Murderer of Sennacherib." Pages 171–82 in *Death in Mesopotamia: Papers Read at the XXVIe Recontre Assyriologique*. Edited by Bendt Alster. Mesopotamia 8. Copenhagen: Akademisk Forlag, 1980.

Paul, M. J. "Hilkiah and the Law (2 Kings 22) in the 17th and 18th Centuries: Some Influences on W M L De Wette." Pages 9–12 in *Das Deuteronomium: Entstehung, Gestalt und Botschaft*. Edited by Norbert Lohfink. BETL 68. Leuven: Leuven University Press, 1985.

———. "King Josiah's Renewal of the Covenant (2 Kings 22–23)." Pages 269–76 in *Pentateuchal and Deuteronomistic Studies: Papers Read at the XIIIth IOSOT Congress, Leuven 1989*. Edited by C. Brekelmans and J. Lust. BETL 94. Leuven: Leuven University Press, 1990.

Pyper, Hugh S. "Swallowed by a Song: Jonah and the Jonah-Psalm Through the Looking-Glass." Pages 337–58 in *Reflection and Refraction: Studies in Biblical Historiography in Honour of A. Graeme Auld*. Edited by Robert Rezetko, Timothy H. Lim, and W. Brian Aucker. VTSup 113. Leiden: Brill, 2006.

Renteria, Tamis Hoover. "The Elijah/Elisha Stories: A Socio-Cultural Analysis of Prophets and People in Ninth-Century BCE Israel." Pages 75–126 in *Elijah and Elisha in Socioliterary Perspective*. Edited by Robert B. Coote. SemeiaSt 22. Atlanta: Scholars Press, 1992.

Robertson, D. "Micaiah Ben Imlah: A Literary View." Pages 139–46 in *The Biblical Mosaic: Changing Perspectives*. Edited by Robert Polzin and Eugene Rothman. Philadelphia: Fortress, 1982.

Rofé, Alexander. "Elisha at Dothan (2 Kings 6:8–23): Historico-Literary Criticism Sustained by the Midrash." Pages 345–53 in *Ki Baruch Hu: Ancient Near Eastern, Biblical, and Judaic Studies in Honor of Baruch A. Levine*. Edited by Robert Chazan, William W. Hallo, and Lawrence H. Schiffman. Winona Lake, IN: Eisenbrauns, 1999.

Rüterswörden, Udo. "Die Prophetin Hulda." Pages 234–42 in *Meilenstein: Festgabe für Herbert Donner zum 16. Februar 1995*. Edited by Manfred Weippert. Aegypten und Altes Testament 30. Wiesbaden: Harrassowitz, 1995.

Scharbert, Josef. "Die Fürbitte im Alten Testament." Pages 91–109 in *"Diener in eurer Mitte": Festschrift für Dr. Antonius Hofmann, Bischof von Passau zum 75. Geburtstag*. Edited by Rainer Beer, August Leidl, Karl Mühlek, and Friedrich Schröger. Schriften der Universität Passau: Reihe Katholische Theologie. Passau: Passavia Universitätsverlag, 1984.

Schenker, Adrian. "La Cause de la Chute du Royaume d'Israël Selon le Texte Massorétique et Selon la Septante Ancienne: Une Différence et ses Conséquences pour l'histoire du Texte des Livres des Rois." Pages 151–71 in *Traduire la Bible Hébraïque de la Septante la Nouvelle Bible Segond*.

Edited by Robert David and Manuel Jinbachian. Sciences Bibliques: Études. Montreal: Médiaspaul, 2005.

———. "The Relationship Between the Earliest Septuagint and the Masoretic Text in the Book of Kings in Light of 2 Kgs 21:2–9." Pages 127–49 in *Traduire la Bible Hébraïque: De la Septante à la Nouvelle Bible Segond.* Edited by Robert David and Manuel Jinbachian. Sciences Bibliques: Études. Montreal: Médiaspaul, 2005.

———. "Die Textgeschichte der Königsbücher und ihre Konsequenzen für die Textgeschichte der Hebräischen Bibel, Illustriert am Beispiel von 2 Kön 23:1–3." Pages 65–79 in *Congress Volume: Leiden, 2004*. Edited by André Lemaire. VTSup 109. Leiden: Brill, 2006.

Segert, Stanislav. "Symmetric and Asymmetric Verses in Hebrew Biblical Poetry." Pages 33–38 in *Proceedings of the Ninth World Congress of Jewish Studies. Division A: The Period of the Bible*. Edited by Raphael Giveon, H. Jacob Katzenstein, and Moshé Anbar. Jerusalem: World Union of Jewish Studies, 1986.

Siebert-Hommes, Jopie. "The Widow of Zarephath and the Great Woman of Shunem: A Comparative Analysis of Two Stories." Pages 231–50 in *On Reading Prophetic Texts: Gender-Specific and Related Studies in Memory of Fokkelien Van Dijk-Hemmes*. Edited by Bob Becking and Meindert Dijkstra. Biblical Interpretation Series 18. Leiden: Brill, 1996.

Smelik, Klaas A. D. "Distortion of Old Testament Prophecy: The Purpose of Isaiah 36 and 37." Pages 70–93 in *Crises and Perspectives: Studies in Ancient Near Eastern Polytheism, Biblical Theology, Palestinian Archaeology and Intertestamental Literature*. Edited by Johannes C. de Moor, N. Poulssen, and Graham I. Davies. OtSt 24. Leiden: Brill, 1986.

———. "The New Altar of King Ahaz (2 Kings 16): Deuteronomistic Re-Interpretation of a Cult Reform." Pages 263–78 in *Deuteronomy and Deuteronomic Literature: Festschrift C. H. W. Brekelmans*. Edited by M. Vervenne and J. Lust. BETL 133. Louvain: Leuven University Press, 1997.

———. "The Representation of King Ahaz in 2 Kings 16 and 2 Chronicles 28." Pages 143–85 in *Intertextuality in Ugarit and Israel: Papers Read at the Tenth Joint Meeting of the Society for Old Testament Study and Het Oudtestamentisch Werkgezelschap in Nederland En Belgie*. Edited by Johannes C. de Moor. OtSt 40. Leiden: Brill, 1998.

Smyth, Françoise. "When Josiah Has Done His Work or the King Is Properly Buried: A Synchronic Reading of 2 Kings 22.1–23.28." Pages 343–58 in *Israel Constructs Its History: Deuteronomistic Historiography in Recent Research*. Edited by Albert De Pury, Thomas Römer, and Jean-Daniel Macchi. JSOTSup 306. Sheffield: Sheffield Academic, 2000.

Solomon, Ann M. Vater. "Jehoash's Fable of the Thistle and the Cedar." Pages 126–32 in *Saga, Legend, Tale, Novella, Fable: Narrative forms in Old Testament Literature*. Edited by George W. Coats. JSOTSup 35. Sheffield: JSOT Press, 1985.

Stavrakopoulou, Francesca. *King Manasseh and Child Sacrifice: Biblical Distortions of Historical Realities.* BZAW 338. Berlin; New York: Walter De Gruyter, 2004.

Talstra, Eep. "A Hierarchy of Clauses in Biblical Hebrew Narrative." Pages 85–118 in *Narrative Syntax and The Hebrew Bible: Papers of the Tilburg Conference 1996.* Edited by E. J. Van Wolde. Leiden: Brill, 1997.

Tarlin, Jan. "Toward a 'Female' Reading of the Elijah Cycle: Ideology and Gender in the Interpretation of 1 Kings 17–19,21 and 2 Kings 1–2:18." Pages 208–17 in *Feminist Companion to Samuel and Kings.* Edited by Athalya Brenner. FCB 5. Sheffield: Sheffield Academic, 1994.

Thiel, Winfried. "Jahwe und Prophet in der Elisa-Tradition." 93–103 in *Alttestamentlicher Glaube und biblische Theologie: Festschrift für Horst Dietrich Preuss zum 65. Geburtstag.* Edited by Jutta Zobel and Hans-Jürgen Hausmann. Stuttgart: Kohlhammer, 1992.

Timm, Stefan. "Wird Nebukadnezar Entlastet? Zu 2Kön 24,18–25,21." Pages 359–89 in *"Sieben Augen auf einem Stein" (Sach 3,9): Studien zur Literatur des Zweiten Tempels: Festschrift für Ina Willi-Plein zum 65. Geburtstag.* Edited by Friedhelm Hartenstein and Michael Pietsch. Neukirchen-Vluyn: Neukirchener Verlag, 2007.

Trebolle Barrera, Julio C. "Recensión y Redacción de 2 Re 17,7–23 (TM LXXuB & LXXuL VL)." Pages 215–28 in *Simposio Biblico Español 1982, Salamanca.* Edited by Natalio Fernandez Marcos and Julio C. Trebolle Barrera. Madrid: Universidad Complutense, 1984.

Uehlinger, Christoph, and Bruce Wallace. "Was There a Cult Reform Under King Josiah? The Case for a Well-Grounded Minimum." Pages 279–316 in *Good Kings and Bad Kings: The Kingdom of Judah in the Seventh Century BCE.* Edited by Lester L. Grabbe. LHBOTS 393. London: T&T Clark International, 2005.

Vanoni, Gottfried. "Beobachtungen zur deuteronomistischen Terminologie in 2 Kön 23,25–25,30." Pages 357–62 in *Das Deuteronomium: Entstehung, Gestalt und Botschaft.* Edited by Norbert Lohfink. BETL 68. Leuven: Leuven University Press, 1985.

Walsh, Jerome T. "2 Kings 17: The Deuteronomist and the Samaritans." Pages 315–23 in *Past, Present, Future: The Deuteronomistic History and the Prophets.* Edited by Johannes C. de Moor and H. F. Van Rooy. OtSt 44. Leiden: Brill, 2000.

Weems, Renita J. "Huldah, the Prophet: Reading a (Deuteronomistic) Woman's Identity." Pages 321–39 in *God So Near: Essays on Old Testament Theology in Honor of Patrick D. Miller.* Edited by Brent A. Strawn and Nancy R. Bowen. Winona Lake, IN: Eisenbrauns, 2003.

Williams, Peter J. "Lying Spirits Sent by God? The Case of Micaiah's Prophecy." Pages 58–66 in *Trustworthiness of God: Perspectives on the Nature of Scripture.* Edited by Paul Helm and Carl R. Trueman. Grand Rapids: Eerdmans, 2002.

Williamson, H. G. M. "Hezekiah and the Temple." Pages 47–52 in *Texts, Temples, and Traditions: A Tribute to Menahem Haran*. Edited by Michael V. Fox, Victor Avigdor Hurowitz, Avi Hurvitz, Michael L. Klein, Baruch J. Schwartz, and Nili Shupak. Winona Lake, IN: Eisenbrauns, 1996.

Wöhrle, Jakob. "Die Rehabilitierung Jojachins: Zur Entstehung und Intention von 2 Kön 24,17–25,30." Pages 213–38 in *Berührungspunkte. Studien zur Sozial- und Religionsgeschichte Israels und seiner Umwelt. Festschrift für Rainer Albertz zu seinem 65. Geburtstag*. Edited by R. Schmitt, I. Kottsieper, and J. Wöhrle. AOAT 350. Münster: Ugarit-Verlag, 2008.

Wright, J. Edward. "Whither Elijah? The Ascension of Elijah in Biblical and Extrabiblical Traditions." Pages 123–38 in *Things Revealed: Studies in Early Jewish and Christian Literature in Honor of Michael E. Stone*. Edited by Michael E. Stone, Esther G. Chazon, David Satran, and Ruth A. Clements. Supplements to the Journal for the Study of Judaism 89. Leiden: Brill, 2004.

Xella, Paolo. "Sur la Nourriture des Morts: Un Aspect de l'Eschatologie Mésopotamienne." Pages 151–60 in *Death in Mesopotamia: Papers Read at the XXVIe Recontre Assyriologique*. Edited by Bendt Alster. Mesopotamia 8. Copenhagen: Akademisk forlag, 1980.

Yannai, Y. "Elisha and the Shunammite (II Kings 4:8–37): A Case of Homoeoteleuton, or a Text Emendation by Ancient Masoretes?" Pages 123–35 in *Estudios Masoreticos (V Congreso de la IOMS): Dedicados a Harry M. Orlinsky*. Edited by Emilia Fernandez Tejero. Textos y Estudios "Cardenal Cisneros" 33. Madrid: Instituto "Arias Montano" CSIC, 1983.

Young, Robb Andrew. *Hezekiah in History and Tradition*. VTSup 155. Leiden: Brill, 2012.

Yun, Ilsung Andrew. "Different Readings of the Taharqa Passage in 2 Kings 19 and the Chronology of the 25th Egyptian Dynasty." Pages 169–81 in *From Babel to Babylon: Essays on Biblical History and Literature in Honor of Brian Peckham*. Edited by Joyce Rilett Wood, Mark Leuchter, and John E. Harvey. LHBOTS 455. New York: T&T Clark, 2006.

Zakovitch, Yair. "'Elisha Died … He Came to Life and Stood Up' (2 Kings 13:20–21): A Short 'Short Story' in Exegetical Circles." Pages 53*–62* in *"Sha'arei Talmon": Studies in the Bible, Qumran, and the Ancient Near East Presented to Shemaryahu Talmon*. Edited by Emanuel Tov, Michael A. Fishbane, Shemaryahu Talmon, and Weston W. Fields. Winona Lake, IN: Eisenbrauns, 1992. (Hebrew).

Articles (2 Kings)

Abrams, Judith Z. "Metzora(at) Kashaleg: Leprosy: Challenges to Authority in the Bible." *JBQ* 21, no. 1 (1993): 41–45.

Ackroyd, Peter R. "Interpretation of the Babylonian Exile: A Study of 2 Kings 20, Isaiah 38–39." *SJT* 27, no. 3 (1974): 329–52.

Ahlström, Gösta W. "Kung So och Israels Undergång." *Svensk Egetisk Årsbok* 54 (1989): 5–19.
Alexandre, Jean. "Des Enfants et du Pain: Deux Récits de Purification dans le Cycle d'Élisée: II Rois 2,19–25 et 4,38–44." *Foi et Vie* 104, no. 4 (2005): 36–47.
Alfrink, Bernardus Cardinal. "Die Gadd'sche Chronik und die Heilige Schrift." *Bib* 8, no. 4 (1927): 385–417.
Allen, Leslie C. "Cuckoos in the Textual Nest at 2 Kings 20:13, Isa 42:10, 49:24, Ps 22:17, 2 Chr 5:9." *JTS* 22, no. 1 (1971): 143–50.
———. "More Cuckoos in the Textual Nest: At 2 Kings 23:5; Jeremiah 17:3, 4; Micah 3:3; 6:16 (70); 2 Chronicles 20:25 (70)." *JTS* 24, no. 1 (1973): 69–73.
Amit, Yairah. "A Prophet Tested: Elisha, The Great Woman of Shunem, and the Story's Double Message." *BibInt* 11, nos. 3–4 (2003): 279–94.
———. "The Shunammite, the Shulamite and the Professor Between Midrash and Midrash." *JSOT* 93 (2001): 77–91.
Amr, Abdel J. "A Nude Female Statue with Astral Emblems." *PEQ* 117 (1985): 104–11.
Anbar, Moshé. "Kai Pou Eisin Hoi Theoi Tēs Chōras Samareias 'et Où Sont les Dieux du Pays de Samarie?' " *BN* 51 (1990): 7–8.
Asensio, Félix. "Restauración de la Dinastía Davídica en la Persona de Joás (2 Rey 11=2 Cr 22:10–23:21)." *EstBib* 2, no. 4 (1943): 475–506.
Asurmendi, Jesús M. "Elisée et la Guerre: 2 R 3:4–27." *BibInt* 13, no. 1 (2005): 1–12.
———. "Eliseo, Justicia y Política, y el Relato Ficticio." *EstBib* 53, no. 2 (1995): 145–64.
———. "En torno a la Serpiente de Bronce." *EstBib* 46, no. 3 (1988): 283–94.
Avioz, Michael. "Josiah's Death in the Book of Kings: A New Solution to an Old Theological Conundrum." *ETL* 83, no. 4 (2007): 359–66.
———. "What Happened at Megiddo? Josiah's Death as Described in the Book of Kings." *BN* 142 (2009): 5–11.
———. "When Was the First Temple Destroyed, According to the Bible?" *Bib* 84, no. 4 (2003): 563–65.
Axskjöld, Carl-Johan. "Altaret Från Damaskus: En Ideologisk Förståelse. " *SEÅ* 67 (2002): 19–25.
Baker, David W. "The Wind and the Waves: Biblical Theology in Protology and Eschatology." *ATJ* 34 (2002): 13–37.
Bakon, Shimon. "Zedekiah: Last King of Judah." *JBQ* 36, no. 2 (2008): 93–101.
Barr, James. "Why the World Was Created in 4004 BC: Archbishop Ussher and Biblical Chronology." *BJRL* 67, no. 2 (1985): 575–608.
Barrick, W. Boyd. "Burning Bones at Bethel: A Closer Look at 2 Kings 23,16a." *SJOT* 14, no. 1 (2000): 3–16.
———. "Elisha and the Magic Bow: A Note on 2 Kings 13:15–17." *VT* 35, no. 3 (1985): 355–63.

Becking, Bob. "Theologie na de Ondergang: Enkele Opmerkingen bij 2 Koningen 17." *Bijdragen* 49, no. 2 (1988): 150–74.
Begg, Christopher T. "2 Kings 20:12–19 as an Element of the Deuteronomistic History." *CBQ* 48, no. 1 (1986): 27–38.
———. "Ahaz, King of Judah According to Josephus." *SJOT* 10, no. 1 (1996): 28–52.
———. "The Death of Josiah: Josephus and the Bible." *ETL* 64, no. 1 (1988): 157–63.
———. "The Deuteronomistic Retouching of the Portrait of Hezekiah in 2 Kgs 20:12–19." *BN* 38–39 (1987): 7–13.
———. "'DTRP' in 2 Kings 25: Some Further Thoughts." *RB* 96, no. 1 (1989): 49–55.
———. "Filling in the Blanks: Josephus' Version of the Campaign of the Three Kings: 2 Kings 3." *HUCA* 64 (1993): 89–109.
———. "Hezekiah's Display (2 Kgs 20:12–19)." *BN* 38–39 (1987): 14–18.
———. "Hezekiah's Display: Another Parallel." *BN* 41 (1988): 7–8.
———. "Hezekiah's Illness and Visit According to Josephus." *EstBíb* 53, no. 3 (1995): 365–85.
———. "Joash and Elisha in Josephus, Ant 9:117–185." *AbrN* 32 (1994): 28–46.
———. "The Reading at 2 Kings 20:13." *VT* 36, no. 3 (1986): 339–41.
———. "'Sennacherib's Second Palestinian Campaign': An Additional Indication." *JBL* 106, no. 4 (1987): 685–86.
———. "The Significance of Jehoiachin's Release: A New Proposal." *JSOT* 36 (1986): 49–56.
———. "Unifying Factors in 2 Kings 1:2–17a." *JSOT* 32 (1985): 75–86.
———. "Uzziah (Azariah) of Judah According Josephus." *EstBíb* 53, no. 1 (1995): 5–24.
———. "Zedekiah and the Servant." *ETL* 62, no. 4 (1986): 393–98.
Ben Zvi, Ehud. "The Account of the Reign of Manasseh in II Reg 21:1–18 and the Redactional History of the Book of Kings." *ZAW* 103, no. 3 (1991): 355–74.
———. "Once the Lamp Has Been Kindled: A Reconsideration of the Meaning of the MT Nîr in 1 Kgs 11:36; 15:4; 2 Kgs 8:19 and 2 Chr 21:7." *ABR* 39 (1991): 19–30.
———. "Tracing Prophetic Literature in the Book of Kings: The Case of II Kings 15:37." *ZAW* 102, no. 1 (1990): 100–05.
———. "Who Wrote the Speech of Rabshakeh and When." *JBL* 109, no. 1 (1990): 79–92.
Berlyn, Patricia J. "The Wrath of Moab." *JBQ* 30, no. 4 (2002): 216–26.
Beyerle, Stefan. "Die 'Eherne Schlange' Num 21,4–9: Synchron und Diachron Delesen." *ZAW* 111, no. 1 (1999): 23–44.
Blake, Ian. "Jericho (Ain Es-Sultan): Joshua's Curse and Elisha's Miracle: One Possible Explanation." *PEQ* 99 (1967): 86–97.
Boogaart, Thomas Arthur. "Elisha's Prayer: O Lord, Open Their Eyes." *RefR* 53, no. 2 (1999): 128–43.

Branch, Robin Gallaher. "Athaliah, A Treacherous Queen: A Careful Analysis of Her Story in 2 Kings 11 and 2 Chronicles 22:10–23:21." *In die Skriflig* 38, no. 4 (2004): 537–59.

Brettler, Marc. "2 Kings 24:13–14 as History." *CBQ* 53, no. 4 (1991): 541.

———. "Ideology, History and Theology in 2 Kings 17:7–23." *VT* 39, no. 3 (1989): 268–82.

Brodie, Thomas L. "The Departure for Jerusalem (Luke 9:51–56) as a Rhetorical Imitation of Elijah's Departure for the Jordan (2 Kgs 1:1–2:6)." *Bib* 70, no. 1 (1989): 96–109.

———. "Towards Unraveling the Rhetorical Imitation of Sources in Acts: 2 Kgs 5 as One Component of Acts 8:9–40." *Bib* 67, no. 1 (1986): 41–67.

Brosh, Bat-Sheva. "The Contribution of Chronological Displacement to the Design of the Characters of Solomon and Hezekiah." *Bet Mikra* 53, no. 2 (2008): 5–26. (Hebrew).

Brown, Sally A. "2 Kings 23:1–20." *Int* 60, no. 1 (2006): 68–70.

Brueggemann, Walter. "2 Kings 5: Two Evangelists and a Saved Subject." *Missiology* 35, no. 3 (2007): 263–72.

———. "2 Kings 18–19: The Legitimacy of a Sectarian Hermeneutic." *HBT* 7, no. 1 (1985): 1–42.

———. "Breaking the Cycle of Enmity: A Case Study." *Living Pulpit* 13, no. 1 (2004): 10–12.

———. "A Brief Moment for a One-Person Remnant (2 Kings 5:2–3)." *BTB* 31, no. 2 (2001): 53–59.

———. "A Culture of Life and the Politics of Death." *Journal for Preachers* 29, no. 2 (2006): 16–21.

———. "The Embarrassing Footnote." *ThTo* 44, no. 1 (1987): 5–14.

Brunet, Gilbert. "L'Hébreu Kìlìb." *VT* 35, no. 4 (1985): 485–88.

———. "Le Terrain aux Foulons." *RB* 71, no. 2 (1964): 230–39.

———. "La Prise de Jérusalem sous Sédécias: Les Sens Militaires de l'Hebreu Bâqa'." *RHR* 167, no. 2 (1965): 159–76.

Burnett, Joel S. "'Going Down' to Bethel: Elijah and Elisha in the Theological Geography of the Deuteronomistic History." *JBL* 129, no. 2 (2010): 281–97.

Burns, John Barclay. "Why Did the Besieging Army Withdraw? (II Reg 3,27)." *ZAW* 102, no. 2 (1990): 187–94.

Cahill, P. Joseph. "Narrative Art in John 4." *Religious Studies Bulletin* 2, no. 2 (1982): 41–47.

Chapman, William John. "The Problem of Inconsequent Post-Dating in II Kings XV 13, 17 and 23." *HUCA* 2 (1925): 57–61.

Christensen, Duane L. "The Identity of 'King So' in Egypt (2 Kings 17:4)." *VT* 39, no. 2 (1989): 140–53.

Cogan, Mordechai. "For We, Like You, Worship Your God: Three Biblical Portrayals of Samaritan Origins." *VT* 38, no. 3 (1988): 286–92.

———. "'From the Peak of Amanah.'" *IEJ* 34, no. 4 (1984): 255–59.

———. "Sennacherib's Siege of Jerusalem: Once or Twice?" *BAR* 27, no. 1 (2001): 40–45.

Cohn, Robert L. "Convention and Creativity in the Book of Kings: The Case of the Dying Monarch." *CBQ* 47, no. 4 (1985): 603–16.

———. "Reading in Three Dimensions: The Imperative of Biblical Narrative." *Religion and Intellectual Life* 6, nos. 3–4 (1989): 161–72.

Cook, Herbert J. "Pekah." *VT* 14, no. 2 (1964): 121–35.

Couroyer, Bernard. "A Propos de II Rois XIII,14–19." *LASBF* 30 (1980): 177–96.

Davies, Graham I. "Tell Ed-Duweir: Not Libnah but Lachish." *PEQ* 117 (1985): 92–96.

Day, John. "The Problem of 'So, King of Egypt' in 2 Kings XVII:4." *VT* 42, no. 3 (1992): 289–301.

Dearman, J. Andrew. "The Tophet in Jerusalem: Archaeology and Cultural Profile." *JNSL* 22, no. 1 (1996): 59–71.

Deboys, David G. "Quinta E in 4 Reigns." *TynBul* 36 (1985): 163–78.

Delamarter, Steve. "The Death of Josiah in Scripture and Tradition: Wrestling with the Problem of Evil?" *VT* 54, no. 1 (2004): 29–60.

Derby, Josiah. "The Tragic King." *JBQ* 29, no. 3 (2001): 180–85.

Dever, William G. "Recent Archaeological Confirmation of the Cult of Asherah in Ancient Israel." *HS* 23 (1982): 37–43.

DeVries, Simon J. "The Three Comparisons in 1 Kings 22:4b and Its Parallel in 2 Kings 3:7b." *VT* 39, no. 3 (1989): 283–306.

Dietrich, Manfried, and Oswald Loretz. "Ug. bsql 'rgz und Hebr. b sqlnw (2 Reg 4,42), 'gwz." *UF* 18 (1986): 115–20.

Díez Fernandez, Florentino. "Crónica Arqueológica." *EstBíb* 42, nos. 3–4 (1984): 421–28.

Dohmen, Christoph. "Heisst Semel 'Bild, Statue.' " *ZAW* 96, no. 2 (1984): 263–66.

Earl, Douglas. "Moving Beyond Grammatico-Historical Methods: The Value an Application of a Literary-Poetic Approach with Specific Reference to 2 Kings 6:24–7:20." *Evangel* 21, no. 3 (2003): 66–77.

Edelman, Diana. "The Meaning of qiṭṭēr." *VT* 35, no. 4 (1985): 395–404.

Effa, Allan. "Prophet, Kings, Servants, and Lepers: A Missiological Reading of an Ancient Drama." *Missiology* 35, no. 3 (2007): 305–13.

Elayi, Josette. "Name of Deuteronomy's Author Found on Seal Ring." *BAR* 13, no. 5 (1987): 54–56.

Emerton, John A. "'The High Places of the Gates' in 2 Kings xxiii 8." *VT* 44, no. 4 (1994): 455–67.

Eskhult, Mats. "Kung Joash och Pilarna." *SEÅ* 70 (2005): 53–61.

Evans, Craig A. "Luke's Use of the Elijah/Elisha Narratives and the Ethic of Election." *JBL* 106, no. 1 (1987): 75–83.

Fensham, F. Charles. "Possible Explanation of the Name Baal-Zebub of Ekron." *ZAW* 79, no. 3 (1967): 361–64.

Fewell, Danna Nolan. "Sennacherib's Defeat: Words at War in 2 Kings 18:13–19:37." *JSOT* 34 (1986): 79–90.

Frevel, Christian. "Vom Schreiben Gottes: Literarkritik, Komposition und Auslegung von 2 Kön 17:34–40." *Bib* 72, no. 1 (1991): 23–48.
Frolov, Serge. "Evil-Merodach and the Deuteronomist: The Sociohistorical Setting of Dtr in the Light of 2 Kgs 25,27–30." *Bib* 88, no. 2 (2007): 174–90.
Fullerton, Kemper. "The Original Text of 2 K. 20:7–11=I. 38:7, 8, 21 F." *JBL* 44, nos. 1–2 (1925): 44–62.
Galil, Gershon. "Israelite Exiles in Media: A New Look at ND 2443+." *VT* 59, no. 1 (2009): 71–79.
García López, Félix. "Construction et Destruction de Jérusalem: Histoire et Prophétie dans les Cadres Rédactionnels des Livres des Rois." *RB* 94, no. 2 (1987): 222–32.
Gass, Erasmus. "Topographical Considerations and Redaction Criticism in 2 Kings 3." *JBL* 128, no. 1 (2009): 65–84.
Geraty, Lawrence T. "Archaeology and the Bible at Hezekiah's Lachish." *AUSS* 25, no. 1 (1987): 27–37.
Gerhards, Meik. "Die Begnadigung Jojachins: Überlegungen zu 2.Kön 25,27–30 (mit einem Anhang zu den Nennungen Jojachins auf Zuteilungslisten aus Babylon)." *BN* 94 (1998): 52–67.
———. "Die Beiden Erzählungen aus 2. Kön 20 und 2. Kön 20,18 als Ankündigung der Begnadigung Jojachins (2. Kön 25,27–30)." *BN* 98 (1999): 5–12.
———. "Zum Emphatischen Gebrauch der Partikel 'al im biblischen Hebräisch (Notizen zu 2 Kön 6,27; dem 'Al-Tašhet von Ps 57,1 etc; Ps 59,12; Spr 27,10; Hld 1,6; Jer 5,10 Un Jer 18,18)." *BN* 102 (2000): 54–73.
Gibson, George S. "A Jar of Oil." *ExpTim* 96, no. 4 (1985): 112–13.
Goedicke, Hans. "The End of 'So, King of Egypt.'" *BASOR* 171 (1963): 64–66.
Gosse, Bernard. "Du Rejet de Yahvé par Israël au Rejet d'Israël et de Juda par Yahvé dans les Livres de Samuel et les Livres des Rois." *ZAW* 112, no. 4 (2000): 550–63.
Graham, M. Patrick. "A Connection Proposed Between 2 Chr 24:26 and Ezra 9–10." *ZAW* 97, no. 2 (1985): 256–58.
Grohmann, Marianne. "Hulda, die Prophetin (2 Kön 22,14–20)." *CV* 45, no. 3 (2003): 209–16.
Gruenthaner, Michael J. "Two Sun Miracles of the Old Testament." *CBQ* 10, no. 3 (1948): 271–90.
Habel, Norman C. "The Survival of Yahwism." *Point* 6, no. 1 (1977): 186–96.
Halpern, Baruch. "Why Manasseh Is Blamed for the Babylonian Exile: The Evolution of a Biblical Tradition." *VT* 48, no. 4 (1998): 473–514.
Hamori, Esther J. "The Spirit of Falsehood." *CBQ* 72, no. 1 (2010): 15–30.
Haran, Menahem. "Rise and Decline of the Empire of Jeroboam Ben Joash." *VT* 17, no. 3 (1967): 266–97.
Hart, Stephen. "Selaʿ: The Rock of Edom." *PEQ* 118 (1986): 91–95.

Hasel, Michael G. "The Destruction of Trees in the Moabite Campaign of 2 Kings 3:4–27: A Study in the Laws of Warfare." *AUSS* 40, no. 2 (2002): 197–206.

Hauge, Martin Ravndal. "Some Aspects of the Motif 'The City Facing Death' of Ps 68:21." *SJOT* 1 (1988): 1–29.

Hayes, John Haralson. "Historical Reconstruction, Textual Emendation, and Biblical Translation: Some Examples From the RSV." *PRSt* 14, no. 1 (1987): 5–9.

Hayward, Robert. "Some Notes on Scribes and Priests in the Targum of the Prophets." *JJS* 36, no. 2 (1985): 210–21.

Heller, Jan. "Drei Wundertaten Elisas." *CV* 2, no. 1 (1959): 82–85.

———. "Tod im Topfe: 2 Kön 4:38–41." *CV* 10, no. 1 (1967): 71–76.

Heltzer, Michael. "Some Questions Concerning the Economic Policy of Josiah, King of Judah." *IEJ* 50, nos. 1–2 (2000): 105–8.

Henige, David. "Found but Not Lost: A Skeptical Note on the Document Discovered in the Temple Under Josiah." *JHebS* 7 (2007): 2–17. http://www.jhsonline.org/Articles/article_62.pdf.

Hens-Piazza, Gina. "Forms of Violence and the Violence of Forms: Two Cannibal Mothers Before a King (2 Kings 6:24–33)." *JFSR* 14, no. 2 (1998): 91–104.

Herr, Bertram. "Hat das Alte Testament als Quelle der Geschichte Israels Ausgedient? Die Probe auf das Exempel 2 Reg Xii 5–17." *VT* 51, no. 1 (2001): 42–54.

Himbaza, Innocent. "Quelle Massore pour Quel Texte?" *BN* 106 (2001): 33–39.

Hobbs, T. Raymond. "2 Kings 1 and 2: Their Unity and Purpose." *SR* 13, no. 3 (1984): 327–34.

———. "Hospitality in the First Testament and the 'Teleological Fallacy.' " *JSOT* 95 (2001): 3–30.

———. "Man, Woman, and Hospitality—2 Kings 4:8–36." *BTB* 23, no. 3 (1993): 91–100.

Höffken, Peter. "Die Rede des Rabsake vor Jerusalem (2 Kön. xviii/ Jes. xxxvi) im Kontext anderer Kapitulationsforderungen." *VT* 58, no. 1 (2008): 44–55.

———. "Zur Eigenart von Jes 39 par II Reg 20,12–19." *ZAW* 110, no. 2 (1998): 244–49.

Holloway, Steven W. "Antiochan Temporal Interpolations in 2 Kgs 6,24–7,20." *Bib* 78, no. 4 (1997): 543–47.

———. "Smart Mobs, Bad Crowds, Godly People and Dead Priests: Crowd Symbols in the Josianic Narrative and Some Mesopotamian Parallels." *BR* 51 (2006): 25–52.

Holt, Else Kragelund. "' . . . Urged on By His Wife Jezebel': A Literary Reading of 1 Kgs 18 in Context." *SJOT* 9, no. 1 (1995): 83–96.

Hoppe, Leslie J. "The Death of Josiah and the Meaning of Deuteronomy." *LASBF* 48 (1998): 31–47.

Horn, Siegfried H. "Why the Moabite Stone Was Blown to Pieces: 9th Cent BC Inscription Adds New Dimension to Biblical Account of Mesha's Rebellion." *BAR* 12, no. 3 (1986): 50–61.

House, Paul R. "Examining the Narratives of Old Testament Narrative: An Exploration in Biblical Theology." *WTJ* 67, no. 2 (2005): 229–45.

Hulbert, W. G. "Good King and Bad King: Traditions about Manasseh in the Bible and Late Second Temple Judaism." *S-CJ* 11, no. 1 (2008): 71–81.

Hyman, Ronald T. "The Rabshakeh's Speech (II Kg 18–25): A Study of Rhetorical Intimidation." *JBQ* 23, no. 4 (1995): 213–20.

Irvine, Stuart A. "The Southern Border of Syria Reconstructed." *CBQ* 56, no. 1 (1994): 21–41.

Janzen, David. "An Ambiguous Ending: Dynastic Punishment in Kings and the Fate of the Davidides in 2 Kings 25.27–30." *JSOT* 33, no. 1 (2008): 39–58.

Joüon, Paul. "Notes Philologiques sur le Texte Hebreu de 1 Rois 1, 9; 2, 8; 3, 13; 12, 5; 12, 9; 12, 10; 14, 5; 14, 15; 22, 27 (= 2 Chr. 18, 26) et Is. 30, 20." *Bib* 9, no. 4 (1928): 428–33.

Kahn, Dan'el. "The Inscription of Sargon II at Tang-I Var and the Chronology of Dynasty 25." *Or* 70, no. 1 (2001): 1–18.

Kaiser, Leo M. "A New Greek Word and 2 Kings 13:6, 8, 10." *CBQ* 10, no. 4 (1948): 406–7.

Kaiser, Otto. "Die Verkündigung des Propheten Jesaja im Jahre 701: Von der Menschen Vertrauen und Gottes Hilfe, Eine Studie über II Reg 18:17 par Jes 36:1." *ZAW* 81, no. 3 (1969): 304–15.

Kalimi, Isaac. "Robbers on the Road to Jericho: Luke's Story of the Good Samaritan and Its Origins in Kings/Chronicles." *ETL* 85, no. 1 (2009): 47–53.

Kang, Seung Il. "A Philological Approach to the Problem of King So (2 Kgs 17:4)." *VT* 60, no. 2 (2010): 241–48.

Kasher, Rimon. "The *Sitz im Buch* of the Story of Hezekiah's Illness and Cure (II Reg 20,1–11; Isa 38,1–22)." *ZAW* 113, no. 1 (2001): 41–55.

Kaswalder, Pietro Alberto. "Re Ioiachin, una Speranza Perduta (2Re 25,27–30)." *LASBF* 54 (2004): 9–24.

Keulen, P. S. F. Van. "The Meaning of the Phrase Wn'spt 'L-Qbrtyk Bšlwm in 2 Kings XXII 20." *VT* 46, no. 2 (1996): 256–60.

Kim, Jean Kyoung. "Reading and Retelling Naaman's Story (2 Kings 5)." *JSOT* 30, no. 1 (2005): 49–61.

Kim, Yoo-Ki. "In Search of a Narrator's Voice: A Discourse Analysis of 2 Kings 18:13–16." *JBL* 127, no. 3 (2008): 477–89.

Klingbeil, Gerald A. "'Asir los Pies'—2 Reyes 4:27 y el Lenguaje Idiomático en el Antiguo Testamento." *Theol* 12, no. 1 (1997): 2–15.

Klink, Edward W., III. "What Concern Is That to You and to Me? John 2:1–11 and the Elisha Narratives." *Neot* 39, no. 2 (2005): 273–87.

Koch, Klaus. "Aschera Als Himmelskönigin in Jerusalem." *UF* 20 (1988): 97–120.

Koenen, Klaus. "Eherne Schlange und Goldenes Kalb: Ein Vergleich der Überlieferungen." *ZAW* 111, no. 3 (1999): 353–72.

Kunz-Lübcke, Andreas. "Auf dem Stein und zwischen den Zeilen: Überlegungen zu einer kontrafaktischen Geschichte Israels am Beispiel von 2 Kön 3 und der Mescha-inschrift." *BZ* 51, no. 1 (2007): 1–22.

Kuyt, A., and J. W. Wesselius. "A Ugaritic Parallel for the Feast for Ba῾al in 2 Kings 10:8–25." *VT* 35, no. 1 (1985): 109–11.

Laato, Antti. "Hezekiah and the Assyrian Crisis in 701 BC." *SJOT* 2 (1987): 49–68.

Labuschagne, C. J. "Did Elisha Deliberately Lie: A Note on 2 Kings 8:10." *ZAW* 77, no. 3 (1965): 327–28.

Lamb, David T. "The Non-eternal Dynastic Promises of Jehu of Israel and Esarhaddon of Assyria." *VT* 60, no. 3 (2010): 337–44.

Lanner, Laurel. "Cannibal Mothers and Me: A Mother's Reading of 2 Kings 6.24–7.20." *JSOT* 85 (1999): 107–16.

Lasine, Stuart. "Jehoram and the Cannibal Mothers (2 Kings 6:24–33): Solomon's Judgment in an Inverted World." *JSOT* 50 (1991): 27–53.

Lawrence, Paul J. N. "Assyrian Nobles and the Book of Jonah." *TynBul* 37 (1986): 121–32.

Lemaire, André. "Le Pays d'Eden et Le Bît-Adini: aux Origines d'un Mythe." *Syria* 58, nos. 3–4 (1981): 313–30.

Léonard, Jeanne Marie. "Multiplication des Pains: 2 Rois 4:42–44 et Jean 6:1–13." *ETR* 55, no. 2 (1980): 265–70.

Leshem, Yossi. "'Va-Tashem Ba-Puk 'Eneha Va-Tetev et-Roshah' 2 Melakim 9:30." *HUCA* 76 (2005): 1–10. (Hebrew).

Leuchter, Mark. "'The Levite in Your Gates': The Deuteronomic Redefinition of Levitical Authority." *JBL* 126, no. 3 (2007): 417–36.

———. "'The Prophets' and 'the Levites' in Josiah's Covenant Ceremony." *ZAW* 121, no. 1 (2009): 31–47.

Levin, Christoph. "Die Instandsetzung des Tempels unter Joasch Ben Ahasja." *VT* 40, no. 1 (1990): 51–88.

Lightbourn, Francis Chesebrough. "The 'Story' in the Old Testament." *AThR* 21, no. 2 (1939): 94–102.

Lipschits, Oded. "'Jehoiakim Slept with His Fathers' (II Kings 24:6): Did He?" *JHebS* 4 (2002): 1–33. http://www.jhsonline.org/Articles/article_23.pdf.

Liver, Jacob. "Wars of Mesha, King of Moab." *PEQ* 99 (1967): 14–31.

Lohfink, Norbert. "2 Kön 23:3 und Dtn 6:17." *Bib* 71, no. 1 (1990): 34–42.

Long, Burke O. "2 Kings 3 and Genres of Prophetic Narrative." *VT* 23, no. 3 (1973): 337–48.

———. "Framing Repetitions in Biblical Historiography." *JBL* 106, no. 3 (1987): 385–99.

———. "The Shunammite Woman: in the Shadow of the Prophet?" *BRev* 7, no. 1 (1991): 12–19.

Long, Jesse C., Jr. "Elisha's Deceptive Prophecy in 2 Kings 3: A Response to Raymond Westbrook." *JBL* 126, no. 1 (2007): 168–71.

———. "Unfulfilled Prophecy or Divine Deception? A Literary Reading of 2 Kings 3." *S-CJ* 7, no. 1 (2004): 101–17.

Loretz, Oswald, and Werner R. Mayer. "Pūlu-Tiglatpileser III und Menahem von Israel nach Assyrischen Quellen und 2 Kön 15,19–20. " *UF* 22 (1991): 221–31.

Maier, Walter A., III. "The Healing of Naaman in Missiological Perspective." *CTQ* 61, no. 3 (1997): 177–96.

Manor, Dale Wallace. "Gates and Gods: High Places in the Gates." *S-CJ* 2, no. 2 (1999): 235–53.

Margalit, Baruch. "Why King Mesha of Moab Sacrificed His Oldest Son." *BAR* 12, no. 6 (1986): 62–63.

Matthews, Victor H. "Kings of Israel: A Question of Crime and Punishment." *SBLSP* 27 (1988): 517–26.

McCarter, P. Kyle, Jr. "Biblical Detective Work Identifies the Eunuch." *BAR* 28, no. 2 (2002): 46–48.

McCarthy, Dennis J. "2 Kings 13:4–6." *Bib* 54, no. 3 (1973): 409–10.

McKay, J. W. "Further Light on the Horses and Chariot of the Sun in the Jerusalem Temple: 2 Kings 23:11." *PEQ* 105 (1973): 167–69.

McKinlay, Judith E. "Gazing at Huldah." *Bible & Critical Theory* 1, no. 3 (2005).

———. "Negotiating the Frame for Viewing the Death of Jezebel." *BibInt* 10, no. 3 (2002): 305–23.

Menn, Esther. "A Little Child Shall Lead Them: The Role of the Little Israelite Servant Girl (2 Kings 5:1–19)." *CurTM* 35, no. 5 (2008): 340–48.

Mercer, Mark K. "Elisha's Unbearable Curse: A Study of 2 Kings 2:23–25." *Africa Journal of Evangelical Theology* 21, no. 2 (2002): 165–98.

Millard, A. R. "Sennacherib's Attack on Hezekiah." *TynBul* 36 (1985): 61–77.

Minette de Tillesse, Caetano. "Joiaqim, Repoussoir du 'Pieux' Josias: Parallélismes entre II Reg 22 et Jer 36." *ZAW* 105, no. 3 (1994): 352–76.

Mitchell, Christine. "Heart and Mind in the Hebrew Scriptures." *Touchstone* 23, no. 1 (2005): 5–13.

Monroe, Lauren A. S. "A 'Holiness' Substratum in the Deuteronomistic Account of Josiah's Reform." *JHebS* 7 (2007): 42–53.

Montgomery, James A. "The Hebrew Divine Name and the Personal Pronoun HŪ." *JBL* 63, no. 2 (1944): 161–63.

Morschauser, Scott. "A 'Diagnostic' Note on the 'Great Wrath Upon Israel' in 2 Kings 3:27." *JBL* 129, no. 2 (2010): 299–302.

Mullen, E. Theodore. "Crime and Punishment: The Sins of the King and the Despoliation of the Treasuries." *CBQ* 54, no. 2 (1992): 231–48.

Müller, Augustin R. "2 Kön 23:3 deuteronomistisch." *BN* 35 (1986): 26–29.

Müller, Walter W. "Eselfleisch und Taubendreck: Zur Hungersnotspeise in Samaria nach 2 Kön 6:25." *BN* 46 (1989): 17–23.

Mulzer, Martin. "Et Ascenderunt Eunuchi ... Zur Bewertung der Vet-Lat-Fragmente in 2(4) Kön 9,33. " *BN* 73 (1994): 20–26.

Murray, Donald F. "Of All the Years the Hopes—Or Fears? Jehoiachin in Babylon (2 Kings 25:27–30)." *JBL* 120 (2001): 245.

Na᾽aman, Nadav. "Death Formulae and the Burial Place of the Kings of the House of David." *Bib* 85, no. 2 (2004): 245–54.

———. "The Debated Historicity of Hezekiah's Reform in the Light of Historical and Archaeological Research." *ZAW* 107, no. 2 (1995): 179–95.

———. "The Dedicated Treasures Buildings within the House of YHWH Where Women Weave Coverings for Asherah (2 Kings 23,7)." *BN* 83 (1996): 17–18.

———. "The Distribution of Messages in the Kingdom of Judah in Light of the Lachish Ostraca." *VT* 53, no. 2 (2003): 169–80.

———. "Historical and Chronological Notes on the Kingdoms of Israel and Judah in the 8th Century BC." *VT* 36, no. 1 (1986): 71–92.

———. "The Historical Background to the Conquest of Samaria (720 BC)." *Bib* 71, no. 2 (1990): 206–25.

———. "The Kingdom of Judah Under Josiah." *Tel Aviv* 18 (1991): 3–71.

———. "Naboth's Vineyard and the Foundation of Jezreel." *JSOT* 33, no. 2 (2008): 197–218.

———. "New Light on Hezekiah's Second Prophetic Story (2 Kgs 19,9b–35)." *Bib* 81, no. 3 (2000): 393–402.

———. "Three Notes on the Aramaic Inscription from Tel Dan." *IEJ* 50, nos. 1–2 (2000): 92–104.

Nelson, Richard D. "The Altar of Ahaz: A Revisionist View." *HAR* 10 (1986): 267–76.

Nevins, Arthur J. "When Was Solomon's Temple Burned Down? Reassessing the Evidence." *JSOT* 31, no. 1 (2006): 3–25.

Ngan, Lai Ling Elizabeth. "2 Kings 5." *RevExp* 94, no. 4 (1997): 589–97.

Nicholson, Ernest W. "Josiah and the Priests of the High Places (II Reg 23,8a.9)." *ZAW* 119, no. 4 (2007): 499–513.

Nwaoru, Emmanuel O. "The Story of Naaman (2 Kings 5:1–19): Implications for Mission Today." *Svensk Missionstidskrift* 96, no. 1 (2008): 27–41.

O'Brien, D. P. "'Is This the Time to Accept . . .?' (2 Kings V 26b): Simply Moralizing (LXX) of an Ominous Foreboding of Yahweh's Rejection of Israel (MT)?" *VT* 46, no. 4 (1996): 448–57.

O'Brien, Mark A. "The Portrayal of Prophets in 2 Kings 2." *ABR* 46 (1998): 1–16.

Ohm, Andrew Taehang. "Manasseh and the Punishment Narrative." *TynBul* 61, no. 2 (2010): 237–54.

Olyan, Saul M. "2 Kings 9:31—Jehu as Zimri." *HTR* 78, nos. 1–2 (1985): 203–7.

Otto, Susanne. "The Composition of the Elijah-Elisha Stories and the Deuteronomistic History." *JSOT* 27 (2003): 487–508.

Pakkala, Juha. "Zedekiah's Fate and the Dynastic Succession." *JBL* 125, no. 3 (2006): 443–52.

Parker, Edmund A. "Note on the Chronology of 2 Kings 17:1." *AUSS* 6, no. 2 (1968): 129–33.

Parzen, Herbert. "The Prophets and the Omri Dynasty." *HTR* 33, no. 2 (1940): 69–96.

Paton, Lewis Bayles. "The Meaning of the Expression 'Between the Two Walls.' " *JBL* 25, no. 1 (1906): 1–13.

Patterson, Richard D. "It Is So." *Fundamentalist Journal* 2, no. 10 (1983): 53–318.

Paul, Shalom M. "Sargon's Administrative Diction in 2 Kings 17:27." *JBL* 88, no. 1 (1969): 73–74.

Person, Raymond F. "II Kings 18–20 and Isaiah 36–39: A Text Critical Case Study in the Redaction History of the Book of Isaiah." *ZAW* 111, no. 3 (1999): 373–79.

———. "II Kings 24,18–25,30 and Jeremiah 52: A Text-Critical Study in the Redaction History of the Deuteronomistic History." *ZAW* 105, no. 2 (1993): 174–205.

Pyper, Hugh S. "Judging the Wisdom of Solomon: The Two-Way Effect of Intertextuality." *JSOT* 18, no. 59 (1993): 25–36.

Rhee, Syngman. "Second Kings 6:8–23." *Int* 54, no. 2 (2000): 183–85.

Rice, Gene. "Elijah's Requirement for Prophetic Leadership (2 Kings 2:1–18)." *JRT* 59 (2007): 1–12.

Rofé, Alexander. "The Vineyard of Naboth: The Origin and Message of the Story." *VT* 38, no. 1 (1988): 89–104.

Rogland, Max. "Pro or Contra? 2 Kings 6:11." *Presb* 27, no. 1 (2001): 56–58.

Ron, Zvi. "Nivhaz or Nivhan?" *JBQ* 37, no. 4 (2009): 239–42.

Roncace, Mark. "Elisha and the Woman of Shunem: 2 Kings 4.8–37 and 8:1–6 Read in Conjunction." *JSOT* 25, no. 91 (2000): 109–27.

Rösel, Hartmut N. "2 Kön 2:1–18 als Elija- oder Elischa-Geschichte." *BN* 59 (1991): 33–36.

———. "Israel: Gedanken zu seinen Anfängen." *BN* 25 (1984): 76–91.

Rudman, Dominic. "Is the Rabshakeh also Among the Prophets? A Rhetorical Study of 2 Kings XVIII 17–35." *VT* 50, no. 1 (2000): 100–110.

———. "A Note on the Personal Name Amon (2 Kings 21,19–26 // 2 Chr 33,21–25)." *Bib* 81, no. 3 (2000): 403–5.

Runnalls, Donna. "The (Parwār): A Place of Ritual Separation?" *VT* 41, no. 3 (1991): 324–31.

Ruprecht, Eberhard. "Die Ursprüngliche Komposition der Hiskia-Jesaja-Erzählungen und ihre Umstrukturierung durch den Verfasser [Dtr] Geschichtswerkes." *ZTK* 87, no. 1 (1990): 33–66.

Salibi, Kamal S. "The 'Flight' From Jerusalem." *TR* 11, no. 2 (1990): 76–84.

Sánchez Caro, José Manuel. "Esdras, Nehemías y los Orígenes del Judaísmo." *Salmanticensis* 32, no. 1 (1985): 5–34.

Satterthwaite, Philip E. "The Elisha Narratives and the Coherence of 2 Kings 2–8." *TynBul* 49, no. 1 (1998): 1–28.

Schaper, Joachim. "Auf der Suche dach dem Alten Israel? Teil I, Text, Artefakt und 'Geschichte Israel' in der alttestamentlichen Wissenschaft vor dem Hintergrund der Methodendiskussion in den historischen Kulturwissenschaften." *ZAW* 118, no. 1 (2006): 1–21.

Schenker, Adrian. "Man Bittet um das Gegenargument! Von der Eigenart Textkritischer Argumentation." *ZAW* 122, no. 1 (2010): 53–63.
Schipper, Jeremy. "'Significant Resonances' with Mephibosheth in 2 Kings 25:27–30: A Response to Donald F. Murray." *JBL* 124, no. 3 (2005): 521–29.
Schmid, Konrad. "Manasse und der Untergang Judas: 'Golaorientierte' Theologie in den Königsbüchern?" *Bib* 78, no. 1 (1997): 87–99.
Schneider, Nikolaus. "'Melchom, Das Scheusal Der Ammoniter.' " *Bib* 18, no. 3 (1937): 337–43.
Schniedewind, William M. "History and Interpretation: The Religion of Ahab and Manasseh in the Book of Kings." *CBQ* 55, no. 4 (1993): 649–61.
———. "The Source Citations of Manasseh: King Manasseh in History and Homily." *VT* 41, no. 4 (1991): 450–61.
Schöpflin, Karin. "Naaman: seine Heilung und Bekehrung im Alten und Neuen Testament." *BN* 141 (2009): 35–56.
Schulte, Hannelis. "Die Rettung des Prinzen Joaš: Zur Exegese von II Reg 11,1–3." *ZAW* 109, no. 4 (1997): 549–56.
Seitz, Christopher R. "Account A and the Annals of Sennacherib: A Reassessment." *JSOT* 58 (1993): 47–57.
Sergi, Omer. "The Omride Dynasty and the Reshaping of Judahite Historical Memory." *Bib* 97 (2016): 503–26.
Shea, William H. "The Murder of Sennacherib and Related Issues." *Near East Archaeological Society Bulletin* 46 (2001): 25–42.
———. "Sennacherib's Second Palestinian Campaign." *JBL* 104, no. 3 (1985): 401–18.
———. "'So,' Ruler of Egypt." *AUSS* 30, no. 3 (1992): 201–15.
Shemesh, Yael. "Elisha and the Miraculous Jug of Oil (2 Kgs 4:1–7)." *JHebS* 8 (2008): 1–18.
Shields, Mary E. "Subverting A Man of God, Elevating A Woman: Role and Power Reversals in 2 Kings 4." *JSOT* 58 (1993): 59–69.
Siddall, Luis Robert. "Tiglath-Pileser III's Aid to Ahaz: A New Look at the Problems of the Biblical Accounts in Light of the Assyrian Sources." *Ancient Near Eastern Studies* 46 (2009): 93–106.
Smith, Jannes. "Jeremiah 52: Thackeray and Beyond." *BIOSCS* 35 (2002): 55–96.
Smith, Mark S. "The Near Eastern Background of Solar Language for Yahweh." *JBL* 109, no. 1 (1990): 29–39.
Smyth-Florentin, Françoise. "Histoire de la Guérison et de la Conversion de Naaman." *Foi et Vie* 69, no. 3 (1970): 29–43.
Snyman, Gerrie. "Bedreiging en Verlossing in 2 Konings 6:24–7:20—'N Literêr-Teoretiese Benadering. " *In Die Skriflig* 25 (1991): 265–83.
Sperber, Daniel. "Weak Waters." *ZAW* 82, no. 1 (1970): 114–16.
Sprinkle, Joe M. "2 Kings 3: History or Historical Fiction?" *BBR* 9 (1999): 247–70.
Staszak, Martin. "Zu einer Lesart und dem historischen Hintergrund des Fragments B der Stele von Tel Dan." *BN* 142 (2009): 67–77.

Sternberger, Jean Pierre. "L'holocauste à la Frontiìre: Une Lecture de 2 Rois 3." *Foi et Vie* 95, no. 4 (1996): 19–32.

Stipp, Hermann-Josef. "Vier Gestalten einer Totenerweckungserzählung (1 Kön 17,17–24; 2 Kön 4,8–37; Apg 9,36–42; Apg 20,7–12). " *Bib* 80, no. 1 (1999): 43–77.

Stromberg, Jake. "The Role of Redaction Criticism in the Evaluation of a Textual Variant: Another Look at 1QIsa[a] XXXII 14 (38:21–22)." *DSD* 16, no. 2 (2009): 155–89.

Talmon, Shemaryahu, and Weston W. Fields. "The Collocation Mshtyn Bqyr W'tswr W'zwb and Its Meaning." *ZAW* 101, no. 1 (1989): 85–112.

Talshir, Zipora. "The Three Deaths of Josiah and the Strata of Biblical Historiography (2 Kings XXII 29–30. 2 Chronicles XXXV 20–25, 1 Esdras I 23–31)." *VT* 46, no. 2 (1996): 213–36.

Tångberg, K Arvid. "A Note on Ba'al Zĕbūb in 2 Kgs 1:2,3,6,16." *SJOT* 6, no. 2 (1992): 293–96.

Thiel, Winfried. "Examples of Individual and National Restitution in the Books of Kings." *SK* 20, no. 2 (1999): 441–54.

Tiemeyer, Lena-Sofia. "Prophecy as a Way of Cancelling Prophecy: The Strategic Uses of Foreknowledge." *ZAW* 117, no. 3 (2005): 329–50.

Tinker, Christopher. "God's Foreknowledge and Prophecy: An Application. (Part 2)." *Churchman* 118, no. 2 (2004): 139–50.

Toloni, Giancarlo. "'Per Non Entrape nel Tempio' (2 Re 23,11ab): Storia Dell'interpretazione di un Sintagma." *EstBíb* 55, no. 2 (1997): 143–69.

———. "Una Strage di Sacerdoti? Dalla Storiografia alla Storia in 2 Re 23,4b–5." *EstBíb* 56, no. 1 (1998): 41–60.

Trebolle Barrera, Julio C. "La Coronación de Joás (2 Re 11): Texto, Narración e Historia." *EstBíb* 41, nos. 1–2 (1983): 1–16.

———. "La Expedición de Senaquerib contra Jerusalén: Reflexiones en Torno a un Libro Reciente." *EstBíb* 45, nos. 1–2 (1987): 7–21.

———. "Glosas en 2 Re 11:6–10: De la Crítica Textual a la Crítica Literaria e Histórica." *EstBíb* 41, nos. 3–4 (1983): 375–80.

———. "Le Texte de 2 Rois 7:20–8:5 à la Lumiìre des Découvertes de Qumrân (6Q4 15)." *RevQ* 13, nos. 1–4 (1988): 561–68.

Vera Chamaza, G. W. "Literarkritische Beolbachtung zu 2 Kön 18:1–12." *BZ* 33, no. 2 (1989): 222–33.

———. "Sanheribs Letzte Ruhestätte." *BZ* 36, no. 2 (1992): 241–49.

Viviano, Pauline A. "2 Kings 17: A Rhetorical and Form-Critical Analysis." *CBQ* 49, no. 4 (1987): 548–59.

Wagenaar, Jan A. "'Someone Came from Baal-Shalisha ...': The Significance of the Topography in 2 Kgs 4.42–44." *BN* 135 (2007): 35–42.

Wagner, Volker. "Eine antike Notiz zur Geschichte des Pesach (2 Kön 23,21–23)." *BZ* 54, no. 1 (2010): 20–35.

Waldman, Nahum M. "Ahab in Bible and Talmud." *Judaism* 37, no. 1 (1988): 41–47.

Wallace, Howard N. "Oracles Against the Israelite Dynasties in 1 and 2 Kings." *Bib* 67, no. 1 (1986): 21–40.

Walsh, Jerome T. "On HYH in 2 Kings 9:37." *VT* 60, no. 1 (2010): 152–53.

Walton, John H. "New Observations on the Date of Isaiah." *JETS* 28, no. 2 (1985): 129–32.

Washburn, David L. "Perspective and Purpose: Understanding the Josiah Story." *TJ* 12, no. 1 (1991): 59–78.

Watson, Paul L. "A Note on the 'Double Portion' of Deuteronomy 21:17 and II Kings 2:9." *ResQ* 8, no. 1 (1965): 70–75.

Weinfeld, Moshe. "Cult Centralization in Israel in the Light of a Neo-Babylonian Analogy." *JNES* 23, no. 3 (1964): 202–12.

Wénin, André. "La Cohérence Narrative de 2 Rois 3: Une Réponse à Jesús Asurmendi." *BibInt* 14, no. 5 (2006): 444–55.

Westbrook, Raymond. "Elisha's True Prophecy in 2 Kings 3." *JBL* 124, no. 3 (2005): 530–32.

Willson, Patrick J. "2 Kings 22:1–23:3." *Int* 54, no. 4 (2000): 413–15.

Wolff, Hans Walter. "Prophets and Institutions in the Old Testament." *CurTM* 13, no. 1 (1986): 5–12.

Wright, Logan S. "MKR in 2 Kings 12:5–17 and Deuteronomy 18:8." *VT* 39, no. 4 (1989): 438–48.

Würthwein, Ernst. "Die Revolution Jehus: Die Jehu-Erzählung in altisraelitischer und deuteronomisticher Sicht." *ZAW* 120, no. 1 (2008): 28–48.

Wyatt, Nicolas. "The Hollow Crown: Ambivalent Elements in West Semitic Royal Ideology." *UF* 18 (1986): 421–36.

Yeivin, Shmuel. "'Edūth." *IEJ* 24, no. 1 (1974): 17–20.

Younger, K. Lawson, Jr. "The Fall of Samaria in Light of Recent Research." *CBQ* 61, no. 3 (1999): 461–82.

Ziegler, Yael. "'As the Lord Lives and as Your Soul Lives': An Oath of Conscious Deference." *VT* 58, no. 1 (2008): 117–30.

Ziolkowski, Eric J. "The Bad Boys of Bethel: Origin and Development of a Sacrilegious Type." *HR* 30, no. 4 (1991): 331–58.

Zwickel, Wolfgang. "Die Kultreform des Ahas (2 Kön 16,10–18)." *SJOT* 7, no. 2 (1993): 250–62.

Scripture Index

Old Testament

Jeremiah

New Testament

Extra-Canonical